Dictionary of Literary Biography

Dictionary of Literary Biography Documentary Series

Dictionary of Literary Biography Yearbooks

1980 edited by Karen L. Rood, Jean W. Ross, and Richard Ziegfeld (1981)

1981 edited by Karen L. Rood, Jean W. Ross, and Richard Ziegfeld (1982)

1982 edited by Richard Ziegfeld; associate editors: Jean W. Ross and Lynne C. Zeigler (1983)

1983 edited by Mary Bruccoli and Jean W. Ross; associate editor Richard Ziegfeld (1984)

1984 edited by Jean W. Ross (1985)

1985 edited by Jean W. Ross (1986)

1986 edited by J. M. Brook (1987)

1987 edited by J. M. Brook (1988)

1988 edited by J. M. Brook (1989)

1989 edited by J. M. Brook (1990)

1990 edited by James W. Hipp (1991)

1991 edited by James W. Hipp (1992)

1992 edited by James W. Hipp (1993)

1993 edited by James W. Hipp, contributing editor George Garrett (1994)

1994 edited by James W. Hipp, contributing editor George Garrett (1995)

1995 edited by James W. Hipp, contributing editor George Garrett (1996)

1996 edited by Samuel W. Bruce and L. Kay Webster, contributing editor George Garrett (1997)

1997 edited by Matthew J. Bruccoli and George Garrett, with the assistance of L. Kay Webster (1998)

1998 edited by Matthew J. Bruccoli, contributing editor George Garrett, with the assistance of D. W. Thomas (1999)

1999 edited by Matthew J. Bruccoli, contributing editor George Garrett, with the assistance of D. W. Thomas (2000)

2000 edited by Matthew J. Bruccoli, contributing editor George Garrett, with the assistance of George Parker Anderson (2001)

2001 edited by Matthew J. Bruccoli, contributing editor George Garrett, with the assistance of George Parker Anderson (2002)

Concise Series

Concise Dictionary of American Literary Biography, 7 volumes (1988–1999): *The New Consciousness, 1941–1968; Colonization to the American Renaissance, 1640–1865; Realism, Naturalism, and Local Color, 1865–1917; The Twenties, 1917–1929; The Age of Maturity, 1929–1941; Broadening Views, 1968–1988; Supplement: Modern Writers, 1900–1998.*

Concise Dictionary of British Literary Biography, 8 volumes (1991–1992): *Writers of the Middle Ages and Renaissance Before 1660; Writers of the Restoration and Eighteenth Century, 1660–1789; Writers of the Romantic Period, 1789–1832; Victorian Writers, 1832–1890; Late-Victorian and Edwardian Writers, 1890–1914; Modern Writers, 1914–1945; Writers After World War II, 1945–1960; Contemporary Writers, 1960 to Present.*

Concise Dictionary of World Literary Biography, 10 volumes projected (1999–   ): *Ancient Greek and Roman Writers; German Writers; African, Caribbean, and Latin American Writers; South Slavic and Eastern European Writers.*

Dictionary of Literary Biography® • Volume Two Hundred Sixty-Five

American Song Lyricists, 1920–1960

Dictionary of Literary Biography® • Volume Two Hundred Sixty-Five

American Song Lyricists, 1920–1960

Edited by
Philip Furia
University of North Carolina at Wilmington

A Bruccoli Clark Layman Book

GALE®

THOMSON
★
GALE

Detroit • New York • San Diego • San Francisco • Cleveland • New Haven, Conn. • Waterville, Maine • London • Munich

Dictionary of Literary Biography
American Song Lyricists, 1920–1960

© 2002 by Gale. Gale is an imprint of The Gale Group, Inc., a division of Thomson Learning, Inc.

Gale and Design™ and Thomson Learning™ are trademarks used herein under license.

For more information, contact
The Gale Group, Inc.
27500 Drake Rd.
Farmington Hills, MI 48331-3535
Or you can visit our Internet site at
http://www.gale.com

LIBRARY OF CONGRESS CATALOGING-IN-PUBLICATION DATA

American song lyricists, 1920–1960 / edited by Philip Furia.
    p. cm.—(Dictionary of literary biography; v. 265)
"A Bruccoli Clark Layman book."
    Includes bibliographical references (p.) and index.
    ISBN 0-7876-6009-4
    1. Popular music—United States—20th century—Bio-bibliography—Dictionaries. 2. Lyricists—United States—Biography—Dictionaries.
I. Furia, Philip, 1943– II. Series.

ML102.P66 A43 2002
782.42164'092'273—dc21
                                       2002009201

Printed in the United States of America
10 9 8 7 6 5 4 3 2 1

Contents

Plan of the Series

. . . Almost the most prodigious asset of a country, and perhaps its most precious possession, is its native literary product—when that product is fine and noble and enduring.

Mark Twain*

The advisory board, the editors, and the publisher of the *Dictionary of Literary Biography* are joined in endorsing Mark Twain's declaration. The literature of a nation provides an inexhaustible resource of permanent worth. Our purpose is to make literature and its creators better understood and more accessible to students and the reading public, while satisfying the needs of teachers and researchers.

To meet these requirements, *literary biography* has been construed in terms of the author's achievement. The most important thing about a writer is his writing. Accordingly, the entries in *DLB* are career biographies, tracing the development of the author's canon and the evolution of his reputation.

The purpose of *DLB* is not only to provide reliable information in a usable format but also to place the figures in the larger perspective of literary history and to offer appraisals of their accomplishments by qualified scholars.

The publication plan for *DLB* resulted from two years of preparation. The project was proposed to Bruccoli Clark by Frederick G. Ruffner, president of the Gale Research Company, in November 1975. After specimen entries were prepared and typeset, an advisory board was formed to refine the entry format and develop the series rationale. In meetings held during 1976, the publisher, series editors, and advisory board approved the scheme for a comprehensive biographical dictionary of persons who contributed to literature. Editorial work on the first volume began in January 1977, and it was published in 1978. In order to make *DLB* more than a dictionary and to compile volumes that individually have claim to status as literary history, it was decided to organize volumes by topic, period, or

From an unpublished section of Mark Twain's autobiography, copyright by the Mark Twain Company

genre. Each of these freestanding volumes provides a biographical-bibliographical guide and overview for a particular area of literature. We are convinced that this organization—as opposed to a single alphabet method—constitutes a valuable innovation in the presentation of reference material. The volume plan necessarily requires many decisions for the placement and treatment of authors. Certain figures will be included in separate volumes, but with different entries emphasizing the aspect of his career appropriate to each volume. Ernest Hemingway, for example, is represented in *American Writers in Paris, 1920–1939* by an entry focusing on his expatriate apprenticeship; he is also in *American Novelists, 1910–1945* with an entry surveying his entire career, as well as in *American Short-Story Writers, 1910–1945, Second Series* with an entry concentrating on his short fiction. Each volume includes a cumulative index of the subject authors and articles.

Since 1981 the series has been further augmented by the *DLB Yearbooks,* which update published entries, add new entries to keep the *DLB* current with contemporary activity, and provide articles on literary history. There have also been nineteen *DLB Documentary Series* volumes which provide illustrations, facsimiles, and biographical and critical source materials for figures, works, or groups judged to have particular interest for students. In 1999 the *Documentary Series* was incorporated into the *DLB* volume numbering system beginning with *DLB 210: Ernest Hemingway.*

We define literature as the *intellectual commerce of a nation:* not merely as belles lettres but as that ample and complex process by which ideas are generated, shaped, and transmitted. *DLB* entries are not limited to "creative writers" but extend to other figures who in their time and in their way influenced the mind of a people. Thus the series encompasses historians, journalists, publishers, book collectors, and screenwriters. By this means readers of *DLB* may be aided to perceive literature not as cult scripture in the keeping of intellectual high priests but firmly positioned at the center of a nation's life.

DLB includes the major writers appropriate to each volume and those standing in the ranks behind them. Scholarly and critical counsel has been sought in deciding which minor figures to include and how full their entries should be. Wherever possible, useful references are made to figures who do not warrant separate entries.

Each *DLB* volume has an expert volume editor responsible for planning the volume, selecting the figures for inclusion, and assigning the entries. Volume editors are also responsible for preparing, where appropriate, appendices surveying the major periodicals and literary and intellectual movements for their volumes, as well as lists of further readings. Work on the series as a whole is coordinated at the Bruccoli Clark Layman editorial center in Columbia, South Carolina, where the editorial staff is responsible for accuracy and utility of the published volumes.

One feature that distinguishes *DLB* is the illustration policy—its concern with the iconography of literature. Just as an author is influenced by his surroundings, so is the reader's understanding of the author enhanced by a knowledge of his environment. Therefore *DLB* volumes include not only drawings, paintings, and photographs of authors, often depicting them at various stages in their careers, but also illustrations of their families and places where they lived. Title pages are regularly reproduced in facsimile along with dust jackets for modern authors. The dust jackets are a special feature of *DLB* because they often document better than anything else the way in which an author's work was perceived in its own time. Specimens of the writers' manuscripts and letters are included when feasible.

Samuel Johnson rightly decreed that "The chief glory of every people arises from its authors." The purpose of the *Dictionary of Literary Biography* is to compile literary history in the surest way available to us—by accurate and comprehensive treatment of the lives and work of those who contributed to it.

The *DLB* Advisory Board

Editor's Note

DLB 265: American Song Lyricists, 1920–1960 includes the major popular lyricists who wrote for the Broadway theater, the Hollywood motion-picture musical, and the sheet-music and recording industry collectively known as Tin Pan Alley. The period surveyed is generally regarded as the golden age of American songwriting, and there are entries on the most-significant lyricists of this era. Songwriters whose greatest work came before 1920, such as George M. Cohan, are not included, nor are songwriters whose major work occurred after 1960, such as Stephen Sondheim, even though they may have written some songs in the period from 1920 to 1960. Other lyricists who produced significant work during this era are listed, with some of their songs, in an appendix.

Each entry begins with a list of the subject's popular songs (rather than a full catalogue of every song by the lyricist). These songs are divided into three categories:

1. Selected songs from theatrical productions;

2. Selected songs from motion-picture productions;

3. Selected songs written and published independently of theatrical or motion-picture productions.

When a lyricist collaborated on an entire score of songs for a production, his or her collaborator is listed beside the title of the production, as in this example from the entry on Lorenz Hart:

Pal Joey (1941), music by Richard Rodgers—"Bewitched, Bothered, and Bewildered";

When a song was interpolated into an existing score by other songwriters, the lyricist's collaborator is listed beside the title of the song, as in this example from the entry on Jack Yellen:

High Jinks (1924)–"All Aboard for Dixieland" (music by George L. Cobb)

Songs are listed only under the production that introduced them, unless their revival for a later production was historically significant.

I thank all of the contributors who, in the best tradition of songwriting, collaborated imaginatively, meticulously, and cheerfully to bring this book to completion. I thank my wife, Laurie Patterson, for lending her time, research acumen, and computer wizardry to resolve formatting problems so that the various submissions comprised a coherent whole and to cull the vast riches of the Internet for a husband whose technical skills revert to the era of Ira Gershwin and Cole Porter.

—Philip Furia

Introduction

With the publication of *DLB 265: American Song Lyricists, 1920–1960,* writers of song lyrics receive long-overdue recognition as men and women of letters. With a few exceptions, such as Ezra Pound's celebration of the medieval troubadours of Provence, the art of the song lyric has received little attention from literary scholars. That art, as practiced by the lyricists in this volume, is a highly specialized and collaborative one that blends poetry and music into the hybrid art of song. Unlike the art song, in which a composer takes an existing poem and creates a musical setting for it, the art of the lyric often consists of finding syllables, words, and phrases to fit the notes of an existing melody. Lyricists such as Johnny Mercer and Lorenz Hart usually waited until their collaborators had completed a melody before even beginning to work on a lyric. Ira Gershwin, in contrast, sat beside his brother George at the piano as the two worked back and forth between music and lyric, yet Ira always maintained that the art of the lyricist lay in writing *to* music, "mosaically" fitting syllables, words, and phrases to musical notes.

When Ira Gershwin traced the history of his art in *Lyrics on Several Occasions* (1959), he excluded such Renaissance English lute-song writers as John Dowland and Thomas Campion because they wrote poems first and then set them to music. Instead, Gershwin aligned himself with the writers of broadside ballads, who put new words, frequently bawdy and satirical, to existing melodies. He saw the lyricist's art truly flourish in the eighteenth century with John Gay's *The Beggar's Opera* (1728), in which Gay took some forty different traditional airs and wrote new lyrics to them that were tailored to the characters and dramatic situations in the play. By such criteria Robert Burns and Thomas Moore would be considered true lyricists, for they put new words to old Scottish and Irish folk airs, respectively.

Yet, Gershwin's criteria forced him to exclude from his pantheon of forebears the songwriter who might seem to have been his most influential progenitor, as well as that of other modern American lyricists such as Hart, E. Y. "Yip" Harburg, and Dorothy Fields: William Schwenck Gilbert. But in the collaboration between Gilbert and Arthur Sullivan, the words were always written before the music. Gilbert had initially been a light-verse poet who published in *Fun* magazine, a rival of *Punch,* under the pseudonym Bab. In their early collaborations Sullivan took completed poems by Gilbert and set them to music. Over time, Gilbert, who had little ear for music, learned to make his lyrics more singable by softening consonants and providing long, open vowels that enabled performers to sustain notes, but his words always took precedence over the music. Whenever Sullivan was asked that perennial question, "Which comes first—the music or the words?" he invariably snapped, "The words, of course," since it was widely assumed that only if a lyric was written first could it have the quality of poetry and fit the characters and dramatic situation of an operetta.

Gilbert's influence on Gershwin and his fellow lyricists was profound, but they knew him initially as a writer of light verse. In the early decades of the twentieth century, when many of these lyricists were growing up, light verse was enormously popular. All the major New York newspapers ran columns of light verse. The most famous of these was "The Conning Tower," by Franklin Pierce Adams ("F.P.A."), in *The New York World,* but there were others as well, such as Don Marquis's "Sun Dial" in the *New York Sun,* that featured verse and humorous squibs by professional and amateur poets. "We were living," as Harburg put it, "in a time of literate revelry in the New York daily press—F.P.A., . . . Bob Benchley—we wanted to be part of it."

Harburg and Ira Gershwin were classmates in high school and put out their own column of light verse in the school newspaper. They also pored over anthologies of light verse, where they found the ancestors of the newspaper poets they loved in Sir John Suckling, Leigh Hunt, Ben Jonson, and Edward Lear. There they found the "Bab Ballads" of Gilbert. When Yip confessed to Ira that Gilbert was his favorite poet, Gershwin gently informed Harburg that Gilbert's "poems" were also song lyrics. He then invited his friend to the Gershwin home, where he played a recording of Gilbert and Sullivan's *H.M.S. Pinafore* (1878) on the family Victrola. "There were all the lines I knew by heart," Harburg recalled. "I was dumbfounded, staggered."

Harburg dated his ambition to become a lyricist from that moment, but such a dream should have been

United States Postal Service stamps, issued on 21 September 1999, commemorating lyricists and their composer-collaborators

impossible, for, while with Gilbert and Sullivan the words came first, in American songwriting the opposite was the case. The influence of ragtime and jazz on American popular music underscored the primacy of music, particularly music for dancing. With sprightly, syncopated rhythms, these melodies were tricky enough to set with simple, conversational lyrics, much less with witty, sophisticated light verse.

Yet, just as Harburg and other light-verse neophytes such as Ira Gershwin and Hart were about to enter their twenties, American music began to change in ways that made it possible for them to find in songwriting an outlet for their poetic aspirations. What happened might be described as the merger of Tin Pan Alley with Broadway. Tin Pan Alley was the nickname for the sheet-music-publishing industry that had dominated popular song in America since the 1880s. Many of these publishers had their offices on West Twenty-eighth Street in New York (where, so the story goes, the

din of plinking pianos creating, demonstrating, and "plugging" new songs earned the street its sobriquet). Tin Pan Alley had excelled from the first in marketing its songs to the public, rather than waiting, as traditional music publishers had done, for a song to become popular before publishing it. Most of the new publishing firms, such as Witmark and Sons, Remick, and Shapiro, Bernstein, were founded by Jewish immigrants who had started out as salesmen. Believing that if they could sell ties and corsets, they could make people want to buy their songs, they relentlessly plugged pieces until they *made* them popular.

Plugging was particularly important in the new form of variety entertainment known as vaudeville, which had developed alongside Tin Pan Alley. Growing out of minstrel shows and rough variety shows aimed at male audiences, vaudeville appealed to a family audience. In place of an ensemble of minstrelsy, vaudeville featured a "bill," a sequence of individual acts—singers, comedians, acrobats, and animal acts—most of which relied upon popular songs. Tin Pan Alley pluggers, therefore, sought out vaudeville stars to use their firm's songs in their acts, while vaudeville performers hoped a new song would catapult them to stardom. With two vast national circuits of theater houses in which to perform, the eastern Keith's and the western Orpheum, touring vaudeville companies could popularize a new song across American cities in a matter of months.

Yet, while vaudeville and Tin Pan Alley were interlocked, the Broadway musical theater initially had little use for the wares of Tin Pan Alley. Despite George M. Cohan's efforts to inject his Broadway scores with jaunty, ragtime-inspired music and catchy, vernacular lyrics, the American musical still clung to the model of Viennese operetta, either in such imports as Franz Lehár's *The Merry Widow* (1905) or in homegrown imitations such as Victor Herbert's *Naughty Marietta.* (1910). While songs from these scores occasionally became independently popular, such as "Ah! Sweet Mystery of Life," from *Naughty Marietta,* they were far more elevated, musically and lyrically, than the songs of Tin Pan Alley.

But World War I managed to do what not even Cohan had been able to do: Americanize the Broadway musical. Anti-German sentiment made Viennese operetta passé and opened the door to scores that sounded more American. In 1914 the quintessential Tin Pan Alley songwriter, Irving Berlin, tried his hand at his first Broadway score, *Watch Your Step,* and had both a successful "book show" as well as individual hit songs. Writing for Broadway made Berlin, at that time unable to read music or play piano in any but the key of F-sharp, strive for greater sophistication. In "Play a Simple Melody," from *Watch Your Step,* he crafted a contrapuntal song, in which two melodies and two sets of opposing lyrics are sung and played simultaneously in the pyrotechnic manner of Gilbert and Sullivan's patter songs.

While Berlin was raising himself from Tin Pan Alley to Broadway, another young composer, Jerome Kern, proved that a theatrical songwriter could handle the simple formulas of Tin Pan Alley with intricate sophistication. Kern's "They Didn't Believe Me" was interpolated into Paul Rubens and Sidney Jones's *The Girl from Utah* (1914) and became a huge success on Tin Pan Alley through sales of sheet music. When young George Gershwin heard an orchestra play the song at a wedding, he quit his job as a song plugger on Tin Pan Alley and went to work as Kern's rehearsal pianist on Broadway. Kern had shown the younger composer that popular songs emanating from the Broadway theater could be innovative and subtle even though they stayed within the confines of Alley formulas.

Just as Kern inspired younger composers such as George Gershwin and Richard Rodgers, one of his collaborators, P. G. Wodehouse, demonstrated to Ira Gershwin, Hart, and other lovers of light verse that they could ply their wit in song lyrics. In a series of influential musicals (1915–1918), called the "Princess shows" because some were staged at New York's small Princess Theatre, Wodehouse and Kern, along with librettist Guy Bolton, created the first genuinely modern American musical comedies. Unlike bloated Viennese operettas or the equally lavish revues of Florenz Ziegfeld, the Princess shows had small casts and orchestras and simple sets and costumes. The stories and characters were contemporary, with an emphasis on wit and sophistication that appealed to New York's emerging "smart set."

Wodehouse's lyrics were perfect for this new kind of musical. When Kern first asked him to collaborate, however, Wodehouse demurred after he found that he would be writing words after Kern had completed a melody. As an Englishman steeped in the tradition of Gilbert and Sullivan, Wodehouse believed that the words must come first. Still, at Kern's urging he tried setting words to completed melodies and found, to his delight, that he could create rhymes and other witty effects that he would have never imagined had he first written light verse and given it to Kern to set to music. Writing lyrics to music also enabled Wodehouse to create more-conversational lyrics, since the pattern of musical notes, while musically metrical, dictated verbal stresses that did not follow any regular poetic meter. A Gilbert lyric, for example, sounds like poetry in its strict, metrical regularity:

> When I merely from him parted,
> We were nearly broken-hearted;
> When in sequel reunited,
> We were equally delighted.

By contrast, a Wodehouse lyric, following a musical rhythm, sounds like ordinary speech:

> What bad luck, it's
> Coming down in buckets. . . .

Yet, within those musical rhythms Wodehouse was able to insert subtle rhymes ("luck, it's / . . . buckets") that rivaled Gilbert's.

The songs of Wodehouse and Kern thrilled young aspiring writers such as Ira Gershwin, Hart, and Harburg, who saw in them a way to channel their love of light verse into songwriting. When the nineteen-year-old Hart met the sixteen-year-old Rodgers, he launched into an attack on the current state of American songwriting, excoriating lyricists who knew nothing about triple rhymes, feminine rhymes, or slant rhymes and who could only come up with such simple combinations as *slush* and *mush*. Only Wodehouse was exempted from this attack, and when Hart found that Rodgers also adored the Princess shows, their collaboration was sealed.

Still, it took several years for Hart, Ira Gershwin, and Harburg to master the fundamentals of the lyricist's art before they could even try to exercise their talent for light verse in songwriting. One of their first lessons as apprentice lyricists was in how to make a lyric singable: "It takes years and years of experience," Gershwin observed in *Lyrics on Several Occasions,* "to know that such a note cannot take such a syllable, that many a poetic line can be unsingable, that many an ordinary line fitted into the proper musical phrase can sound like a million." They had to learn that liquid and nasal consonants were easier to sing, that a line should not end with words with harsh final consonant sounds (such as *talk* or *drop*), and that long open vowel sounds (*oh, ah, oo*) allowed a singer to sustain and project notes to the back rows of the balcony.

Another trick of the lyricist's trade was one that Harburg called "memorability": "When you're writing a song, where the rhyme falls makes it either hard or easy to remember. There are certain tricks that the skilled lyric writer has to make a song memorable, provided it doesn't become mechanical and the hinges don't stick out. In other words, you want to rhyme as many places as you can without the average ear spotting it as purely mechanical." In addition to end rhymes, lyricists learned to weave subtle internal rhymes through a lyric so that they were barely detectable by the listener. Thus, Berlin could weave the *el* rhyme through a line—"a m*el*ody m*el*low played on the c*el*lo h*el*ps Mister Cupid al*ong*"—while Cole Porter could deftly tie together his *i*-rhymes: "Fl*y*ing too h*igh* with some g*uy* in the sk*y* is m*y* *i*dea of nothing to do."

Above all, these young lyricists had to learn to confine themselves to the strictures of Tin Pan Alley's musical formulas. By 1920 the standard formula for popular songs had become the thirty-two-bar chorus, preceded by a brief introductory verse. This formula displaced the strophic form of song construction that had been dominant in the nineteenth century. In strophic song there is an alternation between verse and chorus (or, as it was often called, the "refrain"). Thus, in a song such as "My Darling Clementine," a series of verses, musically the same but each with a different lyric, carries the narrative ("In a cavern, in a canyon, excavating for a mine / Lived a miner forty-niner and his daughter Clementine"), while a brief refrain, usually of eight or sixteen bars, punctuates each verse with the same music and lyric ("Oh, my darlin', oh, my darlin', / Oh, my darlin' Clementine"). The modern formula, in contrast, made the chorus the primary part of the song, while the verse merely introduced the chorus and was

frequently omitted by singers. Thus, few people would recognize a song from a verse that began "I'm discontented with homes that are rented so I have invented my own," but they would know it instantly once the chorus began: "Picture you upon my knee and tea for two and two for tea."

The modern chorus was itself a sleek, streamlined structure, befitting the Art Deco style of the Jazz Age. Almost always thirty-two bars long, it was divided musically into four eight-bar sections, frequently in an AABA pattern. That is, the melodic phrase in the first eight bars (A) was repeated in the second eight bars. The next eight bars (B) introduced a different melodic phrase, referred to as the release or the bridge since it led into the final eight bars, which restated the initial melody (A). The formula was a superbly crafted structure that introduced a catchy melodic phrase and then repeated it, since listeners, upon hearing a lovely melody, want, like Duke Orsino in William Shakespeare's *Twelfth Night,* to hear "That strain again." Before the repetition becomes cloying, the release introduces a new melody, but after that variation the chorus ends with a welcome return of the original melodic phrase. While the AABA pattern was the most popular, other patterns were also used, such as ABAB, ABAC, and, more rarely, ABCD.

Such musical formulas posed a challenge for lyricists, for it gave them as few as sixty or seventy words in which to develop a theme, which had to follow the structure of the music. Berlin's "Blue Skies" (1926), for example, opens with a brief introductory verse ("I was blue, / Just as blue as I could be . . .") and then moves to an AABA chorus, in which the three A sections open with parallel phrases: "Blue skies / Smiling at me," "Bluebirds / Singing a song," and "Blue days, / All of them gone." The release, by contrast, introduces a new musical and lyrical turn: "Never saw the sun / Shining so bright. . . ." In such a structure the most critical stage is the point at which the release turns back toward the final A section. In "Blue Skies" Berlin handles this transition deftly by having the singer reflect that "[w]hen you're in love, / My how" the days "fly," a sweet-sour Keatsian observation that recognizes the transience of happiness. Then, as the final A section opens with "Blue days, / All of them gone," Berlin turns the connotation of *blue* from the joyous "blue skies" and "bluebirds" to the blues—gone for now but always a threat to return.

Berlin was a master at manipulating this constricting formula, and it is little wonder that he admired the poet Alexander Pope for his ability to handle the equally demanding confines of the heroic couplet. For other Tin Pan Alley lyricists, such as Gus Kahn, the musical formula made a lyricist's task clear: "You gotta say 'I Love You' in thirty-two bars." The musical strictures made love the pervasive theme of popular songs from this period. Given the relatively few approaches one can take to romantic themes, lyricists understandably wondered, as Ira Gershwin and Harburg put it in one of their songs, "What Can You Say In a Love Song (That Hasn't Been Said Before)?" (1934). Writing about love was made even more difficult by the paucity of rhymes for the word *love* in the English language. While a Romance language such as French has fifty-one rhymes for *amour*, English has only five for *love: dove, above, shove, glove,* and *of.*

Lyricists who wrote for the musical theater had still another hurdle to face with each song. The lyric for a theater song had to have what songwriters called "particularity," qualities that tailored it to a specific character and dramatic situation. Theater songs of the 1920s and 1930s, such as "Someone to Watch Over Me" (1926) or "My Funny Valentine" (1937), seldom had the fully integrated character of those of the 1940s and 1950s, when songs such as "The Surrey with the Fringe on Top" (1943) or "The Rain in Spain" (1956) were so completely integrated into the dramatic context that upon hearing the song one instantly recalls the scene from the musical. Still, the "particular" songs from musicals of the 1920s and 1930s had to carry an additional burden of character and drama that sometimes also infused nontheatrical songs, such as Kahn's "It Had To Be You" (1924).

After a long apprenticeship in making lyrics singable and memorable, shaping them to the musical formulas of Tin Pan Alley, and giving them the requisite "particularity" for musical theater, young lyricists who had been reared on light verse began to make themselves heard in the 1920s. If there was one lyric that typified the new character of American popular song, it was Rodgers and Hart's "Manhattan" (1925). Long dismissed by Broadway producers as "too collegiate," Rodgers and Hart were invited to contribute songs to *The Garrick Gaieties* of 1925, a fund-raising revue for the Theatre Guild. Hart's lyrics to "Manhattan" were so witty, intricate, and insouciant, that what was to have been a two-performance run played for several months. From the initial "We'll have Manhattan, / The Bronx and Staten / Island too" to "The city's clamor can never spoil / The charms of a boy and goil," "Manhattan" established a new level of artistry in song lyrics.

F.P.A. took note of Hart's lyrics in his light-verse column, and soon other critics, who had rarely singled out lyrics in their reviews of musicals, devoted their attention to the way, for example, Ira Gershwin's vernacular slang complemented his brother George's jazzy melodies in the 1924 production *Lady, Be Good!* The 30 December 1925 issue of *Variety* magazine proclaimed a "lyrical renaissance," praising Hart, Gershwin, Howard Dietz, and other "newer lyric writers" as bringing a new level of sophistication to American song. Soon even Por-

ter, long dismissed by Broadway producers as being too highbrow, was to gain acceptance with his first hit song: the delightfully naughty "Let's Do It," from the 1928 production *Paris.*

This lyrical renaissance coincided with a series of related technological developments—the electric phonograph, the radio, and the microphone—that altered the character of American popular song. As with so many other aspects of American culture in the 1920s, Americans were becoming consumers rather than producers. The parlor piano of the late nineteenth century, around which the family gathered to play and sing songs, was now replaced by the phonograph, on which they merely listened to songs. Radio, developed in 1921, remained a toy until stations began playing popular songs. Soon listeners tuned in, and radio sales hit $60 million in 1922, doubled in 1923, more than tripled that figure in 1925, and surpassed $500 million in 1926.

Both radio and recording studios employed the microphone, and singers learned to use the device to render a song more casually and intimately. Songwriters sought to imbue their songs with these qualities, and there was a renewed emphasis upon the introspective, romantic lyric, or what was sometimes called the "sob ballad." The master of this form was Irving Berlin, whose 1924 ballads "All Alone" and "What'll I Do" were introduced over the radio; sales of the song recordings exceeded the sheet-music sales. Aimed at the youthful audience of the 1920s, primarily at the many young women who had moved to cities to take jobs in offices and department stores, these songs appealed to romantic longings and lonely reflection.

By playing songs on the air, radio initially helped but ultimately eroded the quality of American popular music. The airing of popular songs had long been a delicate issue for songwriters. On the one hand, the more often a song was heard, the more popular it became, but if it was aired too often, listeners tired of it and looked for another "hit" to replace it. If people bought sheet music and recordings of a song while it was still popular, the songwriters profited, but if listeners could hear the songs on the radio, they might not buy their own copies. A similar problem had led to the creation of the Association of Composers, Authors, and Publishers (ASCAP) in 1914. ASCAP was a licensing organization formed by songwriters to charge and collect fees from restaurants, cabarets, and other establishments that hired singers and musicians to perform popular songs to entertain their customers. Restaurant owners at first refused to pay such fees, arguing that songwriters ought to be grateful that their songs were being performed, since such airing would boost sheet-music and record sales. In 1917, however, U.S. Supreme Court Chief Justice Oliver Wendell Holmes ruled on behalf of ASCAP.

In the 1920s ASCAP protected members by requiring radio stations to pay licensing fees in order to play their songs, though station owners, like restaurateurs the decade before, protested that they should not have to pay for the "free" promotion they were providing for the songs. Some songwriters, notably Berlin, worried that radio undercut their sheet-music and record sales and that the incessant playing of songs wore out their popularity. He feared that in time the quality of songwriting would deteriorate with radio listeners' voracious demand for new hits. Berlin's fears, though prescient, were not realized until the 1940s. Until then, ASCAP songs dominated American popular music. The songwriters of the organization enjoyed a monopoly on American popular song, and they saw little need to alter their successful formula—the thirty-two-bar chorus, the AABA structure, and the light-verse flippancy that gave the songs their sophisticated, urbane (and distinctly urban) character.

Fueled by the prosperity of the Roaring Twenties, the Broadway musical enjoyed its most heady days by showcasing such songs. One indication of how the Great White Way thrived at this time is that in 1927 twenty new shows opened during the week of Christmas—eleven of them premiering on the night of 26 December—including Kern and Oscar Hammerstein 2nd's *Show Boat*, Bert Kalmar and Harry Ruby's *The 5 O'Clock Girl*, and Buddy DeSylva, Lew Brown, and Ray Henderson's *Good News*. The lyrics of these shows looked in two directions. On the one hand, revues and loosely conceived "book shows" presented songs that were designed to become hits on Tin Pan Alley through sheet-music and record sales. On the other hand, lyricists and playwrights were tailoring songs to fit integrally into character and dramatic situation. This move toward full integration of song with story was led by Hammerstein, who, with Kern in *Show Boat*, managed to merge the American musical with European operetta. Hammerstein's achievement was not fully realized until 1943, when his collaboration with Rodgers on *Oklahoma!* established the "integrated" musical on Broadway. Other lyricists and composers were pushing toward integration of music and story in the 1920s, such as Rodgers and Hart, whose *A Connecticut Yankee* (1927) featured songs, such as "Thou Swell," that grew out of the characters and story of Mark Twain's *A Connecticut Yankee in King Arthur's Court* (1889). The Gershwins, working with George S. Kaufman, produced a political satire, *Strike Up the Band* (1930), which stood squarely in the tradition of the comic operettas of Gilbert and Sullivan.

Even as songwriters strove for more integration between songs and story, however, they continued to use the Tin Pan Alley formulas and design their songs for independent popularity beyond the show. Even "Ol' Man River," from *Show Boat*, is built on the thirty-two bar AABA chorus. A typical way to balance integration and popularity was to use the verse of a song to tie it to character and dramatic situation in the musical but keep the chorus more generally expressive, so that it could be sung, as it frequently was, without the verse by singers making recordings or performing in nightclubs. Many songs, such as the Gershwins' "'S Wonderful" (1927), were done in shows as duets, with a "boy" verse for the leading man and a "girl" verse for the ingénue. The lyrics of the chorus, however, were androgynous—a "me" cooing to a "you"—so that the pair could sing the chorus in unison on stage but, more important, so that the song would be suitable for either male or female singers and could go on to independent popularity beyond the show.

This balance between integration and popularity marked theater songs of the 1920s and 1930s. Whereas a composer-lyricist today, such as Stephen Sondheim, would never expect one of his songs, even from a successful show such as *Sunday in the Park with George* (1984), to become independently popular, the Gershwins, Berlin, and Porter considered a show a success only if several of its songs went on to become Tin Pan Alley hits. They were writing for New York theater audiences, who expected wit and sophistication, but they also wrote for the general public, who might embrace a song without ever realizing that it came from a Broadway show. Ultimately, however, these songwriters wrote for the toughest audience of all: themselves. They regularly gathered—at the Gershwins' penthouse, at a Porter soiree—to play their latest songs for one another. As Harburg observed, a lyricist would never dare to sing a poor rhyme in the company of Ira Gershwin and Hart. Never again since that time has the Broadway theater produced such songs that spanned the spectrum from witty elegance to mass appeal.

Broadway, however, was not the only venue for these lyricists. Nightclubs flourished during Prohibition, particularly in Harlem, where white patrons flocked to hear jazz and blues from performers such as Duke Ellington, Ethel Waters, and Louis Armstrong. Nightspots such as the Cotton Club put on spectacular revues filled with songs by lyricists such as Fields, Andy Razaf, Ted Koehler, and Mitchell Parish. While some of these lyricists had also begun as writers of what Fields called "smarty verse," they wrote in a distinctively vernacular idiom designed to match the riff-based melodies of composers such as Fats Waller, Harold Arlen, Hoagy Carmichael, and Jimmy McHugh. Such revues frequently went on to play in Broadway theaters, and after the stock-market crash of 1929 the revue became the dominant musical-theater genre as the Depression made lavish, expensive book musicals unfeasible.

Along with these nightclub revues came the satirical "little" revues that built songs and sketches around topical themes. Newer lyricists, such as Dietz and Harburg, flourished in this format, which called for witty songs that could serve as the basis for a comic sketch or that carried their own self-contained dramatic situation. Asked by his producer to write a song to go with a Parisian set, Harburg, who had never been to Paris, got some travel brochures and built the lyric for "April in Paris" (1932) around the character of a woman sitting at a Parisian café. With his light-verse training, however, Harburg could not rest with the clichéd situation of having her simply recall an old lover: "I doubt that I can ever say 'I Love You' head on," he said. "For me the task is never to say the thing directly, and yet to say it—to think in a curve, so to speak." His curve in this lyric was to portray a woman who has never been in love before ("never missed a warm embrace") but now, in an even greater tribute to the power of Paris in the spring, wishes she had—just so she might enjoy a romantic memory.

Some of the revues of the 1930s, such as Moss Hart and Irving Berlin's *As Thousands Cheer* (1933), were as literate and sophisticated as a traditional book show. "Supper Time"—in which a black woman, who has just learned that her husband has been lynched, struggles to put dinner on the table for her children and wonders how to tell them their father is dead—has as much character and dramatic power as "Ol' Man River" from *Show Boat*. Some of the relatively few book musicals of the early Depression years continued to advance the development of the integrated show, most notably the Gershwins' political satires *Of Thee I Sing* (1931) and *Let 'Em Eat Cake* (1933), both with books by Kaufman and Morrie Ryskind. This development was slowed, however, by the fact that songwriters were leaving Broadway altogether and moving to Hollywood.

When Al Jolson belted out Berlin's "Blue Skies" from the hitherto silent screen in *The Jazz Singer* (1927), it brought the American popular song into the world of motion pictures more fully than it had ever been before. Popular songs had been involved with movies from the earliest days of the nickelodeons, when singers would entertain audiences between reel changes as slides of romantic photographs—and song lyrics—flashed on the screen. Many silent movies had theme songs that helped to promote the picture (as the movie, in turn, would boost sheet-music sales of the song). But in *The Jazz Singer,* for the first time, songs were sung directly from the screen (although the movie was silent except for the song sequences). In the "Blue Skies" sequence in particular, Jolson regales his mother with his talents and also banters with her in an impromptu monologue, revealing how much more intimately and colloquially a song could be presented on screen than in a stage performance.

For the next few years studios satisfied audience appetites for the novelty of sound pictures with a flood of stilted musicals. The 1952 masterpiece *Singin' in the Rain* hilariously details the problems with camera noise, stationary microphones, and poor synchronization between sound and image that plagued early musicals. But an even more fundamental aesthetic problem haunted these movies. Given the inherent realism of motion pictures, producers feared that audiences would simply not accept the convention of characters suddenly bursting into—and out of—song, without even the applause that cushions such transitions in the musical theater. Their solution was to make movie musicals about singers—such as *The Jazz Singer*—in which actors had an "excuse" to sing because they portrayed singers. When they sang, therefore, they were "performing" before an audience in a theater or club, rehearsing, or simply demonstrating their professional talents. Most motion-picture musicals were "backstagers," in which a Broadway troupe struggles to mount a musical or neighborhood kids "put on a show."

There were a few exceptions to the rule that all movie songs had to be presented as performances: cartoon characters could burst into song, as could children, and, in pictures such as *Hallelujah* (1929), black characters could break into song and dance as expressions of their stereotypical "spontaneity." In most early motion-picture musicals, however, songs continued to be portrayed as performances, and this meant that the kind of songs needed for these movies were the same kind of popular songs that had been emanating from Broadway and Tin Pan Alley for more than two decades. Berlin's "Blue Skies," featured in *The Jazz Singer,* was already a hit in 1927, having been interpolated into Rodgers and Hart's score of the 1926 Broadway musical *Betsy.* Thus, the development of sound pictures did not bring with it a new kind of song but provided instead another venue for the type of song that had been first developed on Tin Pan Alley and then adapted for the Broadway musical.

Songwriting teams such as DeSylva, Brown, and Henderson; Kalmar and Ruby; and Arthur Freed and Nacio Herb Brown were some of the first to work in Hollywood. There they made the formulaic simplicity of their songs even more streamlined to meet the demand for songs presented as performances. Soon, however, the novelty of talking pictures wore off, and audiences became bored with the same old backstager plots. By 1930 people were asking at movie box offices if the current feature was a musical and walking away if it was. Studios responded by cutting back drastically on the production of musicals and even taking those that had already been filmed and crudely cutting out the songs before releasing them.

Thus, the first years of the Depression were bleak ones for songwriters, since both Broadway and Hollywood provided few opportunities for writing scores. Only radio, the cheapest form of entertainment for most Americans, provided a major outlet. Berlin, in a creative depression of his own at the same time, had gone for several years without a show on Broadway and had seen his songs for the 1931 movie *Reaching for the Moon* gutted from the final print. Nevertheless, his spirits revived when two of his songs of 1932–"Say It Isn't So" and "How Deep Is the Ocean?"–were made into hits by the radio crooners Rudy Vallee and Bing Crosby, respectively.

Like Berlin, the Hollywood musical made a comeback in 1932. For one thing, technology improved to the point that cameras no longer had to be enclosed in stationary sound-proof boxes, enabling them to be moved during filming. Newer microphones could also follow along with performers, increasing the liveliness of the filmed performance. Finally, the playback was perfected, so that performers could record a song in a sound studio and then lip-synch to their own prerecorded singing during the actual filming, giving songs an even more casual, informal quality. Paramount continued to produce musicals during the early years of the Depression, but instead of making backstagers, they imported European directors of operetta, most notably Ernst Lubitsch and Rouben Mamoulian, to create sophisticated, slightly risqué musicals built around such performers as Maurice Chevalier and Jeanette MacDonald. With the European settings of these movies, audiences accepted the convention that characters broke into song, not as performances, but as effusive expressions of what they were feeling at a given dramatic moment. Thus, in *Monte Carlo* (1930), when MacDonald runs away from her wedding, boards a train, and exultantly sings "Beyond the Blue Horizon" as the engine speeds past rolling fields, the song is intricately woven into the dramatic texture of the movie as no song had been before. Rodgers and Hart worked with Mamoulian on *Love Me Tonight* (1932), creating a brilliant musical in which the songs were integrated into the story, rhymed dialogue eased the transition from speech to song, and the camera helped in the dramatic development of the songs. In movies, Rodgers and Hart believed, the American popular song had found its true home. There, a lyric could be much more casually colloquial than it could ever be on stage, and camera and lighting effects could render a song more intimately–as well as more spectacularly–than any stage performance.

In 1933 Warner Bros. revived the backstager with *42nd Street*. With the choreography of Busby Berkeley and the jazzy songs of Al Dubin and Harry Warren, the tired clichés of Broadway kids putting on a show took on a vibrant and gritty new realism that resonated with the worst period of the Depression. The success of *42nd Street* spawned a series of similar movies–*Dames* (1934) and *Gold Diggers of 1935* (1935)–in which Berkeley, Dubin, and Warren revitalized the backstager formula with songs such as "I Only Have Eyes for You" and "Lullaby of Broadway."

The movie musical was suddenly alive and well, and the most sophisticated Broadway songwriters–Kern, Porter, and the Gershwins–were attracted to Hollywood. The most relished assignment was writing songs for a Fred Astaire musical. RKO, a small studio on the verge of bankruptcy, had paired the aging Broadway star with the saucy Ginger Rogers. Blending the innovations of Paramount and Warner Bros., RKO created musicals, often with European settings, in which contemporary American characters broke into song–and even dance–with a graceful ease that audiences readily accepted. RKO also brought in the finest songwriters to tailor songs for Astaire's casually elegant style, which became the perfect embodiment of the sophistication of the era's best light-verse lyrics. Porter's songs were featured in *The Gay Divorcee* (1934), Berlin's in *Top Hat* (1935), Kern and Fields's in *Swing Time* (1936), and the Gershwins' in *Shall We Dance?* (1937). Writing for Astaire brought out the best in these great lyricists, and his debonair style inspired their finest blends of sophistication ("*la belle–*") and vernacular ease ("the perfectly swell–romance"), as in Kern and Fields's "Never Gonna Dance" (1936). The new technology also meant that lyricists could throw out some of the old rules of songwriting, such as providing singers with long open vowels so that they could project syllables to the back of a theater. With microphones and playbacks, lyricists could use the short vowels and strong consonants that are so common in the English language–"Let's Call the Whole Thing Off," "They All Laughed," "A Fine Romance," "Nice Work if You Can Get It"–making their lyrics even more casually conversational.

Toward the latter part of the 1930s, Broadway musicals gradually made a comeback as well. Shows such as Rodgers and Hart's *Babes in Arms* (1937) and *The Boys from Syracuse* (1938), Porter's *Red, Hot and Blue* (1936) and *Leave It to Me* (1938), and even the Gershwins and DuBose Heyward's opera *Porgy and Bess* (1935) continued to balance the demand for integrating songs into the story of a musical with appealing to the general popular market. With Rodgers and Hart's *Pal Joey* (1940) and *Lady in the Dark* (1941), by Ira Gershwin, Kurt Weill, and Moss Hart, the balance shifted toward the more fully integrated song.

The 1943 production *Oklahoma!* brought the movement toward integration to fulfillment and launched another important phase in the history of musical theater and American popular song. Rodgers had initially proposed writing a musical based on Lynn Riggs's play *Green Grow the Lilacs* (1931), but Lorenz Hart had scoffed at the idea of writing a musical about farmers and cow-boys in Oklahoma. Rodgers then turned to Hammer-stein, who had experienced years of frustration in Hollywood and longed to continue the kind of musical drama he had inaugurated with *Show Boat*. Unlike Hart, Ira Gershwin, and other lyricists of his day, Hammer-stein's early roots were in operetta, and he was skilled at taking a literary work such as a novel or a play and adapting it into a libretto for a musical. By doing both "book" (libretto) and lyrics, Hammerstein could create the most integrated kind of musical, and in *Oklahoma!* the songs were more tightly tied to character and dramatic situation than in any previous show.

The success of *Oklahoma!* also reflected America's embrace of regionalism and the folk past during the try-ing times of World War II. The black-tie, Art Deco ele-gance of the 1930s became a thing of the past, and the deaths of George Gershwin in 1937 and of Lorenz Hart in 1943 marked the end of an era of urbane sophistica-tion. While Porter and Berlin adjusted to the new emphasis upon integrated musicals with shows such as *Kiss Me, Kate* (1948) and *Annie Get Your Gun* (1946), respectively, other lyricists who had flourished in the 1920s and 1930s gave way to younger talents, such as Frank Loesser and Alan Jay Lerner, who wrote songs but, like Hammerstein, could also write or adapt the "book" for a musical, making for remarkable integration of song and story. Musicals from this era, such as Loesser's *Guys and Dolls* (1950) and *The Most Happy Fella* (1956) and Lerner and Frederick Loewe's *Brigadoon* (1947) and *My Fair Lady* (1956), are regularly revived on Broadway, along with those of Rodgers and Hammer-stein, while revivals of musicals from the 1920s and 1930s, such as *Crazy For You*, the 1992 revival of the Gershwins' *Girl Crazy* (1930), frequently require a major overhaul to bring songs and story into alignment.

"Original cast" albums enabled songs closely tied to the story and characters of a musical to become inde-pendently popular. Such albums, originally boxed sets of 78-rpm records that included all of the songs from a musical, enabled individual selections as closely tied to the book of the musical as "The Surrey with the Fringe on Top" and the title song from *Oklahoma!* to be aired on radio and achieve popularity, even for people who had never seen a production of the show. By the late 1940s another development, the "LP" (long-playing) record, allowed an entire Broadway score to be recorded on a single large disk that could be played on new "hi-fi" (high-fidelity) phonographs.

Such LPs also revived many songs—if not entire shows—of the 1920s and 1930s. Initially marketed for the classical-music audience, the LP targeted other "adult" listeners after the 45-rpm record was developed. Now teenagers could purchase "singles" cheaply and play

them on equally cheap record players. Singers from the big-band era, such as Frank Sinatra and Doris Day, had hit singles with contemporary songs such as "Hey! Jeal-ous Lover" (1956) and "Que Será, Será" (1955), respec-tively, but when they recorded LPs, they needed twelve to sixteen songs of high quality. They turned back to the Broadway and Hollywood songs of the 1920s, 1930s, and 1940s by songwriters such as Rodgers and Hart, Porter, Berlin, and the Gershwins, helping to transform those songs into the "standards" still enjoyed today. Sinatra alone could take a handful of songs from Rod-gers and Hart's long-forgotten 1937 show *Babes in Arms*—"My Funny Valentine," "The Lady Is a Tramp," "Where or When," and "I Wish I Were in Love Again"—and turn them into swinging, contemporary hits some twenty years later.

During the period of integration of song and story in Broadway shows, a similar integration in Hollywood musicals was taking place. Lyricist-turned-producer Freed nurtured musicals at M-G-M in which songs were tightly tied to the story and characters, such as *The Wiz-ard of Oz* (1939), *Meet Me in St. Louis* (1944), and *The Har-vey Girls* (1946). He also oversaw movie musicals that took an existing set of songs and wove a story around them—the songs of the Gershwins for *An American in Paris* (1951), those of Dietz and Arthur Schwartz for *The Band Wagon* (1954), and Freed's own songs with composer Nacio Herb Brown for perhaps the greatest motion-pic-ture musical of all, *Singin' in the Rain*.

Even as the musical flowered on stage and screen, however, the character of American song had begun to change once more. In 1941 ASCAP and radio squared off when stations refused to pay the higher fees the orga-nization demanded to renew their licenses to play ASCAP members' songs. Although the dispute was eventually resolved, radio stations sought out other song-writers, primarily from the Midwest and the South, and formed a rival licensing organization, Broadcast Music Incorporated (BMI). These songwriters, many of them black and country musicians, did not write for Broadway or Hollywood but aimed their songs for the record, radio, and new jukebox market. The enormous popular-ity in 1940 of "You Are My Sunshine," a country song built on the old strophic verse-chorus pattern, signaled the demise of the slick, urbane (and urban) song formula of the thirty-two-bar chorus. By the 1950s a wholly new kind of music was emerging that eventually brought an end to the great era of Rodgers and Hart, the Gershwins, Porter, and Berlin.

The movement toward integration of song and plot in the stage and screen musical carried that form away from popular taste, despite the enormous popu-larity of such songs as "The Rain in Spain," from *My Fair Lady,* and "Trouble," from Meredith Willson's *The*

Music Man (1957). New kinds of freestanding songs, from black rhythm-and-blues and white country-and-western sources, continued to "cross over" as mainstream popular music. The Broadway musical became increasingly operatic, so that, today, it is rare for a song from such a musical to become popular. By the mid 1950s the rise of television, along with other economic factors, shut down the creation of original Hollywood musicals and had studios relying upon proven Broadway successes. With only a few exceptions these stage musicals were filmed in stiff and slavish adherence to the Broadway original with only a token cast change, such as Audrey Hepburn for Julie Andrews in the movie version of *My Fair Lady* (1964).

Today, the crafting of lyrics that flourished during that period is almost a lost art. Many performers now write their own music and lyrics, and songs are indelibly linked to a single performer. There is little connection between songs for musical theater and the popular-song market, and spectacular stage effects have diminished the importance of lyrics in contemporary theater songs. Hollywood has made few original musicals since the 1960s, and audiences no longer accept the convention that characters on screen can spontaneously burst into song. Yet, the songs of the 1920s and 1930s did what few popular songs of any other era have done—they transcended their own heyday to become timeless "standards." Heard in Broadway revivals, Hollywood soundtracks, jazz performances, and even in television commercials, these evergreens sound as fresh today as when they were first performed. Interpreted anew by each successive generation of singers and musicians, these songs are the closest thing America has to a vital body of classical music.

The lyricists, who were primarily responsible for the alchemy that blended music and words into song, deserve their place in American literary history. The light-verse poets they emulated in their youth—F.P.A., Marquis, and Witter Bynner—are largely forgotten, while such major poets of the twentieth century as Pound, T. S. Eliot, and Wallace Stevens are hardly read outside of the academic world. When ordinary Americans look for words at some emotional moment in their lives, they are likely to turn to Lorenz Hart ("Your looks are laughable, / Unphotographable, / Yet you're my fav'rite work of art"), Ira Gershwin ("There's a somebody I'm longing to see: / I hope that he / Turns out to be / Someone who'll watch over me"),

or Harburg ("Birds fly over the rainbow / Why then oh why can't I?").

Acknowledgments

This book was produced by Bruccoli Clark Layman, Inc. Karen L. Rood is senior editor. Bland Lawson was the in-house editor.

Production manager is Philip B. Dematteis.

Administrative support was provided by Ann M. Cheschi and Carol Cheschi.

Accountant is Ann-Marie Holland.

Copyediting supervisor is Sally R. Evans. The copyediting staff includes Phyllis A. Avant, Brenda Carol Blanton, Caryl Brown, Melissa D. Hinton, Philip I. Jones, Rebecca Mayo, Nancy E. Smith, and Elizabeth Jo Ann Sumner.

Editorial associates are Michael S. Allen, Michael S. Martin, and Catherine M. Polit.

Amber L. Coker is permissions editor and database manager.

Layout and graphics supervisor is Janet E. Hill. The graphics staff includes Zoe R. Cook and Sydney Hammock.

Office manager is Kathy Lawler Merlette.

Photography supervisor is Paul Talbot. Photography editor is Scott Nemzek.

Digital photographic copy work was performed by Joseph M. Bruccoli.

Systems manager is Marie L. Parker.

Typesetting supervisor is Kathleen M. Flanagan. The typesetting staff includes Patricia Marie Flanagan, Mark J. McEwan, and Pamela D. Norton. Freelance typesetter is Wanda Adams.

Walter W. Ross did library research. He was assisted by Jo Cottingham and the following other librarians at the Thomas Cooper Library of the University of South Carolina: circulation department head Tucker Taylor; reference department head Virginia W. Weathers; reference department staff Brette Barron, Marilee Birchfield, Paul Cammarata, Gary Geer, Michael Macan, Tom Marcil, Rose Marshall, and Sharon Verba; interlibrary loan department head John Brunswick; and interlibrary loan staff Robert Arndt, Hayden Battle, Alex Byrne, Bill Fetty, Marna Hostetler, and Nelson Rivera.

Dictionary of Literary Biography® • Volume Two Hundred Sixty-Five

American Song Lyricists, 1920–1960

Dictionary of Literary Biography

Harold Adamson
(10 December 1906 – 17 August 1980)

Anna Wheeler Gentry

SELECTED SONGS FROM THEATRICAL PRO-
DUCTIONS: *Smiles* (1930), lyrics by Adamson
and Clifford Grey, music by Vincent Youmans–
"I'm Glad I Waited"; "Time on My Hands (You
in My Arms)" (lyrics by Adamson and Mack
Gordon);
Earl Carroll Vanities (1931), music by Burton Lane–
"Have a Heart";
Banjo Eyes (1941), music by Vernon Duke–"Make with
the Feet"; "We're Having a Baby";
As the Girls Go (1948), music by Jimmy McHugh–"As
the Girls Go"; "Father's Day"; "(I Got) Lucky in
the Rain"; "It Takes a Woman to Get a Man";
"It's More Fun than a Picnic"; "Nobody's Heart
but Mine"; "Rock, Rock, Rock"; "There's No
Getting Away from You"; "You Say the Nicest
Things, Baby."

SELECTED SONGS FROM MOTION-PICTURE
PRODUCTIONS: *Dancing Lady* (1933), music by
Burton Lane–"Everything I Have Is Yours";
"Heigh-Ho! The Gang's All Here" (lyrics adapted
by Adamson from D. A. Esrom, music adapted
by Lane from Sir Arthur Sullivan and Theodore
Morse); "Let's Go Bavarian";
Bottoms Up (1934), music by Lane–"I'm Throwin' My
Love Away"; "Little Did I Dream"; "Turn on the
Moon";
Kid Millions (1934)–"Your Head on My Shoulder"
(music by Lane);
Palooka (1934)–"Like Me a Little Bit Less (Love Me a
Little Bit More)" (music by Lane);
Here Comes the Band (1935)–"Tender Is the Night"
(music by Walter Donaldson);

Harold Adamson

Reckless (1935)–"Everything's Been Done Before" (lyr-
ics by Adamson and Edwin H. Knopf, music by
Jack King); "Hear What My Heart Is Saying"
(music by Lane);
Banjo on My Knee (1936), music by Jimmy McHugh–
"There's Something in the Air"; "Where the Lazy
River Goes By"; "With a Banjo on My Knee";

The Great Ziegfeld (1936), music by Donaldson—"It's Been So Long"; "You"; "You Gotta Pull Strings"; "You Never Looked So Beautiful";

Suzy (1936)—"Did I Remember (To Tell You I Adore You)?" (music by Donaldson);

Top of the Town (1936), music by McHugh—"Blame It on the Rhumba"; "Jamboree"; "That Foolish Feeling"; "There's No Two Ways about It"; "Top of the Town"; "Where Are You?";

You're a Sweetheart (1937), music by McHugh—"Broadway Jamboree"; "You're a Sweetheart";

Hitting a New High (1938), music by McHugh—"I Hit a New High"; "Let's Give Love Another Chance"; "This Never Happened Before";

Mad about Music (1938), music by McHugh—"Chapel Bells"; "I Love to Whistle"; "A Serenade to the Stars";

Merry-Go-Round of 1938 (1938)—"You're My Dish" (music by McHugh);

That Certain Age (1938), music by McHugh—"Be a Good Scout"; "(Has Anyone Ever Told You) You're As Pretty as a Picture"; "My Own"; "That Certain Age";

Around the World (1943), music by McHugh—"Candlelight and Wine"; "Don't Believe Everything You Dream"; "Roodle-De-Doo"; "They Just Chopped Down the Old Apple Tree";

Higher and Higher (1943), music by McHugh—"I Couldn't Sleep a Wink Last Night"; "I Saw You First"; "It's a Most Important Affair"; "A Lovely Way to Spend an Evening"; "Minuet in Boogie" (based on Ignacy Paderewski's Minuet in G); "The Music Stopped"; "Today I'm a Debutante"; "You're on Your Own";

Hit Parade of 1943 (1943), music by Jule Styne—"A Change of Heart"; "Do These Old Eyes Deceive Me"; "Harlem Sandman"; "Tahm Boom Bah"; "That's How to Write a Song"; "Who Took Me Home Last Night";

Thousands Cheer (1943)—"Daybreak" (music by Ferde Grofé);

Bathing Beauty (1944)—"I'll Take the High Note" (music by Johnny Green);

Four Jills In a Jeep (1944), music by McHugh—"Crazy Me"; "How Blue the Night"; "How Many Times Do I Have to Tell You?"; "Ohio"; "You Send Me";

The Princess and the Pirate (1944)—"(How Would You Like to) Kiss Me in the Moonlight" (music by McHugh);

Something for the Boys (1944), music by McHugh—"Eighty Miles Outside of Atlanta"; "I Wish We Didn't Have to Say Goodnight"; "In the Middle of Nowhere"; "Wouldn't It Be Nice?";

The All-Star Bond Rally (1945)—"Buy a Bond" (music by McHugh);

Doll Face (1945), music by McHugh—"Chico Chico"; "Dig You Later (A Hubba-Hubba-Hubba)"; "Here Comes Heaven Again"; "Red, Hot and Beautiful"; "Somebody's Walkin' in My Dreams";

Nob Hill (1945), music by McHugh—"I Don't Care Who Knows It"; "I Walked In (With My Eyes Wide Open)";

Do You Love Me? (1946)—"I Didn't Mean a Word I Said" (music by McHugh);

Hit Parade of 1947 (1947), music by McHugh—"I Guess I'll Have That Dream Right Now"; "Is There Anyone Here from Texas?";

Smash-Up (1947), music by McHugh—"Hush-a-Bye Island"; "I Miss That Feeling"; "Life Can Be Beautiful";

A Date with Judy (1948)—"It's a Most Unusual Day" (music by McHugh);

If You Knew Susie (1948)—"My How the Time Goes By" (music by McHugh);

His Kind of Woman (1951)—"You'll Know" (music by McHugh);

The Las Vegas Story (1951)—"My Resistance Is Low" (music by Hoagy Carmichael);

Gentlemen Prefer Blondes (1953), music by Carmichael—"Ain't There Anyone Here for Love"; "When Love Goes Wrong";

Jupiter's Darling (1955), music by Lane—"Don't Let This Night Get Away"; "Hannibal's Victory March"; "I Have a Dream"; "I Never Trust a Woman"; "If This Be Slav'ry"; "The Life of an Elephant";

Three for the Show (1955)—"Down Boy!" (music by Carmichael);

Around the World in 80 Days (1956)—"Around the World" (music by Victor Young);

Strip for Action (1956), music by McHugh—"I Just Found Out about Love"; "Love Me as Though There Were No Tomorrow"; "Strip for Action"; "Too Young to Go Steady";

An Affair to Remember (1957), lyrics by Adamson and Leo McCarey, music by Harry Warren—"An Affair to Remember"; "The Tiny Scout"; "Tomorrow Land"; "You Make It Easy to Be True";

Seven Hills of Rome (1957)—"The Seven Hills of Rome" (music by Young);

Separate Tables (1958)—"Separate Tables" (music by Warren).

SELECTED SONGS PUBLISHED INDEPENDENTLY OF THEATRICAL OR MOTION-PICTURE PRODUCTIONS: "Say the Word" (1931), music by Burton Lane;

Sheet music for the 1936 song, with music by Walter Donaldson, that brought Adamson his first Academy Award nomination (from Marion Short, Hollywood Movie Songs, *1999)*

"Here's Hoping" (1932), music by J. Fred Coots;

"Look Who's Here" (1932), music by Lane;

"Sentimental Rhapsody" (1933), music by Alfred Newman;

"Stringin' Along on a Shoestring" (1933), music by Lane;

"It's a Wonderful World" (1939), music by Jan Savitt and Johnny Watson;

"The Little Man Who Wasn't There" (1939), lyrics adapted from verse by Hughes Mearns, music by Bernard Hanighen;

"720 in the Books" (1939), music by Savitt and Watson;

"The Thrill of a New Romance" (1939), music by Fausto Curbelo and Xavier Cugat;

"Ferry-Boat Serenade" (1940), Italian lyrics by Mario Panzeri, music by Eldo di Lazzaro;

"The Woodpecker Song" (1940), Italian lyrics by Bruno di Lazzaro and Eldo di Lazzaro, music by Eldo di Lazzaro;

"Bim Bam Boom" (1942), music by Noro Morales;

"Manhattan Serenade" (1942), music by Louis Alter, originally published in 1928 as a piano solo;

"Moonlight Mood" (1942), music by Peter De Rose;

"Comin' In on a Wing and a Prayer" (1943), music by Jimmy McHugh;

"Five O'Clock Drag" (1943), music by Duke Ellington;

"Just a Shade on the Blue Side" (1948), music by Hoagy Carmichael;

"A Woman Likes To Be Told" (1950), music by Carmichael;

"I Love Lucy" (1953), music (for television-show theme) by Eliot Daniel.

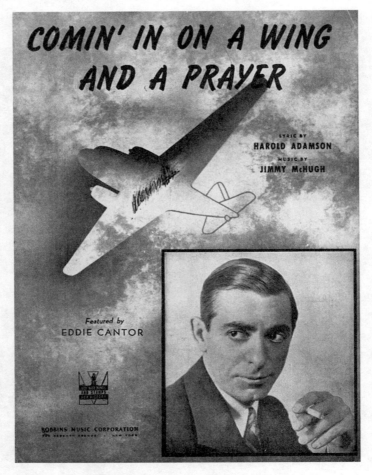

Sheet music for the 1943 patriotic song inspired by a World War II pilot's account of an emergency landing (Bruccoli Clark Layman Archives)

Some lyricists gain notoriety through their association with a particular composer, a series of successful Broadway musicals, or their eccentric and controversial lifestyles. Harold Adamson, by contrast, is relatively unknown to the general public, although he was esteemed by his peers. During the course of his career he collaborated with many composers, most often with Jimmy McHugh but also with Vincent Youmans, Burton Lane, Hoagy Carmichael, Walter Donaldson, Vernon Duke, Sammy Fain, Jule Styne, Victor Young, Eliot Daniel, and J. Fred Coots. A well-mannered, good-natured man, Adamson was temperamentally suited to the collaborative nature of his art. He wrote primarily for Hollywood musicals, for which songwriters were considered much less important than they were on Broadway, where their names usually topped the theater marquee for musicals. Most movie songs, moreover, are less "theatrical" than songs for the musical stage, evincing a more casually colloquial style. Adamson was a master at crafting a simple lyric

around an ordinary catchphrase—as is seen in such song titles as "Time on My Hands (You in My Arms)" (1930), "A Lovely Way to Spend an Evening" (1943), and "It's a Most Unusual Day" (1948)—and many of his more than a thousand song lyrics are still familiar today to people who would not recognize his name.

Harold Adamson was born on 10 December 1906 in Greenville, New Jersey, but he grew up in Brooklyn, New York. His mother, Marion Campbell Adamson, was descended from wealthy Scottish forebears, and his father, James Harold Adamson, was a building contractor who became quite prosperous as Harold, or "Hal," grew up. Adamson attended Brooklyn public schools, where he wrote poems, cultivating an early interest in the use of words, and studied piano, thus preparing him for a career as a songwriter. As a boy of ten he contracted polio, and the disease affected the use of his right side throughout his lifetime. It also confined him even more within the world of reading and writing, but it could not stanch his love of baseball. When he could no longer play the game he became the manager of his school team.

When Adamson was seventeen, his father's fortunes had flourished enough that the family moved to an estate that James Adamson had built on Cedar Island, near Larchmont, New York. Harold enrolled in the Hackle School, a preparatory school in Tarrytown, New York. He dreamed of attending Harvard University, but when his application was denied in 1926, he chose to attend the University of Kansas instead.

While at Kansas, Adamson focused on liberal arts and continued to write poetry, but he also became involved in the university's theatrical productions as both an actor and a writer. In 1926, during his freshman year, he became a member of the Pen and Scroll literary society, for which he served as president in his sophomore year. In 1927 Adamson collaborated on a musical, *Isabel*, with composer Wade Grinstead, which was produced at the university and included such songs as "Alice from Dallas," "China Moon," and "My Sweetie's Half Daffy Over Me." Adamson was also selected to join the MacDowell Fraternity, an organization founded by composer Edward MacDowell to promote interest in painting, music, and literature.

In 1928 Adamson finally realized his boyhood dream and transferred to Harvard. There, his talents as a writer and actor gained recognition in several dramatic organizations. He wrote the book and lyrics for *Close-Up*, a satirical look at Hollywood that was the first musical produced by the Harvard Dramatic Club; the cast for the show included Henry Fonda. During the summers Adamson performed with the University Players Guild in Falmouth, Massachusetts. His lyrics for Harvard's Hasty Pudding Club shows provided him with an opening to Broadway. The budget for these productions generally allowed for lavish scenery, fine costumes, and a professional director. John Boyle, the director of the club's 1930 production, *Face the Music* (which had no connection with Irving Berlin's 1932 show of the same name), was so impressed with Adamson's lyrics that he invited him to meet some colleagues in New York. There Adamson met Youmans, who became his mentor.

Adamson and Youmans, along with co-lyricist Mack Gordon, collaborated on "Time on My Hands (You in My Arms)," which gave Adamson his first commercial success. At the time Youmans was working on *Smiles* (1930), a musical starring Marilyn Miller, Fred and Adele Astaire, Eddie Foy Jr., Virginia Bruce, and Bob Hope. After Adamson's graduation from Harvard in 1930, Youmans introduced

him to Florenz Ziegfeld, the producer of *Smiles*, and "Time on My Hands" was interpolated into the show. It was written for Miller, but she refused to sing it, so it was sung to her in the show by Paul Gregory. Miller did deign to sing one chorus of the melody of "Time on My Hands" but with a lyric written by Ring Lardner titled "What Can I Say?" While *Smiles* closed after ninety-two performances, "Time on My Hands" became an enormous hit and has remained a standard.

Suddenly thrust into the limelight, Adamson gained further exposure on Broadway when "Have a Heart," with his lyrics and music by Lane, was enlisted for the 1931 *Earl Carroll Vanities,* which opened on 27 August of that year at the newly built Earl Carroll Theatre at Fiftieth Street and Seventh Avenue. Lane had become a pianist with a Tin Pan Alley music-publishing firm, Remick, after the cancellation of the *Greenwich Village Follies,* for which he had been composing the score. Adamson met Lane at Remick, and they teamed up for the 1931 edition of the *Earl Carroll Vanities.* As was customary for revues during the 1920s and 1930s, they were only one of several songwriting teams for the show.

Before Adamson had an opportunity to work on a full score for a Broadway musical, he and Lane joined the generational movement of songwriters to Hollywood during the early years of the Depression. In 1933 the two were hired by United Artists to furnish songs for *Palooka* (1934), a boxing comedy starring Jimmy Durante. No sooner had Adamson and Lane moved to Hollywood than production on the movie was halted. It was not released until the following year, but it did feature one of their songs, "Like Me a Little Bit Less (Love Me a Little Bit More)," alongside songs by other composers and lyricists. Faced with this unpredictable production schedule, Adamson and Lane took the opportunity to mix with colleagues at a party. With Lane at the piano and Adamson by his side, they highlighted some of their latest tunes. This informal performance solidified their partnership and led to a contract with M-G-M.

M-G-M assigned Adamson and Lane to write songs for the 1933 motion-picture musical *Dancing Lady,* starring Joan Crawford, Fred Astaire (in his screen debut), Clark Gable, Franchot Tone, Robert Benchley, the Three Stooges, and Nelson Eddy. Adamson and Lane wrote two original songs for the movie, an adaptation of an earlier song, "Heigh-Ho! The Gang's All Here" (from a melody by Sir Arthur Sullivan that was supplied with words in 1917), which was sung and danced by the unlikely team of Astaire and Crawford, and "Everything I Have Is Yours," which was performed by the popular singer/actor Art

Sheet music for a 1943 song that was introduced by Frank Sinatra (Bruccoli Clark Layman Archives)

Jarrett. Through recordings by singers such as Rudy Vallee, Bing Crosby, and Frank Sinatra, the latter song went on to become a standard. While producer David O. Selznick made "Everything I Have Is Yours" the centerpiece of *Dancing Lady,* there were also songs by Richard Rodgers and Lorenz Hart, Arthur Freed and Nacio Herb Brown, and Dorothy Fields and McHugh.

Although Adamson and Lane continued to write movie songs together, they were never given a real opportunity to demonstrate their full capabilities in Hollywood by writing all the songs for a complete movie score. The numbers they composed were either interpolated into movies featuring pieces by other songwriters or used as title songs for dramatic pictures. *Kid Millions* (1934), a musical fantasy offering moviegoers an escape from the reality of the Depression, featured George Murphy and Ann Sothern singing Adamson and Lane's "Your Head on My Shoulder," but the star was Eddie Cantor, and most of the songs he sang in the movie were by Gus Kahn and Donaldson.

The year 1935 was a transitional one in Adamson's life and career. He married Judy Chrisfield, and the couple had a daughter, Eve, but they divorced in 1941. When his songwriting partnership with Lane dissolved, Adamson collaborated with Donaldson on several songs for the 1936 M-G-M production *The Great Ziegfeld,* including "You," which became the number-one song on the radio program *Your Hit*

Director Leo McCarey, Cary Grant, Adamson, Deborah Kerr, and composer Harry Warren going over the title song for the 1957 movie An Affair to Remember *(from Tony Thomas,* Harry Warren and the Hollywood Musical, *1975)*

Parade. An even greater success, from the movie *Suzy* (1936), was "Did I Remember (To Tell You I Adore You)?" Jean Harlow's on-screen rendition of this song was dubbed by Virginia Verrill, but Cary Grant charmingly reprised the tune in his own voice. It held the number-one spot on *Your Hit Parade* for six weeks and garnered Adamson his first Academy Award nomination.

Beginning a long-standing collaboration with McHugh (who had initially come to Hollywood with lyricist Fields), Adamson wrote songs that became recording vehicles for several popular young singers. In 1938 they collaborated on songs for Deanna Durbin, who sang "I Love to Whistle" in *Mad About Music* and "My Own" in *That Certain Age.* Adamson and McHugh wrote five songs for Sinatra for the 1943 movie *Higher and Higher,* including "A Lovely Way to Spend an Evening," which went on to become a standard through recordings by Mel Tormé and June Christy as well as Sinatra. (Tormé made his motion-picture debut in *Higher and Higher,* singing Adamson and McHugh's "Minuet in Boogie".) Jane

Powell introduced Adamson and McHugh's "It's a Most Unusual Day" in *A Date with Judy* (1948).

Although he worked primarily for Hollywood, Adamson occasionally wrote directly for the popular market, and in these songs he again displayed his talent for building a lyric around simple vernacular expression. In 1932 he wrote the lyric for "Here's Hoping," popularized in the 1940s by Frances Langford, and in 1941 the Andrews Sisters made a hit recording of "The Woodpecker Song" (1940). "Daybreak," the music for which is based on the "Mardi Gras" movement of Ferde Grofé's *Mississippi Suite* (1926), was written in 1942 and popularized by Sinatra with Tommy Dorsey and his orchestra. The piece was then used the following year in the patriotic movie *Thousands Cheer* as a vehicle for Kathryn Grayson.

During World War II Adamson, like many of his fellow songwriters, lent his talent to the war effort. Reading about an Army Air Forces pilot's account of an emergency landing, he seized upon the phrase "comin' in on a wing and a prayer" and wedded it to a melody by McHugh. Introduced by Cantor at an

Sheet music for a song from the 1948 musical that inspired the title of the 1997 show-tune revue Lucky in the Rain
(*from Marion Short,* Covers of Gold, *1998*)

Army Air Forces base, the song became a popular and stirring wartime hit:

> "Comin' in on a wing and a pray'r
> "Comin' in on a wing and a pray'r
> "Tho' there's one motor gone, we can still carry on,
> "Comin' in on a wing and a pray'r.
> "What a show–what a fight
> "Yes, we really hit our target for tonight.
> "How we sing as we limp thru the air
> "Look below, there's our field over there
> "With our full crew aboard and our trust in the Lord
> "We're comin' in on a wing and a pray'r."

As a result of his outstanding work and dedication during World War II, Adamson was honored by the U.S. Department of the Treasury, the Canadian government, and the Hollywood Canteen, a Hollywood nightclub founded in 1942 at which movie stars and well-known musical acts entertained servicemen.

During the 1940s Adamson also returned to Broadway. With Duke he wrote *Banjo Eyes* (1941), a musical designed as a vehicle for Cantor that featured such songs as "We're Having a Baby," but Cantor quit the show, cutting short what might have been a long and successful run. In 1948 Adamson tried another stage musical, *As the Girls Go,* with music by McHugh and book by William Roos, which opened at the Winter Garden Theatre. It starred comedian Bobby Clark, who got the bulk of the positive comments in the New York reviews. The show was produced by Mike Todd, who later engaged Adamson to write the adaptation and lyrics for his movie *Around the World in 80 Days* (1956). The plot of *As the Girls Go* was originally based on the format of George and Ira Gershwin's political satire *Of Thee I Sing* (1931), but the story line was changed during its unsuccessful Boston tryout. By the time the production reached New York, it mostly featured the pint-sized Clark (playing the husband of the first female president of the United States) chasing tall showgirls, disguising himself as a female barber, blowing soap bubbles out of a trumpet, and, without looking, tossing his hat across the width of the stage onto a hat rack. In *Opening Night on Broadway* (1990) Steven Suskin states that *As the Girls Go* was one of the "last of the old-style musicals built around star comics. . . . They'd go through all the time-honored routines while a flimsy story unraveled, with ingenue and juvenile singing syrupy ballads in the background. . . . Bobby Clark's final Broadway musical became the first show to lose money despite a full year's run."

After the failure of *As the Girls Go* Adamson remained in Hollywood and continued writing for movies. He married Gretchen Davidson in 1947 and bought a house in Beverly Hills. He also ventured into writing for a new medium when composer Eliot Daniel requested that he supply lyrics for Daniel's already-established theme song for the television comedy series *I Love Lucy* (1951–1956), starring Lucille Ball. When Ball's husband and co-star, Desi Arnaz, learned of the impending arrival of their child, he made a special request to Daniel that words be written to the theme. Thus, the lyrics, completed over one weekend, became one of Adamson's most lucrative ventures. The song was originally recorded in 1953 by Arnaz and his orchestra.

Adamson's other major motion-picture scores during the 1950s included *Jupiter's Darling* (1955), in which Esther Williams introduced "I Have a Dream" in a sumptuous aquatic spectacle. In 1956, at a time when many songwriters of his generation were finding themselves left behind by changing musical tastes, Adamson had two successful songs from movies: "Too Young To Go Steady," from *Strip for Action,* and "Around the World," the title song for *Around the World in 80 Days*. The latter movie was nominated for an Academy Award upon completion, but the title song had not yet been written when the movie was submitted to the Academy of Motion Picture Arts and Sciences, so that while *Around the World in 80 Days* received an Oscar, "Around the World" did not.

One of Adamson's last enduring lyrics was for the title song of the 1957 movie *An Affair to Remember*. Given the soaring, operatic melody by Harry Warren, Adamson, collaborating with lyricist Leo McCarey, employed ardently romantic diction, tone, and imagery, rather than his characteristic colloquial style:

Our love affair is a wondrous thing
That we'll rejoice in remembering.
Our love was born with our first embrace,

And a page was torn out of time and space.
Our love affair, may it always be
A flame to burn through eternity.
So, take my hand with a fervent pray'r,
That we may live and we may share.

Although Adamson continued writing song lyrics for several movies into the 1960s, including *Island of Love* (1963) and *The Incredible Mr. Limpet* (1964), the era of the original Hollywood musical was ending, and the most that songwriters such as Adamson could hope for was an occasional assignment to write a theme song for a dramatic movie.

Adamson's professional and personal life were blended. He loved the company of collaborators such as McHugh, Lane, Carmichael, Donaldson, and Fain. Friends described Adamson as a true gentleman, wonderfully charming and humorous, with a keen sense of morality. His wife, Gretchen, a former Broadway performer for whom he wrote the blues song "A Woman Likes To Be Told" (1950), underscored the importance of the lyricist's art when she said, "A melody remains a melody until the words are put to it, and then it becomes a song." In the course of his career Adamson received five Oscar nominations for his songs, an award from the American Society of Composers, Authors, and Publishers (ASCAP), and an Aggie award from the American Guild of Authors and Composers (now the Songwriters Guild of America), of which he was a member. He was inducted into the Songwriters Hall of Fame in 1972 and was active in ASCAP from 1932 until his death, in Beverly Hills, California, on 17 August 1980.

The best way to identify an Adamson lyric is to describe Adamson himself. He was a true romantic and did not usually employ onomatopoeia, repetition, or comic touches. While he wrote lyrics for many occasions, his songs reflect basic human emotions, always with good nature, much like the unpretentious man writing the words. The titles of some of Adamson's most successful songs—"Did I Remember (To Tell You I Adore You)?" "Everything I Have Is Yours," "How Blue the Night" (1944), "I Couldn't Sleep a Wink Last Night" (1943), "Love Me as Though There Were No Tomorrow" (1956), "A Lovely Way to Spend an Evening," "Manhattan Serenade" (1942), "Moonlight Mood" (1942), "My Resistance Is Low" (1951), "Sentimental Rhapsody" (1933), and "Time on My Hands (You in My Arms)"—suggest the romantic within. He frequently used simple rhyme and uncomplicated meter to encapsulate love, romance, tenderness, and sentimental subject matter. Adamson's method was to write lyrics first and then work with the composer as the words were being set to music. An obvious exception was the occasion for which he was hired to compose words for the *I Love Lucy* television-show theme. Daniel's music had been copyrighted two years prior to that time.

On the front cover of *The Harold Adamson Song Book,* compiled for noncommercial distribution in 1976, close friend and fellow lyricist Stanley Adams (president of ASCAP, 1959–1979) is quoted as having honored Adamson on 22 September 1976 by stating, "*It's A Most Unusual Day* when a lyric of Harold Adamson's is not sung somewhere *Around The World. Everything I Have Is Yours,* he once wrote, and we can all be grateful for the gift. In conclusion, may we say, 'Harold Adamson, *You're A Sweetheart,* and ASCAP salutes you.'"

On 9 July 1997 the Goodspeed Opera House in East Haddam, Connecticut, premiered a new musical, *Lucky in the Rain,* the title of which came from one of Adamson and McHugh's songs from *As the Girls Go,* "(I Got) Lucky in the Rain." The show interpolated several old songs, with music mostly by McHugh and lyrics by Adamson and Fields. There were additional songs by such composers and lyricists as Carmichael, Donaldson, Al Dubin, Ted Koehler, Jan Savitt, and Johnny Watson. *Lucky in the Rain* was set in 1927 Paris and featured period costumes and scenery that paid tribute to both art nouveau and Coco Chanel. Sherman Yellen wove an innovative libretto around the familiar old standards that shimmered with high-fashion elegance. The musical featured characters drawn from real life, such as Gertrude Stein, Josephine Baker, Alice B. Toklas, and Isadora Duncan. Yellen framed

"A Lovely Way to Spend an Evening," "Where Are You?" (1936), "Love Me as Though There Were No Tomorrow," "I Couldn't Sleep a Wink Last Night," "It's a Most Unusual Day," "(I Got) Lucky in the Rain," and other songs by Adamson and McHugh within the context of this musical. Harold Adamson, a lyricist who had never written a successful score for a stage musical, at last had a theatrical showcase for some of his greatest songs.

Bibliography:
The Harold Adamson Song Book, compiled by Stanley Adams (New York: ASCAP, 1976).

Reference:
Roy Hemming, *The Melody Lingers On: The Great Songwriters and Their Movie Musicals* (New York: Newmarket, 1986).

Selected Discography:
Babalu Music! I Love Lucy's Greatest Hits, Columbia, CK48507, 1991;
Classic Movie Musicals of Jimmy McHugh, JJA, 19825, 1982;
Classic Movie Musicals of Walter Donaldson, JJA, 19852, 1985;
The Great Ziegfeld: The Original Motion Picture Soundtrack, Classic International Filmusicals, CIF-3005, 1970;
Higher and Higher, on *Higher and Higher, Step Lively: Original Soundtracks,* Great Movie Themes, 60004, 1997;
Lucky in the Rain: The New Musical, DRG, 12625, 2000;
Remember Marilyn, Twentieth Century, T-901, 1972.

Richard Adler
(3 August 1921 –   )

and

Jerry Ross
(9 March 1926 – 11 November 1955)

Thomas S. Hischak
State University of New York College at Cortland

Unless otherwise indicated, both lyrics and music are by Adler and Ross.

SELECTED SONGS FROM THEATRICAL PRODUCTIONS: *John Murray Anderson's Almanac* (1953)–"Acorn in the Meadow"; "Fini"; "When Am I Gonna Meet Your Mother?"; "You're So Much a Part of Me";

The Pajama Game (1954)–"Hernando's Hideaway"; "Hey There"; "I'll Never Be Jealous Again"; "I'm Not at All in Love"; "Once a Year Day"; "Steam Heat"; "There Once Was a Man"; "Think of the Time I Save";

Damn Yankees (1955)–"The Game"; "Goodbye, Old Girl"; "A Little Brains–A Little Talent"; "Near to You"; "Shoeless Joe from Hannibal Mo."; "Six Months Out of Every Year"; "Those Were the Good Old Days"; "Two Lost Souls"; "Whatever Lola Wants (Lola Gets)"; "Who's Got the Pain?"; "(You Gotta Have) Heart";

Kwamina (1961), lyrics and music by Adler–"Another Time, Another Place"; "The Cocoa Bean Song"; "Did You Hear That?"; "Nothing More to Look Forward To"; "One Wife"; "Ordinary People"; "Seven Sheep, Four Red Shirts, and a Bottle of Gin"; "The Sun Is Beginning to Crow (You Are Home)";

A Mother's Kisses (1968), lyrics and music by Adler–"Don't Live Inside Yourself"; "There Goes My Life"; "When You Gonna Learn?";

The Pajama Game, Broadway revival (1973)–"Watch Your Heart" (lyric and music by Adler);

Music Is (1976), lyrics by Will Holt, music by Adler–"When First I Saw My Lady's Face"; "No Matter Where"; "Should I Speak of Loving You?"

Richard Adler and Jerry Ross (photograph by Talbot)

SONG FROM MOTION-PICTURE PRODUCTION: *Damn Yankees* (1958)–"There's Something about an Empty Chair" (lyrics and music by Adler).

SELECTED SONGS PUBLISHED INDEPENDENTLY OF THEATRICAL OR MOTION-PICTURE PRODUCTIONS: "The Strange Little Girl" (1951);

13

"Even Now" (1953), lyric and music by Adler, Ross, and Dave Kapp (as Dan Howell);

"Rags to Riches" (1953);

"Everybody Loves a Lover" (1958), lyric by Adler, music by Robert Allen;

"Anytime at All" (1961), lyric and music by Adler.

BOOK: *You Gotta Have Heart: An Autobiography,* by Adler, with Lee Davis (New York: Donald I. Fine, 1990).

The team of Richard Adler and Jerry Ross was unusual in the annals of Broadway songwriters in that each man collaborated on both music and lyrics. While several composer-lyricists wrote various songs separately for the same score, Adler and Ross usually sat down at the piano and worked out a song together. As Adler once explained, "It's impossible to say who does what and when. But we've set rules. If I come in with what I think is a beautiful idea, and he says, 'I don't like it,' I can scream, I can rave, but it's out. It obviates arguments. There has to be unanimity in our operation." Theirs was an unusually close collaborative arrangement and fostered many hits. When Ross died, however, Adler was left adrift.

Richard Adler was born in New York City on 3 August 1921, the son of Elsa Adrienne Richard Adler, a noted concert pianist, and Clarence Adler, a piano teacher. But from an early age Richard had little interest in music, especially the classical music that filled his home, and he yearned to be a writer. After taking a few piano lessons from his father, he lost interest. After graduating from New York's Columbia Grammar School in 1939, he enrolled at the University of North Carolina at Chapel Hill, where he studied playwriting with Paul Green. Upon graduation in 1943, Adler joined the navy during World War II and served as a lieutenant on a YP-PC boat in the Pacific Ocean. After his discharge Adler was hired as an advertising copywriter by the Celanese Corporation in 1946, but he also started writing songs, both music and lyrics, in his spare time. His hobby soon got the best of him, and, after being fired for writing lyrics on company time in 1950, Adler devoted all his time and energies to songwriting. Although few of his efforts received the least bit of attention, his 1950 lyric for "Teasin'" (with music by Philip Springer) was recorded by Connie Haines. His real success did not begin, however, until he met Ross in 1950.

Jerry Ross was born Jerold Rosenberg in the East Bronx to a poor family on 9 March 1926. He showed singing and acting talent at a young age; by the time he was ten, he was singing in the synagogue choir and acting with the Bronx Art Theatre, a respected Yiddish company. During his high-school years Ross acted with other Jewish groups around New York. Performing at night and attending high school by day put a strain on his weak health, and he developed chronic bronchiectasis. During his teen years Ross started writing songs, and he pursued his interest by studying music at New York University and taking jobs at summer resorts in the Catskill Mountains, where he wrote original pieces for musical revues and formed a friendship with singer Eddie Fisher. Despite Fisher's help, no song publisher encouraged Ross until he met Adler and the two decided to collaborate.

Composer-lyricist Frank Loesser, with two hit shows—*Where's Charley?* (1948) and *Guys and Dolls* (1950)—to his credit, started his own song-publishing company, Frank Music, in 1951 to handle his works and those of up-and-coming songwriters. The team of Adler and Ross came to his attention because of some numbers they had written for radio programs. Loesser was impressed by the vitality and contemporary sound of their songs and signed them to an exclusive contract. After some modest successes, such as "The Strange Little Girl," recorded by Eddie Howard in 1951, and "Even Now," written with Dave Kapp, which Fisher recorded in 1953, Loesser's hunch paid off when Adler and Ross's "Rags to Riches" went to the top of the charts in 1953 with a recording by Tony Bennett. The success of that song led to their first Broadway assignment: writing songs for the 1953 musical revue *John Murray Anderson's Almanac,* which managed to run for 229 performances on the strength of its stars (Hermione Gingold, Harry Belafonte, and Billy De Wolfe) but did little to bring recognition to the young songwriting team. Nonetheless, before the show even opened, Adler and Ross were signed to write a score for George Abbott, for whom they had been auditioning for some time. When Abbott could not get the overbooked Loesser to write the score for *The Pajama Game* (1954), the assignment fell to Adler and Ross.

The creation of *The Pajama Game* involved many newcomers. It was the first Broadway musical produced by partners Harold Prince and Robert Griffith; it was dancer Bob Fosse's first choreography assignment; and it was Adler and Ross's first opportunity to write a full score for a book musical. While it dealt with the frictions between union workers and management at a pajama factory, little in the show was controversial or thought provoking. But it was a fast-paced musical comedy in the best Abbott tradition and became a major hit, running for 1,063 performances. This time the Adler and Ross songs were hailed by the critics, and several went on to become hits. The score varied in style, from such old-fashioned ballads as "Hey There" to contemporary, jazzy dance numbers such as "Steam

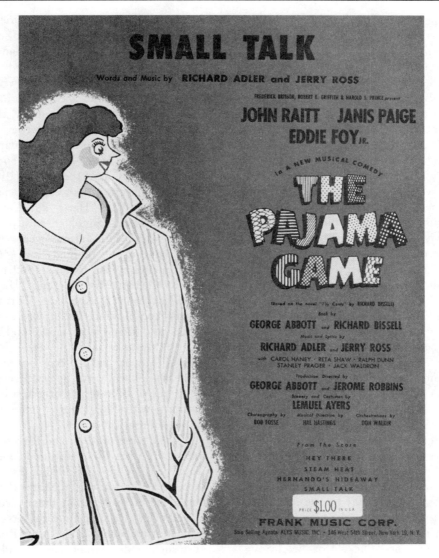

Sheet music for a song from Adler and Ross's 1954 musical about a labor dispute at a pajama factory
(from Lehman Engel, Their Words Are Music, *1975)*

Heat." The team played with Latin rhythms ("Hernando's Hideaway"), merry waltzing ("I'm Not at All in Love"), and even a Western hoedown ("There Once Was a Man"). Adler and Ross were equally at home with a comic character song ("I'll Never Be Jealous Again") and a rousing march ("7½ Cents"). The lyrics were particularly spirited and droll, prompting Leonard Bernstein to label the team "two young Loessers."

Much of the same creative staff reunited in 1955 for *Damn Yankees,* including Abbott, Fosse, Prince, Griffith, and, of course, Adler and Ross. This far-fetched fantasy about a baseball fan who sells his soul to the devil to became a heavy hitter and lead his beloved Washington Senators to the league pennant offered plenty of opportunities for the variety of songs Adler and Ross liked. The

Latin number this time was "Whatever Lola Wants (Lola Gets)," and the hoedown dance was "Shoeless Joe from Hannibal Mo." Comic songs such as "A Little Brains—A Little Talent" and "The Game" were reminiscent of *The Pajama Game* without actually copying it. "(You Gotta Have) Heart" was a rousing barbershop quartet meant to inspire the Senators; "Those Were the Good Old Days" was a delightful soft-shoe number for the devil; and the team satirized the then-current mambo craze with "Who's Got the Pain?" While Gwen Verdon stole the show as Lola, the devil's assistant, and went on to become a star, the score, like that of *The Pajama Game,* was acclaimed and provided hit songs for the record charts. *Damn Yankees* ran almost as long as *The Pajama Game:* 1,019 performances.

With two long-running musicals on Broadway, Adler and Ross were considered the most successful new songwriting team of the 1950s, but their glory was to be short-lived. Six months after *Damn Yankees* opened, Ross suddenly died from an infection caused by his chronic bronchiectasis; he was only twenty-nine years old. One newspaper mistakenly ran Adler's picture with Ross's obituary. It was a chilling portent, for, in many ways, Adler's career was also dead. Although he has had a long and interesting life, Adler has never again enjoyed the level of success that he had with his late partner. Because he wrote both lyrics and music, Adler could continue to write musical scores without a new collaborator, but it proved more difficult in practice than it was in theory.

Collaborating with Robert Allen in 1958, Adler wrote "Everybody Loves a Lover," which Doris Day's recording turned into an enormous success. On 3 January of that same year, Adler married Sally Ann Howes after divorcing his first wife, Marion Hart, whom he had married on 4 September 1951 and with whom he had raised two children. Adler's second marriage ended in divorce in 1966, and he married again on 27 December 1968, but that marriage, too, ended in divorce, in 1976.

After 1958 Adler wrote both lyrics and music for most of his songs. His most accomplished theatrical work after Ross's death was *Kwamina* (1961), an ambitious and thought-provoking musical drama about an English-educated African physician who returns home to lead his people in a fight for independence. There Kwamina falls in love with a white female doctor, but the two are forced to part because the world is not yet ready to accept their relationship. Adler wrote rich, rhythmic numbers such as "The Cocoa Bean Song" and "Seven Sheep, Four Red Shirts, and a Bottle of Gin" for the tribal characters, flowing ballads such as "Nothing More to Look Forward To" and "Ordinary People" for the two pairs of lovers in the musical, and such potent character songs as "Another Time, Another Place" and "Did You Hear That?" Although the ideas in the story were disturbingly serious, Adler still found room for humor, as in the satiric "One Wife" and the ironic "The Sun Is Beginning to Crow (You Are Home)." It was a rich and admirable score, little of it recalling the previous Adler-Ross collaborations, but impressive in its own way. Despite some encouraging notices, audiences stayed away from the controversial musical, and it was forced to close after only thirty-two performances.

Returning to musical comedy, Adler fared even less well with *A Mother's Kisses* (1968), a show about a suffocating Jewish mother, which closed on the road. *Music Is* (1976), Adler's musicalization of William

Shakespeare's *Twelfth Night,* with lyrics by Will Holt, did make it to Broadway, but, despite some commendable songs, it closed after eight performances.

In the 1970s Adler turned to producing on Broadway, but his interracial revival of *The Pajama Game* (1973) and the Richard Rodgers-Sheldon Harnick musical *Rex* (1976), about Henry VIII, both failed. Adler found more recognition writing and coproducing television-musical adaptations of Louisa May Alcott's *Little Women* (1868–1869) and O. Henry's "The Gift of the Magi" (1905), both in 1959. He also wrote music for commercials (he created the catchy jingle "Let Hertz Put You in the Driver's Seat"). Adler was involved with politics in the 1960s and organized fund-raising events and special presentations during the Kennedy and Johnson administrations, including the famous 1962 birthday tribute at which Marilyn Monroe sang "Happy Birthday" to President John F. Kennedy. Turning later to symphonic composition, Adler wrote such instrumental works as "Memory of Childhood" (1978), "Yellowstone Overture" (1980), and "Wilderness Suite" (1983), which have been performed by various orchestras. Thus, while he never recaptured his pinnacle as one of Broadway's brightest hopes in his collaborations with Ross, Adler enjoyed a varied and successful musical career.

The lyrics of Adler and Ross are characterized by their energy, playful vitality, and contemporary quality. The words are rarely subtle but instead call attention to themselves. Part of this quality is their youthful charm but much is owing to a brassy, confident tone that turned even love songs into rousers. There is little that is quiet or meditative in the Adler-Ross song repertoire; even such tender numbers as "Goodbye, Old Girl" and "Near to You," both from *Damn Yankees,* seem to call for a full-voiced delivery. In the songwriting team's love songs, character pieces, and merry chorus numbers, the vivacious spirit rules. The words become their own musical notes, an elongated "steam" in "Steam Heat" adding to the orchestration and the alliterative "Hernando's Hideaway" picking up the tango's percussion section. The lyric itself dances in "Who's Got the Pain?"–the "ugh" sounds lead Fosse's bump-and-grind choreography. The Adler-Ross comic songs rarely fail to deliver, sometimes building in intensity as they catalogue images–"The Game," "I'll Never Be Jealous Again," and "Those Were the Good Old Days," for instance–or playfully elaborate on an idea, as in "What Ever Lola Wants (Lola Gets)" and "Think of the Time I Save," another song from *The Pajama Game.*

Two lyrics from *Damn Yankees* bear close examination. Lola's "I am" song (a song establishing a character's wants or hopes), "A Little Brains–A Little

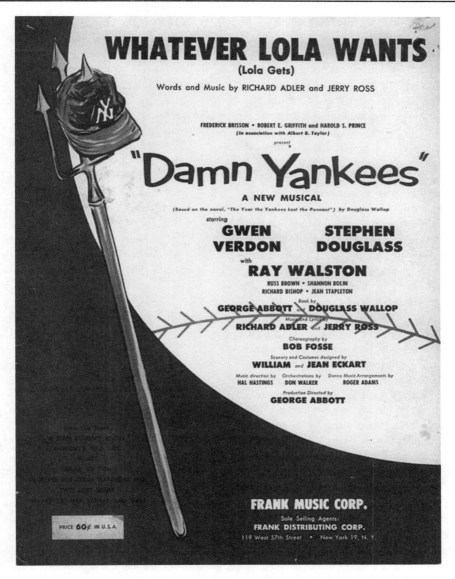

Sheet music for a song from Adler and Ross's 1955 musical comedy about a baseball player who sells his soul to the devil
(Bruccoli Clark Layman Archives)

Talent," is so unusual and tricky that, when added to the show late in tryouts, Verdon was puzzled; she told Adler and Ross that the lines did not rhyme and were impossible to sing. In fact, the stage manager had to whisper some of the lyric to her from behind a curtain so that the nervous performer (it was her first leading role on Broadway) could get through it the first time. Looking at the lyric on the page, it is easy to understand Verdon's confusion. There are few end rhymes, but there is an internal rhyme in nearly every line. These are not subtle or finely hidden interior rhymes such as Oscar Hammerstein might have written but sassy internal rhymes in the manner of Cole Porter—playful and teasing, much as Lola herself is. The rhymes in lines such as "I took the *zing* out of the *King*

of Siam" or "I knocked the *fight* out of a *knight*" are easy to spot on the page, but one has to hear the song sung to catch the rhymes in "tho' *no*body spied him" and "no great *art* gettin' the *heart* of a man." The few end rhymes are often original and striking, such as "farmer" and "armor" or "Lola" and "boffola." There are arch rhymes as well, those silly inaccuracies that charm by their very awkwardness, such as "Nome, Alaska" and "Madagascar." "A Little Brains—A Little Talent" is a comic list song in the Porter tradition and, like the best of its kind, it builds in comic effect as the conceit grows more and more outrageous: Lola claims to have slept with George Washington, so bedding the protagonist, baseball star Joe Hardy, ought to be child's play.

"Two Lost Souls," also from *Damn Yankees,* is another striking lyric. Adler and Ross purposely punch the lyric with musical exclamation points, stopping the words so that the singer may act out the song physically to the music. Whether or not this innovation was suggested by Fosse, such quirky, rhythmic stopping and starting was ideal for his erratic style of choreography. "Two Lost Souls" is a duet sung by Lola and Joe when they think they have been defeated by the devilish Applegate. It is a fatalistic lyric in which even the title is ambiguous, referring to losers in love as well as to damned sinners. The images of a couple of lost siblings, boats, and sheep are carried out nicely, each reference ending with the comforting realization that "we got each other." Again, arch rhymes are plentiful: "ruther" (for *rather*)/"other," "fussin'"/"us'n," and "no rudder"/ "got each udder." Long lines with repetition ("wherever we go, whatever we do") are used to bring out the bluesy flavor of the piece. It is a refreshing version of an old song model: two buddies taking drunken comfort in each other.

While none of the Adler-Ross shows was groundbreaking, they do offer some surprises. The central melodic theme of "Hey There," from *The Pajama Game,* was taken from a Mozart sonata (at the suggestion of Loesser), but the conceit of having it sung into a Dictaphone and then repeated as a duet sung by one man is innovative. The complex "Six Months Out of Every Year" opens *Damn Yankees* in an original way, and the chorus number "7½ Cents" concludes *The Pajama Game* with a pleasant variation on the standard finale. The team of Adler and Ross never ventured into the territory of Rodgers and Hammerstein or even Alan Jay Lerner and Frederick Loewe, but they understood musical comedy and knew how to manipulate its conventions in dazzling fashion.

Adler did enter the milieu of Rodgers and Hammerstein with *Kwamina* (although it was unfavorably compared with their 1951 show *The King and I* by some critics), and he proved to be much more versatile than he had been in his earlier work. Perhaps he and Ross would have taken the Broadway musical into new directions had their collaboration continued. But at least the team left behind two of the brightest shows of the 1950s, both frequently revived and both testaments to musical-comedy panache.

References:

Lehman Engel, *Their Words Are Music: The Great Theatre Lyricists and Their Lyrics* (New York: Crown, 1975), pp. 200–204;

Martin Gottfried, *All His Jazz: The Life and Death of Bob Fosse* (New York: Bantam, 1990), pp. 87–98;

Stanley Green, *The World of Musical Comedy: The Story of the American Musical Stage as Told Through the Careers of its Foremost Composers and Lyricists,* fourth edition (New York: A. S. Barnes, 1980), pp. 270–273;

Thomas S. Hischak, *Word Crazy: Broadway Lyricists From Cohan to Sondheim* (New York: Praeger, 1991), pp. 147–149;

Carol Ilson, *Harold Prince: From Pajama Game to Phantom of the Opera* (Ann Arbor: UMI Research Press, 1989), pp. 13–27;

Ethan Mordden, *Coming Up Roses: The Broadway Musical in the 1950s* (New York: Oxford University Press, 1998), pp. 99–102.

Selected Discography:

Damn Yankees, motion-picture soundtrack, RCA LSO 1047, 1989;

Damn Yankees, 1994 Broadway revival cast, Mercury 314 522 396-4, 1994;

Damn Yankees, original Broadway cast, RCA LSO 1021, 1955;

John Murray Anderson's Almanac and Other Broadway-London Revues, DRG 19009, 1999;

Kwamina, original Broadway cast, Capitol SW 1645, 1961;

The Pajama Game, motion-picture soundtrack, Columbia OL 5210, 1957;

The Pajama Game, original Broadway cast, Columbia S 32606, 1954.

Irving Berlin
(23 May 1888 – 22 September 1989)

Tony L. Hill
University of Minnesota

Unless otherwise indicated, music is by Berlin.

SELECTED SONGS FROM THEATRICAL PRO-
DUCTIONS: *Ziegfeld Follies of 1911* (1911)–
"Woodman, Woodman, Spare That Tree!"
(interpolation; lyrics and music by Berlin and
Vincent Bryant);

The Passing Show of 1912 (1912)–"The Ragtime Jockey
Man" (interpolation);

The Whirl of Society (1912)–"Society Bear" (interpolation);

Along Came Ruth (1914)–"Along Came Ruth" (interpolation);

Watch Your Step (1914)–"Simple Melody/Musical
Demon," later retitled "Play a Simple Melody";

Stop! Look! Listen! (1915)–"The Girl on the Magazine
(Cover)"; "I Love a Piano"; "When I Get Back to
the U.S.A.";

Yip, Yip, Yaphank (1918)–"Mandy"; "Oh! How I Hate
to Get Up in the Morning";

Ziegfeld Follies of 1918 (1918)–"I'm Gonna Pin My
Medal on the Girl I Left Behind" (interpolation);

Ziegfeld Follies of 1919 (1919)–"A Pretty Girl Is Like a
Melody"; "You Cannot Make Your Shimmy
Shake on Tea"; "You'd Be Surprised";

Ziegfeld Midnight Frolic (1919)–"I'll See You in
C-U-B-A";

Ziegfeld Follies of 1920 (1920)–"The Girls of My
Dreams"; "Tell Me, Little Gypsy";

Music Box Revue (1921)–"Everybody Step"; "Say It with
Music";

Music Box Revue (1922)–"Crinoline Days"; "Lady of the
Evening"; "Pack Up Your Sins and Go to the
Devil";

Music Box Revue (1923)–"Learn to Do the Strut"; "Little
Butterfly"; "An Orange Grove in California";
"The Waltz of Long Ago"; "When You Walked
Out, Somebody Else Walked In";

Music Box Revue (1924)–"Tell Her in the Springtime";

The Cocoanuts (1925)–"A Little Bungalow";

Betsy (1926)–"Blue Skies" (interpolation);

Irving Berlin, 1913

Ziegfeld Follies of 1927 (1927)–"It All Belongs to Me";
"Ooh, Maybe It's You"; "Shaking the Blues
Away";

Shoot the Works (1931)–"Begging for Love" (interpolation);

Face the Music (1932)–"I Say It's Spinach (And the Hell
with It)"; "Let's Have Another Cup of Coffee";
"Manhattan Madness"; "Soft Lights and Sweet
Music";

As Thousands Cheer (1933)–"Easter Parade"; "The Funnies"; "Harlem on My Mind"; "Heat Wave";
"How's Chances"; "Lonely Heart"; "Man Bites

Dog"; "Not for All the Rice in China"; "Supper Time";

Louisiana Purchase (1940)–"It's a Lovely Day Tomorrow"; "Louisiana Purchase"; "You Can't Brush Me Off"; "You're Lonely and I'm Lonely";

This Is the Army (1942)–"I Left My Heart at the Stage Door Canteen"; "I'm Getting Tired So I Can Sleep"; "This Is the Army, Mister Jones"; "What the Well-Dressed Soldier in Harlem Will Wear";

Annie Get Your Gun (1946)–"Anything You Can Do"; "Doin' What Comes Natur'lly"; "The Girl That I Marry"; "I Got Lost in His Arms"; "I Got the Sun in the Morning"; "There's No Business Like Show Business"; "They Say It's Wonderful"; "You Can't Get a Man with a Gun";

Miss Liberty (1949)–"Give Me Your Tired, Your Poor"; "Just One Way to Say I Love You"; "Let's Take an Old-Fashioned Walk"; "Paris Wakes Up and Smiles";

Call Me Madam (1950)–"The Best Thing for You"; "Can You Use Any Money Today?"; "The Hostess with the Mostes' on the Ball"; "It's a Lovely Day Today"; "Marrying for Love"; "Once Upon a Time Today"; "They Like Ike"; "You're Just in Love";

Mr. President (1962)–"Empty Pockets Filled with Love"; "This Is a Great Country";

Annie Get Your Gun, revival (1966)–"An Old-Fashioned Wedding."

SELECTED SONGS FROM MOTION-PICTURE PRODUCTIONS: *The Awakening* (1928)–"Marie (The Dawn Is Breaking)";

The Cocoanuts (1929)–"When My Dreams Come True";

Coquette (1929)–"Coquette";

Hallelujah (1929)–"Waiting at the End of the Road";

Lady of the Pavements (1929)–"Where Is the Song of Songs for Me?";

Mammy (1930)–"Let Me Sing and I'm Happy"; "(Across the Breakfast Table) Looking at You"; "To My Mammy";

Puttin' on the Ritz (1930)–"Puttin' on the Ritz"; "With You";

Reaching for the Moon (1930)–"Reaching for the Moon";

Top Hat (1935)–"Cheek to Cheek"; "Isn't This a Lovely Day (To Be Caught in the Rain)?"; "No Strings (I'm Fancy Free)"; "The Piccolino"; "Top Hat, White Tie and Tails";

Follow the Fleet (1936)–"Get Thee Behind Me, Satan"; "I'd Rather Lead a Band"; "I'm Putting All My Eggs in One Basket"; "Let Yourself Go"; "Let's Face the Music and Dance"; "We Saw the Sea";

On the Avenue (1937)–"The Girl on the Police Gazette"; "He Ain't Got Rhythm"; "I've Got My Love to

Keep Me Warm"; "Slumming on Park Avenue"; "This Year's Kisses"; "You're Laughing at Me";

Alexander's Ragtime Band (1938)–"My Walking Stick"; "Now It Can Be Told";

Carefree (1938)–"Change Partners"; "I Used to Be Color Blind"; "The Yam";

Second Fiddle (1939)–"Back to Back"; "I Poured My Heart into a Song"; "I'm Sorry for Myself"; "An Old-Fashioned Tune Always Is New"; "When Winter Comes";

Holiday Inn (1942)–"Abraham"; "Be Careful, It's My Heart"; "Happy Holiday"; "I Can't Tell a Lie"; "I've Got Plenty to Be Thankful For"; "Let's Say It with Firecrackers"; "Let's Start the New Year Right"; "Song of Freedom"; "White Christmas"; "You're Easy to Dance With";

Blue Skies (1946)–"You Keep Coming Back Like a Song";

Easter Parade (1948)–"Better Luck Next Time"; "A Couple of Swells"; "A Fella with an Umbrella"; "It Only Happens When I Dance with You"; "Steppin' Out with My Baby";

White Christmas (1954)–"Count Your Blessings Instead of Sheep"; "Sisters";

Sayonara (1957)–"Sayonara."

SELECTED SONGS PUBLISHED INDEPENDENTLY OF THEATRICAL OR MOTION-PICTURE PRODUCTIONS: "Marie from Sunny Italy" (1907), music by Mike Nicholson;

"My Wife's Gone to the Country (Hurrah! Hurrah!)" (1909), lyrics by Berlin and George Whiting, music by Ted Snyder;

"Sadie Salome (Go Home)" (1909), lyrics and music by Berlin and Edgar Leslie;

"That Mesmerizing Mendelssohn Tune" (1909), music adapted in part from Felix Mendelssohn-Bartholdy's "Frühlingslied" (1844);

"Yiddle, on Your Fiddle, Play Some Ragtime" (1909);

"Call Me Up Some Rainy Afternoon" (1910);

"Grizzly Bear" (1910), music by George Botsford;

"Oh, How That German Could Love" (1910), music by Snyder;

"Oh, That Beautiful Rag" (1910), music by Snyder;

"Piano Man" (1910), music by Snyder;

"Alexander's Ragtime Band" (1911);

"Bring Back My Lovin' Man" (1911);

"Everybody's Doing It Now" (1911);

"Ragtime Violin!" (1911);

"That Mysterious Rag" (1911), music by Snyder;

"When I Lost You" (1912);

"When the Midnight Choo-Choo Leaves for Alabam'" (1912);

"In My Harem" (1913);

"The International Rag" (1913);

"San Francisco Bound" (1913);

"Snookey Ookums" (1913);

"He's a Devil in His Own Home Town" (1914);

"He's a Rag Picker" (1914);

"I Want to Go Back to Michigan (Down on the Farm)" (1914);

"If That's Your Idea of a Wonderful Time (Take Me Home)" (1914);

"This Is the Life" (1914);

"Araby" (1915);

"When I Leave the World Behind" (1915);

"For Your Country and My Country" (1917);

"Let's All Be Americans Now" (1917), lyrics and music by Berlin, Leslie, and George W. Meyer;

"Smile and Show Your Dimple" (1917);

"Goodbye, France (You'll Never Be Forgotten by the U.S.A.)" (1918);

"They Were All Out of Step but Jim" (1918);

"I've Got My Captain Working for Me Now" (1919);

"Nobody Knows and Nobody Seems to Care" (1919);

"Home Again Blues" (1920), lyrics and music by Berlin and Harry Akst;

"All by Myself" (1921);

"All Alone" (1924);

"Lazy" (1924);

"What'll I Do?" (1924);

"Always" (1925);

"You Forgot to Remember" (1925);

"At Peace with the World" (1926);

"Because I Love You" (1926);

"How Many Times?" (1926);

"I'm on My Way Home" (1926);

"We'll Never Know" (1926);

"Russian Lullaby" (1927);

"The Song Is Ended (But the Melody Lingers On)" (1927);

"What Does It Matter?" (1927);

"How about Me?" (1928);

"I Can't Do without You" (1928);

"Roses of Yesterday" (1928);

"To Be Forgotten" (1928);

"The Little Things in Life" (1930);

"How Deep Is the Ocean (How High Is the Sky)" (1932);

"Say It Isn't So" (1932);

"Maybe It's Because I Love You Too Much" (1933);

"God Bless America" (1938);

"The Night Is Filled with Music" (1938);

"Any Bonds Today?" (1941);

"A Little Old Church in England" (1941);

"When That Man Is Dead and Gone" (1941);

"I Threw a Kiss in the Ocean" (1942);

"Love and the Weather" (1947);

"A Man Chases a Girl (Until She Catches Him)" (1949);

"The Ten Best Undressed Women" (1963);

"I Used to Play It by Ear" (1965);

"Wait Until You're Married" (1966);

"Song for the U.N." (1971).

BOOK: *The Complete Lyrics of Irving Berlin,* edited by Robert Kimball and Linda Emmet (New York: Knopf, 2001).

Irving Berlin is regarded—with near universality—as America's most important popular-music composer. This praise has come not only from music critics and fans but also from his contemporary songwriting greats and the country's leaders. When Berlin celebrated his one-hundredth birthday on 11 May 1988, members of the One-hundredth Congress gathered on the steps of the Capitol to sing for him. This tribute was without precedent, but it did resemble many others from late in his life. Many appreciations of Berlin in the 1970s and 1980s—articles, performances, and television documentaries—were written in the second person, referring to him as *you* rather than *he*. He was thus made a part of the audience as much as the subject of the celebration, no doubt because the reclusive songwriter usually refused to cooperate with such projects, despite the uniform reverence they showed for him and his work. By this time Berlin was receiving almost as much publicity for his longevity as for his music. Beginning with his eightieth birthday in 1968—celebrated in a ninety-minute broadcast of *The Ed Sullivan Show* (the only time in its twenty-three-year history that the program ran longer than an hour)—Berlin's birthdays became important national events.

In the course of his long career, Berlin mastered the full range of popular music, writing ballads, marches, rhythmic dance numbers, waltzes, anthems, syncopated songs, and even a rock-and-roll tune. He is one of the few songwriters to have achieved success in all three sectors of American popular music: stage musicals, screen musicals, and the world of "independent" songs that emerged from the recording and sheet-music-publishing industries once known as Tin Pan Alley.

Berlin's music can be divided into three periods. Early Berlin comprises everything he wrote from 1907, the year of his first song lyric, "Marie from Sunny Italy," to late 1914. During this period he was principally a writer of popular songs, although his work was also included in many theatrical productions. While many of his songs from this period were hits, few of them became standards. Berlin is not unusual in this

Sheet music for the 1911 song that revolutionized popular music by employing syncopated rhythms and vernacular American speech
(from Max Wilk, Memory Lane 1890–1925, *1973)*

respect; few songs from the first two decades of the twentieth century are now considered standards.

Middle Berlin starts with the opening of his first complete score for a musical, *Watch Your Step,* at the Globe Theatre in New York on 8 December 1914 and runs through 1931. During this period, Berlin established himself as a Broadway composer, writing complete scores and opening his own Broadway theater, the Music Box. Toward the end of this period Berlin became involved in writing songs and even a few scores for motion pictures. He also continued to write songs independent of productions, although his output of such songs varied greatly throughout this period. Some historians would extend Berlin's early period up to the end of World War I, and possibly to the opening of the Music Box in 1921, but it is worth remembering that he was assigned songwriting duty by the U.S. Army during World War I because by that time he already knew how to write and stage a Broadway show. Further, Berlin's jump to Broadway

in 1914 was a significant departure from what his career had been up to that point, while opening the Music Box was a natural extension of his activities at the time rather than a break with them.

Late Berlin is everything from 1932 on. During this part of his career he reserved his output for scores that were his alone. He wrote relatively few independent songs after 1932, and most of these were tied to some cause: promoting the sale of war bonds, encouraging sympathy for the British at the time when the United States was not yet involved in World War II, and celebrating the return of veterans from the war. Berlin's last wholly original score was for the 1950 Broadway musical *Call Me Madam.* The two motion pictures and the musical that he scored after *Call Me Madam* included substantial portions of music that he had written over a period of years; some of the new songs introduced in the movies *White Christmas* (1954) and *There's No Business Like Show Business* (1954) had been written as early as 1948. For the musical *Mr. Presi-*

Berlin and George M. Cohan during the tour of The Friars' Frolic of 1911
(*from Alexander Woollcott,* The Story of Irving Berlin, *1925)*

dent (1962) Berlin used two songs substantially written in the 1940s and several he wrote in the 1950s. Another song in the show, "Is He the Only Man in the World?" was a rewrite of his 1929 hit "Where Is the Song of Songs for Me?" All of Berlin's twenty-one Broadway shows were successful. Although *Mr. President* and *Miss Liberty* (1949) were panned by critics, both shows ran for hundreds of performances. Berlin never had the indignity of seeing one of his shows close out of town or close after a short Broadway run—things that happened to such luminaries as Cole Porter, Jerome Kern, and Richard Rodgers.

Irving Berlin was born Israel Beilin, the youngest of the eight children of Moses and Leah Lipkin Beilin. There is controversy over both the date and location of his birth. Russia still used the Julian calendar into the Soviet period, so when the boy who grew up to write a song for nearly every important event on the calendar was born, it was 23 May 1888 on the Gregorian calendar used in the West, although to the Beilins it was 11

May. The question of where Berlin was born is the subject of even greater controversy. He always maintained that he was born in the small town of "Temun," somewhere east of the Russian frontier and possibly in Siberia. (There is a Tyumen, east of the Ural Mountains on the West Siberian Plain.)

After Berlin's death, Laurence Bergreen asserted in *As Thousands Cheer: The Life of Irving Berlin* (1990) that the songwriter had really been born in Mohilev, Byelorussia (now Mogilev-Podolskiy, Belarus). Although some scholars have accepted this revised account, Berlin's family still insists that his version is correct, and there is evidence that they are right. Although Tyumen is well outside the Pale of Settlement to which Jews were restricted at that time in Russia, Jews were used as laborers on various projects throughout the empire, including building and maintaining the Trans-Siberian Railway. It is possible that Moses Beilin, a cantor, was sent to the site of one of those projects, with his family, to serve the itinerant Jewish population.

Berlin in his office at the keyboard of his transposing piano, 1914

In any case, the Beilins moved back to the Pale some time in the five years after Berlin's birth, but their village was destroyed in a pogrom staged by the czar's troops. They were living in the Mohilev area when they decided to leave for the United States. The family sailed from Amsterdam on the SS *Rhynland* on 2 September 1893. They traveled in steerage, and Berlin received his first dose of American patriotism when the ship sailed past the recently erected Statue of Liberty. At the immigration station on Ellis Island the Beilins took the name Baline.

The Balines settled into a filthy tenement on Monroe Street on New York's Lower East Side. Before long, Moses Baline's earnings as a *shomer* (kosher meat inspector) and a *malamud* (teacher)—there were no job openings for cantors—made it possible for the family to relocate to a more humane apartment at 330 Cherry Street, near the Manhattan Bridge. After his father's death in 1901, Berlin dropped out of school and left his home to become a street performer, singing on the streets in the hopes that passersby would toss him a few coins. Eventually, he was hired as a singing waiter at the Pelham Café in Chinatown.

Berlin's first song creations may have been wholly extemporaneous. According to some biographies, he was in the habit of singing his own parodies of the day's popular songs, but no record of these parodies survives. The first time Berlin actually set pen to paper and fixed a song in tangible form was in May 1907. Mike Salter, the owner of the Pelham, envied the success of a competing café where the pianist, Al Piantadosi, had written the music for a popular novelty song, "My Mariuccia Take a Steamboat" (1906). Salter goaded the pianist at the Pelham, Mike Nicholson, to write a similar "Italian" song, and Berlin was called upon to write the lyrics. The words that he wrote for "Marie from Sunny Italy" were not of the same caliber as those that later established him as a grand master of songwriting, but they were not terrible, either. As a novelty dialect piece, "Marie from Sunny Italy" filled the bill, although it was not a hit. It is remembered today only because it was Berlin's first song.

According to legend, Berlin made only 37¢ from "Marie from Sunny Italy," but, more important, he received a new name. He was identified as "I. Berlin" instead of "I. Baline" on the sheet music,

Left: Sheet music for the best-known song from Berlin's Yip, Yip, Yaphank *(1918); right: Berlin in his U.S. Army uniform, 1918*
(left: The Joseph M. Bruccoli Great War Collection, Thomas Cooper Library, University of South Carolina; right: courtesy of ASCAP)

supposedly because of a printer's error. The young songwriter liked the new name and decided to let the "I" stand for Irving instead of Israel (or "Izzy," as he was called at the time). He has been known as Irving Berlin ever since.

While Berlin was now a published songwriter, he did not make the writing of additional songs a priority. His next number, "The Best of Friends Must Part," did not come until 1908. It was the first song for which Berlin wrote both words and music. He had picked out tunes on the black keys of the piano in the Pelham and eventually learned to play in the key of F-sharp (which consists mainly of black keys). Eventually, he bought a transposing piano with a lever that would shift the song to other keys while he continued to play in F-sharp. For much of his songwriting career Berlin could neither read nor write music but would play his melodies for a musical stenographer, who would take them down in musical notation. Berlin would then choose from among potential chord voicings played by ear, and the secretary would note these down. Even when Berlin had learned the rudiments of musical notation, sometime in the early 1930s, he maintained the same method of composition with a secretary throughout his life.

Later in 1908 Berlin saw his music performed on Broadway for the first time. "She Was a Dear Little Girl," the first song he wrote with Ted Snyder, who became his publisher and most frequent collaborator in those early years, was sung by Marie Cahill in *The Boys and Betty*. Berlin's next contribution to musical theater brought him into contact with Broadway producers Jake and Lee Shubert, with whom Berlin was to clash many times in the ensuing years on how shows should be produced and theaters run. Berlin and Snyder's song "Oh, How That German Could Love" (1910) was especially noteworthy in that Berlin himself recorded it commercially, and it even showed up on the music charts of the day.

In 1911 Berlin wrote "Alexander's Ragtime Band," the song that, more than any other, revolutionized American popular music. In contrast to the era's watered-down art songs and pieces derived from European operetta, "Alexander's Ragtime Band" took the syncopated rhythms of ragtime and the vernacular speech of black-dialect songs and wove them into an appealing invitation to "Come on and hear, come on and hear." It was the first American song to become an international hit, spreading like wildfire "stateside" and then crossing the Atlantic, "perhaps uniting musically

Berlin with the chorus girls who performed in the first Music Box Revue *(1921)*

the former colonies with their mother land for the first time," as biographer Michael Freedland put it in his biography *Irving Berlin* (1974). Although other songs have been more popular, as an international hit "Alexander's Ragtime Band" is ascribed particular importance, along with other songs similarly revolutionary in popular music, such as W. C. Handy's "St. Louis Blues" (1914) and Kern's "They Didn't Believe Me" (1914). In 1963 "Alexander's Ragtime Band" was named by the American Society of Composers, Authors, and Publishers (ASCAP) as one of its sixteen greatest songs. Two other Berlin songs also made the roster: "God Bless America" (1938) and "White Christmas" (1942).

In 1912 Berlin married Dorothy Goetz, sister of his friend and occasional collaborator E. Ray Goetz. According to legend, Berlin met the nineteen-year-old Dorothy when she and another young singer were supposedly fighting over the right to sing one of his songs. (Edward Jablonski points out in his 1999 biography *Irving Berlin: American Troubadour* that there is no

record of Dorothy's ever having been a performer.) After a whirlwind courtship, Berlin and Dorothy were married in Buffalo.

The Berlins honeymooned in Cuba, but there Dorothy took ill. She was never well again after their return to New York, and what was thought to be a bad cold was soon diagnosed as typhoid fever. Dorothy died on 17 July 1912. Berlin was inconsolable in the wake of these events. He tried to return to a normal life of songwriting, but he found the music would not come. Ray Goetz encouraged him to pour his grief into song. Berlin demurred at first, but he soon wrote "When I Lost You" (1912), the only song he ever acknowledged to have been written from a personal experience. It was his first important ballad. Berlin's idol, George M. Cohan, called it "the prettiest song I ever heard."

Berlin was one of the most active composers on Broadway from 1914, when he wrote the score for *Watch Your Step,* until 1926, when he began to focus more on family life. While Kern and his collaborators

Guy Bolton and P. G. Wodehouse were revolutionizing the American musical with their sophisticated, witty shows (1915–1918) at the Princess Theatre, Berlin was content to turn out show after show with hit tunes, rather than try to reinvent popular song, as he had done with "Alexander's Ragtime Band." Although most of his songs from this period are now forgotten, they were some of the biggest sellers of their time. Musicologist and songwriter Alec Wilder notes in *American Popular Song: The Great Innovators, 1900–1950* (1972) that Berlin moved rather effortlessly among the domains of Broadway, Hollywood, and Tin Pan Alley. Wilder points out that while writers who concentrated primarily on show music—such as Kern, Rodgers, and Porter—strove to make their songs as theatrical as possible, Berlin's theater songs were not much more sophisticated than his popular songs. As a result, many more of his show songs became popular, in terms of short-term sales and the younger market, than did those of his contemporaries.

The most famous Berlin show of this period, *Yip, Yip, Yaphank* (1918), also had the shortest run. He wrote and produced it while he was stationed at Camp Upton on Long Island during World War I. Staged at the Century Theatre in New York, there were only thirty-two performances of the show, but it was an Army fund-raiser that had originally been intended to run for only a week. The highlight of *Yip, Yip, Yaphank* was Berlin himself, singing the song he had written out of his unhappiness with reveille: "Oh! How I Hate to Get Up in the Morning." With its bugle-call melody set to vernacular phrases such as "You gotta get up," the song captured the frustrations of the average soldier. Another hit from the show was "Mandy," sung by soldiers in drag and blackface as an old-fashioned minstrel number. Berlin had originally written "God Bless America" for *Yip, Yip, Yaphank,* but he laid it aside when it seemed there were already enough patriotic numbers in the show.

Serving in the army and writing and producing *Yip, Yip, Yaphank* seemed to produce a remarkable transformation in Berlin; as recently as 1914, he had written a cutting pacifist song, "Stay Down Here Where You Belong," which compared the instigators of war to the devil and soldiers to butchers. The patriotism that colored the rest of Berlin's life may have reflected his decision to become a naturalized citizen of the United States on 6 February 1918, a few months before he was drafted. The run of *Yip, Yip, Yaphank* could probably have continued past the end of the war on 11 November 1918, but the army recalled the show after three weeks of encores.

Berlin's experience producing *Yip, Yip, Yaphank* stood him in good stead after the war when, with copro-

Sheet music for the 1926 Berlin song that was interpolated into the Rodgers and Hart show Betsy *and became the hit of the show (Bruccoli Clark Layman Archives)*

ducer Sam H. Harris, he built the Music Box theater on Forty-fifth Street near Broadway in 1921. The pair spared no expense in making the theater and the productions as lavish as possible. There were four annual Music Box Revues (1921–1924) for which Berlin wrote all the songs. The fact that these shows produced few hits and even fewer standards tends to confirm Wilder's thesis that by making his music more theatrical, Berlin also made it less commercial. During the *Music Box Revue* days, he published only a few independent songs, but a high proportion were big hits, including three from 1924, "Lazy," "All Alone," and "What'll I Do?"

In 1925 the thirty-six-year-old Berlin was the subject of a biography by Alexander Woollcott, *The Story of Irving Berlin.* Kern, in a quotation seemingly as famous as his own songs, was asked by Woollcott to describe Berlin's place in American music. Kern wrote, "the average United States citizen [is] perfectly epitomized in Irving Berlin's music. [Berlin] doesn't attempt to stuff the public's ears with pseudo-original ultra-modernism, but he honestly absorbs the vibrations emanating from the people, manners, and life of his time, and in turn, gives these impressions back to the world—simplified, clarified, glori-

Berlin and his second wife, Ellin Mackay Berlin, shortly after their wedding on 4 January 1926 (Bryant Library Local History Collection, Roslyn, New York)

fied. In short . . . Irving Berlin has no *place* in American music. He *is* American music!"

When Kern evaluated Berlin for Woollcott, Berlin had yet to write many of his most famous songs. Thus, Kern's proclamation was anything but an overstatement, and it indicates that there were many great songs in the overlooked first fifteen years of Berlin's career.

In the mid 1920s, while Berlin was at the height of his professional career, his marriage to Ellin Mackay was easily the most important aspect of his private life. The two met at a dinner party on 23 May 1924–his actual thirty-sixth birthday. Mary Ellin Berlin Barrett, the couple's oldest daughter, recounts in *Irving Berlin: A Daughter's Memoir* (1994) that the first words Ellin spoke to her future husband were "Oh, Mr. Berlin, I do so like your song 'What Shall I Do,'" thus debunking the myth that he had written his greatest waltz, "What'll I Do?," while pining for Ellin. Two other waltzes, "All Alone" and "Remember," were written during this period, and, although Berlin insisted that they were unrelated to his courtship of Ellin, Barrett states firmly that they were "clearly written" for her mother. Ironically, the one song that Berlin admitted to writing for Ellin, "Always," got its start, according to legend, as a lyric he wrote on a lark for

a girl named Mona, who was dating his musical secretary, Arthur Johnston, at the time.

Clarence Mackay, Ellin's wealthy, Catholic father, the head of the Postal Telegraph Company (now ITT), was furious with his daughter's affection for this Jewish songwriter and sent her overseas to forget Berlin, but she was undeterred by her father's machinations. She married Berlin at New York's Municipal Building on 4 January 1926. The newlyweds were mobbed by reporters as they set off for Atlantic City, and there was no letup by the time they returned to New York a few days later to sail for Europe. The Berlins spent most of the year in England, France, and Portugal and returned via Canada in an unsuccessful effort to avoid the press.

Ellin was by this time expecting the couple's first child. Berlin wrote "Blue Skies" on the occasion of the birth of Mary Ellin Berlin, and he was able to use it in the show *Betsy* (1926), for which the remainder of the score was by Rodgers and Lorenz Hart. Belle Baker starred in the production, and she was dismayed that there was nothing in the witty and sophisticated score for her to "belt" in her trademark style. Berlin gave her "Blue Skies" to sing, and the song stopped the show. Even Rodgers, who at the time was outraged at the interpolation of the song into his score, later admitted that "Blue Skies" was superior to anything he and Hart had written for the score. "Blue Skies," another of Berlin's all-time great songs, has been a favorite of popular singers, jazz musicians, and even country-and-western artists such as Willie Nelson and Jim Reeves. In *The Jazz Singer* (1927), the first movie to feature sound (for the musical selections and some dialogue), one of the numbers sung by Al Jolson was "Blue Skies."

Berlin wrote songs for several musicals in the early days of the talkies, notably *Puttin' on the Ritz* (1930), a vehicle for vaudeville star Harry Richman, and *Reaching for the Moon* (1930), best remembered for featuring one of Bing Crosby's first minor screen appearances. The producers of the latter movie cut most of the songs, rendering it effectively a nonmusical, and this experience might have soured Berlin on the motion-picture medium permanently. Only later, when the production of movie musicals was entrusted to people with respect for the music, was Berlin willing to return to Hollywood. He was the only one of the major Broadway songwriters who went on to achieve success in the cinema without moving to California permanently.

Domestic situations were a common theme in Berlin's lyrics from 1926 to 1928, his first years of marriage and fatherhood, with such songs as "At Peace with the World" (1926), "I'm on My Way Home" (1926), "What Does It Matter?" (1927), "I Can't Do without You" (1928), and "Russian Lullaby" (1927). Berlin also wrote torch songs in these years too, vitiating the idea that his

Sheet music for the 1928 waltz version of the song that became a swing-music standard in 1937
(Bruccoli Clark Layman Archives)

songs were based on his life experiences. Some of these have remained in the popular-song repertoire such as "How about Me?" (1928) and "The Song Is Ended (But the Melody Lingers On)" (1927), but others, nearly forgotten, are among his most poignant: "Because I Love You" (1926), "We'll Never Know" (1926), and "To Be Forgotten" (1928)–all waltzes.

The period from 1923 to 1929 was Berlin's most fertile waltz period. Although it is not a well-known fact, even among scholars, his famous song "Marie (The Dawn Is Breaking)" (1928) was originally written in three-quarter time. Only after Tommy Dorsey's swing arrangement of the song–in a 1937 recording featuring Jack Leonard on the vocal and a Bunny Berigan trumpet solo–did "Marie" become a standard.

After this waltz period Berlin entered what came to be known as "the dry spell." From 1929 to 1932 there was little excitement surrounding his output, and he went into a period of personal and professional despondency. Paradoxically, some of the songs written in these

years–"Puttin' on the Ritz" (1930), "Let Me Sing and I'm Happy" (1930), and "Maybe It's Because I Love You Too Much" (1933)–became much bigger hits later on. Berlin also wrote some ballads, such as "With You," "(Across the Breakfast Table) Looking at You," and "The Little Things in Life" (all from 1930), but these were for the most part used in movies that did not showcase them effectively or were interpolated into stage productions over which Berlin had little or no influence. During this dry period Berlin came to fear that he might never write again.

Although Berlin experienced this period of depression and diminished output, he enjoyed unbroken success as a music publisher. From the 1910s until 1944, he was a partner in songwriting companies that published not only his works but also those of others. In his capacity as head of Irving Berlin, Inc., he was involved to some degree in the publication of thousands of songs by others, some of which became standards to rival his own catalogue. The early work of the songwriting team of Buddy DeSylva,

Sheet music for the classic Berlin song introduced in the 1933 stage musical As Thousands Cheer
(University of South Carolina Music Library)

Lew Brown, and Ray Henderson was published by Berlin, as were some of the early scores for Walt Disney's motion-picture musicals. Disney was slow to move into publishing; as a result, some of the songs most closely associated with the Disney organization today, including "When You Wish Upon a Star" (1940), are controlled not by Disney but by the successor to Irving Berlin, Inc., Bourne, Inc.

When Berlin and his business partner, Saul Bornstein, decided to break up Irving Berlin, Inc., in 1943, Berlin kept only his own songs, and Bornstein took everything else. Irving Berlin, Inc., was renamed Bourne, Inc., and is still an active publisher. Berlin set up a new company, the Irving Berlin Music Corporation, and this entity controlled his songs until shortly after his death in

1989, when the administration of the Berlin catalogue was turned over to Williamson Music, Inc., a division of the Rodgers & Hammerstein Organization.

In 1932 came a series of breakthroughs that ended Berlin's period of depression and marked the start of the late period of his career. *Face the Music,* the first musical in seven years to be scored completely by Berlin, had a successful, if brief, run, which was not disappointing, considering how few people had money to spend on the theater in 1932. The show introduced "Manhattan Madness," one of Berlin's most intricate songs, which is quite evocative of New York as it was at that time. Also notable was "I Say It's Spinach (And the Hell with It)." Berlin took the idea for the song from the caption of a *New Yorker* cartoon that showed a mother trying to get a small girl to

Sheet music for a song from the second Berlin movie musical to star Fred Astaire and Ginger Rogers
(from William Zinsser, Easy to Remember, *2000)*

eat her broccoli. Berlin transformed the cartoon into a charming song in which two lovers thumb their noses at the Great Depression.

In 1932 Berlin also published the independent songs "How Deep Is the Ocean (How High Is the Sky)" and "Say It Isn't So," both of which became standards and reminded the world and Berlin himself that he could still write successful songs. The next year brought *As Thousands Cheer,* one of the most inventive of all Berlin's revues, which he wrote with the young playwright Moss Hart. The revue is about a newspaper, with a song for every section. The weather page is represented by "Heat Wave" and the Sunday color section by "Easter Parade." There is even a song about the making of the paper itself, called "Man Bites Dog." (In journalism there is a credo that when a dog bites a man, it is not news; it is news

when a man bites a dog.) This song was not published until 1970, perhaps because it employs the word *bitch.* "The Funnies" is a witty list song that alludes to various newspaper cartoon characters; another list song, "Not for All the Rice in China," is one of Berlin's most amusing catalogues of hyperbolic declarations of love.

In the most memorable scene from *As Thousands Cheer,* Ethel Waters sang a song to accompany a news item about an African American who has been lynched. "Supper Time" expresses the anguish of the lynched man's wife, who has to get a meal on the table as she wonders what she will tell her children about their father. "If one song can tell the whole tragic history of a race," Waters wrote in her autobiography, *His Eye Is on the Sparrow* (1951), "'Supper Time' was that song." It was a disturbing scene, and, had Berlin himself not been the

Bing Crosby singing Berlin's "White Christmas" for Marjorie Reynolds in a scene from the 1942 movie
Holiday Inn *(from Philip Furia,* Irving Berlin: A Life in Song, *1998)*

producer, it probably would have been cut from the show. Waters also showed her enormous versatility by singing and dancing "Heat Wave," an exotic send-up of weather reports, and by impersonating Josephine Baker in "Harlem On My Mind," a song representing the "Paris Report" section of newspapers that provided news on American expatriates.

Berlin went to Hollywood again in 1935, but this time he wrote for movies in which the music was to be primary, not some detail to be tossed about carelessly by the producers. The success of Berlin's first pictures on this return to the medium was owing in no small part to the elegance and professionalism of the stars, Astaire and Ginger Rogers. Their first movie with Berlin was *Top Hat* (1935), long celebrated as one of the best motion-picture musicals. The songs, staging, and even the plot (often a minor detail in movie musicals) cohered into an elegant and charming whole. All of the songs became hits: "Cheek to Cheek," "Isn't This a Lovely Day (To Be Caught in the Rain)?," "The Piccolino," "No Strings (I'm Fancy Free)," and the title song, "Top Hat, White Tie and Tails."

Berlin, Astaire, and Rogers reprised this success with *Follow the Fleet* (1936), which was nearly the equal of

Top Hat. With a larger cast and more-varied production, this movie allowed Berlin greater latitude with his songs. "Let's Face the Music and Dance" is one of his darkest songs, and its gloom is deepened by the dramatic context out of which it emerges. After losing his fortune at a gambling casino, Astaire's character is contemplating suicide when he notices Rogers. The message of the song is that facing the music is at least better than death. *Follow the Fleet* features one of the best integrations of Berlin songs with the story.

Berlin never authorized a filmed biography of his life. Partially to fill the void, three movies were made that were primarily vehicles to showcase old Berlin songs, with a few new ones written for the thin plots: *Alexander's Ragtime Band* (1938), *Blue Skies* (1946), and *There's No Business Like Show Business.* (While the first of these includes some facts from Berlin's life, their inclusion is largely a device to allow the movie to incorporate a maximum number of his old songs and does not serve a biographical purpose.) It would be erroneous to include *Easter Parade* (1948) and *White Christmas* as part of this group, for while each of them featured old songs, they were mostly composed of as yet unused ones, and some of these are among Berlin's most inventive. "A Couple of Swells,"

Berlin performing in his show This Is the Army *(1942) onboard the* USS Arkansas *in the Pacific,
1944 (from Philip Furia,* Irving Berlin: A Life in Song, *1998)*

from *Easter Parade,* is one of the best comic numbers Berlin wrote, and the performances of Astaire and Judy Garland as two tramps in tattered tuxedos who decide to "walk up the avenue" is a classic of the movie musical.

In 1938, with war looming in Europe, Berlin brought out "God Bless America," which he had cut from *Yip, Yip, Yaphank* in 1918. Actually, there is no documentation that the song was written at that time; Berlin did not copyright the then-unpublished "God Bless America," as he did so many of his drafts. The best evidence that the anthem was written in 1918 is an interview that Harry Ruby—who transcribed the song for Berlin—gave to Max Wilk for *They're Playing Our Song: From Jerome Kern to Stephen Sondheim—The Stories behind the Words and Music of Two Generations* (1973). Ruby claimed to be the one who told Berlin that there were too many patriotic songs on the market, whereupon Berlin removed "God Bless America" from the score of *Yip, Yip, Yaphank.* There is an early draft of "God Bless America" in the Irving Berlin Collection at the Library of Congress. This version is a song with a chorus in ABAC

form, in contrast to the ABCD chorus of the song as published. Berlin apparently made this change in the structure of the song when he rewrote it for singer Kate Smith in 1938. The unpublished versions of Berlin's songs establish that virtually every change made from the unpublished to the published version is an improvement, and "God Bless America" is no exception. In an earlier version of the part of the song celebrating foamy oceans, there was a regional reference that would have lessened the universal appeal of the song. Berlin described "God Bless America" as the song that was closest to him emotionally. He did whatever he could to discourage dance bands from using it, although he made a notable exception when Guy Lombardo recorded *Berlin by Lombardo,* an album-length medley of his songs, for Capitol in 1958. Beginning with "God Bless America," Berlin donated the proceeds from his patriotic songs to the Boy Scouts and Girl Scouts. He created a special fund for this purpose. (The organizing documents for the God Bless America Fund state that one trustee must be Catholic; another, Protestant; and a third, Jewish.)

Sheet music for the hit song, from Berlin's longest-running musical, that became a show-business anthem
(Bruccoli Clark Layman Archives)

During this same period Berlin conceived of the idea for a musical built around songs about each of the holidays in a year. The challenging idea came to fruition in 1942 with the movie *Holiday Inn,* starring Crosby and Astaire, with Marjorie Reynolds and Virginia Dale playing opposite them. Berlin had managed to come up with a successful song about every major holiday. For New Year's Day there was "Let's Start the New Year Right"; for Abraham Lincoln's birthday, "Abraham"; for Valentine's Day, "Be Careful, It's My Heart"; and for George Washington's birthday, "I Can't Tell a Lie." For Easter,

naturally, "Easter Parade," originally from *As Thousands Cheer* and already a standard, was interpolated. For Independence Day there was "Let's Say It with Firecrackers"—which Astaire sang and danced amid exploding firecrackers—and "Song of Freedom"; and for Thanksgiving Day, "I've Got Plenty to Be Thankful For."

Actually, *Holiday Inn* produced two Christmas standards: "Happy Holiday" was used in the movie merely as a generic song for celebrating *any* holiday, but it was later seized on by recording artists for inclusion on Christmas albums, which proliferated after development of the LP (long-playing) record in 1948. Berlin's "White Christmas" is now legendary as the most popular song ever written in America, but in 1942 it was just another holiday song in a movie filled with such songs. In Crosby's recording, it became the big hit of the Christmas season that year, and homesick military personnel in World War II, particularly those stationed overseas, took the song to heart.

During World War II Berlin was once again prompted to do a fund-raising soldier show. This time, the cast and crew were drawn not from available troops (as with those at Camp Upton for *Yip, Yip, Yaphank*) but from the many talented friends Berlin had made during his career in show business, such as the director Joshua Logan. *This Is the Army* opened on 4 July, Independence Day, 1942 at the Broadway Theatre and ran for twelve weeks, followed by a national tour and then a world tour. Berlin, now age fifty-four, accompanied the show wherever it went, including to the war zones of Europe, North Africa, and the Pacific, putting his life at risk to entertain the troops. The show featured a rousing title song, "This Is the Army, Mister Jones"; winsome wartime ballads, such as "I Left My Heart at the Stage Door Canteen"; and "What the Well-Dressed Soldier in Harlem Will Wear," a jazzy number for the black members of the cast. (The company that performed in *This Is the Army* was the only integrated unit in the armed forces during World War II.) The showstopper was "Oh! How I Hate to Get Up in the Morning," from *Yip, Yip, Yaphank*, which Berlin himself sang in his World War I uniform (which still fit him). When Warner Bros. made the 1943 motion-picture version of *This Is the Army* (the only time the tight-fisted Berlin ever worked with the tight-fisted Warners—and for a benefit project from which neither profited), Berlin reprised his role from the stage version, singing his trademark song.

After the conclusion of the war Berlin returned to Broadway, but the circumstances that led him to write his greatest score were laced with tragedy. Rodgers and Oscar Hammerstein II, after their triumphs with *Oklahoma!* (1943) and *Carousel* (1945), were trying to expand their musical-production business to include shows written by other people and settled on the idea of producing a show about the western sharpshooter Annie Oakley. The book was to be written by Dorothy Fields and her brother Herbert Fields, with songs by Dorothy Fields and Kern.

Just before he was to begin writing the score for the new musical about Oakley, however, Kern died, at age sixty, collapsing on a Manhattan street and never regaining consciousness. Rodgers and Hammerstein needed a new composer, and Berlin seemed to be the only one who could do it, even though it meant that Dorothy Fields would have to step aside as lyricist. Berlin was at first

Ethel Merman as Mrs. Sally Adams in Berlin's 1950 stage musical Call Me Madam *(Theatre Collection, Museum of the City of New York)*

reluctant because he was in the middle of a string of projects for which his name appeared above the title, a sign of power in the entertainment world: *Holiday Inn, This Is the Army,* and *Blue Skies.* Stepping into this production meant that his name would have to be subordinate to those of Rodgers and Hammerstein. Berlin also expressed some trepidation at writing songs in the new "integrated" idiom (which he termed "situation shows"), but he recognized the importance of the project; the pressing needs of his friends, Rodgers, Hammerstein, and the Fieldses; and the opportunity to step into the shoes of Kern, who had long been acclaimed the supreme composer of the American musical theater.

Still with doubts about whether he could write the kind of folksy songs that would be required of a show about Oakley (particularly after his recent work for the sophisticated Astaire), Berlin took the Fieldses' book to his country place in the Catskill Mountains and wrote several songs, including "Doin' What Comes Natur'lly," "They Say It's Wonderful," and "You Can't Get a Man with a Gun." He found that, as Rodgers had predicted, writing songs for specific characters at various moments of the dramatic action gave him inspiration. Berlin went on to write such songs as "I Got the Sun in the Morning," "The Girl That I Marry," "I Got Lost in His Arms," and, when the second act needed a song to bolster it, "Anything You Can Do."

Although audiences loved *Annie Get Your Gun* when it came out in 1946, the critics were not much better than lukewarm in their response. The show was the longest running of Berlin's career, however, and nearly every song became a hit. *Annie Get Your Gun* produced more hits than any musical before or since, and "There's No Business Like Show Business"—which was nearly dropped from the show in one of the out-of-town tryouts—has become the anthem of the entertainment industry. The success of the show stemmed not only from Berlin's songs but also from the singing of Ethel Merman, who starred as Annie. Merman, too, was playing more of a character than she had in previous shows, and Berlin's array of songs for her fleshed out a character who was brash and cocky but also vulnerable. Merman was unavailable for the movie version of *Annie Get Your Gun* (1950), and Garland was initially cast in the role of Annie. When the studio decided Garland's addictions made her an undependable performer, the movie was produced with Betty Hutton, known more for her comedy than for her singing, but it was still a critical and popular success. *Annie Get Your Gun* continues to be revived, performed, and recorded—a classic of the American musical theater.

Berlin and Merman worked together again in 1950 for *Call Me Madam*. A typical Berlin show in terms of political content and topicality, it was loosely based on the career of Perle Mesta, a Washington socialite and Democratic campaign contributor who was appointed ambassador to Luxembourg by President Harry Truman in 1949. Although the story is somewhat dated, much of the humor transcends the years that have passed since its opening, and the sharp satire still rings true in songs such as "Can You Use Any Money Today?," which presents Berlin's critique of America's generous foreign-aid policies. "They Like Ike" not only promoted Dwight D. Eisenhower—and with the line "I like Ike" created the most successful presidential campaign slogan of the twentieth century—but also aimed barbs at Truman, as well as at Eisenhower's potential Republican opponents. The score included some of Berlin's best songs: "The Best Thing for You," "Marrying for Love," and "Once Upon a Time Today."

While *Call Me Madam* was being tried out on the road, the director, George Abbott, decided it needed a showstopper for the second act. It happened that Berlin's 1914 song "Play a Simple Melody," from his first score, *Watch Your Step,* had again made it to the top of the 1950 pop charts in a new recording by Crosby and his fifteen-year-old son Gary. The song was Berlin's first polyphonic duet—that is, a song with two parts that are sung separately and then together. In

one of his classic all-night songwriting sessions, he wrote another "counterpoint" song, "You're Just in Love," for *Call Me Madam*. As a young diplomat, played by Russell Nype, bemoans his first taste of love—"I smell blossoms and the trees are bare"—Merman's worldly wise character chimes in: "You don't need analyzing / . . . / You're not sick, you're just in love." Berlin and Abbott got the showstopper they wanted, and Berlin wrote more polyphonic songs near the end of his career, including "Empty Pockets Filled with Love," for the 1962 show *Mr. President;* "An Old-Fashioned Wedding," for the 1966 revival of *Annie Get Your Gun;* and "Wait Until You're Married" (1966), which was probably intended for the score of an uncompleted stage-musical project.

Between his successes with Merman, Berlin had written a Broadway score about the girl who posed for the Statue of Liberty. *Miss Liberty,* produced in 1949, was one of his lightest scores, full of such gentle numbers as "Let's Take an Old-Fashioned Walk," "Just One Way to Say I Love You," and "Paris Wakes Up and Smiles." The most famous piece from the show is "Give Me Your Tired, Your Poor," in which Berlin set a stanza of Emma Lazarus's "The New Colossus" (1883), the poem carved on the base of the statue, to music. (Berlin later said that this was the only time he ever deserved to be called a "composer"; otherwise, he was "just a songwriter.")

In the 1950s several Berlin musicals were adapted for the cinema. *Annie Get Your Gun* and *Call Me Madam* were made into movies, in 1950 and 1953, respectively, although Berlin composed no new songs for these adaptations. He drew much of the material for the 1954 movies *White Christmas* and *There's No Business Like Show Business* from music he had composed over the previous decade. During the 1950s rock and roll emerged, but Berlin was not one of those who denounced the music out of hand (although he was reportedly appalled at Elvis Presley's version of "White Christmas"). He even wrote one rock-and-roll song, "The Washington Twist," for *Mr. President*.

It was not simply the advent of rock and roll that displaced Berlin from the top of American music. He became increasingly reclusive in the late 1950s, which gave fuel to many unfounded rumors about his personal life. Not until Barrett published *Irving Berlin: A Daughter's Memoir* in 1994 did the truth become known. Her father had suffered a nervous breakdown, which lasted three years, after his last movie musicals. Berlin had the sense that he was losing his ability. Each time he had an idea for another show, he felt he could write the music but lacked the stamina to fight the battles with those who stood between him and the audience—producers, librettists, directors, conductors, choreographers, backers, and so on—which he had done over the years to ensure that his music was presented as he intended.

In 1962 Berlin recovered his powers enough to provide the score for *Mr. President,* based loosely on the administration of President John F. Kennedy. While Berlin's songs are delightful—five different record albums of them were released at the time—the story was weak, and, while that would not have been a huge detriment to the success of the show in the 1930s, by 1962 the public was used to musicals with strong books and characters. Yet, *Mr. President* was not a complete failure; it ran for a solid 265 performances on Broadway. The gulf between Broadway and the Top 40 had also widened to the point that there was virtually no chance that any of the songs would individually show up on the pop charts.

Mr. President did little to depress Berlin's career; the next year, 1963, he was paid the unprecedented sum of $1 million for the rights to a planned but never completed movie musical, "Say It with Music," which might have been the actual telling of his life story. Berlin composed songs for the movie throughout the 1960s, but the studio canceled the project. There were problems with several aspects of the picture, but the deciding factor was that, in the age of television, the market no longer supported the kind of blockbuster musicals M-G-M had made in its heyday. "I Used to Play It by Ear" (1965), perhaps the best of the songs, was introduced by Robert Goulet on the 1968 tribute to Berlin on *The Ed Sullivan Show.* Some of the other songs intended for "Say It with Music"—notably "The Ten Best Undressed Women" (1963)—showed that the master had not lost his wit.

Another noteworthy song from this period was "Who Needs the Birds and Bees?" (1966), originally intended for the 1966 revival of *Annie Get Your Gun,* which was one of the few strophic verse/chorus songs Berlin ever wrote. The strophic song, in which narrative verses alternate with a brief, eight- or sixteen-bar refrain, or chorus, was the standard song form before 1900.

Berlin's last published song (in his lifetime) was "Song for the U.N." (1971), celebrating the twenty-sixth anniversary of the founding of the United Nations. He was still copyrighting new songs into the 1980s and dictating to his musical secretary, Helmy Kresa, as late as 1987, two years before his death. Berlin lived long enough to see some of his earliest works lapse into the public domain. On 1 January 1987, the copyright on the song that first made him famous, "Alexander's Ragtime Band," expired.

Berlin's one-hundredth birthday in 1988 inspired a celebration of unprecedented magnitude in

Berlin singing a song from his last Broadway production, the 1962 musical Mr. President *(Theatre Collection, Museum of the City of New York)*

the United States, extending to Carnegie Hall and the chambers of Congress. Ellin Mackay Berlin died on 29 July 1988 from a stroke. When Berlin himself died the following year, on 22 September 1989, most newspapers ran the obituary on the front page. The television news program *Nightline* took time out of its coverage of Hurricane Hugo, then devastating South Carolina, to cut to Bobby Short's tribute to the great songwriter at the Carlyle Hotel in New York. Berlin, who had been celebrated and honored by every president since Franklin D. Roosevelt, was eulogized by President George Bush as the country's greatest songwriter. Berlin is buried at Woodlawn Cemetery in the Bronx, alongside his wife of sixty-two years and his infant son, Irving Berlin Jr., who died in 1928. Berlin is survived by his three daughters, Barrett, Linda Berlin Emmett, and Elizabeth Berlin Peters. One of their first acts after their father's death was to turn administration of his song catalogue over to the Rodgers & Hammerstein Organization. Under these auspices, many of Berlin's idiosyncratic business practices have been reversed and brought into line with the rest of music publishing. One of the best developments has been the publication of Berlin songbooks, and the estate has also made previously unpublished material available. After many years when its creator restricted its use, the music of Berlin is now seeing a renaissance in recordings and on the musical stage. As long as there is an America to be blessed, the songs of Irving Berlin will be sung by the American people.

Interview:

Max Wilk, *They're Playing Our Song: From Jerome Kern to Stephen Sondheim—The Stories behind the Words and Music of Two Generations* (New York: Atheneum, 1973), pp. 261–295.

Bibliographies:

Irving Berlin Music Corp., *The Songs of Irving Berlin* (New York, ca. 1957);

Dave Jay, *The Irving Berlin Songography, 1907–1966* (New Rochelle, N.Y.: Arlington House, 1969);

Tommy Krasker and Robert Kimball, *Catalog of the American Musical: Musicals of Irving Berlin, George & Ira Gershwin, Cole Porter, Richard Rodgers & Lorenz Hart* (Washington, D.C.: National Institute for Opera and Musical Theater, 1988), pp. 1–55;

Vince Motto, *The Irving Berlin Catalog* (Quicksburg, Va.: Sheet Music Exchange, 1988);

Motto, *The Irving Berlin Catalog: First Supplement* (Quicksburg, Va.: Sheet Music Exchange, 1990);

Steven Suskin, *Berlin, Kern, Rodgers, Hart, and Hammerstein: A Complete Song Catalogue* (Jefferson, N.C.: McFarland, 1990).

Biographies:

Alexander Woollcott, *The Story of Irving Berlin* (New York: Putnam, 1925);

Michael Freedland, *Irving Berlin* (New York: Stein & Day, 1974);

Ian Whitcomb, *Irving Berlin and Ragtime America* (London: Century-Hutchinson, 1987);

Laurence Bergreen, *As Thousands Cheer: The Life of Irving Berlin* (New York: Viking, 1990);

Mary Ellin Barrett, *Irving Berlin: A Daughter's Memoir* (New York: Simon & Schuster, 1994);

Charles Hamm, *Irving Berlin: Songs from the Melting Pot: The Formative Years, 1907–1914* (New York & Oxford: Oxford University Press, 1997);

Philip Furia and Graham Wood, *Irving Berlin: A Life in Song* (New York: Schirmer, 1998);

Edward Jablonski, *Irving Berlin: American Troubadour* (New York: Holt, 1999).

References:

Caryl Brahms and Ned Sherrin, *Song by Song: The Lives and Works of 14 Great Lyric Writers* (Bolton, U.K.: R. Anderson, 1984), pp. 2–18, 220–225;

David Ewen, *American Songwriters: An H.W. Wilson Biographical Dictionary* (New York: H.W. Wilson, 1987);

Michael Feinstein, "God Bless Irving Berlin," in his *Nice Work If You Can Get It: My Life in Rhythm and Rhyme* (New York: Hyperion, 1995), pp. 209–223;

Philip Furia, "Ragged Meter Man: Irving Berlin," *The Poets of Tin Pan Alley: A History of America's Great Lyricists* (New York & Oxford: Oxford University Press, 1990), pp. 46–71;

Roy Hemming, *The Melody Lingers On: The Great Songwriters and Their Movie Musicals* (New York: Newmarket Press, 1986), pp. 29–54;

Thomas S. Hischak, "As Thousands Cheered: Irving Berlin," in his *Word Crazy: Broadway Lyricists from Cohan to Sondheim* (New York: Praeger, 1991), pp. 9–17;

William G. Hyland, *The Song Is Ended: Songwriters and American Music, 1900–1950* (New York & Oxford: Oxford University Press, 1995), pp. 17–32, 146–159, 201–205, 260–266;

Gerald Mast, *Can't Help Singin': The American Musical on Stage and Screen* (Woodstock, N.Y.: Overlook Press, 1987), 39-48;

Steven Suskin, *Show Tunes, 1905–1991: The Songs, Shows, and Careers of Broadway's Major Composers,* revised and enlarged third edition (New York & Oxford: Oxford University Press, 2000), pp. 37–56;

Mark White, *"You Must Remember This—": Popular Songwriters 1900–1980* (New York: Scribners, 1985), pp. 32–38;

Alec Wilder, *American Popular Song: The Great Innovators, 1900–1950,* edited, with an introduction, by James T. Maher (New York: Oxford University Press, 1972), pp. 91–120.

Selected Discography:

Always: Great Songs of Irving Berlin, World's Most Beautiful Melodies, Reader's Digest, RS7-017-1, 1994;

Annie Get Your Gun, original Broadway cast, MCA, 10047, 1946;

Annie Get Your Gun, motion-picture soundtrack, M-G-M, E-509, 1950;

Annie Get Your Gun, studio cast, Pickwick, 1050, 1957;

Annie Get Your Gun, television soundtrack, Angel, 64765, 1957;

Annie Get Your Gun, studio cast, Columbia, 2360, 1962;

Annie Get Your Gun, revival cast, RCA, 1124, 1966;

Annie Get Your Gun, revival cast, Angel, 56812, 1999;

As Thousands Cheer, revival cast, Varèse Sarabande, 5999, 1998;

Fred Astaire, *The Irving Berlin Songbook,* Verve, 829172, 1986;

Bobbi Baird and Mike Renzi, *Let's Go Back To the Waltz,* Premier, 1007, 1990;

Ben Bagley's Irving Berlin Revisited, Painted Smiles, 118, 1990;

Tony Bennett, *Bennett/Berlin,* Columbia, 44029, 1987;

Jay Blackton, *Let Me Sing and I'm Happy: The Best of Irving Berlin,* Epic, 3408, 1957;

Blue Skies, motion-picture soundtrack, MCA, 25989, 1946;

Teresa Brewer, *American Music Box: The Songs of Irving Berlin,* Signature, 40231, 1991;

Call Me Madam, original Broadway cast members and Dinah Shore, RCA, 2032, 1950;

Call Me Madam, studio cast, Pickwick, 1050, 1957;

Call Me Madam, revival cast, DRG, 94761, 1995;

Capitol Sings Irving Berlin: Puttin' on the Ritz, Capitol, 98477, 1992;

Rosemary Clooney, *Rosemary Clooney Sings Irving Berlin,* Concord Jazz, 4255, 1984;

Frank DeVol, *The Columbia Album of Irving Berlin,* Columbia, 1260, 1959;

Easter Parade, motion-picture soundtrack (1948), Rhino, 71960, 1995;

Michael Feinstein, *Remember: Michael Feinstein Sings Irving Berlin,* Elektra, 60744, 1987;

Ella Fitzgerald, *The Irving Berlin Songbook,* volume 1, Verve, 829 534, 1958; volume 2, Verve, 829 535, 1958;

Holiday Inn, motion-picture soundtrack (1942), MCA, 25205, 1988;

How Deep Is the Ocean?: The Irving Berlin Songbook, Verve, 537 701-2, 1997;

Dick Hyman, *Face the Music: A Century of Irving Berlin,* Musical Heritage Society, 512213, 1988;

Irving Berlin, American Songbook Series, Smithsonian Collection of Recordings, RD 048-1/Sony Music Special Products, A 22403, 1992;

Irving Berlin: A Hundred Years, Columbia, 40035, 1988;

Irving Berlin in Hollywood, Rhino, 75614, 1999;

The Irving Berlin 100th Anniversary Collection, MCA, 39324, 1988;

An Irving Berlin Songbook, Concord Jazz, 45132, 1997;

Guy Lombardo, *Berlin by Lombardo,* Capitol, 1019, ca. 1960s;

Louisiana Purchase, revival cast, DRG, 94766, 1996;

Patti LuPone, *Heat Wave: Patti LuPone Sings Irving Berlin,* Philips/PolyGram, 446 406-2, 1995;

Andrea Marcovicci, *Always, Irving Berlin,* Cabaret, 5014, 1994;

Ethel Merman, *12 Songs from Call Me Madam,* MCA, 10521, 1950;

Miss Liberty, original Broadway cast, Columbia, 4220, 1949;

Joan Morris and William Bolcom, *Blue Skies: Songs,* Nonesuch, 79120, 1985;

Morris and Bolcom, *The Girl on the Magazine Cover,* RCA, 3089, 1979;

Mr. President, original Broadway cast, Columbia, 48212, 1962;

Mr. President, Perry Como and others, RCA, 2630, 1962;

Benjamin Sears and Bradford Connor, *Come On and Hear!: Early Songs by Irving Berlin, 1909–1915,* Oakton, 0001, 1994;

Sears and Connor, *Keep on Smiling: Songs by Irving Berlin, 1915–1918,* Oakton, 0003, 1996;

The Song Is—Irving Berlin, ASV Living Era, 5068, 1989;

The Swingle Singers, *Nothing but Blue Skies: 100th Birthday Tribute to Irving Berlin,* Platinum, 5822, 1996;

Kiri Te Kanawa, *Kiri Sings Berlin,* Angel, 56415, 1997;

This Is the Army, motion-picture soundtrack, Hollywood Soundstage, 4009, 1943;

Unsung Irving Berlin, Varèse Sarabande, 5632, 1995;

Sarah Vaughan and Billy Eckstine, *The Irving Berlin Songbook,* EmArcy, 822 526-2, 1958;

Elisabeth Welch, *The Irving Berlin Songbook,* Verve, 835 491, 1988.

Johnny Burke

(3 October 1908 – 25 February 1964)

Frederick Nolan

Music is by Jimmy Van Heusen unless otherwise indicated.

SELECTED SONGS FROM THEATRICAL PRODUCTIONS: *Nellie Bly* (1946)–"Harmony"; "Just My Luck";

Carnival in Flanders (1953)–"For a Moment of Your Love"; "Here's That Rainy Day"; "It's an Old Spanish Custom"; "That Man Is Doing His Worst to Make Good"; "The Very Necessary You";

Donnybrook! (1961), lyrics and music by Burke–"The Day the Snow Is Meltin'"; "Donnybrook"; "Ellen Roe"; "He Makes Me Feel I'm Lovely"; "I Have My Own Way"; "Sez I"; "When It's Summer" (music by Nat King Cole); "Wisha Wurra."

SELECTED SONGS FROM MOTION-PICTURE PRODUCTIONS: *Let's Go Places* (1930)–"Boop-Boop-a-Doopa-Doo Trot" (music by George A. Little);

Go West Young Man (1936), music by Arthur Johnston–"Go West Young Man"; "I Was Saying to the Moon"; "On a Typical Tropical Night";

Pennies from Heaven (1936), music by Johnston–"Let's Call a Heart a Heart"; "One, Two, Button Your Shoe"; "Pennies from Heaven"; "Skeleton in the Closet"; "So Do I";

Double or Nothing (1937), music by Johnston–"All You Want to Do Is Dance"; "It's the Natural Thing to Do"; "The Moon Got In My Eyes";

Doctor Rhythm (1938), music by James V. Monaco–"My Heart Is Taking Lessons"; "On the Sentimental Side"; "Only a Gypsy Knows"; "This Is My Night to Dream"; "The Trumpet Player's Lament";

Sing You Sinners (1938), music by Monaco–"Don't Let That Moon Get Away"; "I've Got a Pocketful of Dreams"; "Laugh and Call It Love"; "Where Is Central Park?";

Johnny Burke (AP/Wide World Photos)

East Side of Heaven (1939), music by Monaco–"East Side of Heaven"; "Hang Your Heart on a Hickory Limb"; "Sing a Song of Sunbeams"; "That Sly Old Gentleman from Featherbed Lane";

The Star Maker (1939), music by Monaco–"An Apple for the Teacher"; "Go Fly a Kite"; "A Man and His Dream"; "Still the Bluebird Sings";

That's Right–You're Wrong (1939)–"Scatterbrain" (lyrics and music by Burke, Frankie Masters, Kahn Kean, and Carl Bean);

If I Had My Way (1940), music by Monaco–"April Played the Fiddle"; "I Haven't Time to Be a Millionaire"; "Meet the Sun Halfway"; "The Pessimistic Character (With the Crab Apple Face)";

Love Thy Neighbor (1940)–"Dearest, Darest I?"; "Isn't That Just Like Love?"; "Do You Know Why?";

Rhythm on the River (1940), music by Monaco–"Ain't It a Shame about Mame?"; "Only Forever"; "That's for Me"; "When the Moon Comes Over Madison Square";

Road to Singapore (1940)–"Captain Custard" (music by Victor Schertzinger); "Kaigoon" (music by Monaco); "The Moon and the Willow Tree" (music by Schertzinger); "Sweet Potato Piper" (music by Monaco); "Too Romantic" (music by Monaco);

Playmates (1941)–"How Long Did I Dream?"; "Humpty Dumpty Heart"; "Que Chica"; "Romeo Smith and Juliet Jones"; "Thank Your Lucky Stars and Stripes";

Road to Zanzibar (1941)–"Birds of a Feather"; "It's Always You"; "On the Road to Zanzibar"; "You Lucky People, You"; "You're Dangerous";

My Favorite Spy (1942)–"Got the Moon in My Pocket"; "Just Plain Lonesome";

Road to Morocco (1942)–"Ain't Got a Dime to My Name"; "Constantly"; "Moonlight Becomes You"; "The Road to Morocco";

Dixie (1943)–"A Horse That Knows His Way Back Home"; "If You Please"; "Kinda Peculiar Brown"; "Miss Jemima Walks By"; "She's From Missouri"; "Sunday, Monday, or Always";

And the Angels Sing (1944)–"Bluebirds in My Belfry"; "For the First Hundred Years"; "His Rocking Horse Ran Away"; "How Does Your Garden Grow?"; "It Could Happen to You"; "When Stanislaus Got Married";

Belle of the Yukon (1944)–"Belle of the Yukon"; "Ev'ry Girl Is Diff'rent"; "Like Someone in Love"; "Sleigh Ride in July";

Going My Way (1944)–"The Day after Forever"; "Going My Way"; "Swinging on a Star";

Lady In the Dark (1944)–"Suddenly It's Spring" (interpolation);

The Bells of St. Mary's (1945)–"Aren't You Glad You're You?";

Duffy's Tavern (1945)–"The Hard Way";

The Great John L. (1945)–"A Friend of Yours"; "He Was a Perfect Gentleman";

Cross My Heart (1946)–"Does Baby Feel All Right?"; "How Do You Do It?"; "It Hasn't Been Chilly in Chile (Since Lilly O'Reilly's Around)"; "Love Is the Darndest Thing"; "That Little Dream Got Nowhere";

My Heart Goes Crazy (1946)–"The 'ampstead Way"; "Any Way the Wind Blows"; "Hyde Park on a Sunday"; "My Heart Goes Crazy"; "So Would I"; "You Can't Keep a Good Dreamer Down";

Road to Utopia (1946)–"Good Time Charlie"; "It's Anybody's Spring"; "Personality"; "Put It There, Pal"; "Welcome to My Dream"; "Would You";

Road to Rio (1947)–"Apalachicola, Fla."; "But Beautiful"; "Experience"; "You Don't Have to Know the Language";

Welcome Stranger (1947)–"As Long as I'm Dreaming"; "Country Style"; "My Heart Is a Hobo"; "Smile Right Back at the Sun";

The Emperor Waltz (1948)–"The Emperor Waltz" (music by Johann Strauss); "Friendly Mountains" (traditional music); "Get Yourself a Phonograph"; "The Kiss in Your Eyes" (music by Richard Heuberger);

Mystery in Mexico (1948)–"At the Psychological Moment"; "I Could Get Along Without You"; "Rolling in Rainbows"; "Something in Common";

A Connecticut Yankee in King Arthur's Court (1949)–"Busy Doing Nothing"; "If You Stub Your Toe on the Moon"; "Once and for Always"; "When Is Sometime?";

Top o' The Morning (1949)–"The Donovans"; "Oh, 'Tis Sweet to Think"; "You're in Love with Someone";

Mr. Music (1950)–"Accidents Will Happen"; "And You'll Be Home"; "High on the List"; "Life Is So Peculiar"; "Wasn't I There?"; "Wouldn't It Be Funny?";

Riding High (1950)–"The Horse Told Me"; "Someplace on Anywhere Road"; "Sunshine Cake"; "(We've Got a) Sure Thing";

Road to Bali (1952)–"Chicago Style"; "Hoot Mon"; "Moonflowers"; "The Merry-Go-Runaround"; "To See You";

Little Boy Lost (1953)–"A Propos de Rien"; "Cela M'est Egal";

The Vagabond King (1956), music by Rudolf Friml–"Bonjour"; "A Harp, a Fiddle, and a Flute"; "One, Two, Three, Pause"; "This Same Heart"; "Watch Out for the Devil."

SELECTED SONGS PUBLISHED INDEPENDENTLY OF THEATRICAL AND MOTION-PICTURE PRODUCTIONS: "Shadows on the Swanee" (1933), music by Harold Spina;

"Annie Doesn't Live Here Anymore" (1933), lyrics by Burke and Joe Young, music by Spina;

"The Beat of My Heart" (1934), music by Spina;

"You're Not the Only Oyster in the Stew" (1934), music by Spina;

"My Very Good Friend, the Milkman" (1935), music by Spina;

"Oh, You Crazy Moon" (1939);

"What's New?" (1939), music by Bob Haggart;

"Imagination" (1940);

"Polka Dots and Moonbeams" (1940);

"Misty" (1955), music by Erroll Garner.

*Sheet music for the title song from Burke and Arthur Johnston's
score for a 1936 movie (Bruccoli Clark Layman Archives)*

John Francis "Johnny" Burke was born on 3 October 1908 in Antioch, California. His parents were William Earl Burke, a structural engineer, and Mary Agnes Mungovan Burke, a schoolteacher. The Burke family moved to Chicago when Johnny was still a boy. He studied piano and drama as a youth and graduated from Lindblom High School in 1924. He was a student at Crane College in Chicago for one year and then attended the University of Wisconsin, Madison, where he played piano in the orchestra. Burke went to work in Chicago as a staff pianist and song plugger for the Irving Berlin Music Corporation in 1926. In his spare time he played piano in dance bands and vaudeville houses.

Irving Berlin Music eventually moved Burke to their office in New York, where he continued to work as a pianist and earned additional income as a vocal coach. He was already writing song lyrics and came up with his first hit, written with composer Harold Spina and co-lyricist Joe Young, in 1933. The song was "Annie Doesn't Live Here Anymore," popularized by Fred Waring's Pennsylvanians. Burke and Spina collaborated on several more songs through 1935, some of which were hits. Fats Waller made a commercially successful recording of "You're Not the Only Oyster in the Stew" in 1934. Another Burke-Spina hit was "My Very Good Friend, the Milkman" (1935), also introduced by Waller. Burke is also said to have appeared in the *Ziegfeld Follies* and short musical movies produced at the Warner Bros. Vitaphone Studio in New York.

In 1936 Burke signed a contract to work for Paramount Pictures. At first he was teamed with com-

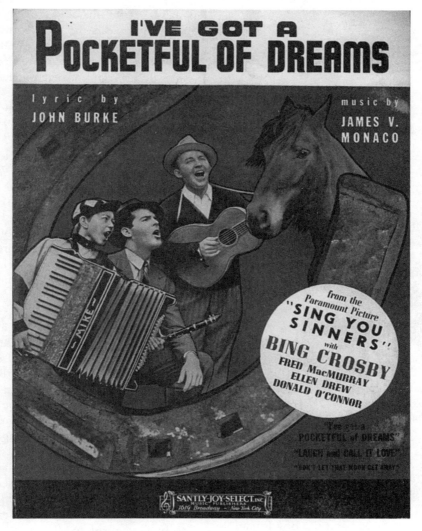

*Sheet music for a song from Burke and James V. Monaco's
score for a 1938 movie (Bruccoli Clark Layman Archives)*

poser Arthur Johnston, who had until 1931 been Irving Berlin's personal arranger, pianist, and musical assistant. With lyricist Sam Coslow, Johnston had written "Cocktails for Two" (1934) and Bing Crosby's first big success, "Just One More Chance" (1931).

Burke's first big break came when he and Johnston were asked to write a song for a Crosby movie. Months went by without their hearing whether the song, "Pennies from Heaven" (1936), would even be used. Only when Burke saw a screening, in which the song title also appeared as the movie title, did he learn that Crosby liked it. "Pennies from Heaven" became a huge hit and a Crosby standard. It was nominated for a 1936 Academy Award for best original movie song, but it lost to Jerome Kern and

Dorothy Fields's song "The Way You Look Tonight," from *Swing Time*.

Johnston and Burke gave Crosby another success with "The Moon Got In My Eyes," featured in the 1937 movie *Double or Nothing*, in which Crosby costarred with Martha Raye. Burke's lyric for the song had a charming ruefulness that perfectly matched Crosby's artless delivery:

Out of the darkness you suddenly appeared
And took my heart completely by surprise.

I guess I should have seen right through you
But the moon got in my eyes.

Also in the score was the popular but more upbeat "It's the Natural Thing to Do."

Burke (right) with Jimmy Van Heusen, who became his main songwriting partner in 1940 (UCLA Music Library Special Collections)

The following year, when Johnston left Paramount to work at 20th Century-Fox, Burke teamed up with James V. "Jimmy" Monaco, a veteran composer who had written the music for such hits as "Row, Row, Row" (1912), "Me and the Boy Friend" (1924), and "You Made Me Love You (I Didn't Want to Do It)" (1913). Together they went on to write a large part of Crosby's movie-song repertoire from 1938 to 1940, beginning with "I've Got a Pocketful of Dreams" featured in *Sing You Sinners* (1938). For *The Star Maker* (1939) Burke and Monaco gave Crosby another enduring hit, "An Apple for the Teacher." "Sing a Song of Sunbeams," "That Sly Old Gentleman from Featherbed Lane," and the title tune were further hits in the 1939 movie *East Side of Heaven*.

During 1939 Burke did a little moonlighting himself, collaborating with Frankie Masters, Kahn Kean, and Carl Bean on the lyrics and music for "Scatterbrain," a clever lament about a giddy woman. That same year, working with composer Bob Haggart, Burke produced the unique and haunting "What's New?" The lyric is a dramatic monologue, one side of a conversation between two former lovers who meet by chance. Burke created a flat, strained, small-talk conversation as a counterpoint to the emo-

tionally soaring melody. The tension between lyric and music reveals the lover's unspoken ardor, right down to his nervously cheery "Adieu!" Only his prosaic reversal of the catchphrase "You haven't changed a bit" to "I haven't changed" releases his suppressed "I still love you so."

Burke and Monaco's "Only Forever," sung by Crosby to Mary Martin in the 1940 movie *Rhythm on the River,* was nominated for an Academy Award for best original song but lost out to Ned Washington and Leigh Harline's "When You Wish Upon a Star," from *Pinocchio.* Also in the same sprightly score for *Rhythm on the River* were "Ain't It a Shame about Mame?" and "When the Moon Comes Over Madison Square," the mock lament of a singing cowboy who is preparing to marry an heiress. "There'll be no more beans and pork," he yodels, "Because the gal owns half New York / So let the moon come over Madison Square."

Burke and Monaco were to write the songs for two more Crosby movies before artistic and personal differences brought about a parting of ways. *If I Had My Way* (1940), in which Crosby costarred with Gloria Jean, featured four songs by Burke and Monaco. "I Haven't Time to Be a Millionaire" and "Meet the Sun Halfway" were probably the most successful of the four, although the novelty number "The Pessimistic Character (With the Crab Apple Face)" was popular at the time.

Burke and Monaco last collaborated on *Road to Singapore* (1940), the first in the series of *Road* movies featuring Crosby, Bob Hope, and Dorothy Lamour. A ballad called "Too Romantic," carefully crafted for Crosby's troubadour delivery, is notable for its appealingly diffident lyric:

You shouldn't let me dream, 'cause I'm too romantic,
Moonlight and stars can make such a fool of me,
You know you're much too near, and I'm too romantic,
Wouldn't I look a fool on a bended knee?

Thrown in for good measure were the sprightly "Sweet Potato Piper," with its piped obbligato harmonies, and "The Moon and the Willow Tree," with music by the director of the movie, Victor Schertzinger, and a suitably Lamour-like lyric by Burke. The main characters—Lamour's moon-eyed sarong girl, Crosby's easygoing lover boy, and Hope's wisecracking, cowardly dupe—were not fully developed, but *Road to Singapore* became one of the most successful movies of 1940.

Burke next teamed up with Jimmy Van Heusen, with whom he went on to have some of his greatest successes. As Van Heusen later recalled, Burke "just

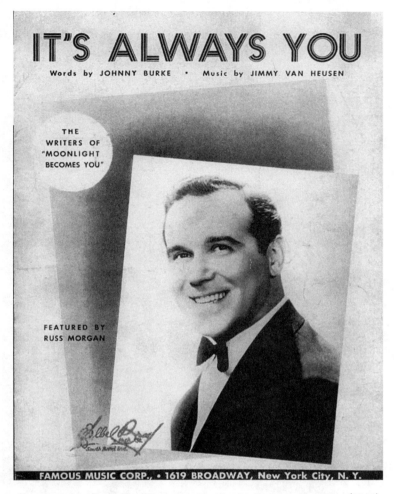

Sheet music for a Burke-Van Heusen song introduced in Road to Zanzibar *(1941),
the second in the series of "Road" movies starring Bing Crosby and Bob Hope
(Bruccoli Clark Layman Archives)*

came into the office"—Remick's, or, more accurately, Warner Bros. Music Holding Corporation—"to shoot the breeze. He said to me, 'Got any tunes?' I said, 'Sure!' So we went and wrote 'Oh, You Crazy Moon.' The next time he was in, we did 'Polka Dots and Moonbeams.' Soon after that came 'Imagination.'" The Tommy Dorsey Orchestra recorded "Polka Dots and Moonbeams" (1940) with Frank Sinatra, giving the singer his first major hit. "Imagination" (1940) was introduced by Fred Waring and His Pennsylvanians, and The Glenn Miller Orchestra's recording of the song became a success on the weekly radio program *Your Hit Parade*.

Together, Burke and Van Heusen wrote some of the finest songs of the 1940s. According to lyricist Sammy Cahn in his autobiography, *I Should Care: The Sammy Cahn Story* (1974), Burke, "the Irish poet," and

Van Heusen would take weeks to write a song. Lyrics came quite slowly to Burke, a painstaking worker. "He always started at the bottom," Cahn said. "He'd lay out a key idea, and then he'd write from the line backwards. [As a result] the songs were lacier, more fragile." Burke put it more simply. All he had to do, he said, was "to listen to Bing's conversation and either take my phrases directly from him or pattern some after his way of putting phrases together."

Mark Sandrich, director of the movies starring Fred Astaire and Ginger Rogers, had fallen in love with "Imagination" and signed Van Heusen to a two-picture contract, initially intending for him to work on the Crosby movie *Love Thy Neighbor* (1940) with Frank Loesser, who was also under contract to Paramount. But Burke—who had long since become a top lyricist for Crosby's movie songs—took a large

Sheet music for a Burke-Van Heusen song from the third of the "Road" movies, released in 1942
(from Marion Short, Hollywood Movie Songs, *1999)*

reduction in his usual salary in order to work on the project with Van Heusen. Although *Love Thy Neighbor* was not a success–the ongoing radio feud between its stars, Jack Benny and Fred Allen, did not work on-screen– Burke and Van Heusen again teamed up when Crosby personally asked Van Heusen to write the songs for his next Paramount picture, another *Road* movie.

Road to Zanzibar (1941) was filmed immediately, again directed by Schertzinger (who died soon after completing the movie). The formula was the same as in *Road to Singapore*. Crosby and Hope are two carnival performers and con artists who sell a phony diamond mine to gangsters and flee to the island of Zanzibar, with Lamour and Una Merkel as two con women with whom they become entangled. Burke

and Van Heusen tapped the right melodic vein with a Crosby ballad, "It's Always You," that boasted another of Burke's lyrical flights:

> If a breeze caresses me,
> It's merely you walking by,
> If I hear a melody,
> It's merely the way you sigh.

Also in the score was the popular but less successful "You're Dangerous." *Road to Zanzibar* was among the four top-grossing movies of 1941. By this time Crosby was such a fan of the Burke-Van Heusen team that he called them his Gold Dust Twins. In 1946 he paid the pair $150,000, making them the highest-paid songwriting partners in Hollywood.

*Sheet music for the Oscar-winning hit song from Burke and Van Heusen's score for
a 1944 movie (from Marie-Reine A. Pafik and Anna Marie Guiheen,*
The Sheet Music Reference and Price Guide, *1992)*

Unusually for those times, Burke spent almost his entire career with one studio, Paramount, taking whatever assignments came his way. "In those days at Paramount, you didn't ask for an assignment, any more than a doctor goes after a wealthy patient," Coslow, who worked there with Johnston, wrote in *Cocktails for Two: The Many Lives of Giant Songwriter Sam Coslow* (1977). "Sometimes you got the one you wanted. Other times the dice came up with someone else's number." Nevertheless, of the forty-one movies on which Burke worked, twenty-five starred Crosby. Burke became one of the few lyricists able to claim that he had written seventeen songs that made *Your Hit Parade* and that he had received an Oscar nomination with each of his composer-collaborators.

Burke and Van Heusen were next assigned to score two turkeys, the first a sad mishmash called *Playmates* (1941), starring John Barrymore and Lupe Velez, and the second an equally forgettable vehicle for Kay Kyser's band, *My Favorite Spy* (1942)—not to be confused with the better-known 1951 movie of the same name starring Hope and Hedy Lamarr. But then came *Road to Morocco* (1942), and, back on familiar ground, Burke and Van Heusen excelled even themselves. The story—a spoof on the exotic *Arabian Nights* fantasies so beloved of Hollywood—was tailor-made for the triumvirate of Crosby, Hope, and Lamour. The gags were clever (even the camels cracked jokes), and Crosby's big love song, "Moonlight Becomes You," turned out to be an enormous hit. Once again, Burke employed his best winsome style:

Sheet music for a song from Burke and Van Heusen's score for a 1944 movie
(from William Zinsser, Easy to Remember, *2000)*

You're all dressed up to go dreaming,
Now don't tell me I'm wrong.
And what a night to go dreaming!
Mind if I tag along?

Burke also wrote a particularly clever conclusion to the title song, "The Road to Morocco," that was good enough to be included in *The Oxford Dictionary of Quotations:* "We certainly do get around / Like *Webster's Dictionary,* we're Morocco-bound." Like *Road to Zanzibar,* the movie was a box-office smash.

In 1943, while Hope was working on a movie of the Cole Porter musical *Let's Face It* (1941), Crosby and Lamour were assigned to a largely fictitious biopic about blackface minstrel Dan Emmett, composer of the popular song "Dixie" (1860), for which Burke and Van Heusen were tapped to write the score. One of the big-

gest box-office hits of the year and Crosby's first movie in color, *Dixie* featured such songs as "Sunday, Monday, or Always" and "If You Please." The former was a big success for Crosby and an even bigger one for Sinatra, who was beginning to threaten Crosby's hold on the crooning business. Far more charming than "Sunday, Monday, or Always" but nowhere near as successful, "If You Please" again demonstrated Burke's delicate skill with a lyrical line:

Did I feel cool September rain just then?
If you please, touch my cheek with your hand again.
When you are near me, I can dream with ease,
And I'm yours, my darling, if you please.

In his next movie Crosby went for a change of pace, playing the priest Father O'Malley in what was to become one of his best-loved pictures, *Going My Way* (1944). Based on an original story by Leo McCarey, it had to do with the problems encountered by a younger priest taking over from an older one (played by Barry Fitzgerald) and the way each adapts to the other. During shooting, producer-director McCarey told Burke and Van Heusen he wanted a song for Crosby to sing with a group of troubled boys. He specified, as if it were a perfectly reasonable request, that the song should be something like the Ten Commandments in rhythm. Burke, never a fast worker, was still wrestling with the problem when, one night during dinner at Crosby's house, the singer's son became stubborn about going to school next day, and Burke chided the boy for acting like a mule. The remark prompted a useful idea: a song about a kid who refuses to better himself because he is as stubborn as a mule. Although it never quite answered McCarey's Ten Commandments requirement, out of the idea grew Burke and Van Heusen's Oscar-winning "Swinging on a Star," which has been recorded in more than two hundred versions.

"Swinging on a Star" and, to a lesser degree, an interpolation, "Too-Ra-Loo-Ra-Loo-Ra," with lyrics and music by James Royce Shannon, were so successful that they completely overshadowed another charming Burke-Van Heusen ballad, "The Day after Forever," and the title song. Not only did "Swinging on a Star" receive the 1944 Academy Award for best original song, but *Going My Way* also garnered the Oscars for best picture, best actor (Crosby), best supporting actor (Fitzgerald), best director and original story (both for McCarey), and best screenplay (by Frank Butler and Frank Cavett).

Burke and Van Heusen's next project was *And The Angels Sing* (1944), a vehicle for the frenetic Betty Hutton, about the four Angel sisters, whose vocal talents are discovered by a conniving bandleader, played by Fred MacMurray. The bandleader swindles the sisters—Hutton, Lamour, Diana Lynn, and Mimi Chandler—but ends up safely in Lamour's arms. Burke and Van Heusen contributed nine songs to *And the Angels Sing,* two of them tailored to Hutton's talents: "Bluebirds in My Belfry" and "His Rocking Horse Ran Away." The movie did not do well at the box office, and as a result, "It Could Happen to You," a charming ballad that further illustrates Burke's whimsically romantic approach to a lyric, was overlooked in the process:

Hide your heart from sight,
Lock your dreams at night,
It could happen to you.
Don't watch stars or you may stumble,

Someone drops a sigh, and down you tumble.
Keep an eye on Spring,
Run when church bells ring,
It could happen to you.
All I did was wonder how your arms would be,
And it happened to me!

Van Heusen and Burke next worked on another *Road* picture, this time about two vaudeville performers hoping to strike it rich at an Alaskan gold mine. Norman Panama and Melvin Frank's screenplay was witty and original, and the songwriters came up with songs to match: "Personality" for Lamour, "It's Anybody's Spring" and "Welcome to My Dream" for Crosby, and two duets for Hope and Crosby, the better of which was undoubtedly "Good Time Charlie," which they rendered with vaudevillian panache. As events transpired, everyone had to wait two years for the movie to be released, but at the 1946 Academy Awards ceremony, *Road to Utopia* won its writers an Oscar. *The New York Times* ranked the picture second in its list of the year's ten best movies.

On loan to RKO, Van Heusen and Burke had meanwhile come up with "Sleigh Ride in July" (1944), which featured another of Burke's winsomely witty lyrics: "A mockingbird was whistling a sentimental tune / And I didn't know enough to come in out of the moonlight." "Sleigh Ride in July," introduced by Dinah Shore in the 1944 movie *Belle of the Yukon,* brought the songwriters another Academy Award nomination in 1945, with "Ac-cent-tchu-ate the Positive," by Johnny Mercer and Harold Arlen; Cahn and Jule Styne's "Anywhere" and "I Fall in Love Too Easily"; and Yip Harburg and Kern's "More and More" among the nominees. (Oscar Hammerstein and Richard Rodgers took the trophy for "It Might as Well Be Spring.") Lost in the shuffle was a fine ballad that Burke and Van Heusen had written for *Belle of the Yukon,* "Like Someone in Love," which later became a Sinatra standard.

There were to be two further major hits for Burke and Van Heusen, both introduced by Crosby: "Life Is So Peculiar," in the movie *Mr. Music* (1950); and "Sunshine Cake," in *Riding High* (1950), a remake of Frank Capra's *Broadway Bill* (1934). With Eddie Cantor, a popular star of the 1920s, as their producer, Burke and Van Heusen collaborated on a 1946 Broadway musical, *Nellie Bly,* about the reporter of the same name who set out to beat the fictional "record" for circumnavigation of the world set by Phileas Fogg in Jules Verne's novel *Around the World in Eighty Days* (1873). When Nellie (Joy Hodges) is assigned by her newspaper to beat Fogg's record, a rival newspaper hires dastardly Phineas Fogarty (Victor Moore) to thwart her. The show opened at the

Adelphi Theatre on 21 January 1946, but it found no favor with the public and sank without a trace, as Gerald Bordman unsympathetically put it, in far less time than it took its heroine to make her trip. One of the songs, "Harmony," was used for a Hope-Crosby duet in a 1947 compendium movie, *Variety Girl,* which featured just about everyone on the Paramount lot.

For *The Bells of St. Mary's* (1945), a sequel to *Going My Way* that again featured Crosby and Fitzgerald, with the added ingredient of Ingrid Bergman as a nun, Burke and Van Heusen wrote "Aren't You Glad You're You?" (There were further sequels: *Welcome Stranger* in 1947, which featured Burke and Van Heusen's "Country Style," and *Top o' The Morning* in 1949, but by this time the charm was wearing off the Father O'Malley series.) In 1946 Burke and Van Heusen worked on only one movie together, a Hutton vehicle called *Cross My Heart,* which inspired nothing remarkable either in song or box-office sales. The following year Burke found himself putting lyrics to the music of Johann Strauss and "Im Chambre Separée," from Richard Heuberger's operetta *Der Opernball* (1898), for a piece of gemütlichkeit called *The Emperor Waltz,* starring Crosby and Joan Fontaine.

Burke and Van Heusen were back on track for their next outing, with a quartet of songs for the fourth movie of the *Road* series, *Road to Rio.* Crosby sang a charmingly philosophical ballad, "But Beautiful," and the Andrews Sisters backed him in a sassy rhumba, "You Don't Have to Know the Language." Lamour had a specialty number called "Experience." The Crosby-Hope duet, done in an appropriately cheesy vaudeville style, was "Apalachicola, Fla.":

> Magnolia trees and blossoms and a pretty South'n gal
> Are better than the orange trees in Cucamonga, Cal.
> We'll sail once more
> Along that Apalachicola shore.
> We may linger on a levee for some hominy grits
> Or pass through Tallahassee if the weather permits.
> We're on our way
> To Apalachicola, F-L-A!
> F-L-O-R-I-D-A
> Apalachicola, F-L-A!

Burke and Van Heusen's next Crosby assignment was a movie remake of Mark Twain's *A Connecticut Yankee in King Arthur's Court* (1889), a story that Herbert Fields, Rodgers, and Lorenz Hart had successfully adapted as the musical *A Connecticut Yankee* in 1927. With Crosby as Sir Boss, who brings Yankee know-how to medieval times, and Rhonda Fleming as his love interest, *A Connecticut Yankee in King Arthur's Court* (1949) was a mild success that featured the Crosby-style ballad "Once and for Always," the

lighter-hearted "If You Stub Your Toe on the Moon," the moodily introspective "When Is Sometime?" sung by Fleming, and, best of all, "Busy Doing Nothing," sung by the highly unlikely trio of Crosby, William Bendix, and Sir Cedric Hardwicke.

The last two movies for which Burke and Van Heusen wrote songs were *Road to Bali* (1952) and *Little Boy Lost* (1953). Neither the ballad "To See You" nor the Hope-Crosby duet "Hoot Mon," both from *Road to Bali,* were up to their usual standard; however, the movie did well. In 1953, Burke and Van Heusen were working as composers and coproducers on another Broadway musical, *Carnival in Flanders,* with book by Preston Sturges. Based on the 1935 movie *La Kermesse Héroïque,* the show opened on 8 September 1953 and starred John Raitt and Dolores Gray. A heavy-handed plot set in seventeenth- century Flanders and a score that failed to scintillate doomed the project, which closed in the same week it opened. Of the songs in the show—which included "For a Moment of Your Love," "It's an Old Spanish Custom," "The Very Necessary You," and "That Man Is Doing His Worst to Make Good"—only one, the hauntingly sad "Here's That Rainy Day," survived to become a favorite ballad of such discriminating singers as Sinatra and Tony Bennett. It also earned Cahn's accolade as one of the ten greatest songs ever written. Van Heusen's complex melody, with its frequent key changes, is as shifting and uncertain as Burke's rueful, reflective lyric:

> Maybe
> I should have saved those leftover dreams;
> Funny,
> But here's that rainy day.
> Here's that rainy day
> They told me about,
> And I laughed at the thought that it might turn out this way.

Throughout 1954 and 1955 Burke's heavy drinking made it almost impossible for him to do any sustained writing, creating a serious problem for Van Heusen, who was under contract to write exclusively with Burke for the publishing house they had founded, Burke and Van Heusen, Inc. This situation compelled Van Heusen to write with other lyricists—such as Mack Gordon, Buddy Kaye, and Sammy Gallop—under a series of pseudonyms.

In 1955 Van Heusen teamed up with Cahn to write "The Tender Trap" for Sinatra. Cahn was "on his lowers," as he himself put it, after the breakup of his successful partnership with Styne, when Burke and Van Heusen's partnership started to falter. As Cahn recalled,

One day the phone rang and it was Sinatra saying "I'd like you to do a song with Van Heusen." I said, "No, no, he's a team with Burke." They were joined at the hip. But Van Heusen called, so I agreed. Came the first writing session over at his place. Suddenly the doorbell rang and Johnny Burke came in. For a lyric-writer that's like being caught with somebody else's wife. . . . Here I was working with a man who had been inseparable from Burke for more than a decade. We made some small talk. . . . I wasn't overly fond of Burke, although I did later come to feel some empathy for him, as did two other Van Heusen aficionados, Ada Kurtz [Van Heusen's former girlfriend] and Jackie Gale, who in Johnny Burke's last years did all but save his life–unfortunately neither they nor anybody could manage that, which was a pity, because personal feelings aside, Johnny Burke was a real Irish poet, a real talent.

Burke's last movie work was to put lyrics to new melodies written by Rudolf Friml for a 1956 motion-picture remake of the Broadway hit *The Vagabond King* (1925), for which Friml wrote the original music. These included "Watch Out for the Devil," "Bonjour," "This Same Heart," "A Harp, a Fiddle, and a Flute," and "One, Two, Three, Pause," but none were memorable. Burke made his final bow in 1961 with the music and lyrics for the Broadway musical *Donnybrook!*, based on the John Ford movie *The Quiet Man* (1952) and starring

Art Lund in the role of a boxer (played by John Wayne in the movie) who retires to his native Ireland after killing a man in the ring, with Joan Fagan as costar. In a season that included the openings of *The Unsinkable Molly Brown, Camelot, Carnival,* and the Lucille Ball musical *Wildcat, Donnybrook!* failed to find an audience and closed after sixty-eight performances. Burke died in New York three years later, on 25 February 1964, at age fifty-five.

References:
Sammy Cahn, *I Should Care: The Sammy Cahn Story* (New York: Arbor House, 1974);
Sam Coslow, *Cocktails for Two: The Many Lives of Giant Songwriter Sam Coslow* (New Rochelle, N.Y.: Arlington House, 1977);
Gary Giddins, *Bing Crosby: A Pocketful of Dreams, 1903–1940* (New York: Little, Brown, 2001), pp. 422–424, 460–461.

Selected Discography:
Bing Crosby, *Bing Crosby in Hollywood, 1930–1934,* Columbia, C2L 43, 1967;
Crosby, *Songs from the Movies,* Empress, 895, 1998;
Road to Morocco, on *Holiday Inn-Road to Morocco-Two for Tonight,* motion-picture soundtrack, Great Music Themes, B00000JRML, 1999.

Irving Caesar
(4 July 1895 – 17 December 1996)

Rachel Scharfman
New York University

SELECTED SONGS FROM THEATRICAL PRO-
DUCTIONS: *Hitchy-Koo* (1918)–"You-oo, Just
You" (music by George Gershwin);

Good Morning, Judge (1919)–"I Was So Young" (music
by Gershwin); "There's More to the Kiss than the
X-X-X" (music by Gershwin);

Demi-Tasse Revue (1919)–"Swanee" (music by Gershwin);

Broadway Brevities of 1920 (1920)–"Spanish Love"
(music by Gershwin);

The Perfect Fool (1921)–"My Log Cabin Home" (lyric by
Caesar and Buddy DeSylva, music by Gershwin);
"No One Else but That Girl of Mine" (music by
Gershwin);

Make It Snappy (1922)–"I Love Her, She Loves Me"
(lyric by Caesar and Eddie Cantor, music by
Caesar);

Greenwich Village Follies (1922), lyrics by Caesar and John
Murray Anderson, music by Louis A. Hirsch–
"Nightingale, Bring Me a Rose";

Spice of 1922 (1922)–"The Yankee Doodle Blues"
(music by Gershwin);

Ziegfeld Follies of 1922 (1922)–"Sixty Seconds Every
Minute, I Think of You" (lyric by Caesar and
Anderson, music by Hirsch);

Nifties of 1923 (1923)–"Nashville Nightingale" (music
by Gershwin);

Poppy (1923)–"Someone Will Make You Smile" (music
by Rudolf Sieczynski); "What Do You Do Sundays, Mary?" (music by Stephen Jones);

No, No, Nanette (1925), music by Vincent Youmans–"I
Want to Be Happy" (interpolation); "Tea for
Two" (interpolation); "Too Many Rings around
Rosie" (interpolation); "You Can Dance with
Any Girl at All" (interpolation);

Betsy (1926)–"Stonewall Moskowitz March" (music by
Richard Rodgers);

Hit the Deck (1927)–"Sometimes I'm Happy" (lyric by
Caesar and Clifford Grey, music by Youmans);

Irving Caesar (courtesy of ASCAP)

Here's Howe (1928), music by Joseph Meyer and Roger
Wolfe Kahn–"Crazy Rhythm";

Whoopee (1928)–"My Blackbirds Are Bluebirds Now"
(music by Cliff Friend);

The Wonder Bar (1931), lyrics by Caesar, libretto by
Caesar and Aben Kandel–"Oh, Donna Clara"
(lyric by Caesar and Beda Fritz Loehner, music
by Jerzy Petersburski).

SELECTED SONGS FROM MOTION-PICTURE
PRODUCTIONS: *Crooner* (1932)–"Sweethearts
Forever" (music by Cliff Friend);

George White's Scandals (1934)–"Nasty Man" (lyric by Caesar and Jack Yellen, music by Ray Henderson);

Curly Top (1935)–"Animal Crackers in My Soup" (lyric by Caesar and Ted Koehler, music by Henderson);

Music for Millions (1944)–"Umbriago" (lyric and music by Caesar and Jimmy Durante);

Lover, Come Back (1946)–"Just a Gigolo" (English lyric by Caesar, original German lyric by Julius Brammer, music by Leonello Casucci).

SELECTED SONGS PUBLISHED INDEPENDENTLY OF THEATRICAL OR MOTION-PICTURE PRODUCTIONS: "We're Pals" (1920), music by George Gershwin;

"Yan-Kee" (1920), music by Gershwin;

"Swanee Rose" (1921), lyric by Caesar and Buddy DeSylva, music by Gershwin;

"Lady, Play Your Mandolin" (1930), music by Oscar Levant;

"If I Forget You" (1933), music by Caesar;

"Is It True What They Say about Dixie?" (1936), lyric by Caesar and Sam Lerner, music by Gerald Marks;

"Remember Your Name and Address" (1937), music by Marks;

"Thomas Jefferski" (1946), music by Caesar;

"Tommy Tax" (1946), music by Caesar;

"United Nations" (1946), music by Caesar;

"We Have a Law" (1946), music by Caesar;

"Two Times a Day" (1947), music by Caesar.

A "real lyric writer," Irving Caesar explained to Max Wilk in Wilk's *They're Playing Our Song* (1986), is "a fellow who can't help singing, and he sings through his words." Best known as the lyricist for "Swanee" (1919) and "Tea for Two" (1925), Caesar collaborated with composers such as George Gershwin, Vincent Youmans, Sigmund Romberg, and Rudolf Friml during what he referred to in a 1958 interview as "the golden age of truly inspirational songs."

Caesar was born Isidore Caesar on 4 July 1895 to Morris and Sofia Selinger Caesar. His father, a Romanian immigrant, owned a secondhand bookstore in New York's Lower East Side and taught evening English classes to recent immigrants. While Irving grew up in a literary environment, he exhibited an early talent for music. At the age of five he picked out the tune "On a Sunday Afternoon" (1902) on a local candy store's piano. Those present at his "first concert," Caesar recalled in 1958, hailed him as a child prodigy. His parents were persuaded to pur-

chase a piano, and he was given lessons, which provided little return: "I still play with one finger," he noted. Though he never mastered the piano, over the course of his career Caesar did come to compose the music for several pieces, including a symphony, show tunes, and songs he wrote for children.

Despite these occasional forays into composition, Caesar's specialty was, and always remained, verse. He wrote his first poem at the age of six:

And a little bird swinging on a tree
It sings to me the whole day long
And I love to hear its pretty song.

The lighthearted simplicity found in this poem resonates in many of the more than one thousand lyrics that Caesar published in the decades to come.

After attending grammar school on the Lower East Side, Caesar was sent to the Chappaqua Mountain Institute, a private Quaker school in Chappaqua, New York. How his father raised the funds to send him away to school was a mystery, but of his time there, Caesar recalled, "I just loved it!" He went on to attend Townsend Harris High School, a Manhattan school for gifted students that was also attended by Ira Gershwin and E. Y. "Yip" Harburg. Though only a year older than Gershwin and Harburg, it is unclear whether Caesar knew these fellow future lyricists at the time. Of George Gershwin, his future collaborator, Caesar noted, "I never ran into him very much on the East Side."

One spring while in high school, at his father's urging, Caesar enrolled in evening stenography and typing classes at the Long Island Business College. After graduating from Townsend Harris High School in 1914, he went to City College of New York, but in 1915 he became distracted by news of Henry Ford's plans to send a "peace ship" to Europe in hopes of spreading goodwill and helping to prevent war. Caesar immediately sent Ford a wire in which he offered his clerical skills for the mission. He was accepted and embarked on 4 December 1915, spending nearly a year abroad.

Caesar made a positive impression upon Ford, who wanted to groom him to manage one of his overseas factories. Ford wished him to gain practical experience first, however. Thus, when the ship returned to the United States, Caesar worked on the assembly line at the Ford plant in Long Island instead of going back to City College. After proving his incompetence at greasing rear axles, he was reassigned to Ford's New York offices, located on Fifty-fourth Street in Manhattan. The location was ideal for Caesar, since it was close to Broadway and the

Sheet music for the 1919 song by Caesar and George Gershwin that became Gershwin's most popular song (from Deena Rosenberg, Fascinating Rhythm: The Collaboration of George and Ira Gershwin, *1991)*

famed Remick's music-publishing house, where he spent many of his lunch hours.

Caesar was enchanted by the environment at Remick's, where "all day long all you heard from about eleven o'clock to about six or seven o'clock was the singing of songs, song plugging." On one of his visits to Remick's he met the fourteen-year-old George Gershwin, who, working as a piano demonstrator, was the youngest "song plugger" on Tin Pan Alley. "I loved to hear George play," Caesar recalled in 1958. "He was creative as he played; he found new harmonies and new little rhythms and harmonic niceties and cadences."

Soon Caesar and Gershwin wrote their first song together. "You-oo, Just You" was published in 1918 and interpolated into a Broadway revue, the *Hitchy-Koo* of 1918. Their next pieces, "There's More to the Kiss than the X-X-X" and "I Was So Young," were both interpolated into *Good Morning, Judge* in 1919. That same year two more of Caesar's lyrics, set to tunes by Walter Donaldson, appeared in the show *The Lady in Red*. Caesar was still working at the Ford offices at this point, but the astounding success of his next collaboration with Gershwin put the brakes on his automotive career for good.

The secret to success in the music industry, Caesar had surmised, was to provide the public with songs in styles with which they were familiar and which had already proved popular. In 1919 the favored style was the one-step, and the song "Hindustan" (1918) was all the rage. "Well, one day I said to George, 'Let's write a one-step and see if we can't

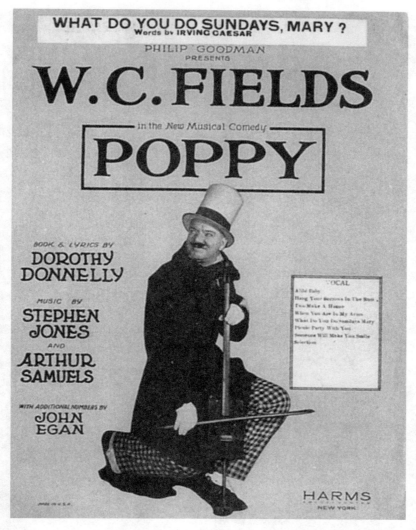

*Sheet music for the song by Caesar and Stephen Jones that was introduced on stage by Luella Gear and Robert Woolsey in 1923
(from Marion Short,* From Footlights to "The Flickers," *1988)*

follow in the wake of 'Hindustan,' because if the public wants one-steps now we ought to write a song in that idiom." The two met to discuss the idea at Dinty Moore's restaurant, located across the street from Remick's, and decided to use an American theme and setting for their song. Thus, "Swanee" (1919) was born. The two left Dinty Moore's, took a bus uptown to Gershwin's family's home, and shortly thereafter completed the song. In 1958, regarding the connection between his songs and his personal experiences, Caesar said, "I never saw the Swanee River. After the song became a hit, I saw the Swanee River. It's a good thing we wrote the song first!"

"Swanee" was first performed in 1919 in *The Demi-Tasse Revue,* the stage show that opened the Capitol Theatre movie house, by chorus girls danc-ing on a darkened stage with light bulbs affixed to their shoes. Despite this innovative introduction, "Swanee" was not yet a hit. That changed as soon as Al Jolson sang it in concert at the Winter Garden Theatre, to thunderous applause. Shortly thereafter, Jolson interpolated it into his 1920 musical *Sinbad.* The song became a huge success and secured the reputation of its two young writers. While watching the popularity of "Swanee" rise, Caesar went to his employers at Ford and said, "Look, if this song is a hit, I can make more money in one year than I can make here in six or seven, and you know I love to write songs." Hedging his bet, he added, "Now, if it's not a hit, can I come back and work here?" The company assured him that he could return if necessary and wished him luck.

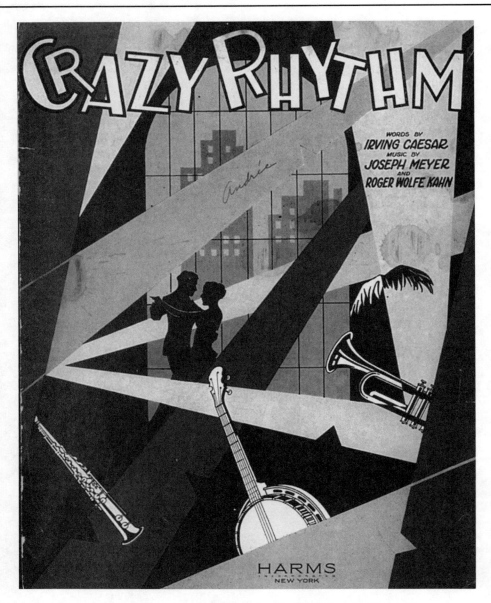

Sheet music for the Caesar song that was introduced in the 1928 musical Here's Howe
(Bruccoli Clark Layman Archives)

Caesar remarked that his entry into full-time songwriting after the success of "Swanee" did not mean "that I started at 9:00 o'clock in the morning and finished at 6:00 o'clock at night. I used to work at the piano in fits and starts." He did so not because he found lyric writing overly difficult. "That's the trouble—when things come too easily, you don't apply yourself as you should. But I just got to be lucky, that's all." Caesar often spoke over the years of his facility with songwriting. "Songs with me are no effort. I write songs effortlessly; that's how I make my living." Regarding the speed with which his most successful lyrics were written, he commented, "most of

the songs I have written that have been huge successes I have written with great facility–'Tea for Two' in about twenty minutes and 'Swanee' in about fifteen minutes."

Caesar's Broadway career took off after "Swanee." From 1919 to 1943, when he was triple-billed as producer, librettist, and lyricist (with Sam Lerner) for *My Dear Public,* he wrote lyrics for more than twenty Broadway shows, and his songs were interpolated into more than thirty-five stage musicals. Among Caesar's most successful lyrics during these years were "Sixty Seconds Every Minute, I Think of You," from the *Ziegfeld Follies of 1922,* written with John Murray Anderson and with music by Louis A. Hirsch; "I Love Her, She Loves Me," written with Eddie Cantor and presented in *Make it Snappy* (1922); "What Do You Do Sundays, Mary?," from *Poppy* (1923), set to music by Stephen Jones; "Sometimes I'm Happy," with words by Caesar and Clifford Grey and music by Youmans, from *Hit the Deck* (1927); and "Crazy Rhythm," introduced in *Here's Howe* (1928), with music by Joseph Meyer and Roger Wolfe Kahn.

Caesar was thrilled with "Crazy Rhythm." Speaking of the lyric to journalist Bob Rusk, he declared, "I love that song, I love that lyric. . . . I think it's the best lyric. I don't mind saying things frankly when I believe them. I do think 'Crazy Rhythm' is the best lyric to a rhythm song ever written. It is almost an intellectual lyric to a down-to-earth rhythm song." Caesar used the melody's repeated two-measure figure to capture the nervous addiction to rhythm that characterized the Jazz Age:

> What's the use of Prohibition?
> You produce the same condition.
> Crazy rhythm,
> I've gone crazy too.

To heighten the frantic pace of the song, Caesar wove insistent rhymes (*use* / prod*uce, you* / *too*) and alliteration (*P*rohibition, *p*roduce) to portray an addict of the era's feverish rhythms.

Most successful of all Caesar's show lyrics were those written for *No, No, Nanette,* which opened on Broadway in 1925. Caesar was not involved with the show at first; Otto Harbach, who was working on the book with Frank Mandel, was the original lyricist. *No, No, Nanette* had played in Detroit in 1924 to negative reviews and public reception. The producer, Harry Frazee, realized that major changes were needed, and, as the production prepared to move to Chicago, efforts were made to bring in new talent. Thus, when Harbach was back in New York and ran into Caesar, he suggested that perhaps Caesar could supply some new lyrics for the show. Of the many requests he received for lyrics to be worked into shows, Caesar commented, "Of course I'd had 'Swanee,' and once you have a hit song and you're a lyric writer—there are so many more composers than there are lyric writers, that you're like the good-looking girl that all the boys woo, because they want you to write lyrics for their tunes."

Caesar agreed to help on *No, No, Nanette* and soon wrote "You Can Dance with Any Girl at All," set to a melody by Youmans, the composer for the show. Caesar was then asked to write a comedy number, and shortly thereafter, Frazee demanded a lyric in the manner of the successful song "I Want to Spread a Little Sunshine," which had been in the show *My Lady Friends* (1919). With *No, No, Nanette* still relatively weak, Youmans and Caesar were now under great pressure to produce. The next morning, borrowing the piano in their hotel's dining room, the two wrote "I Want to Be Happy," which was immediately placed in the show. Like many others, the lyric to this song came quickly to Caesar: "Youmans had a tune. He played the tune for me, and I hit the lyric immediately. Sometimes you do that, you know."

The genesis of the biggest hit in the show, "Tea for Two," was similar, although Caesar had no idea he was "hitting the lyric" at the time. Thanks partly to the countless times he told the story, the genesis of this song has become part of popular-song lore. *No, No, Nanette* had arrived in New York, and Youmans and Caesar were working on songs one evening. That same night Gertrude Lawrence and Beatrice Lillie were in town and were having a party. Caesar wanted to be well rested for the event, so he left Youmans at the piano and went for a nap. "I couldn't have been dozing for more than fifteen minutes," Caesar recalled, "When I felt this tugging at my sleeve." It was Youmans, who declared, "I have a new tune and you must hear it." Reluctantly, Caesar stumbled out of bed and over to the piano. Too tired to set words to the tune, he offered to make up a "dummy lyric," which would serve to mark the rhythmic measures of the tune until he could make something up the next day. Caesar later noted that he could easily have offered the words "Mike and Ike, they look alike, they're out on strike, they own a bike." Instead, however, the first words that came to his mind were the now-famous opening rhymes of the refrain: "Picture you upon my knee, / Just tea for two and two for tea." Youmans was thrilled with the intended "dummy lyrics" and insisted that Caesar continue. The lyricist realized that continuing the pattern of two-measure imitations was not going to work for long: "You sort of run out." So he told Youmans to double the tempo, and he switched from the masculine rhymes of the chorus to feminine rhymes: "Nobody near us to see us or hear us, / No friends or relations on weekend vacations."

Now significantly strengthened with the inclusion of "I Want to Be Happy" and "Tea for Two," *No, No, Nanette* became a hit on Broadway after opening at the Globe Theatre on 16 September 1925. It ran there for more than three hundred performances

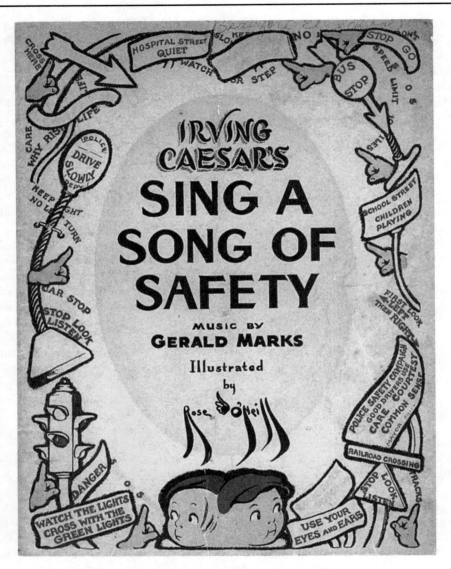

Front cover for a 1937 collection of instructional songs for children
(Collection of Matthew J. Bruccoli)

and doubled that in its subsequent London production. The show was also performed in several other countries. In 1971 a Broadway revival of *No, No, Nanette* was received with great enthusiasm and ran for more than eight hundred performances, proving the staying power of Caesar's lyrics.

While Caesar's career high point might have been reached with his *No, No, Nanette* lyrics, he continued to write steadily throughout the 1930s for both movie and stage musicals. Among the movies featuring his lyrics were *Crooner* (1932), *The Kid from Spain* (1932), and, most notable, the 1935 Shirley Temple vehicle *Curly Top*. Temple's rendition of Cae-

sar's lyric for "Animal Crackers in My Soup" made the novelty song an enormous success.

In the later 1930s and the 1940s Caesar turned from concentrating on commercially successful songs to writing songs for schoolchildren. Gerald Marks provided music for most of the songs in the first collection, *Sing a Song of Safety* (1937), but Caesar wrote both words and music for all the songs in *Sing a Song of Friendship* (1946), and *Songs of Health* (1947). The songs in the series, such as "Remember Your Name and Address" (1937) and "Two Times a Day" (1947), stress such virtues as politeness, good hygiene, and tolerance. In her introduction to *Sing a Song of Friend-*

ship Fannie Hurst described the collection as "a handbook of charming jingles of social significance." Titles include "Thomas Jefferski" (1946), which seeks to foster a sense of equality across national and racial boundaries: "A name like Thomas Jefferson in some lands o'er the sea, / Would not be Thomas Jefferson but Thomas Jefferski." "Tommy Tax" (1946), another song in the series, stresses the importance of paying taxes and reflected Caesar's lifelong belief in the responsibility of citizenship: "Who paid our loyal soldiers, / Who paid our Waves and Wacs? / WHO? YOU, / And little TOMMY TAX." Offering further encouraging support for the democratic process and equality are "We Have a Law" (1946): "You may be white, you may be dark, you may be brown or pink, / Your skin will never matter if your brain knows how to think!"—and "United Nations" (1946). The songs are optimistic, entertaining, and instructive. Some were significantly ahead of their time in their themes.

Caesar worked hard to promote these songs, touring elementary schools throughout the years. Though they were sung by many thousands of schoolchildren in the 1930s, 1940s, and thereafter, they were not recorded until the 1960s. Because he ceded the copyrights of the songs to charitable organizations, Caesar never profited from the songs. (The copyrights to the safety and friendship series went to the children of Sweden, Denmark, and Norway after the Scandinavian tour of the 1971 *No, No, Nanette* revival.) In 1939 a *New York Post* reporter asked "why [Caesar] gives himself the trouble," if he "gets nothing out of this." "I'm a philanthropist," was his reply. "I'm the poorest philanthropist in the world. I wish I could do something about it, but I can't. It's a germ, I guess. I'm cursed with a social conscience." Caesar told the reporter that he had been spurred to write the songs while reflecting upon his childhood in the Lower East Side.

As Caesar was concerned with children's well-being, so was he concerned with that of songwriters and producers. He was highly active in working to preserve artists' rights over their music, and toward that end he served at one time as president of the Songwriters Protective Association (now the Songwriters Guild of America). Caesar also served on the board of directors of the American Society of Composers, Authors, and Publishers (ASCAP) for forty years. He joined the society in 1920 at the insistence of the music publisher Max Dreyfus, who paid the initial dues for Caesar, George Gershwin, and Buddy DeSylva. Passionate about safeguarding artists' rights to the profits from their music, Caesar gained tremendous satisfaction from ASCAP's work.

He also enjoyed the environment: "They never have a meeting that I do not attend, because I love to attend those meetings, and I love the cigars I smoke there, and I love the conversation. Yes, the cigars are free."

Although in principle, artists' work continued to merit protection, Caesar's comments regarding the direction of American music in the 1960s and 1970s suggest that he might have favored denying recording and performing rights to several newer artists. "Turn on your radio—what do you hear? Music? No. *Noise!*" Caesar exclaimed to Wilk. Caesar steadfastly believed that American popular song had degenerated since the mid 1930s. Much of the decline, he argued, was owing to radio and the rabid commercialism it bred: "The people who have taken over this so-called music business—the jukeboxes, the record business, the mass communications media, radio, TV—they have it tied up tight, and they're peddling junk." Listeners, inundated with what he considered generic, senseless songs, were being numbed, Caesar argued. "Read Pavlov! We're raising a generation of zombies!"

This perceived degeneration of songwriting was so disturbing to Caesar because he had been so deeply invested in the art. He lamented, "there's that indefinable something missing" from rock-and-roll music. "It's a damned shame, when you consider that the popular song of the past half-century had the largest impact on American culture of any so-called art form. Why, for God's sake, the popular song *is* American culture!"

The rise of rock and roll, in Caesar's opinion, was symptomatic of more than a change in musical tastes. It reflected what he viewed as decaying societal values. In 1964 he declared, "Someone once said, 'Tell me what a nation is singing and I'll tell you what it's thinking.' Well, judging by rock 'n' roll, today we're not thinking anything." Ever the optimist, however, Caesar predicted that values would improve. When that time came, he predicted that "[rock and roll] too shall pass." Though he lived to the age of one hundred and one, Caesar did not live to see this prediction come true. He appears never to have become bitter about this, however, for he paid little attention to the artists who were revolutionizing popular music during his later years, which he spent with his wife, Christina Ballesteros. Rather, he continued to grant interviews on the subject of the "golden age" of popular song and always remained ready to launch into renditions of his own lyrics.

In 1990, at the age of ninety-four, Caesar received the ASCAP/Richard Rodgers Award for veteran composers or lyricists of the musical theater.

While he was delighted with the formal recognition, awards and commercial success were secondary in the end for the man who long ago proclaimed, "I was born with a song in my heart." Caesar spent a long life doing precisely what he loved; many years before he died, he admitted, "I always think I'm playing at anything I do. . . . Nothing I do ever seems to be really the thing I should be doing. Everything I do seems to be the thing I want to be doing." In such a comment can be heard a faint echo of "Crazy Rhythm":

> Through all this nightlife I fiddle away
> It's not the right life, but think of the pay.
> Someday I will bid it good-bye,
> I'll put the fiddle away
> And I'll say:
>
> Crazy rhythm, here's the doorway,
> I'll go my way, you go your way.

Interview:

"Interview with Mr. Irving Caesar," *Popular Arts Project,* series 1, volume 1, part 1, conducted and transcribed by the Oral History Research Office, Columbia University, 1958.

References:

Michel Mok, "Irving Caesar Sings a Song of Safety—and Gets a Pocket Full of Publicity," *New York Post,* 27 March 1939;

Bob Rusk, "Hail, Caesar!" *Omnibus* (n.d.): 18;

Max Wilk, *They're Playing Our Song,* revised edition (New York: Zoetrope, 1986), pp. 23–29.

Papers:

Irving Caesar's scrapbook is at the Lincoln Center Library for the Performing Arts, New York.

Selected Discography:

Backstage at No, No, Nanette, Columbia, 21023, 1971;

The Best of Al Jolson, MCA, 10002, 1980;

Irving Caesar, The Songwriter Series, Flapper, 7075, 1995;

Frances Langford, *"Hold My Hand"/"Nasty Man," from George White's Scandals,* Perfect, 12994, 1934;

No, No, Nanette, 1971 revival cast, Columbia, 30563, 1971;

Songs of Safety, Decca, 9-90042, ca. 1960s.

Sammy Cahn

(18 June 1913 – 15 January 1993)

Frederick Nolan

SELECTED SONGS FROM THEATRICAL PRO-
DUCTIONS: *Glad to See You* (1944), music by
Jule Styne–"I Guess I'll Hang My Tears Out to
Dry";

High Button Shoes (1947), music by Styne–"Can't You
Just See Yourself?"; "I Still Get Jealous"; "On a
Sunday by the Sea"; "Papa, Won't You Dance
with Me?"; "You're My Girl";

Skyscraper (1965), music by Jimmy Van Heusen–
"Ev'rybody Has the Right to Be Wrong"; "Haute
Couture"; "I'll Only Miss Her When I Think of
Her";

Walking Happy (1966), music by Van Heusen–"How
D'ya Talk to a Girl?"; "I Don't Think I'm in
Love"; "Use Your Noggin"; "Walking Happy";

Look to the Lilies (1970), music by Styne–"Follow the
Lamb"; "I, Yes, Me! That's Who!"

SELECTED SONGS FROM MOTION-PICTURE
PRODUCTIONS: *Sing for Your Supper* (1941),
music by Saul Chaplin–"Why Is It So?";

Time Out for Rhythm (1941), music by Chaplin–"Twid-
dlin' My Thumbs";

Johnny Doughboy (1942), music by Jule Styne–"All Done
All Through"; "Baby's a Big Girl Now"; "It
Takes a Guy Like I"; "Victory Caravan";

Youth on Parade (1942), music by Styne–"Cotcha Too ta
Mee"; "I've Heard That Song Before"; "If It's
Love"; "You Got to Study Buddy"; "You're So
Good to Me";

Crazy House (1943), music by Chaplin–"I Ought to
Dance";

Lady of Burlesque (1943), music by Harry Akst–"So This
Is You"; "Take It Off the E String";

Let's Face It (1943), music by Styne–"Who Did? I Did–
Yes, I Did";

Thumbs Up (1943), music by Styne–"From Here On
In"; "Love Is a Corny Thing"; "Who Are the
British?";

Carolina Blues (1944), music by Styne–"Poor Little
Rhode Island"; "Thanks a Lot, Mr. Beebe" (lyric

Sammy Cahn

by Cahn and Dudley Brooks); "There Goes That
Song Again"; "You Make Me Dream Too
Much";

Follow the Boys (1944), music by Styne–"A Better Day Is
Coming"; "I'll Walk Alone";

Jam Session (1944), music by Styne–"Vict'ry Polka";

Step Lively (1944), music by Styne–"And Then You
Kissed Me"; "As Long as There's Music"; "Ask

61

the Madame"; "Come Out, Come Out, Wherever You Are"; "Some Other Time"; "Where Does Love Begin?"; "Why Must There Be an Opening Song?";

Anchors Aweigh (1945), music by Styne—"The Charm of You"; "I Begged Her"; "I Fall in Love Too Easily"; "We Hate to Leave"; "What Makes the Sunset?";

Tell It to a Star (1945), music by Styne—"You're So Good to Me";

Thrill of a Romance (1945)—"I Should Care" (music by Paul Weston and Axel Stordahl);

Tonight and Every Night (1945), music by Styne—"Anywhere"; "The Boy I Left Behind"; "Cry and You Cry Alone"; "Tonight and Every Night"; "What Does an English Girl Think of a Yank?"; "You Excite Me";

Cinderella Jones (1946), music by Styne—"Cinderella Jones"; "If You're Waiting I'm Waiting Too"; "When the One You Love Simply Won't Love Back"; "You Never Know Where You're Goin' till You Get There";

Earl Carroll Sketchbook (1946), music by Styne—"I Was Silly"; "I've Never Forgotten"; "Lady with the Mop"; "Oh Henry"; "What Makes You Beautiful, Beautiful?";

The Kid from Brooklyn (1946), music by Styne—"Hey, What's Your Name?"; "I Love an Old-Fashioned Song"; "Josie"; "Sunflower Song"; "Welcome Burleigh"; "You're the Cause of It All";

Sweetheart of Sigma Chi (1946)—"Five Minutes More" (music by Styne);

Tars and Spars (1946), music by Styne—"After the War, Baby"; "Don't Call on Me"; "He's a Hero"; "I Always Meant to Tell You"; "I Have a Love in Every Port"; "I Love Eggs"; "I'm Glad I Waited for You"; "Kiss Me Hello, Baby"; "Love Is a Merry-Go-Round"; "When I Get to Town";

It Happened in Brooklyn (1947), music by Styne—"The Brooklyn Bridge"; "I Believe"; "It's the Same Old Dream"; "The Song's Gotta Come from the Heart"; "Time after Time"; "Whose Baby Are You?";

Ladies' Man (1947), music by Styne—"Away Out West"; "I Gotta Gal I Love (In North and South Dakota)"; "I'm as Ready as I'll Ever Be"; "What Am I Gonna Do about You?";

Romance on the High Seas (1948), music by Styne—"It's Magic"; "It's You or No One"; "Put 'Em in a Box, Tie 'Em with a Ribbon and Throw 'Em in the Deep Blue Sea"; "Run, Run, Run"; "The Tourist Trade";

Always Leave Them Laughing (1949)—"Always Leave Them Laughing" (music by Milton Berle); "Say

Farewell" (music by Ray Heindorf); "You're Too Intense" (music by Berle);

It's a Great Feeling (1949), music by Styne—"At the Café Rendezvous"; "Blame My Absent-Minded Heart"; "Fiddle Dee Dee"; "Give Me a Song with a Beautiful Melody"; "It's a Great Feeling"; "That Was a Big Fat Lie"; "There's Nothin' Rougher than Love";

The Toast of New Orleans (1950), music by Nicholas Brodszky—"The Bayou Lullaby"; "Be My Love"; "Boom Biddy Boom Boom"; "I'll Never Love You"; "The Tina Lina";

The West Point Story (1950), music by Styne—"By the Kissing Rock"; "It Could Only Happen in Brooklyn"; "The Corps"; "Long Before I Knew You"; "The Military Polka"; "Ten Thousand Four Hundred and Thirty Two Sheep"; "You Love Me";

Double Dynamite (1951), music by Styne—"It's Only Money"; "Kisses and Tears";

Rich, Young and Pretty (1951), music by Brodszky—"L'Amour Toujours (Tonight for Sure)"; "Dark Is the Night"; "I Can See You"; "Wonder Why";

Two Tickets to Broadway (1951)—"Let's Make Comparisons" (music by Bob Crosby);

April in Paris (1952), music by Vernon Duke—"Give Me Your Lips"; "I Ask You"; "I Know A Place"; "It Must Be Good"; "That's What Makes Paris Paree";

Because You're Mine (1952), music by Brodszky—"Be My Love"; "Because You're Mine";

Three Sailors and a Girl (1953), music by Sammy Fain—"Face to Face"; "Home Is Where the Heart Is"; "Kiss Me or I'll Scream"; "The Lately Song"; "My Heart Is a Singing Heart"; "Show Me a Happy Woman (And I'll Show You a Miserable Man)"; "There Must Be a Reason"; "You're but Oh So Right";

Three Coins in the Fountain (1954)—"Three Coins in the Fountain" (music by Styne);

Ain't Misbehavin' (1955)—"I Love That Rickey Tickey Tickey" (music by Johnnie Scott);

How to Be Very, Very Popular (1955)—"How to Be Very, Very Popular" (music by Styne);

Love Me or Leave Me (1955)—"I'll Never Stop Loving You" (music by Brodszky);

Pete Kelly's Blues (1955)—"Pete Kelly's Blues" (music by Heindorf);

The Tender Trap (1955)—"The Tender Trap" (music by Jimmy Van Heusen);

The Court Jester (1956), music by Sylvia Fine—"Baby, Let Me Take You Dreaming"; "Life Could Not Better Be"; "My Heart Knows a Love Song"; "Outfox the Fox";

The Opposite Sex (1956), music by Brodszky–"Now, Baby, Now!"; "The Opposite Sex"; "A Perfect Love"; "The Rock and Roll Tumbleweed";

Pardners (1956), music by Van Heusen–"Buckskin Beauty"; "Me 'n' You 'n' the Moon";

Serenade (1956), music by Brodszky–"My Destiny"; "Serenade";

Beau James (1957)–"His Honor, the Mayor of New York" (music by Joseph J. Lilley);

The Joker Is Wild (1957)–"All the Way" (music by Van Heusen);

Ten Thousand Bedrooms (1957), music by Brodszky–"Money Is a Problem"; "Only Trust Your Heart"; "Ten Thousand Bedrooms"; "You I Love";

Kings Go Forth (1958)–"Monique" (music by Elmer Bernstein);

Rock-A-Bye Baby (1958), music by Harry Warren–"The Land of La La La"; "Love Is a Lonely Thing"; "Why Can't He Care for Me";

Some Came Running (1958)–"To Love and Be Loved" (music by Van Heusen);

A Hole in the Head (1959), music by Van Heusen–"All My Tomorrows"; "High Hopes";

Say One for Me (1959), music by Van Heusen–"Chico's Choo-Choo"; "The Girl Most Likely to Succeed"; "I Couldn't Care Less"; "The Night That Rock and Roll Died"; "The Secret of Christmas"; "You Can't Love 'Em All";

High Time (1960), music by Van Heusen–"The Second Time Around"; "Showmanship";

Pocketful of Miracles (1961)–"Pocketful of Miracles" (music by Van Heusen);

The Road to Hong Kong (1962), music by Van Heusen–"Let's Not Be Sensible"; "The Road to Hong Kong"; "Teamwork"; "Warmer than a Whisper";

Papa's Delicate Condition (1963)–"Call Me Irresponsible" (music by Van Heusen);

The Pleasure Seekers (1964), music by Van Heusen–"The Pleasure Seekers"; "Something to Think About";

Robin and the 7 Hoods (1964), music by Van Heusen–"All for One and One for All"; "Any Man Who Loves His Mother"; "Bang! Bang!"; "Charlotte Couldn't Charleston"; "Don't Be a Do-Badder"; "Give Praise! Give Praise! Give Praise!"; "I Like to Lead When I Dance"; "Mister Booze"; "My Kind of Town"; "Style";

Where Love Has Gone (1964)–"Where Love Has Gone" (music by Van Heusen);

Thoroughly Modern Millie (1967), music by Van Heusen–"The Tapioca"; "Thoroughly Modern Millie";

Star! (1968)–"Star!" (music by Van Heusen).

SELECTED SONGS FROM TELEVISION PRODUCTIONS: *Our Town* (1955), music by Jimmy Van Heusen–"The Impatient Years"; "Love and Marriage";

The Night the Animals Talked (1970), music by Jule Styne–"The Greatest Miracle of All"; "Let's Not Behave Like People."

SELECTED SONGS PUBLISHED INDEPENDENTLY OF THEATRICAL, MOTION-PICTURE, OR TELEVISION PRODUCTIONS: "Bei Mir Bist Du Schoen" (1933), English lyric by Cahn and Saul Chaplin, Yiddish lyric by Jacob Jacobs, music by Sholom Secunda;

"Shake Your Head from Side to Side" (1933), music by Cahn and Chaplin;

"Rhythm Is Our Business" (1935), lyric by Cahn and Jimmie Lunceford, music by Chaplin;

"Blue Notes" (1936), music by Chaplin and Nat Gardner;

"It Will Have to Do (Until the Real Thing Comes Along)" (1936);

"Shoe Shine Boy" (1936), music by Chaplin;

"Please Be Kind" (1938), music by Chaplin;

"Saturday Night Is the Loneliest Night of the Week" (1944), music by Jule Styne;

"Day by Day" (1945), music by Paul Weston and Axel Stordahl;

"It's Been a Long, Long Time" (1945), music by Styne;

"Let It Snow! Let It Snow! Let It Snow!" (1945), music by Styne;

"The Things We Did Last Summer" (1946), music by Styne;

"Teach Me Tonight" (1953), music by Gene de Paul;

"Christmas Waltz" (1954), music by Styne;

"Hey! Jealous Lover" (1956), lyric and music by Cahn, Kay Twomey, and Bee Walker;

"Come Fly with Me" (1958), music by Jimmy Van Heusen;

"It's Nice to Go Trav'ling" (1958), music by Van Heusen;

"The Last Dance" (1958), music by Van Heusen;

"Only the Lonely" (1958), music by Van Heusen;

"Come Dance with Me" (1959), music by Van Heusen;

"The September of My Years" (1965), music by Van Heusen;

"Let Me Try Again" (1973), lyric and music by Cahn, Paul Anka, and Caravelli.

BOOKS: *I Should Care: The Sammy Cahn Story* (New York: Arbor House, 1974);

Songs with Lyrics by Sammy Cahn (Ft. Lauderdale, Fla.: Cahn Music, 1982);

*Sheet music for the 1933 song that Cahn and Saul Chaplin adapted from a Yiddish song by Sholom Secunda and Jacob Jacobs
(Bruccoli Clark Layman Archives)*

Sammy Cahn's Rhyming Dictionary (Secaucus, N.J.: Warner Bros., 1983).

Sammy Cahn applied a ruthless yardstick when judging the success of a songwriter. "Sing me his medley," he would say, ticking off tunes according to their admissibility: "That's not a hit, you can't include that." Even under those rules, it would take a long time indeed to sing Cahn's medley. He was one of the most successful lyricists—both in artistic and financial terms—of his own or any other generation, winning four Oscars (out of twenty-six Academy Award nominations), two Emmys, and several gold records.

Sammy Cahn—born Samuel Cohen—was the son of Abraham and Elka Riss Cohen, who had immigrated to America from Galicia in Poland. Sammy was born in a drab Cannon Street tenement on New York's Lower East Side on 18 June 1913, the only boy of five children. For some reason his mother believed the piano

was a woman's instrument; thus, while his four sisters—Sadye, Pearl, Florence, and Evelyn—studied the piano, Sammy went to violin lessons. These lessons stood him in good stead; soon after his bar mitzvah he joined a small Dixieland band called the Pals of Harmony, which performed at resorts in the Catskills (the so-called Borscht Belt) during the summer and at private parties and social functions during the winter. Once Cahn discovered music, his parents' hopes that he would become a professional man were doomed.

Cahn played violin in a theater-pit orchestra, worked at a meat-packing plant, and served as a movie-house usher, tinsmith, freight-elevator operator, restaurant cashier, and porter at a bindery. One day, when he was about sixteen, he was in a vaudeville theater—he had been a fan since the age of ten—watching a performer named Jack Osterman sing one of his own songs, and the thought occurred to Cahn that there might be a future in songwriting. On his way home from the theater he wrote his first lyric, "Like Niagara

Falls, I'm Falling for You." "I think a sense of vaudeville is very strong in anything I do, anything I write," he said years later. "They even call it 'a vaudeville finish,' and it comes through in many of my songs. Just sing the end of 'All the Way' or 'Three Coins in the Fountain'—'Make it mine, *make it mine,* MAKE IT MINE!' If you let people know they should applaud, they *will* applaud."

Around this time Cahn invited a piano player named Saul Kaplan to audition for him at the Henry Street Settlement, a community center on the Lower East Side. When the six-foot-tall Kaplan strode into the audition in a raccoon coat and a black derby hat, from under which shocks of long blond hair protruded, to Cahn he looked like King Gustav of Sweden. "I'd learned a few chords on the piano, maybe two," Cahn recalled, "so I'd already tried to write a song. Something I called 'Shake Your Head from Side to Side.'" A few days later, Kaplan brought in an arrangement of the tune. Cahn was amazed, and then and there they became a team: "Saulie" was to write the music; Sammy, the words.

"There was a legendary outfit on West 46th Street, Beckman and Prasky . . . they were the MCA, the William Morris of the Borscht Belt. I got a room in their offices, and we started writing special material," Cahn said. "For anybody who'd have us—at whatever price." Cahn and Kaplan did not make much money, but they got to work for several up-and-coming people, including Milton Berle, Danny Kaye, Phil Silvers, and Bob Hope. One day, Cahn bumped into a childhood friend, Lou Levy, who had graduated from neighborhood bum to blackface dancer with the Jimmie Lunceford Orchestra. When Levy told them Lunceford was opening at Harlem's Apollo Theatre and was looking for special material, Cahn and Kaplan went to work on a song. They came up with "Rhythm Is Our Business" (1935), which had a catchy tune and equally catchy, vernacular lyrics: "Rhythm is our business, rhythm is what we sell / Rhythm is our business, business sure is swell."

Although it was hardly sophisticated, musically or lyrically, "Rhythm Is Our Business" quickly became the Lunceford Orchestra's signature song. Cahn and Kaplan went on to write special material for Glen Gray's Casa Loma Orchestra for its first appearance at New York's Paramount Theatre, and before long the songwriting team was being sought out by other bandleaders. For Andy Kirk and his Clouds of Joy they wrote "It Will Have to Do (Until the Real Thing Comes Along)" (1936); Kirk's successful recording brought both the band and the writers to the attention of the music world.

Cahn, Louis Armstrong, and Saul Chaplin working on "Shoe Shine Boy" (1936), a song Cahn and Chaplin wrote for Armstrong to perform in a show at the Cotton Club in Harlem (photograph by Stan Krell)

At this juncture, Cahn, saying that they did not want to sound "like some dress firm on Seventh Avenue," insisted that Kaplan change his last name to Chaplin. Soon they acquired a reputation for rapidly turning out clever sketches, skits, and songs. Hired to write for a show at the Cotton Club in Harlem, they were told that one number had to be performed in blue costumes, so they quickly wrote a song called "Blue Notes" (1936). When the Cotton Club booked Louis Armstrong in 1936, Cahn and Chaplin gave him "Shoe Shine Boy," which became a big hit. But the team's biggest hit was just around the corner.

Chaplin and Levy heard a Yiddish number performed at the Apollo Theatre that had a stunning effect on the predominantly black audience. The song, called "Bei Mir Bistu Shein" (To me you're beautiful), was written by Yiddish songwriters Sholom Secunda and Jacob Jacobs, who had signed over the rights to J. & J. Kammen. Levy was convinced that if Chaplin adapted

*Frank Sinatra, Cahn, and Jule Styne backstage at the Paramount Theatre
in New York, 1943 (Jule Styne Productions)*

the melody to the standard Tin Pan Alley thirty-two-bar-chorus format and Cahn wrote English lyrics for it, the song would be a hit, and he bought the rights for $150. Cahn was against the whole idea: in his experience, songwriters could not make a hit with a Yiddish song. Levy persisted, and the first lines popped into Cahn's head: "Bei mir bist du schoen / Please let me explain / Bei mir bist du schoen means that you're grand." In about fifteen minutes the rest of the lyric fell neatly into place, along with references to two other popular songs of the moment, "Tutta Bella, Tutta Bella, Umbrella Man," and "Voonderbar" (not the 1948 Cole Porter tune): "I could say 'Bella, Bella,' even say 'Wunderbar!' / Each language only helps me tell you how grand you are."

Levy then approached the Andrews Sisters, a trio of close-harmony singers of Greek descent who were struggling to get bookings in New York. He brought them to Cahn's apartment, and they fell in love with the Yiddish song. Together they persuaded Jack Kapp of Decca Records to produce a recording, and "Bei Mir Bist Du Schoen" became the biggest novelty record of 1938, selling more than a million copies and making stars of Patti, Maxine, and LaVerne Andrews.

Impressed by the success of "Bei Mir Bist Du Schoen," Herman Starr of Warner Bros. Music Holding Corporation, which had taken over the music-publishing houses of Remick and Witmark, offered Cahn and Chaplin a contract to write songs for two-reel "shorts" at Warner's Vitaphone Studios in Brooklyn. For one of these movies they wrote "Please Be Kind" (1938), which might well have been the only song from any two-reeler ever to make

Sheet music for the Oscar-nominated 1944 song about a woman who vows to remain faithful to her boyfriend while he is serving in World War II (Bruccoli Clark Layman Archives)

it onto the radio program *Your Hit Parade.* (It was also banned by NBC because of its opening line, "This is my first affair.") In 1940, when the New York studio was closed, Warner transferred Cahn and Chapin to Hollywood, where they went for two years without a single songwriting assignment. "In desperation, we went to an agent named Al Kingston," Cahn recalled, "and asked him to get us an audition with every studio—only when every studio had turned us down would we go back to New York." They wound up at Republic Pictures, the poorest of the Hollywood studios, and then went on to work at Columbia Pictures, writing story lines as well as utterly forgettable songs for such derivative movies as *Rookies on Parade* (1941), a cheap imitation of Bud Abbott and Lou Costello's *Buck Privates* (1941), and a dull compendium called *Time Out for Rhythm* (1941) that "starred" Ann Miller, Rudy Vallee, and the Three Stooges. These projects

marked the end of the Cahn-Chaplin partnership. "Three years went by, and the well ran dry," as Cahn put it.

"When it seemed I'd hit bottom," Cahn said, "the phone rang." The caller was Cy Feuer of Republic, later a famous Broadway producer. He asked if Cahn would be interested in working with Jule Styne, who had met Cahn on the set of *Rookies on Parade.* "Feeling like I do right now, I'd work with Hitler," Cahn told him. Styne's version of how they came to be songwriting partners was different. Styne had already received an Academy Award nomination for "Who Am I?," featured in the 1940 movie *Hit Parade of 1941.* While on loan from Republic to Paramount, he and lyricist Frank Loesser had successes with "I Don't Want to Walk without You" (1941) and "I Said No" (1942), which spent twenty and twelve weeks, respectively, on the popular-music charts. In Styne's version of the story, Cahn, who was desperate for work, approached Albert J. Cohn, producer of *Sis*

Hopkins (1941), a big-budget ($500,000 was a big budget for Republic) Judy Canova musical with songs by Styne and Loesser. Cohn was a known soft touch for anyone with a hard-luck story. He called in Styne and suggested that he work with Cahn. Styne was hesitant: he told Cahn honestly that he had written two highly successful songs, and he had to maintain that level of artistry. Cahn begged for a week's trial, and Styne agreed to give it a try.

Styne sat down at the piano and played the first thing that came into his head, a melody for which Loesser had never been able to come up with a lyric. Desperate Cahn might have been; tactful he was not. As Styne played the tune, Cahn said, "I've heard that song before." Styne slammed his hands on the keys. "What the hell are you, some kind of tune detective?" he snapped. "You *never* heard that song before!" "It's not a criticism," said Cahn, backpedaling as fast as he knew how. "It's a title. 'It seems to me I've heard that song before.'" They finished the tune before midnight, and "I've Heard That Song Before" went into Cohn's new movie, *Youth on Parade* (1942), where it was performed by the Bob Crosby Orchestra, but it was the Harry James recording, with a Helen Forrest vocal, that took it onto the pop charts for ten weeks. The record sold a million copies and the song was nominated for an Academy Award.

If it had not been for the hit recording of "I've Heard That Song Before," Cahn believed, Styne would have ended their collaboration. Indeed, in spite of the way Cahn presents it in his jaunty autobiography, the relationship was always edgy. Cahn was interested only in writing hits. Styne had higher musical aspirations; he wanted to write at the level of Porter, Jerome Kern, and Richard Rodgers. Thus, for the next few years, Cahn and Styne worked together occasionally (frequently at the request of Frank Sinatra) but never exclusively. They wrote songs for three movies in 1943, but Cahn also worked (although no more successfully) with Chaplin and Harry Akst. The following year Cahn, who had envied Loesser's success with "I Don't Want to Walk without You, Baby," suggested that he and Styne write a similar number, and "I'll Walk Alone," featured in the movie *Follow the Boys* (1944), soared onto the popular-music charts and was nominated for an Academy Award. That same year Cahn and Styne wrote "Come Out, Come Out, Wherever You Are" and "Some Other Time" for *Step Lively* and "There Goes That Song Again" for *Carolina Blues*.

In 1943 Cahn and Styne agreed to write the score for a stage musical called *Glad to See You,* which was to star comedian Phil Silvers (the title was his catchphrase) and the "Mexican spitfire," Lupe Velez. The legendary Busby Berkeley was to direct the show, but by the time it went into rehearsal, Silvers was unavailable and Velez had been found dead from suicide. Nightclub entertainer Eddie Davis was drafted to replace Silvers, and former child star Jane Withers took the Velez role. Then Davis was injured in an automobile accident, and Cahn himself took over the leading role for the premiere in Philadelphia. But the reviews were terrible. Eddie Foy Jr. replaced Cahn, and the production moved to Boston, but again the show was a disaster, opening and closing on the same night, 31 December 1944. *Glad to See You* never got anywhere near Broadway, but at least Cahn and Styne were able to salvage the surprisingly touching "I Guess I'll Hang My Tears Out to Dry" from the score. They also had an independent hit with "Saturday Night Is the Loneliest Night of the Week" (1944), a jaunty tune with a morose lyric.

One day in 1944, while he was sharing an apartment with Sinatra's arranger, Axel Stordahl, and composer-arranger Paul Weston, Cahn heard them play a melody they had come up with and asked them what they called it. They said it did not have a name. "It does now!" Cahn told them and rattled off the lyric for another hit, "I Should Care." (Cahn also used "I Should Care" as the title for his 1974 autobiography.) In 1945 he teamed up with Stordahl and Weston again for yet another massive hit, recorded by Weston's wife, Jo Stafford: "Day by Day." That same year Cahn and Styne had a handsomely profitable trio of independent hits: a "homecoming" song, "It's Been a Long, Long Time"; a novelty number, "Vict'ry Polka" (introduced in the 1944 movie *Jam Session*), which sold several million Bing Crosby-Andrew Sisters records; and a Christmas number that Vaughn Monroe made into a million-selling hit, "Let It Snow! Let It Snow! Let It Snow!"

Sinatra showcased a scintillating series of Cahn-Styne songs in M-G-M's *Anchors Aweigh* (1945): "I Begged Her," "What Makes the Sunset?," "The Charm of You," and "I Fall in Love Too Easily." The last of these was nominated for an Academy Award, as was "Anywhere," featured in Columbia's *Tonight and Every Night* (1945), which starred Rita Hayworth, although the song was sung by another character, played by Janet Blair. "I Should Care" was interpolated into another M-G-M picture, *Thrill of a Romance,* featuring Van Johnson and Esther Williams. Blair appeared again in *Tars and Spars* (1946), a confection from Columbia that also featured songs by Cahn and Styne, but they were off form except for one number, "I'm Glad I Waited for You." Their movie track record for 1945 was poor, not a single hit emerging from any of the four projects for which they wrote songs. The reasons may well have been twofold: in September 1945 Cahn, then thirty-two, had married nineteen-year-old Gloria Delson, and

*Sheet music for the 1945 movie song whose title Cahn used for his
1974 autobiography (Bruccoli Clark Layman Archives)*

she was expecting their first child. Moreover, Cahn and
Styne had become deeply enmeshed in the early preparations for another stage musical. Even under that pressure, they still managed to write two songs that were
big hits for Sinatra: "The Things We Did Last Summer" (1946) and "Five Minutes More" (1946).

Cahn always cited "Five Minutes More" as a perfect example of lyric-writing chutzpah. He said that
when he first showed the lyric to Styne, the composer
said, "What's wrong, you got a stammer?"

> Give me five minutes more,
> Only five minutes more,
> Let me stay, let me stay in your arms.
> Here am I begging for
> Only five minutes more
> Only five minutes more of your charms.

All week long I dream about our Saturday date,
Don't you know that Sunday morning
You can sleep late?

"And what do I follow that with?" Cahn grinned:

> Give me five minutes more,
> Only five minutes more,
> Let me stay, let me stay in your arms.

By 1945 Cahn was well on his way to becoming a
millionaire, but Styne was giving most of his money to
bookies. Styne's yearning to write something closer to
standards, rather than just hits, had grown even stronger after he met Kern. Kern's influence became apparent in the longer melodic lines in the songs for the next
Cahn-Styne assignment, another Sinatra movie called *It*

Sheet music for the 1945 Cahn-Styne composition that became a Christmas standard (from Marie-Reine A. Pafik and Anna Marie Guiheen, The Sheet Music Reference and Price Guide, *1995)*

Happened in Brooklyn, filmed early in 1947. A major rift opened between the lyricist and the composer when Cahn's agent approached Sinatra on the set and told him Cahn would like to work with Harry Warren for the singer's next movie. Sinatra, who had always been intensely loyal to Styne, lied that he had already arranged for Warren to work with Ira Gershwin on his next movie. Although Cahn and Styne continued to work together, things were never quite the same between them again.

Styne's graceful, Kern-like melodies for *It Happened in Brooklyn* required Cahn to work with a new simplicity. To his credit, he managed it beautifully with the lyrics for "Time after Time" and "It's the Same Old Dream." Drawing once again on his vaudeville associations, Cahn also came up with a charming duet for

Sinatra and Jimmy Durante: "The Song's Gotta Come from the Heart."

Even as *It Happened in Brooklyn* premiered, the songwriters were at work on their new project, a stage musical based on Stephen Longstreet's *The Sisters Liked Them Handsome* (1946), a period piece about Longstreet's New Jersey family. Again, Silvers was to star. This time, although the usual hitches and glitches occurred, it all came together. Starring Silvers and Nanette Fabray, *High Button Shoes* opened at the Century Theatre on 9 October 1947 and immediately became the season's biggest hit, remembered not only for its Jerome Robbins–choreographed Keystone Kops routine but also for the charming "I Still Get Jealous" and a foot-stomping polka, "Papa, Won't You Dance with Me?" Though hugely successful—it ran for 727 performances and won the Donaldson Award for best musical,

Sheet music for the song by Cahn and Nicholas Brodzsky that was nominated for an Oscar in 1951
(from Marie-Reine A. Pafik and Anna Marie Guiheen, The Sheet Music Reference and
Price Guide, *1995)*

overshadowing even *Allegro,* the new show by Rodgers and Oscar Hammerstein 2nd—*High Button Shoes* effectively marked the end of the Cahn-Styne partnership. Styne had found that he really wanted to write for Broadway; Cahn preferred what Styne called "rickey-tickey tunes" and the Hollywood lifestyle. "I'm too old and thin for those out-of-town arguments," Cahn said.

Cahn and Styne had a few contractual obligations to work off before they could go their separate ways. Styne, who had become friendly with Jack Warner, found himself in the middle of a set of deals. The songwriters ended up working on an old Warner Bros. property, scripted by Philip and Julius Epstein and directed by Michael Curtiz as *Romance on the High Seas* (1948). When Betty Hutton turned down the lead role, Cahn arranged for Doris Day to audition for the director (who did not know that Warner had already vetoed her as sexless), and Day was

hired. Wanting a "big" song for the movie, Styne played one of his "warm-up" tunes, a tango he had written four or five years earlier. Cahn told Styne to play it more slowly, then more slowly still. "Magic!" Cahn said. "It's magic, it's magic." He started pecking out the words on his portable typewriter and produced the big song they had been looking for. "It's Magic" received an Oscar nomination and became an enormous hit that was forever identified with Day. The box-office success of *Romance on the High Seas* made her a star.

After writing the score for another Day movie called *It's a Great Feeling* (1949)—and again garnering an Oscar nomination, this time for the title song—Cahn and Styne did not work together again until 1954. They had already completed the score for a 1950 James Cagney vehicle, *The West Point Story.* It featured the charming "Long Before I Knew You," but neither the song nor the movie made any permanent impression. Cahn and Styne had also written the songs for *Double Dynamite* (1951), a movie starring Sinatra and Jane Russell that was filmed in 1948 but was so bad that RKO delayed its release for three years.

If the breakup with Styne bothered Cahn, he did his best not to let it cramp his style, moving to M-G-M to collaborate with composer Nicholas Brodszky on songs for producer Joe Pasternak's *The Toast of New Orleans* (1950), starring Mario Lanza and Kathryn Grayson. Cahn and Brodszky's first song together, "Be My Love," was an immediate hit that made Lanza a star and brought Cahn another Academy Award nomination.

Over the next few years Cahn worked with various composers: he received another Oscar nomination for "Wonder Why," one of the songs he wrote with Brodszky for a Jane Powell musical, *Rich, Young and Pretty* (1951). Cahn wrote the original story for *Two Tickets to Broadway* (1951) and had the chastening experience of seeing the assignment for the songs go to Styne and Leo Robin. Cahn collaborated with Vernon Duke on a Doris Day-Ray Bolger movie called *April in Paris* (1952); for *Because You're Mine* (1952), which featured Lanza, he and Brodszky wrote the title song and received another Academy Award nomination. Because Sinatra wanted them, and only them, for his next project, Cahn and a reluctant Styne agreed to work for 20th Century-Fox on "Pink Tights," a major production in which Sinatra was to costar with Marilyn Monroe. The songwriters quickly finished the songs and began rehearsing Monroe after she finished *There's No Business like Show Business* (1954). The new movie was supposed to start production just as soon as the other was completed, but, without warning, Monroe left for Japan with Joe DiMaggio, and "Pink Tights" was never made. The Cahn-Styne score has never been performed.

In 1954 Cahn and Styne, still on salary at 20th Century-Fox, were called into producer Sol C. Siegel's office. He said he had produced a "god awful" movie, tentatively called "We Believe in Love," and he wanted them to write a theme song. After seeing it, Styne suggested they return to the title of the source work, novelist John Secondari's *Three Coins in the Fountain* (1952). Siegel asked, "Could you write a song with that title?" "We can write you a song called 'Yeccch' if you want us to," Cahn replied. He sat down at his typewriter and started typing. Twenty minutes later he had a lyric, and Styne created a melody for it with what he called a "Mascagni feeling." Sinatra, who was on the lot, was brought in to make a recording because Siegel felt that the studio's business office would approve the movie only if it had a major star presenting the theme song. Cahn and Styne's "Three Coins in the Fountain," fea-

tured in the movie of the same title, won the 1954 Academy Award for best original song.

Except for a few more songs and one show, the Cahn-Styne partnership was over for good. Meanwhile, Cahn worked with Sammy Fain on *Three Sailors and a Girl* (1953); with Brodszky again on "I'll Never Stop Loving You," sung by Day in *Love Me or Leave Me* (1955); and with Sylvia Fine on *The Court Jester* (1956), starring her husband, Danny Kaye. Cahn was also now celebrated for his ability to make a lyric out of just about any movie title the studios could invent: "How To Be Very, Very Popular" (1955), "Pete Kelly's Blues" (1955), "Serenade" (1956), "The Opposite Sex" (1956), and "Ten Thousand Bedrooms" (1957).

A whole new career, however, was just around the corner for Cahn. Late in 1955 Sinatra called him and told him he was making a new movie, *The Tender Trap*. "I'd like you to do the songs with Jimmy Van Heusen," Sinatra told him. Cahn pointed out that Van Heusen was a team with Johnny Burke. "But Van Heusen called, so I agreed," Cahn explained in his obituary for Van Heusen, who died in 1990. "Came the first writing session over at his place. Suddenly the doorbell rang and Johnny Burke came in. For a lyric-writer, that's like being caught with somebody else's wife. . . . Here I was working with a man who had been inseparable from Burke for more than a decade."

Van Heusen and Cahn were a "natural" team, and "The Tender Trap" (1955), their first song together, was a big—if atypical for both of them—hit, perhaps the first in the "swingin'" style that Sinatra was to make his trademark:

> You see a pair of laughing eyes,
> And suddenly you're sighing sighs.
> You're thinking nothing's wrong,
> You string along, boy,
> Then snap!
> Those eyes, those sighs,
> They're part of the tender trap.

With Burke out of the picture owing to ill health, Cahn and Van Heusen's next project, again for Sinatra, in a movie loosely based on the life of nightclub comic and singer Joe E. Lewis, was even bigger. "All the Way," from *The Joker Is Wild* (1957), went straight to the top of *Your Hit Parade* and won the writers the 1957 Academy Award for best original movie song. From this point on, they were Sinatra's songwriters of choice. If the singer was making a "theme" album, Cahn and Van Heusen were called in, writing "Come Fly with Me" and "It's Nice to Go Trav'ling" for *Come Fly with Me* (1958); "Only the Lonely," for *Frank Sinatra Sings for Only the Lonely* (1958); and "The September of My Years," the title song for a 1965 album that won two Grammy Awards (album of the year and

Sheet music for the 1954 song that earned Cahn his first Academy Award (from Marie-Reine A. Pafik and Anna Marie Guiheen,
The Sheet Music Reference and Price Guide, *1995)*

best album notes). In 1959 Cahn and Van Heusen won another Oscar, for "High Hopes," from the Sinatra movie *A Hole in the Head.* "The Second Time Around," sung by Bing Crosby in *High Time* (1960), was an Oscar nominee.

Cahn, who had always found writing "special material" easy, rewrote "High Hopes" as the presidential campaign song of John F. Kennedy. As a result, he and Van Heusen were invited to write the music for the inaugural gala. Cahn became and remained the special-material specialist for all occasions. There was no mel-

ody he could not parody, as he demonstrated with lines spoofing the 1913 standard "You Made Me Love You (I Didn't Want to Do It)": "You made me love you / You woke me up to do it."

In 1963 Cahn and Van Heusen won a third Oscar, for "Call Me Irresponsible," a song from a Jackie Gleason movie, *Papa's Delicate Condition.* One of the few Cahn-Van Heusen songs that might be classed as a standard (they were more interested in writing current hits that might not endure beyond their initial period of popularity), "Call Me

Irresponsible" had actually been written seven years earlier for Fred Astaire. "My Kind of Town," from *Robin and the 7 Hoods,* was nominated for an Academy Award in 1964, and the title song from *Thoroughly Modern Millie* was nominated in 1967. In 1968 the title song from a Julie Andrews vehicle, *Star!* (produced by Cahn's first collaborator, Chaplin), was nominated for an Oscar. Other Cahn-Van Heusen songs receiving nominations were "To Love and Be Loved" (1958), "Pocketful of Miracles" (1961), and "Where Love Has Gone" (1964).

Over their years together, Cahn and Van Heusen wrote title songs for many movies, including *Pardners* (1956), *Indiscreet* (1958), *They Came to Cordura* (1959), *Say One for Me* (1959), *Career* (1959), *This Earth Is Mine* (1959), *Night of the Quarter Moon* (1959), *Holiday for Lovers* (1959), *Wake Me When It's Over* (1960), *Who Was That Lady?* (1960), *The World of Suzie Wong* (1960), *Let's Make Love* (1960), *Boys' Night Out* (1962), *The Road to Hong Kong* (1962), *Come Blow Your Horn* (1963), *Under the Yum-Yum Tree* (1963), *4 for Texas* (1963), *My Six Loves* (1963), *Johnny Cool* (1963), *Honeymoon Hotel* (1964), and *Where Love Has Gone* (1964).

In 1965 Cahn and Van Heusen turned to Broadway with *Skyscraper,* an adaptation of Elmer Rice's 1945 play *Dream Girl,* produced by Feuer and Ernest Martin and starring Julie Harris in her first musical role. The show was a moderate success that featured the song "Ev'rybody Has the Right to Be Wrong," but in his autobiography Cahn described putting the show together as "a devastating experience." Nevertheless, Cahn and Van Heusen tried again a year later, but this time the show, *Walking Happy,* starring English knockabout comic Norman Wisdom, was a flop, bringing to an end the hitherto successful producing partnership of Feuer and Martin.

Walking Happy was not the end of Cahn's Broadway ambitions, however; in 1970 he teamed up again with Styne for *Look to the Lilies,* a musical based on the William E. Barrett novel *The Lilies of the Field* (1962), which had already been adapted as a successful Sidney Poitier movie, *Lilies of the Field* (1963). Directed by Joshua Logan and starring Shirley Booth and Al Freeman Jr. (Styne had wanted Ethel Merman and Sammy Davis Jr.), *Look to the Lilies* opened at the Lunt-Fontanne Theatre in New York on 29 March 1970 and closed after only twenty-five performances. "I . . . never dreamed I would do a show without one successful song coming out of it," Cahn said later. "*Look to the Lilies* was what I believe is known as a humbling experience. I hoped I'd had my quota."

Characteristically, Cahn bounced right back. On 2 August 1970, the fifty-seven-year-old lyricist married thirty-two-year-old Tita Basile Curtis. (His marriage to Gloria had ended in 1964.) In 1972 Cahn appeared in one of Maurice Levine's "Lyrics and Lyricists" evenings at the Kaufmann Concert Hall of the 92nd Street Y in New York. That same year, Cahn was inducted into the Songwriters Hall of Fame. (He had helped to establish the Hall of Fame in 1970 and served a term as its president.)

In 1974 producer Alexander Cohen put a show together with Cahn, three singers, and pianist Richard Leonard, giving it the title *Words & Music.* (Cahn, well aware that this title had been used for a 1948 biopic about Rodgers and Lorenz Hart, loved slyly pointing out to audiences that there was no copyright on titles). The show opened at the John Golden Theatre on 16 April 1974, and Cahn suddenly found himself starring in a Broadway hit that, off and on, he "toured with" for the rest of his life. That same year, he published his autobiography, *I Should Care: The Sammy Cahn Story,* promoting it with the same chutzpah with which he plugged his own songs. In his later years Cahn worked as a sort of "goodwill ambassador" for the perfume house Fabergé.

In 1992 Cahn told *Pulse!* magazine that he would love to write songs for such singers as Michael Bolton or Madonna. "My opinion of the music of today is simply put," he said. "Whatever the number one song in the world is at this moment, I wish my name were on it." Cahn died of congestive heart failure at the Cedars-Sinai Medical Center in Los Angeles on 15 January 1993. The marker on his grave in Westwood Memorial Park reads, "Sleep with a smile."

Interview:

Al Kasha and Joel Hirschhorn, *Notes on Broadway: Conversations with the Great Songwriters* (Chicago: Contemporary Books, 1985), pp. 37–47.

Reference:

Theodore Taylor, *Jule: The Story of Composer Jule Styne* (New York: Random House, 1979).

Selected Discography:

Capitol Sings Sammy Cahn: It's Magic, Capitol, 38620, 1995;

The Court Jester, on *Hans Christian Andersen; The Court Jester,* motion-picture soundtracks, Decca, 5433, 1952;

An Evening with Sammy Cahn, DRG Records, 5172, 1978;

Frank Sinatra Sings the Select Sammy Cahn, Capitol, 38094, 1996;

Frank Sinatra Sings the Songs of Sammy Cahn and Jule Styne, Vintage Jazz Classics, 1045, 1993;

The Sammy Cahn Songbook, RCA, LRL1-5079, 1974;

Step Lively, on *Higher and Higher; Step Lively,* motion-picture soundtracks, Great Movie Themes, 60004, 1997.

Betty Comden
(3 May 1915 –   )

and

Adolph Green
(2 December 1915 –   )

Thomas S. Hischak
State University of New York College at Cortland

See also the entries on Comden and Green in *DLB 44: American Screenwriters.*

SELECTED SONGS FROM THEATRICAL PRODUCTIONS: *Three After Three* (1939)–"The Baroness Bazooka";

On the Town (1944), music by Leonard Bernstein–"Come Up to My Place"; "I Can Cook, Too" (lyrics by Comden, Green, and Bernstein); "I Get Carried Away"; "Lonely Town"; "Lucky to Be Me"; "New York, New York"; "Some Other Time"; "Ya Got Me";

Billion Dollar Baby (1945), music by Morton Gould–"Bad Timing"; "Broadway Blossom"; "Dreams Come True"; "Faithless"; "One Track Mind"; "Pals"; "There I'd Be":

Two on the Aisle (1951), music by Jule Styne–"Give a Little, Get a Little"; "Hold Me–Hold Me–Hold Me"; "If You Hadn't, but You Did";

Wonderful Town (1953), music by Bernstein–"Conga!"; "It's Love"; "A Little Bit in Love"; "Ohio"; "One Hundred Easy Ways"; "A Quiet Girl"; "Wrong Note Rag";

Peter Pan (1954), music by Styne–"Captain Hook's Waltz"; "Distant Melody"; "Never Never Land"; "Oh, My Mysterious Lady";

Bells Are Ringing (1956), music by Styne–"I'm Going Back"; "It's a Perfect Relationship"; "It's a Simple Little System"; "Just in Time"; "Long Before I Knew You"; "The Party's Over";

A Party With Betty Comden and Adolph Green (1958)–"Catch Our Act at the Met" (music by Styne); "The Reader's Digest";

Betty Comden and Adolph Green (from Lehman Engel, Their Words Are Music, 1975)

Say, Darling (1958), music by Styne–"Dance Only with Me"; "It's the Second Time You Meet That Matters";

Do Re Mi (1960), music by Styne–"Adventure"; "All of My Life"; "Cry Like the Wind"; "I Know about Love"; "It's Legitimate"; "Make Someone Happy";

Subways Are for Sleeping (1961), music by Styne–"Be a Santa"; "Comes Once in a Lifetime"; "Girls Like Me"; "I Just Can't Wait"; "Ride through the Night";

Fade Out–Fade In (1964), music by Styne–"Call Me Savage"; "My Fortune Is My Face"; "The Usher from the Mezzanine"; "You Mustn't Be Discouraged";

Hallelujah, Baby! (1967), music by Styne–"Being Good Isn't Good Enough"; "Feet, Do Yo' Stuff"; "My Own Morning"; "Not Mine"; "Now's the Time"; "Talking to Yourself";

Lorelei (1974), music by Styne–"Men";

A Party With Comden and Green, revival (1977)–"The Banshee Sisters"; "I Said Good Morning" (music by André Previn);

On the Twentieth Century (1978), music by Cy Coleman–"Life Is Like a Train"; "Mine"; "Never"; "On the Twentieth Century"; "Our Private World"; "Repent"; "She's a Nut";

A Doll's Life (1982), music by Larry Grossman–"Learn to Be Lonely"; "No More Mornings"; "There She Is";

The Will Rogers Follies (1991), music by Coleman–"Give a Man Enough Rope"; "My Big Mistake"; "Never Met a Man I Didn't Like"; "Our Favorite Son"; "Presents for Mrs. Rogers"; "Willomania."

SELECTED SONGS FROM MOTION-PICTURE PRODUCTIONS: *Good News* (1947), music by Roger Edens–"The French Lesson";

On the Town (1949), music by Edens–"Count on Me"; "Main Street"; "Prehistoric Man";

Take Me Out to the Ball Game (1949), music by Edens–"It's Fate, Baby, It's Fate"; "O'Brien to Ryan to Goldberg"; "The Right Girl for Me"; "Strictly U.S.A."; "Yes, Indeedy";

It's Always Fair Weather (1955), music by André Previn–"Baby, You Knock Me Out"; "I Like Myself"; "Thanks a Lot, but No Thanks"; "Time for Parting";

Bells Are Ringing (1960), music by Styne–"Better Than a Dream";

What a Way to Go! (1964), music by Styne–"I Think That You and I Should Get Acquainted."

BOOK: *The New York Musicals of Comden and Green* (New York: Applause, 1997)–comprises the librettos for *On the Town, Wonderful Town,* and *Bells Are Ringing.*

The American theater and Hollywood have boasted many songwriting teams known for working together closely over a long period of time. But no team has worked more closely and over a longer period of time than lyricist-librettists Betty Comden and Adolph Green. Not only have they written librettos, lyrics, and screenplays together over a period of fifty years, they never worked with anyone but each other. Their composer-

collaborators changed, but the words were always by Comden and Green. Whenever they wrote an article, preface, introduction, or tribute, it was cowritten. They often performed together and were nearly always interviewed together. It seemed as though one did not exist without the other. No wonder so many theatergoers mistakenly thought that they were married to each other. (In 1995 Comden published *Off Stage,* a memoir that proved there was a Comden without a Green and that she actually had a personal life separate from his.) Because they worked so closely together over so many decades, it would be futile to try to separate their talents and determine who provided what in their work. They are simply "ComdenandGreen."

One always knows where one is in a lyric by Comden and Green. The setting may be Coney Island or Never Land or a train, but one knows one is really smack in the middle of Broadway. Comden and Green's reality is a Broadway reality, not only because all of their musicals (save one or two) are bright comedies, but also because their characters have a Broadway sensibility. They seem to exist only in the limelight, and each one is a performer as well as a character. Perhaps this characteristic comes from the fact that both Comden and Green were performers first and never totally gave it up. This experience made them ideally suited to write the librettos and/or lyrics for star vehicles. It also enabled them to create particular personas for their characters: people as Broadway types. Comden and Green began in the musical-revue genre, and, although they concentrated on book musicals throughout their careers, some of the revue mentality remained. Both the characters and the lyrics in their shows are sketched quickly, broadly, and clearly. Few of their characters actually grow or develop; they simply are. This tendency can be seen as both a weakness in the team's work and the key to their showmanship.

Betty Comden was born Elizabeth Cohen in Brooklyn on 3 May 1915 (though some sources state she was born in 1919), the daughter of Leo Cohen, an attorney, and Rebecca Sadvoransky Cohen, a schoolteacher. Comden attended the Brooklyn Ethical Culture School and Erasmus Hall High School and went on to graduate from New York University. Adolph Green was born on 2 December 1915 in the Bronx to Daniel and Helen Green. He attended DeWitt Clinton High School and, briefly, a New York community college.

Both Comden and Green became involved in theater by way of collegiate productions. In the 1930s several small theater nightclubs sprang up in Greenwich Village and in other New York neighborhoods, forming a sort of musical fringe years before the Off-Off-Broadway venue existed. Both Comden and Green hoped to become professional performers, and these clubs were ideal showcases for new talent. The two began working together as part of an act called the Revuers, with Judy Holliday in the group and Green's college roommate, Leonard Bernstein, there to provide encouragement. Comden and Green started writing sketches and songs for themselves, hoping to interest casting agents because their material was fresh and different. This backdoor approach to writing may be the reason why their work was always so performer oriented and pleasantly unpretentious.

By 1938 Comden and Green were appearing in more-prestigious clubs uptown, and producers were impressed by their material, if not always by their performing skills. The two were asked to write three songs for the Broadway-bound revue *Three After Three,* but it closed in New Haven after opening there on 24 November 1939. On 4 January 1942 Comden married Stephen Kyle, a businessman; they had a daughter, Susanna, and a son, Alan.

Bernstein suggested Comden and Green as lyricists and librettists in 1944 when he and choreographer Jerome Robbins planned to turn their ballet of that year, *Fancy Free,* into a full-scale Broadway musical. Many accomplishments in *On the Town* (1944), as the project was retitled, have gone into the musical-theater history books: the innovative use of extended dance sequences, the oft-copied premise of servicemen on leave in a place filled with romantic possibilities, the unrealistic yet evocative scenery, George Abbott's brisk and zestful direction, and the vibrant Bernstein score. But it is also worth recalling that *On the Town* was the first Broadway show for Bernstein, Robbins, Comden, and Green. Robbins had danced in the choruses of a few musicals, and Abbott was already an old hand at directing, but, for the most part, the production marked a refreshing and dazzling debut by a group of newcomers. Both Comden and Green appeared in leading roles, another first for them, and most of the rest of the cast were young unknowns as well.

In many ways *On the Town* seemed like a college or summer-stock musical that landed on Broadway with all of its pluck and charm intact. The story line about three sailors on twenty-four-hour leave in Manhattan provided plenty of opportunities for dance and a setting for a variety of songs. There were juicy comic numbers such as "I Can Cook, Too," "I Get Carried Away," and "Come Up to My Place," balanced by such tender ballads as "Lonely Town" and "Lucky to Be Me." Some songs exploded with enthusiasm, as in "New York, New York" and "Ya Got Me," while the quartet "Some Other Time" is quiet and bittersweet. Bernstein's vigorous music is matched by Comden and Green's spirited lyrics.

Comden as Claire de Loon and Green as Ozzie in the 1944 musical On the Town, *which they wrote with composer Leonard Bernstein (Museum of the City of New York)*

In 1945 Comden, Green, Robbins, and Abbott teamed up again for a more ambitious show, a "Musical Play of the Terrific Twenties" called *Billion Dollar Baby.* This time Morton Gould was the composer, and the score was more interesting than likable. The musical managed to include many of the clichés of the Roaring Twenties, from Charleston contests to speakeasies to bathtub gin, and Comden and Green's lyrics echoed the brash optimism of the Jazz Age. "Broadway Blossom" is a mocking nightclub number for a worldly-wise flapper, while the title song is an empty-headed paean sung at a beauty contest. The comic numbers included a tale of vengeance and murder called "Pals," a greedy duet titled "There I'd Be," and a merry tango, "Faithless." Even a plaintive "I am" number (a song establishing a character's wants and hopes), "Dreams Come True," and a jazzy torch song, "Bad Timing," were far

Leonard Bernstein, choreographer Jerome Robbins, Comden, and Green in 1944 at work on On the Town *(Photofest)*

from somber. All in all, *Billion Dollar Baby* was high-flying nonsense that garnered mostly favorable reviews. Yet, audiences were wary; 1920s frivolity seemed an inappropriate topic just after World War II, and the musical played for only seven weeks.

In 1947 Comden and Green's *Bonanza Bound,* with music by Saul Chaplin, was Broadway bound but never made it there, closing in Philadelphia. When the Broadway offers dried up, the two songwriters headed to Hollywood, where they wrote the screenplays for such motion-picture musicals as *The Barkleys of Broadway* (1949) and *Singin' in the Rain* (1952). With composer Roger Edens they provided a song for *Good News* (1947) and wrote a full original score for *Take Me Out to the Ball Game* (1949). For the former, they wrote a delicious duet called "The French Lesson," and, for the latter, the slaphappy ditties "O'Brien to Ryan to Goldberg" and "Yes, Indeedy"; the sly, seductive "It's Fate, Baby, It's Fate"; the dreamy "The Right Girl for Me"; and the patriotic "Strictly U.S.A."

Back in New York, Comden and Green worked for the first time with the man who was to become their most frequent composer-collaborator, Jule Styne. Their initial team effort was the 1951 revue *Two on the Aisle,* which featured Bert Lahr and Dolores Gray. Lahr provided the laughs, but Gray stopped the show twice with the sassy "Give a Little, Get a Little" and the comic "If You Hadn't, but You Did." When the two lyricists teamed with Bernstein again, the result was the splen-

did musical comedy *Wonderful Town* (1953). The story of two Ohioan sisters trying to make it big in Manhattan during the 1930s came from the popular play *My Sister Eileen* (1940), by Joseph A. Fields and Jerome Chodorov, both of whom wrote the libretto for the musical. Comden and Green's lyrics captured the zany charm of the farcical tale, and the exceptional score included the wistful duet "Ohio"; a comic specialty number for Rosalind Russell called "One Hundred Easy Ways"; the ballads "It's Love" and "A Quiet Girl"; and the raucous ensemble numbers "Wrong Note Rag" and "Conga!"

When the musical *Peter Pan* opened on Broadway in 1954, the lyrics for half of the songs were written by Comden and Green, with Styne providing the music. These songs were added to the score and in some cases replaced numbers written by the original songwriters for the show, lyricist Carolyn Leigh and composer Mark Charlap. J. M. Barrie's classic 1904 play provided an ideal setting for one of Comden and Green's most effective ballads, "Never Never Land." But they also wrote the mock-operatic duet "Oh, My Mysterious Lady," for the stars of the show, Mary Martin and Cyril Ritchard, and the satirical "Captain Hook's Waltz."

Back in Hollywood in 1955, Comden and Green wrote the screenplay and lyrics (with music by André Previn) for *It's Always Fair Weather,* an ambitious and rather dark story about a reunion of three army buddies who realize that their former camaraderie is dead. In some ways it was a bitter-tasting sequel to *On the Town,* and the lyrics reflected this bitterness. The slinky "Thanks a Lot, but No Thanks" and the rhythmic "Baby, You Knock Me Out" were playful enough, but there was a wounded melancholy in "Time for Parting" and a shadowy subtext to "I Like Myself" that created a somber mood.

Comden and Green's biggest Broadway hit was *Bells Are Ringing* (1956), a vehicle for their former fellow Revuer Holliday. Comden and Green wrote the first-class score, with music by Styne, as well as the original libretto about telephone-answering-service worker Ella Peterson, who keeps becoming involved with her clients, in particular a floundering playwright, Jeff Moss, who knows her only by her voice and calls her "Mom." The show relied heavily on the star quality of Holliday, but Comden and Green created an original and delectable character for their star in both script and song. From Ella's plaintive "It's a Perfect Relationship" to the heartfelt "Long Before I Knew You" to the determined "I'm Going Back," Comden and Green proved again that they knew how to write for a star. "Just in Time" and "The Party's Over" were the two hits from the musical, but the whole score revealed the songwriters at their best.

Allyn Ann McLerie, Comden, Green, Cris Alexander, Nancy Walker, and John Battles in
the 1944 production of On the Town *(photograph by Van Damm)*

When Comden and Green teamed up again with Styne for *Say, Darling* (1958), a backstage comedy with songs, the result was disappointing. But the same trio wrote an expert score for *Do Re Mi* (1960), an unusual musical comedy about the pop-music industry. The best-selling song from the show was "Make Someone Happy," but the ballad "I Know about Love" and the comic specialty number "Adventure" were also quite proficient. There was much to recommend in *Do Re Mi*, and once again Comden and Green provided top-drawer material for the two stars, Nancy Walker and Phil Silvers. In the same year that *Do Re Mi* premiered, Green married actress Phyllis Newman. The couple had two children, Amanda and Adam.

In 1961 Comden and Green wrote another unusual stage musical with Styne, *Subways Are for Sleeping,* about a handful of Manhattan drifters who have dropped out of conventional society. It was an oddly unsatisfying story (Comden and Green provided the libretto as well as the lyrics), but some of the songs were memorable, especially "Comes Once in a Lifetime" and "Be a Santa." Less known but quite skillful in their own way were the touching character song "Girls Like Me"

and the revealing chorus number "Ride through the Night." Comden and Green drew on their Hollywood experiences (and plenty of Tinseltown clichés) for their libretto and lyrics for *Fade Out–Fade In* (1964), also with music by Styne. It was set in the 1930s, and the story recalled the kind of broad Hollywood satire that the team had provided for the movie *Singin' in the Rain.* The star this time was Carol Burnett, who played usherette Hope Springfield, a character who dreams of movie stardom and, through a bureaucratic mistake, becomes one. The score included a Shirley Temple-Bill "Bojangles" Robinson spoof called "You Mustn't Be Discouraged," which Burnett performed with Tiger Haynes; an emotive song of yearning, "The Usher from the Mezzanine"; and the sparkling "Call Me Savage." Yet, much of the rest of the score was rather routine.

There was nothing routine about the experimental *Hallelujah, Baby!* (1967), an innovative attempt to trace the social history of African Americans in show business from the early days of ragtime to the Civil Rights movement in the 1960s. Arthur Laurents wrote the bold libretto, and Comden and Green provided the eclectic score, with music by Styne. Some of the num-

Green and Comden with M-G-M producer Arthur Freed discussing the screenplay for the 1952 movie Singin' in the Rain
(from Hugh Fordin, MGM's Greatest Musicals: The Arthur Freed Unit, *1996)*

bers, such as "Feet, Do Yo' Stuff," were pastiches of past eras. But the songwriting trio also came up with piercing character songs, such as "Being Good Isn't Good Enough," "Not Mine," and the hopeful "My Own Morning." "Now's the Time" is their own version of a 1960s protest song. But *Hallelujah, Baby!* was more adventurous than it was accomplished, and it failed on the stage.

Comden and Green did have a hit in 1970 when they wrote the libretto (but not the lyrics) for *Applause,* a successful musical based on the movie classic *All About Eve* (1950). They also supplied some new lyrics for *Lorelei* (1974), a revised and inferior version of the 1949 musical *Gentlemen Prefer Blondes.* But they were in top form again when they wrote the commendable libretto and lyrics for *On the Twentieth Century* (1978), a mock operetta with music by Cy Coleman. Based on Ben Hecht and Charles MacArthur's 1932 comic play *Twentieth Century,* about the love and rivalry between a

down-and-out theater producer and a temperamental Hollywood star, the tale was set on the famous luxury train of the title, and Coleman's music had the rushing excitement of a locomotive. Comden and Green captured the silly operetta bombast of former times in their delicious lyrics, from the overblown "Mine" and "Repent" to the cleverly repetitive "She's a Nut" and "Never." Buried in all the theatrics was a beautiful love song, "Our Private World," that proved quite tender when performed out of the context of the show. But *On the Twentieth Century* had trouble appealing to 1970s audiences despite some glowing reviews and a superb production. Regardless, it remains one of the team's most underrated works. A year after *On the Twentieth Century* reached the stage, Comden's husband, Kyle, died on 10 October 1979.

Comden and Green's next project was their least typical: a dark musical play called *A Doll's Life* (1982),

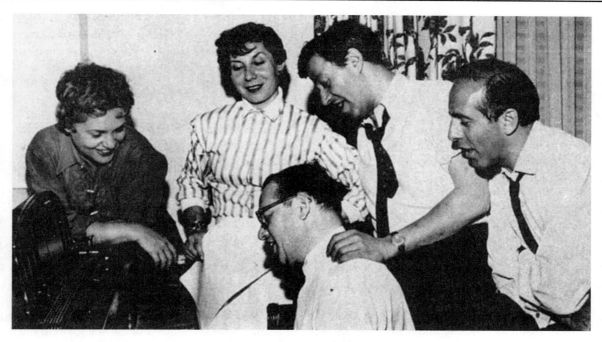

*Judy Holliday, Comden, Jule Styne (at the piano), Green, and Jerome Robbins rehearsing songs
from the 1956 musical* Bells Are Ringing *(photograph by B. C. Mittleman)*

which ventured to guess what happened to Nora Helmer after she left her husband, Torvald, in Henrik Ibsen's landmark drama *A Doll's House* (1879). Comden and Green wrote the book and lyrics while Larry Grossman provided some engaging music. "Learn to Be Lonely" was a delicate and moving ballad, but most of the rest of the score was too closely tied to the plot for any one song to get noticed. The critics trounced *A Doll's Life,* and it closed after five performances, the biggest flop of Comden and Green's career. But it remains a fascinating failure and a curious accomplishment in the saga of the songwriting team. Also unsuccessful was *Singin' in the Rain* (1985), a stage version of their celebrated 1952 screenplay.

Comden and Green returned for one more Broadway hit with *The Will Rogers Follies* (1991), writing lyrics for Coleman's music. The musical biography took the form of a *Ziegfeld Follies* revue, and the songs were often pastiches of numbers from those glory days. "My Big Mistake" was the requisite torch song; "Our Favorite Son," a risible political-campaign song; "Give a Man Enough Rope," a country-flavored number; and "Presents for Mrs. Rogers," an elaborate production number. The quality of the lyrics did not compare favorably to Comden and Green's better work, and the assets of the show were mainly dancing and spectacle.

In addition to their theater and movie work, Comden and Green stayed in the public eye through their many appearances on stage, screen, and television.

Their two-person Broadway revue, *A Party With Comden and Green,* was quite popular in 1958, and they staged a revised version of it in 1977. Both appeared on screen in *Greenwich Village* (1944) and *Garbo Talks* (1984). Comden was featured in *Slaves of New York* (1989) and *The Teddy Bear Habit* (1990), and Green was seen in *Simon* (1980) and *My Favorite Year* (1982). As frequent guests on televised talk and variety shows, the two had a wider visibility than most Broadway songwriters. Just as they often wrote for celebrities, they themselves were celebrities. It was all part of their Broadway persona.

At their best, Comden and Green's lyrics are brash, playful, and entertaining. The Broadway sensibility in their writing did not limit them. In fact, this show-business point of view, narrow as it might seem at first, allowed them to approach each lyric with a showy, cockeyed panache that more-polished or heartfelt lyricists lacked. This quality is most clearly seen in their comic numbers. A Comden and Green comedy song usually stands on its own quite well. It may be character driven, such as the ribald "I Can Cook, Too," or determined by a situation, as in "Conga!," but the song usually is a set piece that can be successfully picked up and performed outside of the context of the musical. This independent quality obviously comes from the authors' early days writing revue material. Once they made it to the big time, the two lyricists only wrote one more revue, *Two on the Aisle,* but they never abandoned the revue mentality.

One of Comden and Green's earliest efforts, going back to their days with the Revuers in the late 1930s, is "The Reader's Digest." The song has a simple premise: in this fast-paced world one does not need to read the classics any longer, just the condensed versions readily available. The lyric then turns into a merry list song in which the plots of literary works such as Leo Tolstoy's *War and Peace* (1865–1869) and William Shakespeare's *Romeo and Juliet* (1597) are reduced to a couplet or four-line synopsis, and the complex ideas of Sigmund Freud and Adolf Hitler's *Mein Kampf* (1925–1927) become punch lines. "The Reader's Digest" is a bright and slapstick lyric, clearly the work of beginners, but there is a polish in its humor that survives. In fact, Comden and Green used the song in both the 1958 and 1977 versions of *A Party With Comden and Green.* Another early Revuers song, "The Baroness Bazooka," is a good example of the twosome's talent for pastiche, something that was to show up in many of their comic numbers. This early effort lampoons European operetta, with a thick-headed goatherd warbling about his goats in the manner that most operetta heroes reserved for their sweethearts. It is a broad and silly spoof but a noteworthy one, for in it can be seen the seeds for such later pastiche songs as "Oh, My Mysterious Lady," "You Mustn't Be Discouraged," and most of the score for *On the Twentieth Century.*

Some of Comden and Green's finest comic lyrics take the form of a soliloquy or a humorous lament. A character's frustration becomes comedy gold when handled correctly, as seen in "One Hundred Easy Ways," sung by Ruth Sherwood, one of the two sisters in *Wonderful Town.* Ruth is too smart for the average man, so she goes through life saying or doing the wrong thing (romantically speaking). The lyric takes the form of a lesson and brilliantly mixes prose and song as Ruth's examples of ways to lose a man build in hilarity. "If You Hadn't, but You Did" from *Two on the Aisle* is another fine example of a comic lament. The singer lists all the reasons she bumped off her husband, her frustration growing as the list continues. Because Comden and Green often performed together, they knew the potential of a comic duet, and their scores are filled with them. The two lyricists themselves sang "I Get Carried Away" in *On the Town,* but that same show boasts an even better example of a comic duet, "Come Up to My Place" (sometimes called "The Taxi Number"). The cliché of a cigar-smoking male cabbie trying to pick up (in more ways than one) a pretty female fare is turned on its head as the eager cabdriver Hildy tries to seduce Chip, a sailor on leave. Unlike the traditional sailor on the make, Chip simply wants to see the sights of New York mentioned in his out-of-date guide book, many of which are no longer there. Hildy offers an alternative,

filled with good-natured lust, to each of his requests. "Come Up to My Place" features a classic comedy lyric that only Comden and Green could have written.

While a good proportion of Comden and Green's songs are comic (just as most of their shows were musical comedies rather than musical dramas), they have written their fair share of romantic ballads, torch songs, and quiet, dreamy numbers as well. Consider the gentle but thrilling duet "Ohio" or the delicate parting song "Some Other Time." In the former, from *Wonderful Town,* the two sisters move from feeling homesickness for their Ohio home to mild disgust at what they have left behind and then back to homesickness. It is an expert lyric that shifts moods and rhymes "Ohio" with "why oh?" without breaking the lullaby tone. The quartet "Some Other Time," sung by two couples at the end of *On the Town* when two of the sailors on leave must return to their ship, is an understated little wonder. All overt signs of passion or melodrama are abandoned as the four list the little things that they never had the chance to experience during their twenty-four-hour romance, such as the women seeing their men shave in the morning or the women washing and drying the dishes together after a meal shared by the two couples. Bernstein's music gently rises and falls, and Comden and Green's lyric concludes with a resigned "oh well" as the melody drops an octave. "Some Other Time" is a marvel of music and words working together and one of the lyricists' most-inspired creations.

One must also consider the many hit songs that came from Comden and Green's scores. Styne always composed with an eye on one or two numbers in a show that would interest top singers and might become best-selling records. The Styne-Comden-Green scores boast several such Tin Pan Alley hits, including "The Party's Over," "Make Someone Happy," "Comes Once in a Lifetime," and "Just in Time." All of these songs have "traveled"; that is, they have proved just as potent outside the context of the musical as on the stage. Some of this success is no doubt owing to the independent quality of the lyrics. They are written with enough of the character in mind to give the words individuality but, at the same time, are general enough that other male or female singers can perform and record them.

Comden and Green rarely wrote directly for Tin Pan Alley, but they certainly understood the qualities that made a song a hit beyond Broadway. Many times a Las Vegas performer had success with a Comden and Green song but managed to weaken it in the process. A delicate character song such as "The Party's Over," from *Bells Are Ringing,* in which Ella sees the end of a night out as a metaphor for the end of her relationship with Jeff, loses something when it is sung as a jazzed-up torch song. As popular as some of Comden and

Sheet music for a hit song from Comden and Green's 1956 musical, which was adapted for the screen in 1960
(Bruccoli Clark Layman Archives)

Green's songs have become in other settings, they are usually at their most potent when performed as part of a complete show.

One must remember, however, that many of Comden and Green's songs were written for stars. Celebrities often requested the team because they knew they would come up with material that would highlight their specials talents. The impressive list of stars who had lyrics written specifically for them by Comden and Green includes Lahr, Holliday, Russell, Martin, Frank Sinatra, Gene Kelly, Carol Channing, and Leslie Uggams. When these people appeared in a stage or screen vehicle, they needed songs that had been carefully tailored for them. Yet, in a way, every song Comden and Green wrote can also be seen as a vehicle. Whether a star was employed or not, the words were usually a performer's words. Deep pro-

fundity may have been sacrificed for charm, heart, or even laughs, but Comden and Green were always highly professional in their writing and understood how to create honest charm, heart, and laughs. The sketch-like tone of their lyrics may have limited them in terms of depth, but it rarely kept them from exhibiting reputable entertainment values in their work. They are show business personified; no one writes that way any more. Some see this change as an advancement in musical theater, but the American musical lost something when Comden and Green's animated kind of writing disappeared.

Bibliography:

Alice M. Robinson, *Betty Comden and Adolph Green: A Bio-Bibliography* (Westport, Conn.: Greenwood Press, 1994).

Biography:

Betty Comden, *Off Stage* (New York: Simon & Schuster, 1995).

References:

Lehman Engel, *Their Words Are Music: The Great Theatre Lyricists and Their Lyrics* (New York: Crown, 1975), pp. 128–137;

Stanley Green, *The World of Musical Comedy: The Story of the American Musical Stage as Told through the Careers of its Foremost Composers and Lyricists,* fourth edition (San Diego: A. S. Barnes, 1980), pp. 249–261;

Thomas S. Hischak, *Word Crazy: Broadway Lyricists from Cohan to Sondheim* (New York: Praeger, 1991), pp. 107–112;

Al Kasha and Joel Hirschhorn, *Notes on Broadway: Conversations with the Great Songwriters* (Chicago: Contemporary, 1985), pp. 63–73;

Richard Chigley Lynch, *Broadway on Record: A Directory of New York Cast Recordings of Musical Shows, 1931–1986* (New York : Greenwood Press, 1987);

Lynch, *Movie Musicals on Record: A Directory of Recordings of Motion Picture Musicals, 1927–1987* (New York: Greenwood Press, 1989);

Max Wilk, *They're Playing Our Song: Conversations with America's Classic Songwriters* (New York: Da Capo, 1997), pp. 111–115.

Selected Discography:

Bells Are Ringing, original Broadway cast, Columbia, 2006, 1956;

Bells Are Ringing, motion-picture soundtrack, Capitol, 1453, 1960;

Bells Are Ringing, Broadway revival cast, Varèse Sarabande, 302 062 115 2, 2001;

Billion Dollar Baby, studio recording, World Premier, 4304, 2000;

Comden and Green Perform Their Own Songs, Heritage, H0057, 1953;

The Comden & Green Songbook, Sony Broadway, 48202, 1992;

Blossom Dearie, *Blossom Dearie Sings Comden and Green,* Verve, MG V-2109, ca. 1959;

Do Re Mi: Original Cast Recording, RCA Victor, LOCD-2002, 1961;

Do Re Mi, studio recording, DRG, 94768, 1999;

A Doll's Life, original Broadway cast, Bay Cities, 3031, 1985;

Fade Out–Fade In, original Broadway cast, ABC-Paramount, ABCS-OC-3, 1964;

Good News, motion-picture soundtrack, Columbia, AK-47025, 1947;

Hallelujah, Baby! original Broadway cast, Sony Broadway, 48218, 1992;

It's Always Fair Weather, motion-picture soundtrack, MCA, 25018, 1986;

Lorelei, original Broadway cast, M-G-M, 5097, 1973;

Sally Mayes, *Our Private World: Sally Mayes Sings Comden & Green,* Varèse Sarabande, 5529, 1994;

On the Town, motion-picture soundtrack, Caliban, 6023, 1949;

On the Town, studio recording with some members of the original cast, Columbia, 2028, 1961;

On the Town, studio recording, Deutsche Grammophon, 437-516-2, 1993;

On the Twentieth Century, original Broadway cast, Sony Broadway, 35330, 1978;

A Party With Comden and Green, original Broadway cast, Capitol, 1197, 1959;

A Party With Comden and Green, revival cast, Stet, S2L 5177, 1977;

Peter Pan, original Broadway cast, RCA, 1019, 1954;

Say, Darling, original Broadway cast, RCA, 1045, 1958;

Subways Are for Sleeping, original Broadway cast, Columbia, KOS 2130, 1962;

Take Me Out to the Ball Game, motion-picture soundtrack, Curtain Calls, 100/18, 1949;

Two on the Aisle: A Broadway Production, original Broadway cast, Decca, 8040, 1951;

The Will Rogers Follies, original Broadway cast, Columbia, 48606, 1991;

Wonderful Town, original Broadway cast, Decca, 79010, ca. 1953;

Wonderful Town, television production, Columbia, 2008, 1958.

Buddy DeSylva

(27 January 1895 – 11 July 1950)

and

Lew Brown

(10 October 1893 – 5 February 1958)

Philip Furia
University of North Carolina at Wilmington

Unless otherwise indicated, lyrics are by DeSylva and Brown and music is by Ray Henderson.

SELECTED SONGS FROM THEATRICAL PRO-DUCTIONS: *Hitchy-Koo* (1917), lyrics by Brown, music by Albert Von Tilzer–"I May Be Gone for a Long, Long Time";

Sinbad (1918)–"I'll Say She Does" (lyric and music by DeSylva, Al Jolson, and Gus Kahn); "'N' Everything" (lyric and music by DeSylva, Jolson, and Kahn);

La, La, Lucille (1919), lyrics by DeSylva and Arthur Jackson, music by George Gershwin–"Tee-Oodle-Um-Bum-Bo"; "Nobody but You";

Linger Longer Letty (1919)–"Oh, by Jingo! Oh, by Gee! (You're the Only Girl for Me)" (lyric by Brown, music by Von Tilzer);

Zip Goes a Million (1919)–"Whip-Poor-Will" (lyric by DeSylva, music by Jerome Kern);

Sally (1920)–"Look for the Silver Lining" (lyric by DeSylva, music by Kern);

Silks and Satins (1920)–"Chili Bean" (lyric by Brown, music by Von Tilzer);

Bombo (1921)–"April Showers" (lyric by DeSylva, music by Louis Silvers); "Arcady" (lyric and music by DeSylva and Jolson); "Avalon" (lyric by DeSylva and Jolson, music by Vincent Rose); "California, Here I Come" (interpolated 1924; lyric by DeSylva and Jolson, music by Joseph Meyer); "Yoo-Hoo" (lyric by DeSylva, music by Jolson);

The Midnight Rounders of 1921 (1921)–"Dapper Dan" (lyric by Brown, music by Von Tilzer);

The French Doll (1922)–"Do It Again" (lyric by DeSylva, music by George Gershwin);

George White's Scandals (1922), lyrics by DeSylva, music by Gershwin–"Argentina"; "Blue Monday Blues"; "Cinderelatives"; "I'll Build a Stairway to Paradise" (lyric by DeSylva and Ira Gershwin [as Arthur Francis]); "Where Is the Man of My Dreams?" (lyric by DeSylva and E. Ray Goetz);

The Greenwich Village Follies (1922)–"Georgette" (lyric by Brown, music by Henderson);

Orange Blossoms (1922), lyrics by DeSylva, music by Victor Herbert–"A Dream of Orange Blossoms"; "A Kiss in the Dark"; "The Lonely Nest"; "This Time It's Love";

The Yankee Princess (1922), lyrics by DeSylva, music by Emmerich Kalman–"I Still Can Dream"; "In the Starlight"; "Roses, Lovely Roses";

George White's Scandals (1923), lyrics by DeSylva, music by George Gershwin–"Let's Be Lonesome Together" (lyric by DeSylva and Goetz); "The Life of a Rose"; "There Is Nothing Too Good for You" (lyric by DeSylva and Goetz); "You and I (In Old Versailles)" (lyric by DeSylva, Goetz, and Ballard Macdonald; music by George Gershwin and Jack Green);

Ziegfeld Follies of 1923 (1923)–"Annabelle" (lyric by Brown, music by Henderson);

George White's Scandals (1924), lyrics by DeSylva, music by George Gershwin–"Somebody Loves Me" (lyric by DeSylva and Macdonald);

Big Boy (1925), lyrics by DeSylva, music by Meyer and James F. Hanley–"As Long as I've Got My Mammy"; "Hello 'Tucky"; "It All Depends on You" (lyric and music by DeSylva, Brown, and Henderson); "If You Knew Susie" (music by Meyer); "Keep Smiling at Trouble" (lyric by DeSylva and Jolson, music by Lewis Gensler);

Buddy DeSylva and Lew Brown (AP/Wide World Photos)

Captain Jinks (1925), lyrics by DeSylva, music by Gensler—"Fond of You"; "I Do"; "Kiki"; "Sea Legs";

George White's Scandals (1925)—"Fly, Butterfly"; "Give Us the Charleston"; "I Want a Lovable Baby"; "What a World This Would Be"; "The Whosis-Whatsis";

Tell Me More (1925), lyrics by DeSylva and Ira Gershwin, music by George Gershwin—"Kickin' the Clouds Away"; "My Fair Lady"; "Tell Me More!"; "Three Times a Day"; "Why Do I Love You?";

George White's Scandals (1926)—"The Birth of the Blues"; "Black Bottom"; "The Girl Is You and the Boy Is Me"; "Lucky Day";

Queen High! (1926), lyrics by DeSylva, music by Gensler—"Cross Your Heart"; "Gentlemen Prefer Blondes"; "Everything Will Happen for the Best"; "You'll Never Know";

Good News (1927)—"The Best Things in Life Are Free"; "Flaming Youth"; "Good News"; "He's a Ladies' Man"; "Just Imagine"; "Lucky in Love"; "The Varsity Drag";

Manhattan Mary (1927)—"The Five-Step"; "It Won't Be Long Now"; "Manhattan Mary";

George White's Scandals (1928)—"I'm on the Crest of a Wave"; "Pickin' Cotton"; "(A Real) American Tune"; "What D'Ya Say?";

Hold Everything (1928)—"Don't Hold Everything"; "To Know You Is to Love You"; "Too Good to Be True"; "You're the Cream in My Coffee";

Three Cheers (1928)—"Because You're Beautiful"; "Maybe This Is Love"; "Pompanola";

Follow Thru (1929)—"Button Up Your Overcoat"; "I Want to Be Bad"; "My Lucky Star"; "You Wouldn't Fool Me, Would You?";

Flying High (1930)—"Good for You, Bad for Me"; "Red Hot Chicago"; "Thank Your Father"; "Wasn't It Beautiful While It Lasted?"; "Without Love";

George White's Scandals (1931), lyrics and music by Brown and Henderson—"Life Is Just a Bowl of Cherries"; "My Song"; "That's Why Darkies Were Born"; "This Is the Missus"; "The Thrill Is Gone";

Hot-Cha (1932), lyrics and music by Brown and Henderson—"You Can Make My Life a Bed of Roses";

Take a Chance (1932), lyrics by DeSylva, music by Nacio Herb Brown and Richard Whiting—"Eadie Was a Lady"; "Should I Be Sweet?" (music by Vincent Youmans); "Rise 'n' Shine" (music by Youmans); "Turn Out the Light"; "You're an Old Smoothie";

Strike Me Pink (1933), lyrics and music by Brown and Henderson–"Let's Call It a Day";

Yokel Boy (1939), lyrics by Brown and Charles Tobias, music by Sam H. Stept–"Comes Love"; "Beer Barrel Polka" (English Lyric by Brown, music by Jaromir Vejvoda; based on the Czech song "Skoda Lasky," lyric by Vasek Zeman and Wladimir A. Timm); "Let's Make Memories Tonight."

SELECTED SONGS FROM MOTION-PICTURE PRODUCTIONS: *The Singing Fool* (1928)–"Sonny Boy";

Sunny Side Up (1929)–"If I Had a Talking Picture of You"; "(I'm a Dreamer) Aren't We All?"; "Sunny Side Up"; "Turn on the Heat";

Just Imagine (1930)–"(There's Something about an) Old-Fashioned Girl";

Show Girl in Hollywood (1930)–"My Sin";

Indiscreet (1931)–"Come to Me";

Stand Up and Cheer (1934), lyric by Brown, music by Jay Gorney–"Baby, Take a Bow";

The Music Goes Round (1936), lyrics by Brown and Harry Richman, music by Victor Schertzinger–"Life Begins When You're in Love";

Strike Me Pink (1936), lyrics by Brown, music by Harold Arlen–"The Lady Dances";

Vogues of 1938 (1937)–"That Old Feeling" (lyrics by Brown, music by Sammy Fain);

Love Affair (1939)–"Wishing" (lyric and music by DeSylva);

Private Buckaroo (1942)–"Don't Sit Under the Apple Tree (With Anyone Else but Me)" (lyric by Brown and Charles Tobias, music by Sam H. Stept);

Du Barry Was a Lady (1943)–"I Love Your Crepes Suzettes" (lyric by Brown and Ralph Freed, music by Burton Lane);

Thousands Cheer (1943)–"I Dug a Ditch in Wichita" (lyric by Brown and Freed, music by Lane).

SELECTED SONGS PUBLISHED INDEPENDENTLY OF THEATRICAL OR MOTION-PICTURE PRODUCTIONS: "I'm the Lonesomest Gal in Town" (1912), lyric by Brown, music by Albert Von Tilzer;

"Kentucky Sue" (1912), lyric by Brown, music by Von Tilzer;

"Please Don't Take My Lovin' Man Away" (1912), lyric by Brown, music by Von Tilzer;

"The Honolulu Hicki-Boola-Boo" (1916), lyric by Brown and Charles McCarron, music by Von Tilzer;

"Au Revoir but Not Good-bye, Soldier Boy" (1917), lyric by Brown, music by Von Tilzer;

"Give Me the Moonlight, Give Me the Girl" (1917), lyric by Brown, music by Von Tilzer;

"I Used to Love You but It's All Over Now" (1920), lyric by Brown, music by Von Tilzer;

"How Ya Gonna Keep Your Mind on Dancing?" (1922), lyric by Brown, music by James F. Hanley;

"Last Night on the Back Porch" (1923), lyric by Brown, music by Carl Schraubstader;

"Seven or Eleven" (1923), lyric by Brown, music by Walter Donaldson;

"Alabamy Bound" (1924), lyric by DeSylva and Bud Green, music by Henderson;

"Memory Lane" (1924), lyric by DeSylva, music by Con Conrad and Larry Spier;

"Shine" (1924), lyric by Brown and Cecil Mack, music by Ford T. Dabney;

"Don't Bring Lulu" (1925), lyric by Brown and Billy Rose, music by Henderson;

"When Day Is Done" (1926), English lyric by DeSylva, music and German lyric by Robert Katscher;

"Just a Memory" (1927);

"One Sweet Letter from You" (1927), lyric by Brown and Sidney Clare, music by Harry Warren;

"For Old Times' Sake" (1928);

"The Song I Love" (1928), lyric by DeSylva and Brown, music by Henderson and Conrad;

"Together" (1928);

"Don't Tell Her What's Happened to Me" (1930);

"You Try Somebody Else" (1931);

"An Old Sombrero" (1947), lyric by Brown, music by Henderson;

"On the Outgoing Tide" (1950), lyric by Brown, music by Mabel Wayne.

No songwriting team captured the spirit of the 1920s more perfectly than that of Buddy DeSylva, Lew Brown, and Ray Henderson. Although the three worked together for only six years, they wrote songs that embodied the giddiness, naughtiness, and optimism of the Jazz Age. While all three men had independent songwriting careers before and after their collaborative period, their fame rests primarily on their work as a team between 1925 and 1931, when they wrote songs for Broadway shows and Hollywood motion pictures. One of the few successful three-way collaborations in the history of American popular music, DeSylva, Brown, and Henderson shared credit for both lyrics and music, although Henderson was primarily responsible for the music and Brown and DeSylva for the lyrics. Together, they managed to wed catchphrases of the day–"keep your sunny side up,"

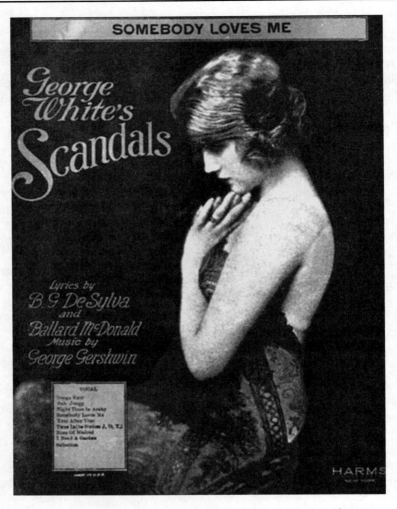

Sheet music for a song that was used in George White's Scandals *of 1924*

"button up your overcoat," "the best things in life are free"—to jazzy rhythms that gave words and music an enduring character. While their songs were written to reflect the spirit of their era, many have endured as standards of American popular music.

The linchpin of the trio was Buddy DeSylva, who was born George Gard DeSylva in New York on 27 January 1895. His father, Aloysius Joseph DeSylva, had been a vaudeville performer, using the name Hal de Forest. (The last name was the English equivalent of his Italian surname.) But when he proposed to Georgetta, her father, who was the sheriff of Azusa, California, insisted that Aloysius find a respectable occupation before marrying his daughter. DeSylva went to law school, moved to Los Angeles with his wife and infant son in 1897, and opened a legal practice. Although his own show-business career was over, DeSylva was determined to make his son a star. George made his debut in a song-and-

dance routine at the age of four and briefly toured on the Keith vaudeville circuit. But Georgetta's father still had considerable influence, and he insisted that his grandchild grow up with a standard education. The boy, who was known as Buddy from the time he entered school, went to elementary school in the Los Angeles area and graduated from Citrus Union High School in Azusa.

Buddy DeSylva worked as a shipping clerk and wrote songs to support himself at the University of Southern California, where he and three classmates formed a singing group, The Hawaiians, accompanying themselves on ukuleles. They played at local nightclubs, and DeSylva began writing songs. In 1917 the group's performance of his song "'N' Everything" was heard by Al Jolson, who bought the musical rights so that his own name appeared on the sheet music alongside DeSylva's. Such buyouts were common in the popular-music business, in which young or impecunious composers often sold the rights to their work outright for a lump sum of money to an established songwriter or performer, who then listed himself as composer and collected royalties from sheet-music and record sales.

Jolson also brought in the more experienced Gus Kahn as a co-lyricist, but even this early lyric bears the hallmark of DeSylva's style. The title phrase carries with it a winking suggestiveness ("She's got a pair of eyes that speak of love–'n' everything") that colors many of his later lyrics. Jolson recorded "'N' Everything" in 1917 and then interpolated the song into *Sinbad*, which he performed at New York's Winter Garden Theatre in 1918. The success of "'N' Everything" prompted Jolson to ask the young songwriter for more lyrics, and DeSylva complied with several songs, including "I'll Say She Does," again with Kahn and Jolson listed as his collaborators. In this lyric, too, DeSylva uses a coyly suggestive title to underscore a risqué series of questions:

> Can she twist?
> Does she do a lot of things I can't resist?
> Does she?
> I'll say she does!

In 1919, while he was still a sophomore at the University of Southern California, DeSylva received a royalty check for $16,000, which prompted him to quit school and head for New York, where he became a staff lyricist for the music publisher J. H. Remick. DeSylva collaborated with some of the best songwriters on Broadway and Tin Pan Alley. In 1919 he and Arthur Jackson wrote lyrics to George Gershwin's music for *La, La, Lucille,* the first Broadway show for which Gershwin wrote all the music. Although neither the show nor its songs, such as "Tee-Oodle-Um-Bum-Bo" and "Nobody But You," were successful, the twenty-four-year-old DeSylva had established himself in the musical theater.

The following year, DeSylva had the opportunity to collaborate with Jerome Kern on the hugely successful *Sally* (1920), starring Marilyn Miller and Leon Erroll, which ran for 520 performances. Most of the lyrics were written by Clifford Grey, but DeSylva contributed the words for the classic "Look for the Silver Lining." In a musical comedy a Pollyanna song such as "Look for the Silver Lining" was usually sung to cheer up a despondent heroine by reminding her that her romantic troubles, like gloomy weather, would soon pass. DeSylva, like so many lyricists who worked with Kern's soaring, gor-

geous melodies, reached for a more elevated style and portentous philosophizing:

> A heart full of joy and gladness
> Will always banish sadness
> And strife,
> So always look for
> The silver lining
> And try to find the sunny side of life.

In 1921 DeSylva pulled out even more sentimental stops for another Pollyanna song, "April Showers," which he wrote with composer Louis Silvers:

> So if it's raining,
> Have no regrets,
> Because it isn't raining rain, you know,
> It's raining violets.
> And where you see clouds
> Upon the hills,
> You soon will see crowds
> Of daffodils[.]

Jolson, who interpolated "April Showers" into his show *Bombo* (1921), was so taken with the song and its watered-down allusion to William Wordsworth's "I Wandered Lonely as a Cloud" (1804) that he would declaim the lyric as if it were the profoundest poetry. His recording turned "April Showers" into an enormous hit.

DeSylva evinced a lighter touch in another interpolation for *Bombo,* "Avalon" (1921), which he wrote with Jolson and composer Vincent Rose, although Giacomo Puccini successfully brought a suit for copyright infringement against the songwriters, charging that the melody had been plagiarized from one of his arias in *Tosca* (1900). Yet, the lyric, with its triple rhymes ("Avalon / travel on") was unquestionably a DeSylva original that established California as a mythical land for songs, along with the Carolinas and Alabama as invoked by Tin Pan Alley writers who had never traveled farther south than Atlantic City. But when DeSylva wrote of Avalon, California, "beside the bay" and "tuna clippers," he was writing about a world he had grown up in, and his lilting words have an authentic ring of familiarity. *Bombo* went on the road three years later, with another interpolation, "California, Here I Come" (1924), with lyrics by DeSylva and Jolson and music by Joseph Meyer, that further established California as a "land of dreams" in the idiom of popular song. On Jolson's recording of "California, Here I Come," DeSylva accompanies the star adroitly on the ukulele.

By 1922 DeSylva had proved that he could write lyrics for a variety of musical styles, ranging from Victor Herbert's operetta *Orange Blossoms* (1922),

Sheet music for the 1925 song on which DeSylva, Brown, and Ray Henderson collaborated for the first time
(Bruccoli Clark Layman Archives)

which included the sumptuous waltz "A Kiss in the Dark," to Gershwin's jazzy melodies for the 1922 *George White's Scandals*. For the latter, DeSylva and Ira Gershwin, who was writing under the pseudonym of Arthur Francis, crafted a rhythmic lyric to "I'll Build a Stairway to Paradise" that culminated in the jazzily syncopated phrase "with a new step every day." That year's edition of *George White's Scandals* also incorporated a one-act operetta, *Blue Monday,* for which DeSylva wrote the libretto and lyrics to George Gershwin's music. Despite its maudlin Frankie-and-Johnnie plot, (when the hero, who has just learned of his mother's death, is killed by his jealous lover, his dying aria begins, "I'm gonna see my mother, mother mine, / Lord, how I miss my mother, mother mine"), this operetta was a foreshadowing of the Gershwins' *Porgy and Bess* (1935). George White, against George Gershwin's strenuous insistence, refused to cast blacks in the roles, using white actors in blackface.

Also in 1922, DeSylva wrote one of his most suggestive lyrics for another George Gershwin melody, "Do It Again":

> Oh,
> Do it again,
> I may say "No, no, no, no, no"
> But do it again. . . .
> Oh, no one is near,
> I may cry, "Oh, oh, oh, oh, oh,"
> But no one will hear.

"Do It Again" was sung by Irene Bordoni, a French star who specialized in risqué songs, in the play *The French Doll.*

For the 1924 *George White's Scandals* DeSylva teamed with Ballard Macdonald to write the lyrics for one of George Gershwin's classic standards, "Somebody Loves Me." With its deceptively simple musical and lyrical repetitions and variations,

"Somebody Loves Me" illustrates how deftly lyricists could work within musical constraints. For the first eight-bar melody, the lyric starts off with the title phrase but immediately gives that romantic cliché a clever twist by posing the question "I wonder who, / I wonder who he can be." The singer who emerges from that line is at once absurdly romantic and yet admirably self-assured in her speculations. When the next eight bars open with the same melody, the lyric parallels it: "Somebody loves me, / I wish I knew. . . ." But then, when the melody takes a different, more urgent turn, the lyric reworks the initial "I wonder who he can be" into the comically troubled "who can he be worries me." In the next eight bars, the "release," or bridge, the melody shifts to more-rhythmic phrases, and the lyric portrays the singer, who started out so whimsically coy, in a nearly frantic quest:

> For every boy who passes me
> I shout, "Hey! maybe,
> You were meant to be my lovin' baby."

With the fourth eight-bar section, the music returns to the opening phrase, and the lyric repeats the original lines—"Somebody loves me, / I wonder who," but, coming after the release, the line, musically and lyrically, sounds almost despondent, as if the singer has given up her search. Then Gershwin's music abruptly truncates the song with a new phrase of four long notes, and DeSylva and Macdonald give the lyric yet another turn by having the singer, once more hopeful of finding her unknown lover, directly confront the listener with a more coyly understated version of the question she shouted to men on the street: "Maybe it's you."

In 1925 profound changes occurred in DeSylva's personal and professional life. On 15 April of that year he married Marie Wallace, a Ziegfeld chorus girl, and, while the couple had no children of their own, DeSylva helped to raise Marie's son, David Shelley. Then, after the success of George and Ira Gershwin's score for *Lady, Be Good!* (1924), George turned to writing for book shows, in which songs had to be tailored to the character and plot of a narrative, rather than the loose revues he had done with DeSylva for *George White's Scandals*. DeSylva joined the Gershwins on their next book show, *Tell Me More* (1925), and his experience as a lyricist helped Ira set words to his brother's tricky melodies. One song from the show that bears DeSylva's stamp is the suggestively titled "Three Times a Day," featuring a sweet, flowing melody by George Gershwin:

> I'll call 'round about three times a day,
> Maybe I could make it four.
> You may throw me out three times a day,
> But I'll come right back for more.

But as the lyric unfolds, the listener finds that the singer is imagining being married to his beloved and sharing three meals a day with her: "For I long to see your smiling face / Across the table, dear, three times a day." *Tell Me More* was the last show on which DeSylva collaborated with George Gershwin.

It was not difficult for DeSylva to find another collaborator in Henderson. Henderson had written the music for several hits, such as "Five Foot Two, Eyes of Blue" (1925) and "I'm Sitting on Top of the World" (1925), with the lyricists Sam Lewis and Joe Young. One of DeSylva and Henderson's first efforts, with co-lyricist Bud Green, was another Jolson hit, "Alabamy Bound" (1925), which was also interpolated by Eddie Cantor into *Kid Boots,* a musical that had opened in 1923. DeSylva crafted another of his naughty lyrics, "If You Knew Susie" (1925), to a melody by Henderson and Meyer. Jolson sang the song in his 1925 revue *Big Boy,* but it was Cantor who made "If You Knew Susie" one of his signature numbers. He would skip and clap his hands in a child-like erotic frenzy and roll his eyes at such suggestive lines as

> We went riding,
> She didn't balk.
> From the Yonkers
> I'm the one who had to walk!

and

> At a party,
> She's meek and mild
> But in a taxi,
> Mother, dear, come save your child!

Such lyrics reflected the image of the freewheeling 1920s flapper.

Since Henderson had already been collaborating with Brown, it seemed natural to form a triumvirate with DeSylva. "If you look at the Tin Pan Alley writers," noted Howard Henderson, the composer's son,

> They all worked with one another. It was a huge, tangled plate of spaghetti with everybody having worked with everybody else. I once counted the number of lyricists my father worked with and came up with thirty-five. The publishers in New York had little rooms with pianos in them and they would work in these rooms. It's like it was a big club. They could wander from one of these publisher's offices where they were writing a song to the next office and write another song with another writer at the same time.

Sheet music for the 1927 song whose title also was used for a 1956 movie about DeSylva, Brown, and Henderson (from William Zinsser, Easy to Remember, *2000)*

DeSylva, Brown, and Henderson tried working together on another song for *Big Boy*. Their first collaborative effort had a casual, insouciant charm. Like so many songs of the era, it took an ordinary catchphrase—"It All Depends"—and gave it a romantic twist by adding "on You." From the start, DeSylva, Brown, and Henderson managed to breathe subtle variations into the repetitive musical and lyrical style of the 1920s. For the first part of the chorus, the lyric of "It All Depends on You" (1925) follows a short melodic pattern, which is repeated at slightly higher and lower intervals:

> I can be happy,
> I can be sad,
> I can be good,
> I can be bad[.]

In the next section, however, while the melodic phrases are repeated, the lyric stretches over them both in a single extended passage: "I can be lonely / Out in a crowd. . . ." Then it again follows the double melodic phrases: "I can be humble, / I can be proud. . . ." In the release Henderson varies the repetitive melody by substituting a rest for the initial note in alternating phrases and raising the melody nearly an octave higher. The syncopated effect created by the rests and the rise in pitch are reflected in the lyric by a greater emotional intensity that still evinces a casual shrug:

> I can save money,
> [rest] Or spend it,
> Go right on living,
> [rest] Or end it.

For the final section of the chorus the lyric at first follows the repeated melodic pattern: "I can be beggar, / I can be king. . . ." But then, in an exultant, yet still off-hand, assertion, the lyric and melody form a single phrase: "I can be almost any old thing. . . ." Such interplay between music and lyric set DeSylva, Brown, and Henderson's songs apart from the simple, repetitive numbers of the 1920s, in which the lyric follows the melodic contour in lockstep fashion.

The three-way partnership lasted until 1931—the only major songwriting triumvirate of that era. "The three men worked so intimately and harmoniously," David Ewen writes in *All the Years of American Popular Music* (1977), "that it was not always clear where the work of one ended and that of the other two began. There were times when the composer, Ray Henderson, helped to write lyrics, and when the two lyricists provided ideas to the composer . . . consequently, in talking about the songs of DeSylva, Brown, and Henderson it is necessary to speak of all of them as a single creative entity."

Much of the magic in DeSylva, Brown, and Henderson's songs comes from their varied backgrounds. In contrast to DeSylva's Italian heritage, California upbringing, and university education, Brown was born in Odessa, then part of Russia, and grew up in New York. Henderson had been an Episcopalian choirboy in Buffalo. When Hollywood made a movie about the trio, *The Best Things in Life Are Free* (1956), the studio tried to capture their varied sensibilities by casting the wholesome Gordon MacRae as DeSylva, Dan Dailey as a dapper Henderson, and, to play Brown, the burly Ernest Borgnine.

Brown was born Louis Brownstein on 10 October 1893 to Jacob and Etta Hirsch Brownstein. In 1899, when he was five, the Brownstein family moved from Odessa to the United States. They first lived in New Haven, Connecticut, and then moved to New York, where Lew Brown attended DeWitt Clinton High School. While working as a lifeguard at Rockaway Beach in Queens, Brown wrote parodies of popular songs, as well as original lyrics, and he was confident enough of his ability to quit high school and try to sell his lyrics on Tin Pan Alley. The experienced composer Albert Von Tilzer, who wrote the music for "Take Me Out to the Ball Game" (1908), took some of Brown's lyrics and set them to music, and in 1912 the nineteen-year-old Brown sold his first songs. A music publisher gave him $7.00 outright for "I'm the Lonesomest Gal in Town" (1912), and the vaudeville star Belle Baker sang his "Please Don't Take My Lovin' Man Away" (1912).

Brown and Von Tilzer worked together for several years, producing such songs as "The Honolulu Hicky-Boola-Boo" (with lyricist Charles McCarron) and two World War I songs, "I May Be Gone for a Long, Long Time," sung by Grace LaRue in the 1917 *Hitchy-Koo* revue, and "Au Revoir but Not Good-bye, Soldier Boy" (1917). They also collaborated on "Give Me the Moonlight, Give Me the Girl" (1917); "Oh, by Jingo! Oh, by Gee!," sung by Charlotte Greenwood in *Linger Longer Letty* (1919); "I Used to Love You but It's All Over Now" (1920); and "Dapper Dan," performed in *The Midnight Rounders of 1921.*

Music publishers recognized Brown's talents, which were far more in keeping with the vernacular idiom of the 1920s than was the music of Von Tilzer. Brown was one of several lyricists brought in, uncredited, to work on the most popular novelty song of the decade, "Yes, We Have No Bananas" (1923). Louis Bernstein, of the music publisher Shapiro and Bernstein, suggested that Brown collaborate with one of the firm's younger composers, Henderson. The two had some success with "Georgette," which was introduced in the 1922 *Greenwich Village Follies,* and they placed "Annabelle" in the *Ziegfeld Follies of 1923,* but Brown continued to collaborate with other songwriters. With Walter Donaldson he wrote "Seven or Eleven," which Cantor made into a hit in 1923. That year Brown also wrote "Last Night on the Back Porch," with music by Carl Schraubstader. The song had the same kind of coyly suggestive lyric that DeSylva had mastered: "I love him in the mornin' and I love him in the fall, / But last night on the back porch I loved him best of all. . . ." In 1924 Brown worked with composer Ford T. Dabney and lyricist Cecil Mack on "Shine," a blackface caricature that Louis Armstrong sang throughout his career and that was revived by Frankie Laine in 1948.

Brown's biggest hit up to 1925 came when, with Billy Rose's assistance (which was normally quite minimal on songs for which the feisty entrepreneur was listed as a lyricist), he wrote "Don't Bring Lulu," with music by Henderson:

> Lulu always wants to do
> What we boys don't want her to.
> When she struts her stuff around,
> London Bridge is falling down.

With its winking suggestiveness, its slangy energy, and its simple turnaround ending ("I'll bring her myself"), Brown's lyric echoed the style of DeSylva, and that resemblance may have prompted White to unite DeSylva, Brown, and Henderson to write the score for the next *George White's Scandals.*

Despite the artistic chemistry of the three collaborators, their first complete score, for the 1925 *George White's Scandals,* produced only one modest hit, "I Want a Lovable Baby," sung by Helen Morgan. Still, the show ran for 171 performances, nearly as many as for the 1920 *George White's Scandals,* the longest-running in the series with music by George Gershwin. For the next *George White's Scandals* DeSylva, Brown, and Henderson wrote a score with several hits: "Lucky Day," "The Girl is You and the Boy is Me," and "Black Bottom," which sparked a raucous new dance craze. The most enduring song from the show, however, was "The Birth of the Blues." To match Hender-

Lobby card for the 1929 movie for which DeSylva, Brown, and Henderson wrote all the songs (from John Kobal and V. A. Wilson, Foyer Pleasure: The Golden Age of Cinema Lobby Cards, *1982)*

son's sinuous and driving melody, DeSylva and Brown wove extended images that resembled the surreal metaphors of modern poetry:

> From a whippoorwill
> Out on a hill
> They took a new note,
> Pushed it through a horn,
> 'Til it was worn
> Into a blue note!

The obstetrical metaphor unfolds against the melodic cadences with colloquial ease. The 1926 *George White's Scandals* ran for 424 performances, far eclipsing any previous edition of the revue.

Because White did not produce a 1927 edition of his *Scandals,* DeSylva, Brown, and Henderson were free to write the score for a book musical, the highly successful *Good News* (1927), which used college life and sports as a hook on which to hang youthful, pleasant, enthusiastic songs: "Flaming Youth," "The Varsity Drag," "Good News," and another standard, "The Best Things in Life Are Free." Here again, there was a

seamless match of musical and verbal phrasing. In the first three lines of the release, for example, DeSylva and Brown set five syllables to Henderson's five-note phrases:

> The flowers in spring,
> The robins that sing,
> The sunbeams that shine[.]

In the final phrase of the release, however, Henderson truncated his melody to four notes, and DeSylva and Brown followed step with a lyric phrase of four syllables that, with its colloquial contractions, is a perfectly conversational counterpart to the musical contraction: "They're yours, they're mine."

Good News, with a libretto by DeSylva and Laurence Schwab, was undoubtedly the artistic high point of the DeSylva-Brown-Henderson collaboration. Starring Mary Lawlor, John Price Jones, Gus Shy, and Inez Courtney, the show ran for 557 performances and was described by Walter Winchell as "flip, fast, furious, free, and flaming festive"–an embodiment of the Jazz Age itself. After seeing the show, Rose Gershwin asked her son George, "Why can't you write hits like DeSylva, Brown, and Henderson?"

In contrast, another collaboration by the songwriting team for White, *Manhattan Mary* (1927), opened a few weeks after *Good News* but was not successful. Although it starred Ed Wynn and featured such songs by DeSylva, Brown, and Henderson as "The Five-Step" and "It Won't Be Long Now," the book (by William K. Wells and White) was too weak to hold the show together. Despite such setbacks, the three were so confident of their continuing success as a team that they established their own publishing company, DeSylva, Brown, and Henderson, in 1927. From that point on, they would receive all the profits from sheet-music sales of their Broadway and Hollywood songs, as well as independent numbers such as "Just a Memory" (1927), "The Song I Love" (1928), and "Don't Tell Her What's Happened to Me" (1930).

In 1928 White returned to staging revues, and DeSylva, Brown, and Henderson wrote the songs for that year's *George White's Scandals,* which ran for 240 performances and featured such songs as "I'm on the Crest of a Wave" and "What D'Ya Say?" This was the last revue DeSylva, Brown, and Henderson wrote; they continued their work on book shows with *Hold Everything* (1928), which took boxing as its theme. With Bert Lahr making his debut in musical comedy playing a punch-drunk boxer, the show featured such songs as "Don't Hold Everything," "To Know You Is to Love You," "Too Good to Be True," and one of DeSylva, Brown, and Henderson's biggest hits, "You're the Cream in my Coffee." In this song DeSylva and Brown develop a catalogue of images within the repetitive melodic phrases of Henderson's music:

You're the cream in my coffee,
You're the salt in my stew.
You will always be
My necessity,
I'd be lost without you.

Here, the ordinary complements of cream and salt are turned into a refreshing compliment that enlivens that tiredest of romantic staples, the inventory of the beloved's beauties, a device that was already stale when William Shakespeare wrote, "My mistress' eyes are nothing like the sun." It is not surprising that such a lyric would garner the praise of Cleanth Brooks in *The Well Wrought Urn: Studies in the Structure of Poetry* (1947). Brooks compared the imagery in "You're the Cream in My Coffee" to the striking metaphysical images used by such modern poets as T. S. Eliot. Under the influence of John Donne and other seventeenth-century poets, Brooks observed, modern poets were

striving for wit, paradox, "ironical tenderness," and a "sense of novelty and freshness with old and familiar objects"—all features of "You're the Cream in My Coffee." *Hold Everything* also pleased audiences, running for 413 performances.

Since book shows on sporting themes had worked with *Good News* and *Hold Everything*, DeSylva, Brown, and Henderson wrote the score for a musical about golfing, *Follow Thru* (1929), again with a book by Schwab and DeSylva. The show included such songs as "You Wouldn't Fool Me, Would You?," "My Lucky Star," and "I Want to Be Bad," which captured the image of the Jazz Age flapper expressing her social and sexual liberation:

If it's naughty to rouge your lips,
Shake your shoulders and twist your hips,
Let a lady confess,
I want to be bad. . . .

Helen Kane made a hit recording of "I Want to be Bad" with her patented "boop-boop-be-doop" inflections.

In another hit from *Follow Thru,* "Button Up Your Overcoat," DeSylva and Brown again used witty imagery to capture the youthful rebellion of the Jazz Age, advising young men to "[G]et to bed by three" and "[K]eep away from bootleg hooch," while cautioning young women, "Don't go out with college boys," and

Oo-oo! Don't sit on hornet's tails,
Oo-oo! Or on nails,
Oo-oo! Or third rails. . . .

Follow Thru was nearly as successful as *Hold Everything,* running for 403 performances.

By 1927 sound had come to Hollywood, and Jolson left vaudeville to star in *The Jazz Singer,* a silent movie of that year with song sequences in synchronized sound. Warner Bros. had initially intended to use the new sound technology to add musical soundtracks to silent movies, eliminating the need for theaters to hire a pianist, organist, or, in the case of big-city theaters, a full orchestra to provide sound accompaniment to motion pictures. But the thrilled reaction of audiences to hearing Jolson sing—and talk—from the hitherto silent screen engendered the "talkies." Studios rushed sound pictures, especially musicals, into production, and by 1928 Jolson was filming his first truly "talking picture," *The Singing Fool.* When he needed a number for a scene in which his character is devastated by the death of his three-year-old son, Jolson called DeSylva, Brown, and Henderson in New York and asked them to produce a song overnight for filming the next day. "Al Jolson called from California," recalled Howard Henderson, "and said 'I'm doing a movie and I need a song and

Sheet music for a hit song from DeSylva, Brown, and Henderson's score for a 1929 musical about golfing
(from William Zinsser, Easy to Remember, *2000)*

nobody out here seems to be able to come up with something. And you guys gotta do it for me.' And Buddy DeSylva said, 'We gotta do it because I owe Jolson my start.' My father said it took less than half an hour to write and by the time they finished writing they were laughing hysterically because they thought it was so terrible and maudlin that they couldn't stand it."

In "Sonny Boy" (1928) DeSylva, Brown, and Henderson dredged up every cliché from Tin Pan Alley tearjerkers, from "gray skies" to "a heaven for me right here on earth." Because of time pressure for filming, they sang the song to Jolson over the phone the next day, but when they sent the sheet music to the studio, they tried to distance themselves from it by ascribing it to "Elmer Colby." When Jolson sang the song, he poured his heart into it, and "Sonny Boy" became a big hit. It sold more than two million copies of sheet music and more than a million records—the most successful song, commercially, ever written by DeSylva, Brown, and Henderson.

In 1929 Fox Studios asked DeSylva to work on another Jolson picture, *Sunny Side Up,* for which he and his two partners wrote their first complete score for a movie musical. It included "If I Had a Talking Picture of You," "(I'm a Dreamer) Aren't We All?," and "Sunny Side Up." The title song is a refreshing transformation of the Tin Pan Alley genre of Pollyanna weather songs:

> Keep your sunny side up, up!
> Hide the side that gets blue. . . .
> Stand upon your legs!
> Be like two fried eggs!
> Keep your sunny side up!

The surreal imagery and the vernacular phrasing mesh perfectly with Henderson's abruptly syncopated melody. Always in touch with the times, the songwriters turned the new phenomena of sound movies into a romantic fantasy in "If I Had a Talking Picture of You," in which a lover yearns for a motion picture of his beloved so he can "give ten shows a day and a midnight matinee."

In 1930 DeSylva, Brown, and Henderson returned to New York for their next and final show, *Flying High,* a musical about aviation. Starring Lahr and Kate Smith, *Flying High* ran for 347 performances. The three men then went back to Hollywood, where they wrote such songs as "Come to Me" for a movie starring Gloria Swanson, *Indiscreet* (1931), their final collaborative project. The last song they worked on together as a team was published in 1931 with the ironic title, "You Try Somebody Else":

> You try somebody else, I'll try somebody else,
> And when we do, we'll both be blue,
> And be back together again.

But DeSylva, Brown, and Henderson never worked together again as a songwriting team. Brown and Henderson returned to Broadway, but DeSylva remained in California.

With the breakup of the songwriting team and the sale of their music-publishing house to Warner Bros., DeSylva concentrated on motion-picture production. At 20th Century-Fox (Fox merged with 20th Century Pictures in 1935) he produced several of Shirley Temple's movies, such as *The Little Colonel* (1935) and *Captain January* (1936). At Universal, DeSylva produced such pictures as *Bachelor Mother* (1939), which starred Ginger Rogers, and, at RKO, *Love Affair* (1939), which starred Irene Dunne and featured "Wishing," a song that DeSylva had written in 1924 that now enjoyed a new popularity.

Back on Broadway, Brown and Henderson wrote the songs for *George White's Scandals of 1931,* starring Ethel Merman and Rudy Vallee. Among the songs were "This Is the Missus," "The Thrill Is Gone," "My Song," "That's Why Darkies Were Born," and the standard "Life Is Just a Bowl of Cherries." Taking another cue from the surreal imagery used by contemporary poets, Brown turned the title phrase into a lyrical shrug at the Depression:

> Life is just a bowl of cherries,
> Don't make it serious—life's too mysterious.
> You work, you save, you worry so,
> But you can't take your dough
> When you go, go, go.

With a wry philosophical look at the losses suffered by so many, the lyric counseled in trenchant vernacular phrases:

> The sweet things in life
> To you were just loaned,

> So how can you lose
> What you've never owned.

This 1931 edition of *George White's Scandals* was so successful that all five of its songs were recorded by Bing Crosby and the Boswell sisters, the first time that all the major songs from a Broadway musical were recorded on a single disc.

In 1932, Brown and Henderson wrote the score for *Hot-Cha* (1932), which starred Jimmy Durante and the Latin firebrand, Lupe Velez, and featured such songs as "You Can Make My Life a Bed of Roses." Then, in 1933, they produced and wrote the libretto and score for *Strike Me Pink* (1933), also starring Jimmy Durante, with such songs as "Let's Call It a Day," another ironic title in light of the fact that Brown and Henderson were seldom to collaborate again. From that point on, each man collaborated with other songwriters, Brown working primarily in Hollywood and Henderson on Broadway.

Buddy DeSylva also returned to Broadway in 1932 to produce *Take a Chance* with Lawrence Schwab. He also wrote the songs, with composers Richard A. Whiting, Nacio Herb Brown, and Vincent Youmans. The show starred Jack Haley, Ethel Merman, Jack Whiting, June Knight, and Sid Silvers. Among its songs were "Rise 'n' Shine," "Eadie Was a Lady," and "You're an Old Smoothie," which contained DeSylva's characteristically surreal and subtly erotic imagery:

> You're an old smoothie,
> I'm a big softy
> I'm just putty
> In the hands of a boy like you.

DeSylva continued to produce on Broadway as well as in Hollywood throughout the 1930s and at the end of the decade enjoyed the distinction of being the first producer since Florenz Ziegfeld to have three successful musicals playing on Broadway simultaneously: Cole Porter's *Du Barry Was a Lady,* which opened in 1939, starred Ethel Merman and Burt Lahr, and ran for 408 performances; Irving Berlin's *Louisiana Purchase,* which opened in 1940 and ran for 444 performances; and, later in 1940, another Cole Porter musical, *Panama Hattie,* which also featured Ethel Merman and ran for 501 performances. DeSylva also wrote the librettos, together with Herbert Fields, for both Cole Porter musicals.

After such impressive success on Broadway, DeSylva returned to Hollywood to become executive producer of Paramount Studios in 1941. There he produced such movies as *Birth of the Blues* (1941), which starred Bing Crosby and featured the classic DeSylva, Brown, and Henderson song. DeSylva also

*Sheet music published at the time of the 1947 motion-picture adaptation of
DeSylva, Brown, and Henderson's 1927 musical
(Bruccoli Clark Layman Archives)*

produced *For Whom the Bell Tolls* (1943) and *The Stork Club* (1945), for which he also wrote the screenplay. In 1942 he provided songwriter Johnny Mercer and record-store-owner Glenn Wallichs with $25,000 to start a new record company, the first on the West Coast. Despite competition from such established firms as Columbia, Victor, and Decca; a wartime shortage of shellac that was needed for manufacturing records; and a strike by the national musicians union, Capitol thrived and featured such talents as Jo Stafford, Peggy Lee, Stan Kenton, and Nat "King" Cole.

At the peak of his success, DeSylva's health deteriorated rapidly, and he had to resign his position at Paramount. He continued to serve as the first chairman of the board at Capitol, but he was so weak the company had to install an elevator for him to get to his second-floor office. His health continued to fail, and he died of a heart attack on 11 July 1950 in Los Angeles, at the age of fifty-five.

Brown also became a Hollywood as well as a Broadway producer. His 1933 production of *Stand Up and Cheer,* for which he wrote "Baby, Take a Bow," with music by Jay Gorney, was the first feature movie for Shirley Temple, who then went on to star in motion pictures produced by Buddy DeSylva. In 1938 Brown wrote one of his most enduring standards, "That Old Feeling," to Sammy Fain's music, for *Vogues of 1938,* which he also produced. Brown's title phrase beautifully matches Fain's melodic figure—"I saw you last night and got that old feeling"—deftly placing long open and closed vowels and liquid and nasal consonants over the arching, sustained notes. "That Old Feeling" was yet another instance of Brown's finding the exact words and phrases to bring out the latent emotional meaning of a melody.

In 1939 Brown and Charles Tobias wrote the lyrics to "Don't Sit under the Apple Tree," with music by Sam H. Stept, for the Broadway musical *Yokel Boy*, starring Judy Canova and Buddy Ebsen, another show produced by Brown. The song, which originally was titled "Anywhere the Bluebird Goes," was also sung by the Andrews Sisters in the 1942 movie *Private Buckaroo*. With its upbeat plea for fidelity at a time when many lovers were separated, "Don't Sit Under the Apple Tree" became one of the most popular songs of World War II. Also in 1939, Brown wrote an English lyric, "Beer Barrel Polka," for a Czech drinking song, and the song was interpolated into *Yokel Boy* to boost the flagging show. A later recording, again by the Andrews Sisters, made it another of the most successful songs of World War II.

Brown wrote lyrics to his last hit song, "On the Outgoing Tide," in 1950 with composer Mabel Wayne, and a recording by Perry Como made it popular. Although he retired from songwriting, during the 1950s Brown continued to write comedy scenes for motion pictures and sketches for the new medium of television. He lived long enough to see the 1956 movie, *The Best Things in Life Are Free*, which portrayed the songwriting team of DeSylva, Brown, and Henderson in their heyday. Lew Brown died at age sixty-four of a heart attack on 5 February 1958 in his New York City apartment at the Navarro Hotel.

He was survived by his second wife, June, and two daughters from his first marriage. Ray Henderson, the longest surviving member of the group, retired from songwriting in the late 1940s and returned to his home in Greenwich, Connecticut, where he died on 31 December 1970. Although their collaboration lasted only six years, it is primarily by the songs they wrote together that DeSylva, Brown, and Henderson are remembered.

References:

David Ewen, *All the Years of American Popular Music* (Englewood Cliffs, N.J.: Prentice-Hall, 1977);

Philip Furia, *The Poets of Tin Pan Alley: A History of America's Great Lyricists* (New York: Oxford University Press, 1990), pp. 87–94.

Selected Discography:

Ben Bagley's DeSylva, Brown, and Henderson Revisited, Painted Smiles, 144, 1993;

Ben Bagley's DeSylva, Brown, and Henderson Revisited, Vol. II, Painted Smiles, 145, 1993;

The Best Things in Life Are Free: The Songs of Ray Henderson, ASV, 5207, 1997;

Good News, studio cast, TER, 1230, 1995;

Just Imagine: The Music of DeSylva, Brown, and Henderson, Stomp Off, 1285, 1994.

Howard Dietz
(8 September 1896 – 30 July 1983)

Thomas S. Hischak
State University of New York College at Cortland

Unless otherwise indicated, lyrics are by Dietz and music is by Arthur Schwartz.

SELECTED SONGS FROM THEATRICAL PRO-
DUCTIONS: *Poppy* (1923), music by Arthur
Samuels–"Alibi Baby";

Dear Sir (1924), music by Jerome Kern–"A Houseboat
on the Harlem"; "If We Could Lead a Merry
Mormon Life";

Merry-Go-Round (1927), lyrics by Dietz and Morrie Ryskind, music by Jay Gorney and Henry Souvaine–
"Hogan's Alley" (music by Gorney);

The Little Show (1929)–"Hammacher Schlemmer, I
Love You"; "I Guess I'll Have to Change My
Plan"; "Moanin' Low" (music by Ralph Rainger);

Three's a Crowd (1930)–"The Moment I Saw You";
"Right at the Start of It"; "Something to Remember You By";

The Band Wagon (1931)–"Confession"; "Dancing in the
Dark"; "High and Low"; "Hoops"; "I Love Lou-
isa"; "Miserable with You"; "New Sun in the
Sky"; "Sweet Music";

Flying Colors (1932)–"Alone Together"; "Louisiana
Hayride"; "A Shine on Your Shoes"; "Smokin'
Reefers";

Revenge With Music (1934)–"If There Is Someone Lovelier Than You"; "You and the Night and the
Music";

At Home Abroad (1935)–"Get Yourself a Geisha"; "Got a
Bran' New Suit"; "Hottentot Potentate"; "Love Is
a Dancing Thing"; "Paree"; "Thief in the Night";

Between the Devil (1937)–"By Myself"; "I See Your Face
before Me"; "Triplets";

Inside U.S.A. (1948)–"Come, O Come to Pittsburgh";
"Haunted Heart"; "Rhode Island Is Famous for
You"; "We Won't Take It Back";

The Gay Life (1961)–"Come A-Wandering with Me";
"For the First Time"; "Magic Moment"; "Some-
thing You Never Had Before"; "Who Can? You
Can!";

Howard Dietz (AP/Wide World Photos)

Jennie (1963)–"Before I Kiss the World Goodbye";
"Waitin' for the Evening Train."

SELECTED SONG FROM MOTION-PICTURE
PRODUCTION: *The Band Wagon* (1953)–
"That's Entertainment."

BOOK: *Dancing in the Dark* (New York: Quadrangle,
1974).

Howard Dietz was a masterful lyricist and
librettist who, with his composer partner Arthur
Schwartz, wrote some of the most memorable songs

*Sheet music for a song from the 1929 show that marked the beginning of Dietz's collaboration
with composer Arthur Schwartz and became a standard torch song
(Bruccoli Clark Layman Archives)*

to come out of that long-gone genre, the original Broadway musical revue. Aside from Irving Berlin, no one contributed better scores to these sophisticated and timely forms of entertainment than Dietz and Schwartz. Yet, success in the field of book musicals eluded the team, and Dietz's lyrics were only rarely heard coming from a character in a musical play. Nonetheless, his lyrics were often incisive and sometimes created succinct minidramas within the framework of a single song.

Dietz's output during a career that lasted forty years was somewhat limited because his energies were divided into two quite different directions: in addition to writing lyrics, librettos, and sketches for Broadway and Hollywood, he was also a topflight creator of advertising and a major movie-studio executive for much of those forty years. The two talents were not as dissimilar as they first appear. Dietz's wit, charm, and brooding sophistication were sometimes

evident in both fields, and he rose to the top of both professions.

Howard Dietz was born in New York on 8 September 1896 to working-class immigrant parents, Herman and Julia Blumberg Dietz. Herman Dietz came from Russia by way of various European countries and went into the jewelry business when he settled in New York. The family prospered and moved several times, and Howard grew up in various New York neighborhoods. He first experienced live theater when the housemaid took him to see Richard Mansfield in *Monsieur Beaucaire* (1901). Later, Dietz had his first taste of musical theater with such period novelties as *The Sunshine Girl* (1912), with Julia Sanderson. When he was fifteen and a student at Townsend Harris, a high school for gifted pupils, Dietz was hired as a copyboy for the *New York American*. He attended Columbia University, where he earned a degree in journalism. His fellow students at Columbia included

*Schwartz and Dietz during the 1930s (from Howard
Dietz,* Dancing in the Dark, *1974)*

Oscar Hammerstein II and Lorenz Hart, and Dietz
worked with them on the student theatricals that
proved a training ground for so many future lyricists.

While not drawn to performing, Dietz loved the
theater and wrote sketches and lyrics for these original revues and musical comedies at Columbia. He
also contributed light verse to the many publications
that featured such work in the 1910s and 1920s. Don
Marquis's "Sun Dial" column in the *New York Sun* and
Franklin P. Adams's column, "The Conning Tower,"
in *The New York World,* were among the most famous,
and Dietz had several comic pieces published in both
under the pen name of Freckles. He also submitted
jingles and ideas to advertising companies, and when
he won a $500 prize in a contest for a slogan for
Fatima cigarettes, his new career was launched.

After graduating from Columbia, Dietz took a
job with an advertising firm. The United States
entered World War I in April 1917, and on 15 September, while waiting to be called into service, Dietz
married Elizabeth Hall, a former Barnard College student. Dietz served in the navy during the war and,
after the armistice, worked for New York newspapers
before returning to advertising, eventually obtaining
a job as publicity director for the new Goldwyn Pictures movie company. In 1924 Goldwyn merged with
Metro Pictures, and Dietz retained his position with
the newly formed Metro-Goldwyn-Mayer (M-G-M).
One of the young publicist's first assignments was to
create a campaign for the new Hollywood studio.

Dietz developed the Leo the Lion trademark and its
slogan, "Ars Gratia Artis." (The idea sprang from his
student days: a lion was the mascot at Columbia,
where he first came across Oscar Wilde's aesthetic
motto "Art for Art's Sake.")

The year 1924 was also an important one
regarding Dietz's other career. He had been writing
lyrics since his student days and sending them to various theatrical producers. "Alibi Baby," a song he
wrote with composer Arthur Samuels, was interpolated into the W. C. Fields vehicle *Poppy* (1923), and it
gained considerable attention on Broadway when it
was sung by Luella Gear. But Dorothy Donnelly, the
lyricist for the rest of the score, did not allow authors
of interpolated songs to be publicly acknowledged,
and Dietz's name did not appear in either the show
program or the sheet music published later.

Also in 1924, composer Jerome Kern, who had
been reading Adams's column for years, sought out
"Freckles" and asked him to write the lyrics for his
next Broadway musical, *Dear Sir* (1924). The
twenty-eight-year-old lyricist was in awe of the
renowned composer and nervously tried to please
Kern, who requested twelve lyrics for the new show.
Asked to return in two days, Dietz labored for fifty
hours straight and completed the dozen songs, only
to find out that Kern meant that only one of the
twelve was needed for their next meeting.

Dear Sir was a lightheaded comedy of manners
concerning a man about town (played by Oscar
Shaw) and his problems in winning the heart of a
working girl (played by Genevieve Tobin). Kern's
music was pleasant but unmemorable, and some of
Dietz's lyrics seemed stiff and uneasy. But there were
two numbers, both based on pieces of light verse
Dietz had written years before, that sparkled. "If We
Could Lead a Merry Mormon Life" extols a life of
polygamy (which Dietz rhymed with "bigamy" and
"pig o' me"), and "A Houseboat on the Harlem" sar-
castically describes the joys of living on a vessel stuck
in the riverside muck. *Dear Sir* managed to run for
only two weeks, and Dietz never worked with Kern
again, but it was an auspicious Broadway debut for
the young lyricist to collaborate with the premiere
composer in American musical theater.

Running a few months longer was the revue
Merry-Go-Round (1927), in which Dietz contributed
sketches created with Morrie Ryskind and songs written with composers Henry Souvaine and Jay Gorney.
Newcomer Libby Holman made a splash singing
"Hogan's Alley," and Dietz got his first taste of working in the revue format on Broadway. Among those
impressed with the witty nature of the lyrics in the
show was young composer Arthur Schwartz, looking

Sheet music for a song from the 1931 show that is considered the best Broadway revue of the 1930s
(from Marion Short, From Footlights to "The Flickers," *1998)*

for a collaborator who had the snappy and irreverent nature of a Hart. (Schwartz had known Hart for some time and had hoped to work professionally with him, but Richard Rodgers first teamed up with Hart in 1925, and their career together was flourishing.) The Brooklyn-born Schwartz was educated at New York University and Columbia Law School, but writing popular songs was his passion. A few of his melodies were heard on Broadway in *The Grand Street Follies* (1926) and *The New Yorkers* (1927), both revues with modest runs, and he was willing to give up the law if he could find the right collaborator. Dietz seemed the perfect match, but the lyricist suggested that each find a more experienced partner to work with, someone who could open doors for each of them. But Schwartz besieged Dietz with letters, phone calls, and telegrams until the lyricist agreed to get involved with a small and intimate revue called *The Little Show* (1929).

There was nothing small about the effect *The Little Show* had on Broadway and the musical revue. The appeal of the large and lavish revues of the past, from the *Ziegfeld Follies* to *George White's Scandals,* was waning, and satiric little revues such as the *Garrick Gaieties* (1925) had shown the way to a more cerebral kind of variety entertainment. *The Little Show* had both the wit of the collegiate satires and the sophistication and professionalism of Broadway. The revue was an immediate hit, running for 321 performances, and launching a golden age for the genre. While there were many authors involved with *The Little Show,* Dietz wrote most of the lyrics and sketches. With composer Ralph Rainger, he contributed the sultry "Moanin' Low," which Holman and Clifton Webb performed as an exotic dance of death. The best of the Dietz-Schwartz collaborations were the wry tribute to the manufacturers of hardware, called "Hammacher Schlemmer, I Love You," and the breezy torch song "I Guess I'll Have to Change My Plan."

The revue was so popular that the next year the producers presented the inevitable *The Second Little Show* (1930), and again Dietz collaborated with a handful of composers. Better Dietz-Schwartz songs were heard in *Three's a Crowd* (1930), a revue that reunited much of the cast and authors of *The Little Show*. The outstanding songs by the team were "The Moment I Saw You," "Right at the Start of It," and "Something to Remember You By." This show was a hit, running for 271 performances, and Dietz and Schwartz were ready to score an entire revue on their own.

The Band Wagon (1931) is generally considered the finest Broadway revue of the 1930s, if not the best the genre has ever produced. A top-notch cast, innovative technical elements, hilarious sketches, and a superior score made *The Band Wagon* the fondly remembered show that it is. The songs by Dietz and Schwartz provided comedy, romance, and spectacle, creating a tapestry of emotions usually reserved for the finest book musicals. Fred Astaire introduced the jaunty "New Sun in the Sky" and then joined his sister, Adele, as a pair of bratty French kids for the comic song "Hoops." John Barker sang the hypnotic "Dancing in the Dark" while Tilly Losch danced on an undulating mirrored set, and he performed the flowing duet "High and Low" with Roberta Robinson. The whole cast rode on a Bavarian carousel for "I Love Louisa." Somehow the large and dazzling show retained the tone of the smaller, intimate revues, and *The Band Wagon* entranced audiences for 260 performances during the worst days of the Depression.

The next year brought another Dietz-Schwartz revue, *Flying Colors* (1932), for which Dietz wrote all the sketches and lyrics. With Schwartz he provided the sultry "Alone Together," the bright dance number "A Shine on Your Shoes," and the happy-go-lucky "Louisiana Hayride." Although the revue played for 188 performances, Dietz and Schwartz felt that the true artistry on Broadway was in book musicals, so they next embarked on an operetta-like project called *Revenge With Music* (1934). Based on a familiar Spanish folktale about a governor who tries to seduce the wife of a miller, only to have the miller make more successful advances on the governor's wife, *Revenge With Music* featured a book by Dietz that provided few surprises but created useful opportunities for songs, two of which became romantic standards: "You and the Night and the Music" and "If There Is Someone Lovelier Than You." While much of the score was laudable, little of it seemed Spanish in tone, and Dietz had not fully incorporated the plot with the songs. The musical was a modest success at 158 perfor-

mances, but the team was discouraged with their effort and returned to the revue format with *At Home Abroad* (1935).

In *At Home Abroad* Dietz and Schwartz used the premise of a world tour to unify the songs and sketches, and there was much merriment displayed by Ethel Waters claiming to be the "Hottentot Potentate" in Africa and by Beatrice Lillie advising the audience to "Get Yourself a Geisha" in Japan. Other notable Dietz-Schwartz numbers included "Paree," "Love Is a Dancing Thing," and "Got a Bran' New Suit." The team scored one more project in the 1930s, the book musical *Between the Devil,* which opened in 1937. Again, the plot was shopworn (a British bigamist tries to shuffle between a French and an English wife), and again, the score did not always mesh with the story. But there were three standout songs that came from the musical: the wry "By Myself," the dreamy "I See Your Face Before Me," and the hilarious trio "Triplets." Also in 1937, Dietz, now divorced, married Tanis Guinness Montague, with whom he had his only child, Liza.

Eleven years passed before Dietz and Schwartz collaborated again. The composer worked with lyricist Dorothy Fields in the 1940s and 1950s. Meanwhile, Dietz became more involved with his duties at M-G-M (where he became a vice president in 1947) but found time to score three unsuccessful book musicals with Vernon Duke: *Dancing in the Streets* (1943), which got no farther than tryouts in Boston; *Jackpot* (1944); and *Sadie Thompson* (1944). No memorable songs came from Dietz's collaborations with Duke, and some felt that Dietz without Schwartz lost his lyrical magic.

By World War II, the revue format had for the most part been exhausted, and, especially after Rodgers and Hammerstein's *Oklahoma!* (1943), integrated book musicals reigned. Dietz and Schwartz reunited for one last revue, *Inside U.S.A.* (1948), and it was, at 399 performances, the longest-running show of their careers. The premise this time was a tour across the nation, and both the songs and the sketches shone brightly. Lillie sang of the joys of industry in "Come, O Come to Pittsburgh," Jack Haley comically praised his true love with "Rhode Island Is Famous for You," and John Tyers and Estelle Loring introduced the surging love song "Haunted Heart."

A related career for Dietz involved writing for opera. He wrote English lyrics for the Metropolitan Opera's production of Johann Strauss's *Die Fledermaus* (1874) in 1950 and Giacomo Puccini's *La Bohème* (1896) in 1952, and they were used, on and off, for several years. A few songs by Dietz had made their way into movie musicals as early as 1928, but he had never enjoyed the songwriting success that many of

Sheet music for a song from Dietz and Schwartz's score for a 1932 revue
(*from Marion Short,* From Footlights to "The Flickers," *1998*)

his colleagues had in Hollywood. In 1953, however, the songs of Dietz and Schwartz were used for the movie musical *The Band Wagon* (not related to the 1931 Broadway revue except for some of the numbers), and America fell in love with the old standards all over again. In the movie, featuring Fred Astaire, Cyd Charisse, Nanette Fabray, Oscar Levant, and the English variety star Jack Buchanan, such old standards as "I Guess I'll Have to Change My Plan," "Dancing in the Dark," and "By Myself" took on a new luster. Dietz and Schwartz wrote only one new song for the movie, the delightful paean to show business "That's Entertainment," which remains to this day one of their most recognized works.

In 1957 Dietz retired from M-G-M and pursued other projects. His third wife, Lucinda Ballard, whom

he had married in 1951 after the end of his second marriage, was one of Broadway's top costume designers, so he was still involved in the theater world. Schwartz had met with modest success writing the book musicals *A Tree Grows in Brooklyn* (1951) and *By the Beautiful Sea* (1954) with Fields, and he was eager to work again with his old partner, Dietz. Their first effort, *The Gay Life* (1961), had a superb score but suffered from a problematic book. The rakish adventures of the playboy Anatole, based on a play by Austrian playwright Arthur Schnitzler, could have made for a potent musical comedy, but the book was heavy-handed, and the leading man (the miscast Walter Chiari) offered no charm. For this show Dietz did successfully advance plot and characters with his lyrics, and Schwartz provided enticing period melodies. "Magic Moment" and "Who Can? You Can!" (both sung by Barbara Cook) were scintillating character songs, and there was also much to appreciate in "For the First Time," "Come A-Wandering With Me," and "Something You Never Had Before." But few Broadway tunes became popular hits in the 1960s, and the Viennese-flavored score was little noticed outside of its 114 performances.

Dietz and Schwartz's collaboration (and each of their careers) came to a disappointing close with the short-lived musical *Jennie* (1963). A vehicle for Broadway favorite Mary Martin, the book musical told of the adventures of a touring actress based loosely on Laurette Taylor. There was a spark of the team's former glory in "Before I Kiss the World Goodbye" and "Waitin' for the Evening Train," but much of the show was an overproduced embarrassment. Dietz retired and pursued his hobby of painting until Parkinson's disease immobilized him. He completed his autobiography, *Dancing in the Dark,* in 1974 and lived until 30 July 1983, cheating the disease by becoming, as he put it, "a guinea pig" for some experimental new drugs that proved successful.

Dietz is often compared with Hart, the latter always outshining him in the comparison. But Dietz was much more than a poor man's Hart. He had a distinctive voice, a superb sense of craftsmanship, and an air of mystery about his words that made him a master in his own right. Although he rarely wrote songs for characters in a full-length story line, he always created characters in situations in each of his songs, and the situations were rarely simple or obvious. Dietz was able to create a sense of ambiguity in his lyrics that even Hart could not rival. Consider the mixed emotions present in a song such as "By Myself." It is a torch song of sorts; yet, the singer has a breezy kind of optimism in his attitude. Instead of the smiling-through-my-tears syndrome, Dietz captures both the sense of relief and of regret in the singer's perplexed situation of finding himself without a sweetheart. Schwartz's music helps with its rhythmic and surging pace, but it is the ambiguous lyric that develops the interesting situation. Many of Dietz's love songs have a similar complexity. In "I See Your Face Before Me" one cannot quite tell if the singer is happy or disturbed by the haunting image of his love's face appearing every time he closes his eyes. Is it a lost love come to remind him or a hoped-for love yet to be fulfilled? The lyric allows for both interpretations.

Even such a passionate love song as "Dancing in the Dark" has a bittersweet quality to it. The picture of two lovers waltzing in the dark is highly romantic, but there is also a sense of foreboding, a feeling that when the music inevitably ends there will be just darkness. The lyric insists that time is hurrying by and that there is always an end to everything. Schwartz's captivating music certainly helps to set up this desperate kind of grasping for happiness, but Dietz's lyric, far from gloomy yet hardly fancy-free, expertly conveys the ambiguous quality of the song. A similar sense of unease can also be found in "Something to Remember You By," "You and the Night and the Music," and "If There Is Someone Lovelier Than You," all three romantic standards and all three filled with a bittersweet flavor.

Dietz could write a joyous or optimistic song that compared favorably to those of the best lyricists of his day, but few could create the mystery that he did in his love songs. "Haunted Heart" is a good example. Again, it is a torch song, and again, mixed emotions abound. The departed lover (Has the couple been separated against their will? Is the affair over? Has the remaining lover been abandoned?) is seen as a ghost that haunts the singer. The singer's reaction to the situation is both disturbing and thrilling, wanting to let go and yet enjoying the constant haunting. Hart often wrote torch songs in which the singer is "glad to be unhappy" (as in his 1936 song of that title), and he knew how to add a painful subtext in his lyrics; but Dietz knew how to be vague enough in creating dramatic situations that the sense of mystery overshadowed any simple and overt emotion. If despair and heartbreak flowed from Hart's torch songs, then a wistful sense of ambiguity pervaded Dietz's lyrics.

Another area in which Dietz and Hart may be compared is their comic songs. Along with Ira Gershwin and Cole Porter, Dietz and Hart wrote the wittiest comedy numbers of the 1930s. Just as he was able to do in the dozens of sketches he wrote for musical revues, Dietz built his comic songs on situation and character rather than jokes or oversized emotions. The comic numbers stand well on their own today because they were written and first presented as free-standing entertainment pieces. The classic "Triplets" was written for a book musical, but the song is sung by a trio in a cabaret and has nothing to do with the plot. The outrageous characterization of three babies with quite adult attitudes is a farcical one-act play in itself. "Get Yourself a Geisha" and "Confession" (1931) have the risqué tone of a Porter song, and "That's Entertainment" (written for Hollywood many years after the golden age of the Broadway musical revue) has the economic wit of a Gershwin lyric, slyly relating the plots of *Oedipus Rex* and *Hamlet* in three lines each:

> It could be *Oedipus Rex,*
> Where a chap kills his father
> And causes a lot of bother. . . .

*Sheet music for the song Dietz and Schwartz wrote for a 1953 motion picture that also included several of their songs
from the 1931 revue of the same title (from Marion Short,* Covers of Gold, *1998)*

Some great Shakespearean scene,
Where a ghost and a prince meet,
And everyone ends in mincemeat. . . .

Dietz's comic timing and his ability to jump from the elegant to the lowdown and farcical provided Broadway with some of the wittiest songs of the era: in "Hoops," as in "Triplets," a child's point of view is employed to make adult observations; "Hottentot Potentate" brings Harlem street savvy to the African jungle; and "We Won't Take It Back" (1948) wryly satirizes a modern world that Native Americans want nothing to do with. Dietz can be silly, satiric, lighthearted, or sarcastic, but many of his comic gems have fallen by the wayside because musical revues are seldom revived, and few of the songs were ever interpolated into movies.

Like Gershwin, Dietz was a meticulous craftsman, and his lyrics provide sterling examples of sound construction and use of imagery. Because many of the songs create their own situation and character, they are often structured like stories or theatrical sketches. Dietz's verses set up the situation succinctly and vividly, allowing a character to develop his or her emotional quandary in the refrain. Sometimes, as in "Miserable with You" (1931) and "Confession," the song takes the form of a musical conversation, with two characters engaged in sparkling lyrical dialogue. At other times, a whole world is created, as in the haunting "Smokin' Reefers" (1932), in which an unhappy Harlem resident resignedly escapes from a despondent reality through drugs. From the expansive joy of "New Sun in the Sky" to the self-destructive "Moanin' Low," Dietz, with the craft of a seasoned playwright, imparted a dramatic tone to his lyrics.

Dietz was particularly adept at rhyme, and, while he rarely dazzled with showy rhyming, as did Porter and

Hart, Dietz was capable of ingenious internal rhymes and arch rhymes. In many of his love songs he avoided rhyming as much as possible, instead employing similar sounds and identities. "Dancing in the Dark," for example, includes no hard rhymes with the word "dark" but instead plays with alliteration (as in the title phrase) and long consonant sounds. "By Myself" is filled with "eye" sound repetitions, and "I Love Louisa" is a playful collection of "ee" sounds. Dietz also searched for that one perfect word that best conveyed the mood or tone he was after, as in "guess," which colors the whole premise of the jaunty torch song "I Guess I'll Have to Change My Plan," or the oxymoronic title "Alone Together," which gives that song its unique charm.

Surveying the career of Dietz, one is puzzled that he was able to forge new ground in his musical revues and yet failed (commercially speaking) in his book musicals. Most songwriters of the time were able to find some success in each genre, except for Dietz. His few ventures into the book musical were marked with inferior librettos (the cause of most musical failures), but there was more at stake than bad luck or ill timing. Perhaps he flourished with revue scores because his songs were such individual and self-reliant pieces of entertainment that they gained their full force from not being connected to a longer story or a larger context. It is possible that the wonderful ambiguity and complex emotions in Dietz's lyrics could not fit in with a boy-meets-girl story line. To say this is not to suggest that his work was too good for much of the musical-comedy material of his day; certainly, the level of the material did not stop Porter or Berlin, who mostly worked with quite thin librettos. But the book musicals of the 1930s might have had trouble incorporating Dietz's minidramas into their structure. Perhaps his sense of mysterious vagueness only caused problems in an art form where clearly defined characters and a swiftly moving plot were essential.

Even in Dietz's two musicals of the 1960s—*The Gay Life* and *Jennie*—there are some superb lyrics in the post-*Oklahoma!* style, but, again, the songs are such satisfying set pieces in themselves that they are better enjoyed apart from the problematic librettos. The scintillating "Magic Moment" and the wistful "Before I Kiss the World Goodbye" conjure up many situations, characters, and emotions, too many for one story, perhaps. Dietz's kind of ambiguity might have been ideal for the "concept" musical that was developed in the 1970s. Musicals such as *Company* (1970) and *A Chorus Line* (1975) are less

bound to plot and more fluid in structure than the traditional book musical and weave together metaphoric songs filled with conflicting emotions, in contrast to the simple, direct expression of characters' feelings found in a traditional narrative musical.

Whether or not Dietz's lyrics from revues of the 1930s anticipated the concept musicals of the 1970s, there is no question that he was truly a theatrical lyricist. Berlin's revue scores succeeded because they were filled with the kind of hits he provided for Tin Pan Alley. But Dietz's lyrics are dramatic, overflowing with character and painting vivid pictures. He was one of the finest lyricists to work on Broadway, and that includes the Broadway of book musicals, such as *My Fair Lady* (1956), as well as Dietz's own world of revues.

References:

Lehman Engel, *Their Words Are Music: The Great Theatre Lyricists and Their Lyrics* (New York: Crown, 1975), pp. 62–71;

Philip Furia, *The Poets of Tin Pan Alley: A History of America's Great Lyricists* (New York: Oxford University Press, 1990), pp. 195–203;

Stanley Green, *The World of Musical Comedy: The Story of the American Musical Stage as Told through the Careers of its Foremost Composers and Lyricists,* fourth edition (New York: Da Capo Press, 1980), pp. 161–171;

Thomas S. Hischak, *Word Crazy: Broadway Lyricists from Cohan to Sondheim* (New York: Praeger, 1991), pp. 71–75.

Selected Discography:

Arthur Schwartz: A Musical Life in Concert, DRG, 17005, 1981;

At Home Abroad, archival reconstruction of 1935 production, Smithsonian, 024, 1981;

The Band Wagon, archival reconstruction of 1931 production, Smithsonian, 021, 1980;

The Band Wagon, motion-picture soundtrack (1953), Rhino, 46197, 1996;

Flying Colors, selections, original Broadway cast (1932), JJA, 1977, 1979;

The Gay Life, original Broadway cast (1961), EMI, 64763 2 2, 1993;

Inside U.S.A., selections, original Broadway cast, Columbia, C-162, 1948;

Jennie, original Broadway cast, RCA Victor, 1083, 1963.

Al Dubin

(10 June 1891 – 11 February 1945)

Michael Lasser

Unless otherwise indicated, music is by Harry Warren.

SELECTED SONGS FROM THEATRICAL PRO-
DUCTIONS: *Broadway and Buttermilk* (1916)–
"'Twas Only an Irishman's Dream" (lyric by
Dubin and John J. O'Brien, music by Rennie Cor-
mack);

Greenwich Village Follies (1921)–"Sundown Brings Back
Memories of You" (lyric by Dubin and Paul Cunningham, music by Charles Edmonds);

Charlot Revue (1926)–"A Cup of Coffee, a Sandwich,
and You" (lyric by Dubin and Billy Rose, music
by Joseph Meyer);

The Streets of Paris (1939), music by Jimmy McHugh–"Is
It Possible?"; "South American Way";

Laffing Room Only (1944)–"Feudin' and Fightin'" (lyric
by Dubin and Burton Lane, music by Lane).

SELECTED SONGS FROM MOTION-PICTURE
PRODUCTIONS: *Gold Diggers of Broadway*
(1929), music by Joe Burke–"Painting the Clouds
with Sunshine"; "Tip Toe through the Tulips";

In the Headlines (1929)–"Love Will Find a Way" (music
by Burke);

Sally (1929), music by Burke–"If I'm Dreaming, Don't
Wake Me Up Too Soon"; "What Will I Do without You?";

The Crooner (1932)–"Three's a Crowd" (lyric by Dubin
and Irving Kahal);

Footlight Parade (1933)–"By a Waterfall"; "Honeymoon
Hotel"; "Shanghai Lil";

42nd Street (1933)–"42nd Street"; "Shuffle Off to Buffalo"; "You're Getting to Be a Habit with Me";
"Young and Healthy";

Gold Diggers of 1933 (1933)–"I've Got to Sing a Torch
Song"; "Pettin' in the Park"; "Remember My Forgotten Man"; "We're in the Money";

Roman Scandals (1933)–"Build a Little Home"; "Keep
Young and Beautiful"; "No More Love";

Dames (1934)–"I Only Have Eyes for You";

Al Dubin in the early 1940s (from Patricia Dubin McBride,
Lullaby of Broadway, *1983)*

Moulin Rouge (1934)–"The Boulevard of Broken
Dreams"; "Coffee in the Morning, Kisses at
Night";

Twenty Million Sweethearts (1934)–"I'll String Along with
You";

Wonder Bar (1934)–"Goin' to Heaven on a Mule";

Broadway Gondolier (1935)–"Lulu's Back in Town";
"The Rose in Her Hair";

Go into Your Dance (1935)–"About a Quarter to Nine";
"Go into Your Dance"; "She's a Latin from Manhattan";

Gold Diggers of 1935 (1935)–"I'm Goin' Shoppin' with You"; "Lullaby of Broadway";

Page Miss Glory (1935)–"Page Miss Glory";

Shipmates Forever (1935)–"Don't Give Up the Ship";

Stars over Broadway (1935)–"Where Am I?";

Cain and Mabel (1936)–"I'll Sing You a Thousand Love Songs";

Gold Diggers of 1937 (1936)–"With Plenty of Money and You";

Melody for Two (1937)–"September in the Rain";

Mr. Dodd Takes the Air (1937)–"Remember Me?";

San Quentin (1937)–"How Could You?";

The Singing Marine (1937)–"The Song of the Marines";

Garden of the Moon (1938), lyrics by Dubin and Johnny Mercer–"The Girl Friend of the Whirling Dervish";

Gold Diggers in Paris (1938)–"I Wanna Go Back to Bali"; "The Latin Quarter"; "A Stranger in Paree";

The Santa Fe Trail (1940)–"Along the Santa Fe Trail" (music by Will Grosz);

'Til We Meet Again (1940)–"Where Was I?" (music by W. Franke Harling);

Stage Door Canteen (1943), music by James V. Monaco–"American Boy"; "She's a Bombshell from Brooklyn"; "We Mustn't Say Goodbye."

SELECTED SONGS PUBLISHED INDEPENDENTLY OF THEATRICAL OR MOTION-PICTURE PRODUCTIONS: "Prairie Rose" (1909), music by Morris Siltmitzer;

"Sunray" (1909), music by Charles P. Shisler;

"Oh, You Mister Moon" (1911), music by Joe Burke;

"All the World Will Be Jealous of Me" (1917), music by Ernest R. Ball;

"Come Down to Tony Spagoni's Cabaret" (1917), music by Clarence Gaskill;

"The Dream of a Soldier Boy" (1917), music by James V. Monaco;

"'Tis an Irish Girl I Love" (1919), lyric by Dubin and J. Keirn Brennan, music by Ball;

"They Didn't Think We'd Do It, but We Did" (1920), music by Fred Rath;

"Tripoli" (1920), lyric by Dubin and Paul Cunningham, music by Irving Weill;

"Crooning" (1921), music by William Caesar;

"Just a Girl that Men Forget" (1922), music by Rath and Joe Garren;

"I Don't Care What You Used to Be (I Know What You Are Today)" (1924), music by Jimmy McHugh;

"My Kid" (1924), music by McHugh and Irwin Dash;

"What Has Become of Hinky Dinky Parlay Voo?" (1924), lyric and music by Dubin, McHugh, Irving Mills, and Dash;

"Cross Words, Why Were They Spoken?" (1925), music by Gaskill and F. Henri Klickmann;

"The Lonesomest Girl in Town" (1925), music by McHugh and Mills;

"Nobody Knows What a Red-Headed Mama Can Do" (1925), lyric by Dubin and Mills, music by Sammy Fain;

"Too Many Kisses in the Summer Bring Too Many Tears in the Fall" (1925), lyric by Dubin and Billy Rose;

"Waters of the Perkiomen" (1925), music by Klickmann;

"My Dream of the Big Parade" (1926), music by McHugh;

"All by My Ownsome" (1927), music by Roger Wolfe Kahn;

"Heaven Help a Sailor on a Night Like This" (1927), lyric by Dubin and Willie Raskin, music by Burke;

"Half Way to Heaven" (1928), music by J. Russel Robinson;

"I Must Be Dreaming" (1928), music by Pat Flaherty and Al Sherman;

"Memories of France" (1928), music by Robinson;

"Dancing with Tears in My Eyes" (1930), music by Burke;

"For You" (1930), music by Burke;

"Crosby, Columbo, and Vallee" (1931), music by Burke;

"If You Should Ever Need Me" (1931), music by Burke;

"Many Happy Returns of the Day" (1931), music by Burke;

"Only a Voice on the Air" (1931), music by Russ Columbo;

"Pagan Moon" (1931), music by Burke and Alfred Bryan;

"To Have and Hold You in My Arms" (1931), music by Burke;

"When the Rest of the Crowd Goes Home" (1931), music by Burke;

"Too Many Tears" (1932);

"You're an Education" (1938);

"Indian Summer" (1939), music by Victor Herbert;

"I Never Felt This Way Before" (1940), music by Duke Ellington;

"The Angels Came Thru" (1941), music by Ernest Lecuona;

"The Anniversary Waltz" (1941), music by Dave Franklin;

"It Happened in Hawaii" (1941), music by Mabel Wayne.

Throughout the 1930s Al Dubin set edgy, smart-guy lyrics to jittery, rhythmic melodies by composer Harry Warren. Their collaboration created the characteristic movie-musical sound of that decade–urban, eager, and sassy–and was instrumental in establishing the style and tone of the Warner Bros. musicals. Dubin wrote his best songs during the darkest days of the

Sheet music for a hit song from a 1929 movie with a score by Dubin and Joe Burke
(Bruccoli Clark Layman Archives)

Great Depression, and when the Depression ended, so, for all practical purposes, did Dubin's career.

Alexander Dubin was born on 10 June 1891 in Zurich, Switzerland, to Simon and Minna Dubin. In the face of rampant anti-Semitism, Simon Dubin had fled from czarist Russia to Switzerland to continue his medical studies in Bern, where he met and married his wife (her maiden name is unknown). A chemist, Minna Dubin consistently placed her career above her maternal responsibilities. At a time when women rarely worked, she returned to teaching six weeks after giving birth to her son. When the young woman hired to look after the baby took ill, Minna tied her son to his crib rather than miss work.

In the summer of 1896, when Dubin was five, his family immigrated to Philadelphia. By 1900 Simon Dubin was the gynecology chief of the dispensary staff at Mt. Sinai Hospital, later renamed Albert Einstein Medical Center, and was especially interested in improving medical care for immigrants. Minna Dubin worked as a seamstress until she was able to find work as a chemist.

Al Dubin felt himself an outsider in school. The family spoke Yiddish, Russian, and German at home, so he had to learn English. His busy parents gave him unlimited freedom, which his daughter and biographer, Patricia Dubin McGuire, suggests that he perceived as a lack of caring on their part. When Al was ten, his mother gave birth to an unplanned second child,

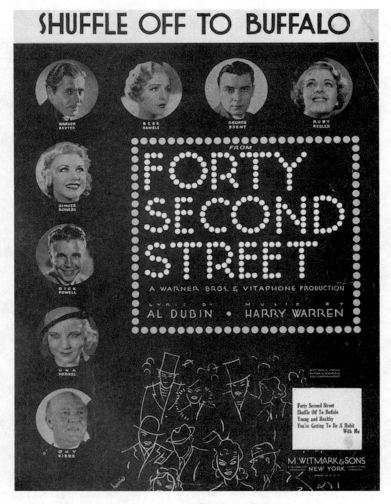

Sheet music for a song by Dubin and Harry Warren that was featured in an
innovative 1933 Warner Bros. movie musical
(Bruccoli Clark Layman Archives)

Joseph. When his Uncle David noticed that Al enjoyed reading, he gave the boy a subscription to *St. Nicholas* magazine. Al soon began to enter the magazine's monthly contests for best drawing, painting, story, and poem. He eventually won a first prize for poetry and discovered that he had a knack for meter and rhyme.

Dubin also loved to walk the streets of Philadelphia. Munching on a kosher pickle, he would listen to the song pluggers pounding out new tunes in the stores. He began to wonder if he could write lyrics like that. He bought sheet music and took it to the house of a friend, Herman Goldberg, because the Goldbergs had a piano. Meanwhile, Simon Dubin insisted that his son become a bar mitzvah, even though neither parent was religious, but Al and his friend Herman, who was also receiving religious instruction, found Hebrew school boring and began to cut classes. During those late afternoons when they were supposed to be study-

ing, Herman taught Al the rudiments of reading music until he could pick out tunes with one finger. Soon Dubin began to write new lyrics to songs to see if he could improve them.

By the time he got his first pair of long pants at the age of twelve, Dubin was a starter on the school baseball team, but he often cut classes to take the train to New York to see Broadway shows and try to sell his material to vaudeville performers. He made his first sale, at age fourteen, to a long-forgotten singer and soon decided on songwriting as a career. Dubin was also overeating and beginning to frequent saloons and brothels. He was still trim and attractive and looked older than he was. By the time he was in his early twenties, he was selling lyrics with some regularity but was regarded as a hard-drinking, tobacco-chewing, gluttonous gambler with a passion for sports. Dubin's overindulgence, combined with a deep anarchic streak that made it impossible for him to accept either criticism or external authority, later destroyed both his career and his marriage.

Simon Dubin, who expected Al to become a physician, became concerned about the direction his older son's life was taking. Though they quarreled, Al realized that he was still dependent on his father and agreed to enter Northeast Manual Training High School in Philadelphia to learn a trade in order to support himself while he wrote lyrics. Always unhappy in school, Dubin refused to return the following fall because M. Witmark and Sons had published two of his songs, "Prairie Rose" (1909) and "Sunray" (1909). His increasingly desperate father suggested a private boarding school as an alternative. Dubin entered Perkiomen Seminary in Pennsburg, Pennsylvania, in the fall of 1909, at the age of eighteen. Although the school was run by a German protestant sect, the Schwenkfelders, the Jewish boy from Philadelphia loved it—especially the girls, the athletics, the yearbook, and the newspaper. Dubin wrote stories and poems for the paper and provided an alma mater that is still sung at the school. He also cut class, drank, and sneaked out of the dormitory after hours.

Rather than take summer school courses to improve his academic record, Dubin went off with a friend to Arden, Delaware, where a colony of writers, artists, and philosophers had gathered to lecture and discuss the arts. Dubin appeared in their production of *Romeo and Juliet,* and a mutual interest in baseball led to a brief friendship with novelist Upton Sinclair. Both men spent a few hours together in a local jail when they were arrested for playing baseball on a Sunday afternoon. Back at Perkiomen in the fall, Dubin continued to defy authority until the school finally expelled him two weeks before graduation.

Dubin then worked as a singing waiter and wrote lyrics that he attempted to sell to Welch and Wilsky, a Philadelphia music-publishing firm. He lived in a furnished room that was always a mess. He said it did not matter: "You do what you can do best. For me, that's lyrics. And the rest of the time you enjoy yourself, have a good time. One hundred years from today, who the hell will care if you made your bed or washed out your socks?" The following year Dubin began collaborating with a struggling young composer named Joe Burke. They published "Oh, You Mister Moon" in 1911 and became close friends, though they did not publish another song together for five years.

In the meantime, Dubin had some luck with other collaborators. He wrote with no particular style or originality in those early years but simply copied the formulaic songs that were typical of Tin Pan Alley. He wrote everything from ethnic songs to sentimental ballads,

and many of his lyrics were maudlin and mawkish. With co-lyricist John J. O'Brien and composer Rennie Cormack, Dubin had his first moderate success in 1916 with an ethnic song, "'Twas Only an Irishman's Dream." The following year he wrote "All the World Will Be Jealous of Me" (1917) with composer Ernest R. Ball, best known for the music for such sentimental Irish ballads as "Mother Machree" (1910) and "When Irish Eyes Are Smiling" (1912). Around this time Dubin read a newspaper article announcing his parents' divorce and his father's intent to marry another woman. He refused to attend his father's wedding and treated the marriage as if it had never taken place.

Soon afterward, Dubin and Burke moved to New York to be closer to Tin Pan Alley. Dubin arranged with music publishers Jack and Irving Mills to set lyrics to the standard melodies in their catalogues, including "Cielito Lindo" and "O Solo Mio," as well as to such light classics as Antonín Dvořák's Humoresque in G-flat (1894) and Nikolay Rimsky-Korsakov's "Song of India" (1899). When America entered World War I, Dubin was drafted and assigned to training at Camp Upton on Long Island, the same base where Sergeant Irving Berlin wrote and produced *Yip! Yip! Yaphank,* his all-soldier show of 1918. While in Manhattan on a weekend pass, Dubin saw a vaudeville act featuring two men and an exceptionally beautiful woman named Helen McClay, whom Dubin began to date.

At this time Dubin was sent overseas with the army. According to some accounts, he saw action with the 305th Field Artillery of the 77th Division and was gassed so severely that his lungs were permanently damaged. Other reports say that he was part of an entertainment unit and saw no combat. During his service, Dubin wrote several patriotic songs, including "The Dream of a Soldier Boy" (1917), with James V. Monaco; "Your Country Needs You Now" (1917), with Rennie Cormack and George B. McConnell; and "They Didn't Think We'd Do It, but We Did" (1920), with Fred Rath, which was published by the 77th Division Association.

Shortly after his father died of a heart attack in 1919, Dubin married McClay, even though her divorce from her first husband was not final. She persuaded Dubin to convert to Roman Catholicism, and they were remarried in church on 19 March 1921. Dubin helped to raise Marie April Kintner, Helen's daughter from her first marriage. He and Helen had one son, Simon Joseph, who died in infancy, and a daughter, Patricia. The marriage was often strained because Helen was a much more conventional person than her husband, and there were frequent separations.

That same year "Sundown Brings Back Memories of You" (1921), a song with lyrics by Dubin and

Lobby card for a 1933 musical for which Dubin and Warren provided the songs (from John Kobal and V. A. Wilson,
Foyer Pleasure: The Golden Age of Cinema Lobby Cards, *1982)*

Paul Cunningham and music by Charles Edmonds, was used in a Broadway revue, *Greenwich Village Follies*. Dubin also joined the American Society of Composers, Authors, and Publishers (ASCAP) and became friendly with composer Jimmy McHugh, with whom he collaborated again near the end of his career. One of the thirty-one songs Dubin wrote in 1924, when he was on the wagon, was "My Kid," a collaboration with McHugh and Irwin Dash in honor of Dubin's baby daughter and McHugh's infant son. In 1925, with F. Henri Klickmann, Dubin wrote "Waters of the Perkiomen."

Later in 1925 Dubin met Harry Warren, who was to become his chief collaborator, in the Oyster Bar in Grand Central Station. Their first song, "Too Many Kisses in the Summer Bring Too Many Tears in the Fall" (1925), flopped, and they went their separate ways. But Dubin finally had a hit in 1926, when Gertrude Lawrence sang the playfully sweet and sexy "A Cup of Coffee, a Sandwich, and You" in *Charlot Revue*. Though Billy Rose is credited as co-lyricist, composer Joseph Meyer said that Dubin was responsible for the title and most of the lyric. Dubin's inspiration came

from the most famous line of one of his favorite poems, Edward FitzGerald's "The Rubáiyát of Omar Khayyám" (1859). He altered "A jug of wine, a loaf of bread—and Thou" into the witty colloquial title of the song. The lyric has an easy charm and a youthful intimacy but lacks the bite of Dubin's later work.

In 1926 Dubin wrote a lyric on the back of a gas-bill envelope. In debt and looking for some quick cash for a poker game, he sold it to lyricist Edgar Leslie (best known for the 1917 song "For Me and My Gal") for $25. "Among My Souvenirs" (1927), with music by Lawrence Wright, quickly became a standard and earned a fortune for Leslie. Dubin would often sell lyrics for anywhere from $5 to $50 to support his various habits, but this song was the only one he ever complained about because it was so successful. He wrote songs for two 1927 Broadway musicals. *White Lights,* with music by J. Fred Coots, flopped, but *Take the Air,* with music by Con Conrad, ran for 206 performances. Dubin also collaborated with Burke on several songs, including "Heaven Help a Sailor on a Night Like This" (1927).

114

Soon after the advent of the talkies in 1927, Dubin was one of the first New York songwriters to journey to Hollywood. He was an established professional, even though he had had few hits and even fewer songs of any distinction. But he was good enough to land a contract with Warner Bros., largely because the studio had purchased T. B. Harms, along with some other important music-publishing firms. Warner Bros. now paid Dubin $500 per week. As people around the country were losing their jobs with the arrival of the Depression in 1929, Dubin was making more money than ever and living in a large house in Beverly Hills.

Among Dubin's first collaborators on the West Coast were M. K. Jerome and Monaco. Mainly, however, he continued to work with Burke. Although he loved Southern California, Dubin soon felt the pressure of working for the studios. They had little regard for songwriters, adding and subtracting songs from pictures at will and demanding as many as four or five songs a week. In New York, Dubin had been used to spending at least twice that long on a single lyric. Despite this pressure, Dubin and Burke wrote the whimsical "Tip Toe through the Tulips" (1929), made into a hit by the ukulele-strumming crooner Nick Lucas, who sang the song in the 1929 movie *Gold Diggers of Broadway*. An admirer of the alliteration in "The Bells" (1849), by his favorite poet, Edgar Allan Poe, Dubin consciously wrote "Tip Toe through the Tulips" as an exercise in alliteration. He and Burke also provided a second song for *Gold Diggers of Broadway*, "Painting the Clouds with Sunshine."

By the end of 1930 Dubin and Burke had written songs for ten additional movies, including *In the Headlines* (1929), *Sally* (1929), *Dancing Sweeties* (1930), and *She Couldn't Say No* (1930). They also wrote two other hit songs of that year, "For You" and "Dancing with Tears in My Eyes," which Dubin said was inspired by a night on the town at the famous Hollywood restaurant the Coconut Grove. He noticed many young women dancing with men old enough to be their fathers—pairings that were called "gold diggers and sugar daddies." Dubin wondered if he were seeing true love or whether these couples were together because the men could support the young women in luxury, especially during the Depression. Surely, he thought, there were young men somewhere whom these women really loved. He wrote the lyric from the point of view of one of the young women, who speaks in an apostrophe to the boy she misses:

For I'm dancing with tears in my eyes,
'Cause the boy in my arms isn't you.
Dancing with somebody new,
When it's you that my heart's calling to.

Dubin, choreographer Busby Berkeley, and Warren during rehearsals for the 1933 movie Roman Scandals (from Tony Thomas, Harry Warren and the Hollywood Musical, 1975)

The heartsick melody of the song is better than the painstakingly obvious and clumsy lyric. Dubin was not at his best in writing conventional love ballads.

In 1931, at about the time Warner Bros. chose not to renew Burke's contract, he and Dubin wrote one of their last songs together, "Crosby, Columbo, and Vallee," in recognition of the three crooners' enormous popularity. Dubin knew all three stars personally. He had the box next to Bing and Dixie Crosby's at Del Mar Racetrack, and he had written "Only a Voice on the Air" (1931) with Russ Columbo a few years before the singer's death at age twenty-six from an accidental shooting in 1934.

With Burke's departure, the studio paired Dubin with Warren. The songs they wrote between 1933 and 1938 helped to define both the Warner Bros. musicals and the Depression itself. They are an indelible part of how that era is known and remembered. Learning from its tough-guy crime movies, starring such distinctive actors as James Cagney and Edward G. Robinson, Warner Bros. applied the same hard-boiled, urban spirit to its backstage musicals. The characters in most

Sheet music for a song from a 1933 Samuel Goldwyn movie musical with a score by
Dubin and Warren (from Tony Thomas, Harry Warren
and the Hollywood Musical, 1975)

of these movies—mainly unknowns trying to make it on Broadway—seemed to be talking out of the sides of their mouths in a kind of wiseacre slang, suggesting that these ambitious, nearly desperate youngsters had taken some hard knocks and were still fighting back.

Warner Bros. made working-class musicals, unlike the elegant, escapist musicals starring Fred Astaire and Ginger Rogers and produced by RKO—romantic comedies set in shimmering white boudoirs and dazzling art deco cabarets where Astaire and Rogers danced the night away. But in drafty dressing rooms or cramped apartments overlooking concrete courtyards, the smart alecks in the Warner Bros. musicals sang the sharp songs by Dubin and Warren that gave voice to their ambitions, their sassy wit ("She only

said no once, and then she didn't hear the question"), and their desire for stardom or love, whichever came first. They wore sweaty rehearsal clothes rather than evening gowns, and they tap-danced as if their lives depended on it.

Dubin and Warren's songs were rarely integrated into the story line of the movies. The songs seldom revealed character or advanced the plot. Rather, they were performance numbers, pure and simple, that let audiences look in on rehearsals or attend opening night. Neither songwriter was a product of the Broadway theater; both made a career of turning out individual songs. In fact, they often finished their work before the screenwriters finished theirs. Yet, the songs were perfectly attuned to the characters who sang them and to

Advertisement for one of three 1933 Warner Bros. movie musicals to feature songs by Dubin and Warren
(from Tony Thomas, Harry Warren and the Hollywood Musical, *1975)*

Busby Berkeley's expansive, surreal choreography, in which dancers sometimes stood nearly still while the camera whirled.

The period of collaboration between Dubin and Warren began quietly, with two songs in 1932: "Too Many Tears" and, for a movie called *The Crooner,* "Three's a Crowd." The next year, they wrote four songs for the legendary musical *42nd Street:* the title song, "You're Getting to Be a Habit with Me," "Shuffle Off to Buffalo," and "Young and Healthy." The movie starred Ruby Keeler, Dick Powell, Bebe Daniels, George Brent, and Warner Baxter, and featured Ginger Rogers, Ned Sparks, Guy Kibbee, and the quintessential gold digger, Una Merkel. It is the story of an overbearing star who breaks her ankle just before opening night. Unless the show opens, the director, played by Baxter, will be ruined. Keeler, playing a chorus girl who is appearing in her first show, steps in to save the day, going onstage a youngster but coming back a star.

With *42nd Street* the movie musical changed forever. It broke out of the flat, stage-bound conventions that initially confined it. Even though much about

42nd Street is dated, one can still sense the exhilaration audiences must have felt as it moved at what was then a furious pace. The restless camera is everywhere, leaving ordinary reality far behind as the dancers, like the camera, cavort on the roof of a taxicab as well as atop a skyscraper.

For Warren's punchy melody to the title song, "42nd Street," Dubin wrote brief, sharply drawn sketches, characterized by internal rhymes that make the lines seem even shorter and sharper than they really are:

> Little nifties from the Fifties, innocent and sweet;
> Sexy ladies from the Eighties, who are indiscreet.
> They're side by side, they're glorified,
> Where the underworld can meet the elite,
> Forty-second Street.
> Naughty, bawdy, gaudy, sporty
> Forty-Second Street.

The language is hip and ironic, but the song revels in what it portrays; it is a New York point of view.

Because *42nd Street* was such a big hit, it established the new conventions of the Warner Bros. musi-

Dubin and Warren (at the piano), going though the sheet music for their 1937 song "September in the Rain" (from Tony Thomas, Harry Warren and the Hollywood Musical, *1975)*

cal: an innocent love story set backstage at a new Broadway show, partially developed subplots involving comic sexual innuendo, sharp dialogue, a sassy performing style, and a batch of new Dubin and Warren songs. Many of these movies portrayed unknown performers aching for success, a full complement of sugar daddies to assist them in one way or another, financial dilemmas in an ever deepening Depression, and a last-minute rescue that ensured a long run for the show and enabled the juvenile, Powell, to win the ingenue, Keeler.

The savvy songs of Dubin and Warren caught the dark, driven feeling of the Depression, and the inventive production numbers of Berkeley let audiences escape their troubles, if only for a few minutes. *42nd Street* premiered at Grauman's Chinese Theatre in Hollywood and was voted one of the top ten movies of 1933. A successful Broadway adaptation in 1980 won a Tony for best musical of that year, and the show was revived in 2001.

The team of Dubin and Warren was next assigned to write songs for *Gold Diggers of 1933* (1933), which had a cast and a backstage plot reminiscent of *42nd Street.* Like *Gold Diggers of Broadway,* it was derived from Avery Hopwood's 1919 play *The Gold Diggers.* Of all the Dubin-Warren movies, this one most directly showed the effects of the Depression, both in the difficulties the characters

encounter in raising money to put on a new show and in the final production number, "Remember My Forgotten Man." Like Yip Harburg and Jay Gorney's classic "Brother, Can You Spare a Dime?" (1932), this large-scale production number expressed the shattered hopes of those who had fought in World War I. Harburg's lyric let one man speak for all those who had lost their jobs and were reduced to begging, while Dubin's invents a loyal woman who bemoans the fate of the man she loves. Set to Warren's insistent, dirge-like march, the words are blunt and clumsy, yet powerful:

> Remember my forgotten man,
> You had him cultivate the land;
> He walked behind the plow,
> The sweat fell from his brow,
> But look at him right now!

In a backhanded tribute to the power of the song, some radio stations banned it, fearing it would undermine American morale.

Paradoxically, *Gold Diggers of 1933* opens with one of Warren and Dubin's jauntiest songs. Sung fetchingly by Rogers and chorus girls covered only by large coins, "We're in the Money" is a perky number that announces the end of the Depression, as if saying so could make it so. It has the snappy, staccato style of Dubin's best lyrics: "Let's spend it, lend it, send it / Rolling along!" The score's other numbers include "I've Got to Sing a Torch Song" and "Pettin' in the Park."

In most of their songs, Dubin's lyrics matched Warren's rhythmic melodies with their own pulsating vitality. But in their love ballads, Dubin played off against the driving music with deceptively simple, conversational lyrics. He was clearly not a poet, but he knew how to turn a phrase that had some zing to it, and he knew how to connect a lyric to the emotions of ordinary people. His ear was also attuned to the Depression. He wrote about simple pleasures—less about trips to the stars than downing cups of coffee, less about forever than today, as in "I'll String Along with You" (1934):

> You may not be an angel,
> 'Cause angels are so few,
> But until the day that one comes along,
> I'll string along with you.

Dubin's best ballads eventually come down to earth, both in outlook and in the feel of everyday talk that gives them conviction.

The years 1933 to 1935 were a time of unrelenting pressure for both Dubin and Warren. In addition to the *Gold Diggers* movies and *42nd Street,* they wrote songs for several musicals of different kinds, for a total

Sheet music for the 1937 song that is regarded as one of Dubin and Warren's best
(from William Zinsser, Easy to Remember, *2000)*

of seventeen scores in three years. They continued to write for such backstage musicals as *Footlight Parade* (1933), with Cagney and Keeler, which featured such Berkeley production numbers as "Shanghai Lil," "Honeymoon Hotel," and the spectacular water ballet "By a Waterfall"; *Twenty Million Sweethearts* (1934), starring Rogers, Powell, and Pat O'Brien and featuring such songs as "I'll String Along with You"; *Dames* (1934), which included the tender ballad "I Only Have Eyes for You"; and *Broadway Gondolier* (1935), which featured the rousing "Lulu's Back in Town." For *Moulin Rouge* (1934), a naughty musical comedy, Dubin and Warren wrote "The Boulevard of Broken Dreams," and they provided songs for several star vehicles as well.

In addition to their work for Warner Bros., Dubin and Warren were also writing songs for the movies of independent producer Samuel Goldwyn, including *Roman Scandals* (1933), an Eddie Cantor farce that included "Keep Young and Beautiful," "No More Love," and "Build a Little Home." "No More Love," written for torch singer Ruth Etting, was filmed as a production number featuring a dozen beautiful blonde slaves, dressed in body stockings but apparently naked and covered only by their long hair. They swayed erotically, their hands and feet in chains. In the midst of all this activity, on 30 April 1934, Dubin and his wife, Helen, formally separated.

Back at Warner Bros., Dubin and Warren provided songs for two Al Jolson vehicles. *Wonder Bar* (1934) included a grotesquely racist production number, "Goin' to Heaven on a Mule," complete with a tree that grew pork chops and blackface angels with watermelons. The best things about the static *Go into Your Dance* (1935) are the comic "She's a Latin from Manhattan," and "About a Quarter to Nine," an ebullient song of anticipation: "The stars are gonna twinkle and shine, / This evening about a quarter to nine." Dubin and Warren also wrote songs for the first of two service musicals, *Shipmates Forever* (1935), about the son of an admiral who reluctantly enters the U.S. Naval Academy. One of their songs, "Don't Give Up the Ship," made the weekly radio program *Your Hit Parade* and was formally adopted by the Corps of Midshipmen. Dubin and Warren's second service musical, *The Singing Marine* (1937), starred Powell; one number, "The Song of the Marines," was adopted by the U.S. Marine Corps.

One night in 1935, by far their busiest and most productive year, Dubin called Warren to say he had written a song for him because he knew how much Warren missed New York. The song was "Lullaby of Broadway," which became the big production number in *Gold Diggers of 1935* (1935) and won the team their only Oscar for best original movie song. Studio head Jack Warner did not like it and wanted it replaced. Warren fought for the lyric because he said it went so well with the offbeat melody he had written and would be difficult to replace. He and Dubin were never close personal friends, but they were loyal to one another and stood together against the injustices of the studio system.

Berkeley filmed the "Lullaby of Broadway" sequence with hundreds of dancers, tapping en masse, ferociously but impersonally, on a huge, almost featureless set that dwarfs the dancers. As an image of the mid 1930s, it appears oppressive and ominous. The dancers provided the background for an ambitious minimusical telling the story of a girl about town who eventually falls to her death from a skyscraper window. As with "42nd Street," Dubin's lyric creates a series of witty images and equally vivid vignettes in a portrait of the high rollers and lowlifes who populate New York:

> The rumble of a subway train,
> The rattle of the taxis,
> The daffy-dills who entertain
> At Angelo's and Maxie's. . . .
> "Hush-a-bye, I'll buy you this and that,"
> You hear a daddy saying,
> And baby goes home to her flat
> To sleep all day.

The angle of vision and the turn of phrase in the song capture the spirit of New York. Other such Dubin-Warren songs as "About a Quarter to Nine" and "Lulu's Back in Town" are active and energetic:

> Gotta get my old tuxedo pressed,
> Gotta sew a button on my vest,

> 'Cause tonight I've gotta look my best,
> Lulu's back in town.

Something is either happening or about to happen. The songs are eager and confident. They feel as if they sprang up from Harlem, Broadway, or Grand Central Station. Concrete is their natural habitat.

Warren once described his and Dubin's working arrangements to an interviewer:

> Al Dubin—he was a terrific eater, weighed about three hundred pounds—he'd disappear on me. Carried a little stub of a pencil, wrote lyrics on scrap paper. I'd write a tune and hand him a lead sheet and then I'd never hear a word. All of a sudden, he'd come back and he'd have the lyric. Once he brought in "Shuffle Off to Buffalo" on the back of a menu from a restaurant. There weren't too many good restaurants here in those days. I always say that with all the wonderful ones we have now, if Al were only alive he could be doing some great lyrics!

On one occasion Dubin disappeared while he and Warren were working on songs for *Stars over Broadway* (1935). Several days later, Warren's phone rang at 2:30 in the morning. It was Dubin. First, he said that he was eating quail and that it was delicious; then, he said that he was in a Mexican brothel, where he had gotten an idea for a song; he then read the lyric. It became "Where Am I?" and reached *Your Hit Parade*. Dubin and Warren had seven other songs on *Your Hit Parade* in 1935: "Lullaby of Broadway" (at number one), "About a Quarter to Nine," "She's a Latin from Manhattan," "Lulu's Back in Town," "The Rose in Her Hair," "Page Miss Glory," and "Don't Give Up the Ship."

Warren and Dubin's major songs during their remaining years at Warner Bros. were "I'll Sing You a Thousand Love Songs" from the 1936 motion picture *Cain and Mabel* (Dubin disliked the lyric and was surprised when it rose to the top of *Your Hit Parade*); "With Plenty of Money and You," from *Gold Diggers of 1937* (released in 1936); "Remember Me?," from *Mr. Dodd Takes the Air* (1937); and "September in the Rain," from *Melody for Two* (1937). "September in the Rain" was one of their loveliest songs and reflected a rarer lyrical strain in Dubin's work:

> The leaves of brown came tumbling down, remember?
> In September, in the rain,
> The sun went out just like a dying ember,
> That September in the rain,
> To ev'ry word of love I heard you whisper,
> The raindrops seemed to play a sweet refrain,
> Though spring is here, to me it's still September,
> That September in the rain.

Usually, when Dubin wrote this kind of ballad, it was unoriginal and even banal, but this song's imagery was compellingly wistful.

In 1938 Dubin had surgery for a fistula. He received morphine for the pain and soon became addicted to the drug, though he managed to pull himself together to write the songs for the fifth and final *Gold Diggers* movie, *Gold Diggers in Paris* (1938). Since *42nd Street* he had written eighty-eight songs for twenty-eight movies. During that same year Warner Bros. assigned Johnny Mercer to work with Warren and Dubin as a co-lyricist. Although he liked Mercer and they became good friends, Dubin resented the studio's action and felt humiliated by their treatment of him. Nonetheless, he and Mercer collaborated on the playful "The Girl Friend of the Whirling Dervish" from *Garden of the Moon* (1938).

Dubin demanded that Warner Bros. buy out his contract so he could return to New York. Back on Broadway in 1939, he and McHugh contributed "South American Way" to the successful revue *The Streets of Paris*. The show made Carmen Miranda a star and won her a Hollywood contract. That same year Dubin wrote a bathetic lyric to a Victor Herbert melody, "Indian Summer," which rose to the top spot on *Your Hit Parade*. Dubin and McHugh also wrote songs for two revues, *Keep Off the Grass* (1940) and *Laffing Room Only* (1944), the latter starring the madcap comedy team of Ole Olsen and Chic Johnson.

During these years Dubin began living with a nurse, Gladys Perrin, who was providing him with drugs. He began an affair with her fifteen-year-old daughter, Edwina Coolidge. Dubin's stormy relationship with both women lasted for most of the rest of his life. He was often broke, and most of his songs were now second-rate. He spent the next few years moving back and forth between the coasts, trying to reestablish himself. Dubin wrote a Western-style title song for the 1940 movie *The Santa Fe Trail* and added Edwina's name as co-lyricist so she would receive some money from its sales. He also wrote a hit song, "Where Was I?," with composer W. Franke Harling for the motion picture *'Til We Meet Again* (1940), and the song received an Oscar nomination.

In 1943 Warner Bros. signed Dubin to work with Monaco on *Stage Door Canteen*. The dozen lyrics he finished testify to the decline in his talents. On 23 February 1943 Dubin married Edwina, even though he had never divorced Helen. He was so dependent on drugs by now that he could rarely work. Five months later Helen sued him for divorce. In January 1945 Dubin called composer Gerald Marks to say that he had written several lyrics for which he wanted Marks to write melodies. Going to meet with Marks, he collapsed on a New York street and was taken to Roosevelt Hospital. Two days later, on 11 February 1945, Dubin died of pneumonia. An autopsy found barbiturates in his bloodstream. He was fifty-three.

Dubin was Dubin only with Warren, and that had been the case for less than a decade. Nevertheless, the songs they wrote together defined the 1930s, and many have endured as standards. Al Dubin was elected to the Songwriters Hall of Fame in 1971.

Biography:

Patricia Dubin McBride, *Lullaby of Broadway* (Secaucus, N.J.: Citadel, 1983).

References:

Richard Barrios, *A Song in the Dark: The Birth of the Musical Film* (New York: Oxford University Press, 1995), pp. 371–407;

Philip Furia, *The Poets of Tin Pan Alley: A History of America's Great Lyricists* (New York: Oxford University Press, 1990); pp. 237–240;

Roy Hemming, *The Melody Lingers On: The Great Songwriters and Their Movie Musicals* (New York: Newmarket Press, 1986), pp. 253–277;

Gerald Mast, *Can't Help Singin': The American Musical on Stage and Screen* (Woodstock, N.Y.: Overlook Press, 1987), pp. 116–137;

Max Wilk, *They're Playing Our Song: The Truth behind the Words and Music of Three Generations* (Mt. Kisco, N.Y.: Moyer Bell, 1991), pp. 118–133.

Selected Discography:

Lullaby of Broadway: The Best of Busby Berkeley at Warner Bros., Rhino, 72169, 1995.

Ray Evans
(4 February 1915 –)

and

Jay Livingston
(28 March 1915 – 17 October 2001)

Graham Wood
Coker College

Unless otherwise indicated, both lyrics and music are by Evans and Livingston.

SELECTED SONGS FROM THEATRICAL PRODUCTIONS: *Oh Captain!* (1958)–"All the Time"; "Femininity"; "It's Never Quite the Same"; "Life Does a Man a Favor (When It Gives Him Simple Joys)"; "The Morning Music of Montmartre"; "Surprise"; "We're Not Children"; "You Don't Know Him"; "You're So Right for Me";

Let It Ride! (1961)–"Everything Beautiful"; "Hey Jimmy, Joe, John, Jack"; "His Own Little Island"; "Just an Honest Mistake"; "Let It Ride"; "Love, Let Me Know";

Sugar Babies (1979)–"The Sugar Baby Bounce."

SELECTED SONGS FROM MOTION-PICTURE PRODUCTIONS: *I Accuse My Parents* (1944)– "Are You Happy in Your Work?"; "Love Came between Us"; "Where Can You Be?";

On Stage Everybody (1945)–"Stuff Like That There";

The Stork Club (1945)–"A Square in the Social Circle";

Why Girls Leave Home (1945)–"The Cat and the Canary";

To Each His Own (1946)–"To Each His Own";

Golden Earrings (1947)–"Golden Earrings" (music by Victor Young);

My Favorite Brunette (1947)–"Beside You"; "My Favorite Brunette";

Dream Girl (1948)–"Dream Girl"; "Drunk with Love";

Isn't It Romantic? (1948)–"At the Nickelodeon"; "I Shoulda Quit When I Was Ahead"; "Indiana Dinner"; "Miss Julie July"; "Wond'rin' When";

The Paleface (1948)–"Buttons and Bows"; "Meetcha 'Round the Corner";

The Great Lover (1949)–"Lucky Us"; "A Thousand Violins";

My Friend Irma (1949)–"Here's to Love"; "Just for Fun"; "My One, My Only, My All";

Captain Carey, U.S.A. (1950)–"Mona Lisa";

Copper Canyon (1950)–"Copper Canyon";

Fancy Pants (1950)–"Home Cookin'";

My Friend Irma Goes West (1950)–"Baby, Obey Me!"; "The Fiddle and Gittar Band"; "I'll Always Love You (Querida Mía)";

Sunset Boulevard (1950)–"Sunset Boulevard";

Here Comes the Groom (1951)–"Bonne Nuit (Good Night)"; "Misto Christofo Columbo"; "Your Own Little House";

The Lemon Drop Kid (1951)–"It Doesn't Cost a Dime to Dream"; "Silver Bells"; "They Obviously Want Me to Sing";

My Favorite Spy (1951)–"Just a Moment More";

Aaron Slick from Punkin Crick (1952)–"Chores"; "I'd Like to Baby You"; "Life Is a Beautiful Thing"; "Marshmallow Moon"; "My Beloved"; "Purt' Nigh, But Not Plumb"; "Saturday Night in Punkin Crick"; "Soda Shop"; "Step Right Up"; "Still Water"; "Why Should I Believe in Love?";

Somebody Loves Me (1952)–"Honey, Oh, My Honey"; "Love Him"; "Thanks to You";

Son of Paleface (1952)–"California Rose"; "What a Dirty Shame"; "Wing-Ding Tonight";

What Price Glory? (1952)–"My Love, My Life";

Here Come the Girls (1953)–"Ali Baba (Be My Baby)"; "Girls"; "Heavenly Days"; "It's Torment"; "Never So Beautiful"; "See the Circus"; "When You Love Someone"; "Ya Got Class";

The Stars Are Singing (1953)–"Haven't Got a Worry to My Name"; "I Do! I Do! I Do!"; "Lovely

122

Ray Evans and Jay Livingston (AP/Wide World Photos)

Weather for Ducks"; "My Heart Is Home"; "My Kind of Day"; "Rruff Song" (music by Juventino Rosas);

Thunder in the East (1953)—"The Ruby and the Pearl";

Casanova's Big Night (1954)—"Pretty Mandolin (Tic-a-Tic-a-Tic)";

Red Garters (1954)—"Bad News"; "Brave Man"; "A Dime and a Dollar"; "Good Intentions"; "Lady Killer"; "Man and Woman"; "Meet a Happy Guy"; "Red Garters"; "The Robin Randall Song"; "This Is Greater Than I Thought"; "Vaquero";

Istanbul (1956)—"I Was a Little Too Lonely (And You Were a Little Too Late)";

The Man Who Knew Too Much (1956)—"Whatever Will Be, Will Be (Que Será, Será)";

The Scarlet Hour (1956)—"Never Let Me Go";

The James Dean Story (1957)—"Let Me Be Loved";

Omar Khayyam (1957)—"The Loves of Omar Khayyam";

Tammy and the Bachelor (1957)—"Tammy";

The Big Beat (1958)—"As I Love You"; "I Waited So Long";

Houseboat (1958)—"Almost in Your Arms"; "Bing! Bang! Bong!";

Once Upon a Horse (1958)—"Once Upon a Horse";

Raw Wind in Eden (1958)—"Magic Touch";

Saddle the Wind (1958)—"Saddle the Wind";

This Happy Feeling (1958)—"This Happy Feeling";

Vertigo (1958)—"Vertigo";

The Blue Angel (1959)—"Lola-Lola";

A Private's Affair (1959), lyrics and music by Evans, Livingston, and Jimmy McHugh—"The Same Old Army"; "36-24-36"; "Warm and Willing";

All Hands on Deck (1961)—"All Hands on Deck"; "I Got It Made"; "Somewhere There's a Home"; "There's No One Like You";

Dear Heart (1964)—"Dear Heart" (music by Henry Mancini);

Those Calloways (1964)—"Angel" (music by Max Steiner);

Harlow (1965)—"Lonely Girl"; (music by Neal Hefti);

Never Too Late (1965)—"Never Too Late" (music by David Rose);

The Third Day (1965)—"Love Me Now" (music by Percy Faith);

The Night of the Grizzly (1966)—"Angela";

The Oscar (1966)—"The Glass Mountain" (music by Faith);

This Property Is Condemned (1966)—"Wish Me a Rainbow";

What Did You Do in the War, Daddy? (1966)—"In the Arms of Love" (music by Mancini);

Wait until Dark (1967)—"Wait until Dark" (music by Mancini).

SELECTED SONGS FROM TELEVISION PRODUCTIONS: *Bonanza* (1959–1973)—"Bonanza";

Mister Ed (1961–1966)—"Mister Ed";

Sheet music for the 1946 song that was Evans and Livingston's
first big success (Bruccoli Clark Layman Archives)

To Rome with Love (1969–1971)–"To Rome with Love."

BOOKS: *Great Songs by Jay Livingston and Ray Evans*
(New York: Famous Music, 1955);
The Songs of Livingston and Evans (Milwaukee: MCA
Music, 1993).

For a fifteen-year period from the mid 1940s to
the late 1950s, Ray Evans and Jay Livingston were one
of the most successful songwriting teams in Hollywood.
Their names appeared as a double credit for lyrics and
music at the head of almost all of their published sheet
music. They won three Oscars for best original movie
song, and they were both inducted into the Songwriters
Hall of Fame in 1977. Their most famous songs include
"To Each His Own" (1946), "Buttons and Bows"
(1948), "Mona Lisa" (1950), "Silver Bells" (1951),
"Whatever Will Be, Will Be (Que Será, Será)" (1956),
"Tammy" (1957), and "Dear Heart" (1964).

Raymond Bernard Evans was born on 4 February 1915 in Salamanca, New York, to Philip and
Frances Lipsitz Evans. In high school he played clarinet
and saxophone in the school orchestra. After graduating in 1931, he enrolled at the University of Pennsylvania, where he majored in banking and finance, played
football and track, and received a B.S. in economics in
1936. Jay Harold Livingston was born 28 March 1915
in Pittsburgh to Maurice and Rose Wachtel Livingston.
He studied piano, which he played with the school
orchestra and a local band. After he graduated from
McDonald High School in 1933, he enrolled at the University of Pennsylvania and received a B.A. in journalism in 1937.

Evans and Livingston first met as undergraduates at the University of Pennsylvania, where Livingston led a dance band. Evans played saxophone and
clarinet in various ensembles, including Livingston's.
During summers and spring holidays, the two played

Sheet music for the 1948 song that earned Evans and Livingston their first Academy Award
(Bruccoli Clark Layman Archives)

in bands on cruise liners. After Livingston graduated in 1937, they tried to break into songwriting in New York. Livingston worked as a pianist for NBC and for Ole Olsen and Chic Johnson's Broadway revue *Hellza-poppin'* (1938), while Evans worked as an accountant and statistician. During the early part of World War II, Livingston served in the army while Evans worked in a defense plant.

In 1944 Olsen and Johnson invited Evans and Livingston to Hollywood, and soon they were writing movie songs for the Producers Releasing Corporation and for Paramount Pictures. After some early successes, Paramount hired them as staff writers in 1945. Famous Music, the music-publishing arm of Paramount, following the practice of other studio firms, had begun buying up Tin Pan Alley publishers in the 1930s. Typically, songs were released several months

in advance of the premiere of a movie as a promotional device; once the movie was released, it helped to continue popularizing the songs. For additional marketing purposes, Paramount also signed radio stars who had recorded the songs.

Evans and Livingston's work for Paramount ranged from single theme songs for essentially nonmusical movies, such as "Whatever Will Be, Will Be (Que Será, Será)," for *The Man Who Knew Too Much* (1956), to the fully integrated score for *Red Garters* (1954). Sometimes songs were used only in instrumental versions, but most of them were published with lyrics and marketed as theme songs from a movie. Evans and Livingston stayed at Paramount for a decade. Their first composition for the studio was "A Square in the Social Circle," for the movie *The Stork Club* (1945), starring Betty Hutton as a suddenly wealthy hatcheck girl. The

Sheet music for Evans and Livingston's second Oscar-winning song, from a 1950 movie (Bruccoli Clark Layman Archives)

lyrics recall Lorenz Hart and Richard Rodgers's socially out-of-place protagonist in "The Lady is a Tramp" (1937):

> I've ditched the "rich in sable" set
> To join the "kitchen table" set. . . .
> I've dined and clubbed, I've elbow rubbed,
> From Yonkers to Cheyenne.

The melody and rhythm of the song have a brash, syncopated, vaudeville quality that resembles the style of George M. Cohan and would indeed have been out of place in the Stork Club. Another early success for Evans and Livingston was "The Cat and the Canary," written for *Why Girls Leave Home* (1945). It was nominated for an Academy Award for best original movie

song but lost to Rodgers and Oscar Hammerstein's "It Might as Well Be Spring," from *State Fair* (1945).

Evans and Livingston's first major success was "To Each His Own," which sold three million records in 1946 alone. Although the song was written to promote the 1946 motion picture of the same title, it was not actually used in the movie (the sheet music says "inspired by the Paramount Picture"). The song was, however, used in instrumental versions in several other movies. Eighth-note triplets give a lilting melodic and rhythmic contour to the opening lines: "A rose must remain with sun and the rain." As the chorus becomes more passionate, the triplets double in duration: "If a flame is to grow there must be a glow." The careful placement of quarter-note rests highlights parallel phrases that are melodically, rhythmically, and tex-

Sheet music for the 1951 Evans and Livingston song that became a Christmas standard (from Ronny S. Schiff, ed.,
Paramount on Parade: Famous Music from Paramount Films, *1996)*

tually similar and that coincide with important phrases of the song:

> [rest] And my own is you. . . .
> [rest] For me there's you. . . .
> [rest] One and only you.

Several versions of "To Each His Own" appeared in the popular music charts in 1946. The first was by big-band singer Eddy Howard, whose version reached the number-one spot, followed by a recording by Freddie Martin and His Orchestra, which also reached the top spot. A rendition by the Ink Spots remained the number-one song for eight weeks. Paula Kelly and the Modernaires' version reached the number-three position, while Tony Martin's recording of "To Each His

Own" reached number four. Among subsequent successful versions was a recording by The Platters, which reached number twenty-one in 1960.

Livingston once described his and Evans's unusual style of collaboration, citing the composition of "To Each His Own" for an example of their method:

> Our general approach to writing is for Ray Evans to write lyrics—sometimes with many different titles—for a particular assignment. We then get together and I see what strikes me as something that would fit the situation best and lead into a good melody, sometimes using only a line or two from pages of lyrics, and then we both sit down and write a melody to a set lyric. . . . I can write a stronger melody if I am free to go on with it where I like. A good example is "To Each His Own." One line caught my eye: "Two lips must insist on two more to be kissed."

This gave me the opening phrase of the song and I went on to write the melody from there. We then got together and wrote the lyrics for this melody. Often we take ideas from Ray's original lyrics if they fit the new melody. It gives him extra work to do, but it has proved successful and we still work more or less that way.

Soon after the success of "To Each His Own," Livingston married Lynne Gordon, on 19 March 1947, and Evans married Wyn Ritchie, on 19 April of that year. Both men collaborated as lyricists with composer Victor Young on the title song for *Golden Earrings* (1947), a movie starring Marlene Dietrich as a gypsy who assists a British agent during World War II. Cast in the minor mode, and with altered second and seventh scale degrees, the melody of "Golden Earrings" has all the stereotypical markers of one intended to sound "Jewish," "oriental," or otherwise non-Western. Such musical traits appeared in the early songs of Irving Berlin, particularly in the verses of his Jewish novelty songs, but they later became a broadened musical code used by many Tin Pan Alley writers to signify various kinds of exoticism. The bridge, or release, of the chorus is the most interesting part of the song, with its twisting, descending contour and two long-held whole notes followed by a cascade of eighth notes: "By the burning fire they will glow with ev'ry coal / You will hear desire whisper low inside your soul." The lyrics are deftly arranged in this parallel phrase pair to produce a complex triple rhyme: "fire"/"glow"/"coal" and "desire"/"low"/"soul." The lines also emphasize the parallel of smoldering embers and metaphorical passion caused by the golden earrings themselves. Although sung by Murvyn Vye in the movie, it was Peggy Lee's version that reached the number-one slot on the popular-music charts early in 1948.

A gypsy exoticism is also suggested in "A Thousand Violins," written for *The Great Lover* (1949), by the use of the minor mode and a sinuously chromatic melody. Through the influence of Berlin and, later, George Gershwin and Cole Porter, such musical gestures had become an accepted part of the language of popular song as a way of musically coding a whole spectrum of non-Western or otherwise immigrant nationalities, cultures, and situations. In a similar vein, "The Ruby and the Pearl," from *Thunder in the East* (1953), also uses the minor mode, augmented intervals, and an ornamented accompaniment to suggest an exotic quality. The lyrics are filled with such deliberately melodramatic phrases as "come close and cling to my kiss."

After working on several Paramount shorts—small-scale, minimusical features lasting up to thirty minutes—Evans and Livingston wrote their first

Academy Award–winning song, "Buttons and Bows," for *The Paleface* (1948). The movie starred Bob Hope as a former dentist, now a disoriented cowboy lamenting his decision to leave the East. Jane Russell has married Hope as a ruse to capture some outlaws. Hope and Russell sing "Buttons and Bows" while driving a covered wagon but end up taking a wrong turn (as in the song) that leads them into an ambush. As Don Tyler has noted in *Hit Parade: An Encyclopedia of the Top Songs of the Jazz, Depression, Swing, and Sing Eras* (1985), the song "has a distinct western flavor in lyrics and melody" and must be seen in the context of the musical idioms of the stage musicals *Oklahoma!* (1943) and *Annie Get Your Gun* (1946). Nevertheless, "Buttons and Bows" is also in the tradition of such Western parody songs as Rodgers and Hart's "Way Out West (on West End Avenue)" (1937), in which a city dweller draws on the musical codes of the cowboy song but undercuts the visual imagery of the West with an ironic urban twist. The main melodic strain of "Buttons and Bows" is based on a pentatonic scale common to many European folk traditions, thus lending it an ersatz authenticity, while the rhythmic "clip-clop" of the accompaniment recalls Rodgers and Hammerstein's "The Surrey With the Fringe on Top" from *Oklahoma!* In addition, the twelve-measure A sections (instead of the usual eight measures) suggest an expansive prairie.

Hope's character, however, is as out of place in the prairie as his deliberately poor grammar ("I have chose") and misplaced verbal accents ("prai-*rie*' and "*ce*-ment") would be humorous in the city. One can feel, or rather hear, the roughness of the wagon ride: "My bones denounce the buckboard bounce." This line is filled with patterned alliteration ("*b*ones"/"*b*uck"/"*b*oard"/"*b*ounce") and assonance ("den*ounce*"/"*bounce*"), while spiky *t*s prick the following line: "And the cac*t*us hur*t*s my *t*oes." Indeed, the construction of the title phrase "buttons and bows" seems to generate several closely matched pairs of words and images that sound like the things to which they refer: "rings and things," "buckboard bounce," "silks and satins," "rocks the room," "high silk hose."

"Buttons and Bows" was later used in *Sunset Boulevard* (1950), sung by Evans and Livingston in a brief cameo appearance, and, with additional lyrics, in *Son of Paleface* (1952). Successful cover versions included a million-selling recording by Dinah Shore, which stayed in the number-one slot for ten weeks from November 1948 to January 1949, and a version by the Dinning Sisters with the Art Van Damme Orchestra. Gene Autry's rendition reached number six on the country-and-western charts. A later Evans-

Sheet music for Evans and Livingston's third Oscar-winning song, featured in a 1958 Alfred Hitchcock movie (Collection of Paul Talbot)

Livingston song that recalls the mood of "Buttons and Bows" and was also sung by Hope, although this time with Lucille Ball, is "Home Cookin'," from the movie *Fancy Pants* (1950). The rhythm of the melody and lyrical humor makes this song a close cousin to "Buttons and Bows." Like the earlier song, "Home Cookin'" recalls the rustic jaunt of a cowboy ballad: "I climb this hill, I try this dale, / And then I step on a rusty nail." This rustic parody style culminated in the 1954 movie musical *Red Garters,* in which the most successful number, "A Dime and a Dollar," is much in the same vein as "Buttons and Bows" and "Home Cookin'." Though visually stylish and full of tongue-in-cheek humor, this set-bound movie could not compete with the outdoor open spaces and earnestness of the movie version of *Oklahoma!,* which was released the following year.

Evans and Livingston's second Oscar-winning song was "Mona Lisa," written for the 1950 movie *Captain Carey, U.S.A.* The melody (originally titled "Prima Donna") was apparently written by Livingston on his way to the studio one morning. In the movie, it is heard only in fragments and with Italian lyrics, so that a blind accordionist on a street corner can warn hero Webster Carey (played by Alan Ladd) and his allies, a group of Italian partisans, of approaching Nazis. Evans and Livingston begged Nat King Cole to record the song, and it stayed at number one for eight weeks, selling more than three million copies. Of the many subsequent cover versions, at least eight were also released in 1950, including those by Harry James, Dennis Day, Ralph Flanagan, Art Lund, Moon Mulligan, Charlie Spivak, Jimmy Wakely, and Victor Young. Addressing an enigmatic woman who has been compared to the Mona Lisa of Leonardo Da Vinci's famous painting, the singer asks, "Do you smile to tempt a lover, Mona Lisa, / Or is this your way to hide a broken heart?" The bold leaps and wide span of the melody are more characteristic of nineteenth-century Italian bel canto than of Tin Pan Alley songs, but they perfectly suit the impassioned protagonist here.

The repetition of the name Mona Lisa at the opening of the chorus is echoed in the next few lines by a pattern of *l*s and a symmetrically reversible pattern of vowel sounds (i-a-o-a-i):

> You're so *l*ike the *l*ady with the mystic smile,
> Is it on*l*y 'cause you're *l*one*l*y
> They have b*l*amed you
> For that Mona Lisa strangeness in your smi*l*e?

The smooth rolling *l*s return in perhaps one of the most eloquently interrogative endings in a popular song: "Are you warm, are you real, Mona Lisa, / Or just a cold and lonely, lovely work of art?" In the entire chorus there are only four harsh consonants: "'*c*ause," "bro*k*en," "*c*old," and "wor*k*," two of them in the final phrase, and they jar in a verbal texture that is mostly extremely mellifluous. The "broken" heart is surrounded by a cushion of *h*s—"*h*ide a bro*k*en *h*eart"—but the "cold" of the last line is highlighted because it is placed on a metrical downbeat near the end of the chorus. All of this hints at a coldness beneath the warm, fleshy surface. The closing phrase encapsulates the paradox of all beautiful works of art that can be admired and loved but that are incapable of returning the emotion.

"I'll Always Love You (Querida Mía)," from the movie *My Friend Irma Goes West* (1950), is a romantic ballad with a flowing quarter-note triplet figure and placement of all five open vowels ("day"/"dear"/"wine"/"so"/ "you") on the longest notes of the melody. The opening line—"Day after day I'll always love you"—sets the tone for the rest of the chorus. Although a full-blooded, passionate tenor could sing his heart out with this song, in the movie it was sung by crooner Dean Martin, along with Corinne Calvet.

Evans and Livingston received their third Oscar in 1956, for "Whatever Will Be, Will Be (Que Será, Será)," which was written for Alfred Hitchcock's *The Man Who Knew Too Much.* Sung by Doris Day, the song is integral to the plot of the movie. Day's recording reached number one on the popular-music charts. This triple-time waltz song has a European, operetta-like elegance, particularly in the matching of the title phrase ("Que será, será") to a dotted quarter note beginning on the second beat of a measure, following a quarter-

note rest. This upbeat, characteristic of Viennese waltzes, is used only once and thus highlights the transition from the verse to the chorus. The title phrase, given in Spanish and English in the last two lines of the chorus—"Que será, será, / Whatever will be, will be"— are separated musically and rhythmically from the rest of the song by a rhythmic pattern of a quarter-note rest followed by two quarter notes. Thus, this philosophical reflection is made to stand out. Alliteration abounds in the lyric, providing sonic concordance between the verse and chorus. For example, the *w* sounds in the chorus ("*w*hatever"/"*w*ill"/"*w*hat") are matched in the verse ("*w*hen"/"*w*hat"/"*w*ill"). Evans and Livingston were not afraid to repeat words, but their patterned repetition never seems gratuitous. In a sense, the chorus, if not the whole song, is just one big shrug—"Who knows?"— expressed lyrically in a series of childlike questions and laconic adult responses that acknowledge the uncertainty of the future but also the value of enjoying the present. The pervasive use of the waltz rhythm suggests a youthful energy that only too quickly slips away.

Evans and Livingston wrote several other waltzes, although most do not have the ballroom sweep of "Whatever Will Be, Will Be (Que Será, Será)." One example is the leisurely "Silver Bells," which was featured in *The Lemon Drop Kid* (1951). Hope plays a racetrack spy who must pay off a huge gambling debt to a gangster by Christmas Eve. He enlists his friends to stand on street corners with bells to collect money. The song describes an urban Christmas, in contrast to a more familiar rural holiday setting, and the refrain cleverly features a long-held note, so that there is space to add tinkling bells in the accompaniment. Even more simple is the naive, childlike waltz "Life Is a Beautiful Thing," sung by Shore and Minerva Urecal in *Aaron Slick from Punkin Crick* (1952).

Perhaps Evans and Livingston's most charmingly innocent triple-time song is "Tammy" from the movie *Tammy and the Bachelor* (1957), as sung by Debbie Reynolds. The melody is simple, consisting rhythmically almost entirely of quarter notes, especially in the A sections of this AABA-pattern chorus. To this nursery-rhyme-like tune are added naive phrases: "Wish I knew if he knew what I'm dreaming of!" The use of Tammy's name as the refrain to each A section of the chorus underscores the overall effect of simplicity by suggesting that she is singing to herself and using her name symbolically to express her feelings. Reynolds's recording of the song reached number one on the popular-music charts, while a later version by the Ames Brothers reached the number-five spot.

In "Never Let Me Go," from *The Scarlet Hour* (1956), an anxious lover doubts the constancy of his beloved; the minor-mode melody is set with some of

*Sheet music for Evans and Livingston's hit that was the title song
for a 1957 movie (Bruccoli Clark Layman Archives)*

the most forlorn lyrics that Evans and Livingston ever wrote. The sweeping melody underscores the singer's anguish and his heartfelt entreaties: "There's no place for me without you. / Never let me go. / I'd be so lost if you went away. . . ." As the bridge leads into a musical return of the opening A section of the chorus melody, an additional anticipatory link provides a seamless lyrical and melodic dovetailing into the final section of the song: "Because of one caress" (end of the bridge) "my world was overturned" (the final A section begins). Indeed, "Never Let Me Go" features an unusual chorus structure, in which an eight-measure A section is followed by an eight-measure bridge and is rounded off by a twelve-measure section based on A. This is not the expected thirty-two measure chorus in either the AABA or ABAC pattern typical of the majority of commercial

popular songs from the first half of the twentieth century, and this foreshortened structure perhaps suggests disorientation or loss on the part of the singer.

When their contract with Paramount expired in 1956, Evans and Livingston wrote on an independent basis for various studios. They also established their own music-publishing firm. Ever versatile in their range of song styles, they sometimes alluded to earlier songwriters. In "I Was a Little Too Lonely (And You Were a Little Too Late)," from *Istanbul* (1956), the quarternote rest that begins the chorus before "you promised me" is a typical Gershwin move, while the Jazz Age humor of the lyric certainly suggests Berlin and Cohan. Certainly, the song exhibits Jazz Age humor: "You thought that I'd be here to run to, / Now I'm gonna do to you as I was done to!"

As the popularity of the Hollywood musical waned in the late 1950s, Evans and Livingston turned to Broadway. They wrote the scores for *Oh Captain!* (1958), a musical based on the British movie *The Captain's Paradise* (1953), and for *Let It Ride!* (1961), a musical adaptation of John Cecil Holm and George Abbott's play *Three Men on a Horse* (1935), but neither show was successful. Evans and Livingston also worked in the medium of television and wrote the theme songs for two popular programs, *Bonanza* (1959–1973) and *Mister Ed* (1961–1966). The former capitalizes on a galloping-horse rhythm for its effect, while the latter has a Yip Harburg quality to its lyrics. Indeed, "Mister Ed" could be a song dropped from *The Wizard of Oz* (1939), particularly in its repetition of "a horse / of course" and its skipping rhythm.

Evans and Livingston continued to write movie songs during the 1960s, working as co-lyricists with such composers as Henry Mancini, Percy Faith, and Neal Hefti. Their greatest success during this period came with Mancini on the title song for *Dear Heart* (1964), which became a hit recording for Andy Williams. The use of the colloquial vacation-postcard greeting "wish you were here" in the opening line of the chorus is the only hint of humor in this largely sentimental song. Evans and Livingston also had an autumnal stage success with two songs in *Sugar Babies* (1979), a Broadway revue about burlesque that starred Ann Miller and Mickey Rooney. Most of the songs in the show were by Jimmy McHugh and Dorothy Fields. Evans and Livingston contributed a new song, "The Sugar Baby Bounce," and an old one, "Warm and Willing," written with McHugh and first used in the movie *A Private's Affair* (1959). *Sugar Babies* was funny enough to remain on the stage three years.

After the death of his wife, Lynne, in 1991, Jack Livingston married actress Shirley Mitchell in 1992. He died in Los Angeles on 17 October 2001, at the age of eighty-six. He was survived by his wife and his daughter from his first marriage, Travlyn Livingston Talmadge. Ray Evans is still living in Los Angeles.

Evans and Livingston's most successful songs combined an eloquent humanity with simplicity of expression, directness of emotion, and a touch of humor. They produced expertly crafted songs with wide appeal.

References:

David Ewen, *American Songwriters* (New York: Wilson, 1987);

Ronny S. Schiff, ed., *Paramount on Parade: Famous Music from Paramount Films* (Milwaukee: Hal Leonard, 1996);

Don Tyler, *Hit Parade: An Encyclopedia of the Top Songs of the Jazz, Depression, Swing, and Sing Eras* (New York: Quill, 1985).

Selected Discography:

Nat King Cole, "Mona Lisa," on *The Greatest Hits of Nat King Cole*, EMI-Capitol, GZS-1127, 1994;

Doris Day, *Que Sera Sera*, Cleopatra, 452, 1999;

Ink Spots, "To Each His Own," on *Favorites*, Universal Special Products, 088112049-2, 1999;

Dinah Shore, *Buttons & Bows*, ASV Living Era, 5317, 2000;

Andy Williams, *Dear Heart/The Shadow of Your Smile*, Sony, 33819, 1999.

Dorothy Fields

(15 July 1905 – 28 March 1974)

Deborah Grace Winer

SELECTED SONGS FROM THEATRICAL PRO-
DUCTIONS: *Hot Chocolates* (1927), music by
Jimmy McHugh–"Freeze an' Melt"; "Harlema-
nia"; "Hottentot Tot";

Blackbirds of 1928 (1928), music by McHugh–"Diga
Diga Doo"; "Doin' the New Low-Down"; "I
Can't Give You Anything but Love"; "I Must
Have That Man";

The International Revue (1930), music by McHugh–
"Exactly Like You"; "On the Sunny Side of the
Street";

The Vanderbilt Revue (1930), music by McHugh–"Blue
Again";

Radio City Music Hall Opening (1932), music by
McHugh–"Hey Young Fella! (Close Your Old
Umbrella)";

Clowns in Clover (1933), music by McHugh–"Don't
Blame Me";

Stars in Your Eyes (1939), music by Arthur Schwartz–
"I'll Pay the Check"; "A Lady Needs a Change";

Up in Central Park (1945), music by Sigmund Romberg–
"April Snow"; "Close as Pages in a Book";

Arms and the Girl (1950), music by Morton Gould–"A
Cow and a Plough and a Frau"; "Nothin' for
Nothin'"; "There Must Be Something Better
Than Love";

A Tree Grows in Brooklyn (1951), music by Schwartz–
"Growing Pains"; "He Had Refinement"; "I'll
Buy You a Star"; "Look Who's Dancing"; "Love
Is the Reason"; "Make the Man Love Me";

By the Beautiful Sea (1954), music by Schwartz–"Alone
Too Long"; "Happy Habit"; "I'd Rather Wake
Up by Myself";

Redhead (1959), music by Albert Hague–"'Erbie Fitch's
Twitch"; "Merely Marvelous"; "The Right Finger
of My Left Hand"; "The Uncle Sam Rag";

Sweet Charity (1966), music by Cy Coleman–"Baby,
Dream Your Dream"; "Big Spender"; "I Love to
Cry at Weddings"; "I'm a Brass Band"; "I'm the
Bravest Individual"; "If My Friends Could See
Me Now"; "The Rhythm of Life"; "Sweet Char-

Dorothy Fields

ity"; "There's Gotta Be Something Better than This";
"Where Am I Going?"; "You Should See Yourself";

Eleanor (1970; unproduced), music by Coleman–"After
Forty It's Patch, Patch, Patch";

Seesaw (1973), music by Coleman–"I'm Way Ahead";
"It's Not Where You Start"; "Nobody Does It
Like Me"; "Poor Everybody Else."

SELECTED SONGS FROM MOTION-PICTURE
PRODUCTIONS: *Love in the Rough* (1930),
music by Jimmy McHugh–"Go Home and Tell
Your Mother";

Cuban Love Song (1931), music by McHugh–"Cuban Love Song";

Every Night at Eight (1935), music by McHugh–"I Feel a Song Comin' On" (lyrics by Fields and George Oppenheimer); "I'm in the Mood for Love";

I Dream Too Much (1935), music by Jerome Kern–"I Dream Too Much";

In Person (1935), music by Oscar Levant–"Don't Mention Love to Me";

Roberta (1935), music by Kern–"I Won't Dance" (lyrics by Fields and Oscar Hammerstein 2nd); "Lovely to Look At";

Swing Time (1936), music by Kern–"Bojangles of Harlem"; "A Fine Romance"; "Never Gonna Dance"; "Pick Yourself Up"; "The Way You Look Tonight";

Joy of Living (1938), music by Kern–"You Couldn't Be Cuter";

One Night in the Tropics (1940)–"Remind Me" (music by Kern);

Excuse My Dust (1951), music by Arthur Schwartz–"That's for Children";

The Big Song and Dance (1952), music by Schwartz–"Where Do I Go from You?";

Lovely to Look At (1952), music by Kern–"Opening Night."

SELECTED SONG FROM TELEVISION PRODUCTION: *Junior Miss* (1957), music by Burton Lane–"I'll Buy It."

SELECTED SONGS PUBLISHED INDEPENDENTLY OF THEATRICAL OR MOTION-PICTURE PRODUCTIONS: "Collegiana" (1928), music by Jimmy McHugh; "April Fooled Me" (1956), music by Jerome Kern; "Pink Taffeta Sample, Size 10" (1966), music by Cy Coleman.

As the only major woman lyricist of the golden age of American popular song and musical theater, Dorothy Fields stood virtually alone among men for almost fifty years after she began her career in the 1920s, writing lyrics for Harlem's Cotton Club revues. Teamed with more than a dozen of the most prominent composers of popular music–primarily, Jimmy McHugh, Jerome Kern, and Cy Coleman–she was responsible for hit songs that have become part of the fabric of American culture. Yet, the fame of Fields's signature songs, such as "I Can't Give You Anything but Love" (1928), "On the Sunny Side of the Street" (1930), and "Big Spender" (1966), far surpasses her personal renown. In her lifetime she often encountered people who would

suddenly exclaim in realization, "*You* wrote *that?*"–a situation about which, publicly anyway, she used to joke.

The trademark of a Fields lyric is her use of slang and colloquial speech, for which she had a keen ear. It was a gift that enabled her, in a career that lasted into the 1970s, to produce lyrics that were not only fresh and sophisticated but also genuinely current. Thus, the twenty-three-year-old who in 1928 wrote, "Gee, I'd like to see you looking swell, baby" (from "I Can't Give You Anything but Love") was also the sixty-year-old lyricist who in 1966 declared (in "You Should See Yourself," from *Sweet Charity*),

> You're a blockbuster, buster,
> You got class,
> And when you make a pass,
> Man, it's a pass.

Because of her ear for current slang, Fields was, in fact, the only lyricist among her contemporaries to remain a viable commodity well past the arrival of rock and roll. Toward the end of her career, she reflected on her craft: "Sounds and rhyming can be beguiling only when they state exactly what you should say. Don't fall in love with what you believe is a clever rhyme–it can throw you. Think about what you want to say and then look for the most amusing or graceful way you can say it."

Tall, with dark hair and eyes and a slim appearance, Fields remained a beacon of impeccable grooming and taste throughout her life, representing the urbane wit that epitomized creative circles in New York during the Jazz Age. But instead of displaying the acid cynicism of Dorothy Parker, Fields combined her unsentimental sophistication with a romantic optimism. She came of age not in the rarified New York literary world but in the commercial theater and Tin Pan Alley. There, Ira Gershwin and Lorenz Hart were already winning over the public with a fresh, new voice: a slangy sophistication that was literary but in a more colloquial idiom than the ardent poetry of the operetta-driven theater that had dominated until recently. Their protagonists were not proclaiming undying passion in songs such as "I Love You Truly" (1901). Gershwin and E. Y. "Yip" Harburg read that as "You're a Builder-Upper." Hart's idea of romance was to "go to Coney and eat baloney." For the young Fields, a lover's undying devotion translated into a wish to buy his "baby . . . diamond bracelets Woolworth doesn't sell."

Other women would have had more difficulty breaking into a business that was hardly considered the province of young ladies of the time. But Fields came to show business naturally, born into a theatrical dynasty founded by her father, Lew Fields, vaudeville star,

Sheet music for the early song that is considered one of Fields's signature numbers
(Bruccoli Clark Layman Archives)

manager, and producer. He was half of the legendary comedy team of Weber and Fields, who are credited with originating the custard-pie-in-the-face routine and the joke that begins, "Who was that lady I saw you with last night?" Later, as a producer, he became a predecessor of Florenz Ziegfeld and widely influenced musical comedy in the early twentieth century. Between 1896 and 1927 six Broadway theaters bore Fields's name, and among his discoveries were Richard Rodgers and Hart, whose early shows he produced. His own stardom aside, the profession was still disreputable enough for Lew and his wife, Rose Harris Fields, to keep their family away from it. Nevertheless, three of

their four children not only ended up in show business but also scored major successes, flourishing on Broadway in the 1940s. Herbert teamed with Dorothy on the book for Irving Berlin's *Annie Get Your Gun* (1946). He was the librettist for the early Rodgers and Hart shows and collaborated with Vincent Youmans on *Hit the Deck* (1927) and with Cole Porter on *Panama Hattie* (1940). Dorothy's eldest brother, Joseph, was a playwright responsible for a string of hits, including *My Sister Eileen* (1940), written with Jerome Chodorov. With Anita Loos, Joseph wrote the book for the 1949 musical version of Loos's 1926 play *Gentlemen Prefer Blondes* (from her 1925 novel of the same name).

Having himself grown up poor on Manhattan's Lower East Side (like many of Dorothy's songwriter contemporaries), Lew Fields, born Lewis Maurice Schoenfeld, had elevated himself and was able to offer his family a life of privilege, raising his children in Manhattan's "Gilded Ghetto"–the affluent, largely Jewish neighborhood along West End Avenue. Dorothy, born 15 July 1905 in Allenhurst, New Jersey, was sent to the Benjamin School for Girls, in order to be groomed for a good marriage into a "nice" family. (This goal had already been accomplished with her sister, Frances.) Rose Fields used to admonish the family, "You have to be more polite than other children, because your father is an actor."

Still, Dorothy was drawn to the more exhilarating world offered not only by her father but also by her older brother Herbert and his Columbia University friends Richard Rodgers and Lorenz Hart. Together, the group formed the nucleus of a youthful and energetic social network, entering the profession by way of amateur revues for which Rodgers and Hart wrote songs, Herbert Fields wrote sketches, and Dorothy, who aspired to be an actress, played the lead role. Like many other hopefuls, they worshiped the Princess Theatre shows (1915–1918)–Kern's efforts, with Guy Bolton and P. G. Wodehouse, to wrest the musical theater from the nineteenth-century European operetta and make it truly contemporary, with modern settings and characters, topical plots, and scaled-down production values.

After Lew Fields sabotaged Dorothy's budding acting career by intercepting a letter of acceptance into summer stock, her talents for turning a smart phrase were brought to the fore. As Gershwin and others had done, she published some light verse (known at the time as "smarty verse") in Franklin Pierce Adams's column, "The Conning Tower," in *The New York World*. In 1924 Fields wed J. J. Wiener, a surgeon, but the marriage lasted only seven months. After a cousin introduced her to J. Fred Coots–composer of "Santa Claus Is Coming to Town" (1934) and "You Go to My Head" (1938)–Fields began, with Coots's encouragement, to write lyrics. Her earliest efforts, she said later, were blighted by her affinity for imitating Hart. But, shepherded by Coots, she gained some assignments on Tin Pan Alley at Mills Music, earning a reputation in the cigar-chomping world of music publishing as "The Fifty-Dollar-a-Night-Girl," for her success at quickie assignments in setting lyrics to existing melodies.

Coots then introduced Fields to McHugh, a gregarious veteran composer, ten years her senior, who had worked his way up from song plugger to manager at Mills. Their first effort, "Collegiana" (1928), was a success. "Collegiana" owed its existence to the college style in fashion and the Charleston dance craze, and

specifically to Buddy DeSylva, Ray Brown, and Henderson's "The Varsity Drag" (1927). Though Fields's writing still showed the influence of such heroes as Hart and Gershwin, with the slangy, smart interior rhymes and a matter-of-fact style, her distinct voice began to show for the first time: "Miss Pollyanna never was glad / Till she grabbed an undergrad." She touted another rhyme from the song as the one she was sure had gotten McHugh's attention:

Honor students and every pedagogue
All go to bed agog
At night.

When Fields announced at the dinner table one night that McHugh had asked her to write a show with him for Harlem's famed Cotton Club, her family was no less horrified than the day she went to work on Tin Pan Alley. "Ladies don't write lyrics," her father admonished her, to which Fields came back, "I'm no lady, I'm your daughter."

The trendy nightspot in the center of Harlem featured the cream of black performers entertaining well-heeled white patrons from downtown. The *Hot Chocolates* revue for which Fields and McHugh came up to write was the same one with which Duke Ellington had made his New York debut. In a manner that mirrored the contradictions of the restrictive yet hedonistic 1920s, the Cotton Club and all-black revues that began to move downtown to Broadway were a peculiar amalgam of racial segregation and a genuine opportunity for black performers to be appreciated by white audiences. The Cotton Club was owned by the gangsters Herman Stark and Owney "The Killer" Madden (Prohibition still being in effect), who made sure that Fields was treated as the little sister at all times. Every afternoon, rehearsals would stop and tea and cookies would be served; swearing was forbidden. For the revue, which opened to a glittering crowd on 4 December 1927, Fields and McHugh had written such songs as "Hottentot Tot," "Freeze an' Melt," and "Harlemania."

It was another song, however, that made Fields and McHugh's fortunes. Thanks to the latter's fast talking, "I Can't Give You Anything but Love" had been given to the impresario Harry Delmar for his *Revels* (1927), where it had been sung by the then-unknown Bert Lahr and Patsy Kelly. A disaster on opening night, the song had been thrown out by Delmar after one performance. But it found its way into Fields and McHugh's next show, Lew Leslie's *Blackbirds of 1928*, which starred Bill "Bojangles" Robinson. Despite one reviewer's reference to it as "a sickly, puerile song," "I Can't Give You Anything But Love" was the crowning hit of a score that yielded two other instantaneous hits,

"Doin' the New Low-Down" and "Diga Diga Doo." The torchy, bluesy "I Must Have That Man" became a standard, with its colloquial black English in the same vein as Kern and Oscar Hammerstein's "Can't Help Lovin' Dat Man" (1927):

> Don't want my mammy, I don't need a friend,
> My heart is broken, it won't ever mend,
> I ain't much carin' just where I will end,
> I must have that man.

In the songs from *Blackbirds of 1928,* along with a wit that was at once urbane and earthy, Fields's growing deftness with language and rhyming was beginning to show itself–especially in the interior rhyming that was to become an elegant trademark, as well as the triple end rhymes she favored ("friend"/"mend"/ "end"). In "I Must Have That Man" the plain-spoken, slangy English ("Don't want" rather than "I don't want," and "I ain't much carin'") is juxtaposed not only with the high-tone declarative "I must" but also with the sonority of the internal phrasing ("Don't"/ "don't"/"broken"/"won't").

Nobody was prepared for the success of "I Can't Give You Anything but Love." With this song Fields's voice was established, in fluid lines such as "*Gee, I*'d *like* to *see* you looking swell, baby" (again, subtle internal rhymes and vernacular expressions such as "Gee," "swell," and "baby"); the catchy repetition of "baby"; the conversational, colloquial language; and the poignantly straightforward expression of flat-out poverty:

> I can't give you anything but love, baby,
> That's the only thing I've plenty of, baby.
> Dream awhile, scheme awhile,
> We're sure to find
> Happiness, and, I guess
> All those things you've always pined for.

"I Can't Give You Anything but Love" went on to become such a rage that in late 1928, when sheet-music sales determined hit status, a copy of the song sat on many pianos in America, and phonographs blared the number-one recording made by Cliff "Ukulele Ike" Edwards. The title became such a catchphrase that it appeared everywhere–from advertisements and cartoons to the cover of *Life* magazine. The song has been used in many movies–notably, as sung by Katharine Hepburn and Cary Grant to a leopard in *Bringing Up Baby* (1938) and by Judy Holliday in the famous gin-rummy scene of *Born Yesterday* (1950). "I Can't Give You Anything but Love" not only made the twenty-three-year-old Fields rich but also brought her national fame. She and McHugh went on to write

Fields with her father, vaudeville comedian, manager, and producer Lew Fields, circa 1928 (Harry Ransom Humanities Research Center, University of Texas at Austin)

the scores for *Hello Daddy* (1928), produced by and starring her father, and two 1929 editions of the *Ziegfeld Midnight Frolic. Hello Daddy* was unremarkable except for the fact that it was Fields's first nonrevue "book show," and it whetted her fascination with lyrics that build continuity of character, a type of lyric writing that she pursued later.

But Hollywood immediately began to call. If in the 1920s George and Ira Gershwin, Rodgers and Hart, and their contemporaries were the first to export New York sophistication to middle America with songs that seeped into everyday consciousness, then the 1930s exodus to Hollywood of Broadway's best composers and lyricists escalated the process to a mass scale. Kern, the great figure of American popular song, went, as did Berlin, Harburg, Hammerstein, and Harold Arlen–as well as the Gershwins, Rodgers and Hart, and Fields and McHugh. Hollywood needed them to keep up with the growth in popularity of the "talkies"–which meant musicals. These talented songwriters were lured by money, opportunity, guaranteed insulation from the rest of the country's misery, and the cosmopolitan company of their peers. In the new development of Beverly Hills, Dorothy, Herbert, and the rest of the Fields family set up a household, which became the same gathering place for the theatrical and musical elite as the family's New York apartment had been.

Cover for a collection of songs Fields and Jimmy McHugh wrote for a 1930 musical revue (from Deborah Grace Winer,
On the Sunny Side of the Street: The Life and Lyrics of Dorothy Fields, *1997)*

At M-G-M and RKO, Fields and McHugh worked by typical studio rules, turning out songs for vehicles over which they had no control, and their songs often shifted from one picture to another. Some writers, such as Hammerstein, hated it. He had relatively little success in Hollywood; neither did Rodgers and Hart, both of whom soon headed back to New York. Others, such as Burton Lane and Frank Loesser, stayed for decades. In the years between 1930 and 1935, Fields and McHugh prolifically turned out hits–many of which became standards–for movies that were largely forgettable. The first movie for which they wrote, *Love in the Rough* (1930), featured "Go Home and Tell Your Mother"–all bouncy innocence, into which Fields casually tossed her sly raciness (with her characteristic triple end-rhyme):

Then ask her what she did,
Ask father what he did
When both of them needed
A darned sight more than kisses.

With McHugh's great musical facility, the team worked in an easy, back-and-forth style and often finished a song in an afternoon. When asked which came first, the music or the lyric, Fields's reply would always be "the title." Elaborating on this statement, she once explained that a good title "has to be catchy and if possible contain some exciting new combination of familiar words used in a declarative sentence." In fact, Fields's titles generally tended to be plain or colloquial declarative statements (or fragments), rather than poetical abstractions: "I'm in the Mood for Love" (1935), "You

138

Couldn't Be Cuter" (1938), "If My Friends Could See Me Now" (1966), "Nobody Does It Like Me" (1973). The signature Hammerstein-Kern ballad was "All the Things You Are" (1939); the title of a Fields-Kern ballad announced more-specific concerns: "The Way You Look Tonight" (1936).

The poetry in a Fields ballad (though she never considered her lyrics poetry) is found in the perceptive eye for detail, spoken of matter-of-factly, that touches the precise truth of a common human experience:

> Someday, when I'm awfully low,
> When the world is cold,
> I will feel a glow just thinking of you
> And the way you look tonight.

Fields's language and imagery are simple and unsentimental, not high-flown, though the expression, rhyming, and repetition are elegant, and her perspective is distinctly feminine.

Exceptions to this typical Fields style were some of the lyrics for her "opera singer" assignments, movie vehicles for such stars as Lawrence Tibbett, Grace Moore, and Lily Pons, for whom she took on an uncharacteristically fervent "poetic" voice. These songs, such as "Cuban Love Song" (1931), and "I Dream Too Much" (1935), are remote from the jazzy, jaunty "I Can't Give You Anything but Love" and "On the Sunny Side of the Street," or the sensuous "I'm in the Mood for Love." Although popular in their day, these atypical songs have worn less well than most of the Fields canon. Forty years later, Fields herself derided her ardent lyric for "Cuban Love Song," dissecting it before an audience at New York's 92nd Street Y for a talk in the "Lyrics and Lyricists" series: "'"I love you"—that's what my heart is saying.' Ridiculous! Your lips say the words. Your heart may dictate them, but hearts don't talk, they beat."

Fields and McHugh shuttled back to Broadway for such shows as *The International Revue* (1930), *Clowns in Clover* (1933), and the gala opening of Radio City Music Hall, for which they wrote and performed in 1932. Along with the standard "Exactly Like You," *The International Revue* included "On the Sunny Side of the Street," which went on to become one of the most memorable popular songs ever written. Stephen Sondheim, citing Fields's "use of colloquialism and effortlessness," has called "On the Sunny Side of the Street" "just perfect as a lyric." Her carefully crafted breeziness is again in evidence in this song:

> Grab your coat, and get your hat,
> Leave your worry on the doorstep.
> Just direct your feet
> To the sunny side of the street.

Fields and McHugh performing on radio (from William Zinsser, Easy to Remember, *2000)*

Beginning with the first word of the chorus ("grab") every line and image is colloquial, yet smooth and vivid. This everyday speech continues to the bridge—"I used to walk in the shade / With my blues on parade"—and to the end: "If I never have a cent / I'd be rich as Rockefeller. . . ."

In Hollywood, Fields and McHugh's songs continued to be interpolated into motion pictures. "Don't Blame Me," introduced in *Clowns in Clover,* was reused in the movie *Meet the Baron* (1933), and it became another of the team's most enduring standards. McHugh's straightforward melody is set off by Fields's lyric, which again exhibits her penchant for casual interior rhyme ("I'm under your *spell* but how can I *hel*p it"; "If I can't conc*eal* the thrill that I'm *feel*ing"). It is fitting that some of Fields's finest standards are associated with Fred Astaire. In a sense, their talents were similar: both practiced obsessive craftsmanship to achieve a result that appeared to be tossed off, both derided pretension, and both were utterly American. Fields was a perfectionist in her search for just the right rhyme, shade, or image. In the days before rock and roll slackened things to the point that such words as "mind" and "time" became acceptable rhymes, the craftsmanship of a lyric was of the utmost importance. The quality and

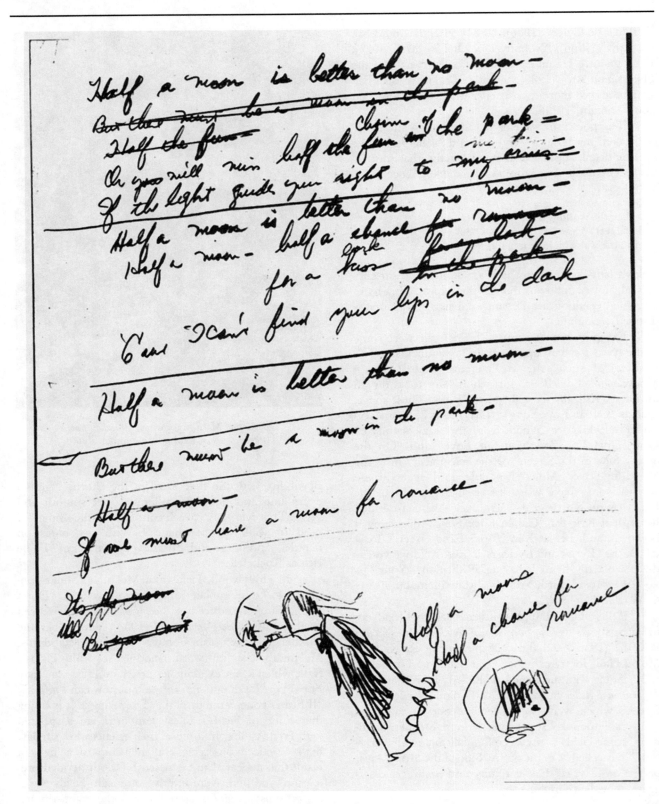

Draft for a lyric (from Deborah Grace Winer, On the Sunny Side of the Street: The Life
and Lyrics of Dorothy Fields, *1997)*

Fields and composer Jerome Kern, with whom she began collaborating in 1935
(from William Zinsser, Easy to Remember, *2000)*

placement of rhymes, stresses, and vowels, the relationship of a word to note values—all of these elements were labored over by lyricists such as Hammerstein, who sometimes took three weeks to write a lyric, and Ira Gershwin, who was nicknamed "The Jeweler." Fields's artistry is apparent in "A Fine Romance" (1936), which she wrote so that the stress on the syllables in the word *romance* fits the musical accents ("RO-mance") but does not follow the standard pronunciation of the word ("ro-MANCE"). The mispronunciation reflects the singer's irritation with the disappointing course of her romance.

Fields was not the only woman songwriter contributing to the spate of movies the studios churned out in the golden age of Hollywood, although the sheer volume of her work at the top of the charts far outstripped that of any others of her sex, who had at most only a handful of enduring hits. In 1933, the year that "Don't Blame Me" was introduced, "Who's Afraid of the Big Bad Wolf?"written by Ann Ronnell with composer Frank E. Churchill for the animated short *The Three Little Pigs,* caused a sensation, becoming a Depression anthem. Ronnell had already produced a hit the previous year, writing both the words and music for "Willow Weep for Me." There were other female songwriters as well: Kay Swift wrote the music for "Can This Be Love?" and the title song for the musical *Fine and Dandy* (1930), collaborating with her lyricist husband, banker James P. Warburg (writing as Paul James). Swift and Warburg also wrote "Can't We Be Friends?" (1929), a top hit, but, apart from "Fine and Dandy," Swift's only enduring standard. In the 1940s Doris Fisher collaborated on words and music with Allan Roberts for about eight notable songs, particularly "Put the Blame on Mame," "Into Each Life Some Rain Must Fall," and "You Always Hurt the One You Love," all from 1944. Dana Suesse wrote the music for "You Oughta Be in Pictures" (1934) and "My Silent Love" (1932). Other women, such as Sylvia Fine (writing for her husband, Danny Kaye) and Kay Thompson, wrote predominantly comedy and special material (Fine's 1958 song "Lullaby in Ragtime" is a notable exception). Though witty and brilliant, these songs

Fred Astaire and Ginger Rogers in a scene from the movie
Swing Time (1936), for which Fields and Kern wrote
the songs (from Deborah Grace Winer, On the
Sunny Side of the Street: The Life and
Lyrics of Dorothy Fields, *1997)*

failed to attain lasting fame in the way of Noel Coward's comic classics, such as "Mrs. Worthington (Don't Put Your Daughter on the Stage)" (1935).

A generation earlier, Fields had two major predecessors. Dorothy Donnelly wrote lyrics and librettos with Sigmund Romberg, most famously for *The Student Prince* (1924), with its memorable "Drinking Song" and "Deep in My Heart, Dear." Donnelly also collaborated with Romberg on *Blossom Time* (1921) and *My Maryland* (1927). Ann Caldwell had been Kern's collaborator for such shows as *Good Morning, Dearie* (1921) and *The Stepping Stones* (1923). Donnelly and Caldwell represented the small group of "lady writers" who thrived in this world of operetta.

Unlike vaudeville- and jazz-tainted musical comedy, operetta was civilized, ennobled, and imbued with family values. Fields wrote with Kern only a decade after Caldwell had, but Fields was a generation and a universe away from her predecessor. Though Fields's work revealed a distinctly feminine perspective on life, it was as bold and edgy as the work of any of her leading male contemporaries, generally too ironic and brash to exude any of the "old-fashioned" female qualities (such as sentimentality or self-sacrificing nobility) that

were negatively associated with popular "women's creations" of the time.

Fields, who came of age in the flapper era, was a direct product of the freedom women had won for themselves in rebelling against Victorian notions of where they belonged. By the 1920s, chaste, idealized womanhood was out and liberated "moderns" were in; women could be active participants in the world around them, meeting men on their own turf, be it speakeasies or sex. On the other hand, outside of a few cities such as New York or Chicago, the country was hardly ready for this change, particularly after the stock-market crash and the onset of the Depression. The idea that women should be assertive—and, worse, admit that sex held a few charms beyond wifely duty—was in many circles downright alarming. Here was Fields in 1936, writing "I've never mussed the crease in your blue serge pants" in "A Fine Romance," a song that is a series of complaints about a lover "as cold as yesterday's mashed potatoes." Her lyrics, apart from their wit, were sensual, suggestive, and appreciative of sex, though no more risqué than those of contemporaries such as Hart, Porter, or Ira Gershwin; the only difference was that the sentiment was being expressed by a woman.

Certainly, the first half of the twentieth century had a complement of women writers and poets who wore sensuality on their sleeves—and led the requisite lives of bohemian debauchery. But at a time when most women never broke through the confines of home, family, and society's dictates of "appropriateness," Fields's success was significant. Her acceptance was probably aided by the fact that she was a hybrid. She was at once independent as a professional in a man's field; yet, she was given credence by her traditionalism and "respectability"—attractive, feminine, and eventually a wife and mother—and her views were not dismissible as "demimonde morals." Fields paved the way for Betty Comden, Carolyn Leigh, Marilyn Bergman, and, eventually (though she would not have thought of herself as a feminist pioneer), for such feminist songwriters and performers as Carole King, Joni Mitchell, Judy Collins, and Carly Simon. Yet, Fields's position as the lone woman in the top ranks of her profession did not seem to affect her or any of her male colleagues whatsoever. It might well have been different had she been a studio executive or a director battling a bureaucracy. As it was, her track record and facility were well respected, and nobody stopped to think much beyond that, even if this colleague was a manicured lady who continually filled her house with flowers.

The year 1935 was a watershed for Fields. Six of her songs topped the charts; two of them, "I Feel a Song Comin' On" and "I'm in the Mood for Love," both from the movie *Every Night at Eight,* came to count

among her most enduring standards. "I'm in the Mood
For Love" particularly remains a perennial ballad.
There is magic in the Fieldsian teetering between
romanticism ("Heaven is in your eyes, / Bright as the
stars we're under") and offhand glibness ("But for
tonight, forget it").

Three of Fields's biggest hits of 1935–"Lovely to
Look At," "I Won't Dance," and "I Dream Too
Much"–were written not with McHugh but with Kern.
With this collaboration she entered another phase of
her career and the most significant working relationship
of her life. To the generation of songwriters who came
of age in the 1920s and 1930s, Kern was God–though
he was referred to instead as "The Dean." Having
inspired so many with the Princess Theatre shows and
his ensuing career, he commanded awe. Lew Fields
had, in fact, given Kern one of his early breaks in 1904.
Preceding Fields in working with Kern were Otto Harbach, with whom Kern wrote such shows as *Roberta*
(1933), featuring "Smoke Gets in Your Eyes," and Harbach's protégé, Hammerstein, with whom Kern wrote
Show Boat (1927), altering the course of musical history.

Although Kern was a family friend, Fields had
never met him, and their partnership occurred virtually by accident, when *Roberta* was being adapted as a
motion picture in 1935. Kern had been called east, and
he had a sixteen-bar melody that needed a lyric. Pan-
dro S. Berman, the visionary head of production at
RKO who was responsible for the innovative movie
musicals featuring Astaire and Ginger Rogers, called in
Fields to write a lyric for Kern's sixteen-bar fragment,
"Lovely to Look At." It was an odd assignment. The
standard popular-song form was thirty-two bars. At
sixteen bars, this melody defied convention, and then
Fields learned that the song was needed both as a love
song and for a fashion-show scene. With Kern unavailable to approve of her overnight effort, Berman
decided to go ahead and put the song in the movie
anyway. Fields was terrified of incurring the master's
wrath; instead, she got more work from Kern on *Roberta,* redoing an existing Hammerstein lyric for "I
Won't Dance." Astaire wanted the song, first used in a
failed show, *Three Sisters* (1934), "jazzed up." Against
Kern's catchy rhythm, Fields kept the title notion but
changed Hammerstein's basic conceit of a song about
not being able to dance into a sexy refusal on the
grounds that "If I hold you in my arms" there will be
consequences. After all, as the singer declares in one of
Fields's most inspired rhymes at the end of the release,
or bridge, "heaven rest us, / I'm not asbestos."

Kern, impressed by the young lyricist, asked
Fields to collaborate with him on *I Dream Too Much* (pop-
ularly dubbed *I Scream Too Much*), a 1935 movie vehicle
for opera star Pons. Fields and Kern, who was sixteen

*Fields in the early 1940s with her brother Herbert, who collaborated
with her on the libretto for the 1946 Irving Berlin musical* Annie Get
Your Gun *(photograph by Van Damm; Billy Rose Theatre Collection,
New York Public Library for the Performing Arts)*

years her elder, immediately developed a rapport and
deep personal affection for one another. A short, bald-
ing man with a fondness for practical jokes and inciting
arguments at the dinner table just to watch the reaction,
Kern stood a head shorter than Fields. She called him
Junior; he allowed it. He invited her to work with him
again on what was to be the crowning achievement of
both their Hollywood careers, the Astaire-Rogers movie
Swing Time (1936), at first tentatively titled "Never
Gonna Dance."

In addition to initiating great developments in the
movie-musical genre (naturalism, as well as freedom
from the "show within a show" constraint for presenting songs and dances), the Astaire-Rogers movies of the
1930s are perhaps the single most concentrated cinematic repository for bedrock chunks of the American
songbook. Porter, Berlin, and Youmans had all preceded
Fields and Kern in writing songs for Astaire-Rogers movie
musicals. Fields and Kern wrote their score for *Swing
Time* in the first few months of 1936. Astaire wanted
two thoroughly contemporary dance numbers, which
made Kern uneasy, because jazz was not in his musical
vocabulary. For the most part, Kern's music soared; it

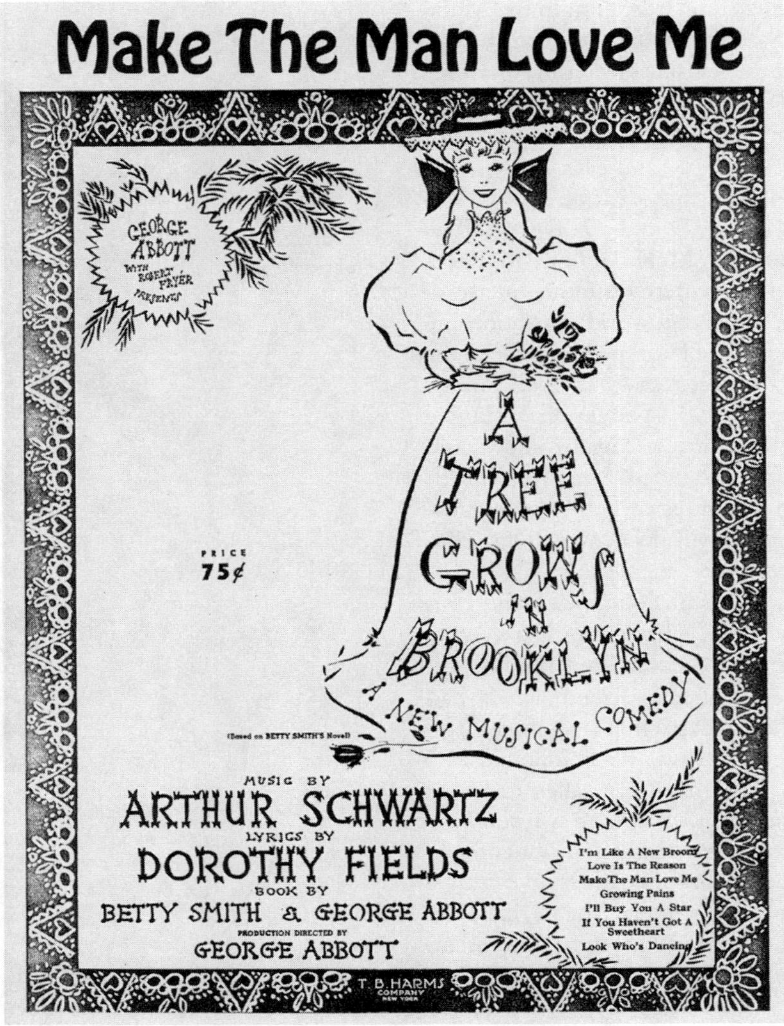

Sheet music for a song from the 1951 stage adaptation, with a score by Fields and Arthur Schwartz, of Betty Smith's 1943 novel A Tree Grows in Brooklyn *(from Lehman Engel,* Their Words Are Music, *1975)*

did not swing. In order to inspire him to write "Bojangles of Harlem," a tribute to Robinson, Astaire spent several afternoons tap-dancing around the rooms and up and down the stairs of Fields's Beverly Hills house so that Kern could get the feel of the syncopated rhythms as he sat at the piano. On two other numbers, Fields also aided the process by breaking with their normal work habits and producing the lyric first. As a result, the catchy verbal rhythms of "Pick Yourself Up" contributed to the syncopation of the melody:

Nothing's impossible, I have found,
For when my chin is on the ground,
I pick myself up,
Dust myself off,
Start all over again.

Just as the score of *Swing Time* brought out more jazz influences in Kern's music, it represented a new development in Fields's lyrical style. She was to return to the glib, edgy voice that had made her early songs with McHugh, such as "I Can't Give You Anything but Love," exceptional. But with Kern, her work became infused with an emotional deepening, sophistication, and sensuality. The direct clarity and appeal of his music brought out the things she did best. The starry-eyed romanticism found in some of their earlier collaborations was rejected for smart, urbane, and sarcasm-tinged expression. "Perhaps I dream too much alone"–from the title song of *I Dream Too Much*–gave way to lines such as "I might as well play bridge with my old maid aunts" (from "A Fine Romance"). "A Fine Romance" was the second *Swing Time* song on which Fields took

Sheet music for the 1951 republication of a Fields-McHugh song introduced in the 1935 movie
Every Night at Eight (Bruccoli Clark Layman Archives)

the first step. When Kern asked her for a "sarcastic love ballad," she returned with an irate rant about a cold lover, with each successive image and rhyme topping the one before. The envy of lyricists for generations to come, these lyrics were Fields at her most brilliant, an amalgam of sophisticated barbs and mundane imagery:

A fine romance! My good fellow!
You take romance! I'll take Jell-O!
You're calmer than the seals in the Arctic Ocean,
At least they flap their fins to express emotion.

Other lines have a seemingly tossed-off quality: "You're just as hard to land as the *Ile de France,* / I haven't got a chance, / This is a fine romance!" The sight of Astaire

and Rogers in the snow, sniping at each other with this sophisticated artillery, is one of the great screen moments of Hollywood musicals in the 1930s.

The melody for "The Way You Look Tonight," with its fluid momentum, resembles Kern's melody for "Smoke Gets in Your Eyes," but whereas Harbach's lyric for that song employs such elevated language as "So I chaffed them, and I gaily laughed," Fields's lyric is restrained, contemplative, and matter-of-fact:

Lovely, never, never change,
Keep that breathless charm,
Won't you please arrange it,
'Cause I love you,
Just the way you look tonight.

*Sheet music for a song from Fields and Cy Coleman's 1966 musical, which was made into a motion picture in 1969
(from Marion Short,* Hollywood Movie Songs, *1999)*

The understated phrasing and rhyming propel the melody. Any other lyricist but Fields would probably have written "*For* I love you," but by choosing the colloquial "'Cause," she not only stamped it as her own but also deflated any sentimental ardor, making the voice more real and thus more poignant. The song won Fields and Kern the 1936 Academy Award for best original movie song.

Sexy and shimmering, the score of *Swing Time* was the culmination of Fields and Kern's work together and seemed to capture, just before it ended, the glow of the Hollywood era that Fields looked back on as the "golden days." Most of the songs from the movie were immediate hits, topped by "The Way You Look Tonight," and including "Bojangles of Harlem," "Pick Yourself Up," "A Fine Romance," and "Waltz in Swing Time." "Never Gonna Dance," the least accessible number, took time to become a standard and includes perhaps the ultimate example of Fields's hallmark blend of sophistication and slanginess: "La belle, / La perfectly swell romance."

Fields and Kern continued to write together, notably for *Joy of Living* (1938), which yielded "You Couldn't Be Cuter" (introduced by Irene Dunne in one of the stiffest renditions that lively number has ever received). But the pall cast by the death of George Gershwin in 1937, a sense of restlessness, and the end of the 1930s drove Fields back to New York. One more

Fields-Kern standard, "Remind Me," found its way to the screen, in the Bud Abbott and Lou Costello movie *One Night in the Tropics* (1940), after being cannibalized from an earlier score. This song presents probably the best argument for the case that Fields's lyrics project a feminine viewpoint. The verse is an anatomy of a woman's "on the other hand" mental process: "Turn off that charm, I'm through with love for a while. / I'm through, and yet You have a fabulous smile." This conceit culminates in the last line of the song with a surprising, deft mental turnaround that "buttons up" the end: "Don't let me kiss you, please remind me, / Unless, my darling, you forget."

In 1938 Fields married clothing manufacturer Eli D. Lahm, with whom she had two children. David, born in 1941, grew up to become a jazz pianist; Eliza, born in 1944, became an artist. Fields spent the rest of her career on Broadway, a busy professional and a respectable society matron. There were several long-distance movie assignments, for which she collaborated with such composers as Arlen, Harry Warren, and Arthur Schwartz. Mainly, though, Fields spent her efforts in pursuit of the integrated musical, the kind of show in which song lyrics emerge from character and plot. She and Schwartz wrote *Stars in Your Eyes,* a vehicle for Ethel Merman and Jimmy Durante, immediately upon her return east in 1939. It included the comedy song "A Lady Needs a Change," as well as the rueful ballad "I'll Pay the Check."

Following *Stars in Your Eyes* Fields went through a period of writing librettos, in collaboration with her brother Herbert, for a trio of Porter shows: *Let's Face It* (1941), *Something For the Boys* (1943), and *Mexican Hayride* (1944). Her pinnacle as a librettist came in 1946 with *Annie Get Your Gun.* Conceived at her inspiration as a Merman vehicle, Fields expected to collaborate on the score with Kern, but his sudden death prompted the show's producers, Rodgers and Hammerstein, to engage Berlin. Not until 1945 did Fields work again as lyricist for a show. *Up in Central Park* was set in nineteenth-century New York. (Until *Sweet Charity* in 1966, all of her shows were period pieces). With a score by the "Operetta King," Sigmund Romberg, the lyrics matched the Romantic-period musical style, and the show produced one standard, "Close as Pages in a Book." Amid the "operatic" ardor of the lyric—"Your life is my life, / And while life beats away in my heart"—a hint of the "other" Fields creeps in with a glib tweaking of the language that does not quite go with the rest of the song: "Darling, as the strongest book is bound, / We're bound to last."

A collaboration in 1950 with Morton Gould, *Arms and the Girl,* was perhaps Fields's least successful theatrical work, showing the lyricist in a bucolic,

"Hammerstein" vein ("A Cow and a Plough and a Frau") that she would have been more suited satirizing. (The show included two more-typical Fields songs, sung by Pearl Bailey: "Nothin' for Nothin'" and "There Must Be Something Better Than Love.") In all, Fields collaborated with eighteen composers, which may partly explain why she never gained the fame that comes of being half of a recognizable team, such as George and Ira Gershwin, Rodgers and Hart, or Rodgers and Hammerstein.

Fields and Schwartz's score for *A Tree Grows in Brooklyn* (1951) was one of the most successful achievements of both their careers, even if the run of the show, which starred Shirley Booth, was a disappointment. "I'll Buy You a Star" became a hit, and "Make the Man Love Me" became one of the most celebrated songs in the Broadway repertory, with its balance of sincere longing and elegantly phrased simplicity:

I must try to make the man love me,
Make the man love me now.
By and by, I'll make the man happy,
I know how.

The comic "He Had Refinement" is the perfect specimen of a character lyric. It is an ode to the gentility of an "ex," delivered in delicate Brooklynese, with each of the lyricist's comic turns topping the one before:

He was shy and awfully modest
He was so high bred,
If the wind blew up my bloomers,
Would his face get red.
He undressed with all the lights off,
Until we was wed.
He had refinement.

Schwartz and Fields followed up with another, less successful vehicle for Booth, *By the Beautiful Sea,* in 1954. The hit Broadway comedy *Junior Miss* (1941), by her brother Joseph and Chodorov, served as the basis for a 1957 television musical of the same name for which Fields teamed with composer and longtime friend Burton Lane. Two years later she collaborated with Albert Hague on *Redhead,* set in a Victorian London wax museum, which garnered the 1959 Tony Awards for best musical, best actress (Gwen Verdon), best actor (Richard Kiley), and best choreographer (Bob Fosse, who also directed). *Redhead* included a tuneful score and some verbal calisthenics, as in the cockney tongue twister "'Erbie Fitch's Twitch." But at the time of preparations for *Redhead,* Fields's personal life was at an all-time low: both her brother Herbert and her husband, Eli, had died in 1958. Her alcoholism, kept at bay during disciplined morning work hours of writing with Black Wing pencils on a yellow legal pad, grew worse.

As the 1960s progressed, Fields went into the same downward spiral of professional obsolescence and neglect experienced by most of her contemporaries in light of the arrival of rock and roll and a new generation of Broadway talent that included Jerry Bock and Sheldon Harnick, John Kander and Fred Ebb, and Jerry Herman. She had never found another collaborator like Kern, for whom she still mourned. In the mid 1950s Fields had set lyrics to some of Kern's "trunk" melodies (melodies left at his death that had not yet been given lyrics), notably "April Fooled Me" (1956), one of the loveliest songs of the Fields-Kern canon. The uneven phrase lengths reflect Kern's trademark soaring melodic line. At fifty-one, Fields's experience and maturity showed in the way she handled that musical line. The song begins with the poetic imagery of an "April" song:

> Once April fooled me,
> With an afternoon so gold, so warm, so beguiling,
> That I thought the drowsy earth
> Would wake up smiling.

Unlike Fields's earlier forays into the poetic, however, there is an expert economy and specificity at work. She turns the thought to a sophisticated, knowing analogy, deftly making an unexpected turn in the last line (as in "Remind Me"):

> It was not really spring,
> Or really love.
> You were alike, you two,
> Restless April fooled me,
> Darling, so did you.

Meeting the brash young Broadway composer Coleman at a cocktail party one evening at the home of lyricist Harnick changed the course of Fields's life. Coleman asked her to collaborate. By the next year, 1966, they had produced *Sweet Charity,* the Broadway score for which Fields is best remembered. In a reprise of the *Redhead* team the star was Verdon, and Fosse (now Verdon's husband) was director. Dorothy Fields, at age sixty, was twenty-five years senior to them all. Yet, for the first time in Fields's work, there was a mature synthesis of integrated, character-based lyrics for *Sweet Charity*—a show about the misadventures of a dance-hall hostess—and she was at her most vibrant and natural as a lyricist: colloquial, urban, and ironic. The two biggest hits in the show harked back to the jazzy, slangy feel of Fields's roots with McHugh. One was "Big Spender": "The minute you walked in the joint, / I could tell you were a man of distinction, / A real big spender." The other was "If My Friends Could See Me

Now": "If they could see me now, my little dusty group, / Traipsin' 'round this million dollar chicken coop. . . ." Other songs in *Sweet Charity* included "There's Gotta Be Something Better than This"; a gospel-rock number, "The Rhythm of Life"; the introspective "Where Am I Going?"; "I'm a Brass Band"; "Pink Taffeta Sample, Size 10," which was cut from the show but later became a favorite of cabaret singers; and the infectious polka "I Love to Cry at Weddings," in which Fields employed her casual interior rhyming: "I walk into a *chapel* and get *happily* hysterical."

Fields's mastery of theatrical integration is seen in the way she handled the title character's monologues in *Sweet Charity,* blurring the line between song and rhythmic speech, as in "You Should See Yourself":

> Man! Man, oh man,
> You should see yourself, like tonight
> You're a hundred watt e-lec-a-tric light. . . .

Thanks to Fields's infallible ear and perceptiveness, the language and imagery of the songs in *Sweet Charity* were as germane to the 1960s as "I Can't Give You Anything but Love" was to the 1920s. In Coleman she had found a perfect collaborator. His energy sharpened her contemporary focus, and her experience lent their work polish. In contrast to her situation with both McHugh and Kern, now Fields was the veteran of the songwriting team, and she and Coleman frequently worked out lyrics and melody at the piano, almost simultaneously.

Seesaw, Fields and Coleman's follow-up, reached Broadway in 1973, amid much financial distress that left its lyricist disillusioned about the state of the theater. Her partnership with Coleman again produced a Broadway standard, "I'm Way Ahead," and two songs that could almost have been written with McHugh, but with more hindsight: "Nobody Does It Like Me" and "It's Not Where You Start," which, with its pep-talk optimism (and rhyme scheme) recalls "On the Sunny Side of the Street":

> It's not where you start, it's where you finish,
> It's not how you go, it's how you land.
> A hundred-to-one shot, they call him a klutz,
> Can outrun the favorite, all he needs is the guts.

Fields died on 28 March 1974, a few months short of her sixty-ninth birthday, during rehearsals for the national tour of *Seesaw.* The president of the American Society of Composers, Authors, and Publishers (ASCAP), Stanley Adams, pronounced her the most important female songwriter in the organization's history, and ASCAP continues to assign her work the highest performance rating of any woman on its rolls. Her legacy, perhaps, is that while she was a pioneer for her gender, neither the public nor her colleagues (nor, most importantly, she herself) saw her as a "woman writer." In the business her parents tried so hard to keep her out of, Fields was the author of nineteen Broadway musicals and lyrics for more than thirty movies. In all, she wrote the lyrics for almost five hundred songs. From her early twenties, her career was marked by extraordinarily consistent artistic and financial success, prompting her characteristic quip, "If, God forbid, we ever had a flop, I'd go to Sardi's and cut my throat, quietly, with a grapefruit knife."

Dorothy Fields died while still a hot Broadway commodity, an astounding fact for someone of her generation in the midst of Vietnam and Watergate. Her career represents more than the talent and craft of an individual. By its sheer span, the Fields canon traces not only the history of Broadway, Hollywood, and Tin Pan Alley but also the ways in which America transformed itself from the Jazz Age to the Age of Aquarius.

Interviews:

Henry Kane, *How to Write a Song* (New York: Macmillan, 1962), pp. 157–179;

Max Wilk, *They're Playing Our Song: From Jerome Kern to Stephen Sondheim—the Stories behind the Words and Music of Two Generations* (New York: Atheneum, 1973), pp. 40–50.

Biography:

Deborah Grace Winer, *On the Sunny Side of the Street: The Life and Lyrics of Dorothy Fields* (New York: Schirmer, 1997).

References:

Lehman Engel, *Their Words Are Music: The Great Theatre Lyricists and Their Lyrics* (New York: Crown, 1975), pp. 81–91;

Philip Furia, *The Poets of Tin Pan Alley: A History of America's Great Lyricists* (New York: Oxford University Press, 1990), pp. 213–223;

Thomas S. Hischak, *Word Crazy: Broadway Lyricists from Cohan to Sondheim* (New York: Praeger, 1991), pp. 75–78.

Selected Discography:

Barbara Cook, *Close as Pages in a Book,* DRG, 91412, 1993;

Dorothy Fields, American Songbook Series, Smithsonian, 048-13, 1993;

An Evening with Dorothy Fields, DRG, 5167, 1998;

Lew Leslie's Blackbirds of 1928, studio recording with Adelaide Hall, Bill Robinson, Ethel Waters, and Duke Ellington and His Orchestra, Columbia, OL-6770, ca. 1968;

Sally Mayes, *The Dorothy Fields Songbook,* DRG, 91410, 1992;

Redhead, original Broadway cast, RCA Victor, 1048, 1959;

Seesaw, original Broadway cast, DRG, 6108, 1973;

Stars in Your Eyes, on *Red, Hot and Blue! / Stars in Your Eyes,* 1939 studio cast with Ethel Merman, AEI, 1147, 1991;

Sweet Charity, original Broadway cast, Columbia, KOS 2900, 1966;

Swing Time, motion-picture soundtrack, EMI, EMTC-101, 1974;

A Tree Grows in Brooklyn, original Broadway cast, Columbia, ML 4405, 1951.

Arthur Freed

(9 September 1894 – 12 April 1973)

Michael Lasser

Unless otherwise indicated, music is by Nacio Herb Brown.

SELECTED SONGS FROM THEATRICAL PRO-DUCTION: *The Hollywood Music Box Revue* (1927)–"Singin' in the Rain"; "The Wedding of the Painted Doll."

SELECTED SONGS FROM MOTION-PICTURE PRODUCTIONS: *Broadway Melody* (1929)–"The Boy Friend"; "Broadway Melody"; "The Love Boat"; "You Were Meant for Me";

Hollywood Revue of 1929 (1929)–"Tommy Atkins on Parade";

Marianne (1929)–"Blondy";

The Pagan (1929)–"Pagan Love Song";

Untamed (1929)–"Chant of the Jungle";

Good News (1930)–"Fight 'Em"; "Football"; "If You're Not Kissing Me";

Lord Byron of Broadway (1930)–"A Bundle of Old Love Letters"; "Only Love Is Real"; "Should I?"; "When I Met You"; "The Woman in the Shoe";

March of Time (1930)–"Here Comes the Sun" (music by Harry M. Woods);

Montana Moon (1930)–"Happy Cowboy"; "Love Was in the Air"; "The Moon Is Low";

Those Three French Girls (1930)–"You're Simply Delish" (music by Joseph Meyer);

Blondie of the Follies (1932)–"It Was So Beautiful" (music by Harry Barris);

The Barbarian (1933)–"Love Songs of the Nile";

College Coach (1933)–"Fit as a Fiddle" (music by Al Hoffman and Al Goodhart);

Going Hollywood (1933)–"After Sundown"; "Cinderella's Fella"; "Going Hollywood"; "Our Big Love Scene"; "Temptation"; "We'll Make Hay While the Sun Shines";

Hold Your Man (1933)–"Hold Your Man";

Peg O' My Heart (1933)–"I'll Remember Only You";

Stage Mother (1933)–"Beautiful Girl"; "I'm Dancin' on a Rainbow";

Arthur Freed with actor Howard Keel (left) and composer Harry Warren (right), 1950 (from Tony Thomas, Harry Warren and the Hollywood Musical, *1975)*

Hideout (1934)–"The Dream Was So Beautiful";

Hollywood Party (1934)–"Hot Chocolate Soldiers" (unused);

Sadie McKee (1934)–"All I Do Is Dream of You"; "Please Make Me Care";

Student Tour (1934)–"By the Taj Mahal"; "The Carlo"; "From Now On"; "A New Moon Is Over My Shoulder";

Broadway Melody of 1936 (1935)–"Broadway Rhythm"; "I've Got a Feelin' You're Foolin'"; "On a Sunday Afternoon"; "Sing Before Breakfast"; "This Is the Night"; "You Are My Lucky Star";

China Seas (1935)–"China Seas";
A Night at the Opera (1935)–"Alone";
After the Thin Man (1936)–"Smoke Dreams";
San Francisco (1936)–"Would You?";
Broadway Melody of 1938 (1937)–"Everybody Sing"; "Got a Pair of New Shoes"; "I'm Feelin' Like a Million"; "Your Broadway and My Broadway"; "Yours and Mine";
Thoroughbreds Don't Cry (1937)–"Sun Showers";
Babes in Arms (1939)–"Good Morning";
The Ice Follies of 1939 (1939)–"Something's Gotta Happen Soon";
Strike Up the Band (1940)–"Our Love Affair" (music by Roger Edens);
Two Girls on Broadway (1940)–"My Wonderful One, Let's Dance" (lyrics and music by Freed, Edens, and Brown);
Lady Be Good (1941)–"Your Words and My Music" (music by Edens);
Swing Fever (1943)–"One Girl and Two Boys";
Meet Me in St. Louis (1944)–"You and I";
Yolanda and the Thief (1945), music by Harry Warren– "Angel"; "Coffee Time"; "Yolanda";
Ziegfeld Follies (1946)–"This Heart of Mine" (music by Warren);
Pagan Love Song (1950), music by Warren–"Etiquette"; "Here in Tahiti, We Make Love"; "House of Singing Bamboo"; "The Sea of the Moon"; "Tahiti";
Singin' in the Rain (1952)–"All I Do Is Dream of You" (revival); "Beautiful Girl" (revival); "The Broadway Melody" (revival); "Broadway Rhythm" (revival); "Fit as a Fiddle" (revival); "Good Morning" (revival); "I've Got a Feelin' You're Foolin'" (revival); "Make 'Em Laugh"; "Should I?" (revival); "Singin' in the Rain" (revival); "The Wedding of the Painted Doll" (revival); "Would You?" (revival); "You Are My Lucky Star" (revival); "You Were Meant for Me" (revival);
Light in the Piazza (1962)–"Light in the Piazza" (music by Mario Nascimbene).

SELECTED SONGS PUBLISHED INDEPENDENTLY OF THEATRICAL OR MOTION-PICTURE PRODUCTIONS: "Indiana Moon" (1919), music by Oliver Wallace;
"When Buddha Smiles" (1921), music by Brown and Jack Doll (as King Zany);
"After Every Party" (1922), music by Earl Burtnett;
"Little Church around the Corner" (1922), music by Gus Arnheim and Abe Lyman;
"Louisiana" (1922), music by Wallace;
"When Winter Comes" (1922), music by Harry Carroll;

"I Cried for You" (1923), music by Arnheim and Lyman;
"It Looks Like Love" (1930), music by Harry M. Woods;
"It's Winter Again" (1932), music by Al Goodhart and Al Hoffman;
"Come Out, Come Out, Wherever You Are" (1933), music by Goodhart and Hoffman.

Arthur Freed is more closely linked than any other lyricist to the history and development of movie musicals. Collaborating with composer Nacio Herb Brown, Freed helped to establish the musical at Metro-Goldwyn-Mayer (M-G-M) beginning in 1929. A decade later, at the height of his career as a lyricist, Freed largely stopped writing songs to become the most innovative and successful producer of Hollywood musicals.

Born in Charleston, South Carolina, on 9 September 1894, Arthur Freed was the oldest of Max and Rosa Grossman Freed's eight children. An emigrant from Budapest in the 1880s, Max Freed became an enterprising businessman, dealing in furniture and art in Charleston, Australia, and Vancouver. By 1910 he was successful enough to retire and move his family to Seattle, Washington, where they lived in a large, antique-filled house overlooking Lake Washington.

Music played an important role in Freed's family life. His father was an amateur musician and singer with a robust tenor voice, and all the children took music lessons. Although Freed began to study piano at the age of six and eventually became an accomplished musician, Max Freed did not believe in music as a career and hoped his oldest son would become a lawyer. Most of his children, nevertheless, ended up in the music business. Ralph was a successful lyricist whose songs include "How About You?" (1941), "Hawaiian War Chant" (1940), "Please Don't Say No, Say Maybe" (1945), and "Adios Amigo" (1962). Walter was a serious composer; Sydney and Clarence worked in the recording business; and Ruth played violin, led a trio on the radio, and published several songs. The only Freed children who never went into music were Hugo, who became an accountant, and Victor, who died during World War I. When Freed resisted his father's promptings to prepare for a career in law, Max sent him to the prestigious Phillips Exeter Academy in New Hampshire. During his years at the school, Freed began writing poetry and decided to try writing songs.

After graduating from Phillips Exeter in 1914, Freed returned to Seattle, and his parents urged him to enter the University of Washington. During these tense months at home Freed went one night to the Orpheum Theatre in Seattle to see the famous vaudeville act of

*Sheet music for a 1929 song by Freed and Nacio Herb Brown that became the title song of a classic
1952 movie musical starring Gene Kelly (Bruccoli Clark Layman Archives)*

Gus Edwards. Edwards was also a composer, best known for "In My Merry Oldsmobile" (1905) and "By the Light of the Silvery Moon" (1908). Backstage after the show, Edwards told Freed that his songs had promise, and he offered him a job in one of his touring shows if he would go to New York. Though the story about Edwards's offer may be apocryphal, Freed soon left Seattle to enter show business—in Chicago rather than Manhattan. He worked for the music-publishing company of Waterson, Berlin, and Snyder, playing new songs for vaudeville acts, helping them to rehearse new material, and writing arrangements. This apprenticeship gave Freed a chance to study current song styles and learn the music business.

One day Minnie Marx, the Marx Brothers' mother, came to the office looking for material for her sons. She liked the way Freed played piano and invited him to join her sons' act, then appearing in small-time theaters in the Chicago area. Freed worked with the Marx Brothers as a singer for one season. When they closed for the summer he sang with Edwards's touring company for the next eighteen months. During this time Freed and Louis Silvers, the act's musical director and later the composer of "April Showers" (1921), wrote several songs together. In 1917 some of their songs were used in the revue *Over the Top,* starring Fred Astaire and his sister, Adele, in their Broadway debut.

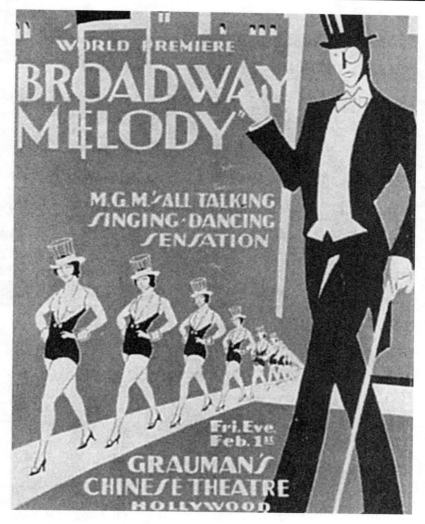

Opening-night program for the 1929 movie musical that featured six songs by Freed and Brown, including "The Boy Friend,"
"Broadway Melody," "The Love Boat," and "You Were Meant for Me" (from Hugh Fordin,
M-G-M's Greatest Musicals: The Arthur Freed Unit, *1996)*

Freed served as an army sergeant during World War I and was in charge of musical shows and entertainment at Camp Lewis in Washington. After the war he supported himself by writing special material for Manhattan cabaret shows. In 1920 one of his songs was included in a Broadway show, *Silks and Satins*. Despite that success, Freed returned to Seattle, where he began a collaboration with a local organist named Oliver Wallace, who later wrote music for Walt Disney Productions. Freed and Wallace had their first successes in 1922 with "Louisiana" and "Cairo." After their attempt to open a music store failed, Freed left for Los Angeles, which became his permanent home. He soon began a collaboration with a successful real-estate salesman named Nacio Herb Brown, who composed melodies as a sideline. Of Freed's approximately 130 published songs, he wrote more than half of them with Brown.

Their first collaboration, "When Buddha Smiles" (1921), with music by Brown and Jack Doll, met with some success, but Freed's first major hit was written with bandleaders Abe Lyman and Gus Arnheim. "I Cried for You" (1923) was an early example of Freed's search for different approaches to familiar material. "A lot of people were writing torch songs," he explained in later years. "I felt, well, I will write one that takes revenge." Yet, a close reading suggests that the lyric, while unusual in its sentiments, is less about revenge than about satisfaction. After bemoaning his lost love, the singer announces that he has fallen in love with someone new, and he relishes his former love's distress:

Now I found two eyes just a little bit bluer,
I found a heart just a little bit truer.

Freed (right) and Brown in 1935 (Bruccoli Clark Layman Archives)

I cried for you,
Now it's your turn to cry over me.

Like most of Freed's lyrics, and like many songs of the 1920s, the language is simple and repetitive, and the sentiment is so clear that it borders on banality. Yet, "I Cried for You" has charm and ironic humor, and its place as a standard remains secure. Judy Garland reprised it in *Babes in Arms* (1939), the first movie for which Freed served as producer.

Freed married Renee Klein on 14 March 1923. They had one child, a daughter named Barbara. Because he and Brown were having problems getting their songs published, Freed returned to vaudeville. He and Renee incorporated their honeymoon into his work as an accompanist for Frances Williams, a singer he had discovered in a San Francisco café. Williams became a star and sang several of his songs at the Palace Theatre in New York. During the mid 1920s Freed returned to Los Angeles to manage the Orange Grove Theatre for four years. The theater had a practice of alternating week-long runs of straight plays and musical revues. Freed and Brown wrote several songs for the original musicals. One of Freed's discoveries was a young Bing Crosby. Crosby and a singer-songwriter named Harry Barris had come to demonstrate their songs. Freed immediately hired the singer for his stage debut in an obscure revue.

Freed then moved on to the Music Box Theatre, also in Los Angeles, where he and Brown wrote songs for

its annual *Hollywood Music Box Revue*. Fanny Brice appeared in the 1927 edition, for which the team wrote their most famous song, "Singin' in the Rain," and "The Wedding of the Painted Doll." Two years later M-G-M hired Freed as a staff lyricist and put him to work with Brown. Their first assignment came when producer Irving Thalberg decided to make a sound movie, which the studio trumpeted as the first motion picture to feature "All Talking! All Singing! All Dancing!" Of Freed and Brown's six songs in the movie, *Broadway Melody* (1929), three became hits: "You Were Meant for Me," "The Wedding of the Painted Doll," and the title song. Actually, they had written most of these numbers for Freed's stage revues at the Orange Grove and Music Box Theatres; he and Brown had a career-long habit of recycling their songs. The movie broke attendance records and won an Oscar as best picture of 1929.

Though *Broadway Melody* has dated badly, it remains a landmark musical. Other movies had used songs, but this was the first true movie musical. It was the first to use original songs and prerecorded sound, the first to use a song as part of the plot ("You Were Meant for Me"), and the first to use large soundstages and two-color Technicolor for the first elaborate musical production number ("The Wedding of the Painted Doll"). The most important song in the score was "Broadway Melody," because it helped to establish the backstage musical plot. This plot device served as the model for hundreds of "backstager" musicals over the next two decades. Yet, even though

Sheet music for a song by Freed and Brown that was featured in a 1935 movie musical (Bruccoli Clark Layman Archives)

Broadway Melody is about two sisters dreaming of Broadway stardom (and about their eventual falling-out when they fall in love with the same rakish songwriter), Freed had had little experience and no success on Broadway. In fact, he had turned down offers to write in New York because he preferred California. The irony was compounded as established Broadway songwriters began flocking to Hollywood to write for movie musicals with the onset of the Depression. They found themselves writing about singers and dancers who long for success on Broadway (rather than in the movies) in a formula established by Freed. Like many lyricists who used formulaic imagery to write about subjects beyond their personal experience, he drew on common knowledge for his anthem-like depiction of Broadway:

A million lights they flicker there,
A million hearts beat quicker there,
No skies of gray on the great White Way,
That's the Broadway Melody.

Freed and Brown's next movie, *Hollywood Revue of 1929,* featured the recycled "Singin' in the Rain," performed by Cliff Edwards and a chorus dressed in slickers while the rain pours down on them. "Singin' in the Rain" is a classic American song, easily sung and remembered, ingratiatingly lilting, and impressed on America's collective memory by Gene Kelly's performance in the 1952 movie of the same title. Yet, the lyric is little more than a grab bag of direct statements that the singer is happy, laughing, and ready for love.

Lobby card for the 1937 movie musical in which Judy Garland introduced Freed and Brown's "Everybody Sing" (from John Kobal
and V. A. Wilson, Foyer Pleasure: The Golden Age of Cinema Lobby Cards, 1982)

What makes the song work is the irrepressible happiness expressed in Brown's ebullient melody and Freed's repetition of the title line, "I'm singin' in the rain," a half dozen times, followed by a leap to ecstasy that is convincing despite its abstraction: "What a glorious feeling, I'm happy again." In fact, Freed's lyrics are often either just this sort of miscellany of references (in "You Were Meant for Me" the loved one is identified as "all the sweet things rolled up in one," "a plaintive melody" the singer cannot get out of his mind, and someone sent by the angels) or an unlikely mix of common speech and formal locutions. In the sweet but bouncy "All I Do Is Dream of You" (1934), the singer states, "And were there more than twenty-four hours a day / They'd be spent in sweet content dreaming away." "You Are My Lucky Star" (1935) includes charming but overwrought lines such as "You opened heaven's portal, here on earth for this poor mortal."

For *Going Hollywood* (1933) Freed assured Crosby's stardom by urging M-G-M to hire the crooner for the lead role because he wanted him to introduce a new song, "Temptation." Sung by Crosby in a seedy saloon as he drunkenly bemoans his inability to escape from a temptress played by Fifi D'Orsay, it became one of his major early hits. The song is overheated and self-pitying, characterized by a studied breathlessness that makes it precious rather than real, but it is also an important part of an exotic strain in Freed and Brown's work. Other songs in this broad category include "The Wedding of the Painted Doll," "Chant of the Jungle" (1929), and "Love Songs of the Nile" (1933). One of the most important of these songs is "Pagan Love Song" (1929), set in a world "where moonbeams light Tahitian skies / And the starlit waters linger in your eyes."

Freed and Brown's other major motion pictures were *Broadway Melody of 1936* (1935), for which they wrote their best score, including "You Are My Lucky Star," "Broadway Rhythm," and "I've Got a Feelin' You're Foolin'"; and *Broadway Melody of 1938* (1937), in which Judy Garland introduced "Everybody Sing." Shortly before this time, Freed had been instrumental in arranging for Garland to sing the James V. Monaco–Joe McCarthy standard, "You Made Me Love You (I Didn't Want to Do It)" (1913), at Clark Gable's thirty-sixth birthday party. Songwriter-arranger Roger Edens had written a new introduction called "Dear Mr. Gable," in which the teenaged Garland confessed her crush on the star by singing to his photograph. It was so successful that the song was added to *Broadway Melody of 1938*.

Freed and Brown collaborated successfully until 1939. Their other songs include "Should I?" (1930), "A Bundle of Old Love Letters" (1930), "Beautiful Girl" (1933), "We'll Make Hay While the Sun Shines" (1933), "Our Big Love Scene" (1933), "After Sundown" (1933), "Hold Your Man" (1933), "A New Moon Is Over My Shoulder" (1934), "Alone" (1935), and "Would You?" (1936). During these same years Freed occasionally collaborated with composers Oskar Strauss, Barris, Al Hoffman, and Al Goodman. *Broadway Melody of 1938* marked the end of Freed and Brown's happy, fruitful collaboration. Brown's contract with M-G-M expired, and Freed was interested in moving on to producing. Although their pulsating songs about New York had helped to create the sound of Hollywood's 1930s backstage musicals, their light, perky numbers were actually reminiscent of the 1920s. Nevertheless, audiences continued to respond favorably to such songs throughout the Great Depression.

By 1939 Freed had tried his hand at a few screenplays and was ready to turn from songwriting to producing, as had lyricists Buddy DeSylva and John Golden before him. Lyricist Ned Washington recalled, "There were a lot of us songwriters working at Metro in those days. We'd all get to the studio at about 11:30 or so, and start working on our songs. All except Arthur Freed, that is. He would get to the studio by 8 or 9 o'clock, and he'd be on the set, learning camera angles and director's set ups, and things like that. To us, it seemed strange for a songwriter to be interested in those things." Freed began his second career as the assistant producer for *The Wizard of Oz* (1939), having persuaded the studio to buy the property because he recognized its potential as a musical. He talked M-G-M studio head Louis B. Mayer out of casting Shirley Temple ("She would have been awful," he said) and into casting Garland, and he was responsible for hiring Harold Arlen and E. Y. "Yip" Harburg to write the score. "Harburg and Arlen didn't want to do a ballad for the picture," Freed explained many

years later. "I talked them into writing 'Over the Rainbow.'" He also convinced the studio executives to keep the song when they seriously considered cutting it from the finished movie.

After the success of *The Wizard of Oz,* Mayer told Freed it was time for him to become a full-time producer and suggested that he find properties suitable for musicals. Freed first chose Richard Rodgers and Lorenz Hart's Broadway hit *Babes in Arms* (1937), because he saw it as a vehicle for Garland and Mickey Rooney. When the movie adaptation, released in 1939, emerged as M-G-M's most successful picture of 1940, Freed's reputation was established. He and Brown added the ebullient "Good Morning" to Rodgers and Hart's score.

As a producer, Freed was notable for surrounding himself with the most talented people he could find and protecting them from studio interference. Among the members of the "Freed Unit" were directors Vincente Minnelli, Stanley Donen, and Charles Walters; choreographer Michael Kidd; writers Betty Comden and Adolph Green; arranger André Previn; and such stars as Garland, Kelly, Astaire, and Cyd Charisse. Freed also discovered Eleanor Powell, Gloria DeHaven, June Allyson, Esther Williams, and Howard Keel. Eventually, Freed became one of Hollywood's most innovative producers, and the "Freed Unit" at M-G-M created some of the most successful musicals in movie history. During his thirty-five years as a producer, he brought Kelly to M-G-M to star with Garland in *For Me and My Gal* (1942); he was the motivational force behind the innovative fifteen-minute ballet sequence in *An American in Paris* (1951); and he purchased the rights to Colette's short story "Gigi" (1944) and persuaded Alan Jay Lerner and Frederick Loewe to forsake Broadway to write the score for the 1958 motion-picture adaptation. Both *An American in Paris* and *Gigi* won Oscars for best picture.

Freed's career as a producer resonated with his work as a lyricist. Many of his song lyrics were about dreams, wishes, and fantasies—for instance, "You Are My Lucky Star," "All I Do Is Dream of You," and "Pagan Love Song." So were many of the best movies he produced. He replaced the gritty, realistic backstage musical of *Broadway Melody* with increasingly lavish productions that created their own imaginative worlds. *Cabin in the Sky* (1943), the best of the all-black musicals, is a fantasy about a woman who negotiates with heaven to save her sinning husband's soul. *Meet Me in St. Louis* (1944) took Americans back to a more innocent time in one of the greatest period musicals. *The Pirate* (1948) is a flamboyant fairy tale about an actor who pretends to be a notorious robber. *Easter Parade* (1948) tells the story of a dancer who loses his partner and, Pygma-

Sheet music for a Freed and Brown song featured in the 1929 stage musical Broadway Melody *and subsequently used in several movie musicals, including* Singin' in the Rain *(Bruccoli Clark Layman Archives)*

lion-like, transforms a chorus girl into someone to dance with and love. *On the Town* (1949) takes three sailors from the dangers of warfare to shore leave in an idyllic New York where, in twenty-four hours, they see the entire city and find love.

Freed also seemed to see his role as producer as an extension of his career as a lyricist. In both roles he was responsible for fitting songs into stories, and he built many of his musicals around the work of individual composers and lyricists. Freed produced three so-called biopics: *Till the Clouds Roll By* (1947), about Jerome Kern; *Words and Music* (1948), about Rodgers and Hart; and *Three Little Words* (1950), about Bert Kalmar and Harry Ruby. He also produced movies with scores drawn from the work of major songwriting teams:

George and Ira Gershwin's songs for *An American in Paris,* Arthur Schwartz and Howard Dietz's for *The Band Wagon* (1953), and his own songs with Brown for *Singin' in the Rain* (1952).

Singin' in the Rain, starring Kelly, Debbie Reynolds, Jean Hagen, and Donald O'Connor, is Freed's greatest musical and is also considered one of the greatest of all movie musicals. His choice to use his and Brown's songs written in the style of the 1920s was perfect for a genial satire that makes nostalgic fun of the early years of talking pictures. Among the songs reprised in the movie are "Fit as a Fiddle" (1933), "You Were Meant for Me," "You Are My Lucky Star," "Should I?," "Would You?," "Good Morning," "Broadway Melody," "Broadway Rhythm," and, of course,

"Singin' in the Rain." Freed later said that the plot of the movie was based loosely on his and Brown's own experiences in making *Broadway Melody*. He and Brown collaborated on one new song for the score, "Make 'Em Laugh," a comic tour de force for O'Connor. Director Donen had asked the team for a song to be used in a sequence in which O'Connor tries to cheer up a melancholy Kelly. When he mentioned Cole Porter's "Be a Clown," from *The Pirate*, Brown and Freed took him all too literally. Their new song resulted in a wonderfully funny scene, but it is dishearteningly close to a plagiarization of Porter's song. Donen later admitted, "None of us had the courage to say to [Freed], it obviously works for the number, but it's a stolen song, Arthur." Freed's other major productions include *Babes on Broadway* (1941), *Du Barry Was a Lady* (1943), *Best Foot Forward* (1943), *Girl Crazy* (1943), *The Harvey Girls* (1946), *Annie Get Your Gun* (1950), *Show Boat* (1951), *The Belle of New York* (1952), *Brigadoon* (1954), *Silk Stockings* (1957), and *Bells Are Ringing* (1960).

In the mid 1940s Freed also returned briefly to songwriting, collaborating with composer Harry Warren on several undistinguished songs for *Yolanda and the Thief* (1945) and *Ziegfeld Follies* (1946). The best of these songs was the romantic ballad "This Heart of Mine," sung by Garland in *Ziegfeld Follies*. In the late 1950s, when the musical genre lost popularity, Freed also produced several minor nonmusical movies. From 1940 to 1953 he had produced thirty-three musicals. In the next decade he produced only seven. In 1962 Freed wrote what was to be his last lyric, the title song for the movie *Light in the Piazza*, with music by Mario Nascimbene. Because of M-G-M's financial decline in the 1960s, Freed's final two projects, a screen biography of Irving Berlin and a musical based on Mark Twain's *Adventures of Huckleberry Finn* (1885), were scrapped.

In 1962 Freed retired from M-G-M and served as president of the Academy of Motion Picture Arts and Sciences from 1963 to 1967. The Academy gave him the Irving Thalberg Award in 1961 and a special Oscar in 1968 in recognition of his achievement as a producer (although he never won an Oscar for best original movie song), and the French Legion d'Honneur made him a chevalier. He was inducted into the Songwriters Hall of Fame in 1972. Freed spent his last months severely handicapped by arthritis and died of a heart attack at age seventy-eight at his home in Bel Air, California, on 12 April 1973.

References:
Hugh Fordin, *The World of Entertainment: Hollywood's Greatest Musicals* (New York: Doubleday, 1975);

Peter Hay, *MGM: When the Lion Roars* (Atlanta: Turner, 1991), pp. 233–246, 313–318;

Roy Hemming, *The Melody Lingers On: The Great Songwriters and Their Movie Musicals* (New York: Newmarket Press, 1986), pp. 324–332;

Gerald Mast, *Can't Help Singin': The American Musical on Stage and Screen* (Woodstock, N.Y.: Overlook Press, 1987), pp. 234–289.

Papers:
Scripts, movie-production information, letters, and memorabilia are in the Arthur Freed Collection at the Cinema-Television Library, University of Southern California, Los Angeles. The collection emphasizes the movie musicals produced by Freed. Material on earlier M-G-M movies for which Freed wrote song lyrics may be found in the library's M-G-M Collection.

Selected Discography:
Singin' in the Rain, 1984 London studio cast, First Night, 6013, 1984;

Singin' in the Rain, 1996 London studio cast, Jay, 1262, 1997;

Singin' in the Rain, motion-picture soundtrack, Rhino, 71963, 1996.

Ira Gershwin

(6 December 1896 – 17 August 1983)

Philip Furia
University of North Carolina at Wilmington

Unless otherwise indicated, music is by George Gershwin.

SELECTED SONGS FROM THEATRICAL PRO-
DUCTIONS: *A Dangerous Maid* (1921)–"Boy
Wanted";

Two Little Girls in Blue (1921), music by Vincent Youmans and Paul Lannin–"Oh Me! Oh My! Oh
You!" (music by Youmans);

George White's Scandals of 1922 (1922)–"(I'll Build a)
Stairway to Paradise" (lyrics by Ira Gershwin and
Buddy DeSylva);

Be Yourself (1924), music by Lewis E. Gensler and Milton Schwarzwald–"Uh-Uh!" (lyrics by Ira Gershwin, George S. Kaufman, and Marc Connelly,
music by Schwarzwald);

Lady, Be Good! (1924)–"Fascinating Rhythm"; "The
Half of It, Dearie, Blues"; "Little Jazz Bird"; "The
Man I Love" (unused); "Oh, Lady Be Good!";

Primrose (1924), lyrics by Ira Gershwin and Desmond
Carter–"Naughty Baby";

Tell Me More (1925), lyrics by Ira Gershwin and
DeSylva–"Three Times a Day";

Tip-Toes (1925)–"Looking for a Boy"; "Sweet and Low-
Down"; "That Certain Feeling"; "These Charming People";

Americana (1926)–"Sunny Disposish" (interpolation,
music by Philip Charig);

Oh, Kay! (1926)–"Clap Yo' Hands"; "Do, Do, Do";
"Someone to Watch over Me";

Funny Face (1927)–"The Babbitt and the Bromide";
"Funny Face"; "He Loves and She Loves"; "Let's
Kiss and Make Up"; "My One and Only"; "'S
Wonderful";

Strike Up the Band (1927)–"Strike Up the Band";

Rosalie (1928), lyrics by Ira Gershwin and P. G. Wode-
house, music by George Gershwin and Sigmund
Romberg–"How Long Has This Been Going
On?" (lyrics by Ira Gershwin, music by George
Gershwin); "Oh Gee! Oh Joy!" (music by George
Gershwin);

Ira Gershwin, 1935 (Van Damm Studio)

Treasure Girl (1928)–"I've Got a Crush on You";
"What Causes That?"; "Where's the Boy? Here's
the Girl!";

Show Girl (1929), lyrics by Ira Gershwin and Gus
Kahn–"Liza";

Girl Crazy (1930)–"Bidin' My Time"; "Boy! What Love
Has Done to Me!" "But Not for Me"; "Could
You Use Me?"; "Embraceable You"; "I Got
Rhythm"; "Sam and Delilah"; "Treat Me
Rough";

Strike Up the Band, revised version (1930)–"Soon";

Of Thee I Sing (1931)–"Love Is Sweeping the Country"; "Of Thee I Sing"; "Who Cares?";

Let 'Em Eat Cake (1933)–"Down with Everyone Who's Up"; "Mine";

Pardon My English (1933)–"Isn't It a Pity?"; "The Lorelei"; "My Cousin in Milwaukee";

Life Begins at 8:40 (1934), lyrics by Ira Gershwin and E. Y. "Yip" Harburg, music by Harold Arlen–"Fun to Be Fooled"; "What Can You Say in a Love Song (That Hasn't Been Said Before)?"; "You're a Builder-Upper";

Porgy and Bess (1935), lyrics by Ira Gershwin and DuBose Heyward–"Bess, You Is My Woman Now"; "I Got Plenty o' Nuthin'"; "I Loves You, Porgy"; "It Ain't Necessarily So" (lyrics by Ira Gershwin); "Oh, Bess, Oh, Where's My Bess?" (lyrics by Ira Gershwin); "Oh, I Can't Sit Down" (lyrics by Ira Gershwin); "A Redheaded Woman" (lyrics by Ira Gershwin); "There's a Boat Dat's Leavin' Soon for New York" (lyrics by Ira Gershwin);

Ziegfeld Follies of 1936 (1936), music by Vernon Duke–"He Hasn't a Thing Except Me"; "I Can't Get Started";

Lady in the Dark (1941), music by Kurt Weill–"My Ship"; "The Saga of Jenny"; "This Is New"; "Tchaikowsky (And Other Russians)";

The Firebrand of Florence (1945), music by Weill–"I Know Where There's a Cozy Nook"; "A Rhyme for Angela"; "Sing Me Not a Ballad";

Park Avenue (1946), music by Arthur Schwartz–"Don't Be a Woman if You Can"; "There's No Holding Me."

SELECTED SONGS FROM MOTION-PICTURE PRODUCTIONS: *Delicious* (1931)–"Blah, Blah, Blah";

A Damsel in Distress (1937)–"A Foggy Day"; "I Can't Be Bothered Now"; "Nice Work if You Can Get It"; "Stiff Upper Lip"; "Things Are Looking Up";

Shall We Dance (1937)–"(I've Got) Beginner's Luck"; "Let's Call the Whole Thing Off"; "Slap That Bass"; "They All Laughed"; "They Can't Take That Away from Me";

The Goldwyn Follies (1938)–"I Was Doing All Right"; "Just Another Rhumba" (unused); "Love Is Here to Stay"; "Love Walked In";

Cover Girl (1944), music by Jerome Kern–"Long Ago (And Far Away)"; "Put Me to the Test";

Where Do We Go from Here? (1945), music by Kurt Weill–"If Love Remains"; "The *Nina*, the *Pinta*, the *Santa Maria*"; "Song of the Rhineland";

The Shocking Miss Pilgrim (1947), music by George Gershwin, posthumously reconstructed by Ira

Gershwin and Kay Swift–"Aren't You Kind of Glad We Did?"; "The Back Bay Polka"; "Changing My Tune"; "For You, for Me, for Evermore";

The Barkleys of Broadway (1949), music by Harry Warren–"My One and Only Highland Fling"; "Shoes with Wings On";

Give a Girl a Break (1953), music by Burton Lane–"Applause! Applause!"; "It Happens Ev'ry Time"; "In Our United State";

The Country Girl (1954), music by Harold Arlen–"Dissertation on the State of Bliss (Love and Learn)";

A Star Is Born (1954), music by Arlen–"Gotta Have Me Go with You"; "The Man That Got Away"; "Someone at Last";

Kiss Me, Stupid (1964), music by George Gershwin, posthumously reconstructed by Ira Gershwin and Roger Edens–"All the Livelong Day (And the Long, Long Night)."

BOOKS: *Lyrics on Several Occasions: A Selection of Stage & Screen Lyrics Written for Sundry Situations, and Now Arranged in Arbitrary Categories: To Which Have Been Added Many Informative Annotations & Disquisitions on Their Why & Wherefore, Their Whom-for, Their How, and Matters Associative* (New York: Knopf, 1959);

Robert Kimball, ed., *The Complete Lyrics of Ira Gershwin* (New York: Knopf, 1993).

In *Lyrics on Several Occasions* (1959) Ira Gershwin described the art of the lyricist as that of fitting words "mosaically" to music, an art that required "the infinite patience of a gemsetter." To answer that perennial question, whether the words or music came first, it was usually the music, or at least the musical germ of a song. "I hit on a new tune," George Gershwin once explained, "and play it for Ira and he hums it all over the place until he gets an idea for a lyric. Then we work the thing out together." Working it out meant finding the precise syllables, words, and phrases that fit the notes of a melody. Sometimes it took Ira all night to find a single word. Once he had to check into a hotel room for three days to find a setting for a tricky string of staccato notes in one of his brother George's melodies; what he came up with–"Come to Papa, come to Papa, do," a line in "Embraceable You" (1930)–shows why, among songwriters, Ira Gershwin was known as "The Jeweler."

While Ira Gershwin is usually associated with George Gershwin's music, he also collaborated over the course of his career with many other composers, each with a distinctive musical style: Harold Arlen, Jerome Kern, Vincent Youmans, Harry Warren, Burton Lane, Arthur Schwartz, Kurt Weill, and even Aaron Copland. With every collaborator he was a consummate

George and Ira Gershwin on the terrace of their twin penthouses at 33 Riverside Drive in New York City, 1929 (The Gershwin Trusts)

crafter of lyrical mosaics, performing that alchemy by which the art of words and the art of music are fused into the hybrid art of song.

Like so many other lyricists of his generation, Ira Gershwin was the son of Jewish immigrants. Moishe and Rose Bruskin Gershovitz married on 21 July 1895 and, after arriving in New York from Russia, they changed their name to Morris and Rose Gershwine. Their first child was born on 6 December 1896 at their apartment on the Lower East Side. Although his birth name was Israel, his parents always called him Izzy, and by the time he learned what his real name was, he had long since gone by Ira. His brother George (whose real name was Jacob, although he was apparently never called that) was born in 1899; another brother, Arthur, in 1900; and, finally, a sister, Frances, in 1906. When George quit school at age fourteen to work on Tin Pan Alley (the music-publishing industry then centered on Broadway and Twenty-eighth Street), he changed his name to "Gershwin," and the entire family followed suit.

Just as they changed names, the Gershwin family changed residences. By the time he turned twenty, Ira estimated, they had moved twenty-eight times. The peripatetic life was prompted by Morris Gershwin's many different business ventures—restaurants, cigar stores, Turkish bathhouses, and pool halls—and his insistence upon living near his business so that he could walk to work. All those moves familiarized Ira Gershwin with his city, and he was proud to be deemed the most knowledgeable pupil in his class at Townsend Harris High School on the subject of New York City. Like most children of immigrants growing up in New York, Ira and George Gershwin learned their English on the streets of New York, where, by 1900, three-fourths of the people were immigrants or the children of immigrants.

Ira Gershwin also imbibed the English language as a voracious reader. Bespectacled and studious, he devoured dime novels and regularly checked out books from the public library by Alexandre Dumas, James Fenimore Cooper, Jules Verne, Arthur Conan Doyle, and, later, Arnold Bennett and John Galsworthy. At Townsend Harris High he also developed a love of poetry. Poetry was then a daily exercise in dramatic, oral performance. One by one, students would troop to the front of the room to recite Henry Wadsworth Longfellow's "The Village Blacksmith" (1841) or "The Wreck of the Hesperus" (1841), replete with dramatic gestures. Not only did students have to memorize, recite, and declaim poetry, they learned to write it. "We received a rigorous training," Ira's classmate lyricist E. Y. "Yip" Harburg recalled, "in the classical poetic forms. We were well-versed in the ballad, the triolet, the rondo, the villanelle." Few high-school and college students today—even those who write poetry—would know those poetic forms, much less be able to write them. What made those forms so demanding was that they came from the poetic tradition of a rhyme-rich language. In French there are fifty-one rhymes for *amour;* in English, *love* rhymes only with *dove, above, glove, shove,* and, as a last resort, *of.* Trying to master the intricate rhyming patterns of the villanelle or rondeau in such a language as English was rigorous training indeed for a future lyricist who would have to ply the mosaic art of fitting words to notes, saying "I love you" in the fifty to seventy words allotted to him in the standard thirty-two-bar chorus of a popular song.

In Ira Gershwin's youth, poetry was not confined to the classroom. All the big New York papers carried regular poetry columns, such as "The Conning Tower," by Franklin Pierce Adams ("F.P.A."), in *The New York World.* "We were living," Harburg exulted, "in a time of literate revelry in the New York daily press—F.P.A., Russell Crouse, Don Marquis, Alexander Woollcott, Dorothy Parker, Bob Benchley. We wanted to be part of it." Together, "Yip" and "Gersh" edited a poetry column titled "Much Ado" for the *Academic Herald,* the Townsend Harris school newspaper. Then, when they

Ethel Merman (center) singing "I Got Rhythm" in the 1930 production of Girl Crazy *(Billy Rose Theatre Collection, New York Public Library for the Performing Arts)*

went on to the City College of New York, they continued it as "Gargoyle Gargles" in *The Campus,* the college's weekly journal. Gershwin occasionally managed to place a poem or a humorous prose squib in other campus publications, as well as in *The New York Mail,* the *New York Sun,* and other newspapers.

One of Ira Gershwin's light-verse efforts from 1916 foreshadows his later work as a lyricist:

A desperate deed to do I crave,
Beyond all reason or rhyme;
Someday when I'm feeling especially brave,
I'm going to bide my time.

In "Bidin' My Time," a song for the 1930 musical *Girl Crazy,* he recast this somewhat stilted and padded bit of verse into charmingly elongated syllables: "I'm bidin' my ti–me, / 'Cause that's the kinda guy I'–m." Their early apprenticeship in light verse, with its metrical discipline and intricate rhymes, later enabled Gershwin and other lyricists to match syllables to intricate musical patterns with colloquial ease.

By the time he was in high school, Ira Gershwin had become a lover of the theater–Henrik Ibsen, J. M.

Barrie, and, of course, W. S. Gilbert and Arthur Sullivan. Fascinated by the literature of the Restoration and eighteenth-century England, he had begun keeping a diary in the manner of Samuel Pepys, which he titled "Every Man His Own Boswell." (Clearly, he took his inspiration from F.P.A.'s similar diary in "The Conning Tower.") Here, Gershwin recorded his enthusiastic responses to performances of some of the legendary Princess Theatre shows, such as *Leave It To Jane* (1917) and *Miss 1917* (1917). He also listened over and over to recordings of songs from these and other shows by Guy Bolton, P. G. Wodehouse, and Kern. Gershwin's diary records his first fledgling attempts, in 1917, at writing lyrics, though it took nearly seven years of apprenticeship before he mastered the craft of wedding words to music.

An early experience at collaborating provided a lesson in the primacy of music over words. While working as a cashier in his father's latest business venture, the St. Nicholas Baths, Ira had written a poem (on company stationery), "The Great American Folk Song (Is a Rag)." He thought it could be turned into a song and approached his brother George, who had already been given a job as a song plugger by the prestigious T. B. Harms publishing firm. When George sat down at the piano with the poem, however, the melody that emerged completely undid the poetic lines, forcing Ira to rewrite the entire lyric so that its syllables were now fitted to the melody. Lines such as "There's a happy, snappy, don't-care-a-rappy sort of / I don't know what to call it" might be fine in light verse, but in a song lyric they had to be whittled down to a simpler and more singable, "A raggy refrain anytime / Sends me a message sublime." The finished song emerged as "The Real American Folk Song (Is a Rag)" and was interpolated into the musical *Ladies First* (1918), in which it was sung by Nora Bayes in out-of-town tryouts, but it was dropped before the show reached New York.

Working mostly with young composers other than his brother George (who in 1919 had the biggest hit of his career with "Swanee," with lyrics by Irving Caesar), Ira Gershwin chose to write under the pseudonym Arthur Francis (the names of his other brother and his sister), so as not to seem to capitalize on George's success. In 1921, with Youmans, Ira wrote a commendable score for *Two Little Girls in Blue,* which featured the wryly tender song "Oh Me! Oh My! Oh You!" Initially the title phrase had been a "dummy" lyric, a temporary working line used to help songwriters remember a melody while they worked on a song. But when Youmans heard the dummy title, he urged Ira to make it the real one, since its long vowels and soft consonants resonated perfectly with the melody. Ira "wrote it up" as what he called a "simple" lyric, in which the words were primarily designed to fit the music, rather than a "comedy" song that displayed the wit of light verse.

During these years Ira Gershwin occasionally collaborated with his brother. "Waiting for the Sun to Come Out" was his first published song, written with George for *The Sweetheart Shop* in 1920. Ira had his first hit, "(I'll Build a) Stairway to Paradise," written with George and co-lyricist Buddy DeSylva, in *George White's Scandals of 1922.* By 1924 Ira Gershwin had emerged as a full-fledged professional in his own right. He dropped the pseudonym Arthur Francis and wrote under his real name when he collaborated with George on *Lady, Be Good!* (1924). Modeled on the Princess Theatre shows, *Lady, Be Good!* inaugurated a series of Jazz Age musicals that featured dynamic dances, snappy gags, and an overall rhythmic thrust that the Gershwin brothers captured perfectly in their songs.

When Ira heard his brother play a melody for the first number they needed for *Lady, Be Good!* he was stumped: "George, what kind of a lyric can I write for *that?*" Then, after a pause, he mused, "Still . . . it is a fascinating rhythm." Suddenly, he had his title phrase—

always the hardest part of a song to come up with—but it still took days to work out the rest of the lyric. "There was many a hot argument between us," Ira recalled, but when "Fascinating Rhythm" was sung by the stars of the show, Fred and Adele Astaire, it sounded exactly like what he said a good lyric should be—"rhymed conversation":

> Fascinating rhythm,
> You've got me on the go!
> Fascinating rhythm,
> I'm all a-quiver.
>
> What a mess you're making!
> The neighbors want to know
> Why I'm always shaking
> Just like a flivver.

Although it was dropped from the score of *Lady, Be Good!* "The Man I Love," Ira Gershwin's first great ballad, exemplified what he had learned in his years of lyrical apprenticeship. For one thing, he could make a lyric "memorable" by stitching together subtle rhymes that wove themselves into the listener's mind:

> *Some* day he'll *come* along,
> The man I love; . . .
> He'll look at me and *smile—*
> *I'll* underst*and;*
> *And* in a little *while*
> He'll take my *hand.* . . .

Another trick of the lyricist's trade was to make the lyric "singable" with long, open vowels a singer could lean on. Near the end of the release, or bridge, of this typical AABA song, Ira deftly wove long, open vowels toward that critical point where the release leads back to the final A section:

> M*aybe* T*ue*sd*ay*
> Will b*e* m*y* g*oo*d n*ew*sd*ay.*
>
> He'll build a little *home,*
> Just meant for *two.* . . .

Even as he demonstrated his mastery of the tools of the lyricist's trade in "The Man I Love," Ira Gershwin showed that he could also throw in witty, light-verse touches, such as the skewed phrasing of "And though it seems absurd, / I know we both won't say a word." Just as the lyric threatens to become cloyingly sentimental, with the singer conjuring up a "little home / . . . / From which I'll never roam," she abruptly turns to her listeners and colloquially inquires, "Who would? Would you?" Above all, Ira gave his lyric a distinctive light-verse "curve," setting it apart from thousands of other love songs,

Page 37 Sc .3.

Kreuger: Billions of dollars were lost us
                            Billions of dollars it cost us
                            Because this viper double crossed us!

Supreme Court:
(To Thrott.)
Wintergreen: Order in the court! Proceed

Kreuger: The score was 8 to 8
                            And we were going great
                                And what did he do ?

Thrott.: (wistfully)   What did I do ?
Kreuger: What did you do!

                            In inning number nine
                            He showed he had no spine
                               And what did he do ?

Thrott.:   What did I do ?
Sup. Ct/   What did you do!

K.   The others were at bat
                          And suddenly like that
All: What did he do
Kreuger: What did I do ?
                    WHAT DID HE DO ?

                He called a foul a fair!
                It was a foul, I swear!

Supreme Court: He knew the ball was foul
Kr.:   He knew it by our howl
                    and that's what he did
All: That's what he did
                    That's what he did!

Su. Ct/   Deny it if you can
              You hypocritical man
                You son of a gun
                You gave the run
Kr.   To the player from Japan

                And so we lost the game
                Our fortune and our name
                This son of a gun
                Gave them the run
              And he's the one to blame

S.Ct.:   Hinky dinky parlay vous
        Things look pretty black for you.

Wint.   You've heard them say you were remiss
        Now what have you got to say to this ?

Throt.:
K: I say the man's a traitor indescribable
        I say they gave him money and he's bribable
        Disgracing all of us who feel we're Aryan
        We want to do away with this barbarian
        The Army wants to handle this barbarian

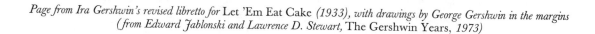

Page from Ira Gershwin's revised libretto for Let 'Em Eat Cake *(1933), with drawings by George Gershwin in the margins*
(from Edward Jablonski and Lawrence D. Stewart, The Gershwin Years, *1973)*

DuBose Heyward and Ira Gershwin working on Porgy and Bess
(Museum of the City of New York)

in the skewed verb tenses of the opening lines. A lesser lyricist would have written "Some day *he'll* come along, / The man *I'll* love," but Ira Gershwin makes the lover of the future seem already present: "Some day *he'll* come along, / The man *I love.*"

In such frothy musicals as *Tip-Toes* (1925), *Oh, Kay!* (1926), *Funny Face* (1927), and *Girl Crazy* (1930), Ira Gershwin took the American vernacular and made it sing. In "Embraceable You" (1930), noting the way Americans added suffixes to words, he concocted "Embrace me, / My sweet embraceable you" and then used the abrupt rests in George's angular melody to separate the suffix from its roots in "embrace-able," "irreplace-able," "silk-and-lace-able," and, even more giddily, in "tip-sy in me" / "gyp-sy in me." In "'S Wonderful" (1927) he toyed with the way Americans clip syllables. Taking his brother's abruptly repeated three-note phrase, he truncated four-syllable phrases to fit them:

'S wonderful! 'S marvelous—
You should care for me!
'S awful nice! 'S paradise—
'S what I love to see!

In "That Certain Feeling" (1925), another of George's musical syncopations afforded Ira a chance to capture the way Americans collapse two syllables onto one:

That certain feeling—
(Beat) *Thefirst* time I met you.
I hit the ceiling;
(Beat) *Icould* not forget you.

In songs such as "Embraceable You," "'S Wonderful," and "That Certain Feeling," the syncopated interplay of words and music reflects the ebullience of love itself.

Ira Gershwin took his lyrics, as he put it, "from thin air, literally and figuratively, by listening to the way Americans spoke to each other—their slang, their clichés, their catchphrases." An expression normally

Sheet music for one of the enduring songs in George and Ira Gershwin's 1935 opera (Music Library, University of South Carolina)

associated with finding one's mate in the arms of another—"How Long Has This Been Going On?" (1927)—became, in his hands, the euphoric exclamation of two jaded lovers experiencing their first truly passionate kiss. The argot of the 1920s, an era intoxicated with language, turns up in Ira's most romantic lyrics, from "It's all bananas" in "But Not for Me" (1930) to "The world will pardon my mush" in "I've Got a Crush on You" (1928). Where other lyricists, such as Lorenz Hart and Cole Porter, rhymed pyrotechnically, Ira Gershwin did it quietly, within the most ordinary expressions, as in these lines from "Someone to Watch over Me" (1926):

Although he may not *be the man some*
Girls think of as *handsome,*
To my heart he'll carry the *key.*

At times, as in "I Got Rhythm" (1930), Ira found he had to abandon rhyme altogether to let one of George's percussive melodies, as he put it, "throw its weight around":

I got rhythm,
I got music,
I got my man—
Who could ask for anything more?

Such a minimalist lyric took Ira Gershwin weeks to create, but, belted out by newcomer Ethel Merman in the first production of *Girl Crazy,* it sounded like the perfectly natural exclamation point to end the Roaring Twenties.

The brothers Gershwin were at the center of the Jazz Age, an era epitomized by George Gershwin's *Rhapsody in Blue,* which he himself premiered at the piano with Paul Whiteman's orchestra in an historic concert at New York's Aeolian Hall on 12 February 1924. The close collaboration between George and Ira, even at the beginning of their careers, is evident from Ira's suggestion that George take a melodic phrase from the second movement of the work and make it his sweeping main theme. Ira also suggested *Rhapsody in Blue* as a title, inspired by his having seen some of James McNeill Whistler's paintings, which had titles such as

Symphony in White and *Nocturne in Black and Gold,* at the Metropolitan Museum of Art. Ira and George lived their entire lives in the same or adjacent houses or apartments, even after Ira married Leonore "Lee" Strunsky on 14 September 1926. Through such lifelong proximity the brothers were able to create a fusion of words and music as seamless as lyricist-composers such as Porter or Irving Berlin did by writing both their own music and lyrics.

Writing for the Broadway musical rather than the straight popular market, Ira Gershwin had to learn another dimension of the lyricist's art that did not concern songwriters on Tin Pan Alley. His lyrics tailored a song to a specific character, dramatic situation, and performer. Ira came to think of his lyrics as "lodgments" that were designed to fit into a particular moment in a musical production, and that particularity is often what inspired the distinctive curve for a lyric. For Ginger Rogers, making her Broadway debut as a tough-talking cowgirl in *Girl Crazy,* Ira opened the verse of "But Not for Me" with these pugnacious lines:

Old Man Sunshine—listen you!
Never tell me dreams come true!
Just try it—
And I'll start a riot.

The Gershwins increasingly sought more integration between song and story. In 1927, working with George S. Kaufman, the premier satiric playwright of his day, they wrote *Strike Up the Band,* a political satire squarely rooted in the tradition of Gilbert and Sullivan. Ira Gershwin was proud that his lyrics actually "carried plot" for long stretches, and there was not a single romantic ballad in the entire score. Yet, audiences were not ready for such experiments and *Strike Up the Band* closed out of town. Still, the enormous success of Kern and Oscar Hammerstein's *Show Boat* that same year showed that the day of the fully integrated musical was not far off.

What delayed its complete arrival was the Depression, which drastically reduced the number and scale of Broadway musicals. What few Broadway productions there were, however, could be more experimental than the boy-meets-girl plots of 1920s musicals. The Gershwins returned to satirical operetta, revising *Strike Up the Band,* which had a more successful run on Broadway in 1930. With audiences more receptive to political satire during the Depression, the Gershwins, working with Kaufman and Morrie Ryskind in 1931, produced a masterpiece in *Of Thee I Sing,* which made fun of the American presidency (and even more of the vice presidency). Modeled closely on Gilbert and Sullivan's spoofs of Victorian institutions and manners, this operetta gave Ira Gershwin another opportunity to write recitatives, patter songs, and choral numbers rather than the standard romantic ballads he had come to feel were so confining. Even the few love songs he was required to supply added to the satire: "Love Is Sweeping the Country" captured the absurd hoopla of political campaigns, while "Who Cares?" managed to laugh at the Depression itself: "Who cares what banks fail in Yonkers, / Long as you've got a kiss that conquers?" The first Pulitzer Prize ever awarded to a musical went to Ira Gershwin, Kaufman, and Ryskind for *Of Thee I Sing* (George Gershwin was deemed ineligible for the purely "literary" award).

Let 'Em Eat Cake (1933), a sequel to *Of Thee I Sing,* was regarded by both critics and the public as too darkly pessimistic, despite the brilliant nihilism displayed in such songs as "Down with Everyone Who's Up." The one successful song to come from *Let 'Em Eat Cake* was "Mine," a clever counterpoint song in the manner of Berlin's "Play a Simple Melody" (1914). For "Mine" George Gershwin concocted an extremely sparse refrain—even for him—that gave his brother only fifty-four notes to fit with syllables. Faced with such parsimony, Ira wrote simple lines for the married lovers in the show to croon with almost mindless bliss: "Mine, more than divine, / To know that love like yours is mine!" To counteract these cloying sentiments and obvious rhymes, George created a countermelody that was sprightly and coy, and Ira gave these lines to the chorus to intone as the lovers are singing the first melody:

It does a person good to see
Such happy domesticity.
The way they're making love, you'd swear
They're not a married pair.

As this second lyric develops, Ira Gershwin indulges in his characteristic pronoun play, contrasting the "mine" of the first melody with third-person "possessive" pronouns:

He says, no matter what occurs,
Whatever he may have is hers;
The point that *she* is making is,
Whatever *she* may have is his.

Not even such bright contrapuntal wit could alleviate the gloom of a story in which America undergoes a fascist takeover, and the failure of *Let 'Em Eat Cake* ended the Gershwins' venture into satirical operetta.

In 1934 George Gershwin was working with the South Carolina writer DuBose Heyward on *Porgy and Bess* (1935), an operatic adaptation of Heyward's novel *Porgy* (1925), and Ira Gershwin turned to satirical revues. Revues thrived on Broadway during the

Depression—not the lavish spectacles of the 1920s but "little" revues that eschewed huge sets and expensive costumes for clever skits and witty songs. With his old friend Harburg and the young composer Arlen, Ira wrote songs and comic sketches for *Life Begins at 8:40* (1934), in which "Gersh" and "Yip" indulged their long-standing love of wordplay:

You're a builder-upper,
A breaker-downer,
A holder-outer,
And I'm a giver-inner;
Sad but true,
I love it, I do,
Being broken by a builder-upper like you!

Featuring Bert Lahr, Ray Bolger, and other comic talents, *Life Begins at 8:40* satirized the New York political scene, Broadway, Hollywood, Tin Pan Alley, and such poets as Edgar Guest and Joyce Kilmer.

In 1936 Ira Gershwin tried his hand at another revue, *The Ziegfeld Follies of 1936*. With Russian composer Vernon Duke (born Vladimir Dukelsky), he wrote songs for such stage luminaries as Fanny Brice, but the best song in the show went to newcomer Bob Hope. A "list" song in the style made popular by Porter, "I Can't Get Started" weaves a lyric out of contemporary allusions, each topping the preceding one in cleverness:

I've flown around the world in a plane,
I've settled revolutions in Spain. . . .
When J. P. Morgan bows, I just nod;
Green Pastures wanted me to play God. . . .

Ira also wrote the skit for the song, which Hope sings to Eve Arden after she refuses to kiss him upon their first meeting. After hearing his lament in the song, however, she relents, only to be overwhelmed by his charms. Once satisfied of his effect on her, however, Hope casually bids her farewell.

In between these stylish revues, Ira Gershwin was called in to help with *Porgy and Bess*, at first polishing Heyward's words for songs such as "Summertime" so that they fit with George's music and then plunging fully into the collaborative process by writing his own lyrics to his brother's music, primarily for the songs sung by the character Sportin' Life. In both Heyward's *Porgy* and the 1927 play that he and his wife adapted from the novel, Sportin' Life was a relatively minor and one-dimensional figure. As Ira's role in the collaboration grew, however, so did the importance of Sportin' Life as a comic but also ominous urban intrusion into the pastoral setting of the opera.

Fred Astaire, George Gershwin, and Ira Gershwin, 1937
(Museum of the City of New York)

"Ira's gift for the more sophisticated lyric," Heyward later observed, "was exactly suited to the task of writing the songs for Sportin' Life." The song that most defines Sportin' Life's big-city condescension toward his country cousins is "It Ain't Necessarily So," which he leeringly delivers to the church folk on their picnic. The form of the song harks back to blues, with the repeated first line of each brief refrain, but Ira also found that George's musical accents formed the metrical pattern of a limerick, and he sensed that the irreverent poetic form was perfect for Sportin' Life's mockery of biblical fundamentalism:

Methus'lah lived nine hundred years,
Methus'lah lived nine hundred years,
But who calls dat livin',
When no gall'll give in
To no man what's nine hundred years?

Ira cast the entire lyric as a 1930s catalogue song, with Sportin' Life debunking one biblical tale after another, such as Moses in the bulrushes: "Ole Pharaoh's daughter / She fished him, she *says,* from dat stream."

Along with Sportin' Life's other great song, "There's a Boat Dat's Leavin' Soon for New York," Ira Gershwin was the primary lyricist for "A Redheaded Woman" and "Oh, I Can't Sit Down." He also worked

Sheet music for a 1924 song by the Gershwins that was later featured in a 1945 movie about the life of George Gershwin (Music Library, University of South Carolina)

closely with Heyward on "I Got Plenty o' Nuthin'," "I Loves You, Porgy," and "Oh Bess, Oh, Where's My Bess?" Ira insisted that Heyward share credit for "Bess, You Is My Woman Now," for while the Gershwins had worked the song out on their own, Ira maintained that he had used several lines from Heyward's libretto. Taking the broken grammar of the vernacular dialect, the lyric transforms it into soaring passion in such exchanges as Porgy's "Bess, you is my woman now, / You is, you is!" and Bess's response: "Porgy, I's yo' woman now! / I is, I is!" Beyond writing his own lyrics and collaborating with Heyward on others, Ira brought to bear on the production the mosaic art of the lyricist, fusing words with his brother's music into a seamless whole that makes *Porgy and Bess* the most enduring of American operatic works.

Like most songwriters, the Gershwins found work during the Depression by heading west to Hollywood. They leapt at the opportunity to write for movies starring Fred Astaire and Ginger Rogers, though some

Hollywood moguls were concerned that, after *Porgy and Bess,* the brothers were too "highbrow" for the movies. But the Gershwins immediately began to explore the genre of the movie musical during one of its most innovative periods. When songwriters wrote for the stage, they had to supply long notes—and open vowels—so that singers could sustain and project phrases to the back of the balcony. In Hollywood, however, where singers sang into a microphone (and frequently lip-synched on-screen to their own prerecorded songs), George Gershwin could write in an even more staccato (or, as he called it, "stenciled") style, and Ira could revel in the short vowels and clipped consonants that are more native to the English language. Writing for the 1937 movies *Shall We Dance* and *A Damsel in Distress,* Ira Gershwin could use such thorny title phrases as "Let's Call the Whole Thing Off," "Stiff Upper Lip," and "Nice Work if You Can Get It."

The Gershwins also used the introductory verse of a song to bridge the gap from spoken dialogue to the singing of the refrain. In the verse for "Things Are Looking Up," from *A Damsel in Distress,* Ira had Astaire apologize for the transition from talking to singing:

> If I should suddenly start to sing,
> Or stand on my head—or anything,
> Please don't think that I've lost my senses;
> It's just that my happiness finally commences.

Even in the refrain, Astaire still seems to be chatting rather than singing:

> Things are looking up!
> I've been looking the landscape over,
> And it's covered with four-leaf clover.

In such movie-song lyrics Ira Gershwin captured the urbane nonchalance that was the hallmark of Astaire's style.

Writing together in Hollywood, Ira and George Gershwin's collaboration grew as intertwined as their lives. "Give me an Irish verse," Ira would ask his mercurial brother, and then marvel as George instantly played a melody that had exactly "the wistful loneliness I meant." When Ira fitted that melody with the words "A foggy day in London," George offered to add another note, which Ira set with "Town," giving the lyric for "A Foggy Day" (1937) the same quaint loveliness as the melody. When George played a four-note phrase for "They Can't Take That Away from Me" (1937), Ira asked for two more notes to accommodate the line "The way you wear your hat" and then added other, wryly tender images, such as "The way you hold your knife" and "The way you sing off-key."

The very difficulties of George Gershwin's "stenciled style" by now had come to inspire his brother. When George started out a melody for "They All Laughed" (1937) with a ten-note phrase, Ira responded with a ten-syllable line: "They all laughed at Christopher Columbus." Then George's melody shortened to seven syllables, and Ira truncated the next line accordingly: "When he said the world was round." George repeated the same initial ten-note phrase, and Ira followed with a parallel ten-syllable line: "They all laughed when Edison recorded." But where another composer would then have given his lyricist another parallel seven-note line, George abruptly stopped short on one note—and Ira stopped with him: "Sound!" While Ira sometimes complained that his brother's tricky rhythms gave a lyricist little room to "turn around," he clearly used those tiny confines inventively.

For "Love Is Here to Stay," used in the 1938 movie *The Goldwyn Follies,* Ira asked George to supply extra notes, deftly placed in the melody, so that he could add the simplest of words:

> The radio *and* the telephone
> *And* the movies that we know
> May just be passing fancies—
> *And* in time may go.

This lovely song was to be the brothers' last. Before they could complete it, George Gershwin died suddenly, on 11 July 1937, from a brain tumor, at only thirty-eight years of age.

Ira Gershwin, who had always guided and protected the younger brother he regarded as the true genius in the family, was devastated by the loss of George. For years, he could not write at all; then, gradually, friends such as Kern and Arlen eased him out of exile. Finally, on New Year's Day 1940, Ira received a call from playwright Moss Hart, inviting him to collaborate on an experimental "play with music" with Weill. *Lady in the Dark* (1941) concerned a brilliant and successful businesswoman, Liza Elliot (played by Gertrude Lawrence in the original stage production), who finds herself coming apart emotionally and seeks out psychiatric help. As she lay on the analyst's couch, the lights would dim, the stage would revolve, and realism would give way to musical fantasy.

For the surreal scenes set in Liza's subconscious, Ira Gershwin wrote such bizarrely brilliant lyrics as "Tchaikowsky (And Other Russians)," in which newcomer Danny Kaye rattled off a song that consisted almost entirely of the names of forty-nine Russian composers. The lyric was actually a piece of light verse Ira had written years before when, browsing through his brother's sheet music, he was bemused by the many advertisements for the music of Russian composers and wove their names into dipodic verse (in which strong and moderately strong beats alternate with weaker ones):

> There's Malichevsky, Rubinstein, Arensky, and Tchaikowsky,
> Sapelnikoff, Dimitrieff, Tscherepnin, Kryjanowsky,
> Godowsky, Arteiboucheff, Moniuszko, Akimenko,
> Solovieff, Prokofieff, Tiomkin, Korestchenko.

Now, in *Lady in the Dark,* the number brought down the house each night and made Kaye, who delivered it in increasingly faster time, a star.

By contrast, Ira Gershwin could work equally dazzling lyrical effects with the simplest of words. In one of her fantasy sequences, Liza encounters a man who feels he has known her in a previous life, and that mix of reincarnation and déjà vu gives an unusual twist to the formulaic song of falling in love at first sight:

Sheet music for the last song George and Ira Gershwin wrote before George's death on 11 July 1937 (from Marion Short,
Covers of Gold, *1998)*

With you I used to roam
Through the Pleasure Dome
Of Kubla Khan. . . .
I lost you through the centuries.
I find you once again. . . .

As the verse leads into the chorus, Ira takes the simple title phrase, "This Is New," and weds it to Weill's musical phrase, which consists of an F, followed by an F#, so that the word "This" is followed by the same sound in "is," but the *s* in "is" is voiced so that it sounds like *z*, the linguistic equivalent of a musical progression from a note to its sharp: "Th*is is* new." He then weaves those verbal chromatics through the chorus as deftly as Weill manipulates his musical intervals, from "I wa*s* merely exi*s*ting" through "I*s* it Venu*s* in*s*isting?" to the final alterations of "Life i*s* bli*ss* and th*is is* new." Thus, with the simplest of

syllables, Ira created a pattern of shifting sounds that enhances the eerie sensation of newness with sameness.

Perhaps Ira Gershwin's most extraordinary achievement in *Lady in the Dark* was to integrate a lyric—indeed, the art of the lyric itself—into Moss Hart's play. During her therapy sessions, Liza struggles to recall the words to a melody remembered from childhood, a melody that plays as a haunting leitmotif throughout the show. The psychiatrist keeps trying to get her to remember the words, feeling that if she can recall them, her cure will begin. Ira saw in her effort to bring the deepest layers of the unconscious to consciousness a parallel to the art of the lyricist, who similarly struggles to find words that will articulate the emotional significance buried in a musical pattern. Liza finally recalls and sings the simple but haunting song "My Ship" at the end of *Lady in the*

*Sheet music for a song from a 1954 motion-picture musical on which
Ira Gershwin collaborated with his old friend Harold Arlen
(from Marion Short,* The Gold in
Your Piano Bench, *1997)*

Dark, concluding the most fully integrated score he had ever written for a Broadway musical.

Such integration, along with Richard Rodgers and Lorenz Hart's *Pal Joey* (1940), anticipated Rodgers and Hammerstein's *Oklahoma!* (1943), which made integration of song with story line the watchword on Broadway from then on. Ira Gershwin, however, played no further role in the development of the American musical. His two other shows, *The Firebrand of Florence* (1945) and *Park Avenue* (1946), failed primarily because of weak books. Unlike Hammerstein and such younger lyricists as Frank Loesser and Alan Jay Lerner, Ira never wrote both book and lyrics for a musical. The consummate specialist and collaborator, he said he "never tried his hand at a script" because he was "no expert at the other man's game."

Instead, Ira Gershwin remained in California. When he, his wife, and George had moved there in 1936, they bought a house at 1019 North Roxbury Drive in Beverly Hills. In 1941 Ira and Lee Gershwin bought the house next door at 1023 Roxbury Drive, which became known as the Gershwin "Plantation," a haven for songwriters and movie performers. After all the housing moves of his youth, Ira cherished his home, seldom venturing beyond it except to work on songs for Hollywood movies. Some of these, such as "Long Ago (And Far Away)," which he wrote with Kern for *Cover Girl* (1944), starring Gene Kelly, were successful, and others marked genuine advances in the Hollywood musical. For *Where Do We Go from Here?* (1945), Ira and Weill wrote a miniature operetta that included such witty patter numbers as "Song of the Rhineland":

Leonore and Ira Gershwin at their Beverly Hills home, 14 June 1959 (The Gershwin Trusts)

Where the wine is winier,
And the Rhine is Rhinier,
And the Heine's Heinier,
And what's yours is minier!

While he worked with many great composers in Hollywood, however, Ira never again established the kind of long-term collaborative relationship he had had with his brother.

For some movies, such as *The Shocking Miss Pilgrim* (1947), Ira Gershwin even tried, with the help of composer Kay Swift, setting lyrics to previously unused or fragmentary melodies George had left behind in manuscripts and notebooks. Such a ghostly collaboration produced some tenderly romantic ballads, such as "For You, for Me, for Evermore," as well as a witty satire on Boston manners, "The Back Bay Polka":

No song except a hymn—
And keep your language prim:
You call a leg a "limb"
Or they boot you out of Boston.

Ira Gershwin's work in movie musicals culminated in *A Star Is Born* (1954), on which he worked with composer Arlen and playwright Moss Hart to integrate songs fully into the story. Even though Judy Garland plays a singer and presents each song as a performance, the lyrics are closely tied to her character and the dramatic context. In the greatest of these songs, Ira had to work with what Arlen called one of his "tapeworms"—an unusually long and intricately structured melody. In one of the few times a title came easily to him, Ira murmured, on first hearing the melody, "The Man That Got Away." Taking the most hackneyed of romantic images, he laced them with harsh alliteration that matched Arlen's biting musical accents:

The night is bitter,
The stars have lost their glitter,
The winds grow colder
And suddenly you're older—
And all because of the man that got away.

The rhymes in the lyric are either starkly simple or embedded in catchphrases: "The man that *won* you / Has *run* off and *un*done you." Some are by-products of Ira's characteristic play with contractions and suffixes: "The road gets rougher, / It's lonelier and tougher." At the climax of this torch song, the double rhymes seem to build up: "With hope you burn up– / Tomorrow he may turn up." But then he drops rhyme altogether for a prosaic wail whose poetic power comes from two colloquial compound words: "There's just no *letup* the *live-long* night and day!"

"The Man That Got Away," one of Ira Gershwin's greatest lyrics, was also his swan song. By the mid 1950s a new musical style was taking over popular music, and the Hollywood studios were dismantling their musical-production units in the face of competition from the new medium of television. Except for a brief stint writing lyrics for three of George's unused melodies for *Kiss Me, Stupid* (1964), a darkly comic movie directed by Billy Wilder, Ira spent his time being what his brother George had always called him–"Ira, the scholar." He edited manuscripts and other Gershwin papers (his own as well as George's); compiled a collection of his own lyrics, *Lyrics on Several Occasions;* and helped to establish archives at the Library of Congress and the Museum of the City of New York. On 17 August 1983 Ira Gershwin died as quietly, peacefully, and pleasantly as he had lived, shortly after eating some of his favorite chocolates.

Biography:

Philip Furia, *Ira Gershwin: The Art of the Lyricist* (New York: Oxford University Press, 1996).

References:

Philip Furia, *The Poets of Tin Pan Alley: A History of America's Great Lyricists* (New York: Oxford University Press, 1990), pp. 126–152;

Thomas S. Hischak, *Word Crazy: Broadway Lyricists from Cohan to Sondheim* (New York: Praeger, 1991), pp. 45–54;

William G. Hyland, *The Song Is Ended: Songwriters and American Music, 1900–1950* (New York: Oxford University Press, 1995), pp. 77–88, 109–121, 136–145, 221–234;

Edward Jablonski, *Gershwin* (New York: Doubleday, 1987);

Jablonski and Lawrence D. Stewart, *The Gershwin Years* (Garden City, N.Y.: Doubleday, 1958; revised and enlarged, 1973);

Robert Kimball and Alfred Simon, *The Gershwins* (New York: Atheneum, 1973);

Deena Rosenberg, *Fascinating Rhythm: The Collaboration of George and Ira Gershwin* (New York: Dutton, 1991).

Papers:

Ira Gershwin's manuscripts, letters, and other papers are deposited at the Library of Congress and at the Ira and Leonore Gershwin Trusts in Los Angeles. Additional papers can be found at the Museum of the City of New York and the University of Texas at Austin.

Selected Discography:

Michael Feinstein, *Pure Gershwin,* Elektra, 60742-1, 1987;

Funny Face, London studio cast, Smithsonian, R 019, 1980;

Gershwin Rarities, Citadel, 7017, 1979;

Frances Gershwin Godowsky, *Frances Gershwin: For George and Ira,* Monmouth Evergreen, MES/7060, ca. 1973;

Ira Gershwin Loves to Rhyme, Mark 56 Records, 721, 1976;

Lady, Be Good!, London studio cast, Smithsonian, R 008, 1977;

Lady in the Dark, original Broadway cast, Columbia, COS 2390, n.d.;

Oh, Kay!, London studio cast, Smithsonian, R 011, 1978;

Oh, Kay!/Girl Crazy/Of Thee I Sing, Time-Life, AM09, 1982;

Porgy and Bess, original Broadway cast, Odyssey, 32 36 0018, 1968;

Bobby Short, *Bobby Short is K-ra-zy for Gershwin,* Atlantic, 2-608, 1973;

A Star Is Born, motion-picture soundtrack, Columbia Harmony, HS-11366, ca. 1960s;

Starring Fred Astaire, Columbia, SG-32472, 1973;

We Like a Gershwin Tune, Monmouth Evergreen, MES-7061, ca. 1973.

Haven Gillespie

(6 February 1888 – 3 March 1975)

Shannon D. McCreery
University of North Carolina at Wilmington

SELECTED SONGS FROM THEATRICAL PRODUCTIONS: *The Jollies of 1922* (1922), music by Egbert Van Alstyne–"Oo-La-La";

The Passing Show of 1923 (1923), music by Van Alstyne–"Nearer and Dearer";

Earl Carroll's Vanities (1932), music by Charles Rosoff and Henry Tobias–"Along Came Love"; "Somebody Sweet"; "Who Needs the Moonlight When You Got Somebody to Love";

Earl Carroll's Vanities (1934)–"I've Taken a Likin' To You" (lyrics and music by Gillespie, Rosoff, Charles Tobias, and Henry Tobias);

Hollywood Holiday (1935)–"Dream Shadows" (lyric and music by Gillespie, J. Fred Coots, and Mitchell Parish).

SELECTED SONGS FROM MOTION-PICTURE PRODUCTIONS: *Girl of the Golden West* (1923), music by Charley L. Cooke–"Girl of the Golden West"; "Weddin' Blues";

Secrets (1924)–"Secrets" (lyric and music by Gillespie, Egbert Van Alstyne, and Al Sobler).

SELECTED SONGS PUBLISHED INDEPENDENTLY OF THEATRICAL OR MOTION-PICTURE PRODUCTIONS: "Harbor of Love" (1917), music by Henry Marshall;

"Old Kentucky Moonlight" (1920), music by Egbert Van Alstyne;

"Right or Wrong" (1921), music by Arthur L. Sizemore;

"You're in Kentucky Sure as You're Born" (1923), lyric and music by Gillespie, George A. Little, and Larry Shay;

"Drifting and Dreaming" (1925), music by Van Alstyne, Erwin R. Schmidt, and Loyal Curtis;

"Breezin' along with the Breeze" (1926), lyric and music by Gillespie, Seymour Simons, and Richard A. Whiting;

"Beautiful" (1927), music by Shay;

"Tin Pan Parade" (1927), music by Whiting;

"Honey" (1928), lyric and music by Gillespie, Simons, and Whiting;

"Who Wouldn't Be Jealous of You?" (1928), music by Shay;

"Fiddlin' Joe" (1929), music by Mabel Wayne;

"Do Ya Love Me Just a Little Bit, Do Ya?" (1930), music by Wayne;

"Let Me Kiss Your Tears Away" (1930), music by Van Alstyne;

"Sleepy Town Express" (1930), lyric and music by Gillespie;

"Fool Me Some More" (1930), lyric and music by Gillespie;

"Beautiful Love" (1931), music by Victor Young, Wayne King, and Van Alstyne;

"By the Sycamore Tree" (1931), music by Pete Wendling;

"Sweetest Little Kid" (1931), lyric and music by Gillespie and Lamont Gillespie;

"Santa Claus Is Comin' to Town" (1934), music by J. Fred Coots;

"Louisiana Fairy Tale" (1935), lyric by Gillespie and Mitchell Parish, music by Coots;

"Whose Honey Are You?" (1935), music by Coots;

"It's the Little Things That Count" (1938), music by Simons;

"Let's Stop the Clock" (1938), music by Coots;

"There's Honey on the Moon Tonight" (1938), lyric by Gillespie and Mack David, music by Coots;

"You Go to My Head" (1938), music by Coots;

"The Old Master Painter" (1945), music by Beasley Smith;

"Stay as Long as You Like" (1947), music by Larry Vincent;

"They're Laying Down the Law Today" (1947), music by Vincent;

"Winky Blinky Peek-a-Boo" (1947), music by Vincent;

"That Lucky Old Sun" (1949), music by Smith;

"God's Country" (1950), music by Smith;

"Kiss" (1952), music by Lionel Newman;

"You Happened to Me" (1956), music by Coots;

"It Takes So Long to Say Goodbye" (1958), music by Shay;

"This Holy Love" (1958), lyric and music by Gillespie.

Haven Gillespie, holding the sheet music of his song "Santa Claus Is Comin' to Town" (1934), with his grandchildren, James and Carole Gillespie, 1930s (from William E. First, Drifting and Dreaming, *1998)*

Haven Gillespie, best known for writing the lyrics to the holiday standard "Santa Claus Is Comin' to Town" (1934) and "You Go to My Head" (1938), was more than a two-hit wonder. A consistent songwriter, Gillespie wrote more than a thousand songs, eventually securing a place in the Songwriters' Hall of Fame. An uneducated, untrained risk taker with the ability to play music by ear, the tenacious and prolific Gillespie once likened his career to trying to beat gambling odds. "A songwriter is like a race horse," he said. "If they bet on you once and you lose, they won't bet on you again." His persistence and enduring talent enabled him to live and die a professional songwriter whose music is still being recorded.

James Haven Gillespie was born to William and Anna (Riley) Gillespie on 6 February 1888 in Covington, Kentucky—a river town neighboring Cincinnati, Ohio. One of nine children, Haven grew up poor, hailing from an Irish clan notorious for having music in

their blood and, according to William First in *Drifting and Dreaming: The Story of Songwriter Haven Gillespie* (1998), "whiskey bottles all over the house." Haven's older brother, Irwin, was musically trained and played the calliope on the *Island Queen* riverboat that tooled up and down the Ohio River. While Haven received no formal musical training and dropped out of school in the fourth grade (poverty forced most of the Gillespie children to leave school to work), Irwin's success and local notoriety inspired Haven to dream of a career in music.

As a child, Haven was enterprising in taking odd jobs to earn money. He swatted flies off horses and ran errands for his Uncle Frank, who owned a saloon. Gillespie knew he needed a professional trade, however. His first real job was working as a printer's devil at the Cuneo Press in Chicago, where he had moved upon encouragement from his older sister Lillian, who had relocated there in 1920. In Chicago, Gillespie

*Gillespie and his wife, Corene Parker Gillespie, on their honeymoon
in Chicago, 1909 (from William E. First,*
Drifting and Dreaming, *1998)*

received not only an early exposure to the printed word
but also an informal introduction to the music of Tin
Pan Alley. Gillespie worked at Cuneo for five years
until the Printer's Union went on strike, forcing him to
return to Kentucky, where he wooed his neighborhood
sweetheart, Corene Parker. They married on 9 March
1909 and returned to Chicago, where Gillespie continued to work as a printer while moonlighting as a song
peddler.

Initially, Gillespie had little luck in the songwriting business, and Corene, pregnant with their first and
only child, Lamont (born 10 January 1910), desired the
security and familiarity of Kentucky. In 1910 the family
returned home. Gillespie, temporarily putting his songwriting dreams aside, worked at the *Cincinnati Times-
Star.* While the Gillespies preferred life in the Ohio
River valley, his career often required that they live
elsewhere, including New York, Chicago, and Los
Angeles. Cincinnati, a short jaunt across the river from
Gillespie's native Covington, Kentucky, had an active
music and theater scene. In 1911 he collaborated with
Roy Stevenson and published seven songs on the Keith
vaudeville circuit, including "You're the Girl I've Met
in My Dreams," "When I'm Gone," and "Winter Time
Is Coming around Too Soon." Locally, Gillespie's
songwriting reputation soon spread, and he developed
a relationship with Louis Mentel—owner of a road-

house, ragtime composer, and president of the Associated Music Company in Cincinnati. Besides writing
songs, Gillespie was also known for frequenting saloons
such as the one owned by Mentel. Not surprisingly,
Mentel and his organization were first to support
Gillespie, publishing many of his early lyrics—some of
them heard for the first time at Mentel's roadhouse
after a few rounds of drinks. During this period
Gillespie also sought the help of his brother Irwin, who
taught him to read and write music. While Cincinnati's
vaudeville scene kept Gillespie busy, he was still unable
to make a steady living writing music. Doggedly, he
kept his day job at the *Cincinnati Times-Star.* Charles
Phelps Taft, the publisher of the newspaper, took an
interest in Gillespie's musical career and helped him get
a job at *The New York Times.* There, Gillespie could be at
the center of the songwriting business—Tin Pan Alley.

With only $80 in his pocket and holes in his
shoes, Gillespie moved Corene and their son to
Brooklyn. He plugged his music on the streets of New
York from eleven o'clock in the morning until five
o'clock in the evening, when he would then head off
to work the third shift as a printer for the *Times.* Often
he was so poor that he could not afford the trolley fare
to get to work. Rough times such as these most likely
inclined Gillespie to hang on to his membership in the
International Typographic Union for sixty-seven
years. When he could not support himself in the songwriting business, he could always return to printing.
Eventually, Gillespie forged connections in New York.
He met with vaudeville composer Henry Marshall,
and the duo collaborated on patriotic tunes popular
during World War I, including "Harbor of Love"
(1917), "Somebody's Going to Get the Bee," and "Go
Lad and May God Bless You." Just as Gillespie's luck
was improving, the influx of polio in New York City
frightened Corene. Once again, the Gillespies relocated, this time to Chicago, where Gillespie resumed
employment at Cuneo and managed the Majestic
movie theater at night.

While Gillespie had not made any money in
New York, he had begun a valuable relationship with
the Remick Publishing Company, which also had
offices in Chicago. Nearly broke, Gillespie showed up
at Remick's one day to check on his royalty payments.
Much to his surprise, he was handed a check for
$12,000 (Gillespie's salary at that time was around
$1,000 a year). "Harbor of Love" had made it to num-
ber three on the pop charts. He quit Cuneo immediately. After this stroke of luck, Gillespie took another
gamble and began to plug his songs full-time on the
streets of Chicago.

Another important connection, perhaps
Gillespie's biggest, was forged in 1919 when Egbert

Sheet music for Gillespie's favorite of his own songs, published in 1925
(Bruccoli Clark Layman Archives)

Van Alstyne, a well-established Tin Pan Alley figure, became his mentor. Through Van Alstyne, Gillespie gained exposure to the intricacies of the songwriter's craft. According to First, Van Alstyne taught Gillespie to "write around the vowels" and never to "end a line on M or S because if you spit on the orchestra leader he'll louse up your act." Van Alstyne and Gillespie then collaborated on a series of successful songs, including "Old Kentucky Moonlight" (1920) as well as songs for musical revues, such as "Oo-La-La" for *The Jollies of 1922* (1922) and "Nearer and Dearer" for *The Passing Show of 1923* (1923). Gillespie later teamed up with Charley L. Cooke to write "Weddin' Blues" and "Girl of the Golden West" for Edwin Carewe's silent movie of the same name in 1923.

Often Gillespie wrote his lyrics in short bursts, sometimes while riding the trolley. "You're in Kentucky Sure as You're Born" was created in such a fashion in 1923 and later became the first of Gillespie's songs to sell more than a million records. In 1925 he wrote his own personal favorite, "Drifting and Dreaming," with Van Alstyne, Erwin R. Schmidt, and Loyal Curtis. "Drifting and Dreaming" became the signature song for noted bandleader Orin Tucker. Gillespie published eighty-eight songs in the eight years he lived in Chicago. Al Jolson popularized "Breezin' along with the Breeze," which Gillespie wrote in 1926 with Seymour Simons and Richard A. Whiting. With its jaunty rhythm and colloquial lyrics, "Breezin' along with the Breeze" was interpolated into several motion pictures, such as *Pete Kelly's Blues* (1955) and *The Helen Morgan Story* (1957). In 1929 Rudy Vallee made a hit out of "Honey" (1928), which Gillespie, again collaborating with Simons and Whiting, wrote for Corene as a twentieth-anniversary present. Both songs exemplify the lessons in vowel and consonant placement Gillespie had absorbed from Van Alstyne. "Honey" alternates between masculine rhymes of a single accented syllable with long open vowels (*too*/*do*/*true*) and two-syllable feminine rhymes with the same nasal consonant and closed vowels on unaccented syllables (hon*ey*/fun*ny*/sun*ny*). In "Breezin' along with the Breeze" he places the same long vowels on accented notes to bring out the melodic pattern in "*trail*in' the *rails* / the *sky* is the only roof *I* have / Mother *Na*ture *makes* me a bed."

Gillespie had by this time made a name for himself on Tin Pan Alley, but, like many other songwriters during this period, he saw the future of music gravitating to Hollywood with the advent of sound movies. Once again the Gillespies decided to take a gamble and made a move to the West Coast. Old friend and collaborator Whiting had signed with Paramount Studios. Neil Moret, another long-standing connection for Gillespie, had opened the first West Coast music publishing company in San Francisco. With Moret, Gillespie wrote for several movies, including *The Last Dance* (1930), *Varsitans* (1931), and *Peacock Alley* (1930). Mabel Wayne, a talented composer, teamed up with Gillespie to create the songs "Fiddlin' Joe" and "Do Ya Love Me Just a Little Bit, Do Ya?"

In 1929 Disney Studios pursued Gillespie because they liked his catchy lyrics and thought he had a penchant for novelty and children's tunes. Gillespie preferred the independence of freelance work, however, and refused Disney's handsome offer. In the meantime he wrote "Sleepy Town Express" (1930), whose playful lyrics foreshadow those in "Santa Claus Is Comin' to Town." Despite Gillespie's success, the lush life in Hollywood did not sit well with his modest personal style. Homesick and unwilling to lock himself into binding studio contracts, he returned to what was familiar: Kentucky and the printing press. Back home, Gillespie had more energy to devote to his two careers and eventually merged them by forming the Gillespie Publishing Company. He published his own work, including a song he had written years earlier with Van Alstyne, "Let Me Kiss Your Tears Away" (1930). While having his own publishing company was convenient, Gillespie dabbled in publishing more as a lark than a serious business venture.

In 1930 he wrote more successful songs. Among them was "Fool Me Some More." Then, reunited with Van Alstyne in 1931, Gillespie created the lyric for the hit "Beautiful Love," which was popularized by Bing Crosby and used in the movie *Sing a Jingle* (1943). Gillespie also collaborated with his son, Lamont, during this period on the song "Sweetest Little Kid" (1931), as well as with Charles Rosoff and Henry Tobias on songs for *Earl Carroll's Vanities,* starring Milton Berle. Songs from this 1932 show included "Along Came Love," "Somebody Sweet," and "Who Needs the Moonlight When You Got Somebody to Love."

On 18 September 1934 Gillespie's brother Irwin, his music teacher and inspiration, died suddenly of bronchial pneumonia. Gillespie was on his way to New York at the time, ready to peddle another portfolio of songs. A few days later, in New York City, Edgar Bittner of Leo Feist commissioned him to write a children's song for Christmas. The sheet-music publishers had been impressed with "Sleepy Town Express" and his other two children's songs, "Sweetest Little Kid" and "Tin Pan Parade" (1927), which he cowrote with Whiting. Gillespie resisted, arguing that September was too late to be writing a song for December, especially since the song could easily be forgotten after the holidays. Bittner persisted, however, and Gillespie recalled the assignment as one "Any songwriter would have traveled on his hands and knees from Hollywood to Timbuktu to get." He was still doubtful, though, about his ability to write a happy holiday lyric with Irwin's death heavy on his mind. He and composer J. Fred Coots caught the subway to begin their collaboration for the holiday tune. As they headed uptown, Coots recited the street names to Gillespie as they passed by, hoping they would trigger an idea. Gillespie's creative wheels began to turn as he recalled Christmases past and his mother's admonition, "If you don't wash behind your ears, Haven, Santa won't come to see you. You better be good." He pulled a soggy piece of paper out of his shoe, which he had placed there to soak up the dampness from the New York streets, and began to write. By the time they reached Forty-ninth Street, the lyrics for "Santa Claus Is Comin' to Town," Gillespie's best-known song, were complete. Although promotional manager Johnny White at Feist accused Gillespie of throwing "corn all over Broadway," Bittner loved the playful nature of the song and Gillespie's clever use of onomatopoeia in such lines as "With little tin horns and little toy drums / Rooty-toot-toots and rummy-tum-tums." The song aired on Eddie Cantor's 1934 Thanksgiving Day radio show because Cantor's wife liked it so well. "Santa Claus Is Comin' to Town" was an overnight sensation, eventually selling twenty-five thousand copies a day. For Gillespie, however, the

Sheet music for Gillespie and J. Fred Coots's standard 1934 Christmas song
(Bruccoli Clark Layman Archives)

success was bittersweet. He could not get over the loss of his brother.

After the financial success of "Santa Claus Is Comin' to Town," Gillespie was able to spend more time in Kentucky while also maintaining his reputation in such larger venues as Chicago and New York. In Covington a favorite haunt was Kern Aylward's saloon. Gillespie had long regarded alcohol as an aid to his creativity, and Aylward's saloon became a sort of workshop for him. One night in 1936, staring at a row of bourbon bottles at the saloon, Gillespie noted that the bottle "can get you as crazy as the girl you can't get." Minutes later he

began composing the seductive lyrics of "You Go to My Head," a tune that compares love to a slow, sweet intoxication:

> You go to my head and you linger like a haunting refrain
> And I find you spinning 'round in my brain
> Like the bubbles in a glass of champagne.

Here Gillespie borrows the image of a "haunting refrain" that "runs around my brain" from Irving Berlin's "A Pretty Girl Is Like a Melody" (1919) but fuses it with the alcoholic imagery implicit in the catchphrase title.

In the second section of the lyric Gillespie comes down in elegance from champagne to ordinary wine and a strong American potable:

> You go to my head like a sip of sparkling Burgundy brew
> And I find the very mention of you
> Like the kicker in a julep or two.

Although he drops the alcoholic imagery in the release, he returns to it subtly in the final section by reminding listeners that alcohol, like mercury, rises in thermometers:

> You go to my head with a smile that makes my temperature rise,
> Like a summer with a thousand Julys,
> You intoxicate my soul with your eyes.

The crisp consonants of "intoxicate" then slide into the mellifluous *m, s,* and *l* sequence around the long open and closed vowels.

With the lyric completed, Gillespie felt inspired to contact Coots in New York. Coots happened to have a wordless piece of music that fit Gillespie's lyrics. Because of a ban against songs that mentioned alcohol—a holdover from Prohibition, which ended in 1933—it was several years before the song made it to the radio. Billie Holiday, Peggy Lee, Lena Horne, and other singers made this torch song a standard, and it became Gillespie's second biggest hit after "Santa Claus Is Comin' To Town." Historians and critics consider this to be, stylistically, Gillespie's pinnacle piece. It peaked on the charts at number three in 1938. It was also selected as one of the Golden One Hundred in *Variety Musical Cavalcade* (1962).

Gillespie's luck continued in 1938. He had two more top-twenty hits that year, "There's Honey on the Moon Tonight" and "Let's Stop the Clock." He was also honored by his native city of Covington with "Haven Gillespie Night," an outdoor concert featuring Sophie Tucker. It was a plentiful period for the songwriter, and he was drinking plentifully as well. The physical reality of his creative aid, the inspiration for the lyrics to one of his biggest hits, was catching up with him, however. Gillespie was deteriorating and arthritic, and he often took respite in Hot Springs, Arkansas, with Corene. The Gillespies were in Covington the summer of 1940, and Gillespie was still writing and drinking. Sobering up from a binge one day, he was inspired by the sun as it hit the bell towers of a local church near his backyard. He got the idea of plantation workers in cotton fields and wrote "That Lucky Old Sun" (1949). A year later, he took the lyrics to New York but could not find a composer.

With the advent of World War II, Gillespie returned to his old reliable standby, printing. He once again worked at the *Cincinnati Times-Star*. In comparison to his prolific song output during the 1930s, the 1940s were less eventful. He did enjoy some success, however. In addition to "That Lucky Old Sun," he had also written the lyrics to "The Old Master Painter" (1945)—a song that encapsulates a spiritual rendering of the sunset:

> The Old Master Painter from the far blue hills
> Painted the vi'lets and the daffodils,
> Did the scenery for the sunset show,
> Sprayed the silver in the moonlight glow.
> He tinted the murals on the summer skies,
> Painted the devil in my darlin's eyes,
> Did a Technicolor garden for a big bouquet,
> The Old Master Painter from the far blue hills.

In 1945 an old friend, Billy White at Feist Music in Cincinnati, suggested Gillespie meet with composer Beasley Smith, who then wrote the music for "The Old Master Painter." By 1950 the song was a hit, and Smith proved an invaluable connection during the rest of the decade. Another old friend, pianist and composer Larry Vincent, collaborated with Gillespie in 1947 and recorded three songs on Smith's Dot record label—"They're Laying Down the Law Today," "Winky Blinky Peek-a-Boo," and "Stay as Long as You Like"—but none of these songs was a major success.

In 1949 Gillespie retired from the printing business and began drinking even more heavily. Corene, fearful for his health, asked Smith if he would meet with Gillespie in Nashville to consider the lyrics for "That Lucky Old Sun." Smith told him that it would never amount to anything but reluctantly composed music for it. Gillespie took the song to New York, but his previous publishers told him it was too much like "Old Man River" to ever make the market. Mitch Miller at Mercury Records felt enthusiastic about the song, however. It was recorded in April 1950 by Frankie Laine and released in August. Three weeks later it jumped to number one and stayed on the charts for twenty-two weeks. Gillespie and Smith had also collaborated on another song shortly thereafter, "God's Country" (1950). Like "That Lucky Old Sun" and "The Old Master Painter," its focus is on nature: "Ain't I got the song of the robin? Ain't I got a roof in the sky? / Wonder why my heart keeps athrobbin', athrobbin'—a son of God's country am I." "God's Country" made the charts, was recorded by Al Jolson, and won a Freedom Foundation Award in 1951 for "preserving the American way of life." While Gillespie wrote a handful of successful songs in the late 1940s, fifteen of his songs failed

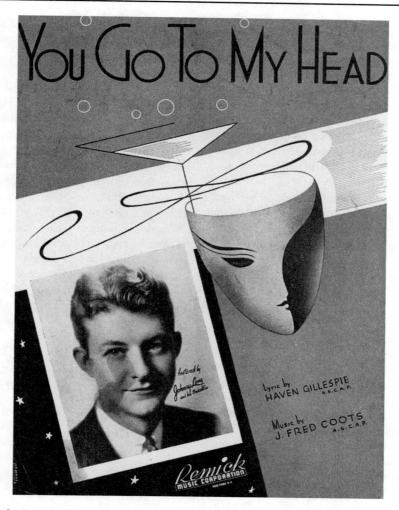

Sheet music for the 1938 Gillespie and Coots song that was introduced by Glen Gray and the Casa Loma Orchestra
(Bruccoli Clark Layman Archives)

to become popular, and the decade was, by and large, a series of unsuccessful ventures.

Despite Gillespie's stamina, he was feeling the effects of age and of years of drinking. At the age of sixty-two he grew so arthritic he could no longer play the piano. He thought a warmer climate would be good for his hands, so he and Corene once again moved out west. While life in Kentucky was comfortable, Gillespie had missed the connections of his friends who had stayed in Los Angeles and was excited about being there again. He and Corene moved into an apartment in Hollywood, and in two years he produced fifty-eight published songs. His collaborators included Max Steiner and Victor Young of Paramount, Larry Shay of M-G-M, Coots, and Smith. In 1952 Gillespie wrote the lyrics for a Marilyn Monroe feature motion picture, *Niagara,* released the next year. His song, "Kiss," was recorded by Monroe and released after her death in 1962. He continued to write at a prolific rate for the studios, but he also continued to drink heavily. "I always thought I had to be drunk to write," he said. "I thought I couldn't write sober." Corene, however, was in failing health and restless. On their way west, they had purchased property across from a hot spring in Las Vegas with the intent to retire there. Once again, in 1954, the Gillespies moved. Waiting to build on their property, they leased an apartment on the Vegas Strip. Gillespie welcomed release from the grind of studio deadlines, but the ease and convenience of casinos and bars did little to improve his relationship with alcohol. His drinking reached a point that it was taking a toll on Corene's health and their relationship. While Gillespie sought comfort in the bottle, she sought haven in the casinos. In 1956 and 1957 Gillespie was making about $50,000 annually, but, according to First in *Drifting and Dreaming,* Corene reportedly lost $70,000 during those same years on the slot machines.

Eventually, Gillespie was hospitalized for his drinking. He then joined Alcoholics Anonymous and remained sober for the last seventeen years of his life. "If I had a billion dollars," he said, "I would spend it to get people off alcohol." Sober, Gillespie surprised himself by writing three songs in 1957. Just as his early professional luck was offset by a personal tragedy when his brother Irwin died, he again encountered misfortune when Corene died of a heart attack in 1958. Gillespie was surprised to find he was not the beneficiary of her life insurance policy. She left everything to their son, Lamont, except for $500 in a white envelope for her husband. Desperate, Gillespie flew to New York to ask for an advance on his royalties. He was able to collect $15,000 in accumulated royalties and a $10,000 advance. Once back in Vegas, Gillespie met with Nat King Cole and gave him a copy of a new song, "This Holy Love" (1958) Cole recorded it for Capitol Records in 1958, and Dean Martin recorded another one of Gillespie's songs, "It Takes So Long to Say Goodbye." Gillespie subsisted on royalties and his retirement benefits from the printer's union. ("Santa Claus Is Comin' to Town" alone provided a substantial portion of his royalty income.) His restlessness never left him, however. Without Corene, Gillespie found Las Vegas unbearable and moved back to Covington, where he married Josephine Krumpelman in November 1962. He and his new bride (twenty-six years his junior) maintained dual residencies in Las Vegas and Covington. In order to give her a wedding gift, Gillespie sold his rights to "You Go to My Head" for $10,000. He continued writing and was excited about a collaboration with Coots on a new interpretation of their song "You Happened to Me" (1956), a song written in imitation of "You Go to My Head" and Cole Porter's "I've Got You Under My Skin." This collaborative effort brought only frustration, however. At age seventy-eight, Gillepie's health was rapidly deteriorating, and it destroyed his second marriage, which ended in divorce in 1968.

Haven Gillespie published his last song in 1972. Soon after, he was diagnosed with cancer. Prior to his death on 3 March 1975 he had arranged for his tombstone to read "Drifting and Dreaming"—the title to his favorite song. "Some of the modern singers are ruining my music," Gillespie said in later life, but in spite of this complaint his songs are still being recorded. "Right or Wrong" (1921) was popularized by George Strait in 1985 and received an ASCAP Nashville Country Song Award. That same year, "Santa Claus Is Comin' to Town," a song that never seems to tire of new interpretations, also received an award for being an ASCAP standard. A writer of more than one thousand songs, Gillespie's catchy and memorable lyrics made an indelible mark not only on Tin Pan Alley but on at least one generation of Americans.

Biography:

William E. First, *Drifting and Dreaming: The Story of Songwriter Haven Gillespie* (St. Petersburg, Fla.: Seaside, 1998).

Selected Discography:

Billie Holiday at Storyville, Black Lion, BLCD 760921, 1988;

The Four Lads, *Breezin' Along,* Columbia, CS 8035, 1959;

Mary Cleere Haran and Richard Rodney Bennett, *Pennies from Heaven: Movie Songs from the Depression Era,* Angel, 56625, 1998;

Frank Sinatra, *The Voice,* Golden Sounds, 1999.

Mack Gordon

(21 June 1904 – 1 March 1959)

Michael Lasser

Unless otherwise indicated, music is by Harry Revel.

SELECTED SONGS FROM THEATRICAL PRO-DUCTIONS: *Smiles* (1930)–"Time on My Hands, You in My Arms" (lyric by Gordon and Harold Adamson, music by Vincent Youmans);

Ziegfeld Follies of 1931 (1931)–"Help Yourself to Happiness" (lyric by Gordon and Harry Richman); "Cigarettes, Cigars!";

Everybody's Welcome (1931)–"I'm All Wrapped Up in You" (lyric by Gordon and Adamson); "One in a Million";

Fast and Furious (1931)–"Doing the Dumbbell"; "Fast and Furious"; "Frowns"; "Hot Feet"; "Rumbatism"; "Shadows on the Wall"; "Walkin' on Air"; "Where's My Happy Ending" (lyric by Gordon and Adamson);

Meet My Sister (1931)–"Do Something Different"; "I Like You"; "I Stumbled Over You and Fell in Love"; "I've Fallen Out of Love"; "If You Want to Be Successful in the Cinema"; "Lonely Little Extras"; "There Will Be a Girl (There Will Be a Boy)";

Marching By (1932), music by Revel and Jean Gilbert–"Finery"; "For You"; "Forward March into My Arms"; "I've Gotta Keep My Eye on You"; "Leave It to Love"; "Light Up"; "On Through the Night"; "To the Victor Belongs the Spoils"; "We're on Our Way to Hell";

Smiling Faces (1932)–"Bootblack Blues"; "Bread and Kisses"; "Can't Get Rid of Me"; "Cane Dance"; "Do Say You Do" (lyric by Gordon and Adamson); "Falling Out of Love"; "In Havana"; "In a Little Stucco in the Sticks"; "It's Just an Old Spanish Custom"; "Landlord at My Door!"; "Poor Little, Shy Little, Demure Little Me"; "Quick Henry, the Flit!"; "Shakin' the Shakespeare"; "Smart Set"; "Something to Think About"; "Sport a Sport"; "Sweet Little Stranger"; "Thank

Mack Gordon (AP/Wide World Photos)

You, You're Welcome, Don't Mention It"; "Think of My Reputation."

SELECTED SONGS FROM MOTION-PICTURE PRODUCTIONS: *Pointed Heels* (1929)–"Ain'tcha" (music by Max Rich);

Sitting Pretty (1933)–"Did You Ever See a Dream Walking?"; "You're Such a Comfort to Me"; "Good Morning Glory";

Broadway Thru a Keyhole (1933)–"You're My Past, Present and Future"; "Doing the Uptown Lowdown";

The Gay Divorcee (1934)–"Don't Let It Bother You"; "Let's K-nock K-nees";

We're Not Dressing (1934)–"Love Thy Neighbor"; "Once in a Blue Moon"; "May I?"; "She Reminds Me of You"; "Good Night, Lovely Little Lady";

Shoot the Works (1934)–"With My Eyes Wide Open I'm Dreaming"; "Were Your Ears Burning?";

College Rhythm (1934)–"Stay as Sweet as You Are"; "Take a Number from One to Ten"; "College Rhythm"; "Let's Give Three Cheers for Love";

She Loves Me Not (1934)–"Straight from the Shoulder"; "I'm Hummin'–I'm Whistlin'–I'm Singin'";

Love in Bloom (1935)–"Here Comes Cookie" (music by Gordon); "My Heart Is an Open Book" (music by Gordon); "Got Me Doin' Things" (music by Gordon); "Let Me Sing You to Sleep with a Love Song";

Paris in the Spring (1935)–"Paris in the Spring";

Two for Tonight (1935)–"From the Top of Your Head to the Tip of Your Toes"; "Without a Word of Warning"; "Takes Two To Make a Bargain (What's the Answer–What's the Verdict–How's About It Baby?)"; "I Wish I Were Aladdin"; "Two for Tonight";

Stolen Harmony (1935)–"Would There Be Love?";

Big Broadcast of 1936 (1936)–"It's the Animal in Me";

Collegiate (1936)–"I Feel Like a Feather in the Breeze"; "You Hit the Spot";

Poor Little Rich Girl (1936)–"When I'm with You"; "Oh, My Goodness"; "You've Gotta Eat Your Spinach, Baby"; "But Definitely";

Stowaway (1936)–"Goodnight, My Love"; "One Never Knows, Does One?"; "You Gotta S-M-I-L-E to Be H-A-Double-P-Y";

Head over Heels in Love (1937)–"Through the Courtesy of Love"; "May I Have the Next Romance with You?"; "Looking around Corners for You";

You Can't Have Everything (1937)–"Please Pardon Us–We're in Love"; "Afraid to Dream"; "The Loveliness of You"; "Danger–Love at Work";

Wake Up and Live (1937)–"Never in a Million Years"; "There's a Lull in My Life"; "I'm Bubbling Over"; "Wake Up and Live"; "It's Swell of You";

Love and Hisses (1937)–"Sweet Someone"; "I Wanna Be in Winchell's Column";

Ali Baba Goes to Town (1937)–"Broadway's Gone Hawaiian"; "I've Got My Heart Set on You";

This Is My Affair (1937)–"I Hum a Waltz";

In Old Chicago (1937)–"In Old Chicago";

My Lucky Star (1938)–"I've Got a Date with a Dream"; "Could You Pass in Love?";

Love Finds Andy Hardy (1938)–"Meet the Beat of My Heart";

Sally, Irene and Mary (1938)–"Sweet as a Song";

Josette (1938)–"Where in the World?"; "In Any Language";

Rebecca of Sunnybrook Farm (1938)–"An Old Straw Hat";

Thanks for Everything (1938)–"Thanks for Ev'rything";

Rose of Washington Square (1939)–"I Never Knew Heaven Could Speak";

Down Argentine Way (1940), music by Harry Warren–"Down Argentina Way"; "Two Dreams Met";

Tin Pan Alley (1940), music by Warren–"You Say the Sweetest Things, Baby";

Young People (1940), music by Warren–"I Wouldn't Take a Million";

Star Dust (1940)–"Secrets in the Moonlight" (music by Gordon);

Johnny Apollo (1940)–"This Is the Beginning of the End" (music by Gordon);

Little Old New York (1940)–"In an Old Dutch Garden" (music by Wilhelm Grosz);

Sun Valley Serenade (1941), music by Warren–"Chattanooga Choo-Choo"; "I Know Why (And So-Do-You)"; "It Happened in Sun Valley";

That Night in Rio (1941), music by Warren–"I Yi Yi Yi Yi (I Like You Very Much)"; "Chica Chica Boom Chic"; "Boa Noite (Good Night)";

Week-End in Havana (1941), music by Warren–"Tropical Magic";

The Great American Broadcast (1941), music by Warren–"Long Ago Last Night";

Orchestra Wives (1942), music by Warren–"I've Got a Gal in Kalamazoo"; "Serenade in Blue"; "At Last";

Springtime in the Rockies (1942), music by Warren–"I Had the Craziest Dream";

Iceland (1942), music by Warren–"There Will Never Be Another You";

Song of the Islands (1942), music by Warren–"Sing Me a Song of the Islands";

Hello, Frisco, Hello (1943), music by Warren–"You'll Never Know";

Sweet Rosie O'Grady (1943), music by Warren–"My Heart Tells Me (Should I Believe My Heart?)";

Sweet and Low-Down (1944), music by James Monaco–"I'm Making Believe";

Pin-Up Girl (1944), music by Monaco–"Time Alone Will Tell"; "Once Too Often";

The Dolly Sisters (1945), music by Monaco–"I Can't Begin to Tell You";

Diamond Horseshoe (1945), music by Warren–"The More I See You"; "I Wish I Knew"; "In Acapulco";

Three Little Girls in Blue (1946), music by Josef Myrow–"You Make Me Feel So Young"; "Somewhere in the Night"; "On the Boardwalk (In Atlantic City)";

The Razor's Edge (1946)–"Mam'selle" (music by Edmund Goulding);

Mother Wore Tights (1947), music by Myrow–"You Do"; "Kokomo, Indiana";

When My Baby Smiles at Me (1948), music by Myrow–"By the Way"; "What Did I Do?";

Come to the Stable (1949)–"Through a Long and Sleepless Night" (music by Alfred Newman);

The Beautiful Blonde from Bashful Bend (1949), music by Myrow–"Every Time I Meet You";

It Happens Every Spring (1949), music by Myrow–"It Happens Every Spring";

Wabash Avenue (1950), music by Myrow–"Wilhelmina"; "Baby, Won't You Say You Love Me?"; "May I Tempt You with a Big Red Rosy Apple?";

Summer Stock (1950), music by Warren–"If You Feel Like Singing, Sing"; "Friendly Star";

Call Me Mister (1951), music by Sammy Fain–"I Just Can't Do Enough for You, Baby";

I Love Melvin (1953), music by Myrow–"A Lady Loves";

Young at Heart (1954)–"You, My Love" (music by Jimmy Van Heusen).

SELECTED SONGS PUBLISHED INDEPENDENTLY OF THEATRICAL OR MOTION-PICTURE PRODUCTIONS: "Such Is Life, Such Is Love" (1931);

"Underneath the Harlem Moon" (1932);

"I Played Fiddle for the Czar" (1932);

"Listen to the German Band" (1932);

"A Boy and a Girl Were Dancing" (1932);

"And So to Bed" (1932);

"An Orchid to You" (1933);

"It's Within Your Power" (1933);

"It Was a Night in June" (1933);

"A Tree Was a Tree" (1933);

"There's a Bluebird at My Window" (1933);

"A Star Fell Out of Heaven" (1936);

"To Mary, With Love" (1936);

"Speaking of Heaven" (1939), music by Jimmy Van Heusen;

"You Will Find Your Love in Paris" (1958), music by Guy LaFarge.

Mack Gordon turned out musical hits for Hollywood with almost machine-like regularity. In the 1930s, with composer Harry Revel, and in the 1940s, with composers Harry Warren and Josef Myrow, he wrote lyrics to nearly 120 hit songs, more than any other movie lyricist. Most of his best work was in the characteristic styles of the day–either generic romantic ballads or songs designed for the stars who introduced them. They were hummable and easily remembered but not complicated or especially sophisticated.

Born Morris Gittelson in Warsaw, Poland, on 21 June 1904, Gordon came to the United States with his family when he was three years old. His father, Benjamin, owned a grocery store in Brooklyn, where Mack attended elementary school. He went to high school in the Bronx and had odd jobs as a butcher boy, a runner for a Wall Street brokerage house, and an errand boy for a department store. He had one brother, Harry, who eventually worked at 20th Century-Fox, and a sister, Ida. Gordon's parents were horrified at the thought that he might want to enter show business, but he sang on street corners and acted in school plays. During World War I he was asked to sing in Times Square in New York for a Liberty Bond program. He eventually dropped out of school to appear as a boy soprano in Honey Boy Evans's Minstrels, until his voice changed. Later, he became an end man (occupying either end of the line of performers) in Gus Hill's touring minstrels. Because his parents were so upset when he joined a minstrel show, he called himself Mack Gordon.

Eventually, Gordon moved up to vaudeville as a singing comedian and began to write songs in his spare time. He first tried writing for the movies in the late 1920s. Although his initial attempt failed and he soon returned to New York, he and composer Max Rich wrote one song, "Ain'tcha," that Helen Kane introduced in the movie *Pointed Heels* (1929). Soon after his return, he and co-lyricist Harold Adamson put words to a melody by Vincent Youmans. Marilyn Miller introduced their song, "Time on My Hands, You in My Arms" in the 1930 Broadway musical *Smiles*. Youmans had scribbled some notes on the back of a restaurant menu while waiting for his date to return from the ladies' room, and Gordon and Adamson added the lyric afterward. Miller disliked the song, however, and refused to sing it. The producer of the musical, Florenz Ziegfeld, agreed with her. They finally decided to use it, but neither the song nor the show attracted any public interest. Only when Marion Harris recorded it successfully in England in 1930 and crooner Russ Columbo followed with an American release the following year did "Time on My Hands" become a standard.

Gordon met his major collaborator of the 1930s, composer Harry Revel, in the New York offices of Harms, Inc., an important song publisher. Billy Rockwell, the manager of music publishing for the company, urged the two men to try working together. According to one story, probably true in its outlines, Revel, just back from Europe, was improvising at the piano, and Gordon, just finishing a vaudeville tour of the Midwest, went over and began to sing, improvising lyrics as he went along. Suddenly Gordon shouted, "Gotta catch a boat!" and dashed out the door. Revel pursued him, found the boat, and an hour later was on board, heading up the Hudson River. Gor-

*Illustration by Alberto Vargas for the sheet music of one of the songs by Gordon and Harry Revel
featured in the* Ziegfeld Follies of 1931 *(from Marion Short,* Covers of Gold, *1998)*

don did not think much of songwriting as a career, how-ever, and did not want to do anything that might hurt his vaudeville bookings. It took most of the boat ride for Revel to convince him to try it.

During the next two weeks, while Gordon was appearing in Utica, New York, he and Revel wrote nine-teen songs together. Some versions of the story also say that Revel become Gordon's accompanist but eventually talked him into giving up vaudeville for full-time songwrit-ing. Indisputably, however, they cemented their partner-ship despite their differences. Revel was the more sophisticated of the two. He had been raised in London and had traveled in Europe many times.

Gordon and Revel wrote quickly and were extremely prolific, even at the start of their careers, when they had many more failures than successes. A studio press release from the mid 1930s reported they had no set method for working. As Gordon explained, "Sometimes Harry gets an idea for a tune and hums it to me, and

maybe I like it and write a lyric. Or maybe I get the idea, and we work it up from there. Or maybe one of us hits on a good title, and we get a song out of it. Or maybe it hap-pens some other way. But anyway, we write a song." Once they finished a song, Gordon would promote it. Revel said Gordon was "the best song demonstrator in the country . . . Look, you ask Bing Crosby. When it comes to taking suggestions on how to put a song across, Mack's the only man he ever listens to."

Revel and Gordon began their collaboration by writing their first hit, "Underneath the Harlem Moon" (1932). They had previously signed with Ziegfeld, who hired them to contribute songs to the *Ziegfeld Follies of 1931,* the first of six Broadway musicals in which their songs appeared and the last edition of the *Follies* produced by Ziegfeld before his death in 1932. Their songs for the *Fol-lies* included "Cigarettes, Cigars!," introduced by Ruth Etting, and "Help Yourself to Happiness," introduced by Harry Richman, who was also co-lyricist. That same year

Sheet music for four of Gordon's movie songs of the 1930s (upper left, right: Bruccoli Clark Layman Archives; bottom left, right: Collection of Paul Talbot)

Sheet music for Gordon and Harry Warren's song that was nominated for an
Academy Award in 1941 (Collection of Paul Talbot)

they wrote "Such Is Life, Such Is Love" for Etting and wrote their first Broadway score together for *Fast and Furious,* an all-black revue that ran for only six performances. In 1932 they wrote the scores for two more Broadway flops, *Marching By* and *Smiling Faces.* Revel and Gordon never again wrote for the stage, but they bounced back quickly. Later that same year they wrote "And So to Bed" and "I Played Fiddle for the Czar," introduced by the popular bandleader Ben Bernie. In 1933 they wrote "It's Within Your Power" and "An Orchid for You," dedicated to the gossip columnist and radio personality Walter Winchell, who had praised their early songs. In 1937 they honored him more directly with the song "I Wanna Be in Winchell's Column" for the movie *Love and Hisses.*

By 1933 musicals had established themselves as an important genre in the movies, mainly at Warner Bros. and M-G-M. Such musicals as *Broadway Melody* (1929), *42nd Street* (1933), and *Gold Diggers of 1933* (1933) had

been popular successes. Paramount Studios, eager to produce musicals of its own, offered Revel and Gordon a contract in 1933. Their first assignment was writing for *Sitting Pretty* (1933), featuring Ginger Rogers. The biggest hit from the movie, "Did You Ever See a Dream Walking?," was a typical Revel-Gordon collaboration and their first major song together. Gordon lacked the wit and inventiveness of such lyricists as Dorothy Fields and Frank Loesser, but he had their keen ear for the slangy rhythms of everyday American urban speech. He was also especially skillful at investing his lyrics with a punchy quality that made them feel both conversational and musical, especially when joined with Revel's bouncy tunes. "Did You Ever See a Dream Walking?" efficiently sets up a series of questions and answers that culminates in a happy ending. The song becomes personal only in the answers; its use of "Well, I did" even suggests a kind of self-satisfied one-upmanship:

Helen Forrest singing Gordon and Warren's "I Had the Craziest Dream" with Harry James and His Orchestra in Springtime in the Rockies *(1942) (from Tony Thomas,* Harry Warren and the Hollywood Musical, *1975)*

Did you ever see a dream walking?
Well, I did.
Did you ever hear a dream talking?
Well, I did.

Gordon relied on that kind of conversational turn of phrase in both the perky uptempo numbers and the romantic ballads he and Revel wrote throughout their collaboration.

Gordon's lyrics are smart-alecky and streetwise. The songs are sharp, quick, and breezy, often with titles that reveal an irreverent sense of humor. Because of their flirtatious and self-confident qualities, and because Gordon never took himself too seriously, they also feel youthful. He may have written in Hollywood, but he brought a New York sensibility to his compositions. Among the songs that demonstrate these attributes are "Let's K-nock K-nees" (from *The Gay Divorcee,* 1934), "Take a Number from One to Ten" (from *College Rhythm,* 1934), "Straight from the Shoulder" (from *She Loves Me Not,* 1934), "From the Top of Your Head to the Tip of Your Toes" (from *Two for Tonight,* 1935), "It's the Animal in Me" (from *Big Broadcast of 1936,* 1936), and "Never in a Million Years" (from *Wake Up and Live,* 1937). Perhaps the best of them is "You Make Me Feel So Young," written with Myrow in 1946 for the motion picture *Three Little Girls in Blue:*

The moment that you speak,
I wanna go play hide and seek!
I wanna go and bounce the moon
Just like a toy balloon.

"You Make Me Feel So Young" is more innocent than Gordon's usual streetwise lyrics, giddily transforming memories of childhood play into the delights of love.

At the same time, because Gordon usually wrote quickly and because he was reaching for the widest possible audience, most of his ballads tend to use abstract language. He did, however, return to certain allusions and references. He often wrote about dreaming, specifically how dreams become embodied and reachable. The word *dream* appears in at least a half dozen of his titles, and his lyrics often express the magical idea that the impossible can become real through love. In addition to "Did You Ever See a Dream Walking?," he wrote "With My Eyes Wide Open I'm Dreaming" for the movie *Shoot the Works* (1934), "I've Got a Date with a Dream" for *My Lucky Star* (1938), and "I Had the Craziest Dream" for *Springtime in the Rockies* (1942). He also wrote "I Wish I Were Aladdin" (for *Two for Tonight,* 1935), "I Never Knew Heaven Could Speak" (for *Rose of Washington Square,* 1939), and "There Will Never Be Another You" (for *Iceland,* 1942), which further develop the theme of fantasy becoming reality.

Darryl F. Zanuck, the head of production at 20th Century-Fox, was so impressed by Gordon and Revel's work that he arranged to have them write the score for the Fox musical *Broadway Thru a Keyhole* (1933). Their songs included "You're My Past, Present and Future," introduced by Columbo, and "Doing the Uptown Lowdown," a jazzy dance tune with an insinuating beat and an earthy, suggestive lyric. Like several similar songs that preceded it—the Gershwins' "Sweet and Low-Down" (1925), James

Gordon, Alice Faye, and Harry Warren on the set of Hello, Frisco, Hello *(1943) (from Tony Thomas,*
Harry Warren and the Hollywood Musical, *1975)*

McHugh and Dorothy Fields's "Doin' the New Low-Down" (1928), and Irving Berlin's "When the Folks High-Up Do That Mean Low-Down" (1930)—the music and lyrics reflect the embrace of jazz and the slang of the Harlem Renaissance of the 1920s.

Over the next seven years, Revel and Gordon contributed songs to more than thirty movies, including "Love Thy Neighbor" and "Once in a Blue Moon" in *We're Not Dressing* (1934), the title song for *College Rhythm,* and "It's the Animal in Me." Fourteen of their songs were featured on the radio program *Your Hit Parade* and three made the top spot—the title song for *Paris in the Spring* (1935); "When I'm with You," introduced by Shirley Temple and Tony Martin in *Poor Little Rich Girl* (1936); and "Goodnight, My Love," introduced by Alice Faye in *Stowaway* (1936). Among the other fourteen are "Without a Word of Warning" from *Two for Tonight,* "I Feel Like a Feather in the Breeze" and "You Hit the Spot" from *Collegiate* (1936), "Afraid to Dream" from *You Can't Have Everything* (1937), and "There's a Lull in My Life" from *Wake Up and Live.* Their Paramount contracts also allowed them to write songs for one picture a year for other studios. As a result, they wrote "Let's K-nock K-nees," sung by Betty Grable and Edward Everett Horton, and "Don't Let It Bother You" for *The Gay Divorcee,* and "Looking around Corners for You" and "May I Have the Next Romance with You?" for English star Jesse Matthews in *Head over Heels in Love* (1937). During those same years, Revel and

Gordon also wrote songs to be introduced by the stars under contract to Paramount. They wrote romantic ballads for Bing Crosby, who remained the most important musical star at Paramount for twenty-five years, and also provided songs regularly for such performers as Shirley Temple, Francis Langford, Alice Faye, Jack Oakie, and Jack Haley. Their songs for Crosby include "Love Thy Neighbor," "May I?" (also from *We're Not Dressing*), and "I Wish I Were Aladdin." For Temple, they wrote "When I'm with You," and another song for *Poor Little Rich Girl,* "You've Gotta Eat Your Spinach, Baby." On occasion, Gordon wrote both words and music. In 1935 he wrote "Here Comes Cookie" and "My Heart Is an Open Book" for *Love in Bloom,* and at 20th Century-Fox he wrote "This Is the Beginning of the End" in 1940 for *Johnny Apollo.*

Though Gordon was known as a jovial man with a penchant for practical jokes, he was also alleged to have treated his wives badly. He insulted them, was rarely home, and he was accused of striking Rose Gittler, his first wife, on several occasions. She divorced him in 1936. They had a son and a daughter. On 14 January 1939 Gordon married his second wife, the former Elizabeth Cook. They had one son, Roger, and divorced rancorously in 1949, the same year he legally changed his name to Mack Gordon.

When Gordon and Revel's contract with Paramount expired in 1939, the team signed for one year with 20th Century-Fox. By then it was clear that Gordon no

*Sheet music for the 1943 song that brought Gordon his only Academy Award
for best original movie song (Collection of Paul Talbot)*

longer wanted to write with Revel, who soon moved on to RKO. Fox now needed to find a composer for Gordon. Harry Warren had recently left Warner Bros. after working with lyricist Al Dubin for many years. Although Warren planned to return to New York, Fox head Zanuck persuaded him to sign with the studio. When Fox teamed him with Gordon, it was the second major collaborative partnership for both men. Warren and Gordon's first movie, *Down Argentine Way* (1940), made Grable a star and introduced Carmen Miranda to American audiences. Its hit songs were "Two Dreams Met" and the title song, which received the first of Gordon's nine Oscar nominations. Set against a background of rancheros and racetracks, the movie tells a familiar story of an American woman who finds romance in an exotic locale. Its success convinced Zanuck that revitalizing the movie musical required a combination of good songs and glamorous locations photographed in vivid technicolor. Even during World War II, Warren and Gordon wrote songs for mov-

ies about Americans vacationing in such places as Rio, Havana, and Sun Valley. These musicals were pure escapism, with the heroine departing on a steamship or airplane, to the tune of such diverse songs as the Oscar-nominated swing classic "Chattanooga Choo-Choo" (from *Sun Valley Serenade,* 1941), the Latin-style novelty "Chica Chica Boom Chic" (from *That Night in Rio,* 1941), the seductive rhumba "Tropical Magic" (from *Week-End in Havana,* 1941), and the big-band ballad "I Had the Craziest Dream."

As he had with Revel, Gordon wrote love ballads and slangy up-tempo numbers with Warren, often recorded by such swing bands as Glenn Miller's and Harry James's. The love songs were slower and more romantic than his previous efforts, however. During the war years ballads became especially dreamy; the songs of the time affirmed the permanence of love but focused on parting, separation, and the longing for return. Among Gordon's sweetest and most ardent wartime ballads are "I

Sheet music for a 1946 song by Gordon and Edmund Goulding
(Collection of Paul Talbot)

Had the Craziest Dream," "You'll Never Know" (1943), "My Heart Tells Me (Should I Believe My Heart?)" (1943), "The More I See You" (1945), and "I Wish I Knew" (1945). In addition to their musicals set in resorts and exotic locales, Warren and Gordon also wrote songs for period musicals set at the turn of the twentieth century. These nostalgic movies touched a public chord with their uncomplicated re-creations of safer, more innocent times, giving audiences a vision of the United States worth fighting for. The best of these musicals is *Meet Me in St. Louis* (1944), produced by M-G-M, but Fox made more of them than anyone else, first starring Faye, then Grable, and finally June Haver. Because Warren and Gordon wrote for both "tourist" and period musicals, their songs are more varied than Gordon and Revel's are. In addition to a full complement of slow ballads, they also wrote such gimmicky swing tunes as the Oscar-nominated "I've Got a Gal in Kalamazoo"

(from *Orchestra Wives,* 1942), Latin songs for Miranda's fractured English such as "I Yi Yi Yi Yi (I Like You Very Much)" (from *That Night in Rio*), and vaudeville songs such as "Kokomo, Indiana" (*Mother Wore Tights,* 1947).

The first of the Fox period musicals was *Tin Pan Alley* (1940), which featured the Warren-Gordon hit "You Say the Sweetest Things, Baby." Their most important song for a period musical was "You'll Never Know," which was written for *Hello, Frisco, Hello* (1943). It reached the top on *Your Hit Parade* and earned Gordon his only Academy Award for best song. The song is considered one of the loveliest, most important ballads of the war years, sentimental yet convincing despite the abstraction of the lyric. Because it has little imagery and almost no story, it relies almost entirely on a sustained tone of private longing made persuasive through a combination of hushed romanticism and whispered passion:

You went away and my heart went with you.

I speak your name in my ev'ry prayer.

If there is some other way to prove that I love you,

I swear I don't know how.

You'll never know if you don't know now.

Even though Fox's period musicals are set in a time of horse-drawn carriages and bustles, they always include at least one up-to-date song that was aimed squarely at *Your Hit Parade*. In *The Dolly Sisters* (1945), for example, Grable and John Payne sing Gordon and James Monaco's Oscar-nominated "I Can't Begin to Tell You" five different times between them. By the time Crosby recorded it, it was well on its way to success. During the years of his collaboration with Warren, Gordon also occasionally wrote with Monaco. Their songs include the Oscar-nominated "I'm Making Believe" (from *Sweet and Low-Down*, 1944) and "Time Alone Will Tell" and "Once Too Often" (from *Pin-Up Girl*, 1944).

During World War II Gordon organized shows to entertain servicemen as early as 1942, thereby preceding USO shows and the Stage Door Canteen. He typically would take a group of songwriters to sing their own songs for the troops. Warren and Gordon had an unusual but productive way of working together. According to Warren, "I worked during the day and would get the tunes. Then Mack would come around late in the afternoon, pick up the lead sheet, and go off to work with a piano player on the words. He'd call from time to time to ask what I thought. It made for long days." Among their other hits are "Long Ago Last Night" (from *The Great American Broadcast*, 1941), "My Heart Tells Me" (from *Sweet Rosie O'Grady*, 1943), and "The More I See You" and "I Wish I Knew" (from *Diamond Horseshoe*, 1945).

When Warren left Fox after completing work on *Diamond Horseshoe*, Gordon wrote for the next six years with Myrow. Even though musicals were out of favor in the years after the war, he continued to work productively. In 1946 he and Myrow collaborated on the score to *Three Little Girls in Blue*, which Gordon also produced, and followed it in 1947 with songs for one of the last and best of the Fox period musicals, *Mother Wore Tights*. The score included the Oscar-nominated "You Do," which reached the top spot on *Your Hit Parade* for one week. The movie presents it twice, once as a brassy vaudeville turn by Dan Dailey and once as a tender ballad by Grable. Gordon's use of a question-and-answer format in the lyric is reminiscent of "Did You Ever See a Dream Walking?" Myrow and Gordon also wrote "By the Way" and "What Did I Do?" for *When My Baby Smiles at Me* (1948); "Wilhelmina," the last of Gordon's nine Oscar-nominated songs, for *Wabash Avenue* (1950); and "A Lady Loves" for *I Love Melvin* (1953). Gordon also moved to M-G-M for one picture in 1950, collaborating with Warren once again on "If You Feel Like Singing, Sing" and "Friendly Star" for *Summer Stock*.

Because movie musicals were temporarily unpopular in the late 1940s, Gordon wrote individual songs for nonmusical movies, including "Mam'selle" with Edmund Goulding (for *The Razor's Edge*, 1946) and the Oscar-nominated "Through a Long and Sleepless Night" with Alfred Newman (for *Come to the Stable*, 1949). "Mam'selle" was featured on *Your Hit Parade* fourteen times. At Frank Sinatra's request, Gordon wrote "You, My Love" for the movie *Young at Heart* (1954) to a melody by Jimmy Van Heusen, who was composing under the name of Arthur Williams. In 1958, for "You Will Find Your Love in Paris," he wrote new English lyrics to a melody by French composer Guy LaFarge.

Mack Gordon was still active when he died on 1 March 1959 at the Roosevelt Hospital in New York City after a short illness. He was fifty-four and had written songs for eighty-one movies over a span of twenty-nine years.

References:

Philip Furia, *The Poets of Tin Pan Alley: A History of America's Great Lyricists* (New York & Oxford: Oxford University Press, 1990), pp. 240–243;

Roy Hemming, *The Melody Lingers On: The Great Songwriters and Their Movie Musicals* (New York: Newmarket, 1986), pp. 280–284;

William G. Hyland, *The Song Is Ended: Songwriters and American Music, 1900–1950* (New York: Oxford University Press, 1995), pp. 206–220;

James Robert Parish, *The Fox Girls* (New Rochelle, N.Y.: Arlington House, 1971).

Selected Discography:

Rose of Washington Square, Uni/Varèse Sarabande, 302 066 089 2, 1939;

Rose of Washington Square / The Dolly Sisters / Gold Diggers of 1933, Great Movie Themes, CD 60009, 1997;

Song Is Harry Warren, ASV Living Era, 5139, 1995.

Papers:

The Margaret Herrick Library, Academy of Motion Picture Arts and Sciences, Los Angeles, has press releases, interviews, and newspaper articles related to Mack Gordon's motion pictures. The 20th Century-Fox collection at the University of Southern California Cinema-Television Library contains script material for most of the motion pictures for which Gordon wrote songs, including the one movie he produced, *Three Little Girls in Blue* (1946).

Oscar Hammerstein 2nd
(12 July 1895 – 23 August 1960)

Stephen Citron

SELECTED SONGS FROM THEATRICAL PRO-
DUCTIONS: *Always You* (1920), music by Her-
bert Stothart–"Always You"; "My Pousse-Cafe";
"Syncopated Heart"; "The Tired Business Man";

Tickle Me (1920), lyrics by Hammerstein and Harbach,
music by Stothart–"I Don't Laugh at Love Any
More"; "If a Wish Could Make It So"; "Tickle
Me";

Jimmie (1920), lyrics by Hammerstein and Otto Har-
bach, music by Stothart–"Below the Macy-Gimbel
Line"; "I Wish I Was a Queen"; "Some People
Make Me Sick";

Daffy Dill (1922), music by Stothart–"Fair Enough";
"My Little Redskin"; "Prince Charming";

Queen o' Hearts (1922), lyrics by Hammerstein and Sidney Mitchell, music by Louis Gensler and Dudley
Wilkinson–"Dreaming Alone"; "Marriage C.O.D.";

Mary Jane McKane (1923), lyrics by Hammerstein and
William Cary Duncan, music by Vincent You-
mans and Stothart–"Mary Jane McKane"; "The
Rumble of the Subway"; "Speed"; "Stick to Your
Knitting";

Wildflower (1923), lyrics by Hammerstein and Harbach,
music by Youmans and Stothart–"April Blossoms"; "Bambalina"; "I Love You, I Love You, I
Love You"; "Wild-Flower";

Rose-Marie (1924), lyrics by Hammerstein and Harbach,
music by Rudolf Friml and Stothart–"Indian
Love Call"; "Only a Kiss"; "Rose Marie"; "Song
of the Mounties"; "Totem Tom-Tom";

Song of the Flame (1925), lyrics by Hammerstein and
Harbach, music by George Gershwin and Stot-
hart–"Song of the Flame"; "Wander Away";
"Woman's Work Is Never Done";

Sunny (1925), lyrics by Hammerstein and Harbach,
music by Jerome Kern–"D'Ye Love Me?"; "Let's
Say Goodnight 'Til It's Morning"; "Sunny";
"Who?";

The Desert Song (1926), lyrics by Hammerstein and Harbach, music by Sigmund Romberg–"The Desert

*Oscar Hammerstein 2nd (Rodgers and Hammerstein
Organization, New York City)*

Song"; "It"; "One Alone"; "The Riff Song";
"Romance";

The Wild Rose (1926), lyrics by Hammerstein and Harbach, music by Friml–"It Was Fate"; "Lovely
Lady"; "One Golden Hour";

Golden Dawn (1927), lyrics by Hammerstein and Har-
bach, music by Emmerich Kalman and Stothart–
"Here in the Dark"; "Jungle Shadows"; "When I
Crack My Whip";

Show Boat (1927), music by Kern–"Bill" (lyric by Ham-
merstein and P. G. Wodehouse); "Can't Help
Lovin' Dat Man"; "I Might Fall Back on You";
"Life upon the Wicked Stage"; "Make Believe";

"Ol' Man River"; "Where's the Mate for Me?"; "Why Do I Love You?"; "You Are Love";

The New Moon (1928), music by Romberg–"Lover, Come Back to Me"; "One Kiss"; "Softly, as in a Morning Sunrise"; "Stouthearted Men"; "Wanting You";

Rainbow (1928), music by Youmans–"I Like You as You Are";

Sweet Adeline (1929), music by Kern–"Don't Ever Leave Me"; "Here Am I"; "Play Us a Polka, Dot"; "'Twas Not So Long Ago"; "Why Was I Born?";

East Wind (1931), music by Romberg–"East Wind"; "It's a Wonderful World";

Free for All (1931), music by Richard A. Whiting–"Free for All"; "Just Eighteen";

Music in the Air (1932), music by Kern–"And Love Was Born"; "I've Told Ev'ry Little Star"; "In Egern on the Tegern See"; "The Song Is You"; "There's a Hill beyond a Hill";

Three Sisters (1934), music by Kern–"I Won't Dance"; "Lonely Feet";

May Wine (1935), music by Romberg–"Just Once around the Clock";

Gentlemen Unafraid (1938), lyrics by Hammerstein and Harbach, music by Kern–"Gentlemen Unafraid"; "Our Last Dance";

Very Warm for May (1939), music by Kern–"All in Fun"; "All the Things You Are"; "Heaven in my Arms"; "In the Heart of the Dark";

American Jubilee (1940), music by Arthur Schwartz–"Tennessee Fish Fry";

Sunny River (1941), music by Romberg–"Sunny River";

Carmen Jones (1943), music by Georges Bizet–"Beat Out Dat Rhythm on a Drum"; "Dat's Love"; "My Joe"; "Stan' Up and Fight";

Oklahoma! (1943), music by Richard Rodgers–"All er Nothin'"; "The Farmer and the Cowman"; "I Cain't Say No"; "Kansas City"; "Lonely Room"; "Many a New Day"; "Oh, What a Beautiful Mornin'"; "Oklahoma"; "Out of My Dreams"; "People Will Say We're in Love"; "Pore Jud Is Daid"; "The Surrey with the Fringe on Top";

Carousel (1945), music by Rodgers–"Blow High, Blow Low"; "The Highest Judge of All"; "If I Loved You"; "June Is Bustin' Out All Over"; "Mister Snow"; "A Real Nice Clambake"; "Soliloquy"; "What's the Use of Wond'rin'"; "When the Children Are Asleep"; "You'll Never Walk Alone"; "You're a Queer One, Julie Jordan";

Allegro (1947), music by Rodgers–"A Fellow Needs a Girl"; "The Gentleman Is a Dope"; "Money Isn't Everything"; "One Foot, Other Foot"; "So Far"; "Yatata, Yatata, Yatata"; "You Are Never Away";

South Pacific (1949), music by Rodgers–"Bali Ha'i"; "Bloody Mary"; "Carefully Taught"; "A Cock-eyed Optimist"; "Dites-Moi"; "Happy Talk"; "Honey Bun"; "I'm Gonna Wash That Man Right Outa My Hair"; "Some Enchanted Evening"; "There Is Nothin' Like a Dame"; "This Nearly Was Mine"; "Twin Soliloquies"; "A Wonderful Guy"; "Younger Than Springtime";

The King and I (1951), music by Rodgers–"Getting to Know You"; "Hello, Young Lovers"; "I Have Dreamed"; "I Whistle a Happy Tune"; "My Lord and Master"; "A Puzzlement"; "Shall I Tell You What I Think of You?"; "Shall We Dance?"; "Something Wonderful"; "We Kiss in a Shadow"; "Western People Funny";

Me and Juliet (1953), music by Rodgers–"The Big Black Giant"; "Keep It Gay"; "Marriage Type Love"; "Me and Juliet"; "No Other Love"; "That's the Way It Happens";

Pipe Dream (1955), music by Rodgers–"All at Once You Love Her"; "All Kinds of People"; "Everybody's Got a Home but Me"; "The Man I Used to Be"; "Suzy Is a Good Thing"; "Sweet Thursday";

Flower Drum Song (1958), music by Rodgers–"Chop Suey"; "Don't Marry Me"; "Grant Avenue"; "A Hundred Million Miracles"; "I Am Going to Like It Here"; "I Enjoy Being a Girl"; "Love, Look Away"; "Sunday"; "You Are Beautiful";

The Sound of Music (1959), music by Rodgers–"Climb Ev'ry Mountain"; "Do-Re-Mi"; "Edelweiss"; "How Can Love Survive?"; "The Lonely Goatherd"; "Maria"; "My Favorite Things"; "An Ordinary Couple"; "Sixteen Going on Seventeen"; "So Long, Farewell"; "The Sound of Music."

SELECTED SONGS FROM MOTION-PICTURE PRODUCTIONS: *Viennese Nights* (1930), music by Sigmund Romberg–"You Will Remember Vienna";

Children of Dreams (1931), music by Romberg–"Oh, Couldn't I Love That Girl";

The Night Is Young (1935), music by Romberg–"The Night Is Young"; "Vienna Will Sing"; "When I Grow Too Old to Dream";

Give Us This Night (1936), music by Erich Wolfgang Korngold–"Music in the Night";

High, Wide, and Handsome (1937), music by Jerome Kern–"Can I Forget You?"; "The Folks Who Live on the Hill"; "High, Wide, and Handsome";

The Great Waltz (1938), music by Johann Strauss II, arranged and adapted by Dimitri Tiomkin–"I'm in Love with Vienna"; "One Day When We

Marilyn Miller and Jack Donohue in Sunny *(1925), the first musical on which Hammerstein worked with composer Jerome Kern (Museum of the City of New York)*

Were Young"; "Only You"; "Tales from the Vienna Woods";

The Lady Objects (1938), music by Ben Oakland—"When You're in the Room";

State Fair (1945), music by Richard Rodgers—"It Might As Well Be Spring"; "It's a Grand Night for Singing"; "Our State Fair"; "That's for Me."

SELECTED SONGS FROM TELEVISION PRODUCTION: *Cinderella* (1957), music by Richard Rodgers—"Do I Love You Because You're Beautiful (Or Are You Beautiful Because I Love You?)"; "Impossible"; "In My Own Little Corner"; "A Lovely Night"; "The Prince Is Giving a Ball"; "Ten Minutes Ago."

BOOK: *Lyrics* (New York: Simon & Schuster, 1949; revised and enlarged edition, Milwaukee: Hal Leonard, 1985).

Oscar Hammerstein 2nd was one of the most prolific lyricist-librettists ever to have been a part of the American musical theater. His landmark collabo-

rations with Richard Rodgers—*Oklahoma!* (1943), *Carousel* (1945), *South Pacific* (1949), and *The King and I* (1951)—spring instantly to mind; yet, one must not overlook the seminal work he did with Jerome Kern, the rhythmic verve of his shows with Vincent Youmans, and the charming operettas he turned out with Rudolf Friml, George Gershwin, and Sigmund Romberg. *Show Boat* (1927) and *Music in the Air* (1932), Hammerstein's two most successful collaborations with Kern, are filled with stylish songs. The former even has a credible plot—at least for the times. Then there are the individual songs from his operettas, such as "Lover, Come Back to Me" (1928), "Indian Love Call" (1924), "The Desert Song" (1926), "Stouthearted Men" (1928), and "When I Grow Too Old to Dream" (1935), which have become part of American song literature. Still, Hammerstein's achievement in the seventeen years he worked with Richard Rodgers so revolutionized the lyric stage as to eclipse his earlier output unjustly. Perhaps it was because Hammerstein learned the craft of play construction early in his career, when his uncle Arthur Hammerstein, a Broadway producer, sent him on the road to stage manage and look after the creaky plays he was producing. There Oscar Hammerstein had the chance to learn the craft of libretto writing, which came easily to him. Lyric writing, however, did not—at least in his early years—but he persisted. Thus, when the mature Hammerstein had the opportunity to write for characters and dramatic situations, he created his most-apt lyrics, which were set to music by Rodgers, whose compositional talents were also then at their peak.

Hammerstein could work easily with Rodgers in part because he was able to write lyrics that Rodgers would then set to music, whereas Kern, Youmans, and the European operetta composers, Hammerstein's previous colleagues, wrote their music first, and the lyricist filled in the words. He found that this method of having a blank page on which he could initiate a song (always after lengthy discussion of the concept with Rodgers) gave him a free canvas for poetic vision. In this fresh way Hammerstein was able to hone a plot for dramatic strength and believability, and he and Rodgers could shape the songs to build character. Then they inserted them into the fabric of the libretto, sometimes eliminating whole patches of dialogue. Other songwriters were to copy this incisive method, and the end result of this turnabout in construction was enough to transform musical comedy, or operetta, into a wholly American product: the musical play.

Oscar Hammerstein 2nd was born in New York City on 12 July 1895 to William and Alice Nimmo Hammerstein. He was named after his distinguished paternal grandfather, but he preferred to sign "2nd" after his name rather than the pretentious "II." Oscar Hammerstein I had been a poor immigrant who rose to become a legendary impresario of opera and the owner of many theaters and much real estate in the New York of the 1870s. Though beloved of opera fans, Oscar I's ruinous passion for grand opera and lavish productions were the bane of his sons, who managed his theaters. They were often left penniless after their father swooped down on the box office to scoop up the week's receipts in order to reward a diva. Arthur Hammerstein pulled away and became a well-known producer. William Hammerstein, although he managed the "old man's" theaters, tried to keep his own sons away from what he called "the humbug of show business." Oscar's mother alone encouraged her son's theatricality and home recitations. Stimulated by her, he soon became involved during his high-school days in writing amateur theatrical productions, although his father tried to root out his theatrical leanings by sending him to Columbia University to study law.

After two years at Columbia, the hopelessly inept, gangly law clerk went to his uncle Arthur, by that time an eminently successful producer of musicals, for a job, but he was turned away. Perhaps out of desperation, he tried to join the army when the United States entered World War I in 1917, but he was rejected for being underweight. After the death of his father, Hammerstein approached his uncle Arthur again—this time announcing his impending marriage to Myra Finn, with whom he was to have two children, and claiming that he was desperate for some employment to support his family. Arthur relented and considered letting his nephew stage-manage his current Broadway hit, *You're In Love* (1917). The surrogate father warned his young protégé that he was to absorb the technique of play-writing from stage managing and attending performances but that he was not to try his hand at writing a script for at least a year. Before the year was up, Arthur, who had a taste for the melodramatic and the pretentious, suggested that Oscar adapt a senti-mental story he had found. Called *The Light* (1919), it was a total failure, closing down during its pre-Broadway performances and ever afterward referred to by its author as "the light that failed."

Oscar Hammerstein was young and optimistic, and Arthur Hammerstein, realizing his nephew's promise as a dramatist, decided to pair him with his resident music director, Herbert Stothart. Stothart's output was prodigious, but his scores never rose above mediocrity. Their first show, *Always You* (1920), was called "conventional but competent" by the critics, which led Arthur Hammerstein to con-clude that his nephew needed further seasoning. He called Otto Harbach, the acknowledged master of the lyric and the libretto, who had written twelve shows for Arthur, and asked him to let Oscar sit in on his collaboration with Stothart so that he might learn the creative process. The show, *Tickle Me* (1920), written as a vehicle for the comic Frank Tinney, had mostly been completed, and Oscar could do little more than watch the way Harbach supervised the rehearsals. Nevertheless, he was delighted at the reception of *Tickle Me* and Harbach's generous offer to split royal-ties with him. Hammerstein's relationship with Har-bach, twenty-two years his senior, was ideal. The two got along famously and developed a unique way of working together that was—for creative people—amaz-ingly without ego. Harbach would generally suggest a concept and point out how the song would fit into the play. Then he would usually give Hammerstein the title, as if it were an assignment. Hammerstein would work on the lyric, returning it to his mentor to polish. Once it was finished, neither man chose to remember who wrote which line, so deep was their collaboration and trust.

With Frank Mandel working out the plot, Ham-merstein and Harbach turned out their first true col-laborative work, *Jimmie*, in 1920. Like most of the shows he and Harbach wrote from 1920 to 1924, it was not a hit, but it was serviceable. The team's only real success during this period was *Wildflower* (1923), which ran for nearly 500 Broadway performances. The music, mostly by Youmans, was quite catchy, and the show produced a hit song, "Bambalina." The majority of the lyrics are stagy, but some of Hammer-stein's homespun simplicity was starting to show through in a letter song called "I Love You, I Love You":

> "Do write soon, I miss you so, Long to hug and kiss you so. Dearest, can you read my silly scrawl?"

In April 1924 Arthur Hammerstein sent Oscar and Harbach to Montreal to research a musical built on a legend about an ice palace that was turned into a molten river. He had heard of this Native American myth and thought it would make a stunning climax to a new musical. The collaborators found the story groundless, but they did concoct a story that involved a prospector, a true-blue heroine, an Indian, a low comic, a titled Englishwoman, and a troop of Mount-ies. Rudolf Friml and Stothart wrote the music. *Rose-Marie* (1924) features the first song written for an American musical that was truly integral to the dra-matic story and characters. "Indian Love Call" was

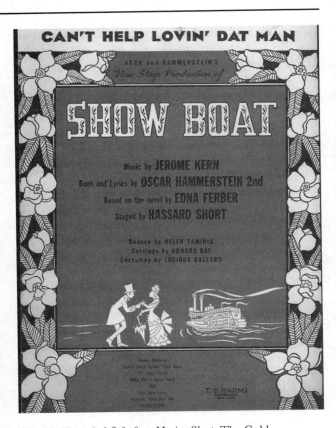

Sheet music for two songs from Hammerstein and Kern's groundbreaking 1927 musical (left: from Marion Short, The Gold in Your Piano Bench, *1997; right: Music Library, University of South Carolina)*

written as a yodel-like theme that the heroine uses to warn her lover, as Harbach put it, "to get the hell out of here because they're after you." The show ran for 557 New York performances and succeeded in London as well, holding the record at Drury Lane until the advent of *Oklahoma!* nearly twenty years later.

With a genuine hit to his credit, Hammerstein was delighted when Harbach introduced him to Kern, with whom they were slated to do *Sunny* (1925), a musical built around the Broadway star Marilyn Miller. Two of the songs in the show were created without the participation of Harbach. For one of them, Kern, who considered his music sacrosanct, gave Hammerstein a long-held musical note, and Hammerstein used it for the line "Who-o-o-o-o-o-o stole my heart away?" in his first solo song hit, "Who?" After a brief collaboration with George Gershwin on *Song of the Flame* (1925), for which Stothart wrote most of the music, Hammerstein and Harbach turned out *The Desert Song* (1926). The lyric for the title song, however, perhaps inspired by Romberg's exotic melody, was the masterful work of Hammerstein alone:

Blue heaven and you and I
And sand kissing a moonlit sky,
A desert breeze whispering a lullaby,
Only stars above you to see I love you. . . .

The Desert Song was a huge success, and although Hammerstein was to work with Harbach on three more shows, because he had done so much of *Desert Song* alone, it sounded the death knell of their collaboration.

Kern, who had appreciated Hammerstein's work on *Sunny,* sensed that a younger viewpoint than Harbach's was necessary for his new project and asked Hammerstein to collaborate with him on an adaptation of Edna Ferber's sprawling novel *Show Boat* (1926). The result was a masterpiece that marked a turning point in the history of musical theater. Hammerstein and Kern's *Show Boat,* the plot of which includes miscegenation, alcoholism, and desertion, is a total musical play for which the songwriters abandoned their formulaic approach to the musical. It might well have opened the door to the fully integrated musical long before *Oklahoma!* did so in 1943, had not Hammerstein and Kern turned their backs in succeeding works and retreated into writing operettas. The songs in *Show Boat,* with few exceptions, are integral to the plot. With the opening lines (the verse of "Ol' Man River"), "Niggers all work on de Mississippi / Niggers all work while de white folks play," Hammerstein announced a controversial play, and Kern supported that idea with his greatest score. From the thematic "Ol' Man River," a force that unifies this sprawling show, to the ballad "Can't Help Lovin' Dat Man," a song that fits neatly into the story, there is hardly a melody or lyric that can be excised. The latter song is taught to the young heroine, Magnolia, by Julie, the star of the floating theater. Julie is a mulatto who passes for white, and her song, with its twelve-bar-blues verse, shows Hammerstein at his most open and elemental: "Fish got to swim and birds got to fly, / I got to love one man till I die." With so many numbers that have since become standards, *Show Boat* stands out as a seminal work in American musical theater.

The late 1920s were a heady time for Hammerstein, for he now took his future life in hand. He divorced his first wife, Myra, and in 1928 met the love of his life, Dorothy Blanchard, whom he married in 1929. She was just the kind of mate he needed—someone who would show him how to relax and not to worry, especially through the next decade, when his kind of romantic lyrics began to seem passé. Hard on the heels of Hammerstein's success with *Show Boat,* he returned to operetta with *The New Moon* (1928), with music by Romberg. Except for one song from the show, "Lover, Come Back to Me," he wallowed in soaring sentiments, with such lines as "longing to hold you close to my eager breast," from "Wanting You," and a title, "Softly, as in a Morning Sunrise," which for decades has been the butt of critics who cite its redundancy: "as distinguished from an evening sunrise?"

The decade of the 1930s was Hammerstein's artistic nadir. Every show he touched seemed to collapse; when he tried Hollywood, the romantic movies for which he wrote lyrics and scenarios left little mark. Fortunately, he was able to coast for the first years of the decade on his royalties from *Show Boat* and his still-popular operettas. But when he and Kern tried to repeat their *Show Boat* success with a turn-of-the-century, semiserious operetta—this time to star Helen Morgan, the dramatic singer who had triumphed as Julie in *Show Boat*—they were stymied by their own masterpiece. Although they did not sense it at the time, Hammerstein and Kern had pushed the musical in a new direction and could not return to the comfortable operetta genre. Called *Sweet Adeline* (1929), the show had only two songs, "Why Was I

Hammerstein and Kern in the orchestra pit of the Alvin Theatre in New York during a rehearsal of their 1932 show, Music in the Air *(photograph by Van Damm)*

Born?" (the answer: "to love you") and "Don't Ever Leave Me," to recommend it.

After three successive flops, *Ballyhoo* (1930), *Free for All* (1931), and *East Wind* (1931), Hammerstein realized that his ambition was overtaking him; he was writing too fast. He made an effort to fight his tendency of dealing with the superficial but ignoring the fundamental. For the rest of his life he more often than not remembered to work slowly and to concentrate on basic emotion. For their next show Hammerstein and Kern turned to a story they knew, an operetta about songwriters, *Music in the Air,* which premiered in 1932. It had some lovely songs, but Hammerstein, always deferring to Kern, whose literary tastes were quite old-fashioned, turned out a show that is unrevivable today. It was mildly successful, and its hit song, the lovely "I've Told Ev'ry Little Star," sounds like the sentiments of a man deeply in love. Even more so was he able to juxtapose singing and love in a kind of *preislied,* or panegyric, "The Song Is You": "I hear music when I touch your hand, / A beautiful melody from some enchanted land."

For the rest of the 1930s Hammerstein produced nothing of great consequence, except for his and Kern's songs for the movie *High, Wide, and Handsome* (1937), which included a gem called "The Folks Who Live on the Hill." A harbinger of the simple kind of lyric Hammerstein was to write with Rodgers, it is just a step away from "When the Children Are Asleep," from *Carousel:*

> Our veranda will command a view of meadows green;
> The sort of view that seems to want to be seen.
> And when the kids grow up and leave us,
> We'll sit and look at the same old view
> Just we two,
> Darby and Joan,
> Who used to be Jack and Jill. . . .

Rumblings of the war in Europe brought the 1930s to a close while Hammerstein floundered, looking for projects that would suit him. Hollywood, except for the climate and the presence of Kern—now his closest friend and collaborator—held little appeal for him. He was eager to do another Broadway show with Kern. They started and quickly abandoned work on a show based on the adventures of Marco Polo before settling on a plot concerning the struggles of a young singer trying to extricate her father from gangsters to whom he is heavily indebted. The story, even before it was written, was already old hat. What appealed to Hammerstein was the possibility of a show-within-a-show format, which had been so successful in *Show Boat, Sunny,* and *Music in the Air*.

Hammerstein and his wife left the West Coast and settled in New York, eventually buying a farm in Bucks County, Pennsylvania, but the musical he and Kern completed, *Very Warm for May* (1939), eked out only fifty-nine performances. Still, it did include a gem, "All in Fun," which showed that Hammerstein could turn out a sophisticated lyric in the manner of Cole Porter:

> All in fun, this thing is all in fun
> When all is said and done, how far can it go?
> Some orchids, some cocktails, a show or two,
> A line in a column that links me with you. . . .

The other songs in the show, including the standard "All the Things You Are," showed a return to the operetta style. Hypercritical of his own work, Hammerstein labored to no avail on the ending of the song, attempting to avoid the rhyme of "divine" with "mine": "And someday, I'll know that moment divine, / When all the things you are are mine." At last he reluctantly accepted the trite rhyme, hoping that Kern's rueful melody would somehow make the song a hit. It did.

With war on the horizon, Hammerstein settled down on his "gentleman's farm," hoping to sit out the conflict, growing vegetables, and writing when it pleased him. He found a silent collaborator in Georges Bizet, whose opera *Carmen* (1875) he began to adapt as

Carmen Jones (1943), conceiving it to be performed by an all-black cast. Transforming the toreador into a prizefighter and moving the action from a cigarette factory in Seville to a southern wartime parachute factory (peopled only with blacks) would, Hammerstein thought, make the story timely enough. Now he could work at his own pace, and he avoided all the inverted or forced rhymes so prevalent in much of his earlier work. Perhaps because he was writing about ordinary black people, he was able to recapture some of the naturalness that characterized his songs for blacks in *Show Boat*. When he finally finished *Carmen Jones,* good as it was, nobody saw fit to produce it at first because of its black cast and Hammerstein's heady record of flops.

Hammerstein had hardly delivered *Carmen Jones* to producer Max Gordon (on whose desk it lay for months) when Rodgers called, asking him to look at Lynn Riggs's *Green Grow the Lilacs* (1931), a play Rodgers had been asked to adapt as a musical by the Theatre Guild. Hammerstein had no need to read the play, because, as he told Rodgers, he had already read it "three or four times" and "would love to do the play." He added, however, that he would participate in the project only if Rodgers's longtime collaborator, Lorenz Hart, was not interested in it. It was well known among the Broadway community that Rodgers and Hart had come to the end of their twenty-four- year collaboration because of Hart's heavy drinking; he would frequently go on a bender and stay away for days at a time. Rodgers loved nothing better than writing music and leading an orderly life, but there may have been more to the parting of ways between him and Hart. Perhaps Rodgers sensed the untapped creative springs in himself that would make his work with Hammerstein so different from his writing with Hart. Rodgers also knew and respected the poetry in Hammerstein's lyrics, and if the plots he chose were old-fashioned, no one could say they were not well constructed. Hart usually concentrated on lyrics and left the book of a musical to others, so there was little true integration between song and story in Rodgers and Hart musicals. In leaving Hart, Rodgers lost the witty, flippant lyrics that Hart created to match the syncopation in his melodies. But something far more important surfaced. Now all was more orderly and straightforward. Exit the musical comedy; enter the musical play.

Oklahoma! and all of Rodgers and Hammerstein's succeeding shows proved to be work that both men reveled in. Hammerstein could take all the time he needed to craft his lyrics and then give them to Rodgers. For his part, the Julliard-trained Rodgers could set the lyric, often more like a poem, as he would a Heinrich Heine ballad. Even in their first song, "Oh,

Director Rouben Mamoulian, Hammerstein, production supervisor Theresa Helburn, and composer Richard Rodgers planning their 1943 musical Oklahoma! *(Museum of the City of New York)*

What a Beautiful Mornin'," Hammerstein agonized over whether to include the "Oh" or not. But its inclusion is not so important to their work as the fact that Rodgers knew how to set the words like a jeweler setting diamonds. He put the word "mor-nin'" on a flattened, or blue, note (D-flat in the key of E-flat) and saved the brighter D-natural for the word "feel-in'": "I got a beautiful feelin' / Everything's goin' my way." Such a setting makes the end of the song feel as though the sun has come out and the play has started.

Another example of this serendipitous collaboration is found in "The Surrey with the Fringe on Top." Rodgers knew exactly the kind of barnyard, henpecking melody necessary for making the fowl scurry away from the country carriage that Hammerstein's lyric described: "Chicks and ducks and geese better scurry, / When I take you out in the surrey." Even the negative love song, "People Will Say We're in Love" ("Don't throw . . . / Don't laugh . . .") was fresh and fit beautifully into the simple story of two shy young lov-

ers. *Oklahoma!* opened on 31 March 1943 and became a hit of enormous proportions (2,212 performances in its first run), so Hammerstein had no trouble securing a production of *Carmen Jones* before 1943 was out and was easily back on top with two successes restoring luster to his name.

Rodgers and Hammerstein's next show, the 1945 musical *Carousel,* based on Ferenc Molnár's *Liliom* (1909), the story of a carousel barker and the woman who loves him, was their personal favorite. But since a brusque, self-centered protagonist was the hero of the original play, Hammerstein told Rodgers that they could not go forward with the project unless he could find a way to make Billy, the barker who strikes out at everyone, even the wife he loves, sympathetic. After much searching, they came up with the idea of a long monologue that would center on this ne'er-do-well's assumption of responsibility with his approaching fatherhood. They wrote "Soliloquy," an eight-minute aria-scene with a stream-of-consciousness lyric—unprec-

Poster for the original production of the 1943 musical that marked the beginning of Hammerstein's long and successful collaboration with Rodgers (from Amy Henderson and Dwight Blocker Bowers, Red, Hot & Blue, *1996)*

edented for a Broadway musical. After envisioning his child as a son, Billy realizes it may turn out to be a girl:

> I got to get ready before she comes
> I got to make certain that she
> Won't be dragged up in slums
> With a lot of bums—
> Like me.
> She's got to be sheltered and fed, and dressed
> In the best that money can buy.
> I never knew how to get money,
> But I'll try—
> By God! I'll try!
> I'll go out and make it,
> Or steal it or take it
> Or die!

As masterful as this lyric is, one must not overlook the other glories on display in *Carousel:* the exquisite "bench scene" early in the play, built around "If I Loved You," as tentative and unexpected as "People Will Say We're in Love" in *Oklahoma!;* and the inspiring finale, "You'll Never Walk Alone":

> Walk on through the wind,
> Walk on through the rain,
> Though your dreams be tossed and blown.

Rodgers and Hammerstein's next show was not an adapted story, as *Oklahoma!* and *Carousel* had been. Titled *Allegro* (1947), it was intended to be staged with the simplicity of Thornton Wilder's play *Our Town* (1938). Hammerstein conceived the story of a young doctor's life from birth to midlife crisis. He is full of humanitarian ideals, but along the way his ideals are subverted by success and a loveless marriage. En route to the stage, as it turned out, the production acquired a large amount of complicated scenery, as well as a pretentious chorus in the style of Greek drama, that weighed the show down. The score, too, lacked inspiration, featuring only one hit song, "The Gentleman Is a Dope," a lament by the nurse who loves the doctor from afar, but even this confession is strangely out of keeping with the rest of the show. With its predictable punch line, "He doesn't belong to me," and the vernacular "Dope" in the title, the song smacks more of musical comedy than musical drama.

The list of song hits from the 1949 musical *South Pacific,* the team's next offering, indicates how easily Rodgers and Hammerstein were able to bounce back from *Allegro.* They adapted two stories from James Michener's *Tales of the South Pacific* (1947): "Fo' Dolla," the tale of a straitlaced naval lieutenant and his affair with the daughter of an island woman called Bloody Mary, and "Our Heroine," about the romance of an army nurse with an expatriate French planter. To add a touch of levity, Hammerstein conceived the idea of a comic con man and linked him with the harridan Bloody Mary. With the plot of the nurse and planter in the forefront and the two subplots, Hammerstein created the kind of color and background he had not employed since *Show Boat.*

Perhaps the most impressive song in the score, which shows the lyricist-librettist and the composer at their peaks, is one that suggests the exoticism of the South Pacific. The melody of "Bali Ha'i," first heard in the overture, haunts the audience from the outset. The octave skip, descending a half step, sets up the nirvana of life on the wartime outpost of Bali Ha'i. Hammerstein's lyric does little but repeat the title; yet, that title resonates throughout the play.

In "Twin Soliloquies" a drama unfolds between the silent thoughts of the lovers Nellie Forbush and

Emile De Beque, played by Mary Martin and Ezio Pinza, respectively, in the original production:

> NELLIE: Wonder how I'd feel
> Living on a hillside
> Looking at an ocean
> Beautiful and still. . . .
>
> EMILE: This is what I need
> This is what I've longed for
> Someone young and smiling
> Climbing up my hill. . . .

These hesitant soliloquies then swell into the passionate strains of "Some Enchanted Evening."

Hammerstein was a political activist who fought religious and ethnic prejudice. The inclusion of his anti-discrimination song, "Carefully Taught," was to become a cause célèbre, but Hammerstein was adamant that it be used in the show:

> You've got to be taught to be afraid
> Of people whose eyes are oddly made
> And people whose skin is a different shade,
> You've got to be carefully taught.

Although he gave the lyric an anemic musical setting, Rodgers stood with Hammerstein against a majority of colleagues who felt that "Carefully Taught" would limit the number of theaters into which *South Pacific* could be booked. But since Rodgers and Hammerstein themselves were the producers, the song was retained. Perhaps the most ravishing song in the show was the love ballad "Younger Than Springtime," a new lyric for the song "My Wife," which had been cut from *Allegro*. It was to become one of the glories of the score.

West and East met again in *The King and I,* Rodgers and Hammerstein's 1951 musical about Anna Leonowens, an Englishwoman who moved to Siam (now Thailand) in 1862 to tutor the king's children. But there was an added theme: the triumph of democratic teaching over autocratic rule. Using Margaret Landon's novel based on Leonowens's experiences, *Anna and the King of Siam* (1944), and a 1946 movie adaptation of the book, Hammerstein tackled the libretto with a bold hand, leaving hardly any detail of either version of the story unchanged. In the end he created a true distillation of the original, although it was greatly different in episode. Rodgers's music avoided the pentatonic and other Oriental scales in favor of more bizarre chordal juxtaposition, unorthodox voice-leading, and open fourths and fifths to create a Siamese atmosphere. But this musical approach did not mean that the score lacked popular appeal. Three songs—"Hello, Young Lovers," "Getting to Know You," and "Shall We Dance?"—were to become standards, and others, such as "I Whistle a Happy Tune," "We Kiss in a Shadow," and "Something Wonderful," were integral to the score.

Early in *The King and I* the Eastern/Western theme is established with "Hello, Young Lovers." Anna talks lovingly about her late husband in the early couplets, and then, as though she were recalling love through Siamese eyes, sings: "Hello, young lovers, whoever you are / I hope your troubles are few. / All my good wishes go with you tonight," in a 6/8, quasi-Eastern rhythm. Then, slipping back into her nostalgic three-quarter-time English waltz world, she adds, "I've been in love like you." "Getting to Know You," with its juxtaposed triplets, now accented on the fourth, now on the first, beat of the measure, was written for *South Pacific* but not used in the show.

The climactic moment of *The King and I* occurs when Anna, teaching the king to dance, is on the brink of falling in love with him. Both are exhilarated by an infectious polka and spin around the library with great abandon. Hammerstein wrote a perfectly simple lyric, enlivened by Rodgers's music, which included spaces for the king to count out the beat he was to step to:

> ANNA: Shall we dance?
> KING: One, two, three, and . . .
> ANNA: On a bright cloud of music shall we fly?
> KING: One, two, three, and . . .

The combination, with these pauses, instead of sounding sophomoric, takes on an Oriental intensity.

Rodgers and Hammerstein's next two shows, *Me and Juliet* (1953) and *Pipe Dream* (1955), were the least successful of their working partnership. The former, a backstage musical in which the writers tried to avoid cliché by setting the action in various parts of the theater while the performance of a hit show is going on, was full of shallow characters in mundane situations. As for the "hit show," a stylized musical titled *Me and Juliet* requiring five songs, the scenario left only seven numbers divided among as many principals to flesh out the characters—an impossible task. Besides, it was the weakest score of Rodgers and Hammerstein's collaboration. Only "The Big Black Giant," a title referring to the nightly theater audience, deserves special mention because its witty catalogue captures the performer's point of view:

> One night it's a laughing giant
> Another night a weeping giant
> One night it's a coughing giant
> Another night it's a sleeping giant.

Sheet music for Rodgers and Hammerstein's Oscar-winning 1945 song (Bruccoli Clark Layman Archives)

From its inception, Rodgers and Hammerstein's next show was also bound for failure. Hammerstein, who had no heart or talent for squalor, blithely chose *Sweet Thursday* (1954), John Steinbeck's sequel to his sordid novel *Cannery Row* (1945), in which the protagonist is Dora, a hardhearted prostitute. The sequel features Dora's sister, Fauna, a madam who teaches her prostitutes, for example, which fork to select from the silverware at a formal dinner they will certainly never be invited to, instead of giving them lessons in the amorous arts. *Cannery Row* has three suicides, several fights, and a healthy dash of profanity. *Pipe Dream,* the musical adaptation of *Sweet Thursday,* lacked all of these. The story climaxes in a masquerade at which the denizens of the whorehouse and flophouse arrive dressed as Snow White and the Seven Dwarfs. To make matters worse, Rodgers and Hammerstein chose Metropolitan Opera diva Helen Traubel as their lead. She could not dance or act and was the only principal who had to use a concealed microphone to be heard. Except for the mildly successful "All at Once You Love Her," the score featured not a single hit and expired after 246 performances, the shortest run of any Rodgers and Hammerstein show.

The next year, Rodgers and Hammerstein wrote an adaptation of the Cinderella story for television. Created for Julie Andrews, *Cinderella* (1957) did much to restore family audiences to the Rodgers and Hammerstein camp, now somewhat tarnished by their involvement with *Pipe Dream*. The telecast was watched by 107 million viewers—far more people than had collectively seen all of their previous musicals. Hammerstein said he did not want *Cinderella* to have a "tricked up" script; he would cling to the fairy tale but would discard the traditional ways of telling the story. The fairy godmother would be young and beautiful, and the stepsisters and their mother more comic than downright evil. But the greatest change would be in Cinderella herself. She is a spirited, atypical fairy-tale heroine whose imagination takes her far beyond pretty things and marriage. She has enough ingenuity to spawn the idea for the pumpkin coach and its rodent attendants. The fairy godmother merely says, "Impossible things are happening every day." Hammerstein made his heroine work to achieve the supernatural. The score includes songs with an almost Freudian edge, such as "Do I Love You Because You're Beautiful (Or Are You Beautiful Because I Love You?)." Rodgers was back in peak form with a raft of swirling waltzes, and even the stepsisters were given an amusing song.

Early in 1958, when Hammerstein was on the West Coast supervising the filming of *South Pacific,* librettist Joseph Fields mentioned a book he had optioned and thought would make a splendid musical. Titled *The Flower Drum Song* (1957), by C. Y. Lee, it was a novel about a college-age Chinese American man and his efforts to satisfy his own romantic nature while kowtowing to the traditions of his wealthy and implacable father. Hammerstein and Fields decided to collaborate on the libretto and on production of the musical. Unfortunately, in adapting the novel they trivialized the plot by adding minor characters and tying everything up with a ribbon for a happy ending. The plot of *Flower Drum Song* (1958) deals with one of Hammerstein's favorite themes: the breakdown of the old social order, as seen in *Oklahoma!* and *The King and I*. It also resembled the latter, as well as *South Pacific,* in its East-West rapprochement. The score includes a variety of songs, from the simple sentiment of "You Are Beautiful" to the almost operatic "Love, Look Away." One of Hammerstein's most poetic lyrics, "I Am Going to Like It Here," paints a picture not unlike a classical Chinese brush drawing:

I am going to like it here,
There is something about the place,
An encouraging atmosphere,
Like a smile on a friendly face.

There is something about the place,
So caressing and warm it is,
Like a smile on a friendly face,
Like a port in a storm it is.

With a sexy song, "I Enjoy Being a Girl"; a silly song, "Chop Suey"; and the brash, noisy "Grant Avenue," *Flower Drum Song* was a crowd pleaser that enjoyed a considerable run.

Just as Gertrude Lawrence, England's first lady of the musical stage, and her agent were the first to bring *Anna and the King of Siam* to Rodgers and Hammerstein's attention, it was Martin, America's favorite musical-theater star, and her agent, Vincent Donehue, who brought Rodgers and Hammerstein their last production, *The Sound of Music* (1959). Martin had optioned the life stories of the Trapp family of folk singers, who had fled the Nazis during World War II by crossing the Alps. She wanted Rodgers and Hammerstein to add "a couple of folk songs" to the story, which was to be adapted by Hammerstein's old friends Russell Crouse and Howard Lindsay. Rodgers and Hammerstein told Martin that if she could wait until they had staged *Flower Drum Song,* they might be able to provide her with a full score. Martin decided to wait.

At age sixty-four, Hammerstein lacked the energy to tackle both libretto and lyrics, and while the libretto Lindsay and Crouse wrote was no more than serviceable, it allowed Hammerstein to concentrate on his collaboration with Rodgers. Their score ranged from religious music to Austrian *ländler,* and the cast featured seven precocious children and the mature Martin, who somehow made audiences believe that she was a young nun. The 1965 motion-picture version of *The Sound of Music,* which was shot in Salzburg, Austria, featured a young, vibrant Andrews and was one of the most successful movies of all time.

The Sound of Music became one of Rodgers and Hammerstein's most successful scores. Hammerstein is often criticized for his pseudoreligiosity, his "lark who is learning to pray" (a line from the title song), but he is not given enough credit for coming up with the answer in a song such as "Maria" to the almost unanswerable question "How do you solve a problem like Maria?" He understands that there is no answer by raising a more-ephemeral question: "How do you hold a moonbeam in your hand?" Hammerstein showed his inventiveness in the simple "Do-Re-Mi," the scale-syllable song that was obligatory in a show about teaching children to sing. He used "Do" as a deer, "Re" as sunlight, "Mi" as myself, "Fa" as "far to run," and "Sol" as "Sew" in "Sew, a needle pulling thread." When he reached "La," which apparently had no associative word, he was at the point at which other lyricists would have

Yul Brynner as the King of Siam and Gertrude Lawrence as Anna Leonowens dancing to "Shall We Dance?" in the original stage version (1951) of Rodgers and Hammerstein's The King and I *(Museum of the City of New York)*

stopped and, realizing the scheme was not going to work, given up. Hammerstein insouciantly brushed the problem aside, defining "La" merely as "a note to follow So(l)." If there is one single quatrain that illustrates the true poet in Hammerstein, it is the simple lead-in for "Sixteen Going on Seventeen" as reprised at the end of the musical by a wiser, older Maria to one of the children in her charge:

A bell is no bell till you ring it,
A song is no song till you sing it,
And love in your heart wasn't put there to stay
Love isn't love till you give it away

This quatrain encapsulates Hammerstein's philosophy, which equates generosity and selflessness with love.

In the fall of 1959 Hammerstein was diagnosed with inoperable cancer. *The Sound of Music,* which opened in November of that year, was to be his last show. (The simple, almost Schubertian "Edelweiss" was to be his last song.) After he died, on 23 August 1960, the lights all over Times Square were dimmed in homage to the man over the course of whose long

*Mary Martin as Maria Rainer performing "Do Re Mi" with the actors portraying the von Trapp
children in the original stage version (1959) of Rodgers and Hammerstein's*
The Sound of Music *(Museum of the City of New York)*

career the American musical had metamorphosed from mindless musical comedy through operetta, finally settling down and coming of age as "the musical play."

Hammerstein's view of humanity can be gleaned by looking at the characters in some of his finest musicals. The protagonists in *Rose Marie, Show Boat, Oklahoma!, Carousel, The King and I,* and even *The Sound of Music* are certainly similar in pattern. The men are generally blustering, domineering, swaggering, and full of braggadocio, while the women are usually brighter than their mates but more retiring in character. It is they who usually save the day and bring about that special quality of ennoblement that is the hallmark of Hammerstein's best work. His moralistic viewpoint of men and women prevailed throughout the first half of the twentieth century. Not only was he responsible for the integrated musical and the believable story, Hammerstein was to have a heavy influence on American moral-

ity and mores. In this way his control over the American musical was to reach far, far beyond his time.

Biographies:

Hugh Fordin, *Getting to Know Him: A Biography of Oscar Hammerstein II* (New York: Random House, 1977);

Stephen Citron, *The Wordsmiths: Oscar Hammerstein 2nd and Alan Jay Lerner* (New York: Oxford University Press, 1995).

References:

Philip Furia, *The Poets of Tin Pan Alley: A History of America's Great Lyricists* (New York: Oxford University Press, 1990), pp. 181–194;

Thomas S. Hischak, *Word Crazy: Broadway Lyricists from Cohan to Sondheim* (New York: Praeger, 1991), pp. 31–43;

Miles Kreuger, *Show Boat: The Story of a Classic Musical* (New York: Oxford University Press, 1977);

Ethan Mordden, *Rodgers & Hammerstein* (New York: Abrams, 1992);

Frederick Nolan, *The Sound of Their Music: The Story of Rodgers and Hammerstein* (London: Dent, 1978);

Richard Rodgers, *Musical Stages: An Autobiography* (New York: Random House, 1975);

Rodgers and Hammerstein Theatre Library <http://www3.rnh.com/theatre/theatre_home.asp>;

Deems Taylor, *Some Enchanted Evenings: The Story of Rodgers and Hammerstein* (New York: Harper, 1953);

Max Wilk, *OK! The Story of Oklahoma!* (New York: Grove, 1993).

Papers:

Oscar Hammerstein 2nd's papers are located in the Rodgers & Hammerstein Collection at the library of Lincoln Center in New York City.

Selected Discography:

Allegro, original Broadway cast (1947), RCA/BMG, 07863–52758–2, 1993;

Cinderella: Original Television Broadcast Soundtrack (1957), Columbia, 60889, 1999;

Rosemary Clooney, *Rosemary Clooney Sings Rodgers, Hart & Hammerstein,* Concord, 4405, 1990;

Conversations with Two Legends of the American Musical Theatre: Richard Rodgers, Oscar Hammerstein II, Facet, 1349181082, 1960;

Barbara Cook, *Oscar Winners: The Lyrics Of Oscar Hammerstein II,* DRG, 91448, 1997;

Flower Drum Song, original Broadway cast, Columbia, 2009, 1959;

A Grand Night For Singing, Varèse Sarabande, 5516, 1994;

Hello, Young Lovers: Capitol Sings Rodgers and Hammerstein, Capitol, 7243 8 28107 2 8, 1994;

The King and I, original Broadway cast, Decca, 9008, 1951;

Me and Juliet, original Broadway cast, RCA Victor, 1012, 1953;

Music in the Air, RCA Victor, LK1025, 1955;

Oklahoma! original Broadway cast (1943), Decca, 9017, 1958;

Pipe Dream, original Broadway cast, RCA Victor, 1023, 1955;

The Rodgers and Hammerstein Collection, MCA, 10775, 1993;

Rodgers and Hammerstein Songbook, Sony, 53331, 1993;

Rodgers & Hammerstein's Carousel: 1994 Broadway Cast Recording, Angel, 5 55199 2 4, 1994;

Rodgers and Hammerstein's The Sound of Music: Original Soundtrack from the 20th Century-Fox Film The Sound of Music, RCA Victor, 2005, 1965;

Show Boat, 1962 studio cast, Sony, 2000;

Show Boat and *Sunny,* on *Show Boat/Sunny/Lido Lady,* Pearl, 9105, 1994;

Sinatra Sings Rodgers and Hammerstein, Columbia/Legacy, 64661, 1996;

The Sound of Music, original Broadway cast, Columbia, 5450, 1959;

South Pacific, original Broadway cast, Columbia, 850, 1949;

Very Warm for May: A Musical Comedy, original Broadway cast, AEI, 008, 1985.

Otto Harbach

(18 August 1873 – 24 January 1963)

Thomas S. Hischak
State University of New York College at Cortland

POPULAR SONGS FROM THEATRICAL PRO-
DUCTIONS: *Three Twins* (1908), music by Karl
Hoschna–"Cuddle Up a Little Closer, Lovey
Mine";

Madame Sherry (1910), music by Hoschna–"Every Little
Movement";

The Firefly (1912), music by Rudolf Friml–"Sympathy";
"Love Is Like a Firefly"; "Giannina Mia";

High Jinks (1913), music by Friml–"Something Seems
Tingle-Ingling"; "All Aboard for Dixie";

Katinka (1915), music by Friml–"Rackety Coo";
"Allah's Holiday";

Going Up! (1917), music by Louis Hirsch–"The Tickle
Toe"; "Going Up"; "If You Look in Her Eyes";

Mary (1920), music by Hirsch–"The Love Nest";

Jimmie (1920), lyrics by Harbach and Oscar Hammerstein, music by Herbert Stothart–"All That I
Want"; "Below the Macy-Gimbel Line"; "I Wish
I Was a Queen"; "Rickety Crickety"; "Some People Make Me Sick"; "Up Is a Long, Long Climb";

Tickle Me (1920), lyrics by Harbach and Hammerstein,
music by Stothart–"Broadway Swell and Bowery
Bum"; "Didja Ever See the Like?"; "I Don't
Laugh at Love Any More"; "Tickle Me"; "You
Never Know What a Kiss Can Mean";

Wildflower (1923), lyrics by Harbach and Hammerstein,
music by Vincent Youmans and Stothart–"Wildflower"; "Bambalina";

No, No, Nanette (1923), lyrics by Harbach and Irving
Caesar, music by Youmans–"No, No, Nanette";

Rose-Marie (1924), lyrics by Harbach and Hammerstein,
music by Friml and Stothart–"Indian Love Call";
"The Mounties"; "Rose-Marie"; "The Door of
My Dreams"; "Totem Tom-Tom";

Sunny (1925), lyrics by Harbach and Hammerstein,
music by Jerome Kern–"Sunny"; "Who?"; "D'Ye
Love Me?";

Song of the Flame (1925), lyrics by Harbach and Hammerstein, music by George Gershwin and Stothart–"Woman's Work Is Never Done"; "Song
of the Flame"; "Wander Away";

Otto Harbach (AP/Wide World Photos)

Criss Cross (1926), music by Kern–"In Araby with You";

The Wild Rose (1926), lyrics by Harbach and Hammerstein, music by Friml–"Lovely Lady"; "It Was
Fate"; "One Golden Hour";

The Desert Song (1926), lyrics by Harbach and Hammer-
stein, music by Sigmund Romberg–"The Desert
Song"; "It"; "One Alone"; "The Riff Song";
"Romance";

Golden Dawn (1927), lyrics by Harbach and Hammer-
stein, music by Emmerich Kalman and Stothart–
"When I Crack My Whip"; "Here in the Dark";
"Jungle Shadows";

The Cat and the Fiddle (1931), music by Kern–"She
Didn't Say 'Yes'"; "Try to Forget"; "The Night

Was Made for Love"; "The Breeze Kissed Your Hair";

Roberta (1933), music by Kern–"Smoke Gets in Your Eyes"; "Yesterdays"; "You're Devastating"; "The Touch of Your Hand";

Forbidden Melody (1936), music by Romberg–"Blame It on the Night"; "How Could a Fellow Want More"; "Lady in the Window"; "No Use Pretending"; "When a Girl Forgets to Scream";

Gentlemen Unafraid (1938), lyrics by Harbach and Hammerstein, music by Kern–"Abe Lincoln Had Just One Country"; "Boy with a Drum"; "Gentlemen Unafraid"; "Sweet as a Rose"; "When You Hear That Humming."

Otto Harbach was one of the most prolific lyricist-librettists of Broadway, writing more than forty musicals between 1908 and 1933 and providing books and lyrics for musical comedies and operettas with such distinguished composers as Rudolf Friml, Vincent Youmans, Sigmund Romberg, and Jerome Kern. At one point in 1925, five Harbach shows were playing on Broadway, a record still to be surpassed. Yet, Harbach is hardly a familiar name, rarely invoked along with Oscar Hammerstein or Alan Jay Lerner, even though he was a major influence on both of them, as well as on other major Broadway lyricists. Harbach's importance lies not in his prolific output or because of a handful of song standards such as "Smoke Gets in Your Eyes" (1933), but because he encouraged a new degree of maturity in musical theater creating librettos and lyrics that were literate, logical, and integrated with character and plot. At a time when many book writers and lyricists were little better than hacks supplying musicals with filler to get from song to song, Harbach took a serious and dedicated approach to the craft and laid the groundwork for *Show Boat* (1927), *Oklahoma!* (1943), and the integrated musical that dominated Broadway for more than three decades.

Otto Ables Hauerbach was born on 18 August 1873, in Salt Lake City, Utah, to Danish parents with the surname of Christiansen. Coming to the United States in the 1830s, the family changed their name to that of their employer's farm, Hauerbach, a common practice at the time. Otto retained the name Hauerbach until World War I, when he shortened it to Harbach to avoid the anti-German sentiment that might damage his career. Although they were simple, rural folk, the Hauerbachs saw to it that the youth was well educated. After his graduation from the Collegiate Institute in Salt Lake City, he attended Knox College in Illinois and received a bachelor of arts in 1895. Harbach found a position as a teacher of English and public speaking at Whitman College in the state of Washington. He

moved to New York City in 1901, not to pursue a theater career but to earn a graduate degree in English at Columbia University. Harbach worked for an insurance firm to pay for his education, then as a copywriter in advertising, and later as a journalist. But soon his money ran out, and he had to leave Columbia without completing his degree.

Harbach told Lerner many years later that his life went in a new direction one day in 1902 when, riding on a streetcar, he saw a billboard with Fay Templeton's picture advertising her appearance in a new Joseph Weber and Lew Fields musical. His previous interest being in the literary classics, he was not much familiar with musical comedy, but after attending a performance he realized the great potential of the lighthearted genre. Harbach's next important turning point in his life was meeting the young musician Karl Hoschna later the same year. Hoschna was born in Kuschwarda in Bohemia in 1877 and grew up in a different world from that of Harbach. He received his musical training at the Vienna Conservatoire and later played the oboe in an Austrian Army band. He immigrated to the United States in 1896 and landed jobs playing in musical theater orchestras, most notably for shows by Victor Herbert. Hoschna was of poor health, however, and, convinced that playing the oboe was making it worse, he sought out other work. Through Isidore Witmark at the Witmark Brothers music publishing firm, Hoschna secured work arranging, recopying, and creating piano reductions of theater music for publication. This position led to composing his own work, and some of his songs were heard onstage.

Harbach and Hoschna began their collaboration with a comic opera, in which they tried to interest producers, but to no avail. Hoschna continued to have his songs interpolated into Broadway shows, but the new team seemed stalled. Then, in 1907, Witmark asked Hoschna to help turn Mary Pacheco's play *Incog* into a musical comedy, and Harbach was brought in on the project. The new work, now titled *Three Twins,* opened in 1908 with Harbach as sole lyricist (the libretto was written by Witmark and Charles Dickson), and he was paid $100 for his contribution. *Three Twins* concerns a young heir (played by Clifton Crawford in the original production) who masquerades as a commoner by passing himself off as the brother to a pair of twins. The Hoschna-Harbach score is a combination of waltzes, choral numbers, and marches, but the hit of the show was "Cuddle Up a Little Closer, Lovey Mine," a ballad that the team had originally written for a vaudeville act but decided to add to the score for *Three Twins.* The musical comedy was an immediate success, running 288 performances, and it launched the new team's career.

Sheet music for a song in a 1912 operetta on which Harbach collaborated with Czech composer Rudolf Friml
(from Dian Zillner, Hollywood Collectibles, *1991)*

Their next project, *Madame Sherry* (1910), was just as popular. Harbach wrote the libretto as well as the lyrics this time, adapting a 1902 German operetta of the same title but giving it a distinctly Broadway flavor. The youthful owner (originally played by Jack Gardner) of a progressive dance school has to try to convince his rich uncle that he is married with two children, so a farcical charade is played out for the old man, complete with a substitute family made up of staff from the school. The score was all new, and the runaway hit was "Every Little Movement," which remains a standard. (The Albert von Tilzer and Junie McCree

song "Put Your Arms Around Me, Honey" was interpolated into the score, and it also was popular.) *Madame Sherry* is just as notable for its tightly constructed libretto, which foreshadowed Harbach's interest in integrating song and story more closely.

Harbach and Hoschna together scored four other shows with varying success before Hoschna's death in 1911 at the age of thirty-four. The short-lived collaboration had made a name for Harbach, so in 1912 he was asked by producer Arthur Hammerstein to provide the lyrics for an operetta called *The Firefly*. The composer was the young Czech musician Rudolf Friml, who had written some songs for Hammerstein but had never scored a full Broadway musical. (Herbert was slated to write the music, but he refused to work with the leading lady, Emma Trentini.) Again Harbach was teamed with a novice composer, and the result was one of the most beloved of American operettas. *The Firefly* is the Cinderella-like story of an Italian street singer who disguises herself as a boy to be near her beloved, eventually becoming a famous operetta diva. Again the libretto was well constructed, and the lush score featured such operetta favorites as "Sympathy," "Love Is Like a Firefly," and "Giannina Mia." Friml and Harbach worked together on eleven more musicals over the years. *High Jinks* (1913) and *Katinka* (1915) were the other two Friml-Harbach shows of the decade, the former featuring the song hits "Something Seems Tingle-Ingling" and "All Aboard for Dixie," and the latter introducing "Rackety Coo" and "Allah's Holiday." Harbach provided the librettos as well as the lyrics, and each show ran for more than two hundred performances.

Working for the first time with composer Louis Hirsch, Harbach had his biggest hit to date with *Going Up!* in 1917. Hirsch was a contemporary of Harbach's who had made a name for himself through his music for revues, including some editions of the *Ziegfeld Follies*. *Going Up!* is a romantic farce about an author (Frank Craven) who has written a book on aviation but knows nothing about flying, and the air race he finds himself involved with in order to win the girl he loves. The musical was based on a 1910 comedy by James Montgomery (who cowrote the libretto with Harbach) and captured the current public fascination with flying. The show ran for 351 performances, toured the country, and was an even bigger hit in London. The Harbach-Hirsch score was filled with contemporary ballads and comic songs, and captivating numbers such as "The Tickle Toe" became popular dance songs. The score also featured the lilting love song "If You Look in Her Eyes" and the rousing title number.

Harbach collaborated with Hirsch on two other occasions, one of them being the long-running *Mary* (1920), which introduced "The Love Nest," a ballad that swept the country as the epitome of domestic bliss. *Mary* is a silly piece about an inventor (Jack McGowan) who plans to make his fortune by selling "portable houses," an idea that amused audiences in the 1920s, before the invention of mobile homes. The out-of-town tryouts were so popular that "The Love Nest" was already a hit by the time the show opened on Broadway. (The ballad served as the theme song for George Burns and Gracie Allen's radio and television shows for many years.)

With *Wildflower* (1923), Harbach worked with composer Vincent Youmans for the first time, and he co-wrote the book and lyrics with Oscar Hammerstein. Hammerstein came from an illustrious theater family but had been encouraged by them to study law. Getting involved with student shows at Columbia, he soon realized his limitations as an actor and started writing plays. Harbach had taken the youth under his wing, teaching him about the importance of precise lyric writing and carefully plotted librettos. They had previously collaborated on *Tickle Me* (1920) and *Jimmie* (1920), but in *Wildflower* the two started to create the integrated musical that they had so often discussed. The plot was another Cinderella variation (a farm girl will inherit a fortune if she can keep her temper for six months), but the songs, as in opera, were integrated into the dialogue and story. (Herbert Stothart composed half of the score, both he and Youmans sharing credit for all the music.) The hit songs included the lively dance number "Bambalina" and the romantic title ballad. Hammerstein always credited Harbach with teaching him everything he knew about writing for the musical theater. Hammerstein and not Harbach, however, eventually brought his teacher's ideas to fruition with *Show Boat* and *Oklahoma!*

Harbach contributed to the book and lyrics for *No, No, Nanette* (1923), considered by many to be the quintessential 1920s musical comedy. The tale of a married Bible salesman (played by Charles Winninger in the original Broadway production) who has been giving money to three ladies and the complications that follow was not at all what Harbach was trying to achieve in the musical theater, and the two biggest hits of the show, "Tea for Two" and "I Want to Be Happy," had lyrics by Irving Caesar. They were added to the show after it opened in Chicago. Youmans was the composer of all of the songs in the show, and Harbach's lyrics were as sharp as ever, if rarely related to the plot. *No, No, Nanette* was a major hit, running a year in Chicago before making it to New York in 1925 and then conquering Europe as well. When the show returned to Broadway in 1971 in a revised version (but with the score largely intact), it was an even bigger hit than it had been more than forty years before, and the songs seemed as fresh as ever.

In 1924, while waiting for *No, No, Nanette* to reach Broadway, Harbach and Hammerstein presented an operetta that was the closest yet to an integrated musical. *Rose-Marie* had music by Friml and Stothart and introduced a handful of classic operetta songs ("Indian Love Call," "The Mounties," "The Door of My Dreams," "Totem Tom-Tom," and the passionate title ballad), but the real innovation was Harbach and Hammerstein's libretto. The authors felt the songs were woven into the story so tightly that they omitted listing the musical numbers in the program. In light of later

*Sheet music for the title song from the 1917 show that marked Harbach's first collaboration with composer
Louis Hirsch (from Max Wilk,* Memory Lane, 1890–1925, *1973)*

musical plays, *Rose-Marie* is not completely integrated, but it was a daring start. The romantic melodrama, set in the Canadian Rockies, hinges on the murder of the villain by his mistress, and there are some chilling moments not usually encountered in comic operetta. The success of *Rose-Marie* (557 performances on Broadway and many more elsewhere) convinced Harbach and Hammerstein that audiences would accept a more serious kind of musical play. Harbach, however, rarely got any closer to his ideal musical than *Rose-Marie.* Too many of his subsequent assignments lacked the kind of stories needed for such an ideal. Harbach wrote many

excellent shows during the rest of his career, however; he continued to strive for precise lyrics and logical librettos, and his efforts often resulted in superior products. *Sunny* (1925) was his first musical with Jerome Kern, who was collaborator for much of Harbach's best work. Collaborating with Hammerstein again on both libretto and lyrics, Harbach helped fashion the story of an American circus performer (Marilyn Miller) who stows away aboard an ocean liner to avoid an unwanted marriage. Much of it was improbable, but the score includes "Who?," "D'Ye Love Me?," and the title song.

Sheet music for a hit song from the 1924 show for which Harbach and Oscar Hammerstein collaborated on the lyrics and libretto (from Marion Short, Hollywood Movie Songs, *1999)*

That same year Harbach worked with composer George Gershwin for the only time. *Song of the Flame* was not typical Gershwin, being a European-like operetta about a subversive group of peasants in rural Russia. Again Hammerstein and Harbach collaborated on libretto and lyrics, and Stothart contributed to the music. Although it produced no operetta standards, *Song of the Flame* was popular enough to run 219 performances.

A Harbach-Hammerstein project that did result in classic operetta was *The Desert Song* (1926), the two men working with Sigmund Romberg for the first time. The show was inspired by events and people in the headlines at the time: a Riff revolt in French Morocco, the well-publicized adventures of T. E. Lawrence, and the fascination of the American public with movie star Rudolph Valentino in the silent movie *The Sheik* (1921). *The Desert Song* concerns a mysteri-

ous Riff rebel (Robert Halliday) and the aristocratic French lady (Vivienne Segal) who loves him. The story allowed for marvelous musical opportunities, if not the fully integrated musical the two authors dreamed of. The Hungarian-born Romberg composed music that seemed to inspire Hammerstein and Harbach, for their score is passionately romantic. "One Alone," "The Riff Song," "Romance," and the enticing title song remain musical theater standards, and *The Desert Song* itself is among the handful of 1920s operettas that can still be produced without apology.

After *The Desert Song,* Hammerstein teamed with Kern for *Show Boat* and Harbach was left to work on a series of routine musicals with composers Stothart, Harry Ruby, Youmans, and Romberg. His career took on a new and promising direction with *The Cat and the Fiddle* (1931). Working alone with Kern, Harbach fashioned a libretto in which music was integral to the plot.

215

Sheet music for one of Harbach and Hammerstein's songs for the 1926 show based on the revolt of the Riffs in French Morocco (from Short, From Footlights to "the Flickers," *1998)*

An American musician (Bettina Hall) meets a dashing Romanian composer (Georges Metaxa) in contemporary Brussels, and the two fall in love while preparing a musical revue. The cast of characters includes chorus singers and dancers, as well as a street singer, so that all of the songs are logically presented as part of the plot. *The Cat and the Fiddle* is full of backstage clichés, but the show strongly ties together its music, plot, and characters. It also includes one of Kern's better scores, which Harbach strongly supported with succinct lyrics throughout. "She Didn't Say 'Yes,'" "The Night Was Made for Love," "Try to Forget," and "The Breeze Kissed Your Hair" are among the standout numbers, and the show managed to run for 395 performances during the depths of the Depression.

The book may not have been much stronger in *Roberta* (1933), Harbach's next project with Kern, but the score was even better and included some of the lyricist's best work. The story concerns an American football hero (Ray Middleton) who inherits a Paris dress shop, and a princess in disguise (Tamara) keeps the plot moving. Every song for the production is exceptional, particularly the unforgettable "Smoke Gets in Your Eyes." "You're Devastating," "Yesterdays," and "The Touch of Your Hand" are all graceful numbers that have stood the test of time. (Another hit from the show, "I'll Be Hard to Handle," had a lyric by Harbach's nephew Bernard Dougall.) *Roberta* was not a runaway hit, but the popularity of "Smoke Gets in Your Eyes" on the radio allowed the show to run for 295 performances. It was Harbach's last Broadway success of any kind. He reteamed with Romberg for the short-lived *Forbidden Melody* in 1936 and one final time, in 1938, with Hammerstein and Kern for *Gentlemen Unafraid,* which got no closer to Broadway than St. Louis.

Sheet music for a song published at the time of the 1935 movie version of a 1933 show by Harbach and Jerome Kern
(Bruccoli Clark Layman Archives)

Unlike many of his colleagues, Harbach did not fare well in Hollywood. Some of his successful operettas were transferred to the screen, but he rarely contributed to new works. Movie studios were even less interested in integrated musicals than Broadway was, and Harbach and his kind of show were considered out of date. If anything, however, Harbach was in many ways ahead of his time. His contribution to the American musical theater is twofold: he moved the Broadway musical in the direction of the integrated musical play, and he brought integrity to the art of lyric writing. The latter point is too often forgotten. Before Harbach, the men and women who wrote the words for musicals were considered (and often were) hacks. Harbach was a literary man in an unliterary field, and the precision, dedication, and care he bestowed on getting the words right was distinctive for his time. He approached the writing of musicals with the slow, exacting, and thorough procedure of an academic. He constantly revised, rewrote, and perfected when most others rushed through their work in the belief that the music, the stars, and the spectacle were the only things that mattered. He taught Hammerstein and others to think about a character or situation for a long time before attempting to write the lyric. Then the accuracy of the actual writing was employed, making sure every rhyme was a true rhyme (a minor consideration at the turn of the twentieth century) and that every line fell into place in a way so that meaning and music coincided effectively. While some of Harbach's lyrics may seem a bit dated or overly romanticized, they are never sloppy or inconsistent.

Aside from this high level of precision, it is difficult to define the Harbach style. He worked with so many different composers and lyricists (sometimes there were as many as three different lyricists scoring the same show) and collaborated on lyrics with Hammerstein, Caesar, and others so often that perhaps only his discipline can be pinpointed. The question of where Hammerstein leaves off and Harbach takes over in a lyric for *Rose-Marie* or *The Desert Song* is difficult to resolve. The best way to look at Harbach's talent as a lyricist is to examine his earliest and his last works, when he was usually writing solo. The lyrics for *The Three Twins,* for example, are slangy and personal. Harbach was never to get as conversational as Ira Gershwin, but there is an informal intimacy in "Cuddle Up a Little Closer, Lovey Mine" that is youthful and even irreverent.

By the time he wrote *The Cat and the Fiddle* and *Roberta,* Harbach had gotten a bit formal and even stuffy at times. Yet, he developed a more mature and poetic way of expressing himself. "The Touch of Your Hand" has the sentiment of a sonnet:

> When you shall see flowers that lie on the plain,
> Lying there sighing for one touch of rain;
> Then you may borrow
> Some glimpse of my sorrow,
> And you'll understand
> How I long for the touch of your hand.

In "Smoke Gets in Your Eyes" the metaphor is that of a dying fire whose smoke climbs up and blinds one with tears. Both images are lush and highly romantic but avoid sentimentality because they are so carefully thought out. Harbach's vocabulary, much wider than the average lyricist of his day, sometimes complicates his lyrics. He occasionally uses words that immediately date him, and he has expressions that distance him from modern audiences. "Sequester'd days" and "Yesterdays" is a superb rhyme, but the formal word *sequester* immediately strikes one as more academic than colloquial. Even as late as the 1930s Harbach used *forsooth* or *thee* in a lyric, and he did not mean to be anachronistic or satirical, as did Lorenz Hart, who tossed in antique words just for fun. Perhaps there was some truth to the claim that Harbach was too old-fashioned for post-Depression Broadway. Nevertheless, Harbach understood, and in fact helped invent, the foundation of good lyric and libretto writing.

Otto Harbach died on 24 January 1963 at the age of eighty-nine. Alan Jay Lerner once related a telling anecdote about Harbach that might sum up the man and his work. When in his eighties, practically blind and confined to a wheelchair, the lyricist complained one morning to his son that he could not sleep the previous night. When his son asked what ailed him, Harbach said that he had just realized what was wrong with the lyric to "Smoke Gets in Your Eyes," a song he had written nearly thirty years before. Such a sense of perfection allowed Harbach to make substantial demands of the American musical, demands that were later met by Hammerstein and others.

References:

Stanley Green, *The World of Musical Comedy: The Story of the American Musical Stage as Told through the Careers of Its Foremost Composers and Lyricists* (New York: Da Capo, 1980), pp. 31–39;

Thomas S. Hischak, *Word Crazy: Broadway Lyricists from Cohan to Sondheim* (New York: Praeger, 1991), pp. 19–24.

Selected Discography:

Americans in London in the 1930s: Original London Cast Recordings from "Follow a Star" (1930), "The Cat and the Fiddle" (1932), "Three Sisters" (1934), Encore, ENBO CD #3/92, 1992;

The Cat and the Fiddle, on *Hit the Deck; The Cat and the Fiddle,* excerpts, Epic, LN3569, 1959;

The Desert Song, RCA Victor, LM2440, 1960;

A Jerome Kern Songbook, Concord Special Products, JAZ45162, 1997;

Jerome Kern's Roberta, Columbia, CL6220, ca. 1952;

Music of Sigmund Romberg EMI/Angel, CD 7 69052 2, 1987;

No, No, Nanette: The New 1925 Musical [1971 revival cast], Sony Classical, SMK 66173, 1973;

Rose Marie, motion-picture soundtrack (1954), Metro, MS-616, 1960;

Show Boat / Sunny / Lido Lady [1928 London casts], Pearl, CD 9105, 1994.

E. Y. "Yip" Harburg

(8 April 1896 – 5 March 1981)

Deena Rosenberg
New York University

and

Harold Meyerson

SELECTED SONGS FROM THEATRICAL PRO-
DUCTIONS: *Americana* (1932)–"Brother, Can
You Spare a Dime?" (music by Jay Gorney);
"Satan's Li'l Lamb" (lyric by Harburg and
Johnny Mercer, music by Harold Arlen);

Ballyhoo of 1932 (1932), music by Lewis Gensler–"Riddle Me This"; "Thrill Me";

The Great Magoo (1932)–"It's Only a Paper Moon"
(lyric by Harburg and Billy Rose, music by
Arlen);

Walk a Little Faster (1932), music by Vernon Duke–
"April in Paris"; "Speaking of Love"; "That's
Life";

Life Begins at 8:40 (1934), lyrics by Harburg and Ira
Gershwin, music by Arlen–"Fun to Be Fooled";
"Let's Take a Walk around the Block"; "Quartet
Erotica (We're Not What We Used to Be)";
"Things!"; "What Can You Say in a Love Song
(That Hasn't Been Said Before)?"; "You're a
Builder-Upper";

Ziegfeld Follies of 1934 (1934)–"I Like the Likes of You"
(music by Duke); "Moon about Town" (music by
Dana Suesse); "What Is There to Say?" (music by
Duke);

The Show Is On (1936)–"Song of the Woodman" (music
by Arlen);

Hooray for What! (1937), music by Arlen–"Buds Won't
Bud" (unused); "Down with Love"; "God's
Country"; "In the Shade of the New Apple
Tree"; "Life's a Dance"; "Moanin' in the Mor-
nin'";

Hold on to Your Hats (1940), music by Burton Lane–
"Don't Let It Get You Down"; "There's a Great
Day Coming Mañana"; "The World Is in My
Arms";

E. Y. "Yip" Harburg (*from Stanley Green,* The World
of Musical Comedy, *1962*)

Bloomer Girl (1944), music by Arlen–"The Eagle and
Me"; "Evelina"; "It Was Good Enough for
Grandma"; "Man for Sale"; "Right as the Rain";
"T'morra', T'morra'";

Finian's Rainbow (1947), music by Lane–"The Begat";
"How Are Things in Glocca Morra?"; "If This
Isn't Love"; "Look to the Rainbow"; "Necessity";
"Old Devil Moon"; "Something Sort of Grand-

ish"; "That Great Come-and-Get-It Day"; "This Time of the Year"; "When I'm Not Near the Girl I Love"; "When the Idle Poor Become the Idle Rich";

Flahooley (1951), music by Sammy Fain–"He's Only Wonderful"; "Here's to Your Illusions"; "The Springtime Cometh"; "Who Says There Ain't No Santa Claus?"; "The World Is Your Balloon";

Jamaica (1957), music by Arlen–"Ain't It de Truth"; "Cocoanut Sweet"; "Hooray for de Yankee Dollar"; "Incompatibility"; "Leave de Atom Alone"; "Little Biscuit"; "Monkey in the Mango Tree"; "Napoleon"; "Push de Button"; "What Good Does It Do?";

The Happiest Girl in the World (1961), music by Jacques Offenbach, arranged by Gorney–"Adrift on a Star"; "Five Minutes of Spring"; "The Glory That Is Greece"; "Never Bedevil the Devil"; "Never Trust a Virgin"; "Shall We Say Farewell?";

Darling of the Day (1968), music by Jule Styne–"Butler in the Abbey"; "Let's See What Happens"; "Panache"; "That Something Extra Special"; "That Stranger in Your Eyes" (unused); "Under the Sunset Tree";

What a Day for a Miracle (1971), music by Larry Orenstein and Jeff Alexander–"When You Have Forgotten My Kisses" (unused); "Who Will Walk with Me?"

SELECTED SONGS FROM MOTION-PICTURE PRODUCTIONS: *Applause* (1929)–"What Wouldn't I Do for That Man?" (music by Jay Gorney);

Leave It to Lester (1930)–"I'm Yours" (music by Johnny Green);

The Singing Kid (1936), music by Harold Arlen–"I Love to Sing-a"; "Save Me, Sister";

Stage Struck (1936), music by Arlen–"Fancy Meeting You";

At the Circus (1939), music by Arlen–"Lydia, the Tattooed Lady"; "Two Blind Loves";

The Wizard of Oz (1939), music by Arlen–"Ding-Dong! The Witch Is Dead"; "If I Only Had a Brain"; "If I Only Had a Heart"; "If I Only Had the Nerve"; "If I Were King of the Forest"; "The Merry Old Land of Oz"; "Munchkinland"; "Optimistic Voices"; "Over the Rainbow"; "We're Off to See the Wizard";

Babes on Broadway (1941)–"Anything Can Happen in New York" (music by Burton Lane);

Ship Ahoy (1942), music by Lane–"I'll Take Tallulah"; "Poor You";

Cabin in the Sky (1943), music by Arlen–"Happiness Is a Thing Called Joe"; "Life's Full of Consequence";

Can't Help Singing (1944), music by Jerome Kern–"Californ-i-ay"; "Can't Help Singing"; "More and More";

Kismet (1944)–"Willow in the Wind" (music by Arlen);

California (1946), music by Earl Robinson–"Said I to My Heart, Said I";

Nellie Bly (1956; unproduced)–"Stay Out of My Dreams" (music by Arlen);

Gay Purr-ee (1962), music by Arlen–"Little Drops of Rain"; "The Money Cat"; "Paris Is a Lonely Town";

Hurry Sundown (1967)–"Hurry Sundown" (unused; music by Robinson).

SELECTED SONGS PUBLISHED INDEPENDENTLY OF THEATRICAL OR MOTION-PICTURE PRODUCTIONS: "Isn't It Heavenly?" (1932), music by Joseph Meyer;

"Then I'll Be Tired of You" (1934), music by Arthur Schwartz;

"Free and Equal Blues" (1944), music by Earl Robinson;

"The Same Boat, Brother" (1945), music by Robinson;

"The Silent Spring" (1963), music by Harold Arlen;

"An African Song" (1964), music by W. Chad Mitchell, Michael Kobluk, Joseph Frazier, and Milton Okun;

"It's a Short, Short Walk to a Long Sleep" (1969), music by Ann Sternberg;

"Goodnight, Mrs. Calabash" (1972), music by Sammy Fain;

"I, Whoever I Am" (1973), music by Fain;

"Looks Like the End of a Beautiful Friendship" (1976), music by Arlen;

"Crazy Old World" (1979), music by Phil Springer;

"Drivin' and Dreamin'" (1979), music by Springer;

"Time, You Old Gypsy Man" (1979), music by Springer;

"Where Have I Seen Your Face Before?" (1981), music by Burton Lane.

BOOKS: *Rhymes for the Irreverent* (New York: Grossman, 1965; republished, New York: Harburg Foundation, 1998);

At This Point in Rhyme (New York: Crown, 1976; republished as *More Rhymes for the Irreverent* (New York: Harburg Foundation, 2000).

"There were three overwhelming passions which governed the life of Bertrand Russell," said E. Y. "Yip" Harburg in 1970, in a talk in the "Lyrics and Lyricists" series at the 92nd Street Y in New York:

The longing for love, the search for knowledge, and unbearable pity for the suffering of mankind. The challenge to the lyricist should be to put these passions into provocative, compelling, entertaining songs. . . . The magic in song only happens when the words give destination and meaning to the music and the music gives wings to the words. Together as a song they go places you've never been before. The reason is obvious. Words make you think thoughts. Music makes you feel a feeling. But a song makes you feel a thought. . . . And that's why . . . you can teach more through song and you can rouse more through song than all the prose in the world or all the poems. Songs have been the not-so-secret weapon behind every fight for freedom: "The Marseillaise," "The Battle Hymn of the Republic," "We Shall Overcome," and many more. . . . Songs are the pulse of a nation's heart. A fever chart of its health. Are we at peace? Are we in trouble? . . . Do we feel beautiful? Do we feel ugly? . . . Listen to our songs. . . . The lyricist, like any artist, cannot be neutral. He should be committed to the side of humanity.

Harburg was one of the preeminent theater-song lyricists and librettists of the Broadway musical stage during its first golden age, the first half of the twentieth century. He was also one of a handful of artists who developed the form of the classic Broadway musical during the 1930s and into the 1940s. His best-known project is M-G-M's 1939 movie *The Wizard of Oz,* for which Harburg not only wrote all the lyrics and edited the final script but also infused the entire picture with his characteristic brand of humor and wordplay and his aptitude for fantasy mixed with reality. *The Wizard of Oz* was the prelude to his stage work that followed, in which Harburg combined his sense of humor and his lyrical genius with a political radicalism otherwise largely absent from Broadway musicals. In such landmark musical plays as *Bloomer Girl* (1944) and *Finian's Rainbow* (1947) and such classic songs as "Brother, Can You Spare a Dime?" (1932), Harburg openly criticized capitalism, racism, and sexism—in what was generally an apolitical, mainstream popular medium—and got away with it.

Alone among his brilliant peers—such as Ira Gershwin, Lorenz Hart, Oscar Hammerstein 2nd, Cole Porter, Dorothy Fields, and Irving Berlin—Harburg was both the house radical and imp: the munchkin politico of his generation. Because he sought to address a broader range of concerns than his peers, many of his greatest songs deal with matters other than romantic love. And they ask a lot of questions: "Why should I be standing in line just waiting for bread?" ("Brother, Can You Spare a Dime?") and "Whom can I run to? What have you done to my heart?" ("April in Paris," 1932). Even "Over The Rainbow," from *The Wizard of Oz,* asks "Why?" While on the surface "Over the Rainbow" may

Harburg at City College of New York, 1915 (from Harold Meyerson and Ernie Harburg, Who Put the Rainbow in The Wizard of Oz? *1993)*

seem to be a ballad of childhood yearning, it emerged from Harburg's profound dissatisfaction with the here and now, his deep belief in the individual's capacity to ask why and to change his society, his abiding passion for freedom, and his ability to "dare to dream." A quick catalogue of his important songs runs well beyond the usual love ballads to contemplations of economic conditions ("Necessity," 1947), class distinctions ("When the Idle Poor Become the Idle Rich," 1947), and rampant consumerism ("Push de Button," 1957), as well as pleas for racial equality ("The Eagle and Me," 1944) and atomic disarmament ("Leave de Atom Alone," 1957). Uniting these songs and Harburg's great love ballads— "It's Only a Paper Moon" (1932), "Old Devil Moon" (1947)—is a distinct radical humanism. He believed in the human capacity for continuous growth, putting a skeptical and celebratory, definitely paradoxical, focus on people's need both to love and to believe as well as to question. Harburg's work, unlike that of his peers, actually has an underlying philosophy—indeed, an underlying cosmology. It even suggests to listeners the Socratic method of asking hard questions for the purpose of solving at least some of them.

Harburg was born Isidore Hochberg to immigrant Russian-Jewish parents in New York City on 8

April 1896. The initial *Y* actually stands for the nickname Yip, short for the Yiddish *yipsl,* or "little squirrel," a name he acquired from the way he scampered around as a child. His father, Louis Hochberg; mother, Mary Ricing Hochberg; and sister, Anna, worked in a ladies'-garment sweatshop. He also had an older brother, Max, who taught college physics but died young, at age twenty-eight. Unlike his future lyricist peers, Harburg grew up in dire poverty: only Berlin had as economically insecure a childhood. As a boy Harburg worked in the sweatshops, too; he also lit and damped the gaslights along Broadway. The Lower East Side apartment at Eleventh Street and Avenue C where he spent much of his childhood was a sixth-floor walk-up with no hot water. He had no bed, sleeping instead on chairs that he and Anna would push together each evening, absorbing (in a line Harburg frequently quoted from his idol, George Bernard Shaw) "the chill of poverty which never leaves your bones."

Out of this combustible mix of poverty and ambition came a radicalism and a drive that were to define Harburg. "I empathized with my father in his sweatshop," he later said, "my mother at her washing and making hair nets for a living on the Lower East Side. I always had hope that someday they would be liberated. It became part of my chemistry—to free them from drudgery." The saving grace was his father's hope, humor, and Jewish socialism. Louis Hochberg and his son pored over the *Jewish Daily Forward* and attended the Yiddish theater often. As Harburg described himself in Bernard Rosenberg and Ernest Goldstein's *Creators and Disturbers: Reminiscences by Jewish Intellectuals of New York* (1982), he was "a New Yorker down to the last capillary." He grew up immersed in the city's rich cultural milieu. At Townsend Harris High School, a school for gifted students, Harburg struck up a friendship, through the system of alphabetical seating, with the young Ira Gershwin. The two shared a passion for the operettas of W. S. Gilbert and Arthur Sullivan, which were lifelong influences for both lyricists.

Gershwin and Harburg wrote a verse-and-humor column for the school newspaper, a collaboration they continued as they moved on to the City College of New York. Their reading included both classical verse and works by the light-verse poets of the time, who commented on current fashions and trends using classical poetic forms. This reading accounts for the eclecticism of the list that Harburg once assembled of the writers who influenced him. "My roots are Shakespeare," he said in a 1978 interview, "Wordsworth, Shelley, Shaw: the English language . . . if you want to write songs and you don't know A. E. Houseman, if you don't know Dorothy Parker, Frank Adams, [Chicago columnist and light versifier Bert L.] Taylor, Gilbert,

you cannot begin to be a good lyric writer." A particularly strong influence on both Harburg and Ira Gershwin was "The Conning Tower," a column by Franklin P. Adams ("F.P.A.") in *The New York World,* which he opened to a generation of young contributors who were later to become some of the leading humorists and lyricists of the interwar years.

Harburg periodically contributed light verse to "The Conning Tower" in the decade following his graduation from City College in 1918—years that he spent primarily, however, as a successful businessman, feeling obliged to lift his family out of poverty. In 1921, with a former classmate, he founded the Consolidated Electrical Appliance Company. He also changed his name from Isidore Hochberg to Edgar Y. Harburg. The appliance company flourished; Harburg married Alice Richmond in 1923; and the couple had two children, Marge and Ernest. Despite his longing to become a writer, he remained in business until the 1929 crash wiped him out. Harburg then turned to songwriting. Ira Gershwin lent him $500 and introduced him to a composer, Jay Gorney, who was looking for a lyricist. "I had my fill of this dreamy abstract thing called business," he quipped to Studs Terkel for *Hard Times: An Oral History of the Great Depression* (1970), "and I decided to face the hard reality of musical theater."

What followed was a three-year apprenticeship during which Harburg learned the lyricist's craft. Working with Gorney and other composers, he wrote lyrics for songs for radio shows; for Paramount musicals filmed at their Astoria, New York, studios; and for such long-forgotten Broadway revues as the eighth *Earl Carroll Vanities* (1929), *The Vanderbilt Revue* (1930), and Billy Rose's *Crazy Quilt* (1931). These songs were often crafted for particular performers or were one-shot numbers in shows. In them one can see Harburg slowly learning how to build a lyric as a dramatic story, how to craft certain vowel sounds to lengthen melody notes, and how to avoid pedestrian rhymes.

During this songwriting apprenticeship, from 1929 through 1932, Harburg wrote songs with twenty-five composers. He was to work with forty-eight overall during his fifty-year career: as he told Morley Safer on the CBS television program *60 Minutes* in 1978, paraphrasing his own lyric "When I'm Not Near the Girl I Love" from *Finian's Rainbow,* "When I'm not near the composer I love, I love the composer I'm near." In 1932 Harburg had more songs on Broadway than any other lyricist. But more important, 1932 was the year that he wrote three of his signature songs: with Gorney, "Brother, Can You Spare a Dime?"; "April in Paris," with music by Vernon Duke; and "It's Only a Paper Moon," with music by Harold Arlen. In particular, what Harburg had learned that burst forth in these

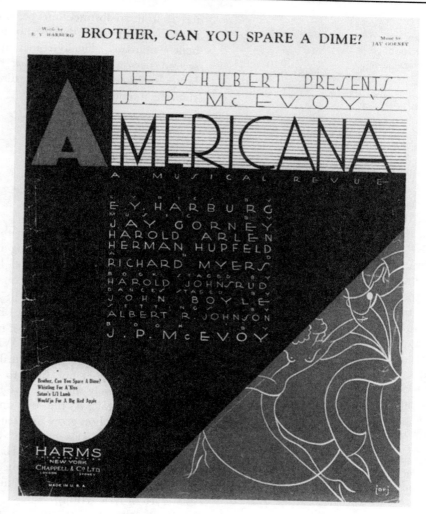

Sheet music for the 1932 song by Harburg and Jay Gorney that is considered an anthem of the Great Depression (from Harold Meyerson and Ernie Harburg, Who Put the Rainbow in The Wizard of Oz? *1993)*

three songs was how to write a song for the theater. "To make the transition from verse writing to song writing," he told Terkel in 1977,

is like a leap from Peter's foot to Satan's knee, or from Satan's foot to Peter's knee. It's an altogether different medium. Verse writing is an intellectual pursuit. [When reading verse] you sit at home with a book; you are quiet; you absorb the thought; you chuckle to yourself. A song done in a theater is an emotional explosion. At the end of it you expect applause. You've got to move an audience, not only with words, but with the emphasis on the music.

"Brother, Can You Spare a Dime?" was written for the 1932 revue *Americana,* with a book by humorist J. P. McEvoy. The show was a largely satiric look at the current events of 1932–the worst year of the Depression. One scene depicted a breadline. Gorney, one of the composers for the show, had in his trunk an unpublished torch song with a banal lyric. Harburg immediately heard something deeper in the melody, something timely and broadly resonant. With Gorney's assent, he set a new lyric to the melody. The chorus in the original lyric began:

I could go on crying
Big blue tears,
Ever since you said we were through. . . .

Harburg's new version of the chorus began:

Once I built a railroad,
Made it run,
Made it race against time.

With an introductory verse he depicted the character who sings the bewildered lament of the chorus:

They used to tell me
I was building a dream,
And so I followed the mob.
When there was earth to plow
Or guns to bear,
I was always there,
Right there on the job.
They used to tell me
I was building a dream
With peace and glory ahead.
Why should I be standing in line,
Just waiting for bread?

"Brother, Can You Spare a Dime?" remains virtually the anthem of the Depression—the only Broadway song of the time that dealt with the broader social context of the 1930s—and carries a message informed by Harburg's leftism. "In 1930, when the dream machine was derailed and the engine wrecked," he said on the 1971 PBS special *The Great American Dream Machine,* "I saw executives driving taxis, engineers selling apples, skilled workers and veterans standing in breadlines. They were not people in revolt or angry, but baffled, bewildered that this big, powerful dream machine could collapse so utterly. The lyric I wrote was not for an underling asking for a handout, but for a proud man asking a vital question":

Once I built a railroad,
Made it run,
Made it race against time.
Once I built a railroad,
Now it's done,
Brother, can you spare a dime?

Harburg's challenge in crafting the lyric for "Brother, Can You Spare a Dime?" was much like the challenge confronting the man on the street, suddenly out of work: to establish that character's individuality and the moral-political basis of his claim. To that end, he slowly escalates the protagonist's claims:

Once I built a tower
To the sun,
Brick and rivet and lime.
Once I built a tower,
Now it's done.
Brother, can you spare a dime?
Once in khaki suits,
Gee, we looked swell,
Full of that Yankee Doodle-de-dum.
Half a million boots went sloggin' through hell,
I was the kid with the drum.

By this point in the lyric, the listener knows that the person singing is a builder and a war veteran. Harburg also builds in an increasing degree of intimacy and self-revelation on the part of the character. The lyric

moves from an abstract third person (" *They* used to tell me / I was building a dream") to first person ("Once *I* built a railroad"). Finally comes the direct address of second person ("Say, don't *you* remember"), which brings the listener and the singer directly together at the climactic moment in the melody:

Say, don't you remember?
They called me Al,
It was Al all the time.
Say, don't you remember,
I'm your pal!
Buddy, can you spare a dime?

The singer shares his past with the listener, he has a name, and the steadily growing intimacy culminates with the substitution of "Buddy" for "Brother" in the last line of the song.

It should be noted that the melody to the first five notes of the chorus ("Once I built a rail[road]") is in a plaintive, minor key. Almost no American theater songs are in the minor mode. While the song reverberates with the 1930s, the word "Once" and those initial notes after it link back to laments of the past that used precisely the same five notes, the beginning of the minor scale. As the song unfolds, the narrative, music, and emotion grow in intensity as they had not in any previous Harburg—or Gorney—song. The moral and political urgency Harburg conveyed in "Brother, Can You Spare a Dime?" sped the development of his craft and propelled him to a much higher standard of lyric writing.

"Brother, Can You Spare a Dime?" broke across Broadway—and then America. Newspaper and magazine notices of revues, which almost never discussed particular songs, did so in this case. The song "has expressed the spirit of these times with more heart-breaking anguish than any of the prose bards of the day," wrote Brooks Atkinson in *The New York Times.* Soon, recordings of the song by both Bing Crosby and Rudy Vallee were heard over the airwaves around the time of the 1932 presidential election, and some stations even banned it. Decades after its composition, "Brother, Can You Spare a Dime?" still stands as the masterpiece among American "social issue" songs. Like the best-known songs of Woody Guthrie and Bob Dylan, it was written to the headlines of its day, but the lyric and music combine to transcend the immediate crisis of 1932, to depict for all time the indignation of the economic outcast, and to state his claim for justice. Like the greatest songs of the American theater, the lyric and music build to tell—really, to unveil—a story; only, in this instance, the story is not that of a jilted lover but of a betrayed citizen.

Sheet music for a song by Harburg and Harold Arlen that was originally written for Ben Hecht's 1932 play
The Great Magoo *(from Harold Meyerson and Ernie Harburg,*
Who Put the Rainbow in The Wizard of Oz? *1993)*

One month after the presidential election, another show for which Harburg wrote lyrics–*Walk a Little Faster* (1932), with music by Duke and book by humorist S. J. Perelman–opened on Broadway. Harburg's collaboration with Duke lasted only four years (1930–1934) and proved difficult for both men, but it was largely in the twenty-five songs Harburg wrote with Duke that his lyrical genius took shape. He became fluent in internal and multisyllabic rhymes; he became comfortable with metaphor; he learned to build both comic and dramatic lyrics; and he learned–and, when necessary, transcended–narration. Ira Gershwin introduced the socialist Harburg to the social-climbing fashion plate Duke. "With my pumpernickel background and his orchid tunes," Harburg later said to Max Wilk for *They're Playing Our Song* (1973), "we made a wonderful marriage." While Duke had visited most of Europe's major cities, Harburg used travel posters and his imagination to conjure up a quite real and evocative Paris for "April in Paris."

Walk a Little Faster starred two great comics of the stage, Beatrice Lillie and Bobby Clark. For the first time, Harburg crafted songs to specific comic personae–a skill at which he became particularly adept, as his later songs for Bert Lahr and Groucho Marx attest. The major ballad in the show, "April in Paris," was, by the standards of 1932, almost an avant-garde work. The lyric is a haiku-like solution for Duke's at once sweeping but parsimonious tone poem–so lush in harmony, but with so few notes in the melody. Narrative would be constricted in these passages, and the best lyrical evocation of this kind of music, Harburg concluded, was to keep the lyric purely imagistic throughout the first stanza. "April in Paris" opens almost as a French symbolist song, Harburg playing Stéphane Mallarmé to Duke's Claude Debussy:

In the last stanza the lines are constructed around two highly charged questions (as noted, a Harburg trademark):

> Till April in Paris.
> Whom can I run to?
> What have you done to my heart?

For these last three lines Duke sweeps the melody dramatically upward, paralleling the initial musical phrase, but higher, to a resolution at the top of the scale. Harburg plunges the lyric into an expression of unexplained dread that underlies all the imagery: "Whom can I run to?" The last lines are that rarity in song lyrics: a genuine climax. The fear—and, reading backward, the emotions and images—are explicated and decoded. The movement from imagery to generalized feeling to personalized feeling takes one last step toward intimacy as the last line uses direct address: "What have *you* done to *my* heart?" Sweeping and concise, enraptured and apprehensive, mysterious and resolved, art song and pop song, "April in Paris" is a masterpiece of American theater song.

Harburg's proclivity for posing questions in song lyrics was not simply a matter of his settling upon an evocative pattern for final lines. It was also a way to implicate the listener directly: "Buddy, can you spare . . . ," "What have you done to. . . ." It allowed him to deal with his more-cosmic concerns: "What is the curse that makes the universe so all bewilderin'?" ("Necessity"), "What's the matter with now?" ("T'morra', T'morra'" 1944), and, of course, "If happy little bluebirds fly / Beyond the rainbow, / Why, oh, why can't I?" Merely expressing such concerns, of course, set Harburg apart from the other lyricists of his generation. By expressing them in this colloquial and quizzical way his characters often seem the children of Sholom Aleichem's Tevye: they may not be in the shtetl, but they are certainly arguing with God.

After "April in Paris" Harburg's awareness of love's complexity and ambivalence received even fuller expression in another song he and Arlen wrote for the 1932 Ben Hecht play *The Great Magoo,* which also opened on Broadway that December. Arlen, whom musical-theater historian Alec Wilder, in his *American Popular Song, 1900–1950: The Great Innovators* (1972), called "the most jazz-oriented of the great theater song composers," had met Harburg in 1930, when Arlen was just beginning to compose standards (with lyricist Ted Koehler) for Harlem's Cotton Club revues. A master of a distinct colloquial style—a studied looseness complete with bluesy harmonies and melodies that could stay close to home or take huge leaps—Arlen, still in his twenties, was also interpolating songs into occa-

Bobby Clark, Beatrice Lillie, and Paul McCullough in Walk a Little Faster *(1932), a show with songs by Harburg and Vernon Duke, including "April in Paris" (from Stanley Green,* The World of Musical Comedy, *1962)*

> April in Paris,
> Chestnuts in blossom.
> Holiday tables under the trees.

And he does so in a mere sixty-four words. The propulsive motion in the song, musically and lyrically, is toward the revelation of the emotion behind these initial images. Harburg's first definition of April in Paris, in the second stanza of the chorus, is deliberately distanced and generalized:

> April in Paris,
> This is a feeling
> No one can ever reprise.

In the next section—the release, or bridge—the harmonies become less exotic, and the emotion is both identified and personalized: first-person narration is employed for the first time:

> I never knew the charm of Spring,
> Never met it face to face,
> I never knew my heart could sing,
> Never missed a warm embrace. . . .

Arlen, seated with his dog Stormy, and Harburg at the Beverly Hills home of opera singer Lawrence Tibbett, which they sublet in the mid 1930s while working on songs for Warner Bros. movie musicals and where they wrote "Last Night When We Were Young" (1935) (from Harold Meyerson and Ernie Harburg, Who Put the Rainbow in The Wizard of Oz? 1993)

sional Broadway shows. Harburg and Arlen wrote "It's Only a Paper Moon" for *The Great Magoo:*

> Say, it's only a paper moon
> Sailing over a cardboard sea,
> But it wouldn't be make-believe
> If you believed in me.

"It's Only a Paper Moon" is not only an illustrious beginning to the Harburg-Arlen collaboration, but it is also the first of Harburg's songs to be concerned with the power of illusion, conviction, and—if Harburg is taken at his word—even ideology. Speaking about the song in 1978, Harburg said, "Eugene O'Neill took five hours to say in *The Iceman Cometh* that man cannot live without illusions. My own belief is that man cannot live with them. Politically, they can be disastrous." Witness the illusion Harburg whimsically demolishes in "It's Only a Paper Moon":

> Yes, it's only a canvas sky,
> Hanging over a muslin tree,
> But it wouldn't be make-believe
> If you believed in me.

At other times, however, Harburg provided a far more conventional interpretation of the lyric for "It's Only a Paper Moon," telling Wilk in 1973, "There's a saving grace called love. Without it, life is all a honky-tonk parade":

> Without your love
> It's a honky-tonk parade.
> Without your love
> It's a melody played
> In a penny arcade.
> It's a Barnum and Bailey world,
> Just as phony as it can be,
> But it wouldn't be make-believe
> If you believed in me.

Harburg's contradictory attitude toward illusion and belief—they are "disastrous," but they are also "a saving grace"—constituted a deep and unresolved tension that marked his lyrics for the duration of his career. Beginning with "It's Only a Paper Moon," he produced a series of ballad lyrics that depicted belief and romance as arbitrary constructions. Many of the images that recur in Harburg's work—that old devil moon, April, spring—are harbingers not only of enchantment but also of entrapment and artifice. Throughout the 1930s in particular, his ballad lyrics were less love songs than songs about love and its complexities—and his lyrics never say "I love you" in so many words. "It's Only a Paper Moon" was the first of his songs to express a search for meaning in a meaningless, or, in this case, utterly artificial, world. "Every person who thinks," he said when speaking of the song in his 1970 "Lyrics and Lyricists" talk,

is confronted with two things in this life: his drive to be related to the universe, but that's a hard thing because there are so many stars and it's very hard to grasp that relationship. So his next best thing is to be related to humanity, but there are a lot of people, and that's hard too. But if he can identify himself, and really relate with one other person, he will relate with all of humanity and he will relate with all the stars.

By the end of 1932 Harburg's status as a major lyricist had received both public and private confirmation. His peers—Ira Gershwin and Hart in particular—showered his work with praise. On 8 January 1933 *The New York Times* profiled "The Lyrical Mr. Harburg" as "a member of the newer school of lyric writers who are giving Broadway audiences these days a series of rhymes somewhat more intelligent than 'June' and 'moon.'" Throughout the 1930s Harburg split his time between Broadway, where he worked on a series of revues (and several musical comedies that anticipated the integrated "book" musicals of the 1940s), and Hollywood, where he contributed songs to motion pictures. Among his more notable early Hollywood achievements was to write the lyric to Burton Lane's music for Frank Sinatra's first major movie song, "Poor You" (1942). The lyric gives a wry twist to the usual formulas of romantic praise:

Poor you,
I'm sorry you're not me,
For you will never know
What loving you can be.

By 1934 Harburg was working increasingly and, by the late 1930s, almost exclusively with Arlen. In 1934, while George Gershwin was orchestrating *Porgy and Bess* (1935), Ira Gershwin had some free time. He and Harburg teamed up as lyricists to collaborate with Arlen on the score for a comic revue called *Life Begins at 8:40*. The chief ballad in the show, "Fun to Be Fooled," takes up where "It's Only a Paper Moon" left off—in the realm of romantic artifice and self-deception. To a somewhat subdued and almost melancholy melody and harmony, Harburg and Gershwin wrote a chorus full

of contradictions from the title on (how can it be "fun" "to be fooled"?), which, however, reveals in a bittersweet way that the singer knows that is how life is:

Fun to be fooled,
Fun to pretend;
Fun to believe
Love is unending.
Thought I was done,
Still, it is fun
Being fooled again. . . .
Fun to be fooled,
Fun to pretend
This little dream won't end.

But *Life Begins at 8:40* was notable chiefly for satiric songs. Some were tailored to the comic persona of Lahr, with whom Harburg was to work repeatedly during the 1930s. For Lahr he crafted several mock art songs that destroyed all manner of cultural pretense. In *Life Begins at 8:40* Lahr transported the audience to the ineffably vague platitudes of Edgar Guest and Joyce Kilmer in "Things!":

Ah, Things! Sweet Happiness of Things!
Things that ease the Rocky Way,
Things that look at God all day!

The revue concluded with an extended mock operetta, "Beautifying the City," in which Lahr played New York's new mayor, Fiorello LaGuardia. The song prefigures Harburg's mini-operettas in *The Wizard of Oz* and is suffused with an affection for both LaGuardia and Franklin D. Roosevelt and respect for the New Deal.

The next year, 1935, Harburg and Arlen shared a house in Beverly Hills while working on movies together. Arlen had written a song with especially intense, disquieting music, with a melancholy melody suspended over a dissonant and ever-shifting harmony. George Gershwin told him the music was too complex for a popular song. Arlen played it for Harburg, who, as with the music for "Brother, Can You Spare a Dime?," heard something profound in the music that immediately elicited a lyric, titled "Last Night When We Were Young." Harburg's lyric with Arlen's melody added up to a song of sudden, transformative, devastating loss:

Last night when we were young,
Love was a star, a song unsung,
Life was so new, so real, so right,
Ages ago, last night.
Today, the world is old,
You went away and time grew cold.
Where is that star that seemed so bright
Ages ago, last night?

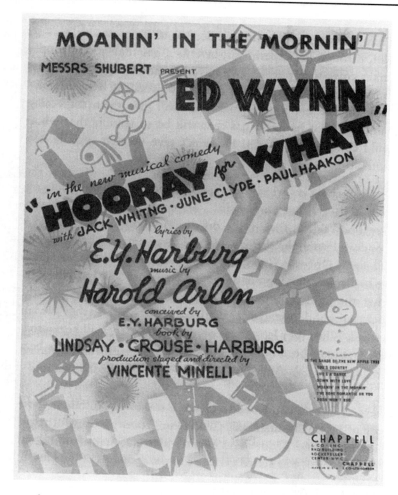

Sheet music for a song from a 1937 show, one of two Broadway musicals that Harburg and Arlen wrote in the late 1930s
(from Harold Meyerson and Ernie Harburg, Who Put the Rainbow in The Wizard of Oz? *1993)*

The final stanza moves from a metaphor of turning old overnight to more-literal physicality, with the recounted memories growing steadily more physical and intimate—and painful:

> So now, let's reminisce
> And recollect the sighs and the kisses,
> The arms that clung
> When we were young
> Last night.

The music moves beyond Arlen's usual blues into something more tragic and less remediable, and Harburg responds with a picture of a disillusioned world. The two songwriters often cited "Last Night When We Were Young" as their personal favorite. It is the only lyric Harburg ever wrote about losing love irrevocably, and it came shortly after his wife, Alice, suddenly left him and his father died.

Twice during the late 1930s Harburg and Arlen went back to Broadway. The two composed songs for the 1936 revue *The Show Is On,* for which they crafted another comic gem, "The Song of the Woodman," for Lahr. In 1937 they turned to a more ambitious project. Harburg had conceived the idea of a musical based loosely on the international armaments business, a particular target of 1930s radicals who laid retrospective blame for World War I on arms makers and looked fearfully at the military buildup of the new fascist powers in Europe. But the kind of integrated "book" musical Harburg was moving toward was not yet something he—or Broadway—was ready for. The show he put together, *Hooray for What!* (1937), did center on an inventor of a deadly gas, but cast as that inventor was the Broadway comic Ed Wynn. Wynn, moreover, did not sing. Still, the show was a hit, and Harburg wrote some witty lyrics, including "God's Country," in which he affectionately contrasted America's benign foibles with Europe's malignant Fascists: "We've got no Mussolini—Got no Mosley, / But we've got Popeye and Gypsy Rose Lee. . . ." Perhaps the most notable result of the show, however, was the effect that one song had on fledgling M-G-M producer Arthur Freed. "In the Shade of the New Apple Tree" combined a certain old-fashioned sentiment with a swinging looseness and modernity. That was enough to convince Freed that Harburg and Arlen should be the songwriters on M-G-M's ambitious new musical project, *The Wizard of Oz,* which, as Aljean Harmetz has argued, was more the product of the studio system than of any one individual—all the more so since the movie had two producers, three directors, and eleven screenwriters. But if one person is responsible for the unique charm and coherence of the musical, it is Harburg.

Freed later became the master producer of M-G-M musicals, but *The Wizard of Oz* was his first musical, and he was only the associate producer in charge of matters musical. His first and best decision was to hire Harburg and Arlen; he saw in Harburg's lyrics "a great sense of fantasy," he later told author John Lahr for *Notes on a Cowardly Lion: The Biography of Bert Lahr* (1969). *The Wizard of Oz* was also to move Harburg one step closer to his preferred musical form: the political parable cloaked in fantasy. The energy behind "Ding-Dong! The Witch Is Dead" is ultimately the result of the joy he took in a song of liberation, more particularly when it took the form of a comic operetta number. Similarly, Harburg wrote the scene at the end of the movie in which the wizard, shown to be a "humbug," is still able to grant the wishes of Dorothy's companions with altogether worldly responses and tells Dorothy that she is free and able to take herself home. *The Wizard of Oz* provided Harburg with the chance to create his first happy ending of demystification.

The Wizard of Oz also provided Harburg with the opportunity to put together a fully integrated entity—that is, a movie in which song and dance, far from interrupting the plotline, as in most Broadway musical comedies up to that time, would be the medium through which plot unfolded and character was delineated. Only a handful of Broadway shows and Hollywood musicals (chiefly the comic operettas of the early 1930s directed by Ernst Lubitsch and Rouben Mamoulian) had taken this form; it had always required the unifying vision of a single producer-director. For *The Wizard of Oz,* lyricist Harburg came close to playing that role. He served as the editor of the script through its many drafts; he excised an exposition scene of Dorothy's arrival over the rainbow and substituted the seven-minute comic operetta "Ding-Dong! The Witch Is Dead"; and he wrote the lines leading into all the songs, integrating them smoothly with the dialogue. Harburg was even instrumental in key casting decisions: Bert Lahr, who had worked with Harburg and Arlen in two revues, became the Cowardly Lion, and Ray Bolger, who had worked with them in *The Show Is On,* became the Scarecrow. Buddy Ebsen, who had worked with Harburg on the *Ziegfeld Follies of 1934,* was cast as the Tin Man, though he soon became sick and had to be replaced by Jack Haley (who had also worked with the lyricist). Harburg crafted the role of the wizard for W. C. Fields (hence the repeated references to balloon ascensions, a running joke in many Fields movies), but M-G-M was unable to sign him.

The Wizard of Oz begins with "Over the Rainbow," the best-known song Harburg and Arlen ever wrote, with each other or anyone else. While they had discussed what the song would say in detail, Harburg, as was his wont, left Arlen free to compose a melody before he imposed any verbal constraints. Finally, Arlen wrote what sounded to Harburg like much too heraldic, heroic music and played it with a complex accompaniment to the melody. Harburg responded, "Oh, no, not for little Dorothy! That's for Nelson Eddy!" Only when Ira Gershwin, called in to provide a third opinion, told Arlen to play the tune more lightly, with a touch more swing and a sparse left hand, did Harburg hear the song as suitable for Dorothy:

> Somewhere over the rainbow,
> Way up high,
> There's a land that I heard of
> Once in a lullaby.

In fact, the song is for "little Dorothy," Eddy, and almost everyone in between. The big octave leap at the start of the melody on the word "Somewhere" and the long vowels on held notes ("*O*-ver the *rain*-bow") put the song in emotional overdrive from the start. In addition, the music and lyrics interact at an even deeper level. Dorothy is home when she starts the song, on the "some" of "somewhere," on the home note and harmony. But when she leaps up to "where," yearning for that unknown place, the harmony turns to a melancholy minor. With one word, "somewhere," and two notes in the melody, the listener knows what Dorothy, the song, even the plot and theme of the movie, are all about. Of course, Harburg and Arlen had to balance the power of that emotion against the poignancy and delicacy of its context. By the third and fourth lines, the musical leaps grow smaller, short vowels (*a, of, once*) supplant the long ones, and the stanza ends on the first clear reference in the song to childhood, the word "lullaby," set to music that sounds like one.

Sheet music for the signature song from the 1939 M-G-M movie musical based on L. Frank Baum's novel
The Wonderful Wizard of Oz *(1900) (from Amy Henderson and*
Dwight Blocker Bowers, Red, Hot & Blue, *1996)*

The tension between the two musical strains (and the thoughts that go with them) runs throughout the song–both the need for a home and the need to leave it:

> Somewhere over the rainbow,
> Skies are blue,
> And the dreams that you dare to dream
> Really do come true.

In the bridge, or release (the B section of the AABA structure of the chorus), Arlen again uses simpler music under the following lines:

> Someday I'll wish upon a star
> And wake up where the clouds are far
> Behind me,
> Where troubles melt like lemon drops,
> Away above the chimney tops,
> That's where you'll find me.

Arlen then uses the first musical phrase (A) for the lines:

> Somewhere over the rainbow
> Bluebirds fly,
> Birds fly over the rainbow,
> Why then oh why can't I?

Harburg and Arlen end the song with the unusual structural decision to bring back the simpler music of the release ("Someday I'll wish upon a star"):

> If happy little bluebirds fly
> Beyond the rainbow
> Why, oh, why can't I?

There had been no reference to a rainbow in L. Frank Baum's *The Wonderful Wizard of Oz* (1900), the novel on which the movie was based; Harburg put the rainbow in *The Wizard of Oz*. In the movie it served as a kind of rhetorical transition from the black and white of Kansas to the Technicolor of Oz, but it was a good deal more than that. For Harburg, the rainbow stood for the act of dreaming, of imagining a better, more multihued world, as well as one in which many cultures could coexist peacefully. He was to return to the rainbow in multiple songs and shows throughout his career.

The first numbers written for *The Wizard of Oz* were "If I Only Had a Brain," "If I Only Had a Heart," and "If I Only Had the Nerve," three songs that establish the characters of the Scarecrow, the Tin Man, and the Cowardly Lion, respectively. They sing their different lyrics and plights to identical music; thus, these distinct but kindred voices take star turns that also serve as bonding ceremonies. Everyone needs a brain and a heart, as well as the courage to use them, Harburg is saying. The songs speak to perceived lacks, distinct needs, and a common human condition.

The section of *The Wizard of Oz* culminating in the song "Ding-Dong! The Witch Is Dead"—the Munchkinland operetta that begins with Glinda, the Good Witch of the North, singing "Come out, come out, wherever you are"—is the first sung section heard when the movie switches to Oz. It is one of the most formally ambitious numbers Harburg ever wrote. The sequence comprises not simply musicalized speech but musicalized speeches—of mayors, councilmen, union leaders, heads of ladies' auxiliaries, coroners, and commoners. Like the numbers in the Gershwins' *Of Thee I Sing* (1931), it is a satire of American public and political rituals, but it is an affectionate satire: "Ding-Dong! The Witch Is Dead" is, after all, a song for the day of deliverance. The lyric begins to run gently amok when Harburg starts placing normally unstressed syllables on emphasized notes—"*Which* was not a healthy *sitch*-uation for a wicked *witch*"—and settles down to a study of how many ways death can be adverbialized: completely, sweetly, neatly, legally, morally, ethically, spiritually, physically, positively, undeniably, absolutely, reliably, not merely, and sincerely. The establishment is smothering fact with ceremony, but it is a little-people's establishment, and Harburg's laughter is finally more empathetic than derisive. Incidentally, again, none of this material is in Baum's book; Harburg created it for the screenplay.

Harburg and Arlen's main battle for *The Wizard of Oz* came after filming was completed, when Louis B. Mayer and his associates wished to excise "Over the Rainbow," which they feared slowed down the picture. The songwriters repeatedly had to have Freed intervene with Mayer to save it. "Over the Rainbow," of course, went on to win the 1939 Oscar for best original movie song and to become one of the most widely known and most beloved songs in the world. The movie itself achieved almost talismanic status by virtue of its annual screenings on network television from the 1950s on. Today many critics regard *The Wizard of Oz* as one of the greatest movies Hollywood ever made, and it played an important role in the evolution of the stage as well as the screen musical. The movie preserved the loose, vaudeville style of Bert Lahr, which was typical of earlier stage musicals, but it placed this style within the newly conceived boundaries and structural advancement of the integrated "book" musical. At the same time *The Wizard of Oz* marked one last, gentle shot at the targets of the cultural wars of the 1920s, at the operas, the poetry, and the stultifying propriety that a Babbitt bourgeoisie had force-fed to Harburg and his peers when they were growing up.

After *The Wizard of Oz* Harburg and Arlen turned their talents to some other M-G-M comics, the Marx Brothers. For *At the Circus* (1939) they crafted a signature song for Groucho Marx, "Lydia, the Tattooed Lady." The number is a lyrical feast of comic incongruities as Harburg catalogues Lydia's tattoos:

Lydia, oh, Lydia
That "encyclopidia,"
Oh, Lydia, the champ of them all.
For two bits she will do a mazurka in jazz,
With a view of Niag'ra that no artist has,
And on a clear day you can see Alcatraz,
You can learn a lot from Lydia.

In 1943 Harburg and Arlen completed work on the last notable motion-picture musical for which they wrote songs: M-G-M's *Cabin in the Sky,* the first all-black movie musical to play to both black and white audiences. *Cabin in the Sky* had been a successful 1940 Broadway musical by Vernon Duke and John LaTouche, but M-G-M producer Freed commissioned new songs from Harburg and Arlen. They wrote two notable songs: the comic number "Life's Full of Consequence," which Eddie "Rochester" Anderson blurts out as he tries to fend off the advances of seductress Lena Horne, and "Happiness Is a Thing Called Joe," a ballad for Ethel Waters. "Life's Full of Consequence" was the first in a series of Harburg songs centering around one-word abstract nouns—to be followed by "T'morra', T'morra'" in *Bloomer Girl,* "Necessity" in *Finian's Rainbow,* and "Incompatibility" in *Jamaica* (1957)—in which some ignoble, manmade creation, be it guilt or capitalism, intervenes to inhibit men or women from following their natural impulses. "That ole devil consequence," Anderson sings as he pushes Horne away, "That's the wrench in the works, / It's consequences that irks."

The success of *Oklahoma!* (1943), Richard Rodgers and Hammerstein's landmark musical that fully

Harburg and Arlen accepting the 1939 Oscar for best original movie song for "Over the Rainbow" (from Harold Meyerson and Ernie Harburg, Who Put the Rainbow in The Wizard of Oz? *1993)*

integrated songs with the story and characters of the "book," allowed Harburg to take his next major step. Since the late 1930s he and Arlen had been pushing the boundaries of the established musical, writing scores of a distinct character from beginning to end and working with thematic material that ran through both the book and the score. In the mid 1940s Harburg proved, first with Arlen and then Lane, that he was able, like Hammerstein, to craft an "integrated" musical. Indeed, his 1944 Broadway score with Arlen, *Bloomer Girl,* was the first post-*Oklahoma!* musical to be called a "folk opera," in critic Arthur Pollock's words—but with political rather than nostalgic themes.

Moreover, from the mid 1940s through the early 1950s Harburg was in a position to control his own shows. For three successive musicals—*Bloomer Girl, Finian's Rainbow,* and *Flahooley* (1951)—Harburg wrote all the lyrics. He also conceived the ideas behind *Finian's Rainbow* and *Flahooley;* initiated and directed *Bloomer Girl;* cowrote, with Fred Saidy, the book for *Finian's Rainbow;* and cowrote (with Saidy),

coproduced, and codirected *Flahooley.* In the assessment of musical historian Stanley Green in *The World of Musical Comedy* (1960), Harburg "was the motivating force behind each production." He served the multiple functions Hammerstein did, but with radical politics, a more fantastical touch, and an array of collaborators. Although the Broadway musical is one of the most collaborative of art forms, Harburg's trilogy constitutes perhaps the most personalized musicals until the rise of Stephen Sondheim.

Bloomer Girl started out as an outline by Harburg's Hollywood acquaintance Lilith James about Civil War–era women's suffragist Amelia Bloomer. In the story he crafted with the librettists, Saidy and Sig Herzig, Amelia's feminist niece, Evelina, not only campaigns against uncomfortable hoopskirts in favor of "bloomers" (which were named for the historical Amelia) but also uses the suffragettes' headquarters as a stop on the Underground Railroad. The show, said Harburg, was about "the indivisibility of human freedom." The musical, set during the Civil War, was written against the backdrop of World War II, as well as the two great demographic shifts in wartime America: the entrance of both women and blacks into the industrial workforce. The libretto gives equal weight to the two struggles. Harburg's sharp political antennae were attuned to the movement for black equality, then led by such figures as A. Philip Randolph, which was given a major boost by the war. Harburg's espousal of the women's movement, however, which was at that time nowhere nearly as developed, was twenty-five years ahead of its time. The main feminist number in *Bloomer Girl* is "It Was Good Enough for Grandma":

> That good old gal
> With her frills and her feathers and fuss.
> It was good enough for grandma,
> Good enough for grandma,
> But it ain't good enough for us!

Later in the show, a runaway slave protected by Evelina and her friends emerges. In the song "The Eagle and Me" the slave, Pompey, explains to his master, Jeff, why he has escaped. His song, characteristically, starts with a question posed at the beginning of the verse: "What makes the gopher leave his hole, / Trembling with fear and fright?" Pompey answers resoundingly in the chorus:

> River it like to flow,
> Eagle it like to fly,
> Eagle it like to feel its wings against the sky.

There had been serious ballads for black characters on the musical stage before, such as Jerome Kern and Hammerstein's "Ol' Man River" (1927) and Irving Berlin's "Supper Time" (1933), that had dealt with the legacy of racism, but both of these are lamentations that take black oppression as a given, as does *Porgy and Bess*, for the most part. "The Eagle and Me," however, is a ballad of the 1940s, when, for the first time, a nascent civil-rights movement was beginning to direct public pressure to curtail institutional racism. A lamentation would no longer suffice. "The Eagle and Me" is the first theater song of the fledgling civil-rights movement. Like "April in Paris," "The Eagle and Me" moves from an imagistic beginning to a personal conclusion. Moreover, the striving for freedom is linked, by image and idea, to some universal life force, some basic natural law. Of all the images, that of the eagle is given special emphasis. There is an almost palpable sense of freedom conveyed by the eagle feeling his "wings against the sky," enhanced by the alliteration and the long vowels on the stressed and longer notes, to the words *flow, fly, feel,* and *sky.* The shock of the lyric comes in the bridge:

> Ever since that day,
> When the world was an onion,
> 'Twas natch'ral for
> The spirit to soar and play
> The way the Lord wanted it. . . .
> We gotta be free,
> The eagle and me.

Here, Harburg turns the song into something of a moral creation epic, moving the basis for freedom from the merely natural to the cosmological. In a 1981 interview with Jonathan Schwartz on WNEW radio in New York, Stephen Sondheim cited part of this passage as his favorite line of lyrics, a "resonant line that implies a whole ethos": "Ever since the day when the world was an onion. . . ." At bottom, Harburg is saying, the civil-rights struggle is about rights as fundamental and incontestable as gravity–about physical laws encoded, like genes in a DNA molecule, in that ancient onion. Even in the sparing use of the imperative mood at the end of "The Eagle and Me," this and other lyrics from *Bloomer Girl* pit the naturally ordained against the socially mandated.

Bloomer Girl also features a comic depiction of the war between society and nature. "T'morra', T'morra'"–a song about self-denial and repression–is given to Daisy, Evelina's maid, who laments the deferring of sex until marriage:

> The present, the present,
> The present is so pleasant.
> What am I savin' it for?. . .
> Utopia, utopia,
> Don't be a dope, ya dope ya,
> Get your Utopia now! . . .
> My dialectics are clear
> I'll havta, I'll havta
> Give up my hereafta
> For what I'm afta here!

The wordplay builds steadily through the choruses to a final rejection of both the political and religious abstractions–utopia and the hereafter–that are used to justify self-repression and self-sacrifice. These two rejections, moreover, stamp "T'morra', T'morra'" as a peculiarly personal song for Harburg. With the death of his beloved older brother, Max, when Harburg was still a child, he had come to reject the idea of the hereafter; with the economic crash of 1929, he had rejected America's promise of a worldly utopia.

Bloomer Girl was a tremendous hit. Critics praised the performances, the spectacle, the dances (which Agnes de Mille choreographed, as she had *Oklahoma!*), Harburg's direction, and, above all, the score, which was widely called the best since *Oklahoma!* the previous year. With *Bloomer Girl*, moreover, critics came to

Lobby card for the 1943 M-G-M musical scored by Harburg and Arlen that was one of the first all-black movie musicals aimed at both black and white audiences (from John Kobal and V. A. Wilson, Foyer Pleasure, *1982)*

believe that Rodgers and Hammerstein's ground-breaking show had not been an aberration, that the American musical had fundamentally changed, and that the integrated book show had arrived to stay. In *Bloomer Girl* Harburg had the kind of musical he had long sought to craft, and the public ratified his judgment: the show ran for 654 performances.

Harburg continued to work as the bard of left liberalism. In 1944 he produced the preelection-night radio broadcast of the Hollywood Democratic Committee, urging Roosevelt's reelection. Performed on the show was a controversial though humorous song Harburg had written with composer Earl Robinson, "Free and Equal Blues," which addressed the resistance that had arisen in the Red Cross and armed forces to mixing the blood pool of whites and blacks. In 1945, for a Norman Corwin CBS broadcast on the eve of the opening of the United Nations' founding conference in San Francisco, Harburg and Robinson wrote "The Same Boat, Brother," a rousing ballad of globalist ideals.

Harburg's next—and greatest—show, the 1947 musical *Finian's Rainbow,* carried on where *Bloomer Girl* left off, encompassing the liberal egalitarianism of the earlier show and adding to it, in the form of a fable, an assault on racism and capitalism. Going well beyond the standard populist assault on wealth and class inequalities, *Finian's Rainbow,* disguised and charming as it may be, is a work of socialist analysis in the form of the mainstream American musical—something that no one else has ever really attempted, let alone realized. It is Harburg's tour de force at "gilding the philosophic pill." It is also the quintessence of Harburg. In its humor and sentiment, its story and songs, all the complexities and contradictions that had permeated his work since "It's Only a Paper Moon" received their fullest expression. All three of the main male characters—Finian, the scheming rainbow chaser; Woody, the union organizer and troubadour; and Og, the lustful leprechaun—are clearly refractions of Harburg himself, an author-character identification all but unheard-of on the classical musical stage. *Finian's Rainbow* is his most complex and fully realized achievement.

The genesis of *Finian's Rainbow* began with Harburg's rage at the repeated wartime racist rants of two congressmen from Mississippi, Senator Theodore Bilbo and Representative John Rankin. Harburg toyed with a play in which such a character—in the show, he is named Billboard Rawkins—could be turned black, to see what the Jim Crow laws felt like firsthand. This idea prompted Harburg to think of magic, of the Irish legend of the three wishes, one of which inadvertently transforms a person. From there, it was but a short leap to the story of the Irishman who steals the leprechauns' gold and comes to America, as Harburg augmented the tale, to bury the crock by Fort Knox, where gold grows especially well. In the end Finian McLonergan's stolen gold turns to dross, but Senator Rawkins, turned black by the leprechaun Og, has been enlightened by his experience as a black man, and the biracial union of tenant farmers has grown richer on Keynesian economics. Finian, having lost his pot of gold, moves on to his next adventure. "Ah, things are hopeless, hopeless," he says in the penultimate moment of the show as the magic and the gold vanish. "But they're not serious!" he roars, recovering himself, and he is off, as the curtain falls, chasing his next rainbow to the next pot of gold, the better world. "That's all man has left," Harburg once said while lecturing on *Finian's Rainbow,* "the rainbow."

What emerged on stage was a quixotic mix of Irish-tinged folk melodies and wit, Southern country egalitarianism, socialist economics, and Broadway sophistication, with a musical score by Lane that is both suitably eclectic and brilliantly unified. Lane was sixteen years Harburg's junior, like Arlen, a George Gershwin protégé who had not yet written a Broadway hit. Harburg turned to Lane when Arlen rejected the show as too political and Robinson proved not to be up to the challenge of writing the music for a Broadway show. Lane was totally prepared to compose a dramatic score, including meeting the demands of composing the nostalgic Irish ballad, "How Are Things in Glocca Morra?" which became the signature song of the show—indeed, a universal cry of all immigrants:

I hear a breeze,
A River Shannon breeze,
It well may be
It's followed me
Across the seas.
Then tell me please. . . .
How are things in Glocca Morra?
Is that willow tree still weeping there?
Does that laddie with the twinklin' eye
Come whistlin' by,

And does he walk away
Sad and dreamy there,
Not to see me there?

So I ask each weepin' willow,
And each brook along the way
And each lad that comes a-whistlin'
"Tooralay,"
How are things in Glocca Morra
This fine day?

If the lyric for "April in Paris" works by association, that for "How Are Things in Glocca Morra?" works almost by incantation. The place-name Glocca Morra functions less in a denotative vein than as some old-world ritual whose original meaning has, in some measure, been lost. In the final stanza the nostalgia in the song becomes even more explicit: Glocca Morra is some lost Arcadian ideal, which the singer can ask about but not revisit. "How Are Things in Glocca Morra?" is reprised several times in the show, featured in the overture and at the final curtain. At the center of the only socialist American musical is a ballad not of worlds to come but of worlds that have been lost.

Or have they? Finian brings his daughter Sharon to America from Ireland to give her a better life, thereby joining thousands of his countrymen in contributing his culture to American life. Glocca Morra—Irish culture—still exists, distinct from but part of the larger American society. In this sense Harburg's philosophy has deepened from that expressed in *The Wizard of Oz*. There, the ultimate destination was Dorothy's original home in Kansas. In *Finian's Rainbow* the Irish look for a new home, in which they can also keep the best of the old. Conceiving the show in 1947, Harburg was decades ahead of those who looked beyond a melting pot to a place where people could be individuals as well as compatriots. Glocca Morra, as he wrote in the script for a 1980 revival of *Finian's Rainbow,* is "that far away place in everyone's heart, a little beyond your reach, but never beyond your hope."

"Look to the Rainbow," Sharon's anthem about her father, comes closest to a definitive statement of the Harburg credo, set to an almost hymn-like Lane melody:

Look, look, look to the rainbow,
Follow it over the hill and stream.
Look, look, look to the rainbow,
Follow the fellow that follows the dream.

Harburg had dealt with this notion eight years before. The original lyric for "Follow the Yellow Brick Road" in *The Wizard of Oz,* not heard in the movie, went:

*Sheet music for a song from a 1944 musical by Harburg and Arlen about nineteenth-century American
women's suffragist Amelia Bloomer (from Harold Meyerson and Ernie Harburg,
Who Put the Rainbow in The Wizard of Oz? 1993)*

Follow the yellow brick road,
Follow the yellow brick road,
Follow the rainbow over the stream,
Follow the fellow who follows a dream.

But *The Wizard of Oz* had not gotten it exactly right. Harburg ultimately did not wish to celebrate whatever it was that lay over the rainbow, much less affirm that there was no place like home. Look to the rainbow, he now asserted, to the dreamer and the very act of dreaming, to the activist and the fight to realize the dream, to idealism, struggle, and all that the rainbow now signified for him.

If "Look To The Rainbow" celebrates dreaming, questing, roaming, and taking action, there is another force at work in the mythical Missitucky valley where *Finian's Rainbow* is set, a force that anchors people just as they start to roam. It is the

"old devil moon" in the song of that title—for which Lane wrote a melody that begins with a complex upward movement:

I look at you and suddenly
Something in your eyes I see
Soon begins bewitching me.

The melody then explodes in downward cascades of joy, to Harburg's sensuous, exultant words and long vowel sounds:

It's that old devil moon
That you stole from the skies,
It's that old devil moon
In your eyes. . . .
Wanna cry, wanna croon,
Wanna laugh like a loon,
It's that old devil moon
In your eyes.

David Wayne (on ladder), who played Og the leprechaun in Finian's Rainbow *(1947), and Harburg at the Columbia cast recording for the Broadway musical (from Harold Meyerson and Ernie Harburg,* Who Put the Rainbow in The Wizard of Oz? *1993)*

Yet, the jubilation of love also leads to romantic entrapment. The coda begins with another Harburg bird, like the happy little bluebirds of "Over the Rainbow," a symbol of freedom. But this bird, the dove, cannot fly free:

> Just when I think I'm
> Free as a dove,
> Old devil moon,
> Deep in your eyes,
> Blinds me with love.

It is an uneasy resolution to an uneasy love song. No one blinded with love looks to the rainbow.

Finian's Rainbow was the first Broadway show to feature a racially integrated chorus—a necessity for depicting the black and white tenant farmers who were

Harburg's collective protagonists. "Necessity" is the name of the song—a mock-portentous, highly secular but church-like blues—in which they lament the socially imposed constraints on their lives, starting with a series of larger-than-life questions:

> What is the curse
> That makes the universe
> So all bewilderin'?
> What is the hoax
> That just provokes
> The folks
> They call God's childerin?
> What is the jinx
> That gives a body
> And his brother
> And everyone aroun'
> The runaroun'?

The all-encompassing answer is:

> Necessity, necessity,
> That most unnecessary thing.
> Necessity.
> What throws a monkey wrench in
> A fellow's good intention?
> That nasty old invention,
> Necessity.

Harburg's Lord is a Lord of begetting and abundance, all carrot, no stick. But his will is thwarted—by capitalism.

> My feet want to dance in the sun,
> My head wants to rest in the shade,
> The Lord says, "Go out and have fun,"
> But the landlord says,
> "Your rent ain't paid."

Thus, people's problems come from basic needs (which cost too much for many)—namely, shelter, food, and clothing:

> Necessity,
> It's plain to see
> What a lovely old world
> This silly old world could be.
> But man, it's all in a mess
> Account of necessity.

The mess of necessity is turned on its head by the first-act curtain number, "That Great Come-and-Get-It Day." Reports of newfound gold have opened the Shears and Robust catalogue spigot to the Missitucky farmers, and they celebrate in another gospel-tinged song:

> On that great come-and-get-it day,
> Won't it be fun when worry is done
> And money is hay? . . .

Sez here!
Sez it in the good book, it sez,
A mighty mornin' is nigh,
Universal Fourth of July!
Gonna get your freedom and pie!

Gradually, people's reasonable material desires are supplanted by the increasingly bizarre wants of a hyped consumer culture, as described in lines set to increasingly and ludicrously more reverential music:

Bells will ring in every steeple.
Come and get your test on the movie screen,
Come you free and equal people,
Come and get your beer and your benzedrine. . . .

Just as "Old Devil Moon" is in part a response to "Look to the Rainbow," so "That Great Come-and-Get-It Day" is an answer to "Necessity," moving from necessity to the realm of freedom. But the revolution that was reshaping America in 1946, when Harburg was writing *Finian's Rainbow,* was hardly a socialist one, and "That Great Come-and-Get-It Day" devolves into a satiric look at the rise of consumer culture, with the chorus upping its requests from washing machines to jukeboxes to helicopters.

The satire continues in the first number of act 2, when the farmers don their improbable high-fashion outfits for "When the Idle Poor Become the Idle Rich." The farmers may have succumbed to consumer excess, but they retain an almost Shavian appreciation of class differences:

When a rich man doesn't want to work,
He's a bon vivant,
Yes, he's a bon vivant,
But when a poor man doesn't want to work,
He's a loafer, he's a lounger,
He's a lazy good for nothing,
He's a jerk!

Nonetheless,

When the idle poor become the idle rich,
You'll never know just who is who
Or who is which,
No one can see the Irish or the Slav in you
For when you're on Park Avenue,
Cornelius and Mike
Look alike.

So why not go all the way?

Let's make the switch.
With just a few annuities
We'll hide those incongruities
In cloaks from Abercrombie-Fitch
When the idle poor become the idle rich,
When the idle poor become the idle rich.

Meanwhile, in another story line, the racist Senator Rawkins has been inadvertently wished into blackness—and liberalism.

Og the leprechaun, who has his own unique lyrical and musical language, also undergoes a transformation as a pixie who turns mortal. Harburg created a lyric for him, "Something Sort of Grandish" (filled with words ending in the suffix *ish*), set to a mock gavotte by Lane:

Something sweet,
Something sort of grandish
Sweeps my soul
When thou art near;
My heart feels
So sugar candish,
My head feels
So ginger beer.

The lyric continues ever more carefree and clever:

Something so dare-ish,
So I don't care-ish,
Stirs me from limb to limb.
It's so terrifish, magnifish, delish,
To have such an amorish, glamorish dish.

Og originally comes to America to reclaim his gold, but as he becomes increasingly mortal and steadily more susceptible to women—all women—he stops caring for gold. He sings, "When I'm Not Near the Girl I Love," one of Harburg's wittiest romantic laments:

Oh, my heart is beating wildly,
And it's all because you're here.
When I'm not near the girl I love,
I love the girl I'm near.

The basic idea of the lyric is strengthened through Harburg's penchant for alliteration:

Every femme that flutters by me
Is a flame that must be fanned.
When I can't fondle the hand that I'm fond of,
I fondle the hand at hand. . . .

To put it in a nutshell,

I'm confessing a confession,
And I hope I'm not verbose.
When I'm not close to the kiss that I cling to,
I cling to the kiss that's close.

"When I'm Not Near the Girl I Love" is what songwriters call an "eleven o'clock number," a song performed near the end of the show, when the composer and lyricist want to rouse the audience for the approaching cur-

Sheet music for the best-known song from Harburg and Burton Lane's 1947 Broadway musical (from Harold Meyerson and Ernie Harburg, Who Put the Rainbow in The Wizard of Oz? *1993)*

tain. Eleven o'clock numbers on Broadway today are often light shows that dazzle the audience. "When I'm Not Near the Girl I Love" dazzles the brain and ear rather than the eye, with a bravura display of near-palindromic virtuosity, with all of Harburg's comedic flair for neologisms, comically long or short lines, emotional veracity, and sheer wordplay:

> Always I can't refuse 'em,
> Always my feet pursues 'em,
> Long as they have a bosom,
> I woos 'em.

Finian's Rainbow ends with the farmers keeping their land, racism banished, boy getting girl, and Finian himself moving on to the next rainbow, the next dream. The musical received rave reviews and ran for 725 performances. Despite their success with this show, however, Harburg and Lane were temperamentally unsuited for one another and never worked together again.

In 1950 McCarthyism caught up with Harburg. While working at M-G-M on the most "American" of projects—a musical version of Mark Twain's *Adventures of Huckleberry Finn* (1885)—for Freed, he was blacklisted from writing for movies or television. There was no questioning Harburg's liberalism, but his personal correspondence during those years shows ample evidence of his detestation of Stalinism. He was not a member of the Communist Party. Nonetheless, Harburg was close to many American "fellow travelers" and had worked on Henry Wallace's 1948 presidential campaign. These associations were enough to get him blacklisted—unless he chose to "name names," an option Harburg repeatedly refused. The blacklist kept him from working on several Hollywood movies—most notably, Judy Garland's "comeback" picture, *A Star Is Born* (1954), which Arlen eventually scored with Ira Gershwin.

Harburg was still free to work on Broadway, which scorned the blacklist, and in 1951, with composer Sammy Fain, he wrote *Flahooley,* his most idiosyncratic musical. Set inside a toy-manufacturing conglomerate, *Flahooley* employs puppets and dolls in a satire of corporate culture and the zeitgeist of witch-hunts and loyalty oaths. More fundamentally, the show is a cautionary parable on the use of atomic energy and, underpinning it all, a comic contemplation of capitalism's tendency toward overproduction and underconsumption.

The overproduced commodity is dolls. "I've come into a world of pure fantasy," one character concludes, as the price of dolls continues to drop,

> Where people magically beget
> All that on which their hearts are set.
> Having got of that a lot,
> They cannot get what they've begot.
> What?

Flahooley was hardly a typical Broadway musical. The nonmusical stage had yet to tackle the problems associated with atomic power; Arthur Miller's assault on McCarthyism, *The Crucible* (1953), was still two years off; and here was the most avant-garde of the political avant-garde playing nightly on the Broadway of Frank Loesser and Berlin. Unfortunately, the show did not live up to the theme: the songs were uneven and the plotline confusing. Still, *Flahooley* was a wildly imaginative and eclectic evening of theater, featuring Bil Baird's marionettes, soprano Yma Sumac, comic Irwin Corey, and Harburg's lyrics. The show received acclaim in its preview run in Philadelphia, but when it reached New York, critics were either disappointed or politically outraged, and the show closed after only forty performances.

In the wake of the failure of *Flahooley,* Harburg was never again to control one of his Broadway shows as he had the previous three. Thereafter, a producer or director was able to change his work or even take it away from him, which was basically what happened on his next show, *Jamaica,* a project that reunited him with Arlen and that opened on Broadway in 1957. Harburg had conceived the musical as an attack on postwar American culture—in particular, its infatuation with atomic power and its dependence on consumerism. The show, he felt, demanded an offshore setting where American culture could intrude on a natural paradise. He originally called the show "Pigeon Island," and by 1956 the production had acquired a major star, Harry Belafonte, and an idiom—calypso—in which both Harburg and Arlen felt comfortable. The book, by Harburg and Saidy, was every bit as political as that of its predecessors but far less fantastical. "Pigeon Island" worked

Fred Saidy, librettist for Harburg's musicals Bloomer Girl *(1944),* Finian's Rainbow *(1947),* Flahooley *(1951), and* Jamaica *(1957), with Harburg (from Harold Meyerson and Ernie Harburg,* Who Put the Rainbow in The Wizard of Oz? *1993)*

as a story, with the action fully sustaining the authors' thematic aspirations.

But it was not "Pigeon Island" that finally reached Broadway. Belafonte suddenly had to undergo surgery on his vocal cords in mid 1956, and he would not be able to sing for a full year. At the command of producer David Merrick, the show was reshaped into a vehicle for Horne. Most of Harburg and Arlen's songs remained, but not the original story. Harburg felt increasingly distant from the emerging product, and he actually left the show shortly before it opened as *Jamaica* on Broadway, where, nonetheless, it was a major hit.

The songs from *Jamaica* were strong. "Push de Button" was a meditation on the automated life:

Sheet music for a song from Harburg and Sammy Fain's 1951 musical that satirized American corporate culture in a story about a toy-manufacturing conglomerate (from Harold Meyerson and Ernie Harburg, Who Put the Rainbow in The Wizard of Oz? *1993)*

Push de button,
Don't be antiquated,
Get de baby
All prefabricated. . . .

"Leave de Atom Alone" anticipated the sardonic spirit of 1980s assaults on nuclear energy. One quatrain certainly prefigures the spirit of the saying "One nuclear bomb can ruin your whole day":

You most exasperated
When radioactivated
And cannot be located
On telephone.

In the same vein was "Napoleon," a humorously cynical look at fame—in the long run:

Napoleon's a pastry,
Bismarck is a herring,
Alexander's a creme de cocoa mixed with rum,
And Herbie Hoover is a vacu-u-um.
Better get your jug of wine and loaf of love
Before that final bow.

The Harburg-Arlen score included one further exhortation to live life to the fullest. "Ain't It de Truth" was a song they had initially written for Horne to sing in *Cabin in the Sky,* but it was not included in the final cut of the movie. (One can easily imagine M-G-M's reluctance in 1943 to screen a song that included a casual denial of the afterlife.) Now, fourteen years later, they resurrected it for her in *Jamaica.* The ethos of the song follows from Harburg's philosophy:

Ricardo Montalban, Lena Horne, and other cast members in a scene from Harburg and Arlen's 1957 musical Jamaica
(from Harold Meyerson and Ernie Harburg, Who Put the Rainbow in The Wizard of Oz? *1993)*

Life is short, short, brother!
Ain't it de truth?
An' dere is no other.
Ain't it de truth?
You gotta rock that rainbow
While you still got your youth.
Oh! Ain't it de solid truth?

In its ecological and antinuclear concerns, Harburg and Arlen's score looked forward to the 1960s (and the 1990s) Left. In fact, some of the songs seem related to the late-1950s non-rock-and-roll rebellion: that fledgling, half-counter, half-straight, folk-music culture that was flourishing on college campuses. But the Broadway theater was not the primary venue for a new, politically oriented audience.

As popular music moved in the direction of rock and roll, and as the songs of Harburg's generation became suddenly and increasingly marginal to music's changing mainstream, he alternately tried to stay current by occasional collaborations with young, more-up-to-date composers, especially the gifted Phil

Springer; continued to write defiantly old-fashioned songs for a diminishing audience; or detoured from the theater altogether to the comforts of light verse. Harburg published one anthology, *Rhymes for the Irreverent,* in 1965 and another, *At This Point in Rhyme,* in 1976. In these he ran the gamut from topical observations to cosmological musings, such as "Adverbs":

WHERE and WHEN
    Are lost in space.
THERE and THEN
    Do not embrace.
So before we disappear
    Come sweet NOW and kiss the HERE.

Furthermore, even though the blacklist was lifted in the early 1960s, Harburg's kind of song was no longer in favor in Hollywood. His only subsequent project there, *Gay Purr-ee* (1962), was an animated movie with some strong songs that he scored with Arlen for such singers as Garland.

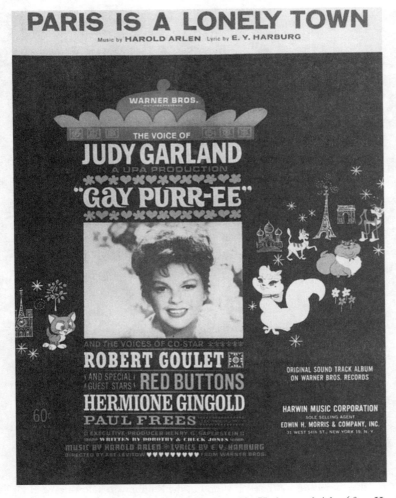

Sheet music for a song from a 1962 animated motion picture scored by Harburg and Arlen (from Harold Meyerson and Ernie Harburg, Who Put the Rainbow in the Wizard of Oz? *1993)*

In 1961 Harburg returned to Broadway with his most defiantly old-style musical yet: *The Happiest Girl in the World,* with lyrics set to the music of Jacques Offenbach, as arranged by Gorney. The musical was an adaptation of Aristophanes' *Lysistrata,* the classic Athenian comedy of women refusing to have sex with their husbands and boyfriends until the men stop their war. Lyrically and politically, *The Happiest Girl in the World* looks forward to the antimilitarism and anti-imperialism of the later 1960s, as in the song "The Glory That Is Greece":

Each backward nation is our protégé and ward,
We bring them culture with our cultivated sword.
We set them free from tyranny,
And woe to the foe who refuses to be free. . . .

Stylistically, however, Offenbach's light-opera music from the 1860s did not jibe with Harburg's lyrics.

The Happiest Girl in the World ran for only ninety-seven performances.

Nonetheless, the use of Offenbach's music gave an older Harburg the opportunity to return to his cosmological concerns—in particular, to the human quest for meaning in a godless, planless universe, a theme he had handled since at least as far back as 1932 with "It's Only a Paper Moon." For *The Happiest Girl in the World* he wrote the lyric "Adrift on a Star" to be set to Offenbach's "Barcarole" (1864)—which, as Harburg pointed out in a *New York Times* interview at the time of the show,

actually means "boat song," and I held on to that idea, but the interpretation I gave it is one which has post-Einsteinian, post-Freudian values:

Here we are
Adrift on a star,
Alone in a silent sky. . . .

The world we now know is a boat drifting in space. We used to think it was the center of the universe, that things revolved around us. Now we know different[ly]:

Lost in space
Together we face
The wonder of where and why. . . .

What I try to do is hit the audience with its everyday philosophy. Man is now preoccupied with his world as never before. Where are we? What are we doing? Can we destroy the world?

Why a sky without an end,
A sea without a chart?
Why the rain and why the rose
And why the trembling heart? . . .

Again, Harburg employed the Socratic method: question answered by question, answered by question.

Withal, Harburg's belief in the human capacity for transformation remained as strong as ever. With Robinson he wrote a title song for the Otto Preminger movie *Hurry Sundown* (1967). As it turned out, Preminger did not use the song, but Peter, Paul, and Mary recorded it, and it became Harburg's only song to reach the popular-music charts during the 1960s. For once, his abiding faith in the dialectic of human progress meshed with that decade's zeitgeist and taste in songs:

Hurry down sundown,
Be on your way.
Weave me tomorrow
Out of today.

For the most part, however, in the 1960s and 1970s Harburg, like most of his surviving contemporaries, was adrift on a sea of changing musical tastes. He occasionally collaborated with Arlen or Lane for individual songs, but Arlen was in declining health and chronically depressed, and Lane and Harburg were still unable to sustain a working relationship.

Harburg wrote one more Broadway musical, *Darling of the Day* (1968), with the composer Jule Styne. Based on *Holy Matrimony* (1943), a comic screen adaptation by humorist Nunnally Johnson of Arnold Bennett's novel *Buried Alive* (1908), the musical was set in Victorian England and concerned a famous painter, Priam Farll, a Gauguin-like figure who returns to England from the tropics, whose dying manservant is mistaken for him, and who proceeds to live in anonymity as the servant, happily painting—until his own talent exposes him. The score includes an unusual love song, "Under the Sunset Tree," written for an older couple. It is a resolution of sorts of Harburg's career-long battle with illusion and with the conflict between staying and straying:

Spring is a young man's fancy
In a world that is fancy free,
But to know the grace of a warm embrace,
When the heart is folly free,
Is to know why the bold leaf turns to gold
Under the sunset tree. . . .

The show also includes "Butler in the Abbey," a first-rate comic courtroom number, straight out of Harburg's Gilbert sensibility, performed by Farll as he endeavors to convince the court that unless they rule that he is his own manservant, they must face the fact that they have buried a butler in the Abbey—that is, in Poets' Corner in Westminster Abbey. If that is the case,

Dickens will be definitely stricken,
Pitt will cry the empire is dissolved,
Gladstone and Disraeli will be singing, "Eli, Eli"
And Darwin wish he never had evolved. . . .

While Harburg and Styne were working on the excellent score, however, the show went through a revolving door of librettists, directors, and stars. It reached Broadway in near chaos, and the uninspired performance of the leading man, Vincent Price, was roundly reviled. Critics such as Walter Kerr welcomed Harburg's lyrics as a throwback to Broadway's great past, but they were not enough to save the show.

Harburg did not lack acclaim. He inaugurated the 92nd Street Y's extremely popular "Lyrics and Lyricists" series and appeared five times in it. He was profiled in 1978 on *60 Minutes,* an episode repeated by popular request, appeared as a guest on late-night talk shows, and lectured at universities. Musical historian Ethan Mordden has hailed him as Hollywood's greatest lyricist. Histories of the Broadway musical rank Harburg with Hart, Porter, Hammerstein, Ira Gershwin, Howard Dietz, Alan Jay Lerner, Sheldon Harnick, and Sondheim. Lines from "Brother, Can You Spare a Dime?," "Over the Rainbow," "The Eagle and Me," and "How Are Things in Glocca Morra?" are quoted in John Bartlett's *Familiar Quotations:*

Once I built a railroad, now it's done.
Brother, can you spare a dime?

Somewhere over the rainbow
Bluebirds fly.
Birds fly over the rainbow—
Why then, oh why can't I?

We gotta be free—
The eagle and me.

How are things in Glocca Morra this fine day?

Dust jackets for two collections of Harburg's lyrics, published in 1965 (right) and 1976 (left)

But it was harder and harder to find composers of Arlen's and Lane's stature and talent as collaborators. Harburg's final song with Arlen, "Looks Like the End of a Beautiful Friendship" (1976), concludes:

> Here's to the end of a beautiful friendship,
> Here's to the stardust we promised to share,
> Here's to our beautiful illusions,
> May they still be there
> For my next affair.

Illusions, even dreams, may die, said Harburg in this song, but dreamers have to move on. He kept working right up to his death. On 5 March 1981 he was on Sunset Boulevard in Hollywood, driving to a story conference for a movie version of Robert Louis Stevenson's *Treasure Island* (1881), when he suffered a heart attack and died instantly. He was one month shy of his eighty-fifth birthday.

Harburg was distinguished by his ability to celebrate dreamers who act and activists who dream; to give voice to dreams, questions, and the quest for answers; and to translate his own indignation and joy into songs of hope, change, humor, and liberation. The man on the breadline, the runaway slave, the young lovers from Paris and Glocca Morra, and the little girl in Kansas all apprehended something better over the rainbow or in a new world they could build. To the lush harmonies of Duke, the show-tune drive of Lane, the old-world laments of Gorney, or the bold, melodic, and jazzy turns of Arlen, Harburg set odes to the human capacity for transformation—celebrations of imagination and decency that have enchanted the world and gotten people to feel, to think, and perhaps to act. "And the dreams that you dare to dream / Really do come true," sang Dorothy in *The Wizard of Oz*. Hundreds of millions around the world joined her in 1990 when the Academy Awards television broadcast closed with a satellite-feed sing-along of "Over the Rainbow" from Los Angeles, Moscow, Buenos Aires, Sydney, Tokyo, and London, apparently on the assumption that if there were such a thing as a global song, "Over the Rainbow" was it.

Interview:

Max Wilk, *They're Playing Our Song: Conversations with America's Classic Songwriters* (New York: Atheneum,

1973; reprint, New York: Da Capo, 1997), pp. 217–232.

Biography:

Harold Meyerson and Ernest Harburg, *Who Put the Rainbow in The Wizard of Oz? Yip Harburg, Lyricist* (Ann Arbor: University of Michigan Press, 1993).

References:

Caryl Brahms and Ned Sherrin, *Song by Song: The Lives and Work of 14 Great Lyric Writers* (Bolton, U.K.: Ross Anderson, 1984);

Lehman Engel, *Their Words Are Music: The Great Theatre Lyricists and Their Lyrics* (New York: Crown, 1975), pp. 72–80;

John Fricke, Jay Scarfone, and William Stillman, *The Wizard of Oz: The Official 50th Anniversary Pictorial History* (New York: Warner, 1989);

Philip Furia, *The Poets of Tin Pan Alley: A History of America's Great Lyricists* (New York: Oxford University Press, 1990), pp. 203–212;

Stanley Green, *The World of Musical Comedy: The Story of the American Musical Stage as Told through the Careers of Its Foremost Composers and Lyricists* (New York: Ziff-Davis, 1960);

Aljean Harmetz, *The Making of the Wizard of Oz* (New York: Knopf, 1977);

Thomas S. Hischak, *Word Crazy: Broadway Lyricists from Cohan to Sondheim* (New York: Praeger, 1991), pp. 79–85;

Stephen Holden, "The Lyrics of Yip Harburg," in *The Yip Harburg Songbook* (Miami: CPP-Belwin, 1994);

Edward Jablonski, *Harold Arlen: Happy with the Blues* (Garden City, N.Y.: Doubleday, 1961);

John Lahr, "The Lemon-Drop Kid," *New Yorker,* 72 (30 September 1996): 68ff;

Lahr, *Notes on a Cowardly Lion: The Biography of Bert Lahr* (New York: Knopf, 1969);

Bernard Rosenberg and Ernest Goldstein, "From the Lower East Side to 'Over the Rainbow,'" in their *Creators and Disturbers: Reminiscences by Jewish Intellectuals of New York* (New York: Columbia University Press, 1982).

Selected Discography:

Bloomer Girl, original Broadway cast (1944), Decca Broadway, 440 013 561-2, 2001;

Cabin in the Sky, motion-picture soundtrack (1943), Rhino, R272245, 1996;

Darling of the Day, original Broadway cast (1968), RCA, 09026-63334-2, 1998;

E. Y. Harburg, American Songbook Series, Smithsonian, RD-048-16, 1994;

Finian's Rainbow, original Broadway cast (1947), Columbia, SK 89208, 2000;

Flahooley, original Broadway cast (1951), Angel, ZDM 7 64764 2, 1993;

The Happiest Girl in the World, original Broadway cast, Columbia, KOS 2050, 1961;

Harold Arlen, American Songbook Series, Smithsonian, RD-048-5, 1992;

Hold on to Your Hats, Painted Smiles Records, 120, 1990;

Jamaica, original Broadway cast (1957), RCA, 09026-68041-2, 1995;

The Wizard of Oz, motion-picture soundtrack (1939), Rhino, R271999, 1995;

Ziegfeld Follies of 1934, live 1934 recording, AEI, 039, 1998.

Sheldon Harnick

(30 April 1924 –)

Michael Lasser

Music is by Jerry Bock unless otherwise indicated.

SELECTED SONGS FROM THEATRICAL PRO-
DUCTIONS: *New Faces of 1952* (1952)–"Boston
Beguine" (lyric and music by Harnick);

Two's Company (1953)–"Merry Little Minuet" (lyric and
music by Harnick);

The Littlest Revue (1956)–"The Shape of Things" (lyric
and music by Harnick);

Shoestring Revue (1957)–"Garbage" (lyric and music by
Harnick); "Medea in Disney Land" (music by
Lloyd B. Norlin); "Someone Is Sending Me Flow-
ers" (music by David Baker);

The Body Beautiful (1958)–"All of These and More";
"Summer Is";

Portofino (1958), lyrics by Harnick and Richard Ney,
music by Will Erwin and Louis Bellson;

Fiorello! (1959)–"Little Tin Box"; "Politics and Poker";
"On the Side of the Angels"; "I Love a Cop";
"When Did I Fall in Love?"; "The Name's La
Guardia"; "'Til Tomorrow"; "The Very Next
Man";

Tenderloin (1960)–"My Miss Mary"; "Good Clean
Fun"; "How the Money Changes Hands"; "The
Picture of Happiness"; "Artificial Flowers"; "The
Army of the Just"; "My Gentle Young Johnny";

She Loves Me (1963)–"She Loves Me"; "A Trip to the
Library"; "Grand Knowing You"; "Ice Cream";
"Perspective"; "Days Gone By"; "Dear Friend";
"A Romantic Atmosphere";

Fiddler on the Roof (1964)–"If I Were a Rich Man"; "Do
You Love Me?"; "Matchmaker, Matchmaker";
"Far from the Home I Love"; "Sunrise, Sunset";
"Anatevka"; "Tradition"; "Now I Have Every-
thing"; "Miracle of Miracles"; "Sabbath Prayer";
"To Life";

To Broadway with Love (1964)–"To Broadway with
Love"; "Beautiful Lady"; "Mata Hari Mine";
"Remember Radio"; "Popsicles in Paris";
"Hawaii;" "Concert," "Finale";

Sheldon Harnick (photograph by Margery Gray Harnick)

The Apple Tree (1966)–"Forbidden Love"; "I've Got
What It Takes"; "What Makes Me Love Him?";
"Here in Eden";

The Rothschilds (1970)–"In My Own Lifetime"; "One
Room"; "Sons";

Rex (1976), music by Richard Rodgers–"Away from
You"; "In Time"; "No Song More Pleasing";

A Wonderful Life (1991), music by Joe Raposo–"Christ-
mas Gifts"; "First Class All the Way"; "I
Couldn't Be with Anyone but You"; "If I Had a
Wish"; "Not What I Expected"; "Panic at the
Building and Loan"; "A Wonderful Life."

SELECTED SONGS FROM TELEVISION PRO-
DUCTIONS: *The Canterville Ghost* (1966)–"I
Worry"; "If You Never Try";

Free to Be You and Me (1974)–"William's Doll" (music
by Mary Rodgers).

Collaborating primarily with composer Jerry Bock, Sheldon Harnick is one of the most gifted lyricists of Broadway musicals. He is a man of the theater, whose songs for such popular shows as *Fiorello!* (1959) and *Fiddler on the Roof* (1964) are wed intrinsically to character and plot. As a result, Bock and Harnick's songs only occasionally appealed to a broader public that was increasingly uninterested in live theater. He emerged as a songwriter as musicals surrendered their primacy in American entertainment to movies and recordings and as rock and roll began its domination of popular music. Nevertheless, Harnick wrote enduring lyrics of trenchant wit, empathetic emotion, and sophisticated charm for musicals that were often innovative and unconventional.

Born in Chicago on 30 April 1924, Harnick was the second of three children of Harry Harnick and the former Esther Kanter. His father, born in the Austro-Hungarian Empire in what is now Romania, came to the United States by himself at the age of fifteen, studied dentistry after working in a cigar-making factory, and settled in Chicago. Harry Harnick loved to sing and to listen to music on the radio. There was also a windup phonograph in the house, along with recordings by such performers as Enrico Caruso, Jascha Heifetz, and Mischa Elman. Esther Harnick was a homemaker who was also a self-taught pianist and violinist with a passion for ragtime. Sheldon Harnick listened to popular songs on the radio but was primarily drawn to serious orchestral music.

Harnick attended Portage Park Grammar School and Carl Schurz High School in Chicago. At the age of eight, in the midst of the Great Depression, he began violin lessons at $1 a session. Like other outstanding lyricists, his musical training helped develop his sensitivity to the music inherent in language. A distant relative with some musical knowledge heard him play at the age of sixteen and said he was gifted but without technique. Harnick then began two years of study at the Boguslawsky Musical College and earned money playing in a small local orchestra at weddings and Bar Mitzvahs. An excellent sight reader, he was also hired to play for amateur productions of operettas by W. S. Gilbert and Arthur Sullivan, where he was enchanted by the linguistic virtuosity of Gilbert's patter songs. Harnick attributes his affection for their light operas to these early experiences. Some of his early songs, such as "The Suave Young Man" (1950), are reminiscent of Gilbert's comic style. During his junior and senior years in high school, Harnick collaborated on parodies and songs with a school friend named Stanley Orzey. He also wrote light verse, as Ira Gershwin and E. Y. "Yip" Harburg did before him. Harnick wrote the music, and he and Orzey collaborated on the words.

Under pressure from his father, who wanted to keep him out of military service, Harnick agreed to study pre-engineering at the Lewis Institute after graduating from high school as class salutatorian in 1942. He lasted a semester before the U.S. Army drafted him in 1943. In 1944, while stationed at Robins Field in Georgia, Harnick appeared as a performer and wrote songs for shows put on by a volunteer Special Services group. He describes the songs as personal in that they dealt with his own experiences in the army. Throughout his career Harnick has measured the success of his songs by their ability to adapt his own emotions to the characters who sing them. Unlike the troops attached to Irving Berlin for the production of *This Is the Army* (1942), Harnick and his fellow soldiers did their performing on their own time. He was also among the first American troops to arrive in Japan after World War II ended. He did not start going to the theater in any purposeful way until he was in the army. He especially remembers being excited by a production of Oscar Hammerstein's *Carmen Jones* (1943). He saw his first Broadway production, *Gentlemen Prefer Blondes* (1949), in 1950, because his brother was in the chorus.

After his discharge in 1946 Harnick worked in the Chicago area as a violinist in Bud Whalen's dance band and entered Northwestern University School of Music, where he majored in violin and contributed songs to the annual student revue, *Waa-Mu*. He graduated with a bachelor of music degree in 1949 and managed to land a job with the Xavier Cugat Orchestra. Cugat fired him after only one show, however, because Harnick improvised on the claves when he had trouble reading the minimal arrangements the orchestra used. He then toured the Midwest and played a long engagement at the Edgewater Beach Hotel in Chicago with Henry Brandon's dance orchestra. When Brandon had to cut three musicians to keep the band going, Harnick was among those let go. He had also begun to suffer from stage fright and a disorder called "violin cramp," which affected his left arm.

By then Harnick had become interested in writing song lyrics for Broadway musicals. If he failed, he thought he would become a librarian or even a tour guide at the United Nations. His serious interest in songwriting had sprung from hearing a recording of the hit 1947 musical *Finian's Rainbow;* Harnick calls the experience his epiphany. A college friend, the future cabaret singer Charlotte Rae, had urged him to listen to it. When he heard Burton Lane and Harburg's score, he suddenly realized that writing lyrics for the musical theater, saying pertinent things in entertaining ways, was a highly desirable career.

With war bonds and some savings to carry him, Harnick and his new wife, the former Mary Boatner, left for New York in 1950. She was his college sweetheart. He looked up an army friend and theatrical agent named Sol Lerner, who got him one of his first jobs, writing a theme song for a new television show, *Dumont's Cavalcade of Stars,* starring a young comedian named Jackie Gleason. During the seven years of their marriage, the Harnicks lived on

Tom Bosley in his Tony Award–winning portrayal of New York mayor Fiorello H. La Guardia
in Harnick and Jerry Bock's 1959 musical Fiorello!

Mary's salary, supplemented by whatever royalties Sheldon's few published songs earned. The couple had no children, and the marriage was annulled in 1957. Through Rae, Harnick met Harburg, who encouraged him but made the disheartening observation that it would take seven years before he would become a first-rate lyricist. "He was wrong," Harnick later observed, "It took nine." Harburg also said there were more good composers than lyricists for the theater and suggested that Harnick write with other composers.

Harnick sold some of his early songs to nightclub singers, such as Rae, Kaye Ballard, and Arte Johnson. Then, despite Alice Ghostley's show-stopping performance of his first Broadway song, "Boston Beguine," from *New Faces of 1952,* Harnick's career made little headway beyond placing individual songs in Broadway and off-Broadway revues. These songs included "Merry Little Minuet" in *Two's Company* (1953), "The Shape of Things" in *The Littlest Revue* (1956), and "Garbage," "Medea in Disney Land" (music by Lloyd B. Norlin), and "Someone Is Sending Me Flowers" (music by David Baker, Harnick's first collaborator) in *Shoestring Revue* (1957). He also placed songs in several of Julius Monk's sophisticated cabaret shows. During those same years he worked on the theater staff at Green Mansions, an Adirondacks Mountains summer resort, and was called in to write additional lyrics for several Broadway shows that eventually flopped, including *Shangri-La* (1956) and *Portofino* (1958). He also wrote the lyrics for his first book show, *Horatio,* with music by David Baker and a book by Ira Wallach. It was first produced at the Margo Jones Theatre in Dallas in 1954 and eventually opened for a short run off-Broadway in 1961 with a new title, *Smiling, the Boy Fell Dead.*

In 1956 Harnick met his major collaborator, composer Jerry Bock. Between 1958 and 1970, seven musicals by them were produced on Broadway: *The Body Beautiful* (1958), *Fiorello!, Tenderloin* (1960), *She Loves Me* (1963), *Fiddler on the Roof, The Apple Tree* (1966), and *The Rothschilds* (1970). Before meeting Bock, Harnick had suffered from clinical depression. He was unable to work until Samuel Liff and Len Bledsow, producers of industrial shows for advertising agencies, asked him to write for them. In 1958 and 1959 he wrote lyrics for such companies as Buick, Standard Oil, Millikin, Columbia Records, and Nabisco.

Although *The Body Beautiful* closed after only sixty performances, it was sufficiently promising for producer Harold Prince to hire the collaborators to write the score for a new musical about the legendary mayor of New

York in the 1930s and 1940s, Fiorello H. La Guardia. While *Fiorello!*, their first success, is a conventional musical comedy, it focuses on La Guardia's early years and culminates in his first election. It also provides a colorful view of life in New York City between 1914 and 1932 and takes a healthily irreverent swipe at politics in such songs as "Politics and Poker" and "Little Tin Box." Other important songs in the score include "On the Side of the Angels," "The Name's La Guardia," "I Love a Cop," and "When Did I Fall in Love?" The show was so skillfully written and vigorously performed (especially by Tom Bosley as La Guardia) that it won the Pulitzer Prize in drama, one of only three musicals to have done so. It ran for 795 performances and also won the Tony and New York Drama Critics Circle Awards. The director was George Abbott, who, Harnick says, taught him the value of writing economically.

Like *Fiorello!*, Bock and Harnick's other major shows demonstrate an affinity for creating bygone worlds populated by ordinary people who often find happiness but who may also suffer the loss of a job, a loved one, or a home. Among the settings for their shows are nineteenth-century Austria (*The Rothschilds*), Russia in 1905 (*Fiddler on the Roof*), and New York City at the turn of the twentieth century and shortly thereafter (*Tenderloin* and *Fiorello!*). Rarely do their shows depend on beautiful chorines and handsome leading men. Rather, they have always written scores that develop character clearly and penetratingly. A typical score by Bock and Harnick combines elements of social justice, comedy, and emotion with Broadway pizzazz. Even though Harnick's deft combining of irony and sentiment has a contemporary feel, he and Bock have also turned for inspiration to the styles of earlier days to match the periods of their shows. For *Fiorello!* their score includes both a nineteenth-century sentimental ballad, "'Til Tomorrow," and a twentieth-century brassy love song of character, "The Very Next Man."

For *Tenderloin* they wrote another nineteenth-century sentimental ballad, "My Miss Mary," as well as a parody of the same kind of song, "Artificial Flowers," which tells the mock-melancholy tale of an orphan girl who makes and sells artificial flowers of wax but eventually succumbs to illness and poverty: "and wiring and waxing, she waned." The song is typical of the effortless punning and wordplay that characterize Harnick's comic lyrics. Unfettered by political correctness, he felt free to make fun of the Victorians' maudlin melancholia over the death of a child. Elsewhere in *Tenderloin* he skewers the preciousness of virginity in the exuberantly amoral "The Picture of Happiness." Even though *Tenderloin* starred English Shakespearean actor Maurice Evans in his first musical role, it ran for only 216 performances. Taking its title from the "Tenderloin," the red-light district in Manhattan at the turn of the twentieth century, its story concerned the

Jack Cassidy and Peg Murphy rehearsing a song from the 1963 Harnick-Bock musical She Loves Me *(from Al Kasha and Joel Hirschhorn,* Notes on Broadway, *1985)*

efforts of a reformist minister to clean up corruption in New York City. The show had a strong score but was hurt by a book that lacked a consistent point of view. Among the noteworthy songs are a satiric number, "How the Money Changes Hands"; a hymn-like anthem, "The Army of the Just"; and the ebullient "Good Clean Fun."

In 1962 Harnick married the comedian and writer Elaine May, but they separated two months later. Three years later he married Margery Gray, a performer he met during the run of *Tenderloin*. Harnick adopted Gray's daughter, Beth. The couple later adopted a son, Matthew, born in 1968. In 1964 Bock and Harnick wrote new songs and adapted standard numbers for a panorama of the American musical theater, *To Broadway with Love*, for the New York World's Fair, and the next year they wrote a musical version of Oscar Wilde's 1887 story "The Canterville Ghost" that aired on the ABC television network in 1966. In their later shows together, Bock and Harnick proved to be especially good at innovating within the conventions and commercial constraints of the Broadway musical. Harnick's early lyrics relied heavily on his talent for wordplay and irony, but they also grew consciously from his own feelings and convictions. His strong sense of social justice led to such clever but biting songs as "Merry Little Minuet," about such man-made disasters as civil war and nuclear explosions. Even in later years, Harnick never lost his sense of humor and often used comedy to spice songs otherwise devoted to the revelation of character.

Harnick's penchant for lyrics that express character was also evident in *She Loves Me,* a small-scale musical that quickly became a cult favorite when it ran for 302 performances in 1963–1964. This succès d'estime, starring Barbara Cook and Daniel Massey, was based on a play, *Illatszertar,* written in 1937 by Miklós László, which was turned into a movie, *The Shop around the Corner,* in 1940 and then into a movie musical, *In the Good Old Summertime,* in 1949. It tells a tale of coworkers who despise one another but are actually in love even though they do not realize it. Set in a Budapest perfumery during the Great Depression, this romantic comedy plays out against the despair engendered by lost jobs, personal betrayal, and unrealized dreams. Though it focuses on the lovers, the score for *She Loves Me* gives six of its seven characters their own songs, including the naive "A Trip to the Library," the timid "Perspective," the nostalgic "Days Gone By," and the cynical "Grand Knowing You." The songs for the lovers are noteworthy for their emotional conviction, directness, and inventiveness, especially the title song and "Ice Cream."

With *She Loves Me* Harnick's work took on a new and convincing simplicity, especially in his writing of love ballads. He says it emerged as he learned to trust his own emotions. As a young man he loved Lorenz Hart's verbal shenanigans and Harburg's barbed social wit, but as he matured and became more secure about his own writing, he says he came to admire the unadorned emotionalism of Hammerstein. The sentiment in such songs as "She Loves Me" and the lilting waltz "Ice Cream" is clear and direct, but each is also a song of character that gives voice to a specific person in a specific circumstance. For example, Harnick's lyric to "She Loves Me" begins:

> She loves me and to my amazement
> I love it knowing that she loves me!
> She loves me! True, she doesn't show it.
> How could she when she doesn't know it.

The song is a sincere yet playful revelation of character. Its mastery lies in its repetitive twisting and turning of a few simple words until it reaches its punch line. At the same time, this one brief bit of lyric embodies the youthful high jinks, giddy confusion, and unpredictable tumbling into love that identify *She Loves Me* as a romantic comedy. Harnick's words, coupled with Bock's ebullient melody, are a direct and irrepressibly jaunty expression of emotion.

Likewise, in "Sunrise, Sunset" from *Fiddler on the Roof,* Tevye and Golde find themselves lost in their own thoughts as their oldest daughter marries. Harnick's lyric expresses their mutual emotions by linking their memories of their daughter's growing up and their recognition of their own aging with the passing of the days—from the personal to the universal. Harnick avoids banality by resting the characters' familiar response on Bock's sweet melody, flavored by Hebrew prayer, and adds his own undercurrent of gentle irony: "I can't remember growing older, / When did they?" Among the funniest and most revealing of the songs from *Fiddler on the Roof* are "If I Were a Rich Man" and "Do You Love Me?" Despite the success of *Fiddler on the Roof,* Bock and Harnick's songs rarely became hits because they are so firmly interwoven with story and character. "Matchmaker, Matchmaker" received some play on the radio, and "Sunrise, Sunset" was a successful recording for Eddie Fisher.

Adapted by librettist Joseph Stein from the short stories of Sholom Aleichem, *Fiddler on the Roof* tells the story of a group of eastern European Jews living in the obscure Russian village of Anatevka in 1905. It emphasizes the experiences of a poor dairyman named Tevye, who must come to grips with a changing world and still marry off his five daughters. Even though their choices in husbands surprise and eventually outrage him, he comes to learn they have chosen well. At the end, Tevye, his family, and all the Jews of Anatevka are banished from their home by an edict of the czar.

The Yiddish-inflected score of *Fiddler on the Roof* begins with a stirring number, "Tradition," that creates the village where Tevye, Golde, and their family and friends live, but it also defines the values by which they live. Harnick calls the number "the guidepost for the show." He adds that director Jerome Robbins influenced his writing by insisting that in addition to being a show about Tevye's family, it is also about the breakdown of tradition and the family's inability to cope with drastic change. Among the other notable songs in *Fiddler on the Roof* are "Matchmaker, Matchmaker," "To Life," "Sabbath Prayer," and "Anatevka." Among the numbers cut from the show is a song that combines ironic humor with deep sadness—for the individuals who must leave Anatevka and for the suffering of the Jewish people. "When Messiah Comes" is a tour de force that confused audiences, who were expecting something with less ambiguous emotion:

> When Messiah comes, He will say to us,
> "I was worried sick if you'd last or not,
> And I spoke to God and said, 'Would that be fair,
> If Messiah came and there was no one there.'"

Bock and Harnick replaced it with the equally emotional but more conventional "Anatevka."

One of the most successful of all Broadway musicals, *Fiddler on the Roof* ran for 3,242 performances during its original production, made Zero Mostel an international star, and won the New York Drama Critics Circle Award. It also won nine Tonys, including best musical. It has played successfully around the world and in 1971 became a successful motion picture starring the Israeli actor Topol. It won platinum records for both its Broadway-cast album and motion-picture soundtrack recordings. Also in 1971, the stage production became the longest-running show in Broadway history, a record it held until 1979, when its run was surpassed by *Grease*. *Fiddler on the Roof* also played a key role in transforming the musical play championed by Richard Rodgers and Hammerstein into something known as the concept musical. Less bound to plot, more fluid in structure, and more like dance than drama, the concept musical found its expression most fully a few years later in such works as *Cabaret* (1966), *Company* (1970), *Follies* (1971), and *A Chorus Line* (1975).

Harnick says his later lyrics reflect his attempts to empathize with what the characters are feeling and his no longer needing to mask his own emotions with wit. "Through a combination of living and therapy," he says, "little by little I got to be able to deal with those simple emotions." That, he says, was when he began to appreciate lyricists such as Hammerstein and Berlin: "I tended to think of Berlin as simple-minded. His simplicity of expression seemed too unsophisticated. The older I got, the more I recognized how difficult that is to achieve."

The Apple Tree, Bock and Harnick's most experimental production, ran for 463 performances. They wrote the book as well as the score for the three one-act musicals that make up the show, each based on a well-known humorous short story: Mark Twain's "The Diary of Adam and Eve," Frank R. Stockton's "The Lady, or the Tiger?" (1882), and Jules Feiffer's "Passionella" (1959). Barbara Harris, who in the original production played a different woman in each act, sang the three principal songs in the score, "Forbidden Love," "I've Got What It Takes," and "What Makes Me Love Him?"

The Rothschilds, Bock and Harnick's final collaboration, was unconventional primarily in its approach to its subject: the rise of poor Mayer Rothschild as the head of the Rothschild banking family in nineteenth-century Germany. The musical is less interested with how he made his fortune than with the emergence of modern European attitudes toward Jews. As usual, the score produced no hits but excellent songs of character, including a stirring soliloquy for Rothschild, "In My Own Lifetime," and his fiancée's yearning for the simple joys of domesticity, "One Room." The show also uses the fluidity of the concept musical in "Sons," which covers fourteen years in just over six minutes. Within the song, the ambitious and idealistic Rothschild realizes he cannot achieve his goals alone. Only sons will allow him to succeed because "Sons refresh a man's purpose, / Sons renew a man's hope," and "There are walls to destroy." The song provides insight into Rothschild's eagerness for fatherhood as well as his drive to succeed. He raises his five sons and instructs them in hon-

Sheet music for a song from the 1964 musical that ran for 3,242 performances on Broadway, thereby becoming one of the most successful musicals of all time (Bruccoli Clark Layman Archives)

esty, family pride, humility, and effort in a now-familiar mix of emotion and humor.

Bock and Harnick's separation occurred as the result of a disagreement over the dismissal of the director of *The Rothschilds* when the show ran into difficulties on the road. Though they continue to see one another, Bock has begun to write his own lyrics and Harnick has developed an interest in opera and has done translations, as well as a variety of projects with different composers. In 1976 he collaborated with Richard Rodgers on *Rex,* a musical based on the life of Henry VIII. Initially a failure, *Rex* was revised extensively by Harnick and Sherman Yellen, who wrote the book for the original version. Subsequently, there have been several successful productions. *Rex* was Harnick's last venture on Broadway.

His other collaborators include Mary Rodgers, with whom he wrote a musical version of *Pinocchio* for the Bil Baird Marionettes in 1973, and a single song, "William's Doll," for a Marlo Thomas television special, *Free to Be You and Me,* in 1974. He also translated the libretto of *The Umbrellas of Cherbourg* for Michel LeGrand in 1979 and collaborated with him on a musical version of Charles Dick-

Zero Mostel, who starred as Tevye in Fiddler on the Roof, *during the recording of the cast album for the musical (Institute of the American Musical, Inc.)*

ens's *A Christmas Carol* (1843) in 1981. He collaborated with composer Joe Raposo on several productions: an adaptation of Lewis Carroll's *Alice's Adventures in Wonderland* (1865) for the Bil Baird Marionettes in 1975, in which Harnick provided the voice of the White Rabbit; a cantata, *Sutter's Gold,* in 1980, which was premiered by the Boston Symphony Orchestra; and *A Wonderful Life* in 1991, a musical based on the Frank Capra movie *It's a Wonderful Life.*

After he and Bock separated, Harnick grew more interested in opera. Though he had gone to occasional performances and had already written the words and music for one opera (*Frustration: A Mini-Opera in One Brief Act,* 1968, performed in 1973 as one of several short operas in a program titled *Fantasies Take Flight*), his interest was kindled by a performance of Gian Carlo Menotti's *The Saint of Bleecker Street* (1954), starring Julia Migenes, an original cast member of *Fiddler on the Roof.* Jack Beeson, a composer of operas who taught music at Columbia University, asked Harnick to work with him on a light-opera adaptation of Clyde Fitch's 1901 play *Captain Jinks of the Horse Marines.* A commission from the Lyric Opera of Kansas City, it premiered in 1975. His other operas with Beeson are *Dr. Heidegger's Fountain of Youth* (1978), based on

Nathaniel Hawthorne's 1837 short story "Dr. Heidegger's Experiment," and *Cyrano* (1980), based upon a Dutch operatic adaptation of Edmond Rostand's play, *Cyrano de Bergerac* (1897). With Thomas Z. Shepard he wrote two one-act operas, "That Pig of a Molette" and "A Question of Faith," performed under the title *Love in Two Counties* in 1991. Opera Delaware commissioned Harnick, Norton Juster, and composer Arnold Black to write an adaptation of Juster's popular children's tale, *The Phantom Tollbooth,* in 1995. He and Henry Mollicone wrote *Coyote Tales,* commissioned by the Lyric Opera of Kansas City in 1998.

Harnick's other translations and adaptations include English-language librettos for works by such composers as Igor Stravinsky, Maurice Ravel, Wolfgang Amadeus Mozart, Johann Sebastian Bach, and Emmanuel Chabrier. His 1977 adaptation of Franz Lehar's *The Merry Widow* (1905) starred Beverly Sills and was premiered by the San Diego Opera Company. A subsequent album of the production won the 1979 Grammy Award for best new opera recording. His translation of the libretto of Georges Bizet's *Carmen* (1875) was commissioned and premiered by the Houston Grand Opera in 1981 and served as the English text for Peter Brooks's acclaimed stage production, *La*

Tragedie de Carmen, in 1984. Harnick's translations of several Yiddish songs were featured in the Los Angeles and New York productions of Joshua Sobol's play *Ghetto* in 1986, and he collaborated on the English libretto for *Cyrano,* a translation/adaptation of a Dutch musical by Od and Koen Van Dijk, in 1993.

Harnick's work for television and movies ranges from songs for the HBO animated movie *The Tale of Peter Rabbit* (1991, music by Stephen Lawrence) to lyrics for the opening number of the 1988 Academy Awards telecast. He wrote the theme songs for two movies, both with music by Cy Coleman: *The Heartbreak Kid* (1972) and *Blame It on Rio* (1984). Harnick has also worked over a long period on two projects, *Dragons* and "Miracles." Based on *The Dragon* (1943) by Russian playwright Yevgeny Schwarz, *Dragons* received its first production at Northwestern University in 1984, though Harnick had been working on the book, music, and lyrics for nearly a dozen years. A fantasy romance, ostensibly about a dragon that tyrannizes a village, *Dragons* is actually about the nature of power. "Miracles" is an unfinished musical based on an idea by librettist Joe Stein. It covers four biblical stories, with lyrics by Harnick and music by a different composer for each: Marvin Hamlish for "Moses," David Shire for "Chanukah," and Stephen Schwartz for "Esther." A fourth section, "David and Goliath," remains unwritten.

Sheldon Harnick is a member of the Dramatists Guild and the Songwriters Guild of America. His awards include the Johnny Mercer Award, presented by the Songwriters Hall of Fame; the Marc Blizstein Memorial Award, presented by the American Academy and Institute of Arts and Letters; and honorary doctorates of humane letters from Illinois Wesleyan University and Muskingum College. He lives with his wife in Manhattan and East Hampton, New York.

Harnick, actress Barbara Harris, and Bock preparing to record the cast album for the 1966 musical The Apple Tree *(photograph by David Gahr)*

Papers:

Some of Sheldon Harnick's papers are located at the University of Wisconsin; others are promised to the New York Public Library.

Selected Discography:

The Apple Tree, original Broadway cast, Sony Broadway, ST 48209, 1992;

Captain Jinks of the Horse Marines, original Broadway cast, RCA Red Seal, ARL2-1727;

Dr. Heidegger's Fountain of Youth, original Broadway cast, Composers Recordings, CRI SD 406;

Fiddler on the Roof, original Broadway cast, RCA, OK-1005 Victor, 1964;

Fiorello! original Broadway cast, Capitol, SWAO 1321, 1959;

The Rothschilds, original Broadway cast, Sony Broadway, SK 30337, 1992;

She Loves Me, original Broadway cast, DRG, DS-2-15008, 1963;

Tenderloin, original Broadway cast, Capitol, SWAO 1492, 1960.

Interviews:

Al Kasha and Joel Hirschhorn, *Notes on Broadway: Conversations with the Great Songwriters* (Chicago: Contemporary, 1985), pp. 153–169;

Max Wilk, *They're Playing Our Song: The Truth behind the Words and Music of Three Generations* (Mt. Kisko, N.Y.: Moyer Bell, 1991), pp. 185–194.

References:

Lehman Engel, *Their Words Are Music: The Great Theatre Lyricists and Their Lyrics* (New York: Crown, 1975), pp. 152–163;

Thomas S. Hischak, *Word Crazy: Broadway Lyricists from Cohan to Sondheim* (New York: Praeger, 1991), pp. 137–144.

Lorenz Hart

(2 May 1895 – 22 November 1943)

Frederick Nolan

See also "The Lorenz Hart Centenary" in Y-95.

Unless otherwise indicated, music is by Richard Rodgers.

SELECTED SONGS FROM THEATRICAL PRO-
DUCTIONS: *A Lonely Romeo* (1919)–"Any Old
Place with You" (interpolation);
Fly with Me (1920)–"A College on Broadway"; "Don't
Love Me Like Othello";
Poor Little Ritz Girl (1920)–"You Can't Fool Your
Dreams";
Helen of Troy, New York (1923)–"Moonlight Lane" (inter-
polation; music by W. Franke Harling);
The Melody Man (1924), lyrics and music by Hart, Rodg-
ers, and Herbert Fields, as Herbert Richard
Lorenz–"I'd Like to Poison Ivy";
Dearest Enemy (1925)–"Bye and Bye"; "Here in My
Arms"; "Here's a Kiss";
The Garrick Gaieties (1925)–"Manhattan";
Betsy (1926)–"Sing"; "This Funny World";
The Fifth Avenue Follies (1926)–"In the Name of Art";
The Garrick Gaieties (1926)–"Mountain Greenery";
The Girl Friend (1926)–"The Blue Room"; "The Girl
Friend";
Lido Lady (1926)–"Atlantic Blues"; "Try Again Tomor-
row";
Peggy-Ann (1926)–"A Little Birdie Told Me So"; "A Tree
in the Park"; "Where's That Rainbow?";
A Connecticut Yankee (1927)–"On a Desert Island with
Thee"; "Thou Swell"; "You're What I Need" (cut
before opening and introduced in *She's My Baby*,
1928);
One Dam Thing after Another (1927)–"My Heart Stood Still";
Chee-Chee (1928)–"Better Be Good to Me"; "Moon of My
Delight";
Present Arms (1928)–"You Took Advantage of Me";
Heads Up! (1929)–"A Ship without a Sail";
Spring Is Here (1929)–"Why Can't I?"; "With a Song in
My Heart"; "Yours Sincerely";
Ever Green (1930)–"Dancing on the Ceiling";

Lorenz Hart during the tryouts for Pal Joey, *1940 (Rodgers
and Hammerstein Organization, New York City)*

Simple Simon (1930)–"He Was Too Good to Me"; "Ten
Cents a Dance";
America's Sweetheart (1931)–"I've Got Five Dollars";
Jumbo (1935)–"Little Girl Blue"; "The Most Beautiful
Girl in the World"; "My Romance";
On Your Toes (1936)–"Glad to Be Unhappy"; "The Heart
Is Quicker Than the Eye"; "It's Got to Be Love";

256

"On Your Toes"; "Quiet Night"; "There's a Small Hotel"; "Too Good for the Average Man";

Babes in Arms (1937)–"Babes in Arms"; "I Wish I Were in Love Again"; "Imagine"; "Johnny One-Note"; "The Lady Is a Tramp"; "My Funny Valentine"; "Way Out West"; "Where or When";

I'd Rather Be Right (1937)–"Have You Met Miss Jones?";

The Boys from Syracuse (1938)–"Falling in Love with Love"; "He and She"; "Sing for Your Supper"; "This Can't Be Love"; "What Can You Do with a Man?"; "You Have Cast Your Shadow on the Sea";

I Married an Angel (1938)–"At the Roxy Music Hall"; "I Married an Angel"; "Spring Is Here";

Too Many Girls (1939)–"Give It Back to the Indians"; "I Didn't Know What Time It Was"; "I Like to Recognize the Tune";

Higher and Higher (1940)–"Disgustingly Rich"; "From Another World"; "It Never Entered My Mind"; "A Lovely Day for a Murder";

Pal Joey (1940)–"Bewitched, Bothered and Bewildered"; "Den of Iniquity"; "I Could Write a Book"; "Pal Joey (What Do I Care for a Dame?)"; "Plant You Now, Dig You Later"; "That Terrific Rainbow"; "What Is a Man?"; "You Mustn't Kick It Around"; "Zip!";

By Jupiter (1942)–"Ev'rything I've Got"; "Nobody's Heart"; "Wait Till You See Her";

A Connecticut Yankee, revival (1943)–"To Keep My Love Alive."

SELECTED SONGS FROM MOTION-PICTURE PRODUCTIONS:

The Hot Heiress (1931)–"Nobody Loves a Riveter";

Love Me Tonight (1932)–"Isn't It Romantic?"; "Love Me Tonight"; "Lover"; "Mimi";

Dancing Lady (1933)–"That's the Rhythm of the Day";

Hallelujah, I'm a Bum (1933)–"You Are Too Beautiful";

Hollywood Party (1934)–"Manhattan Melodrama"; "Prayer";

Manhattan Melodrama (1934)–"The Bad in Ev'ry Man";

The Merry Widow (1934), music by Franz Lehár–"Vilia" (lyric by Hart and Gus Kahn);

Mississippi (1935)–"Down by the River"; "It's Easy to Remember";

Too Many Girls (1940)–"You're Nearer."

SELECTED SONGS PUBLISHED INDEPENDENTLY OF THEATRICAL OR MOTION-PICTURE PRODUCTIONS:

"Chloe, Cling to Me" (1922), lyric by Hart and Herbert Fields, music by Joseph Trounstine;

"The Spanish Dancer" (1924), music by Mel Shauer;

"Terpsichore and Troubadour" (1925);

"Blue Moon" (1934);

"The Bombardier Song" (1942);

"Shorty the Gunner" (1942).

BOOK: *The Complete Lyrics of Lorenz Hart,* edited by Dorothy Hart and Robert Kimball (New York: Knopf, 1986; enlarged edition, New York: Da Capo Press, 1995).

SELECTED PERIODICAL PUBLICATION–UNCOLLECTED: "Perfect Union: Essentials in Lyrics and Music," by Hart and Richard Rodgers, *Variety,* 31 July 1940.

The wistfulness, the wit, the elegant "rightness"–and the essential hopelessness–of these couplets from the 1926 song "Where's That Rainbow?" are immediately identifiable:

> In each scenario,
> You can depend on the end
> Where the lovers agree.
> Where's my Lothario?
> Where does he roam, with his dome
> Vaselined as can be?

These lines can have come from the lyrical lexicon of only one writer: Lorenz Hart. At once irrepressible and sad, insouciant and tragic, reckless and withdrawn, cocky yet insecure, brilliant but unreliable–a kaleidoscope of conflicting inclinations that were simultaneously the wellsprings of his genius and the roots of his downfall–he was one of the most erudite, sophisticated, and talented writers ever to have addressed the subject of the popular song. Yet, more than a century after his birth, he remains nearly forgotten by the general public, the greater part of his work seemingly fated to be forever overshadowed by his former songwriting partner's later collaboration with Oscar Hammerstein 2nd.

Born in Manhattan on 2 May 1895, Lorenz Milton "Larry" Hart was the second son of a shamelessly outrageous self-promoter and main-chancer named Max Hart (originally Hertz), who had come to the United States as a boy from Hamburg, Germany, and Frieda Eisenberg Hart. The couple married in 1886; their first child, James, died in infancy. After "Lorry," as Larry's mother always called him, came another son, grandly named Theodore "Teddy" Van Wyck, for Theodore Roosevelt and for a New York mayor, Robert A. Van Wyck, with whom Max Hart was then friendly.

Family life at the Hart home was at best undisciplined and often a katzenjammer chaos. When times

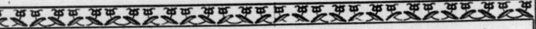

Fire Notice—Look around NOW and choose the Exit nearest your seat. In case of fire walk (not run) to THAT exit. Do not try to beat your neighbor to the street.
THOMAS J. DRENNAN, Fire Commissioner.

The
THEATRE GUILD
presents

The Theatre Guild Jr. Players
in the

Garrick Gaieties

Music by Richard Rodgers   *Lyrics by Lorenz Hart*
Production directed by Philip Loeb.
Settings and costumes designed by Carolyn Hancock.
Orchestra directed by Richard Rodgers.

ACT ONE.

"Soliciting Subscriptions"
In which we let you into one of the business secrets of an Art theatre.
Sterling Holloway, James Norris, Romney Brent, June Cochrane

"Gilding the Guild"
In which we introduce you to Betty Starbuck and the Guild Gaieties Chorus;
(the girls are all college graduates and have undergone a course in the
higher mathematics, which accounts for their keeping time so well.)
Betty Starbuck and Chorus

"The Guardsman"
by B. M. Kaye
(*With apologies to Franz Molnar, Alfred Lunt, Lynn Fontanne and*
Dudley Digges.)
Alfred Lunt, The Actor..Romney Brent
Lynn Fontanne, The Actress..Edith Meiser
Dudley Digges, The Critic...Philip Loeb

"Romantic You and Sentimental Me"
June Cochrane, James Norris, Edith Meiser, and Sterling Holloway

"Working With a Scarf"
Eleanor Shaler

continued on page x

Program of the 1925 revue in which Hart and Richard Rodgers's "Manhattan" was introduced
(from Samuel Marx and Jan Clayton, Rodgers and Hart, *1976)*

were good, the household had two maids, a chauffeur, and even a footman. It was the scene of lavish parties attended by the beau monde of Gilded Age Manhattan: Lillian Russell, Fay Templeton, John Morrissey, Tony Pastor, Willie Hammerstein (Oscar's father), and "Diamond Jim" Brady. But when Max Hart's fortunes waned, as they frequently did, he would hock his wife's jewels, fire the housemaids and the chauffeur, and cut down on the champagne and caviar until things looked up. Such a turnaround did not usually take long: he always had a couple dozen irons in the fire, not all of them legitimate. In fact, as Larry grew up, he took a certain raffish pleasure in telling his friends that his "O.M"–"Old Max" or "Old Man"–was an out-and-out crook. Certainly, Max Hart took perverse pleasure in outraging the sensibilities of his proper middle-class neighbors in tree-lined Harlem, thinking nothing of urinating out of his son's bedroom window.

Larry and Teddy Hart had a bizarre, outrageously spoiled childhood of parties, theatergoing, and outings, balanced only by the more sober proprieties of school and synagogue. By the time he was ten, Larry was already writing poetry. At thirteen he began writing skits, sketches, and songs for shows put on by his fellow summer campers at the Weingart Institute, in Highmount, in upstate New York, and editing the camp magazine, which he characteristically referred to as the "Daily Dope Sheet." (He was to become a lifelong aficionado of the scratch sheet.) Hart attended Columbia Grammar School and enrolled in Columbia University in 1913. He transferred to the Columbia School of Journalism the following year but never took a degree.

Hart took pleasure in being "shocking." "Wherever Larry was there was excitement," his fellow camper Mel Shauer remembered in later years. "He was a laughter-maker, a non-conformist." Hart himself claimed to believe that he had "inherited some inborn rascality from a bacchanalian progenitor" that justified his precocious and avid interest in sex, liquor, a spendthrift lifestyle, and outrageous behavior. It is therefore all the more amazing that he should have chosen as his collaborator, friend, and perhaps also later his own source of constant irritation (to paraphrase Rodgers's characterization of Hart), the young Richard Charles Rodgers, the properly–one might almost say severely–brought-up son of a "society" doctor.

By the time Rodgers first met him in 1918–Hart then twenty-three, Rodgers a mere sixteen–Larry Hart, as he was now widely known, was already recognized as one of the most original young writers in New York, a lyricist of such abundant talent that such an established Tin Pan Alley writer as Billy Rose would pay him $100 a session to come up with ideas. Another would-be Broadway composer, Arthur Schwartz, actu-

Helen Ford as the title character in the prologue to Rodgers and Hart's 1926 show Peggy-Ann *(Billy Rose Theatre Collection, New York Public Library for the Performing Arts)*

ally enrolled in one of the summer camps Hart attended each year just to get a chance to work with him, underlining the awe in which Hart was held by his contemporaries long before anything he wrote had been heard on the Broadway stage. Rodgers, by comparison, was a novice composer who had as yet written nothing outside of a few tunes for camp or club shows. But he had the great good fortune to know Philip Leavitt, son of a paint manufacturer, who dabbled in amateur shows produced for charity. Leavitt liked Rodgers's melodies but "realized Dick needed someone who could write lyrics that approached his music, and I suggested . . . he do a tie-up with Lorry." Rodgers agreed, and a few days later Leavitt took him around to West 119th Street (just a few blocks from the Rodgers home on West 120th Street) and introduced him to Hart. "It was so simple," Leavitt remembered. "Dick sat down at the piano and Lorry said 'What have you written?' and Dick played some of his music, and it was really love at first sight. All that had to be done was [for me to] sit, listen, and let nature take its course."

Sammy White and Eva Puck in Rodgers and Hart's 1926 show
The Girl Friend *(Billy Rose Theatre Collection, New York*
Public Library for the Performing Arts)

Contrary to movie "tradition" about struggling songwriters, the new team of Rodgers and Hart received its first break almost immediately. In the summer of 1919 Leavitt introduced them to producer Lew Fields, of the comedy team Weber and Fields. Rodgers played some of the songs they had written, and Fields selected one of them to be used in *A Lonely Romeo,* a show he was preparing for its Broadway opening. The song was a jaunty number called "Any Old Place with You," and it served notice on Broadway that a new era of lyric writing had begun. In it Hart rhymed "dude a pest" with "Budapest," "corner ya" and "California," and even more outrageously, "I'd go to hell for ya / Or Philadelphia." *A Lonely Romeo* opened on 10 June 1919 and ran for exactly seven weeks. After that hopeful beginning (with the exception of a "score" consisting mostly of revamped amateur-show songs for a 1920 Fields production called *Poor Little Ritz Girl*) it was five years before Rodgers and Hart got another Broadway break.

One by-product of Rodgers and Hart's work with Fields was the close friendship they struck up with his son Herbert, who wrote dramatic sketches and "books" for musicals. Over the next five years, Rodgers, Hart, and Herbert Fields wrote some fifteen complete amateur productions—Columbia Varsity shows, shows for a young men's association called the Akron Club, for the Oppenheim Collins Mutual Aid Associa-

tion of Brooklyn, the Free Scholarship Fund of the New York Child Labor Commission, Mrs. Benjamin's School for Girls (Mrs. Benjamin put up the entire $3,000 so her students could gain some acting experience), the Institute of Musical Art, the Park Avenue Synagogue, and the Evelyn Goldsmith Home for Crippled Children—but none of these led to professional productions. Still, the trio plugged on, producing, under the collective pseudonym "Herbert Richard Lorenz," a short-lived drama called *The Melody Man* (1924), which is remembered solely as the vehicle that introduced Fredric March to Broadway.

Rodgers, Hart, and Herbert Fields next collaborated on a musical play about an episode in the Revolutionary War and managed to interest actress Helen Ford, who had had a big hit in *The Gingham Girl* (1922), in helping them audition it for backers, but no one wanted to put money into a show by complete unknowns. With nothing at all to show for five years of dedicated hard work, it was beginning to look as if the team of Rodgers and Hart was finished before it had ever started. At age thirty, Hart had to start considering other options. Rodgers, who had never held a job, was seriously entertaining the thought of becoming a salesman of baby clothes at $50 a week. Then his phone rang.

The caller, a friend of Rodgers's older brother, Mortimer, told Rodgers the prestigious Theatre Guild was putting on a two-performance Sunday-night benefit and wondered if he would be interested in writing the songs for it. Rodgers said yes, and it was arranged for him to meet a deputation from the guild consisting of actors Romney Brent and Edith Meiser. On the appointed day Brent could not make it, so Meiser auditioned Rodgers and "wasn't terribly impressed" with what she heard. "And then he played 'Manhattan,'" she said, "and I *flipped!* I knew, I knew, this was an enormous, big, hit number."

> We'll have Manhattan,
> The Bronx, and Staten
> Island, too.
> It's lovely going through
> The zoo. . . .
> And tell me what street
> Compares with Mott Street
> In July?
> Sweet pushcarts gently gliding by.
> The great big city's a wondrous toy
> Just made for a girl and boy.
> We'll turn Manhattan
> Into an isle of joy.

The show was *The Garrick Gaieties* (1925), its aim to raise money for tapestries to decorate the auditorium of the theater from which the show took its name. Many years later Rodgers and Hart stood in the auditorium, remembering old times. Hart pointed to the hanging tapestries and said, "Look, Dick, we were responsible for those." And Rodgers replied, "No, Larry, they were responsible for us." In a way he was right, because the little show originally slated for two performances was such a hit that it was held over for a respectable run, during which "Manhattan" became one of the biggest popular songs of the 1920s. The song and its "infectious lyric" were reprinted in newspapers all over the country, heralded as a new breakthrough in the art of songwriting. "Manhattan" also heralded the "arrival" of Rodgers and Hart as a major new theatrical team.

The Rodgers-Hart partnership may be viewed in three slightly overlapping stages. The first covers the years 1926 to 1930, when the songwriters were perfecting their youthful skills in bright, bouncy shows written, as most were in that period, around star performers whose tried-and-true routines had been staple Broadway fare for many years. In the second period, 1930 to 1935, Rodgers and Hart worked as contract writers in Hollywood, where—with one or two exceptions—they had neither control over nor, apparently, much interest in what they were writing. Finally came the triumphant series of innovative, fresh, and utterly original Broadway musicals that the team wrote between 1935 and 1943.

The success of *The Garrick Gaieties* in 1925 triggered the production of Rodgers and Hart's show about the Revolutionary War. *Dearest Enemy* (1925), starring Helen Ford, gave them another substantial success. Already, critics were remarking on how different Hart's approach to lyrics was from the standard Tin Pan Alley, thirty-two-bar, "moon-croon-June" technique. Just how different is apparent in "In the Name of Art," a declamatory opening written for *The Fifth Avenue Follies*, a nightclub show staged by Billy Rose in 1926:

Kind auditors, you see in us
A most unholy Trinity!
Compared to us, Boccaccio's
A doctor of divinity!
Our sins if laid from end to end
Would stretch into infinity!
We earn an honest living
While we rob you of your sleep.
Our manager has warned us
It's the height of asininity
If we'd offend the morals
Of this sacrosanct vicinity!
Our show must please both movie stars
And ladies of virginity!

No American had ever written a lyric like this for the stage before. Audiences of 1926 were used to songs that

Rodgers (middle) and Hart (right) in 1927 with Herbert Fields, who wrote the librettos for their shows from 1925 to 1931 (from Stanley Green, The World of Musical Comedy, *1962)*

were really jingles: "Just tea for two and two for tea, / Just me for you and you for me"; "Your eyes of blue, your kisses, too, / I never knew what they could do"; or "When the red, red robin / Comes bob, bob, bobbin' along." They were not ready for the kind of wit and sophistication that Hart was determined to bring to the Broadway stage.

As a result, during this first decade of their collaboration, Hart and Rodgers had difficulties in getting their kind of work accepted. Even Lew Fields, more sympathetic than most to what they were trying to do, balked when they brought in a lyric for his show *A Connecticut Yankee* (1927) that he felt was altogether too clever. The audience, he protested, would never "get" Hart's eclectic mix of contemporary American and mock–Olde English. After a strenuous argument Fields allowed the song to be included, but only on condition that if the first-night audience did not like it, out it would go. It is not difficult to understand Fields's puzzlement. The second verse opened:

Thy words are queer, sir,
Unto mine ear, sir,
Yet thou'rt dear, sir,
To me.
Thou couldst woo me.
Now couldst thou try, knight.
I'd murmur "Swell," too,
And like it well, too.

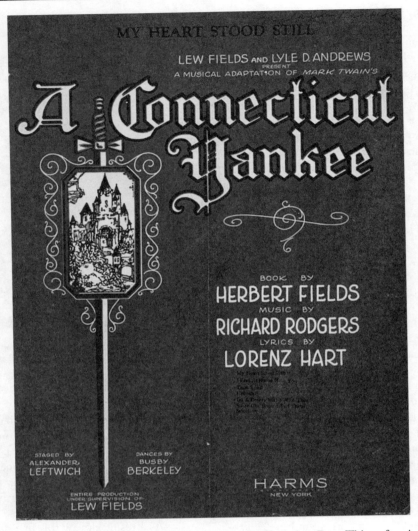

Sheet music for the 1927 Rodgers and Hart song that was introduced in One Dam Thing after Another
and recycled in their second show of that year (Bruccoli Clark Layman Archives)

"Thou Swell" remained in the score, a perfect example of Hart's impeccable ear for singable lines.

Despite such simple and eloquent statements as the deliberately monosyllabic "My Heart Stood Still" (1927) or the mischievous charm of "A Tree in the Park" (1926) many of Hart's songs came all too easily under the criticism voiced by lyricist Howard Dietz, who remarked that "Larry Hart can rhyme anything. And does." But what appeared to be overrhyming was sometimes occasioned by the syncopations of Rodgers's melodies: for instance, in "You're What I Need" (1927), the seemingly forced rhyme "I need/my need" is there because the skip in the melody requires it. Likewise, in "Sing" (1926), the two-note emphasis at the end of each line of music insists that the lyric follow:

When you are blue, sing;
Be sure you do sing;
I'm telling you sing something!
Start in to hum that dumb thing,
"Ta-ra-ta-ra sing boom!"

To fault Hart for trying too hard in his lyrics, however, is to miss the point. Verbal pyrotechnics, puns, in-jokes, slang, brand names, and even the titles of show tunes built into show tunes—that was the whole idea. Hart was intent on "seeing what could be done," on pushing the boundaries of song lyrics outward as far as he could. He did not intend them simply to be sung, but to be acted as part of the play. Most of them were written for a specific spot in a specific show at a specific moment—sometimes with the benefit of time for Hart to

Hart and Rodgers in Makers of Melody *(1929), a movie short*
(The Academy of Motion Picture Arts & Sciences)

reflect on how a song would fit into the show, but far more often because a number was needed here, now, ready to perform. The remarkable thing, then, is not how many sometimes forced or merely adequate quatrains there are in Hart's work, but how few.

What emerges from Hart's lyrics is a constantly surprising range of polysyllabic invention that not only has its own freight of knowing humor but reflects the essence of that moment, that time, that place. Nowhere in his work does the sloppiness of today's writers—rhyming *fine* with *time* or *maybe* with *daisy*—appear. Everything rhymes; the vocabulary is always apt, sometimes elegantly, as in "How we love sequestering / Where no pests are pestering," from "Mountain Greenery" (1926); or outlandishly, as in the first encore from the same song: "You can bet your life its tone / Beats a Jascha Heifetz tone." It was as much a direct result of the charm and elegance of Hart's lyrics as it was of Rodgers's melodies that the "standards" that grew organically out of their shows went on to outlive the vehicles for which they were written and become classics of American popular song.

In 1926, however, shows were written around established performers and acts, and at first, Rodgers, Hart, and Herbert Fields had no choice but to follow that convention. They wrote a show designed around the talents of a popular husband-and-wife team, Eva Puck and Sammy White, a diminutive song-and-dance duo who had been a success in the 1923 edition of *The Greenwich Village Follies*. With Lew Fields as producer, *The Girl Friend* gave the team their first solid Broadway hit and what Alec Wilder, in *American Popular Song: The Great Innovators, 1900–1950* (1972), called "the first wholly distinctive Rodgers song"—"The Blue Room." After the 1926 *Garrick Gaieties* and a London visit, during which they scored a Jack Hulbert musical, *Lido Lady* (1926), Rodgers and Hart returned to Broadway with a successful reworking by Herbert Fields of an old Marie Dressler vehicle, *Tillie's Nightmare* (1910), now adapted as *Peggy-Ann* (1926), with Ford introducing "A Tree in the Park" and the wistful "Where's That Rainbow?"

In a coincidence, *Peggy-Ann* opened on the same night as another Rodgers and Hart show, *Betsy*—a thirty-nine-performance disaster, which dragged a good song, "This Funny World," down with it. Rodgers and

Sheet music for a song in the 1932 movie that also featured the Rodgers and Hart standards "Lover"
and "Isn't It Romantic?" (from Marion Short, Hollywood Movie Songs, *1999)*

Hart returned to London to write a C. B. Cochran–produced revue called *One Dam Thing after Another* (1927), which featured a song allegedly born in a Paris taxicab when a near collision prompted a lady passenger to exclaim "Oh, my heart stood still" and Hart to suggest it would make a good song title. He frequently cited "My Heart Stood Still" when defending himself against the accusation that he overused polysyllabic rhymes, pointing out that in the entire refrain, seventy-one words have only one syllable and the remaining five have two. That same year the song was used in *A Connecticut Yankee,* with a book by Herbert Fields based on Mark Twain's *A Connecticut Yankee in King Arthur's Court* (1889). It was Rodgers and Hart's first big hit, running for 418 performances, and they had their first heady taste of fame. Profiled in the "Times Square Tintypes" column of the New York *Sun,* Hart "revealed" that he hated first nights, radio, vaudeville, plays with a mes-

sage, and home cooking. He loved mountains, good cigars, Beatrice Lillie, tropical scenery, Percy Bysshe Shelley, and chop suey. "Is very nervous at his own opening nights," the paper reported. "Paces the back aisle continuously. Asks standees 'How do you like it?' and won't take no for an answer. During intermission he shaves himself to look neat for the second act. Stays up all night waiting for the reviews."

From 1927 on, Rodgers and Hart embarked upon an exclusively theatrical songwriting career, writing a minimum of two full shows a year—one per season, in Broadway terms. Unlike almost every other songwriting team in the business, they never wrote special material for star vaudeville performers, or would-be "hits" tied to whatever event or personality was in the news. Most of the productions with which they were associated were successful in the sense that a run of more than 150 performances was considered good at a time

Sheet music for the 1934 standard whose melody by Rodgers had three prior lyric settings by Hart
(from Harris Lewine, Black Beauty, White Heat, *1996)*

when a new show opened every single night of the week. Establishing what was to become a sort of Rodgers and Hart "trademark," every score they wrote produced at least one song that became a "standard": "You Took Advantage of Me," from *Present Arms* (1928); "With a Song in My Heart," from *Spring Is Here* (1929); "A Ship without a Sail," from *Heads Up!* (1929); "Ten Cents a Dance," from *Simple Simon* (1930); "Dancing on the Ceiling," from *Ever Green* (1930); and "I've Got Five Dollars," from *America's Sweetheart* (1931).

America's Sweetheart was a mild satire that grew out of Rodgers and Hart's first encounter with Hollywood. With the Great Depression biting hard on Broadway—producers had difficulty raising money to put on shows, and customers were increasingly reluctant to part with $5 to see one—Hollywood offered the only viable alternative. A hundred million Americans were going to the movies every week, and motion-pic-

ture musicals took full advantage of the introduction of sound in 1927. Rodgers and Hart signed to write the songs for two movies for Warner Bros. Hart, in particular, was excited about working in motion pictures. He and Rodgers had ideas they wanted to try, ideas they felt would work only on-screen, where dialogue and song could be integrated in ways that were nearer to opera than the Broadway musical. In spite of their enthusiasm, their first picture, *The Hot Heiress* (1931), starring Ben Lyon and Ona Munson, was a flop. When the studio canceled their contract, Rodgers and Hart headed back East to find the situation there even grimmer.

The chance to score a movie musical for Paramount Pictures with Maurice Chevalier and Jeanette MacDonald brought Rodgers and Hart back to California. Their contribution to the movie was a remarkable one, and as a result, *Love Me Tonight* (1932) was—and still is–original, bold, and witty. Rodgers's music and Hart's lyrics were fresh, apposite, and effervescent. "Lover," "Mimi," "Isn't It Romantic?" and the title song were the cream of a score that made *Love Me Tonight* one of the most endearing of all 1930s motion-picture musicals. It was one of the few things Rodgers and Hart did in their five-year stint in Hollywood that they could look back upon with either pleasure or pride. They wrote a beggar's opera called *Hallelujah, I'm a Bum* (1933) for Al Jolson, whose star was already in the descendant, and *The Phantom President* (1932), a vehicle for George M. Cohan, another star who had not yet accepted his own obsolescence.

Rodgers and Hart's attempts to be innovative were praiseworthy, but the movie industry was not looking for innovation. Songwriters in Hollywood were hired for one reason only: to write "hits" that would pull people into the cinemas. So Rodgers and Hart became contract writers on the M-G-M lot, charged with the job of writing songs for whichever movie might be in the making, or for stars who could not carry a tune–Anna Sten in *Nana* (1934), Joan Crawford in *Dancing Lady* (1933), Marion Davies in *Peg O' My Heart* (1933), and Jean Harlow in *Hollywood Party* (1934). In 1933 Rodgers and Hart worked with Moss Hart on a planned movie for Jeanette MacDonald to be called "I Married an Angel" and produced half a dozen songs before production was canceled. Hart even succumbed to the indignity of writing replacement lyrics to Franz Lehár's music for another MacDonald vehicle, a 1934 motion-picture adaptation of Lehár's 1905 operetta *The Merry Widow*.

One thing Hollywood did do for Rodgers and Hart was to emphasize and perhaps even exacerbate the enormous differences in their approach to life. While Rodgers lived what he described as the life of a retired banker, Hart's revels accelerated–parties, more parties, and still more, in company increasingly déclassé. "Larry was 'respectable' until ten-thirty," one of his friends said. "He would take his mother to a show, or to dinner, or a party. Then they would go home and he'd wait until she went to bed, and he'd be out with his own crowd. Those crazy nights. It was like he never wanted to go to sleep."

One final irony marked the end of Rodgers and Hart's Hollywood hegira. While producing songs for *Hollywood Party,* they had written a stenographer's lament called "Prayer" for Harlow. It was dropped, only to reappear with a new lyric as "The Bad in Ev'ry Man" in *Manhattan Melodrama* (1934). When this version was no more successful than the original one, they put the song into their trunk and forgot about it. But M-G-M's music publisher, Jack Robbins, told them they would have a great song if only they would put a com-

mercial lyric to the melody. "You mean something corny, like 'Blue Moon'?" Hart sneered. "Blue Moon" (1934) became a huge hit, and of all their hits, the only one that did not belong to a show or a movie.

No sooner had Rodgers and Hart quit Hollywood than they were called back to write a score for *Mississippi* (1935), a movie to star crooner Lanny Ross. He was replaced by Bing Crosby, and the nine or ten songs written for the movie were whittled down to four and a half. However, since two of them were "Down by the River" and "It's Easy to Remember," Rodgers and Hart came out of a distinctly unmemorable picture as well as anyone.

Back on Broadway, however, Rodgers and Hart's spotty record in the movies proved no great recommendation to the few producers who were still putting on shows. They wrote several interpolations that made little impression on anyone and then, lacking a better offer, signed up to write the songs for a new extravaganza, part circus, part musical, being produced by Billy Rose. *Jumbo* (1935), as it was called, was a monster in every way, costing a staggering $340,000 to stage, and although it ran seven months, the initial outlay and high overheads ensured that it never recouped even half its cost. But in their first theater songs since 1931 Rodgers and Hart exhibited a sure touch, producing three classics: "The Most Beautiful Girl in the World," "Little Girl Blue," and "My Romance." Actually, four classics resulted, because "There's a Small Hotel" (1936) was also written for *Jumbo* but not used in the show.

After quickly writing a couple of numbers for a forgettable movie called *The Dancing Pirate* (1936), Rodgers and Hart plunged into a new show, *On Your Toes* (1936), which had grown out of an idea they had originally pitched to Fred Astaire in Hollywood, about a vaudeville hoofer who becomes mixed up in ballet. George Abbott, whom they had brought in as director on *Jumbo* so that he could gain some experience in musicals, wrote most of the book, with Broadway star Marilyn Miller in mind. When she dropped out, the ballet part of the story was expanded and George Balanchine was brought in as choreographer. Original and daring, briskly staged by the no-nonsense Abbott and starring Ray Bolger as the hoofer, *On Your Toes* was a ten-month hit, with a score that included not only "There's a Small Hotel" and a wonderfully sharp comic number, "Too Good for the Average Man," but also one of Hart's most touchingly wry lyrics, "Glad to Be Unhappy." Of all the musicals that opened during the 1935–1936 season–and they included George and Ira Gershwin's *Porgy and Bess,* Cole Porter's *Jubilee,* Sigmund Romberg and Oscar Hammerstein's *May Wine, George White's Scandals,* and the last *Ziegfeld Fol-*

*Sheet music for hit songs from four Rodgers and Hart shows (from Samuel Marx
and Jan Clayton,* Rodgers and Hart, *1976)*

lies–the two longest runners were by the "forgotten" Rodgers and Hart. *Jumbo* and *On Your Toes* were but the beginning of an astonishing sequence of successes that within five years was to skyrocket them to the pinnacle of their profession.

In April 1937 *Babes in Arms* opened on Broadway. With a book nominally written by both Rodgers and Hart but largely concocted by Hart, it was completely different from all the shows that had preceded it, featuring a youthfully exuberant cast of largely unknown performers, many of whom–Alfred Drake, Mitzi Green, Ray Heatherton, Dan Dailey, Robert Rounseville, and Wynn Murray–went on to greater things. Balanchine again did the choreography for what *Newsweek* described as "a joyous array of boys and girls who sing and dance and have a wonderful time without much of a story to hamper their frivolity."

Once again, the finest and most enduring feature of the show was the score. *Babes in Arms* shows Hart at his unsurpassable best. With seeming effortlessness, he covered the entire spectrum of emotion, from jaded impatience, as in "Johnny One-Note"–

> Poor Johnny One-Note
> Got in *Aïda*–
> Indeed a great chance to be brave.
> He took his one note,
> Howled like the north wind,
> Brought forth wind that made critics rave,
> While Verdi went round in his grave!

–to the wistful déjà vu of "Where or When":

> It seems we stood and talked like this before,
> We looked at each other in the same way then,
> But I can't remember where or when.

Brash confidence is expressed in "The Lady Is a Tramp":

> I get too hungry for dinner at eight,
> I love the theatre but never come late.
> I never bother with people I hate. . . .
> I'm all alone when I lower my lamp,
> That's why the lady is a tramp.

There is reluctant romanticism in "My Funny Valentine":

> You make me smile with my heart,
> Your looks are laughable,
> Unphotographable,
> Yet you're my fav'rite work of art.
> Is your figure less than Greek?
> Is your mouth a little weak?
> When you open it to speak,
> Are you smart?

"I Wish I Were in Love Again" is slyly cynical:

> When love congeals,
> It soon reveals
> The faint aroma of performing seals,
> The double-crossing of a pair of heels,
> I wish I were in love again.

With *Babes in Arms* the phrase "a Rodgers and Hart show" came to mean a certain kind of musical with a certain kind of song: youthful, original, witty, and unpredictable in its musical harmonies and, more especially, in the twists and turns and sometimes outrageous rhymes of the lyric. As with nearly every Rodgers-Hart score, even the lesser-known numbers were full of wit and melodic style–a spoof of the singing cowboy craze in "Way Out West" or an equally sardonic tilt at all those smile-and-keep-your-chin-up songs in "Imagine," with its octave drop in the third eight-bar section providing a perfect example of how Rodgers achieved his "constantly surprising" refrains (to use Hart's own words in "My Romance").

Broadway princes at last, Rodgers and Hart could not have been closer artistically or personally farther apart. For Rodgers success meant recognition, celebrity, and, most of all, security, the means of giving his family all the sweet fruits of success: a lovely house in Port Washington, New York, cars, society parties, and private tutors for his two daughters. To maintain and continue that success, he became even more disciplined and more work-oriented. He had never been patient with Hart's intemperance, and as their success grew and Hart's unreliability increased, Rodgers found himself in the position of being the bully, the taskmaster, the nagging wife. It was not a role he cared to play, but if the alternative was getting no work whatsoever out of Hart, he was left with little choice.

For Hart success meant "having fun"–parties and vacations, hanging out boozing with his cronies until dawn. Everyone who knew him has acknowledged he was difficult to be with: constantly on the move, simultaneously creative and distractive, inspirational and disruptive. He would be to a partnership what a hyperactive child is to a marriage, a problem simply by reason of his existence. Put Hart to work, and he was brilliant, assured, swift, and always funny. Yet, he was also inescapably noisy and unreliable, a nonstop talker, smoker, and heavy drinker. He was not just a check grabber; he would fight for a check. If others put money on the table, he would throw it back at them. When his drinking really became a problem, there was always the chance that he would disappear for days.

Rolly Pickert, Grace McDonald, Mitzi Green, Ray McDonald, and Wynn Murray, the stars
of Rodgers and Hart's 1937 show Babes in Arms (© Bettmann/Corbis)

Rodgers and Hart's next show was *I'd Rather Be Right* (1937), the hero of which was an "imaginary" president of the United States called Franklin D. Roosevelt. The actor chosen to play the part, George M. Cohan, was himself a once-successful songwriter and one of the most arrogant, bombastic, and egocentric performers ever to strut the Broadway stage. Rodgers and Hart had already collided with Cohan in Hollywood, where he had taken no trouble to conceal his contempt for them. Prevailed upon against their better judgment by producer Sam Harris to cast Cohan in *I'd Rather Be Right,* they quickly found that his contempt for their kind of work had not diminished. When they played the score for him the first time, Cohan listened in silence, his face impassive. At the end he got up to leave, tapped Rodgers on the shoulder, and said, "Don't take any wooden nickels, kid." After that, Cohan continued to display his enmity. "Tell Gilbert and Sullivan to run over to the hotel and see if they can write a decent tune," he would say after dismissing yet another Rodgers and

Hart song as too clever, not clever enough, too difficult, or too simple-minded. His intransigence scaled new heights when, on opening night, he committed the unpardonable sin of reworking Hart's lyrics. Other arguments marred the production. Instead of the customary even split between librettists and composers, George S. Kaufman and Moss Hart insisted on 8 percent to Rodgers and Hart's 5 percent. "Kaufman won in the end," Rodgers said much later. "He was bigger, richer, and older." Although the show was a hit—it ran for 290 performances—the rival generations never exchanged friendly words again.

Pausing only to write a few songs for another movie, *Fools for Scandal* (1938)—most of which ended up on the cutting-room floor or were reduced to background music—and making a personal appearance on a Hollywood radio show, Rodgers and Hart plunged into a theatrical reworking of "I Married an Angel," the shelved movie project they had originally put together in a clapboard bungalow on the M-G-M lot in 1933. *I Married an Angel* opened on Broadway

Vera Zorina and Dennis King in Rodgers and Hart's
I Married an Angel *(1938) (Billy Rose
Theatre Collection, New York Public
Library for the Performing Arts)*

on 11 May 1938 and starred Vera Zorina in the role of an angel who becomes charmingly mortal. Much of the score was unexceptional, although, as usual, Rodgers and Hart came through with one big song to go into their book of standards. The lyric to "Spring Is Here" is probably the one most frequently cited when the question of the autobiographical content of Hart's lyrics arises:

> Spring is here,
> Why doesn't my heart go dancing?
> Spring is here,
> Why isn't the waltz entrancing? . . .
> Maybe it's because
> Nobody loves me.
> Spring is here, I hear.

Also in the score of *I Married an Angel* was "At the Roxy Music Hall," an ineffable, affectionate salute to the landmark New York movie house operated by Sam "Roxy" Rothafel:

> Where an usher puts his heart in what he ushes,
> Where the fountain changes color when it gushes,

> And the seats caress your carcass with their plushes. . . .
> Where the acrobats are whirling on their digits,
> Where the balcony's so high you get the fidgets,
> Where the actors seem to be a lot of midgets. . . .
> Where the spectacle goes on ad infinitum,
> And the picture is a secondary item
> At the Roxy Music Hall!

Around this time Hart's lifestyle began to change from what had been an erratic but still fairly ordered existence into a new and more frenetically self-indulgent mode. "He was spending all his time with [Doc] Bender," producer Leonard Spigelgass recalled, "and a lot of stupid people. Handsome men, but stupid. Bender was kind of a comic. Mrs. Hart hated him. But if you wanted Larry, you took Bender [even though he] was a procurer, a pimp, an arranger, men or women." A pattern that was to dominate the rest of Hart's life was established. Right after New Year's Day he and Bender would take off on a booze-fogged cruise or a long vacation in Florida or California. Then they returned to New York so that Hart could work on the spring show, which would be followed by another vacation in the Caribbean, Mexico, or even Europe. Next was another show in the fall, and then Hart and Bender set off on another spree.

No matter how fast Hart spent his money, more came rolling in. *I Married an Angel* had settled in for what turned out to be a nine-month run; *I'd Rather Be Right* was still playing to full houses; and the movie rights to *Babes in Arms* and *On Your Toes* had been sold. He was earning more than he knew what to do with, anywhere between $60,000 and $100,000 a year. Rodgers and Hart were featured in *The New Yorker*. They were on the cover of *Time* magazine. There were more parties at Hart's apartment or "21" or the Stork Club, more and more booze, and ever madder whirls. "He was the greatest party-giver of all time," his friend Milton Pascal said. "Nobody could ever pick up a check with Larry around. He used to have all these parties, six hundred people, where you met everybody in the business."

The only thing that kept Hart's life together was his family. Max Hart had died in 1928, and Larry had become the provider. He lived in a Central Park West apartment with his mother and his actor brother, whose widow claimed that Teddy shared a room with Hart until she and Teddy married in 1938. If this was the case, Teddy's marriage might well mark the point at which Hart's frenetic life began its long, messy, and unattractive slide. Hart adored—and to an extent dreaded—his mother. She was, as Hart's friend Henry Myers remarked, his anchor. His world revolved around her. For as long as she lived, Hart sublimated his own needs so that nothing she would unquestion-

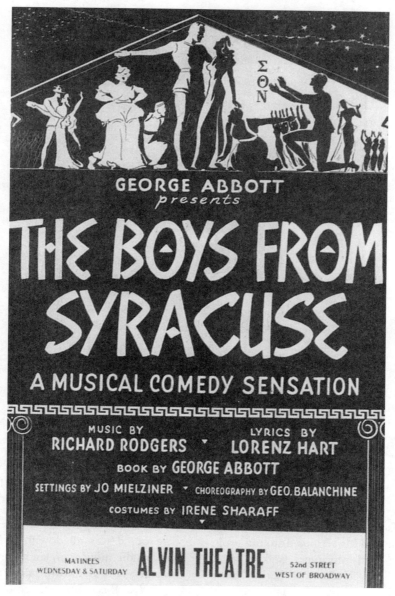

Poster for Rodgers and Hart's second Broadway show of 1938, based on Shakespeare's
A Comedy of Errors *(from Amy Henderson and Dwight Blocker*
Bowers, Red, Hot & Blue, *1996)*

ably have perceived as ugly and unacceptable was allowed to intrude upon Frieda Hart's rosy view of her son's life.

For Rodgers and Hart's next show, which was to be based on William Shakespeare's *A Comedy of Errors,* Hart contacted Abbott and asked him to work up an outline script on which they could then collaborate. Abbott's outline turned out to be so "right" that they decided to go straight ahead and put *The Boys From Syracuse* (1938) into production. Once again, the score was a delight, and once again, Hart's wit and erudi-

tion shone from every line. From the bittersweet romanticism of "Falling in Love with Love" to the throwaway sentiments of "This Can't Be Love," from "He and She" (the tale of a couple so hideously awful that when they died and went to heaven all the angels moved to hell) to the delectably lubricious "Sing for Your Supper," brilliantly arranged as a trio by budding composer Hugh Martin, everything sparkled. Much to Hart's delight, the cast included his brother, Teddy, acting the "twin" of comedian Jimmy Savo, whom he closely resembled. But for the first time in

TIME

The Weekly Newsmagazine

MR. RODGERS AND MR. HART
"If it's good enough for Shakespeare, it's good enough for us."
(See THEATRE)

Volume XXXII

Number 13

Magazine cover featuring Rodgers and Hart at the peak of their fame, 1938 (© Time Inc.)

his life, Larry Hart missed his own opening night. His frenetic, erratic lifestyle and his serious drinking problem overpowered his frail physique, and he was admitted to Mount Sinai Hospital suffering from pneumonia, contracted during the New Haven tryouts and resulting directly from his alcoholism. In mid December 1938, as ebullient as ever, Hart left to convalesce in Miami, full of talk about a new show. Apart from another radio appearance in Chicago, however, he wrote little or nothing until rehearsals began the following September for *Too Many Girls* (1939).

In the summer of 1939 Hart moved with his mother from their old apartment at the Beresford on Eighty-first Street to a large, terraced, twenty-first-floor duplex at the Ardsley, ten blocks uptown. Here the living arrangements were completely different: Frieda had her own place on the top floor, with Hart occupying the lower floor as a bachelor apartment. Immediately after he moved in, he had a soundproofed door installed between the two floors, so that his mother would not be

disturbed by any noise generated by his parties. From here on, it was all downhill. All Hart's cronies and hangers-on moved in, and the unfinished apartment became a sort of uptown saloon and bookie joint.

Too Many Girls was concocted mainly to show-case the talents of Desi Arnaz, a handsome young Cuban who had become a nightclub star. The rest of the cast, as always in an Abbott-Rodgers-Hart production, consisted of bright, gifted newcomers. Once again, the adjectives heaped on the show were the ones a Rodgers and Hart show always attracted—fresh, exhilarating, youthful, and tuneful—and once again the show was a hit. If perhaps not as scintillating as *Babes in Arms,* the score still featured gems, most notably "I Didn't Know What Time It Was" and "I Like to Recognize the Tune," a satire aimed at the swing craze. "Give It Back to the Indians" was a catalogue of modern Manhattan's woes that was the antithesis of Rodgers and Hart's 1925 love song to their hometown, "Manhattan."

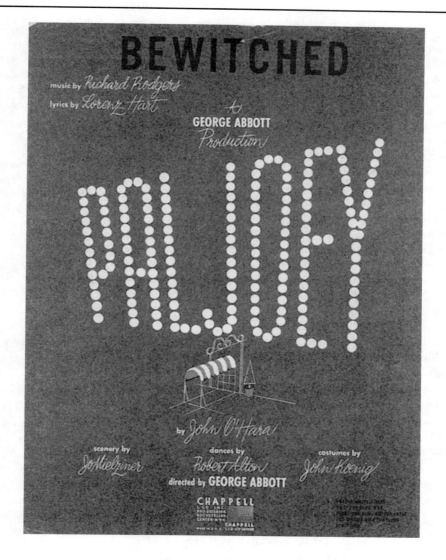

Sheet music for a song from the 1940 Rodgers and Hart musical, with a libretto by John O'Hara
(from William Zinsser, Easy to Remember, 2000)

Renowned on Broadway for never following a formula and never repeating a successful idea, Rodgers and Hart now proceeded to do something nobody expected: they wrote a flop. *Higher and Higher* (1940) was an attempt by producer Dwight Deere Wiman to create a star vehicle for Zorina and repeat the success of *I Married an Angel,* but, by the time director Joshua Logan and his writer, Gladys Hurlbut, had pulled the story line into some kind of believable shape, Zorina had bowed out, and the whole show had to be revamped to accommodate the talents and personality of its new star, Budapest-born Marta Eggerth. "And Larry, although he wrote some marvelous lyrics, really I think deep in his heart didn't like it very much," Logan said, "and began to drink."

Hart's disappearing act had always been a problem. Now he was missing for days at a time. Left with no alternative, Rodgers sometimes had to write both music and lyrics for new songs and additional choruses for existing ones. Which ones he had a hand in and which are clearly Hart's is not difficult to divine in a score that had few highlights. "A Lovely Day for a Murder" and "Disgustingly Rich" had the authentic Hart touch, but much of the rest was merely adequate. As always, however, Hart came up with another unforgettable ballad, "It Never Entered My Mind." Like so many of Hart's love songs, it is full of the ineffable sadness of a man seemingly convinced he was physically too unattractive for anyone to love him.

Higher and Higher folded in June 1940, after 108 performances. Astonishingly, by December of that year, Rodgers and Hart had not only completed and scored another show, but in it produced one of the landmark musicals of the first half of the twentieth century: *Pal Joey* (1940). The show had its genesis in a series of *New Yorker* stories by John O'Hara about a nightclub emcee, Joey Evans, who vents his frustration at being forced to recognize his own lack of success in a series of bitter, vicious letters to his former friend Ted, now a successful bandleader. When O'Hara suggested that his stories might form the basis of a "book show," Rodgers and Hart immediately saw that here was an opportunity to do something totally different from anything they–or for that matter anyone else–had ever done. O'Hara began to write new material for the show, which Abbott was to produce and direct. Writing the kind of cynical, scabrous lyrics needed for characters such as Joey, the man-hungry society matron Vera Simpson, or the sleazy nightclub routines that the show was to feature inspired Hart. From the tawdry "That Terrific Rainbow" to the torrid "Bewitched, Bothered and Bewildered," Rodgers–taking time off halfway through the score to scotch a newspaper report that the songwriting team was splitting up by telling the press he and Hart had been splitting up for twenty-two years and still were–brilliantly matched his partner's every raucous word.

The songs in *Pal Joey* were–for the time–outrageously direct, unabashed, and outspoken. According to Gene Kelly, who starred as Joey, the matinee ladies in the flowered hats did not know how to take them. "They were frigidly cold, they were sub-zero," he recalled. "On some songs they'd just sit there and stare at us and there was hardly a patter of applause." It is hardly surprising. When Vera and Joey, her younger, paid lover, sing about their living arrangement in "Den of Iniquity," no punches are pulled:

> The chambermaid is very kind,
> She always thinks we're so refined.
> Of course she's deaf and dumb and blind–
> No fools, we. . . .
> We're very proper folks, you know,
> We've separate bedrooms *comme il faut,*
> There's one for play and one for show.
> You chase me
> In our little den of iniquity.

Here, as throughout the show, Hart left little to the imagination, as in the even bawdier reveries of "Bewitched, Bothered and Bewildered," in which Vera confesses to being "Hexed again, / Perplexed again, / Thank God I can be oversexed again."

The high point of *Pal Joey* was "Zip!" the specialty number Rodgers and Hart wrote for a hard-bitten reporter, played by Jean Casto, who recounts how she persuaded "intellectual" striptease dancer Gypsy Rose Lee to describe what she thinks about as she disrobes. An exercise in topicality, "Zip!" poked fun not only at Lee's pretensions but at every passing fad and fancy then current in New York:

> Zip! Walter Lippman wasn't brilliant today.
> Zip! Will Saroyan ever write a great play?
> Zip! I was reading Schopenhauer last night.
> Zip! And I think that Schopenhauer was right.
> I don't want to see Zorina,
> I don't want to meet Cobina,
> Zip! I'm an intellectual.
> I don't like a deep contralto
> Or a man whose voice is alto
> Zip! I'm a heterosexual.
> Zip! It took intellect to master my art.
> Zip! Who the hell is Margie Hart?

Every line was an in-joke. Walter Lippman was then America's most respected political columnist and pundit. William Saroyan had just turned down the Pulitzer Prize. Zorina had been the star of *I Married an Angel,* and Cobina Wright was one of the most famous of that season's debutantes. The final punch line was aimed at another stripper, one of Lee's rivals. "Zip!" stopped the show, and more choruses were needed. Up went the now-familiar cry: "Where's Larry? Where's Larry?" "And he came in and said, 'Oh, yes, let me see,' and in four-letter words he wrote down the rhyming scheme to bring it back," Kelly said, "and literally, it was a piece of old wrapping paper. And that night, it was all done . . . as fast as the girl could learn them they went into the show":

> Zip! I consider Dali's paintings passé.
> Zip! Can they make the Metropolitan pay?
> Zip! English people don't say clerk, they say clark.
> Zip! Anybody who says clark is a jark.
> I have read the great Kabala,
> And I simply worship Allah.
> Zip! I am just a mystic,
> I don't care for Whistler's Mother,
> Charlie's Aunt, or Shubert's brother.
> Zip! I'm misogynistic.
> Zip! My intelligence is guiding my hand.
> Zip! Who the hell is Sally Rand?

Pal Joey opened in New York on Christmas Day 1940, and that night Hart threw one of his customary no-holds-barred parties at the Ardsley while waiting for the reviews. The critics were mostly supportive, but the one Hart most wanted to like it had reservations. *New York Times* critic Brooks Atkinson's tough but by no

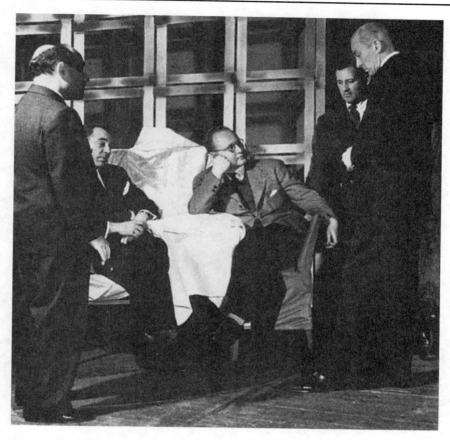

*Hart, Rodgers, choreographer Robert Alton, John O'Hara, and producer-director
George Abbott working on* Pal Joey, *1940 (Billy Rose Theatre Collection,
New York Public Library for the Performing Arts)*

means completely hostile review concluded, "Although it is expertly done, can you draw sweet water from a foul well?" Devastated, Hart left the party and retreated to his own room in tears. With a run of 374 performances, *Pal Joey* was an indisputable success (and a record-setting revival in 1951 was even more triumphant), but it does seem to mark the onset of Hart's last, precipitant decline.

So swift was this decline, so marked, that even Rodgers, riven on the one hand by guilt and on the other by the need for some form of respite, discussed the "Larry Hart problem" with Logan and Abbott, only to learn that their prognosis was even grimmer than his own. Finally, Rodgers discussed his options with one of his and Hart's oldest friends, Oscar Hammerstein. Rodgers and Hart had been offered the chance to adapt Ludwig Bemelmans's *New Yorker* pieces about a fictional Hotel Splendide, but Hart did not want to do the show. In point of fact, he did not want to do anything. He was enmeshed in the classic alcoholic dilemma: the more he drank, the worse his problems became, and the worse his

problems became, the more he drank. He "didn't want to write any more," his sister-in-law, Dorothy Hart, said. "He didn't know what to do with his life or himself. His life had come to an end long before he died."

After writing some songs for a mediocre movie called *They Met In Argentina* (1941), Hart worked on only two more shows. One of them was *By Jupiter,* the biggest hit of 1942 and of Rodgers and Hart's career. The other came a year later, by which time Hart's alcoholic decline had become irreversible. Yet, to the end, his astonishing gifts did not desert him: his lyrics for *By Jupiter* (even though some of them were written while he was hospitalized, nominally for pneumonia but more probably for acute alcoholic poisoning) abound in erudition and wit. As well as "Ev'rything I've Got," the raucous show-stopper he wrote for the "big-voiced" Benay Venuta, he turned in "Wait Till You See Her," an intricately constructed, five-rhyme lyric set to one of Rodgers's most appealing waltzes, and another wistful song called "Nobody's Heart," into which many have read a confession of Hart's own feelings of inadequacy and despair:

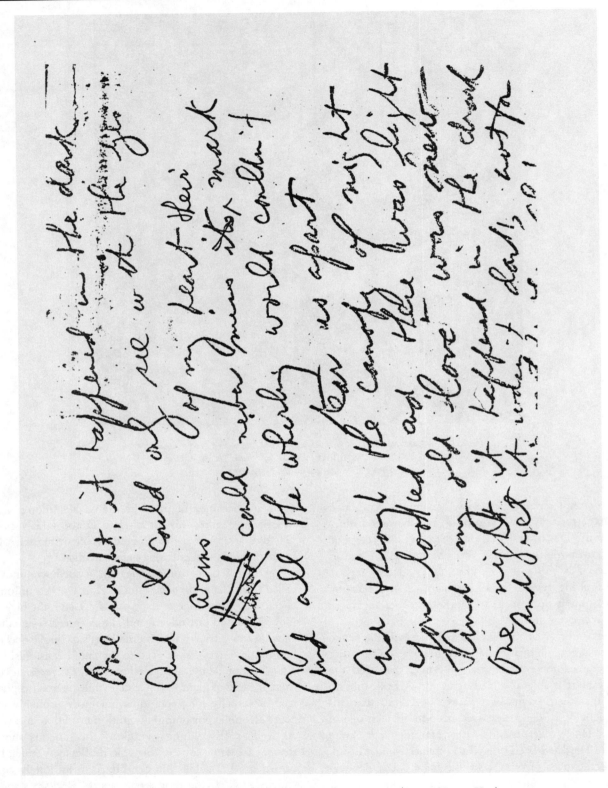

Manuscript for Hart's final lyric, "It Happened in the Dark" (Estate of Lorenz Hart)

Sheet music for the Rodgers and Hart song originally featured in their 1937 show
Babes in Arms *and recycled in a 1955 movie (Bruccoli Clark Layman Archives)*

Nobody's heart belongs to me,
Heigh-ho, who cares?
Nobody writes his songs to me,
No one belongs to me—
That's the least of my cares.
I may be sad at times,
And disinclined to play,
But it's not bad at times
To go your own sweet way.
Nobody's heart belongs to me,
No arms feel strong to me.
I admire the moon
As a moon, just a moon,
Nobody's heart belongs to me today.

By the time the show opened, Hart had become a problem Rodgers could no longer solve and perhaps no longer wished to.

Approached by the Theatre Guild to consider a musical adaptation of the Lynn Riggs play *Green Grow the*

Lilacs (1931) and faced with Hart's adamant assertion that the piece simply was not their style, Rodgers gave Hart an ultimatum: if he would not do the show, Rodgers was going to work with Hammerstein. That Hart offered no protest or argument confirmed the depths to which his self-esteem had sunk. The partnership of Rodgers and Hart was effectively over. Hart did work fitfully on a project called "Miss Underground," based on a Paul Gallico story, with music to be written by Emmerich Kálmán, but it never came to fruition. It was as if Hart had lost not only his way but also any interest in finding it again. On 31 March 1943 Rodgers and Hammerstein's new show, *Oklahoma!,* opened on Broadway. Hart was at the opening with Billy Rose and, as Rose told it, "Every once in a while Larry would lean over and whisper to me: 'It's a flop, isn't it?' and I'd answer 'Sure it's a flop,' knowing all the time it was the most sensational kind of success. But what could I do?"

A month later Frieda Hart died, and Hart's last tenuous hold on any kind of normality disappeared. He was drunk most of the time and seen with such disreputable company that former friends would cross the street to avoid him. An unpublished memoir by Myers depicts how catastrophic was the decline:

> I don't remember precisely where or how I happened to encounter him; I only recall that he was staggeringly, incoherently drunk. That was when I was first aware of his growing compulsion to keep talking. He had liked, a long time before, to sing songs he was writing, but this was not the same thing. Now his words made no sense, and they've left no record with me, only an impression that they weren't addressed especially to me. Or to anyone. To anyone alive, that is. I managed somehow to make him tell me where he lived, and I took him home to bed. He was living alone at 415 Central Park West, in the penthouse.
>
> When Larry was safely put to bed I made a date with him for lunch the next day, at Lindy's at noon, not expecting him to keep it. But he did. I got there a little before noon, and asked a waiter whether Mr. Hart was there. I was told "No," but he would be, and was conducted to what was called "his table." I sat there, and sure enough, exactly at noon, he arrived. He was already totally drunk, and staggering, but he made his way to the table where I was, and sat opposite me, all without saying a word. He just sat. The waiter immediately came to the table, carrying two bottles of beer, which he opened and emptied into two mugs, both of which he set before Larry, who drank them off. Then he took my order, but did not wait for Larry's, evidently knowing he would not want to eat. I made such conversation as I could, and when the waiter returned with my lunch I ate it, not knowing what else to do. Larry said nothing throughout. When I asked for the check the waiter shook his head "No," indicating that Mr. Hart allowed no one to pay the reckoning at his table.
>
> We both got up, and started out. I stopped at the desk for an instant, to get some of what I knew was Larry's favorite brand of cigar, but when I had them, he was gone, I don't know where. I hurried out and looked in all directions, but there was no sign of him. That was the last time I ever saw him.

There was one brief return to something like the old Hart when Rodgers and Herbert Fields persuaded him to work with them on a revival of their 1927 hit *A Connecticut Yankee*. Hart stayed at the Rodgers home in Connecticut and worked regular hours. "I don't think he took a drink the entire time," Rodgers said. "There was no question that he was making a genuine effort to rehabilitate himself and to prove that the team of Rodgers and Hart was still a going concern." The idea of writing for Vivienne Segal, who had starred in several of their shows, was an added incentive, and for her multiply married Morgan le Fay character he fashioned a sardonic number called "To Keep My Love Alive," which, if not in the same league as "Zip!"

or "I Wish I Were in Love Again," was still demonstrably superior to the competition. But by the time the show was in tryouts in Philadelphia, Hart had fallen decisively off the wagon.

A Connecticut Yankee opened at New York's Martin Beck Theatre on 17 November 1943. It was a tempestuous night, with bitter winds and lashing rain. Halfway through the second act, the disturbance Hart was making as he paced up and down at the rear of the theater, repeating the dialogue and singing hoarsely, led to his being removed from the theater. After spending part of the night in his brother's apartment, he disappeared again. Two days later he was found in a semicoma in his apartment and rushed to a hospital. Through the intercession of Eleanor Roosevelt, penicillin, not yet available to the public, was flown in, but it was too late. Shortly after 9:00 P.M. on Monday, 22 November, the troubled spirit of Hart slipped away. He was buried two days later at Mount Zion Cemetery in Queens.

Lorenz Hart never wrote anything autobiographical, and although some believe it is possible to capture some of the essence of who he was and what he was through a comprehensive examination of his lyrics, his "real" self remains elusive. Even when he is present—in photographs or in old home-movie clips—it is almost as if he is just acting at being there. He mugs, grins, and lights his cigar with quick and jerky movements, "always skipping and bouncing," as Hammerstein remembered him, "like an electrified gnome." "Here one minute and around the world in forty seconds," as another contemporary recalled. Only in the songs did Hart seem to present his simple yet complex, poetic inner self—someone quite distinct from the undisciplined, hedonistic figure always intent upon "having fun." Yet, behind that boisterous facade, in the midst of the crowd of hangers-on he attracted, he remained a compellingly lonely figure. "He didn't care where he lived, how much he earned, what the social or financial standing of his friends was, or what row he sat in on opening night," Rodgers said in one of his fonder reminiscences. "He did care tremendously, however, about the turn of a phrase or the mathematical exactness of an interior rhyme." It shows in every line Hart wrote.

Biographies:

Samuel Marx and Jan Clayton, *Rodgers & Hart: Bewitched, Bothered, and Bedeviled: An Anecdotal Account* (New York: Putnam, 1976);

Frederick Nolan, *Lorenz Hart: A Poet on Broadway* (New York: Oxford University Press, 1994).

References:

"The Boys from Columbia," *Time,* 32 (26 September 1938): 35–39;

David Ewen, *Richard Rodgers* (New York: Holt, 1957);

Ted Goldsmith, "One Hart Would Not Stand Still," *Theatre Magazine* (April 1931);

Margaret Case Harriman, "Words and Music," *New Yorker* (28 May 1938): 9–23; "Words and Music" (4 June 1938): 21–25;

Dorothy Hart, ed., *Thou Swell, Thou Witty: The Life and Lyrics of Lorenz Hart* (New York: Harper & Row, 1976);

Frederick Nolan, *The Sound of Their Music: The Story of Rodgers & Hammerstein* (New York: Walker, 1978);

Richard Rodgers, *Musical Stages: An Autobiography* (New York: Random House, 1975);

"Song Writer," *New York Times,* 25 November 1943.

Selected Discography:

Ben Bagley's Rodgers and Hart Revisited, volumes 1–5, Painted Smiles, 116, 139, 106, 126, 140, ca. 1970s–1992;

Tony Bennett, *The Rodgers and Hart Songbook,* DRG, 2102, 1986;

The Boys from Syracuse, 1963 revival cast, Columbia, 2580, 1973;

By Jupiter, 1967 revival cast, RCA, LSO-1137, 1967;

Betty Comden, *Remember These,* includes five songs from *Chee-Chee,* Ava, A-26, ca. 1960s;

A Connecticut Yankee, 1943 revival cast (1955), AEI, 043, 1996;

Barbara Cook, *Barbara Cook Sings from the Heart* (1959), Urania, 2026, 1997;

Dearest Enemy, 1955 television production, AEI, 042, 1996;

Dearest Enemy, studio recording of complete 1925 score, Bayview, RNBW0008, 2001;

Ella Fitzgerald, *Ella Fitzgerald Sings the Rodgers and Hart Songbook* (1956), Verve, 314 519 832-2, 1993;

Fly with Me, 1980 revival cast, Original Cast, 8023, 1980;

The Girl Friend, 1987 revival cast, That's Entertainment, 1148, 1987;

Hollywood Party, studio recording of thirteen unused songs and five songs from other Rodgers-Hart shows, Bayview, RNBW0009, 2001;

I Married an Angel (1938), AEI, 002, 1985;

Jessie Matthews and orchestra, *Ever Green* (1930), Monmouth, MES7049, n.d.;

The Merry Widow, motion-picture soundtrack (1934), on *The Merry Widow; The Love Parade,* Nadine, 260, ca. 1983;

Music from the Soundtrack of the Metro-Goldwyn-Mayer Production Billy Rose's Jumbo (1962), Columbia, 2260, 1973;

Anita O'Day, *Anita O'Day and Billy May Swing Rodgers and Hart,* Verve, 2141, ca. 1961;

On Your Toes, selections (1936), Monmouth, MES7049, 1972;

On Your Toes, 1983 Broadway revival cast, That's Entertainment, 1063, 1988;

Pal Joey, motion-picture soundtrack, Capitol, 912, 1957;

Pal Joey, 1980 London revival cast, That's Entertainment, 1005, 1991;

Pal Joey, original Broadway cast (recorded 1950), CBS, 4364, 1988;

Rodgers and Hart 1927–1942, compilation of original-cast singles, JJA, 19734, 1973;

Rodgers and Hart in Hollywood, volume 1 (1929–1935), JJA, 19766, ca. 1980s;

Rodgers and Hart in Hollywood, volume 2 (1934–1943), JJA, 19821, ca. 1980s;

Rodgers and Hart in Hollywood, volume 3, *Words and Music* soundtrack and outtakes, JJA, 19822, ca. 1980s;

Rodgers and Hart in London: Original Cast Recordings Including Lido Lady, Lady Luck, On Your Toes, World, SH 183, 1973;

Rodgers and Hart's Babes in Arms, 1989 revival cast, New World, NW386-2, 1990;

Bobby Short, *Bobby Short Celebrates Rodgers & Hart,* Atlantic, 2-610, 1975;

Frank Sinatra, *Frank Sinatra Sings Rodgers and Hart,* Capitol, W 1825, ca. 1960s;

The Supremes, *The Supremes Sing Rodgers and Hart,* Motown, MS659, 1967;

Too Many Girls, studio cast recording, Painted Smiles, 104, 1977;

Dawn Upshaw, *Dawn Upshaw Sings Rodgers & Hart,* Nonesuch, 79406-2, 1996;

Frederica Von Stade, *My Funny Valentine: Songs by Rodgers and Hart,* EMI, 7 54071 2, 1990;

Ronny Whyte and Travis Hudson, *It's Smooth, It's Smart: It's Rodgers, It's Hart,* Monmouth/Evergreen, 7069, n.d.;

Lee Wiley, *Lee Wiley Sings Rodgers & Hart and Harold Arlen,* Monmouth/Evergreen, 6807, 1971;

Teddy Wilson, *Teddy Wilson Revamps Rodgers & Hart,* Chiaroscuro, CR 168, n.d.;

Words and Music: Selections from the M-G-M Technicolor Film, M-G-M, E3771, ca. 1949.

Gus Kahn

(6 November 1886 – 8 October 1941)

Marty Minchin
University of North Carolina at Wilmington

SELECTED SONGS FROM THEATRICAL PRO-
DUCTIONS: *The Passing Show of 1916* (1916)–
"Pretty Baby" (music by Tony Jackson and
Egbert Van Alstyne);

Sinbad (1918)–"I'll Say She Does" (lyric and music by
Kahn, Buddy DeSylva, and Al Jolson); "'N'
Everything" (lyric and music by Kahn, DeSylva,
and Jolson);

Bombo (1921)–"Toot, Toot, Tootsie! (Good-bye)" (lyric
and music by Kahn, Ernie Erdman, Ted Fiorito,
and Robert A. King);

The Passing Show of 1922 (1922)–"Carolina in the Morning" (music by Walter Donaldson);

Whoopee (1928), music by Donaldson–"I'm Bringing a
Red, Red Rose"; "Love Me or Leave Me";
"Makin' Whoopee";

Show Girl (1929), lyrics by Kahn and Ira Gershwin,
music by George Gershwin–"Do What You
Do!"; "Liza"; "So Are You!"

SELECTED SONGS FROM MOTION-PICTURE
PRODUCTIONS: *Whoopee!* (1930)–"My Baby
Just Cares for Me" (music by Walter Donaldson);

Flying Down to Rio (1933), lyrics by Kahn and Edward
Eliscu, music by Vincent Youmans–"Carioca";
"Flying Down to Rio"; "Music Makes Me";
"Orchids in the Moonlight";

Peg o' My Heart (1933)–"Sweetheart Darlin'" (music by
Herbert Stothart);

The Prizefighter and the Lady (1933)–"You've Got Everything" (music by Donaldson);

Bottoms Up (1934)–"Waitin' at the Gate for Katy"
(music by Richard A. Whiting);

Hollywood Party (1934)–"I've Had My Moments" (music
by Donaldson);

Kid Millions (1934), music by Donaldson–"An Earful of
Music"; "Okay Toots"; "When My Ship Comes
In";

One Night of Love (1934)–"One Night of Love" (music
by Victor Schertzinger);

Gus Kahn

Operator 13 (1934)–"Sleepy Head" (music by Donaldson);

Riptide (1934)–"Riptide" (music by Donaldson);

Stingaree (1934)–"Tonight Is Mine" (music by W.
Franke Harling);

Escapade (1935)–"You're All I Need" (music by Bronis-
law Kaper and Walter Jurmann);

The Girl Friend (1935)–"Two Together" (music by
Arthur Johnston);

Love Me Forever (1935)–"Love Me Forever" (music by
Schertzinger);

Thanks a Million (1935), music by Johnston–"I'm Sitting
High on a Hilltop"; "I've Got a Pocketful of Sun-

shine"; "New O'leans"; "Sugar Plum"; "Thanks a Million";

Her Master's Voice (1936)–"With All My Heart" (music by Jimmy McHugh);

Let's Sing Again (1936)–"Let's Sing Again" (music by McHugh);

San Francisco (1936)–"San Francisco" (music by Kaper and Jurmann);

Three Smart Girls (1936), music by Kaper and Jurmann–"My Heart Is Singing"; "Someone to Care for Me";

A Day at the Races (1937), music by Kaper and Jurmann–"All God's Chillun Got Rhythm"; "Blue Venetian Waters"; "A Message from the Man in the Moon"; "Tomorrow Is Another Day";

Maytime (1937) "Farewell to Dreams" (unused; music by Sigmund Romberg);

They Gave Him a Gun (1937)–"A Love Song of Long Ago" (music by Romberg);

Girl of the Golden West (1938), music by Romberg–"Shadows on the Moon"; "Soldiers of Fortune"; "Who Are We to Say (Obey Your Heart)";

Honolulu (1939), music by Harry Warren–"Honolulu"; "This Night (Will Be My Souvenir)";

Idiot's Delight (1939) "How Strange" (music by Earl Brent and Stothart);

Lillian Russell (1940)–"Blue Lovebird" (music by Kaper);

Spring Parade (1940), music by Robert Stolz–"It's Foolish but It's Fun"; "Waltzing in the Clouds"; "When April Sings";

Ziegfeld Girl (1941)–"You Stepped Out of a Dream" (music by Nacio Herb Brown).

SELECTED SONGS PUBLISHED INDEPENDENTLY OF THEATRICAL OR MOTION-PICTURE PRODUCTIONS: "My Dreamy China Lady" (1906), music by Egbert Van Alstyne;

"I Wish I Had a Girl" (1907), music by Grace LeBoy;

"Sunshine and Roses" (1913), music by Van Alstyne;

"Everybody Rag with Me" (1914), music by LeBoy;

"On the Good Ship Mary Ann" (1914), music by LeBoy;

"Memories" (1915), music by Van Alstyne;

"Some Sunday Morning" (1917), lyric by Kahn and Raymond B. Egan, music by Richard A. Whiting;

"Where the Morning Glories Grow" (1917), lyric by Kahn and Egan, music by Whiting;

"My Isle of Golden Dreams" (1919), music by Walter Blaufuss;

"You Ain't Heard Nothin' Yet" (1919), lyric by Kahn and Al Jolson, music by Buddy DeSylva;

"Your Eyes Have Told Me So" (1919), lyric by Kahn and Van Alstyne, music by Blaufuss;

"Ain't We Got Fun?" (1921), lyric by Kahn and Egan, music by Whiting;

"Bimini Bay" (1921), lyric by Kahn and Egan, music by Whiting;

"Broken-Hearted Melody" (1922), music by Isham Jones;

"Dixie Highway" (1922), music by Walter Donaldson;

"My Buddy" (1922), music by Donaldson;

"On the Alamo" (1922), lyric by Kahn and Joe Lyons, music by Jones;

"Beside a Babbling Brook" (1923), music by Donaldson;

"No, No, Nora" (1923), music by Ernie Erdman and Ted Fiorito;

"Sittin' in a Corner" (1923), music by George W. Meyer;

"Swingin' Down the Lane" (1923), music by Jones;

"When Lights Are Low" (1923), lyric by Kahn and Ted Koehler, music by Fiorito;

"Charley My Boy" (1924), music by Fiorito;

"I'll See You in My Dreams" (1924), music by Jones;

"It Had to Be You" (1924), music by Jones;

"The Little Old Clock on the Mantle" (1924), music by Fiorito;

"Mindin' My Business" (1924), music by Donaldson;

"Nobody's Sweetheart" (1924), lyric and music by Kahn, Erdman, Billy Meyers, and Elmer Schoebel;

"The One I Love Belongs to Somebody Else" (1924), music by Jones;

"Spain" (1924), music by Jones;

"When You and I Were Seventeen" (1924), music by Charles Rosoff;

"Where Is That Old Girl of Mine?" (1924), music by Jones;

"Why Couldn't It Be Poor Little Me?" (1924), music by Jones;

"Alone at Last" (1925), music by Fiorito;

"Got No Time" (1925), music by Whiting;

"I Never Knew (That Roses Grew)" (1925), music by Fiorito;

"I Wonder Where My Baby Is Tonight?" (1925), music by Donaldson;

"Isn't She the Sweetest Thing?" (1925), music by Donaldson;

"Kentucky's Way of Saying Good Morning" (1925), music by Van Alstyne;

"Sometime" (1925), music by Fiorito;

"That Certain Party" (1925), music by Donaldson;

"Ukulele Lady" (1925), music by Whiting;

"What Do I Care, What Do I Care, My Sweetie Turned Me Down" (1925), music by Donaldson;

"When I Dream of the Last Waltz with You" (1925), music by Fiorito;

"Yes Sir, That's My Baby" (1925), music by Donaldson;

"Barcelona" (1926), music by Tolchard Evans;

"But I Do—You Know I Do" (1926), music by Donaldson;

"For My Sweetheart" (1926), music by Donaldson;

"Just a Bird's Eye View (Of My Old Kentucky Home)" (1926), music by Donaldson;

"Let's Talk About My Sweetie" (1926), music by Donaldson;

"There Ain't No Maybe in My Baby's Eyes" (1926), lyric by Kahn and Egan, music by Donaldson;

"Chloe" (1927), music by Charles N. Daniels (as Neil Moret);

"Dixie Vagabond" (1927), music by Donaldson;

"He's the Last Word" (1927), music by Donaldson;

"If You See Sally" (1927), lyric by Kahn and Egan, music by Donaldson;

"My Ohio Home" (1927), music by Donaldson;

"Persian Rug" (1927), music by Daniels (as Moret);

"Sing Me a Baby Song" (1927), music by Donaldson;

"Beloved" (1928), music by Joe Sanders;

"Coquette" (1928), music by Johnny Green and Carmen Lombardo;

"I'm Sorry, Sally" (1928), music by Fiorito;

"Last Night I Dreamed You Kissed Me" (1928), music by Lombardo;

"Ready for the River" (1928), music by Daniels (as Moret);

"Ten Little Miles from Town" (1928), music by Schoebel;

"Where the Shy Little Violets Grow"(1928), music by Harry Warren;

"Here We Are" (1929), music by Warren;

"Around the Corner" (1930), music by Art Kassel;

"Goofus" (1930), music by Wayne King and William Harold;

"Hangin' on the Garden Gate (Sayin' Good Night)" (1930), music by Fiorito;

"Sweetheart of My Student Days" (1930), music by Seymour Simons;

"The Waltz You Saved for Me" (1930), music by Emil Flindt and King;

"Was I to Blame for Falling in Love with You?" (1930), lyric and music by Kahn, Charles Newman, and Victor Young;

"Building a Home for You" (1931), music by Joseph H. Santly;

"Dream a Little Dream of Me" (1931), music by Fabian André and Wilbur Schwandt;

"Guilty" (1931), music by Harry Akst and Whiting;

"The Hour of Parting" (1931), music by Mischa Spoliansky;

"I'm Thru with Love" (1931), music by Matty Malneck and Joseph A. "Fud" Livingston;

"Now That You're Gone" (1931), music by Fiorito;

"Old Playmate" (1931), music by Malneck;

"I'll Never Be the Same" (1932), music by Malneck and Frank Signorelli;

"Lazy Day" (1932), lyric by Kahn and Earl Martin, music by George Posford and LeBoy;

"A Little Street Where Old Friends Meet" (1932), music by Harry Woods;

"Lovable" (1932), music by Woods;

"A Million Dreams" (1932), music by J. C. Lewis Jr.;

"So At Last It's Come to This" (1932), music by Malneck and Signorelli;

"The Voice in the Old Village Choir" (1932), music by Woods;

"Hi-Ho, Lack-a-day, What Have We Got to Lose?" (1933), lyric by Kahn and Charlotte Kent, music by Louis Alter;

"Dancing in the Moonlight" (1934), music by Donaldson;

"Clouds" (1935), music by Donaldson;

"Footloose and Fancy Free" (1935), music by Lombardo;

"Josephine" (1937), music by Burke Bivens and King;

"Day Dreaming" (1941), music by Jerome Kern.

Gus Kahn, one of the most prolific and successful songwriters of the twentieth century, wrote lyrics to more than two thousand songs, averaging six hits a year for twenty years. Writing the words to songs was a life-consuming passion for him. He would frequently stop whatever he was doing and scribble the words to a new song on any available writing surface, be it a golf scorecard or a napkin. In the middle of conversations he would quickly write down a lyric, then resume the conversation as if he had never left it. Kahn liked to write lyrics for melodies that had already been written, and he matched vernacular phrases to the popular tunes of three decades. His versatility led to success on Broadway in the 1920s and then even more acclaim in Hollywood in the 1930s as a songwriter for movies. Long after their heyday, Kahn's songs have been successfully performed in the musical styles of later decades and become hits again.

Kahn was born Gustav Gerson Kahn in Coblenz, Germany, in 1886, the son of Isaac Kahn and Theresa Mayer Kahn. The Kahn family immigrated to Chicago in 1891, when Gus was five years old. He found the first outlet for his songwriting talent in the vaudeville shows of Chicago. Kahn worked as a clerk in a hotel-supply firm and, later, a mail-order house in Chicago

Sheet music for a 1921 hit song by Kahn, Raymond Egan, and Richard A. Whiting that is
mentioned in F. Scott Fitzgerald's 1925 novel The Great Gatsby
(Bagaduce Music Lending Library)

after dropping out of the city's public-school system, but his songs were so successful that he was soon supporting himself writing lyrics and special material for vaudeville acts.

Kahn broke into big-time songwriting when Egbert Van Alstyne, a composer from New York, chose him to replace his longtime partner, Harry Williams, who had moved to the West Coast. Kahn was able to adapt his lyrics to Van Alstyne's music, which featured the typically opulent melodies of early-twentieth-century popular music. They published their first song, "My Dreamy China Lady," in 1906, beginning a partnership that carried Kahn's career through the 1910s. Kahn had his first major success in 1915 with "Memories," a song with a soaring, wide-ranging melody that echoed Van Alstyne's 1905 hit, "In the Shade of the Old Apple Tree." When the composer came up with a more sprightly, rhythmic melody in 1916, Kahn matched it with the crisply alliterative lyric of "Pretty Baby":

Everybody loves a baby,
That's why I'm in love with you,
Pretty baby.

During this period Kahn also wrote with other composers. In 1907 he published "I Wish I Had a Girl," set to pianist Grace LeBoy's music. The pair wrote "On the Good Ship Mary Ann" in 1914, and on 18 August 1915 they were married, forming a rare marriage partnership of a composer and lyricist. The couple had some other successes with songs such as "Everybody Rag with Me" (1914) and "Lazy Day" (1932). Grace Kahn later wrote the music for "You're My Love," the theme song for Ed Sullivan's television show. She also composed successful ragtime songs.

The Kahns had two children: Donald, born in 1918, and Irene, born in 1923. Gus Kahn would have preferred to continue collaborating with his wife, but, as his success grew, she encouraged him to write with

Sheet music for a popular 1922 song that Kahn wrote with one of his main collaborators of the 1920s (from Ian Whitcomb, Tin Pan Alley: A Pictorial History, *1975)*

others, a generosity reflected in the 1951 biopic of Kahn's life, *I'll See You in My Dreams*. "She loved what he was doing," Donald Kahn said. "She was very proud of him."

Gus Kahn hit his lyrical stride in the 1920s, setting colloquial, truncated, and often ungrammatical words and phrase—frequently vernacular catchphrases—to the repetitive, fragmented, and oscillating melodies of the decade. In 1921 he produced two hit songs that have become standards: "Toot, Toot, Tootsie! (Goodbye)," written with Ernie Erdman, Ted Fiorito, and Robert A. King, and "Ain't We Got Fun?" with a lyric

by Kahn and Raymond Egan and music by Richard A. Whiting. In the latter song, Kahn and Egan abandon syntax for the telegraphic shards of conversation:

> Every morning,
> Every evening,
> Ain't we got fun?
> Not much money,
> Oh, but honey,
> Ain't we got fun?

The lyricists heighten the ragged, ricky-tick phrases with rhymes that fall off and on the beat—*got* against *not,*

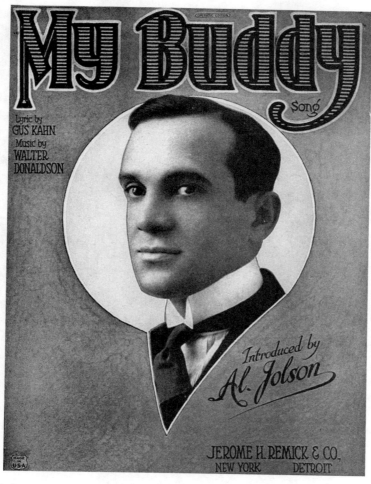

Sheet music for a 1922 song that incorporates notes from a tune played by a toy pig that Walter Donaldson gave to Kahn's son (Bruccoli Clark Layman Archives)

fun against *money* and *honey*. At one point they drop an expected rhyme to underscore the sexual compensations of poverty: "There's nothing surer, / The rich get rich and the poor get children." In place of rhyme, the alliteration—the *ch* of ri*ch* and *ch*ildren—continues the repetitive pattern. When rhyme returns with "In the meantime, / In between time," it reflects the incessant, frenetic nature of the "fun" itself. In F. Scott Fitzgerald's *The Great Gatsby* (1925), when Jay Gatsby is reunited with Daisy Buchanan in the novel, he commands a song from Klipspringer, who responds by playing "Ain't We Got Fun?" at the piano.

Although New York's Tin Pan Alley was the hub of American popular music in the 1920s, Kahn remained in Chicago with his family. There, according to his son, he spent half of his time on the golf course and the other half in the nightclubs, where he was so popular that he was known as the "King of Chicago." Kahn was often the celebrity guest at the College Inn,

one of Chicago's best-known nightclubs in the 1920s. While he frequently traveled to New York to work with composers, sometimes staying as long as a month, he never moved there. As his fame grew, New York composers would often take the train to Chicago to work with him.

Kahn wrote lyrics for several songs with music by bandleader Isham Jones, including "Broken-Hearted Melody" (1922) and "Swingin' Down the Lane" (1923). In 1924 Kahn and Jones wrote three songs that have become standards—"I'll See You in My Dreams," "The One I Love Belongs to Somebody Else," and "It Had to Be You." The first two lyrics resonate with Jones's repetitive melodies by portraying characters who are caught up in a round of lament for a lost love, but "It Had to Be You" is especially artful in the way it links musical repetition to romantic fate. The catchphrase formula, "It had to be," conveys a nonchalant resignation to love that suits the to-and-fro oscillation between

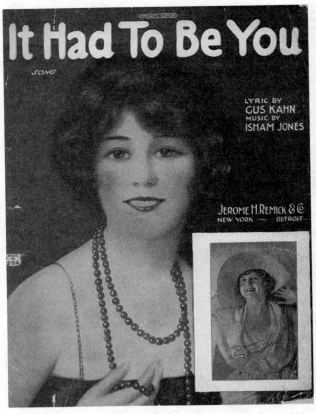

*Sheet music for an original 1924 song and for a tie-in with a 1939 movie in which the song was used
(left: Bruccoli Clark Layman Archives; right: from Marion Short,* Hollywood Movie Songs, *1999)*

two notes in the melody. The power of that fated attraction is also underscored by the way the lyric pushes beyond the musical boundaries of the eight-bar sections of the chorus. The first eight-bar section, for example, closes with the lyric on a dangling relative pronoun: "I wandered around and finally found / The somebody who. . . ." Only in the next eight-bar section is the clause completed: "could make me be true, could make me be blue / And even be glad just to be sad, / Thinking of you." Such an elastic lyric counterpoints the repetitive patterns of the music and gives the song a buoyant drive that makes even fatalistic resignation seem romantic as the singer confesses his helplessness with a wryly backhanded compliment: "Nobody else gave me a thrill / With all your faults, I love you still."

"It Had to Be You" was the title song of a 1947 movie starring Ginger Rogers and Cornel Wilde, and Marie MacDonald danced to the song in the movie *Living in a Big Way,* released the same year. More recently, it has figured prominently in *When Harry Met Sally* (1989) and *A League of Their Own* (1992). Perhaps one of the greatest compliments paid to Kahn's talent

was a comment the songwriter Johnny Mercer made when asked which of his own songs was his favorite. He replied that while he was fond of his own songs, the one he liked best was not one of his own but "It Had to Be You."

Kahn continued to collaborate with Fiorito, whose band helped to popularize such songs they had cowritten as "No, No, Nora" (1923), "Charley My Boy" (1924), "When I Dream of the Last Waltz with You" (1925), and "I'm Sorry, Sally" (1928). Kahn worked with Ira Gershwin on the lyrics for George Gershwin's music in *Show Girl,* a Florenz Ziegfeld musical that opened on 2 July 1929 and ran for 111 performances. Songs from the production include "So Are You!" "Do What You Do!" and another standard, "Liza."

In "Liza" Kahn and Ira Gershwin followed the shifting musical phrases of George Gershwin with colloquial phrasing and playful rhyme and alliteration. Where the music is languorous, the lyric features long vowels that create subtle internal rhymes: "Liza, Liza, skies are gray. . . ." When the music takes a bouncy turn, the lyric follows with a vernacular contraction:

"But if you smile on me, / All the clouds'll roll away." Here the alliterating and near-rhyming liquid consonants smoothly follow sinuous turns of the melody.

Kahn's most successful collaborations in the 1920s were with Walter Donaldson, a New Yorker who became a lifelong friend. One of their first joint ventures came about when Donaldson visited Kahn in Chicago, bringing Kahn's son, Donald, a toy pig. According to Donald Kahn, when Donaldson noticed that the boy loved the tune the pig played when its tail was wound, he sat down at Kahn's piano and incorporated the notes into a song. Gus Kahn stayed up late that night writing the lyric to "My Buddy" (1922), one of the pair's first successes. Kahn and Donaldson went on to collaborate on several songs in which the melody, in the typically repetitive style of the 1920s, moved back and forth between two notes. To offset the monotony, Kahn had to devise various lyrical strategies. In "Carolina in the Morning" (1922) there are off rhymes on *finer* and Caro*lina* to create some variation amid the repetition, but where the melody varies, incessant rhymes are introduced:

Where the *mor*-ning *glor*-ies
Twine around the *door,*
Whispering pretty *stor*-ies
I long to hear once *more.*

With the return of Donaldson's repetitive main melody, Kahn leavens his internal rhymes with alliterating *d*s, *n*s, and *l*s: "If I had Aladdin's lamp for only a day."

While Kahn and Donaldson produced a collection of hit songs, they attempted only one complete Broadway score, *Whoopee,* starring Eddie Cantor, which premiered on 4 December 1928 and had a run of 379 performances. Ziegfeld, the most famous producer on Broadway at the time, originally had misgivings about hiring Kahn, who was then still based in Chicago. Donaldson, however, persuaded Ziegfeld to hire Kahn, who headed to New York. The songwriters soon fell into trouble when Donaldson included Kahn in his lifestyle of parties, golf, and horse racing. When Ziegfeld discovered what the two were doing, he fired them. His telegram to them, written at three in the morning, noted: "All night parties have been important to you. I have not had one line delivered or a note since we have been here and I can't sacrifice Eddie Cantor or my production further. . . . I will get your work done by others at your expense."

Dejected, Kahn returned to Chicago, where he brooded over his failure to succeed with a Broadway show. Ziegfeld called him there and asked him to return to the show, but Kahn hung up, thinking it was a practical joke. Then Cantor called to tell him that Ziegfeld really did want him back, and Kahn caught the next train to New York, where he and Donaldson finished the songs for the production in record time.

Whoopee, presenting the madcap adventures of a hypochondriac who goes West to find a cure for the multiple diseases he believes he has contracted, was written in a time when plot was relatively unimportant to musical theater: shows consisted of songs that did little to advance a story line or create character. Instead, the dialogue between the musical numbers was often sketch material—sometimes even burlesque-style gags—that gave the main actors time to get in place for the next song. The librettist and codirector of *Whoopee,* William Anthony McGuire, gave Donaldson and Kahn a brief synopsis of the show but fed the actual script to them scene by scene as they worked. They continued to write songs until just weeks before opening night, a frequent situation in this type of production, in which a new song or lyric could be requested up to the final dress rehearsal. New material was ordered so often that Kahn and Donaldson joked that they were afraid to go to sleep for fear that they would wake up to find the producers under the bed demanding more songs.

Kahn and Donaldson's preferred method of producing songs was not always conducive to short-order song writing, however. Kahn preferred to set words to a completed melody, one reason why he was able so easily to adapt his talent to different styles of music. When time was a luxury, Donaldson would sit at a piano and play chords, joining them together until he found a melody he liked. He played the melody repeatedly, adding variations each time, until Kahn stopped him and asked him to play the last melody again. Kahn would then jot down words on a paper, often writing the last two lines of a chorus first and then working backward to finish the chorus and write the verse. Sometimes Kahn would sit with Donaldson for days before coming up with an idea, but once inspired, he would write the entire song on the spot.

"Makin' Whoopee," the best-known song from *Whoopee,* reveals Kahn's fondness for slang and his talent for writing to repetitive melodies. Walter Winchell, the New York columnist who declared Broadway the "slang capital of the world" in the 1920s, coined the term *makin' whoopee,* and Kahn used the unusual phrase to counterpoint the commonness of the sex act to which it coyly alludes. The song is a cynical look at sex and marriage, outlining the sequence from a June wedding to a groom who looks for sex elsewhere just a year into a marriage. Kahn's lyric repeats words and rhymes:

Another bride, another June,
Another sunny honeymoon,
Another season, another reason
For makin' whoopee.

Eddie Cantor, as Henry Williams, and the Goldwyn Girls in a scene from the 1930 motion-picture adaptation of Kahn and Donaldson's only Broadway show, Whoopee, *which premiered in 1928 (Samuel Goldwyn Company)*

The to-and-fro rhymes, coupled with Donaldson's jerky melody, mock the repetitiveness of both the marriage vows and sex. Kahn also uses feminine rhymes—"she feels ne*glected,* and he's sus*pected* / Of makin' whoopee"—to emphasize the redundancy of home life that turns the husband adulterous.

While Kahn's slang was certainly relevant in the 1920s, "Makin' Whoopee" has transcended its time and become a hit several times over in later decades. In the 1989 movie *The Fabulous Baker Boys,* Michelle Pfeiffer, wearing a slinky red dress, drapes herself on a piano and croons the song, lounge-singer style. By omitting the opening verse, which takes a jab at marriage with such lines as "I see a fallen brother take a bride," Pfeiffer turns the song into a sultry, sexy lament. Woody Allen gave the versatile song yet another interpretation in his 1996 movie *Everyone Says I Love You,* in which he attempted to recapture the sensibility of 1920s musicals.

"My Baby Just Cares for Me," a Kahn-Donaldson song introduced by Cantor in the 1930 motion-picture adaptation of *Whoopee,* has also been a perennial success. In the lyric the singer lists the many things in which his lover shows no interest—"My baby don't care for shows, / My baby don't care for clothes"—in order to underscore the point made in the title phrase: "My baby just cares for me." The song later became the signature number for singer Nina Simone, who included it on a 1959 album because she needed a "bright, up-tempo" number to complete her recording. "My Baby Just Cares for Me" was also part of Frank Sinatra's 1950s repertoire, and in 1987 it was used as the theme for a

Sheet music for the 1921 song, republished to tie in with the 1949 movie
(from Dian Zillner, Hollywood Collectibles, *1991)*

British television advertisement for Chanel No. 5 perfume.

Faced with the repetitive melody of "Love Me or Leave Me," another song from the stage musical *Whoopee,* Kahn again wrote a lyric telling a story of romantic entrapment, in which the singer delivers an ultimatum to a jealous mate. Using oscillating phrases, Kahn creates a tightly faceted pattern of alliteration (leave/love/believe), assonance (lonely/won't/only), and the grammatical byplay of "let me" and "leave me."

The repetitive insistence even forces a tied rhyme between might/night/right and *my-t*ime:

You *might* find the *night*time
The *right* time for kissing,
But *night*time is *my-t*ime
For just reminiscing.

Caught up in the thrall of romantic fate, the lover confesses, "I'd rather be lonely / Than happy with somebody else," and then swerves into a boast of helplessness: "I intend to be independently blue." The paradoxical characterization of the singer as a helpless yet defiant victim of fate culminates in the stretching of "blue" over three notes.

While many talented lyricists left New York during the Depression for more-lucrative work writing songs for Hollywood, Kahn stayed in Chicago with his family and his ailing mother. While his mother was still alive, he turned down repeated offers from Hollywood to write songs for movies, but the day she died, he accepted a job in California. He moved with his family to Los Angeles in 1933, becoming one of the last of many talented lyricists to make the move west to Hollywood. Kahn never crossed the California border again, as he loved the camaraderie of the movie community there and the weather that allowed him to play golf every day.

From then on, Kahn wrote almost exclusively for motion pictures. He had already contributed lyrics to the 1930 movie version of *Whoopee* (for which an exclamation point was added to the title—*Whoopee!*), and he now worked on such pictures as M-G-M's *Peg o' My Heart* (1933). Kahn's first important job was writing songs with Edward Eliscu and Vincent Youmans for RKO's *Flying Down to Rio* (1933), which starred Fred Astaire and Ginger Rogers in their movie debut as a team. Songs such as "Orchids in the Moonlight," "Carioca," and "Music Makes Me" stimulated the dance pair's career and set a standard for the great movie musicals of the era. During the 1930s Kahn wrote lyrics for more than fifty movies, including the title song for *One Night of Love* (1934), "I've Got a Pocketful of Sunshine" for *Thanks a Million* (1935), and "Tomorrow Is Another Day" for *A Day at the Races* (1937). His collaboration with director Victor Schertzinger on the title song for *One Night of Love* led to an Academy Award, the first Oscar given to a movie for its score.

I'll See You in My Dreams, the 1951 movie about Kahn's life and career, starred Danny Thomas as Kahn and Doris Day as Grace LeBoy Kahn and included many famous Kahn songs, such as "It Had to Be You" and "Nobody's Sweetheart" (1924). While the movie, like most Hollywood biopics about songwriters, may not be an entirely accurate description of Kahn's life, it does capture his easygoing personality and outlook on music.

Kahn's lasting success has come from just that—his ability to write lyrics that have become enduring standards because they say what so many people cannot quite say themselves. "His songs have lasted because they say something and they say it straight up," said Donald Kahn (who has found success himself as the composer of songs such as "Sam's Got Him," 1944; "A Beautiful Friendship," 1956; and "Dream on a Summer Night," 1945). "He had a great feeling for what people think." Gus Kahn, who died of a heart attack at his home in Beverly Hills in 1941, had a similar assessment of his own fame, ascribing his success to his ability to "express colloquially something that every young person has tried to say—and somehow can't."

Reference:

Philip Furia, *The Poets of Tin Pan Alley: A History of America's Great Lyricists* (New York: Oxford University Press, 1990), pp. 75–83.

Selected Discography:

Eddie Cantor, *Makin' Whoopee with Banjo Eyes,* ASV, 5357, 2000;

Cantor, *Whoopee!* Jasmine, 116, 2000;

Doris Day, *I'll See You in My Dreams; Calamity Jane,* Collectables, 6689, 2001;

A Day at the Races, motion-picture soundtrack (1937), Sound Track Factory, 33503, 1999;

Whoopee, archival reconstruction of the 1928 production, Smithsonian, 012, 1978.

Bert Kalmar

(16 February 1884 – 18 September 1947)

Graham Wood
Coker College

Music is by Harry Ruby unless otherwise indicated.

SELECTED SONGS FROM THEATRICAL PRO-
DUCTIONS: *The Whirl of Society* (1912)–"Ghost
of the Violin" (music by Ted Snyder);

One Girl in a Million (1914)–"Moonlight on the Rhine"
(lyric by Kalmar and Edgar Leslie, music by Snyder);

Maid in America (1915)–"I've Been Floating Down the
Old Green River" (music by Joe Cooper);

Ladies First (1918)–"What a Girl Can Do";

Ziegfeld Follies of 1920 (1920)–"I'm a Vamp from East
Broadway" (lyric and music by Kalmar, Harry
Ruby, and Irving Berlin);

Broadway Brevities of 1920 (1920)–"We've Got the Stage
Door Blues" (interpolation);

The Passing Show of 1921 (1921)–"My Sunny Tennessee" (music by Ruby and Herman Ruby);

The Midnight Rounders of 1921 (1921)–"My Sunny Tennessee" (interpolation);

Snapshots of 1921 (1921)–"Memories" (interpolation);

Greenwich Village Follies of 1922 (1922)–"Beautiful Girls"
(interpolation);

Helen of Troy, New York (1923)–"Cry Baby"; "Helen of
Troy, New York"; "I Like a Big Town"; "It Was
Meant to Be"; "Look for the Happy Ending";

No Other Girl (1924)–"I Would Rather Dance a Waltz";

Puzzles of 1925 (1925)–"The Doo-Dab";

The Ramblers (1926)–"All Alone Monday"; "Any Little
Tune"; "California Skies"; "Just One Kiss"; "Like
You Do"; "Oh! How We Love Our Alma
Mater"; "We Won't Charleston"; "Whistle";
"You Smiled at Me";

Twinkle Twinkle (1926)–"Sweeter than You" (interpolation); "Whistle" (interpolation);

Lucky (1927)–"Dancing the Devil Away" (lyric by Kalmar and Otto Harbach); "The Same Old Moon"
(interpolation);

Five O'Clock Girl (1927)–"Happy Go Lucky"; "Thinking
of You"; "Up in the Clouds"; "Who Did?–You
Did!";

Bert Kalmar (from David Ewen,
American Songwriters, *1987)*

Good Boy (1928), music by Ruby and Herbert Stothart–
"Good Boy"; "I Wanna Be Loved by You";
"Some Sweet Someone";

Animal Crackers (1928)–"Hooray for Captain Spaulding"; "Musketeers"; "Watching the Clouds Roll
By"; "Who's Been List'ning to My Heart?";

Top Speed (1929)–"Keep Your Undershirt On";
"Reaching for the Moon"; "What Would I
Care?";

High Kickers (1941)–"Panic in Panama"; "The Time to
Sing"; "Waltzing in the Moonlight"; "You're on
My Mind."

SELECTED SONGS FROM MOTION-PICTURE PRODUCTIONS: *The Cuckoos* (1930)–"Goodbye"; "I Love You So Much"; "I'm a Gypsy"; "Tomorrow Never Comes";

Animal Crackers (1930)–"Why Am I So Romantic?";

Check and Double Check (1930)–"Nobody Knows but the Lord"; "Three Little Words";

Horse Feathers (1932)–"Ev'ryone Says 'I Love You'"; "Whatever It Is I'm Against It";

The Kid from Spain (1932)–"The College Song"; "In the Moonlight"; "Look What You've Done"; "What a Perfect Combination" (lyric by Kalmar and Caesar, music by Ruby and Akst);

Duck Soup (1933)–"The Country's Going to War"; "Hail, Hail Freedonia"; "The Laws of My Administration"; "When the Clock on the Wall Strikes Ten";

Happiness Ahead (1934)–"The Window Cleaners";

Hips, Hips, Hooray (1934)–"Keep on Doin' What You're Doin'"; "Keep Romance Alive"; "Tired of It All";

Kentucky Kernels (1934)–"One Little Kiss";

Movie Queen (1934)–"Puppchen";

Bright Lights (1935)–"She Was an Acrobat's Daughter";

Walking on Air (1936)–"Cabin on the Hilltop"; "Let's Make a Wish" (lyric by Kalmar and Sid Silvers); "My Heart Wants to Dance" (lyric by Kalmar and Silvers);

Everybody Sing (1938)–"Quainty, Dainty Me"; "Why? Because!";

The Story of Vernon and Irene Castle (1939)–"Only When You're in My Arms" (lyric by Kalmar and Con Conrad);

Copacabana (1947)–"Go West, Young Man";

The Egg and I (1947)–"The Egg and I" (lyric and music by Kalmar, Akst, Ruby, and Al Jolson);

The Strip (1951)–"A Kiss to Build a Dream On" (lyric adapted by Oscar Hammerstein from Kalmar and Ruby's 1935 song "Moonlight on the Meadow").

SELECTED SONGS PUBLISHED INDEPENDENTLY OF THEATRICAL OR MOTION-PICTURE PRODUCTIONS: "In the Land of Harmony" (1911), music by Ted Snyder;

"Where Did You Get That Girl?" (1913), music by Harry Puck;

"Hello, Hawaii, How Are You?" (1915), lyric by Kalmar and Edgar Leslie, music by Jean Schwartz;

"If You Can't Get a Girl in the Summertime (You'll Never Get a Girl at All)" (1915), music by Harry Tierney;

"He Sits Around" (1916);

"Since Maggie Dooley Learned the Hooley Hooley" (1916), lyric by Kalmar and Leslie, music by George W. Meyer;

"Hello Wisconsin (Won't You Find My Yonnie Yonson?)" (1917), lyric by Kalmar and Leslie;

"When Those Sweet Hawaiian Babies Roll Their Eyes" (1917);

"All the Quakers Are Shoulder Shakers Down in Quaker Town" (1919);

"Oh! What a Pal Was Mary" (1919), lyric by Kalmar and Leslie, music by Pete Wendling;

"Take Your Girlie to the Movies (If You Can't Make Love at Home)" (1919), lyric by Kalmar and Leslie, music by Wendling;

"You Said It" (1919), lyric by Kalmar and Eddie Cox, music by Henry W. Santly;

"Snoops the Lawyer" (1920);

"So Long! Oo-Long (How Long You Gonna Be Gone?)" (1920);

"Timbuctoo" (1920);

"Where Do They Go When They Row, Row, Row?" (1920);

"Mandy 'n' Me" (1921);

"She's Mine, All Mine" (1921);

"I Gave You Up Just before You Threw Me Down" (1922), music by Ruby and Fred E. Ahlert;

"The Sheik of Avenue B" (1922);

"Roll Along, Missouri" (1923), lyric by Kalmar and Ruby, music by M. K. Jerome;

"Who's Sorry Now?" (1923), lyric by Kalmar and Ruby, music by Snyder;

"Nevertheless (I'm in Love with You)" (1931);

"Getting Away with Murder" (1936);

"The Moon Is in the Sky" (1936);

"Show Me a Rose (Or Leave Me Alone)" (1936);

"Charlie McCarthy" (1937), lyric by Kalmar and Edgar Bergen, music by Ruby and Alfred Newman;

"When You Dream about Hawaii" (1937), lyric by Kalmar and Sid Silvers;

"I've Got to Stop Dreaming of You" (1938), lyric by Kalmar and Silvers;

"Ain't Cha Comin' Out?" (1939).

BOOK: *The Kalmar-Ruby Song Book* (New York: Random House, 1936).

PLAY PRODUCTIONS: *Top Speed,* by Kalmar, Ruby, and Bolton, New York, Chanin's Forty-Sixth Street Theatre, 25 December 1925;

The Ramblers, by Kalmar, Harry Ruby, and Guy Bolton, New York, Lyric Theatre, 20 September 1926;

She's My Baby, book by Kalmar and Ruby, New York, Globe Theatre, 3 January 1928.

PRODUCED SCRIPTS: *Check and Double Check,* motion picture, story by Kalmar and Ruby, RKO, 1930;

Broadminded, motion picture, by Kalmar and Ruby, First National, 1931;

Horse Feathers, motion picture, by Kalmar and Will B. Johnstone, Paramount, 1932;

The Kid from Spain, motion picture, by Kalmar, Ruby, and William Anthony McGuire, Samuel Goldwyn / United Artists, 1932;

Duck Soup, motion picture, by Kalmar and Ruby, Paramount, 1933;

Hips, Hips, Hooray! motion picture, by Kalmar and Edward Kaufman, RKO, 1934;

Kentucky Kernels, motion picture, by Kalmar, Ruby, and Fred Guiol, RKO, 1934;

Circus Clown, motion picture, by Kalmar and Ruby, First National, 1934;

Bright Lights, motion picture, by Kalmar, Ruby, and others, First National / Warner Bros., 1935;

Walking on Air, motion picture, by Kalmar, Ruby, Rian James, and Viola Brothers Shore, RKO, 1936;

The Life of the Party, motion picture, by Kalmar and Ruby, RKO, 1937;

Ship Ahoy, motion picture, story by Kalmar, Matt Brooks, and Bradford Ropes, M-G-M, 1942;

Look for the Silver Lining, motion picture, story by Kalmar and Ruby, Warner Bros., 1949.

Bert Kalmar's lyrics and his songwriting activities encompassed virtually all the musical genres of the time. He wrote popular vernacular hits for Tin Pan Alley, several of which were interpolated into existing shows (mostly revues) alongside songs by his best-known contemporaries; he wrote entire scores for musical comedies and Hollywood musicals; and he wrote scripts for both stage and screen. With composer Harry Ruby, his principal collaborator from 1919 until his death, he wrote dozens of songs and several slapstick comedy scripts, including screenplays for the Marx Brothers. Kalmar and Ruby's songs were performed and recorded by the leading singers of the day, and after becoming standards, they were later reinterpolated into motion pictures. His varied career also included performing (singing, dancing, and magic) and music publishing. Kalmar's broad familiarity with all aspects of musical theater clearly served him well, and he worked alongside many of the leading creative artists of his day. His best work is characterized by a keen ear for catchy vernacular phrases, a directness of emotional expression, a knack for topics that caught the popular mood, and a sure feeling for comic situations.

Like many other famous songwriters of his generation, Kalmar was born into a poor community in the Lower East Side of Manhattan on 16 February 1884. In those days many families, even poorer ones, had pianos. Music was not just an integral part of family life but a

Broadway performer and choreographer Jack Donohue, Kalmar, and Harry Ruby in costume for a comic skit, 6 December 1926 (© Bettman/CORBIS)

potential passport to success. The young Kalmar stayed home from school to perfect new magic tricks and frequently entertained at neighborhood households with his top hat, juggling, and sleight of hand. An accomplished magician by age ten, he ran away from home to join a tent show, and nothing is known about his parents. The honing of his performance skills led him into vaudeville, where he used his theatrical experience to write parody songs with new lyrics, set to the popular song tunes of the day, for himself and older vaudeville performers to use as the climax to their comedy routines. His first big break came during the road production of *Wine, Women, and Song*—a successful burlesque show that had run for a year in New York during the 1907–1908 season—where he scored a hit with his singing and dancing impersonation of George M. Cohan.

While performing in vaudeville, Kalmar teamed up with Jessie Brown (whom he later married), and the duo was featured on both the Orpheum and Keith touring circuits. In the heyday of vaudeville, its audiences accounted for about half the theatergoers in the nation, and male-female comedy teams such as Kalmar and Brown were an extremely popular part of the bill. The duo's performance of Kalmar's own song-and-dance routine, "Nurseryland," earned them a thousand dollars a week and gave Kalmar a reputation as a singing-dancing comedian and writer of skits. Although he continued to perform in vaudeville, a backstage accident during one of his dancing acts resulted in a knee injury that left him unable to continue dancing, so he pursued songwriting full-time.

Some of his earliest songs were written with established composers, either for revues or directly for Tin Pan Alley. "In the Land of Harmony" (1911) was written with Ted Snyder, as was "Ghost of the Violin" (1912), which appeared in *The Whirl of Society* (1912). Other composers Kalmar collaborated with at this time included Harry Puck, with whom he wrote "Where Did You Get That Girl?" (1913), and Harry Tierney, with whom he wrote "If You Can't Get a Girl in the Summertime (You'll Never Get a Girl at All)" (1915). With co-lyricist Edgar Leslie, he wrote "Moonlight on the Rhine" (1914), "Hello, Hawaii, How Are You?" (1915), and "Oh! What a Pal Was Mary" (1919). The style and sentiments of these early songs are typical of Tin Pan Alley and vaudeville. "If You Can't Get a Girl in the Summertime" is somewhat saucy, with its colloquial, earthy expression of amorous pursuit: "At the beaches there's a raft of them, / Lovely peaches, go right after them." Such frankness about sexuality also occurs in "Where Did You Get That Girl?" and "Take Your Girlie to the Movies (If You Can't Make Love at Home)" (1919), both brisk marches reminiscent of the Cohan songs Kalmar was fond of parodying.

The onset of World War I heightened the need for escapist entertainment and began a craze for Hawaiian songs that peaked in 1916. The antithesis of the war-torn fields of Europe, these images of beaches and dancing hula girls on the other side of the world were enough of a distraction to popularize three of Kalmar's songs: "Hello, Hawaii, How Are You?" "Since Maggie Dooley Learned the Hooley Hooley" (1916), and "When Those Sweet Hawaiian Babies Roll Their Eyes" (1917). Twenty years later the Depression rekindled an interest in the exotic aspects of Pacific culture. Among the diverse cultural responses were travel literature, photographs, poetry, Hawaiian-style decorative dinnerware, and, of course, more songs, such as Kalmar and Ruby's "When You Dream about Hawaii" (1937), for which Sid Silvers served as co-lyricist.

After World War I, sentiments in songwriting tended to recall a nostalgic, unspoiled, prewar innocence in which wholesome love and old-fashioned girls were prized. Unlike the energetic marches of the prewar era, songs such as "Oh! What a Pal Was Mary," which

sold more than a million copies; "She's Mine, All Mine" (1921); and "Roll Along, Missouri" (1923) were cast as sentimental waltzes, recalling the mood and tone of Charles K. Harris's "After the Ball" (1892).

The fluid nature of stage shows in the 1910s and 1920s allowed great flexibility in the way songs were performed. Cuts were common, and an interpolation often turned out to be the hit of the show. Interpolations were an important mechanism by which individual songs could reach a wider audience. Notable stage performers, always on the hunt for new material, would often introduce the latest songs in their current shows. A star's interest could make a song an overnight hit. "He Sits Around" (1916) became Belle Baker's signature song and one of Kalmar's first successes with Ruby.

There was a plethora of revues in the early 1920s. The most celebrated was Florenz Ziegfeld's *Follies*. With an emphasis on spectacle and high production values, the sets and costumes were fabulous and glamorous. Ziegfeld's impeccable taste combined with his extravagant expenditure to make the *Follies* a distinctive, if unsustainable, theatrical enterprise. Ziegfeld's main competitors were *The George White Scandals,* the Shubert brothers' *Passing Shows,* John Murray Anderson's *Greenwich Village Follies,* and the somewhat lowbrow *Earl Carroll's Vanities.* In several of these shows, Kalmar's songs appeared alongside those of George Gershwin and Irving Berlin and were often sung by the leading performers of the time. In the *Ziegfeld Follies of 1920* comedienne Fanny Brice stopped the show with "I'm a Vamp from East Broadway," written with Berlin and Ruby, while Eddie Cantor popularized "My Sunny Tennessee" by interpolating it into the rooftop cabaret *The Midnight Rounders of 1921,* the Shubert brothers' response to Ziegfeld's *Midnight Frolics.*

A chance meeting with Ruby began a lifelong association between lyricist and composer. During the 1920s they wrote mostly for the Broadway stage; after 1930, mostly for Hollywood. A skillful pianist and baseball fanatic, Ruby had previously accompanied silent movies in the Bronx, but, as he told *The New York Times* in 1926, he "soon tired of those who read the subtitles out loud" and thereby disturbed his art. Kalmar and Ruby joined publishers Waterson, Berlin, and Snyder as songwriters, and the success of "He Sits Around" was soon followed by "So Long! Oo-Long (How Long You Gonna Be Gone?)" (1920), "My Sunny Tennessee," "I Gave You Up Just Before You Threw Me Down" (1922), "Who's Sorry Now?" (1923), and other songs that were sung in vaudeville by such well-known performers as Gus Van and Joe Schenck.

Like the great lyricists of his day, Kalmar had a knack for turning colloquial, everyday speech into a

The comedians Bob Woolsey (in glasses) and Bert Wheeler with two uncredited actresses performing the 1926 Kalmar-Ruby song "Alma Mater" in the 1930 movie musical The Cuckoos
(from Edward Watz, Wheeler & Woolsey, *1994)*

song lyric. There is an easy, conversational tone to his lyrics, which often seem lifted directly from street corners. Rarely literary in his allusions (unlike his contemporary Lorenz Hart), his frank expressions of emotion and sexuality had a broad appeal yet were often as finely crafted as any lyrics by his colleagues. "So Long! Oo-Long (How Long You Gonna Be Gone?)" is an example of a type of ethnic comedy song perfected by Joseph Weber and Lew Fields and popularized in vaudeville in the 1900s and 1910s. Taking as its point of departure Bob Cole and J. Rosamond Johnson's "coon" song "Under the Bamboo Tree" (1902) (which is directly referred to in the lyrics), the jaunty rhythms and catchy melody of "So Long! Oo-Long" match the quirky yet musical dialogue:

> Please don't be too long,
> Oo-Long,
> So long,
> Hurry back home.

The first line of the chorus of "My Sunny Tennessee," "I wanna be in Tennessee—in my Dixie paradise," uses the same slang contraction as "I Wanna Be Loved by You" (1928). So perfectly does Kalmar match Ruby's melodic line that, without an extraneous word, there is a sense of inevitability to the words of the chorus, as in following "An angel's voice I hear" with "I mean my mammy dear." "I Gave You Up Just Before You Threw Me Down" is an exercise in colloquial speech that could just as easily be spoken as sung, but this simplicity includes subtle rhyming, assonance, and alliteration: "Don't try to deny that you fooled me from the start; / You broke each vow, and I know now you meant to break my heart."

Written in 1923, "Who's Sorry Now?" originally sold more than a million copies of sheet music, and thirty-four years later, in 1957, it helped launch the career of Connie Francis. The sheet music transmits two versions of the song, side by side: first a nostalgic waltz, then a syncopated fox trot—showing the team's versatility. The terse emotional phrases with matching rhymes combine with an insistent repetition of "who's" to suggest a barely contained grief that finally overflows at the words "Just like I cried over you":

Who's sorry now? Who's sorry now?
Whose heart is aching for breaking each vow?
Who's sad and blue? Who's crying too?
Just like I cried over you.

"Who's Sorry Now?" is an anguished torch song, yet it reveals a hint of inner strength in the final line, which replaces the rhetorical question "Who's sorry now?" with the firm assertion, "I'm glad that you're sorry now."

Also in 1923, the team of Kalmar and Ruby embarked on their first full-length Broadway musical, *Helen of Troy, New York*. The book, by George S. Kaufman (writing his first musical) and Marc Connelly, was a satire of business and the advertising industry, and the show was designed as a vehicle for Helen Ford. It had a modest run, but no hit songs emerged. The story of how George Jessel raised the money for the production (told by Frederick Nolan in *Lorenz Hart: A Poet on Broadway*, 1994), with its gangsters and unexpected plot twists, might easily have been the subject of another stage musical. One of Hart's songs was interpolated into the show, probably because of his friendship with Helen Ford. No one remembered the song, "Moonlight Lane" (with music by W. Franke Harling), but perhaps Hart remembered Kalmar and Ruby, since their scripts became the sources for two shows by Hart and Richard Rodgers later that decade: *Lido Lady* (1926) and *She's My Baby* (1928).

The Ramblers (1926) marked Kalmar and Ruby's debut as scriptwriters and featured the comic antics of Bobby Clarke and Paul McCullough. Two songs in particular show Kalmar's increasing maturity as a lyricist: the duet "All Alone Monday," which became a popular blues standard, and "California Skies," a sultry waltz. The Viennese flavor of "California Skies" derives from the deliciously unexpected chromatic twists of its melody and accompaniment, which Kalmar matched with evocative lyrics:

Balmy breezes echo lovers' sighs,
Paradise is calling you
Underneath the blue
California skies.

The combination of soft *l*'s (balmy/lovers/calling/blue/California) and *s*'s (breezes/lovers/sighs/paradise/is) and long-voweled rhymes and assonance (sighs/paradise/skies; you/blue; breezes/underneath) conjure up a sensuously languid verbal haze evocative of the West Coast climate. With nearly three hundred performances on Broadway, *The Ramblers* was Kalmar and Ruby's most successful show to date and was considered by a reviewer for *The New York Times* to be the product of "facile pens" and "minds which are unusu-

ally inventive in the field of gags." The show later became the basis for the motion-picture musical *The Cuckoos* (1930).

More successful than either *Twinkle Twinkle* (1926) or *Lucky* (1927) was *Five O'Clock Girl* (1927), a "fairy tale in modern dress," with a book by Guy Bolton and Fred Thompson, stylishly modern sets by Norman Bel Geddes, and a first-rate number, "Thinking of You." The show was a success in London as well as New York, and this transatlantic triumph is wittily portrayed in *Three Little Words,* the 1950 movie biography of Kalmar and Ruby. Shots of Broadway and West End theaters are intercut with shots of Kalmar and Ruby as audience members enjoying "Up in the Clouds"–first sung in lush Yankee style and then in the brighter tones and clipped diction of an English chorus.

"Thinking of You" is unashamedly romantic; Ruby's bold, descending melodic line–reminiscent of Sergey Rachmaninoff–with its flat seventh providing a touch of the exotic that is matched by Kalmar's soaring lyrics. Wide, open vowels hang over the longest notes–"why," "day," "you"–while the first three syllables of the title phrase are set to a languorous triplet, creating a slowly lilting rhythm not unlike Berlin's "What'll I Do?" (1924). According to Gerald Bordman in *American Musical Theatre: A Chronicle* (1978), although the script "drew laughs from situations implicit in the text or in the social structure of the day," the future of the show was ill-fated: the planned movie version was never released, and the only Broadway revival, in 1981, was unsuccessful.

Kalmar and Ruby's collaborations with Rodgers and Hart were both direct and indirect. An unused script by Kalmar, Ruby, and Bolton was made into a book by Ronald Jeans for the relatively successful London production *Lido Lady*. The script for *She's My Baby,* however, proved to be less than inspired, and this show was one of Rodgers and Hart's least successful, closing after only seventy-one performances.

The most memorable number in their next show, *Good Boy* (1928), "I Wanna Be Loved by You," was sung by Helen Kane to her future husband, Dan Healy, in the original production and is surpassed in popularity only by "Who's Sorry Now?" and "Three Little Words" among the Kalmar and Ruby song canon. In *The First Hollywood Musicals: A Critical Filmography of 171 Features, 1927 through 1932* (1996), Edwin Bradley noted that "I Wanna Be Loved by You" has a "suggestive 'boop-boop-a-doop' lyric, which originated as an ad-lib by the singer [and] became her trademark. Strictly fictional is the account in *Three Little Words,* that the songwriters discovered Kane squeaking out this song on a Bronx sidewalk, although Debbie Reynolds is dubbed by the real Helen Kane." (Kane later became

*Sheet music for the best-known Kalmar-Ruby song, from the 1930 movie
(Bruccoli Clark Layman Archives)*

famous as the voice of the cartoon character Betty Boop). As a title, "I Wanna Be Loved by You" is a colloquial catchphrase, slangier than Hart's "I Didn't Know What Time It Was" (1939) or Ira Gershwin's "How Long Has This Been Going On?" (1928). The insistent repetition of the word *you* (four times in as many lines) matches the deliberately nonliterate and virtually monosyllabic lyric, while the nonsense tags almost reduce the song to incoherent babbling:

I wanna be loved by you,
Just you,
And nobody else but you.
I wanna be loved by you alone,
Poo-poo-pa-doop.

In stark contrast to this elemental simplicity, a self-consciously humorous triple rhyme follows, suggest-

ing, perhaps, that the singer is more knowing and manipulative than it first appears:

I couldn't aspire
To anything higher
Than fill a desire
To make you my own.

Kalmar's neat psychological portrait is achieved with an economy, wit, and verbal playfulness that are entirely appropriate to the character of the singer. Although one usually associates this kind of skill with the sophisticated wit of Cole Porter or the delicious angst of Hart, neither character nor song really do aspire to anything higher than a direct, unmediated appeal for romantic, marital, and, ultimately, economic security.

Kalmar and Ruby's first project with the Marx Brothers gave them ample scope to ply their talent at

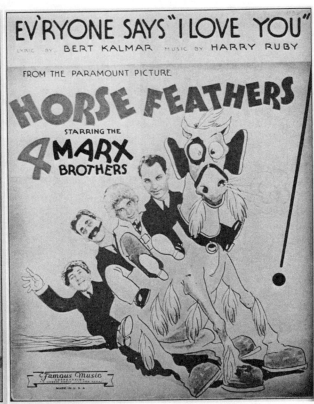

Sheet music for Kalmar-Ruby songs from 1930 and 1932 Marx Brothers movies
(Collection of Paul Talbot)

humorous songs. *Animal Crackers* (1930), with a book by Kaufman and Morrie Ryskind—the team who later won the Pulitzer Prize for *Of Thee I Sing* (1931)—is filled with the anarchic, madcap comedy at which the Marx Brothers excelled, which descended from the comic style of Weber and Fields. The play evinces a barely contained lunacy consisting of loosely strung-together comic dialogue scenes, visual gags, specialty musical numbers, theatrical parodies (in this case of Eugene O'Neill's *Strange Interlude,* 1928), and chorus numbers. When African explorer Captain Spaulding (Groucho Marx) returns to the United States, Mrs. Rittenhouse (Margaret Dumont) throws a party for him in her Long Island home. The whimsical lyric of "Hooray for Captain Spaulding," perhaps the best-known song from the show, parodies a W. S. Gilbert and Arthur Sullivan ensemble with refrain-like choral interjections that ultimately spin wildly out of control, interrupting the captain each time he attempts to speak. The absurdity of a phrase such as Groucho's "Hello, I must be going," according to Richard Barrios, "distills Marxian logic better than any book-length discourse." The following exchange is typical:

All: The Captain is a very moral man.
Jamison: If he hears anything obscene,
He'll natchrally repel it.
Spaulding: I hate a dirty joke I do
unless it's told by someone who
(rest, rest) Knows how to tell it.
All: The Captain is a very moral man.

"Hooray for Captain Spaulding" was later used as the theme for Groucho Marx's radio show and his television quiz show, *You Bet Your Life.* In "Musketeers," another number in the show that harks back to Gilbert and Sullivan, there are playful syntactical shifts, self-conscious rhymes, and knowing wordplay in such lines as "We live by the sword, by the sea, by the way" and "It's one for all and two for five—We're four of the three Musketeers."

Kalmar and Ruby's next venture, *Top Speed* (1929)—a story of the carefree 1920s featuring a speedboat race—was less than welcome right after the Wall Street crash, but it did launch the career of Ginger Rogers. The marriage of a synchronized soundtrack to celluloid created a new genre, the movie musical, whose development was (and still is) influenced by a migration of creative talent and ideas back and forth from East Coast to West Coast. Kalmar and Ruby were among the first wave of songwriters to leave New York and try their luck in Hollywood. The 1927–1928 season on Broadway produced record numbers of plays and more than fifty musicals. Although these figures declined in subsequent years, there was thus no shortage of material for the new sound studios in Hollywood. In addition, entire Tin Pan Alley publishing houses were bought up in order to keep the studios supplied with both old and new songs.

Common sense was often overruled by economics when it came to adapting stage shows. It would have made more sense to keep the songs, which in many cases bound the musicals together, and to adapt or refine their somewhat flimsy plots. The studios often did the opposite, however, keeping the plot and throwing out all but the hit songs and replacing them with inferior ones by staff writers, primarily to avoid royalty payments on the songs they did not own. Such was the case with the movie adaptation of *Top Speed* (1930), for which all Kalmar and Ruby's songs were replaced by a score by Al Dubin and Joe Burke. This not-atypical practice was made even more ludicrous when the studios began to sense that audiences were tiring of the decidedly uneven quality of musicals produced throughout 1929. In a last-ditch effort to salvage current projects, many if not all of the musical sequences were excised in the editing room. *Top Speed* was one casualty in this process; another was *Five O'Clock Girl*, the first try by M-G-M at a traditional musical comedy, starring Marion Davies and Charles King in an adaptation of Kalmar and Ruby's stage show. The project was abandoned in 1929 and remained unreleased because of difficulties with Davies's stammer, her problematic singing, and various technical issues.

In spite of the questionable artistic decisions and technical difficulties that dogged early studio ventures, Hollywood was nevertheless an exciting place to be and a potential gold mine for East Coast songwriters struggling to attract hard up Broadway audiences. Although *Top Speed* and *Five O'Clock Girl* were failures, Kalmar and Ruby scored three comedy hits in 1930, all with movies featuring legendary performers: two were adaptations—*The Cuckoos* and *Animal Crackers*—and the third was their first original movie musical, *Check and Double Check*. *The Cuckoos* starred comic duo Bert Wheeler and Robert Woolsey and was originally titled *Radio Revels* and planned by RKO as the first installment of an annual screen revue. Since audiences were beginning to demand more substance from movie musicals, however, the project eventually emerged as a movie version of *The Ramblers*. The original plot concerns two traveling fortune-tellers who get mixed up with members of a

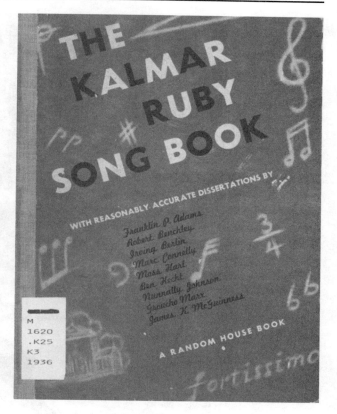

Cover for the 1936 collection of Kalmar and Ruby's songs
(Ralph Brown Draughon Library, Auburn University)

movie company filming in Tijuana. The movie version switches the location to a gypsy camp in California. As was typical with movie adaptations of stage productions, this version includes songs from a variety of sources: some came from the original stage show ("California Skies"), some were newly composed ("I'm a Gypsy" and the endearingly simple "I Love You So Much"), and others were garnered from elsewhere ("Dancing the Devil Away" was lifted from *Lucky* and was one of the earliest sequences shot in Technicolor). The movie version of *Animal Crackers* had most of its original songs removed, but the Marx Brothers' onstage magic translated well to the screen, and it was Paramount's largest moneymaker in 1930.

Another huge success, this time for RKO, was *Check and Double Check*, featuring Amos 'n' Andy (Freeman F. Gosden and Charles J. Correll) in their only screen performance. The movie was filmed from Kalmar and Ruby's first original screenplay, but it was one of their songs that stole the show. "Three Little Words," sung by Bing Crosby (dubbing for Charles Morton) and performed by Duke Ellington and his Cotton Club Orchestra, was almost dropped from the movie but turned out to be its highlight. The apparent

Sheet music for the 1928 song by Kalmar, Ruby, and Herbert Stothart that was used in a 1950 biopic about Kalmar and Ruby's songwriting career in which Astaire portrayed Kalmar
(from Marion Short, Covers of Gold, *1998)*

simplicity of "Three Little Words" exemplifies a style of song that was often successful in Hollywood, one that looked back to the earlier days of Tin Pan Alley. In *The Poets of Tin Pan Alley: A History of America's Great Lyricists* (1992) Philip Furia has noted that Ruby's melody to "Three Little Words" "posed a seemingly insurmountable problem for a Hollywood song": "its main phrase did not fit the usual cookie-cutter pattern that always enabled a lyricist . . . to say 'I love you.' Since it consisted of a four-note phrase, it was too long for the three-syllable standard 'I love you.' What they needed,

in other words, were *four* little words, but they solved their problem–ingeniously, for Hollywood–with the four syllable equation 'three lit-tle words'":

> Three little words,
> Eight little letters,
> Which simply mean
> "I love you!"

The song is about the craft of lyric writing, and in the movie *Three Little Words* humorous play is made of Ruby attempting unsuccessfully to fit "I love you" onto the four-note phrase. Kalmar later supplies the "correct" phrase and not only completes the song but reconciles the quarreling songwriting partners.

"Nevertheless (I'm in Love with You)" (1931) was written around the same time as "Three Little Words" and is equally artful in its use of patterned repetition. The opening four lines, for example, are generated from just seven words. Also, the musical rhythm of the word *nevertheless* is echoed in almost every phrase of the chorus, even in the bridge, so that musically and textually the entire chorus seems derived from that one word. Also masterful are the initially laconic one-measure phrases—

Maybe I'm right,
And maybe I'm wrong
And maybe I'm weak,
And maybe I'm strong

—that ultimately expand into two-measure phrases for the final flowering of emotion in the closing moments of the chorus:

Maybe I'll live a life of regret
And maybe I'll give much more than I get,
But nevertheless I'm in love with you.

More movies followed *Check and Double Check,* including *The Kid from Spain* (1932), which stars Eddie Cantor pretending to be a celebrated bullfighter to evade a mistaken bank robbery charge; *Horse Feathers* (1932); and *Duck Soup* (1933). The latter two feature the Marx Brothers, with Groucho turning authority on its head, first as a college president, then as leader of an unfortunate minor principality. In *Horse Feathers,* the second Marx Brothers movie developed originally for the screen (the first was *Monkey Business,* 1931), the music, lyrics, and performance style constantly undercut one another. As Barrios notes, when "Ev'ryone Says 'I Love You'" is sung to Thelma Todd, "the insipidly sweet lyrics suddenly read as riotously accusatory double-entendres." Similarly, the Sousa-like march tune of "Whatever It Is I'm Against It" is a perfect rhythmic corollary to the title phrase; yet, together music and lyrics humorously represent the blind pomposity of authority that Groucho portrays so well.

Duck Soup, again with a Kalmar-Ruby script, revels in absurdity and is perhaps the quintessential Marx Brothers production. Barrios has noted that "the staid sanity usually targeted by the Marxes appeared here in the form of the ultimate insanity—war—and as the empty politics that foolishly attempt to rule the world." His observations on the music and songs are equally trenchant:

The music is almost entirely ceremonial–Groucho's grand entrance, the hymn to Freedonia, the epic "The Country's Going to War"–and with straightfaced solemnity equates the atrophied pomp of traditional operetta with the insincere pomposity of diplomacy. The concerted choruses, the troupes of ballerinas sprinkling petals, the reckless unreality that shotgun-mates warfare with lyricism à la *Song of the Flame:* all are the stock of operetta that *Duck Soup* assaults with dazzling concentrated force.

This carnival-like juxtaposition of high and low styles is nowhere more explicit than in the grand ensemble finale, "The Country's Going to War." In that number, folk, popular, and classical clichés are punctuated by choral responses and refrains in the manner of Gilbert and Sullivan ("To war, to war") in a rapid-fire succession of march, square dance, barbershop, and darkly menacing folk spiritual ("All God's chillun got guns") that is as disturbing in its effect as it is humorous. This subversive stylistic dissonance is echoed in Groucho's rousing call-to-arms quatrain:

Ride though every village and town,
Wake every citizen uphill and down,
Tell them the enemy comes from afar
With a hey-non-nonny and a ha-cha-cha!

Kalmar's versatility and wit are the perfect complement to Ruby's free-roving kaleidoscope of musical styles and the Marx Brothers' anarchic performance.

Apart from a brief return to Broadway in 1941 with *High Kickers*–George Jessel's look back at the days of vaudeville and burlesque, starring himself and Sophie Tucker–Kalmar and Ruby subsequently wrote fewer full scores for either screen or stage. Kalmar's remaining work focused more on screenplays–*Bright Lights* (1935), *Walking on Air* (1936), and story ideas for *Look for the Silver Lining* (1949), the screen biography of Marilyn Miller–but he did continue to produce such gems as "Cabin on the Hilltop" for *Walking on Air* (1936), and "The Egg and I" (1947) for the motion picture of the same name. In "The Egg and I" the clever egg metaphors (for example, "hardboiled," "such a good egg," and "once you get under his shell") are brought to a climax with a highly unusual word (for a lyric)–*facsimile:* "Here's what we pray for in the sweet bye and bye–A bundle of love, facsimile of the Egg and I." Thus this seemingly effortless wordplay culminates in a highly compact yet evocative final turn of the title phrase.

The Kalmar-Ruby Song Book, published by Random House in 1936, includes eleven songs and witty tributes to the duo by, among others, Groucho Marx, Moss Hart, Berlin, Nunnally Johnson, and Ben Hecht. Apart from "Hooray for Captain Spaulding" and perhaps

"Show Me a Rose (or Leave Me Alone)" (1936), the other songs are not well known and are all parody songs of one sort or another. Unlike *The Rodgers and Hart Song Book* (1951), this collection does not showcase Kalmar and Ruby's best-known songs, though it is a measure of their reputation as writers of comic and parody songs. In addition to those found in *The Kalmar-Ruby Song Book,* their other comic songs include "Where Do They Go When They Row, Row, Row?" (1920), a parody of the 1912 hit song "Row, Row, Row" by William Jerome and James V. Monaco; "The Sheik of Avenue B" (1922), a play on "The Sheik of Araby," by Harry B. Smith, Francis Wheeler, and Ted Snyder; "Ain't Cha Comin' Out?" (1939), a song that plays on the would-be Romeo's lack of singing ability and his relentless repetition of the naive and colloquial title phrase; and "Go West, Young Man" (1947), reminiscent of "Hooray for Hollywood" (1938) in its parody of the old and new West with a humorous mix of cowboys, prairies, orange juice, divorce, and other juxtapositions of frontier and contemporary life.

Kalmar's last hit was the posthumously released "A Kiss to Build a Dream On," performed by Louis Armstrong and Kay Brown in the movie *The Strip* (1951), with lyrics adapted by Oscar Hammerstein. Kalmar's standards also continued to be featured in movies after his death. "Who's Sorry Now?" appeared in such diverse movies as *National Lampoon's Animal House* (1978) and Bob Fosse's *All That Jazz* (1979), while perhaps the most renowned screen performance of a Kalmar song is Marilyn Monroe's rendition of "I Wanna Be Loved by You" in *Some Like It Hot* (1959). In addition to his diverse career, Kalmar maintained his interest in magic (performing card tricks for his friends at Hollywood parties), and, from 1920 onward, was an active member of ASCAP. The fact that he worked with so many of the leading figures in the entertainment industry over his long career suggests that he was well liked as well as versatile.

Kalmar's reputation was solidified in the M-G-M screen biography *Three Little Words,* based on his and Ruby's careers. With excellent performances by Fred Astaire as Kalmar, Red Skelton as Ruby, and Vera-Ellen and Arlene Dahl as their wives, the movie, like the song from which it takes its name, is about songwriting and teamwork. The joining of words and music takes on symbolic proportions when a rift between the collaborators is finally healed only when words are added to music, and Kalmar surprises Ruby with a setting of an old tune to "Three Little Words." The movie is a fitting tribute to a versatile, everyman wordsmith whose skill is often concealed by his wit and the directness of his emotional expression. Bert Kalmar died on 18 September 1947, only a few days after signing the contract for *Three Little Words.*

References:

Richard Barrios, *A Song in the Dark: The Birth of the Musical Film* (New York: Oxford University Press, 1995), pp. 268–269;

Philip Furia, *The Poets of Tin Pan Alley: A History of America's Greatest Lyricists* (New York: Oxford University Press, 1990), pp. 236–237;

"More or Less in the Spotlight: The Rise of Kalmar and Ruby," *New York Times,* 17 October 1926.

Selected Discography:

Eddie Cantor, *The Columbia Years: 1922–1940,* Columbia/Legacy, C2T-57148, 1994;

Three Little Words: Song Hits by Kalmar and Ruby, M-G-M, 53, 1950.

Ted Koehler
(14 July 1894 – 17 January 1973)

Paul Woodbury
University of North Carolina at Wilmington

Music is by Harold Arlen unless otherwise indicated.

SELECTED SONGS FROM THEATRICAL PRO-DUCTIONS: *Brown Sugar* (1930)–"Linda";
Earl Carroll's Vanities of 1930 (1930)–"One Love";
9:15 Revue (1930)–"Get Happy";
Rhythmania (1931)–"Between the Devil and the Deep Blue Sea"; "I Love a Parade";
Cotton Club Parade (1932)–"I've Got the World on a String"; "Minnie the Moocher's Wedding Day"; "That's What I Hate about Love";
Earl Carroll's Vanities of 1932 (1932)–"I Gotta Right to Sing the Blues";
Cotton Club Parade (1933)–"Happy as the Day Is Long"; "Stormy Weather";
Cotton Club Parade (1934)–"As Long as I Live"; "Ill Wind";
Cotton Club Parade, World's Fair Edition (1939), music by Rube Bloom–"Don't Worry 'bout Me"; "The Mayor of Harlem";
Americanegro Suite: Four Spirituals, a Dream, and a Lullaby (1941)–"Big Time Comin'"; "Little Ace o' Spades."

SELECTED SONGS FROM MOTION-PICTURE PRODUCTIONS: *Let's Fall in Love* (1933)–"Let's Fall in Love";
Curly Top (1935)–"Animal Crackers in My Soup" (lyric by Koehler and Irving Caesar, music by Ray Henderson);
The King of Burlesque (1936)–"I'm Shootin' High" (music by Jimmy McHugh);
Artists and Models (1937)–"Laughing Song" (lyric and music by Koehler and the Yacht Club Boys); "Pop Goes the Bubble (And Soap Gets in Your Eyes)" (music by Burton Lane); "Public Melody Number One"; "Stop! You're Breakin' My Heart" (music by Lane);
23 1/2 Hours Leave (1937), music by Sam H. Stept–"Good Night My Lucky Day" (lyric by Koehler and Sidney D. Mitchell); "It Must Be Love" (lyric by Koehler and Mitchell); "Now You're Talking My Language" (lyric by Koehler and Mitchell); "We Happen to Be in the Army" (lyric by Koehler and Mitchell);
Love Affair (1939)–"Sing My Heart";
Hollywood Canteen (1944)–"Sweet Dreams, Sweetheart" (music by M. K. Jerome); "What Are You Doin' the Rest of Your Life" (music by Lane);
Up in Arms (1944)–"Now I Know."

SELECTED SONGS PUBLISHED INDEPENDENTLY OF THEATRICAL OR MOTION-PICTURE PRODUCTIONS: "At the Ragtime Strollers Ball" (1918), lyric and music by Koehler and Spencer Williams;
"Beyond the Stars" (1920), music by Koehler, Frank Magine, and Paul Biese;
"By the Shalimar" (1922), music by Koehler, Magine, and Del Delbridge;
"Dreamy Melody" (1922), music by Koehler, Magine, and Clayton Nacet;
"When Lights Are Low" (1923), lyric by Koehler and Gus Kahn, music by Ted Fiorito;
"America Did It Again" (1927), lyric and music by Koehler and Marty Bloom;
"Wrap Your Troubles in Dreams (And Dream Your Troubles Away)" (1931), lyric by Koehler and Billy Moll, music by Harry Barris;
"When the Sun Comes Out" (1941).

Ted Koehler, lyricist, composer, and pianist, was a prolific writer whose poetic talent fashioned several enduring standards, including "Get Happy" (1930), "Between the Devil and the Deep Blue Sea" (1931), and "I Gotta Right to Sing the Blues" (1932). His best-known song, "Stormy Weather" (1933), is still a mainstay of club performances and recordings.

Ted Louis Koehler was born in Washington, D.C., on 14 July 1894 but grew up in New York and Newark, New Jersey. The son of George Koehler, a photoengraver, and Ethel Goldsboro, Koehler attended

Ted Koehler with his main songwriting partner, Harold Arlen (Arlen Archive)

public schools but dropped out at age fourteen to begin working full-time in his father's photoengraving shop in Manhattan. Koehler's father was an accomplished pianist, and when young Ted demonstrated an interest in music, he was given piano lessons. Before long he was drawn to bars and clubs in Newark, where his nightly piano playing, with his hot, barrelhouse style, became popular. These late-night gigs began affecting his work in the photoengraving shop, and his father, a strict disciplinarian, issued an ultimatum: during the week Ted was to be in bed by midnight—or he could move out of the house and out of the photoengraving plant. Given the choice of giving up his musical moonlighting or moving out, Koehler left home in 1912, at age eighteen.

Putting his budding career as an artist and illustrator in the photography business behind him, Koehler spent the next several years as a pianist in Newark, Brooklyn, and New York. He started as the house pianist at the Sea Shell Theater, a movie house, and then moved from one job to another, providing piano accompaniment for silent films during the day and entertaining in different clubs and cafés at night. He even tried going into business and, with a partner,

opened a motion-picture theater. Koehler played accompaniment while his partner sold tickets, but he was not a businessman, and the venture failed. Returning to the piano circuit, yet seeking a more artistic outlet for his talent, he began writing songs.

Koehler's first song, "At the Ragtime Strollers Ball," was written in collaboration with Spencer Williams and published in 1918. In 1920, working with Frank Magine and Paul Biese, he published "Beyond the Stars," and in 1922, again with Magine, he had two more songs published—"By the Shalimar" (also with Del Delbridge) and "Dreamy Melody" (also with Clayton Nacet). Although none of these songs became standards, they were popular and marked Koehler's acceptance into the company of songwriters. In these early years Koehler also worked as a pianist and accompanist in vaudeville, creating comedy routines and special lyrics to popular songs for such contemporary vaudeville stars as Al Jolson, Eddie Cantor, and Sophie Tucker.

He married in 1923 (his wife's name is unknown), and his first son, George, was born, but Koehler was not ready to settle down; he went on the

*Sheet music for a song introduced in a 1931 revue at Harlem's Cotton Club
(from Marion Short,* The Gold in Your Piano Bench, *1997)*

road with the small bands common in the cafés of that time, traveling to Buffalo, Pittsburgh, and Detroit, and finally ending up in Chicago. There he established himself in the cafés and nightclubs and then added a daytime job, working for the publishing firm of J. W. Stern, rehearsing songs for popular singers and plugging numbers for the publishers. He later switched to the company of Leo Feist and became the manager for the Chicago office.

Koehler also had a talent for staging productions and soon became noted for producing shows for prominent cafés and nightclubs in Chicago, including the Rendezvous, Frolics, and the Marigold Gardens. He had a natural talent for set layout and seemed to know intuitively how to stage a song to its best advantage. Later Koehler applied these skills to staging many of the Cotton Club productions. His tendency to pitch in and work with his hands on set construction won him the nickname of "Willie Westinghouse," the guy who could do it all. On the sets Koehler could apply his talent to satisfy a visual artistic drive, a drive that had not

found outlet earlier in the rigid, black-and-white discipline of his father's photoengraving shop. Koehler's son, Ted Jr., suggested in 1999 that, if modern color photography had been available in those days, his father might have stayed in the photo business and never become a songwriter.

Koehler's songwriting continued to develop during his years in Chicago. He composed, played, and sang his songs in vaudeville theaters and soon published several songs, including "When Lights Are Low" (1923), a collaboration with Gus Kahn and Ted Fiorito, and a song about Charles Lindbergh written with Marty Bloom, "America Did It Again" (1927). Topical and quite popular at the time, these compositions were mostly sentimental ballads and torch songs that bore little resemblance to the jazzy lyrics that later became his hallmark. While still not widely recognized, Koehler became a respected professional among his musical peers, with a solid body of published work to his credit. In 1926 he became a member of the American Society of Composers, Authors, and Publishers (ASCAP). In

1927, now thirty-three years old and divorced from his first wife, Koehler married Elvira Hagen, a dancer in Al Capone's club, The Green Mill, and returned with her to settle in Brooklyn. The couple had a daughter in 1928, Carolyn (Carrie), and two sons, Ted Jr. (1935) and Robert (1941).

Over the next two years Koehler worked as a staff songwriter for the publishing firm of Piantadosi, a subsidiary of Remick's. In July 1929, as a result of improbable coincidences, Koehler was introduced to Harold Arlen. Arlen was filling in for the dance accompanist during rehearsals at the Cosmopolitan Theater for the Broadway musical *Great Day*. The choreographer for the production took frequent breaks to add instructions or corrections. Then he would signal Arlen, who would cue the dancers with a short, two-bar vamp, the "pickup" to warn them to resume their positions. Arlen amused himself by experimenting with the pickup during these breaks, changing it and extending it to produce variations. Harry Warren, a staff composer with Remick Music Corporation, had stopped by to watch the rehearsal and saw members of the cast crowded around the piano as Arlen entertained them with this catchy tune. Convinced that Arlen had the making of a song, Warren told him, "I know the guy to write it up." Warren might have realized that Koehler, with his years of experience and natural affinity for jazz, would be the perfect lyricist to work with the young, inexperienced Arlen and his tune with its jazzy tempo. More probably, he suggested Koehler primarily because Koehler was the most experienced lyricist he knew who was not collaborating with anyone at the time.

From this first effort came the immediately popular song "Get Happy." The nearly overnight success of "Get Happy" arose from several factors, but most of all it was the snappy brashness of the music and the upbeat lyrics that grabbed the listener. Koehler, a master of vernacular idioms and the language of the streets, loaded the song with the hopeful words of Negro spirituals, adapting them to the staccato and fast-ranging music and making the message upbeat, even to the imperative of the title. His title matches the strong three-notes that round out the opening phrase and that are repeated six times in the song. Koehler laced his lyric with a sequence of guttural, dental, and plosive consonants and abrupt imperative phrases that emphasize the verb *get:*

Forget your troubles and just get happy. . .
Get ready for the Judgment Day.

He then filled in the blanks with the familiar words of popular gospel music: "Judgment Day," "the River," and "Wash your sins away with the tide." His lyrics were ideally suited for the tune and for the times. They were a new experience for him, since his prior work gave little hint of his appreciation of the soulful hopefulness reflected in the black culture of the times. Koehler had not only managed to tie lyrics to the challenging music written by Arlen, but his words complemented the strong musical imperatives and turned Arlen's impromptu "riff" into a great song. "Get Happy" has remained a popular song over the years and was recorded by several artists, including Judy Garland in the 1950 movie *Summer Stock*. For Arlen it was the first song he had ever published that brought both artistic and financial rewards; it also gained him a full-time songwriting job. For the older and more experienced Koehler, it was his first major hit and his first successful effort in a jazz idiom. For both of them it was the start of a new creative marriage, the teaming of lyricist and composer.

The immediate popularity of "Get Happy" assured a continuing collaboration between Koehler and Arlen. The team worked together in New York over the next few years, producing several hits, and eventually went to Hollywood. In 1930 they collaborated on the Cotton Club show *Brown Sugar* and on the Broadway show *9:15 Revue,* which featured "Get Happy" in a prime spot as the first-act finale. The show, produced by Ruth Selwyn, opened in Boston and starred Ruth Etting. Etting, who was discovered by Koehler and picked out of the chorus to take a feature role at the Marigold Gardens, was a firm friend from these Chicago days. She was instrumental in the inclusion of "Get Happy" into the score, and this song was the only successful aspect of an ill-conceived and poorly executed show. The stage presentation of "Get Happy"—set on a sunny, sandy beach with Etting clad in a bathing suit—must have seemed absurd to an experienced set designer such as Koehler. The song went over well, however, even though the show itself folded before its Broadway opening.

Koehler and Arlen soon became one of the most sought-after teams in the songwriting world. As the United States entered the 1930s, the aura of danger and excitement associated with Prohibition was reaching a climax and the Great Depression had begun. In an environment of economic uncertainty, a thrill-seeking public thronged to nightclubs such as the Cotton Club in Harlem, where white patrons stood in line to watch black performers. The club owner, Owney Madden, had served time in prison, a fact that added spice to the reputation of the club and helped attract customers—the "Mink Set," as Arlen called them, who came to Harlem in taxis and limousines to be titillated by the racy shows. Cotton Club shows were normally set pieces. The audiences knew there would be a well-staged blues number, a comedy skit, a suggestive ditty, and plenty of scantily dressed girls. The team of Koehler and Arlen soon

Sheet music for a song featured in a 1932 Cotton Club revue
(Bruccoli Clark Layman Archives)

became a fixture at the Cotton Club, writing the words and music for the shows, arranging sequences, designing the sets, and even overseeing the rehearsals. At Arlen's insistence, some of their more risqué, off-color pieces were never published. Other songs were not only published but went on to become major hits and long-term staples for many performers.

The contrast between the two collaborators, their personalities and backgrounds, probably facilitated their creative efforts. Arlen, who was then in the formative stage of his development as a composer, would spontaneously create short segments of music, bits that seemed to have promise. Then, with Koehler listening, he would put together some of these bits, or "jots," as he called them, and play the piece, often switching the arrangement as they worked. As Arlen played the music, Koehler would listen and suggest lyrics. Koehler's working style reflected his easygoing, laid-back personality. He often stretched out on the sofa, eyes closed, listening as Arlen played a segment over and over. Frustrated when

nothing seemed to be working, Arlen often chided Koehler for "sleeping." Koehler responded by urging Arlen to be calm, explaining that he was composing the words in his mind. Slowly, bar by bar and stanza by stanza, the song would emerge. These early songs were often characterized by their strong rhythm, wide melodic range, and unconventional style and form. This result can be attributed, at least in part, to the building-block approach of their development.

If Arlen had found the ideal lyricist to help him solidify his early compositions and develop his craft, Koehler had connected with a gifted composer whose music challenged him. For Koehler, Arlen's wide-ranging music evoked images of the city streets and the working people with whom he grew up. The results were lyrics such as "Between the Devil and the Deep Blue Sea," "I've Got the World on a String" (1932), and "I Gotta Right to Sing the Blues," in which slang, missing pronouns, the truncated *-ing*, and Koehler's favorite guttural verbs, such as *got* and *get*, strengthened the driving rhythms of the music and lent a familiarity that helped the listener to identify with the song. Koehler's lyrics, often invoking heavenly intervention and blues-like laments, created images of the Negro gospels, images that were heightened by Arlen's early affinity for black culture and music.

Although Arlen had grown up in Buffalo, his father had originally come to the United States to sing at a Louisville synagogue. Arlen was certain that during his father's years in the South he had picked up the inflections of black music. He told Max Wilk in *They're Playing Our Song: From Jerome Kern to Stephen Sondheim—The Truth behind the Words and Music of Two Generations* (1973) that he once played a Louis Armstrong record for his father, and at an Armstrong riff, his father demanded to know, in Yiddish, "Where did *he* get it?" While Arlen knew and admired the work of Kern and George Gershwin, he told Wilk that his real beginnings "were never centered on those guys, only jazz." Initially, he wanted to be a singer and developed a style that blended his father's cantorial style with his love of jazz and blues. Koehler's lyrical style was also colloquial, not poetic, and the words he chose tended toward the vernacular. His extensive use of short verbal phrases, alliteration, and internal rhyme also fit Arlen's music, and the simplicity of his words helped make their songs popular.

During the next few years Arlen and Koehler produced many popular songs for the Cotton Club shows, including *Rhythmania* (1931), and for the 1930 and 1932 Broadway productions of *Earl Carroll's Vanities,* in addition to other songs not associated with any show. They wrote nine songs for *Brown Sugar,* but only two were published. One of these, "Linda," was a playfully plaintive song that introduced a new technique—rising or dropping an entire octave in the interval between two notes—that Arlen repeated in later songs and that Koehler and other lyricists had to match with an equally dramatic sequence of two syllables. For the 1930 *Vanities* they wrote the melodious "One Love," a rare waltz for the jazzy team. It was presented as an exotic number, as Earl Carroll, in his attempt to upstage *Ziegfeld's Follies,* had Faith Bacon enter onstage, following the vocal, to dance seductively to the music, costumed with only two large, strategically positioned fans. Word spread, morals charges were brought, and Carroll's show continued to mostly full houses well into the next year. While noteworthy in its own sake and for the recognition it brought its writers, "One Love" soon faded from popularity. Other songs written by Koehler and Arlen during this period proved to be more durable.

Two of the numbers they wrote for *Rhythmania,* "Between the Devil and the Deep Blue Sea" and "I Love a Parade," were not only instant hits but also went on to become widely recorded standards. "I Love a Parade"

was so popular that all subsequent Cotton Club shows were titled *Parades.* These two rhythm songs, however, share little in musical or lyrical style. "I Love a Parade" has a fairly long verse, stressing the first and the final, drawn-out syllables of each bar, followed by the refrain, which, in opposition to the verse, is dominated by the first syllable, the drawn-out pronoun *I.* "Between the Devil and the Deep Blue Sea," on the other hand, has no verse. Its melodic leaps and drops, along with its tempo changes, created different challenges for the lyricist. Koehler responded by using short, stressed verbs in mid bar and relying more on alliteration instead of rhyme to match the energy of the music:

> I should hate you,
> But I guess I love you,
> You've got me in between the devil and the deep blue sea.

"I Gotta Right to Sing the Blues," from the 1932 *Earl Carroll's Vanities,* has one of Arlen's octave drops, which Koehler matches with assonance, having "around" followed by "down around":

> I gotta right to hang around
> Down around the river.

The shift in meaning from the casual "hang around" to the nearly suicidal "Down around the river" intensifies the lyrical contour of that deep melodic drop.

The *Cotton Club Parade* productions of 1932, 1933, and 1934 were productive for the team. "I've Got the World on a String," from the 1932 show, is an especially lovely song. The verse begins "Merry month of May, sunny skies of blue," but escapes cliché by its dreamy nature and its transition into a chorus that retains the gentle feeling while introducing a more solid, realistic world. Koehler again relies on the guttural alliteration found in "Between the Devil and the Deep Blue Sea":

> I've got a song that I sing.
> I can make the rain go.

Here, however, the use is softer and the result more delicate, as in "I'd be a silly so-and-so if I should ever let it go."

From the 1933 Cotton Club show came "Happy as the Day Is Long," a lively rhythm tune similar to, and even concluding on the same musical bar that begins, "Get Happy." The second hit from this show, "Stormy Weather," turned out to be the most enduring song that Koehler and Arlen created together. Written for Cab Calloway, who turned out to be unavailable for the show, "Stormy Weather" was introduced by Ethel Waters, who followed Arlen's instructions for "slow

Sheet music for Koehler and Arlen's best-known song as it was introduced in 1933 and republished as the title song for a 1943 movie (left: from Marion Short, The Gold in Your Piano Bench, *1997; right: Bruccoli Clark Layman Archives)*

lament" and stunned the audience with the intensity of her rendition. The number was an instant success and became Waters's theme song. The version she introduced was published and performed without the twelve-bar interlude that begins "I walk around, heavy hearted and sad." A month later, when she recorded the song, the interlude was added, and it was later restored to the published version. Unconventional, with its unusual thirty-six bars instead of the standard thirty-two, "Stormy Weather" caused consternation in rhythm bands, which were accustomed to playing only eight-measure phrases. It was also different in that it did not repeat a phrase in the first eight bars, a feature that Gershwin pointed out to Arlen, who had never given it a thought. Koehler matched Arlen's innovative melody with a lyric that, while it also avoided repeating any of its abrupt slang phrases, so deftly omitted pronouns and connectives that it gave the song a nervous monotony:

Don't know why there's no sun up in the sky,
Stormy weather, since my man and I ain't together,
Keeps raining all the time.

He intensifies the relentless feel of the lyric with subtle assonance and rhymes—"ain't" with "raining," "rockin' chair" with "walk in the sun once more"—and a wrenching off-rhyme, "can't go on, ev'rything I have is gone."

"Stormy Weather" turned out to be the ticket to Hollywood for Koehler and Arlen. In 1933 they traveled together to the West Coast to write the music for the movie *Let's Fall in Love*. From that endeavor came another hit, the title song, "Let's Fall in Love," which, with its brassy beat and whimsical questions ("Why shouldn't we fall in love?"), became part of the repertoire of many performers.

When the two returned to New York in 1934, the era of nightclub shows was coming to a close. Broadway had been in a deepening slump since the 1929 market crash, and the clubs were being squeezed by the combined forces of the end of Prohibition and the Great Depression. The economic downturn was affecting the entire city as the pair began working on their final *Cotton Club Parade* show together. The credits indicated that the entire production was "conceived and supervised by Ted Koehler," and it proved to be the springboard for two new hit songs,

Sheet music for a 1934 song from the last Cotton Club revue on which Koehler and Arlen collaborated (from William Zinsser, Easy to Remember, *2000)*

"Ill Wind" and "As Long as I Live." Handwritten notes on the bottom of the "Ill Wind" manuscripts tell much about their relaxed, comfortable collaboration at that time. Below the music, Arlen scrawled, "Havin' the time of my life." Under that, Koehler wrote, "Says you." Despite the differences in age and style, Arlen and Koehler worked well together, although their partnership ended shortly thereafter.

Early the next year, Arlen was approached by Ira Gershwin and E. Y. "Yip" Harburg to collaborate with them on a major Shubert Broadway musical, *Life Begins at 8:40.* This was a tremendous opportunity for Arlen, but he worried about Koehler. While each of them had occasionally worked with others during their years together, Arlen saw his planned move as an act of betrayal and was miserable as he sought a way to tell Koehler about it. In the end he wrote Koehler a letter, and Koehler responded by telling him, "You'd be a fool if you didn't do it." As Ted Koehler Jr. explained, "There were never any hard feelings. Dad was always pretty easy-going–

happy-go-lucky. In fact, we all went to California together and remained good friends." Although they continued to collaborate on occasion, for each of them it was time to move on. Arlen wrote new hits with Harburg and, later, with Johnny Mercer and worked alternately in shows and films. Koehler chose Hollywood for his career and moved back there in 1936, taking his family with him. Although he returned to the East Coast a few times to collaborate on songs, including working with Rube Bloom on the last Cotton Club show, the 1939 *World's Fair Edition,* California became home for the Koehler family, and movies became the genre in which he preferred to work.

For many songwriters the fast-paced Hollywood style, with its lack of serious artistic focus, was anathema. Others were upset to find that they were at the bottom of the power hierarchy in the movies and could expect neither fame nor recognition for their work. For Koehler these were not important considerations. He had a lucrative contract with M-G-M, and his work, the pay, and his family were his priorities. Always quiet, Koehler was shy in public and unassuming in relationships with others. Unlike Mercer he was content to leave the limelight to his composer, and he did not miss the public recognition that he had in New York. He joined the small, tight community of other songwriters in California and, like many other writers, took up painting as a hobby. So, while many others returned to New York, Koehler, like Harry Warren, stayed. In 1936 Koehler worked with both Arlen and Burton Lane on the film *Artists and Models* (1937). He also worked with Ray Henderson on *Curly Top* (1935), starring Shirley Temple, and with Sam H. Stept and Sidney D. Mitchell on *23 1/2 Hours Leave* (1937).

In 1938 he joined again with Arlen to work on a spiritual song cycle–an independent effort of uncertain future, since there was no market for spirituals by then. Both of them were busy on other projects at the time: Arlen on *The Wizard of Oz* (1939) and Koehler on *Love Affair* (1939) with Irene Dunne, for which he wrote the graceful "Sing My Heart." Work proceeded slowly on the spiritual songs, as Koehler and Arlen continued with other endeavors, including a few songs together. Among these was the blues ballad "When the Sun Comes Out" (1941), a vintage Koehler-Arlen song that was recorded by many of the big bands of the period. In 1940, fully two years after starting, they completed their sixth and last song of the cycle, which they decided to call *Americanegro Suite*. It was subtitled "Four Spirituals, a Dream, and a Lullaby" and was recorded by Decca in 1941. The songs in the cycle included a melodic lullaby, "Little Ace o' Spades," and the upbeat closing number, "Big Time Comin'." Koehler's earthy lyrics, which received acclaim from both black and white critics in 1940, were considered racist a few decades later. Arlen and Koehler had enjoyed close friendship with many black performers in New York and were more closely attuned to blacks and black culture than most whites. Changing public attitudes, however, dictated that, before the suite could be re-recorded in 1986, the lyrics had to be modified. By this time Koehler had died, so, with Arlen's approval, titles and terms like "Little Ace o' Spades" became "Little Angel Child."

During the period from 1935 until his death in 1973, Koehler collaborated on fifteen movies. In 1944 two of them, *Up in Arms* and *Hollywood Canteen*, on which he had collaborated with Burton Lane, were nominated for Academy Awards. Other movies on which Koehler worked include *Let's Fall in Love* and the 1943 picture named after his most renowned hit, *Stormy Weather*. By the early 1950s Koehler was no longer a significant contributor to group songwriting efforts in the movies, and he tried one last trip back to New York to test the market there. He found a new era with new music, however. Most of his friends were gone, the pace of the city was frenetic, and the weather was cold. Most depressing, in his words, "The music has gone to hell." After a few months he returned to California and shortly thereafter gave up songwriting.

Completely retired by 1955, Koehler took the opportunity to pursue his hobbies. He continued painting, which he had begun a decade earlier, and returned again to his youthful interest in photography. Also, in a reprise of his old days of designing and building stage sets, he handcrafted elaborate model-train systems with finely detailed settings. Koehler suffered a stroke in 1963 and died ten years later, on 17 January 1973, at the age of seventy-eight.

Ted Koehler was a master at selecting and fitting words to fill the tight riffs and wide-ranging melodies of the Tin Pan Alley era. His lyrics of that period were rich with the idioms of the city streets of New York and, when matched with jazz tunes, they mirrored the spirit of that raucous time in the United States. While the bulk of his career was spent in the movie industry, his best-known work was done in the late 1920s and early 1930s, while working on songs for the Cotton Club with Arlen. Not a Broadway writer, Koehler never received the public recognition attained by some of his peers, such as Gershwin or Harburg. Nonetheless, he was one of the great lyricists of the 1920s and 1930s. Many of his songs have become standards in American music. His contributions were respected by his peers, and his impressive body of work received special public recognition on 15 May 1972, when Koehler was inducted into the Songwriters Hall of Fame. The shy and retiring lyricist did not attend.

References:

Philip Furia, *The Poets of Tin Pan Alley: A History of America's Great Lyricists* (New York: Oxford University Press, 1990), pp. 245–250;

Edward Jablonski, *Harold Arlen: Happy with the Blues* (Garden City, N.Y.: Doubleday, 1961).

Selected Discography:

Americanegro Suite: Four Spirituals, a Dream, and a Lullaby, Decca, 170, 1941;

Harold Arlen, *Over the Rainbow,* Pearl, 7095, 1997;

Ella Fitzgerald, *The Harold Arlen Songbook, Vol. 1,* Verve, 8175272, 1988;

Maxine Sullivan Sings the Great Cotton Club Songs of Harold Arlen and Ted Koehler, Stash, ST-C-244, 1984;

Sullivan, *Swingin' Sweet,* Concord Jazz, CCD-4351, 1988;

The Ultimate Billie Holiday, Polygram, 539051, 1997;

Weslia Whitfield, *My Shining Hour,* HighNote, 7012, 1997.

Carolyn Leigh

(21 August 1926 – 19 November 1983)

Deborah Grace Winer

SELECTED SONGS FROM THEATRICAL PRO-
DUCTIONS: *Peter Pan* (1954), music by Mark
Charlap–"I Won't Grow Up"; "I'm Flying";
"I've Gotta Crow"; "Tender Shepherd";
Wildcat (1960), music by Cy Coleman–"Corduroy
Road"; "Hey, Look Me Over"; "One Day We
Dance"; "What Takes My Fancy"; "You've
Come Home";
Little Me (1962), music by Coleman–"Le Grand Boom-
Boom"; "Here's to Us"; "I've Got Your Num-
ber"; "Little Me"; "On the Other Side of the
Tracks"; "Real Live Girl";
How Now, Dow Jones (1967), music by Elmer Bernstein–
"Step to the Rear";
Little Me, revival (1982), music by Coleman–"Don't
Ask a Lady"; "I Wanna Be Yours."

SELECTED SONGS FROM MOTION-PICTURE
PRODUCTIONS: *The Cardinal* (1964), music by
Jerome Moross–"Stay with Me";
Father Goose (1964), music by Cy Coleman–"Pass Me
By."

SELECTED SONGS PUBLISHED INDEPEN-
DENTLY OF THEATRICAL OR MOTION-
PICTURE PRODUCTIONS: "I'm Waiting Just
for You" (1951), music by Henry Glover and
Lucky Millinder;
"Young at Heart" (1953), music by Johnny Richards;
"First Impression" (1954), music by Mark Charlap;
"How Little It Matters, How Little We Know" (1956),
music by Philip Springer;
"Witchcraft" (1957), music by Cy Coleman;
"(Doop Doo-De-Oop) A Doodlin' Song" (1958), music
by Coleman;
"Firefly" (1958), music by Coleman;
"I Walk a Little Faster" (1958), music by Coleman;
"It Amazes Me" (1958), music by Coleman;
"You Fascinate Me So" (1958), music by Coleman;
"The Best Is Yet to Come" (1959), music by Coleman;
"The Rules of the Road" (1960), music by Coleman;

Carolyn Leigh (from David Ewen, American Songwriters, *1987)*

"When in Rome (I Do as the Romans Do)" (1964),
music by Coleman;
"Afterthoughts" (1965), music by Gene De Paul.

Carolyn Leigh was the youngest of the three
female lyricists–along with Dorothy Fields and Betty
Comden–who occupied a central position in the golden
age of American popular music, having produced a
body of work equal in fame and stature to the most
prominent men who ruled the genre. In the time before
rock and roll and a generation of such feminist
singer-poets as Carole King and Joni Mitchell, Fields,
Comden, and Leigh were the voice of their sex and
(because they were in the big leagues) not really

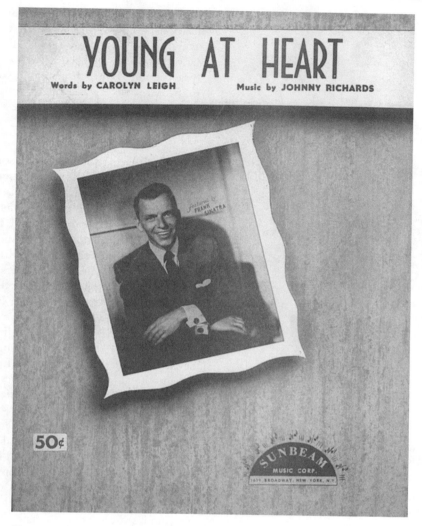

Sheet music for the hit 1953 song that brought Leigh to the attention of a Broadway producer planning to adapt J. M. Barrie's Peter Pan *as a musical (Collection of Paul Talbot)*

"women songwriters" at all but songwriters who happened to be women. Like Fields but even more so, Leigh is underappreciated. The fame of her work is in sharp contrast with the obscurity of her name, even in theatrical circles. Yet, the songs she wrote are ingrained in American daily life. Leigh has hundreds of songs to her credit–including such pop standards as "Young at Heart" (1953), "How Little It Matters, How Little We Know" (1956), "Witchcraft" (1957), "The Best Is Yet to Come" (1959), "Hey, Look Me Over" (1960), and "I've Got Your Number" (1962)–and Broadway scores such as *Peter Pan* (1954) and *Little Me* (1962).

Emotional and bombastic, Leigh was a more tempestuous figure than either Fields or Comden, who were both known for their professional, workaday approach to the creative process. As a personality,

Comden followed closely in Fields's literate, theaterwise image, even possessing the same skill at writing librettos. Yet, because Comden's voice is forever melded with that of her collaborator, Adolph Green, and is never revealed as either individual or feminine, Leigh emerges as Fields's artistic successor. Coming of age in the early 1950s, a full generation after Fields, Leigh was tremendously influenced by her predecessor. The two women had an urbanity, a sexy wit balanced by kitchen-sink imagery, and a flawless ear for colloquial speech. The lyrics of both display a glib irony that masks romantic optimism and a distinctly feminine turn of mind.

Like Fields, Leigh had an astounding facility with words, yet she imbued the result with a satisfying, sensual "rightness." She expressed subtle thoughts and

313

*Mary Martin as Peter Pan and Cyril Ritchard as Captain
Hook in the 1954 musical* Peter Pan, *for which Leigh
wrote most of the lyrics (from Mary Martin,*
My Heart Belongs, *1976)*

emotions with conversational directness. These traits
are encapsulated in Leigh's "simple" chorus of the ballad "It Amazes Me" (1958):

> It amazes me,
> It simply amazes me,
> What he sees in me
> Dazzles me,
> Dazes me.

Everything about these lines is both economical and
complex. The statement itself is plain and matter-
of-fact yet subtly conjures the conflicting emotions of
an average woman marveling at attentions she cannot
quite believe she deserves. The words are short and
unflashy, yet the sonority of the echoing vowels and
consonants in off-kilter patterns and line lengths make
the lines compelling, building tension and then resolv-
ing as quietly as it began. The simplicity is deceptive:
since every line ends in "me," any rhyming is auto-
matically internal. The first two lines voice the same
exclamation. But the third line begins weaving things
together, with the alliterative "sees in me" echoing
both the *z* sound in "amazes" and the "me"s above it.

"Dazzles," in the next line, is jarring as a suddenly
introduced new vowel sound, although the alliterative
*z*s link it to "sees in me" above. By now one wonders
why there has not been a rhyme yet and where the
lyric is going. But then the next two-word line, "Dazes
me," both delivers and neatly resolves, with the echoed *d* and *z* sounds, the long-awaited rhyme for
"amazes," and the buttoned-up "me," ending the line
like all the others.

Both Fields and Leigh had some of their greatest
success teamed with the same composer, Cy Coleman—
Fields at the end of her life in the last of her three major
songwriting partnerships and Leigh in the one major
partnership of her career. But if Leigh shared much
with Fields, she also differed in showing an emotional
rawness that Fields shrank from displaying. Partly, this
difference was a function of personality. Fields was
known for generally concealing her private feelings
even from her closest friends. Her lyrics express honest
poignancy and yearning but are restrained. Unlike
Fields, who came of age with the first wave of liberated
women in the 1920s, Leigh grew up awash in a culture
already used to self-examination. In life she was known
for emotional honesty; in her lyrics she bared her soul,
albeit skillfully and to elegant effect. A Leigh lyric is
witty, wicked, savage, and sexy; yet, her poignancy
cuts right to the core, and underlying the smart exterior
is a darkly shaded, aching vulnerability and unrequited
romanticism akin to Lorenz Hart's. The whiff of personal unhappiness with a snappy vocabulary gives
much of Leigh's work, like Hart's, its haunting, emotional pull. Her witty and rueful reflections on love,
loss, and self-esteem were made for the smoky New
York boîtes of the 1950s and 1960s and the tortured
chanteuses and smart revues they housed. Of her lyricist contemporaries, she is most akin to Sheldon Harnick, their similarity an amalgam of intellect, facility,
and heart.

Leigh had the same huge commercial success at
an early age that Fields had at twenty-three with "I
Can't Give You Anything But Love" (1928). But Leigh
did not grow up among the same privileged theatrical
set as her predecessor had. Born Carolyn Paula
Rosenthal to Henry and Sylvia Rosenthal on 21 August
1926 and raised in a middle-class family in the Bronx,
she was never a glamorous figure, wearing thick glasses
and struggling throughout her life with her weight. But
the young Carolyn showed exceptional gifts from the
start, writing verse by the age of nine. She attended
New York City public schools—the selective Hunter
College High School and Queens College—and later
graduated from New York University. "I wasn't specifically educated for this business," she liked to say.

Sheet music for a 1958 song by Leigh and composer Cy Coleman, one of the songs they wrote in the late 1950s and early 1960s (Collection of Paul Talbot)

"Oddly enough, I don't think you can be. There is no course in writing lyrics."

Leigh began her career by writing announcements at the classical radio station WQXR, later working for an advertising agency and for early television programs—among other things, contributing parodies to *The Phil Silvers Show*. Later in life, she enjoyed telling the story of calling an advertising agency with an idea for a new television show and falling into conversation with the man at the other end of the connection. He asked her if she wrote lyrics, since they happened, at the moment, to be short of lyricists. He invited her to come in for an interview, and she left with a contract. By 1951, the year she turned twenty-five, Leigh is rumored to have written more than two hundred unpublished

songs. That changed with "I'm Waiting Just for You," for which she set a lyric to a melody by Henry Glover and Lucky Millinder. Recorded by the newly famous Rosemary Clooney, the song marked Leigh's first success (it was later recorded by Pat Boone).

Leigh spent her early career setting lyrics to existing melodies handed to her by music publishers. One such tune, a lilting melody by Johnny Richards presented to her in 1953 by Sunbeam Music, changed her life. She handed back the lyric in only three hours, but "Young at Heart" became an instant hit when it was recorded by Frank Sinatra. The song went on to become one of Sinatra's hallmarks. What is striking about "Young At Heart" is not only the poignancy but the precociousness of the lyric. It belies Leigh's youth, dispensing a universal wisdom that seems to come from a much more mature sensibility. Part of the reason for this outlook was that as Leigh was writing the lyric, her father lay gravely ill in the hospital after a heart attack: "Don't you know that it's worth every treasure on earth / to be young at heart?" The message of "Young at Heart" is a mix of mature insight and clear-eyed optimism. The lyric is an amalgam of uncomplicated declarations ("Here is the best part") and sly, sophisticated wording, rhythms, and rhyming (such as the internal rhyme in "If you are among / The very young at heart").

Just this aura of sophisticated naïveté caught Richard Halliday's attention as he listened to "Young at Heart" on his car radio while driving to the Connecticut home he shared with his wife, Mary Martin. A Broadway producer, he was looking for the right lyricist to collaborate on Martin's upcoming vehicle, a new musical version of J. M. Barrie's 1904 play *Peter Pan*. When Leigh received a call from Halliday, she thought it was a gag and almost hung up on him. After being convinced of his sincerity and accepting the job, Leigh later recalled, "I reacted violently—I threw up." On *Peter Pan*, which opened in 1954, Leigh collaborated with the composer Mark "Moose" Charlap. Although seasoned veterans—lyricists Comden and Green and composer Jule Styne—were eventually called in to supply some additional material, the team of Leigh and Charlap was responsible for some of the best-loved songs in *Peter Pan*, particularly "I've Gotta Crow," "I'm Flying," and "I Won't Grow Up."

With her first Broadway show, Leigh demonstrated her versatility in understanding the difference between a pop and a character lyric. While Fields worked for decades to refine the expertise of writing to character that flowered in her lyrics for such shows as *A Tree Grows in Brooklyn* (1951) and *Sweet Charity* (1966), Leigh, at twenty-eight, seemed to swim just by being thrown in the water. Of course, the "integrated," character-driven musical had not fully evolved until later in Fields's career, but it was well established by the time Leigh came along. Direct from the quintessentially pop "Young at Heart," Leigh stepped firmly inside the minds of children, particularly cantankerous little boys, for the songs in *Peter Pan*. She showed not only an innate eye and ear for character observation but also her usual delight in rolling around sounds and rhyming, as in "I've Gotta Crow" (sung by Peter Pan):

> I've gotta crow.
> I'm just the cleverest fella
> T'was ever
> My fortune to know. . . .

> Naturally,
> When I discover
> The cleverness of a
> Remarkable me . . .
> I've gotta let go
> And crow.

"I'm Flying" (from the moment at which Peter gets the Darling children airborne), could not have been more simply constructed, with mostly monosyllabic words that keep directly to the rhythm of the melody and straightforward rhyming:

> I'm flying . . .
> Over bed, over chair,
> Duck your head, clear the air.
> Watch me, everyone
> Oh what lovely fun
> Take a look at me
> And see how easily
> It's done.

"I Won't Grow Up" defines character because the lyric (in which Peter indoctrinates the masses with his creed) rings of little-boy belligerence set in a call-and-response format:

> I won't grow up!
> (I won't grow up!)
> I don't wanna wear a tie
> (I don't wanna wear a tie)
> And a serious expression
> (And a serious expression)
> In the middle of July!
> (In the middle of July!)

Leigh's best stroke of character comes with the bridge: "'Cause growing up is awfuler / Than all the awful things that ever were." "Awfuler" is not a word anywhere but in childhood, just as the generalization that follows is typical of childish grasping for the second half of an analogy that often cannot be found. Leigh's pièce de résistance here is "awful-*er*" as a rhyme for "were" because the stress is on the wrong syllable. That deliberate, one-syllable "mistake" underscores Peter's character.

In 1956, after working on Max Liebman's television version of Johanna Spyri's children's novel *Heidi* (1880–1881), for which she set words to themes by Robert Schumann (she wrote lyrics for other such televised "spectaculars," including adaptations of Franz Lehár's 1905 operetta *The Merry Widow* and Oscar Straus's 1908 operetta *The Chocolate Soldier*), Leigh had her second Sinatra hit. The music to "How Little It Matters, How Little We Know" was written by Philip Springer. The following year she teamed with Coleman, the composer with whom she was to have consis-

*Cover of a songbook featuring selections from the 1960 musical by Leigh and Coleman
(from Dian Zillner,* Hollywood Collectibles, *1994)*

tent success. Leigh began writing with him in 1957, and, almost immediately, they produced "Witchcraft"—another Sinatra hit, and a song that became an enduring standard. The team of Leigh and Coleman became known both for the collaborators' stormy working relationship and for the hits and standards that seemed to come in a continuous stream. They wrote "(Doop Doo-De-Oop) A Doodlin' Song" (1958), which Peggy Lee recorded; "Firefly" (1958) and "I Walk a Little Faster" (1958), both recorded by Tony Bennett; the smart, cabaret-revue standards "It Amazes Me" and "You Fascinate Me So" (1958); and, in 1959, yet another blockbuster for Sinatra, "The Best Is Yet to Come," which was also by recorded by stars from Count Basie and Tito Puente to Clooney, Sarah Vaughan, and Mel Tormé. That same year, Leigh married her second husband, David Wyn Cunningham Jr., an attorney. Leigh and Coleman followed up the suc-

cess of "The Best Is Yet to Come" with another commercial stalwart, "The Rules of the Road" (1960).

Because of this background of commercial successes, Leigh and Coleman were commissioned to write a Broadway vehicle for Lucille Ball. *Wildcat* (1960), which was entirely backed by Ball's company, Desilu, and featured Lucy as an oil prospector, was a flop. Even Ball's star appeal could not keep the show from closing after only 171 performances. The Leigh-Coleman score included a few notable numbers, such as "Corduroy Road" and "What Takes My Fancy." There was also one enormous hit, the ebullient march "Hey, Look Me Over" (a cousin to "If My Friends Could See Me Now," which Coleman wrote with Fields for *Sweet Charity* a few years later).

Leigh and Coleman's next Broadway try, in 1962, fared much better. On *Little Me* they collaborated with the young director-choreographer Bob Fosse and the then little-known playwright Neil Simon. Based on Patrick Dennis's fictitious 1961 memoir of the same title, the story of a promiscuous movie star named Belle Poitrine, *Little Me* starred television comedian Sid Caesar in multiple roles as Belle's lovers. Leigh and Coleman, inspired by the material, came up with an inventive and satiric score that included numbers such as the one sung by Caesar as quintessential French entertainer Val du Val, "Le Grand Boom-Boom." The score produced one major commercial hit, "I've Got Your Number," along with such enduring theater songs as "Here's to Us," "Little Me," and "On the Other Side of the Tracks."

However, it is "Real Live Girl" (which has been recorded by many artists, from Sinatra to Barry Manilow) that has become the standard from *Little Me*. Sung to Coleman's lilting waltz by a myopic World War I doughboy, Leigh's lyrics virtually tumble out:

> Pardon me, Miss,
> But I've never done this
> With a real live girl–
> Strayed off the farm
> With an actual arm-
> Ful of real live girl!

Each successive phrase tops the last in blithe wit. In tying up each one, a characteristic asymmetrical rhyme scheme brings elegant cosmic order out of chaotic sonority:

> I'm simply drowned
> In the sight and the sound
> And the scent
> And the feel
> Of a real live girl!

Leigh skillfully constructed the lyric to give it tension and unpredictable resolution. The first two quoted lines are straightforward end rhymes; in the third, "scent" seems to come from nowhere, and the phrasing of the music causes the word to hang in the air. In the next line, "feel" doesn't help at all, also hanging, unmatched. When resolution arrives with a rhyme for "feel," the rhyme comes as a glossed-over internal rhyme. The subliminal elegance tying it together is in the pure sensuousness of the sounds– *I'm, sight, live, drowned, sound, feel, real*–that jostle each other and then resolve to organic stillness. Later lines twist these values around even more so:

> I'll take the flowering hat
> And the towering heel
> And the squeal
> Of a real live girl!

Now, the first two lines rhyme internally ("hat" just hangs there), the second one launching the main rhyming sound, in "heel," which repeats three times. The rhythm is broken up by a lengthening of the verbal phrases. If this passage adhered to the form of the other corresponding ones, it would read:

> I'll take the flow-
> ering hat and the tow-
> ering heel. . . .

Leigh cared deeply about her lyrics and took great pride in their craftsmanship. She once told an interviewer, "I'm very rarely satisfied with what I've done, and I'll wake up in a cold perspiration about something. But then common sense tells me that if so many people liked a song, it couldn't have been so bad."

Driven by this insecurity and perfectionism, Leigh lovingly and painstakingly labored over her words and felt for them personally. In *All His Jazz: The Life & Death of Bob Fosse* (1990), Martin Gottfried recounts a production meeting for *Little Me* in which Caesar announced to the group his refusal to sing more than one chorus of "Real Live Girl," brusquely dismissing any more as unnecessary. Immediately, Leigh's eyes filled with tears, the slight to her beloved creation wounding her to the core. The additional lines were, in fact, eventually saved, transferred from the unappreciative star to the male chorus, with rousing success. It was not unusual for Leigh to become overwrought in this way. Her neurotic, emotional nature, volatile personality, and deep-seated unhappiness often made collaboration with her a tempestuous affair. One well-known incident came when *Little Me* was in its Philadelphia tryout. Rehearsing in the Erlanger Theatre, a group that included Fosse, Simon, Coleman, and producers Cy Feuer and Ernest H. Martin was attempting to fix the beginning of the second act and a number that was not working, and they momentarily made a lyric change that Leigh had not approved. The teary outburst with which she berated the group–invoking her rights, the Dramatists Guild, and the law–was followed by her disappearance and later reappearance at the rehearsal, with a policeman in tow, demanding that the men all be arrested.

Little Me marked the peak of Leigh's success, but it also spelled the beginning of the end of her collaboration with Coleman, although the two wrote a few more songs together the following year. The storminess of their partnership was acknowledged even in public interviews, such as one in which Coleman jokingly complained about being forced to take

*Sheet music for a song from a 1964 movie that was the last project on which Leigh
and Coleman collaborated (Collection of Paul Talbot)*

a house in the Hamptons to be near Leigh so that they could work: "Snarling on the telephone is empty compared to insults face to face," he said. "Besides, on a phone the other collaborator can always just hang up." After a few more songs together, including the seductive cabaret standard "When in Rome (I Do as the Romans Do)" (1964) and one more hit, "Pass Me By" (another march), written for the 1964 Cary Grant–Leslie Caron movie *Father Goose,* the Leigh-Coleman partnership was formally dissolved. Coleman, fed up with Leigh, approached Fields about collaborating upon meeting her at a cocktail party, and they promptly began a partnership that led to commercial and artistic success (*Sweet Charity* came in 1966, followed by *Seesaw* in 1973) and gave the veteran Fields a new lease on her waning career.

Leigh, however, did not have anywhere near the same success with other songwriting partners.

Subsequent collaborators included Lee Pockriss, Gene De Paul, and the movie-music composer Elmer Bernstein, with whom she wrote her next–and final–Broadway musical, *How Now, Dow Jones* (1967), a commercial and critical failure that Dorothy Parker termed "Standard and poor." The most notable musical moment in the show was the march "Step to the Rear," recorded later by Peggy Lee. Leigh wrote lyrics for Shirley MacLaine's Emmy Award–winning television special *Gypsy in My Soul* (1976). Commissioned by the U.S. Department of Labor, Leigh collaborated with Morton Gould on a revue, *Something to Do: A Salute to the American Worker* (1976), which starred Pearl Bailey. At the time of her death, Leigh had been working with composer Marvin Hamlisch on a musical adaptation of *Smiles.*

Leigh's two marriages were unhappy, and both ended in divorce. A smoker and a hard drinker, she was considered "one of the boys" (and could out-curse any of them). Despite her histrionic episodes, in the man's world of Broadway songwriters in which she lived and worked, she was respected by her peers and held in genuine affection. Leigh is legendary for being the only woman ever to be allowed in Styne's all-male poker games. Before the end of her life, several projects were announced but never came to fruition. She stayed in the spotlight by performing her own work in cabarets, including a date at New York's Michael's Pub in 1980. That same year, Leigh presented her work as a subject of the 92nd Street Y's famed "Lyrics and Lyricists" series and later taught a workshop there on the craft of lyric writing.

Leigh's weight problem, as persistent as the rest of the physical and emotional turbulence that plagued her, led to a heart attack, and she died at New York's Lenox Hill Hospital on 19 November 1983 at the age of fifty-seven. Shortly before her death, she had reunited with Coleman to collaborate on two new numbers for the upcoming Broadway revival of *Little Me*. The resulting songs, "Don't Ask a Lady" and "I Wanna Be Yours," showed Leigh at the top of her form after a long absence, reveling in a level of excellence that had always been her creative norm. The songs stand out in relief from her work on the rest of the score of *Little Me*—sharper, more poignant, and burnished by the maturity of a twenty-year lapse. "Don't Ask a Lady" is an older woman's call for seduction before it is too late:

> Don't ask a lady what the lady did before,
> Ask what the lady's doing now!
> Don't poke around inside the lady's bureau drawer,

> What's here to thrill ya'
> Ain't memorabilia. . . .

With the help of Coleman's progressively building melody, "I Wanna Be Yours" is simultaneously exuberant and aching in its plea for affection, the glib sophistication masking a yearningly vulnerable core: "I want to be tied with velvety strings, / I want to be all those good-for-you-things, . . ." "I Wanna Be Yours" is perhaps the quintessential Carolyn Leigh lyric—the sum of her craft and of her life.

Reference:

Martin Gottfried, *All His Jazz: The Life & Death of Bob Fosse* (New York: Bantam, 1990).

Selected Discography:

Cy Coleman, American Songbook Series, Smithsonian, 048-19, 1994;

Randy Graff, *Doing Something Right: Randy Graff Sings Cy Coleman,* Varèse Sarabande, 5652, 1996;

How Now, Dow Jones, original Broadway cast (1968), RCA, 09026-63581-2, 1999;

Little Me, original Broadway cast (1962), RCA, 09026-61482-2, 1993;

Peter Pan, studio cast, Jay, 1280, 1997;

Peter Pan, original Broadway cast (1954), RCA, 3762-2-RG, 1988;

Peter Pan, television movie soundtrack, Jay, 1352, 2000;

Marilyn Volpe, *You Fascinate Me So: Marilyn Volpe Sings Cy Coleman,* Original Cast, 9618, 1996;

Wildcat, original Broadway cast, RCA, 1060, 1961;

Julie Wilson, *Julie Wilson: The Cy Coleman Songbook,* DRG, 5252, 2000.

Alan Jay Lerner

(31 August 1918 – 14 June 1986)

Stephen Citron

Unless otherwise indicated, music is by Frederick Loewe.

SELECTED SONGS FROM THEATRICAL PRO-
DUCTIONS: *The Day before Spring* (1945)–"The
Day before Spring"; "Forever Young"; "God's
Green World"; "A Jug of Wine"; "My Love Is a
Married Man";

Brigadoon (1947)–"Almost Like Being in Love"; "Briga-
doon"; "Come to Me, Bend to Me"; "Down on
MacConnachy Square"; "The Heather on the
Hill"; "I'll Go Home with Bonnie Jean";

Love Life (1948), music by Kurt Weill–"Economics";
"Green-Up Time"; "Here I'll Stay"; "I Remember
It Well"; "Progress"; "This Is the Life";

Paint Your Wagon (1951)–"Another Autumn"; "I'm on
My Way"; "I Still See Elisa"; "I Talk to the
Trees"; "They Call the Wind Maria";

My Fair Lady (1956)–"Ascot Gavotte"; "Come to the
Ball" (unused); "Embassy Waltz"; "A Hymn to
Him"; "I'm an Ordinary Man"; "I Could Have
Danced All Night"; "I've Grown Accustomed to
Her Face"; "Just You Wait"; "On the Street
Where You Live"; "The Rain in Spain"; "Show
Me"; "Why Can't the English?"; "With a Little
Bit of Luck"; "Wouldn't It Be Loverly?"; "You
Did It";

Camelot (1960)–"Camelot"; "Follow Me"; "I Wonder
What the King Is Doing Tonight"; "If Ever I
Would Leave You"; "The Jousts"; "The Lusty
Month of May"; "The Simple Joys of Maiden-
hood"; "What Do the Simple Folk Do?";

On a Clear Day You Can See Forever (1965), music by Bur-
ton Lane–"Come Back to Me"; "Hurry! It's
Lovely Up Here!"; "Melinda"; "On a Clear Day
You Can See Forever"; "What Did I Have That I
Don't Have?";

Coco (1969), music by André Previn–"Coco"; "The
Money Rings Out Like Freedom"; "Orbach's,
Bloomingdale's, Best and Saks"; "When Your
Lover Says Goodbye";

Alan Jay Lerner (photograph © Roddy McDowell)

Lolita, My Love (1971), music by John Barry–"Sur les
Quais de Ramsdale, Vermont";

Gigi (1973)–"The Contract"; "In This Wide, Wide
World";

1600 Pennsylvania Avenue (1976), music by Leonard
Bernstein–"It's Gonna Be Great"; "The President
Jefferson March"; "Take Care of This House";
"Welcome Home";

321

Carmelina (1979), music by Lane—"It's Time for a Love Song"; "One More Walk around the Garden"; "Someone in April"; "Why Him?";

Dance a Little Closer (1983), music by Charles Strouse—"Anyone Who Loves"; "He Always Comes Home to Me"; "It Never Would Have Worked"; "A Woman Who Thinks I'm Wonderful";

My Man Godfrey (1984, unfinished), music by Gerard Kenney—"Garbage"; "It Was You Again"; "I've Been Married"; "Some People."

SELECTED SONGS FROM MOTION-PICTURE PRODUCTIONS: *Royal Wedding* (1951), music by Burton Lane—"Every Night at Seven"; "How Could You Believe Me When I Said I Loved You When You Know I've Been a Liar All My Life?"; "I Left My Hat in Haiti"; "Too Late Now"; "What a Lovely Day for a Wedding"; "You're All the World to Me";

Gigi (1958)—"Gigi"; "I Remember It Well"; "I'm Glad I'm Not Young Anymore"; "The Night They Invented Champagne"; "The Parisians"; "Say a Prayer for Me Tonight"; "She's Not Thinking of Me"; "Thank Heaven for Little Girls";

The Little Prince (1973)—"Be Happy."

BOOKS: *The Street Where I Live* (New York: Norton, 1978; London: Hodder & Stoughton, 1978);

The Musical Theatre: A Celebration (New York: McGraw-Hill, 1986; London: Collins, 1986).

Alan Jay Lerner had the ability to make words cling inseparably to a melody. But he had more than that: erudition, sophistication, and style. He was also a dogged worker who, after holding up the filming of the movie *Gigi* (1958) for two weeks, fussing with a couplet that finally read "She's so ooh-la-la-la / So untrue-la-la-la," admitted, "It seems hardly worth the effort."

Lyricist, librettist, memoirist, and man-about-town, Lerner's tempestuous personal life was well known to the nontheatrical public, for his eight stormy marriages were often played out on the front pages of the tabloids. The musical world knew Lerner through his collaborations with composer Frederick Loewe, especially *Brigadoon* (1947), *Camelot* (1960), the movie *Gigi,* and his masterpiece, *My Fair Lady* (1956). Lerner was deeply revered by New York theater critic Clive Barnes, who, in writing his obituary, paraphrased Lerner and Loewe: "We shall never see their like again. A pity. I had grown accustomed to their grace."

Lerner was born into wealth. The Lerner Shops, chain stores that became one of America's leading purveyors of women's midpriced clothing throughout the first half of the twentieth century, were founded by his uncle Samuel Lerner. As the business prospered, Samuel soon sought the help of his colorful, flamboyant younger brother Joe Lerner and took him into the firm. Joe was living from hand to mouth, practicing "painless dentistry" on the boardwalk in Atlantic City, when Samuel called him to help expand the family business. Within just a few years Joe had rented an extravagant apartment on New York's Park Avenue, which he furnished with European antiques. Soon he and his wife, Edith, began trying to acquire the patina of culture that had been denied them in the Philadelphia ghetto where they had grown up. Edith spent her days shopping, while Joe had teachers of piano, ballroom dancing, and foreign languages come to the apartment. Somewhat like the title character in Molière's *Le Bourgeois Gentilhomme* (1670), Joe wanted to taste everything cultural in life. Good-looking and with a winning personality, by midlife he looked like a professional on the dance floor, played theater songs acceptably at the piano, and could converse in French and Italian. The now-affluent Lerners never missed an important Broadway opening night and mingled with what they considered "society" but was really café society, since they were barred from the real thing by their Jewishness and nouveau riche status.

Into this milieu Alan Jay Lerner was born on 31 August 1918. His musicality began to evince itself at an early age, and, precocious child that he was, by the time he was six, he had had a year of classical piano instruction. Enrolled in Manhattan's Columbia Grammar School, a long-established liberal private school with impeccable academic standards, he soon began to write essays as well. But stormy scenes began occurring in the Lerner household: strife between the parents because of Joe's philandering and Alan's arguments with his two brothers, Richard and Robert, soon meant that he could generally be found behind his locked door, working on a poem or a piano piece. Money flowed freely in the household; since neither parent put any constraint on what their sons bought, Alan and his brothers seemed to take their chief joy from the position, luxury, and ease their wealth brought them. This spendthrift attitude was to become a lifelong problem for Lerner, as well as a goad to his success.

When Lerner was fourteen, his father sent him to school in England, ostensibly to "improve his abominable English." His term there was enough to awaken Lerner's lifelong interest in etymology and deepen his enduring love for the language. His sense of the sheer beauty of words and rhyme manifests itself in his songs. Shortly after returning from the English odyssey and the obligatory "grand tour," Lerner was enrolled at Choate, in Wallingford, Connecticut, one of the most prestigious preparatory schools in the country.

Because there were only seven Jews attending Choate (four of whom were members of the Lerner clan) out of five hundred students, many considered the school anti-Semitic, but not Lerner. He reinvented himself at the school, sometimes calling himself half Jewish, at other times avowing that he was born a Catholic. Wallingford was near enough to New York for him to be able to attend theater and especially musicals on Broadway, and in those prep-school years Lerner knew the lyrics and "second chorus as well as I did the Lord's Prayer, and I knew them within a week after each show opened." His goal during those days was to become a composer, and he wrote many songs, one of which, "The Choate Marching Song," is still used. The curious thing about that song and others by Lerner at the time is that the lyrics are quite ordinary, but the musical lines are fresh and original. Composer Maury Yeston, who came under the mature Lerner's tutelage, called him "a composer who doesn't write music."

Upon graduation from Choate in 1936, Lerner entered Harvard University, where he majored in sociology. While in Cambridge, his chief interest was the Harvard Hasty Pudding Show, and his words and especially the music to the shows *So Proudly We Hail* (1938) and *Fair Enough* (1939) are more than acceptable. Before finishing his degree at Harvard, he had more study in advanced forms of music during summer terms at the Juilliard School in New York. After graduating from Harvard in 1940, Lerner settled down at the Lambs Club, a theatrical retreat on West Forty-fourth Street in Manhattan. He had no theatrical job, nor did he need one, but living at the Lambs gave him the opportunity to be near enough to see all the latest shows and to pretend to be a member of the theatrical community. In 1940 Lerner also married Ruth O'Day Boyd, with whom he had a daughter, Susan.

One of the denizens of the Lambs was lyricist Lorenz Hart. Frequently at the bar, he became a self-appointed mentor to Lerner. He scanned the verses of the budding lyricist and left a deep mark on his future output, for Lerner's work was to bear far more kinship to Hart's, with its dazzling rhyming and use of the vernacular, than that of any of the many great lyricists of the mid twentieth century. One notes a touch of Howard Dietz's iconoclasm, a bit of Ira Gershwin's erudition, and some of E. Y. "Yip" Harburg's zaniness in Lerner's mature lyrics, but Hart's gentle warmth, his oblique way of looking at life, and his somewhat mystical penchant were to influence the young Lerner most. Hart's lyric for "Where or When" (1937), with its allusions to reincarnation, was Lerner's favorite. Its philosophy that lovers take up with the same partners in the afterlife was to be fully developed in Lerner's *On a Clear Day You Can See Forever* (1965), written with composer

Poster for the Lerner and Loewe 1947 show, their first hit (from Amy Henderson and Dwight Blocker Bowers, Red, Hot & Blue, 1996)

Burton Lane. Yet, Lerner never chose the clever over the meaningful, as Hart was wont to do. As a playwright in the tradition of Oscar Hammerstein 2nd, Lerner imbued his lyrics with character, always being careful that the language he chose was natural to the personality he had created. Perhaps more than any lyricist except Hammerstein, he was careful to be consistent in tone. King Arthur sounds Arthurian and Henry Higgins, Shavian. Lolita sings and speaks in the whiny vernacular of a 1970s preteen and Coco Chanel, as limned by Lerner, is a determined French couturiere.

One evening while he was living at the Lambs, Lerner met his future composing partner, Loewe, who told him simply, "I hear you write good lyrics." Loewe added that he had received an advance of $500 to write a musical—but it needed to be done in two weeks. The musical was an adaptation of *The Patsy*, a 1925 farce by Barry Conners; Loewe and his former lyricist, Earle Crooker, had already written some songs for it, but the score was far from complete. Lerner accepted the challenge of slipping his lyrics into Loewe's already completed music–which more experienced hands would say was a guaranteed way to write a flop. The team of Lerner and Loewe was established, and the two men worked together for the next eighteen years and produced musicals that have become some of the glories of the American musical theater. *The Patsy,* however, was not to be one of them, but at the time it seemed an entrée for the twenty-four-year-old Lerner into Broadway and a last, desperate attempt for the forty-one-year-old Loewe. Retitled *Life of the Party* (1942), it was written and rehearsed in twelve days. The producer kept it open, tinkering with it for nine weeks of previews in Detroit, but he was forced to close the show before it reached New York.

Undaunted, Lerner and Loewe carried on with a vehicle for baggy-pants comedian Jimmy Savo called *What's Up?* (1943). This farce did make it to Broadway and somehow, overcoming dreadful reviews, managed to eke out eight weeks of performances. Now the team decided to make an all-out effort to come up with a successful musical so that they might acquire some of the wealth that genuine hit shows were capable of generating. They decided to rent an office in the theater area. To the detriment of their marriages, they worked practically around the clock on a musical they brought to John C. Wilson, who had recently had a hit with Harold Arlen and Harburg's *Bloomer Girl* (1944). Wilson decided both to produce and direct Lerner and Loewe's *The Day before Spring* in the autumn of 1945.

The original book by Lerner is a rather whimsical, jejune story about an uncompleted college campus tryst. Katherine, now married to Peter, a reliable but plodding businessman, returns with him to their alma mater for their ten-year reunion. Her secret plan is to consummate an interrupted affair with dashing Alex Maitland, now a successful novelist. The tryst began when they were undergraduates. The affair was thwarted when Alex's car broke down on the way to a motel. Peter, then her boyfriend, came along at the propitious moment and repaired the car, but Katherine had by this time lost heart and wanted only to return to campus. Predictably, at the reunion Alex and Katherine sneak away toward the same motel, but, once again, the car breaks down, and Peter comes along searching for his wife. Realizing that Alex will always philander (something that dawns on her during what was then the obligatory second-act ballet), Katherine goes back to safe, lovable Peter.

While Lerner's protagonists in *The Day before Spring* act more like high-school sophomores than college alumni in their thirties, the dialogue has enough dash to be intriguing. As with any artist's early work,

one can notice themes that became lifelong obsessions and recurred in all of Lerner's shows. The time warp was a persistent motif, dominating *Brigadoon* and *1600 Pennsylvania Avenue* (1976) and related to the concept of reincarnation, to be fully developed in *On a Clear Day You Can See Forever*. The lyrics present such romantic concepts, as in "Forever Young": "Let others age and lose the spark, and leave their happy song unsung, / Our life will be a joyous lark–we'll be in love and ever young." They are also characterized by what later became a Lerner trademark, the flip use of syllables, as in "My Love Is a Married Man": "We could have such fun, / Clean or maybe un. . . ."

The concept for their next show, Lerner said, came to him from Loewe's casual remark that "faith can move mountains." "From there," he added, "I went to all sorts of miracles occurring and eventually faith moved a town." The plot of the 1947 musical *Brigadoon* concerns Tommy and Jeff, two American friends on a hunting trip in Scotland, their last before Tommy's impending marriage. Suddenly they hear muted voices chanting a hymn-like melody and see a distant, fog-shrouded village that is not on their map. When they arrive at this quaint place, named Brigadoon, they find a wedding in progress and inhabitants who have never heard of modern conveniences. Tommy falls deeply in love with the bride's older sister, Fiona, while Jeff is seduced by a forward village girl, Meg, who provides the subplot as well as comic relief. As the marriage ceremony takes place, Tommy notices that the groom has signed the Bible with the date of 1746. "What's going on?" he asks Fiona. Reluctantly, she takes Tommy to Mr. Lundie (a figure not unlike the star-keeper in Richard Rodgers and Hammerstein's 1945 musical *Carousel*), who explains that, back in 1746, the minister was so disturbed by encroaching witches that he prayed to God that Brigadoon might vanish into the highlands–but not forever. It would become visible one day every hundred years. "But," the minister warned, "should any of its occupants leave, the spell will be broken and the town will disappear forever." When Tommy, now deeply in love with Fiona, asks if someone from the outside could stay, he is told that he would have to forswear the world forever. Shortly afterward, at the wedding reception, when the bride's rejected suitor, Harry Beaton, kisses her passionately, a fight breaks out between him and the groom. As the first act ends, Harry threatens to leave Brigadoon and thus destroy the miracle.

The second act opens with a balletic chase after Harry. When he is found and accidentally killed by Jeff, the town is saved, but Tommy and Jeff sense the violence directed at outsiders from within the town, and Tommy's resolve to stay forever in Brigadoon with

Fiona is shaken. He and Jeff leave, but back in New York, Tommy realizes that his nagging fiancée will make his life impossible, and once again he postpones his upcoming marriage to return to Scotland. Before long, he and Jeff have found the spot where they originally heard the voices. Seeing no town, they are convinced that the whole episode was a dream. Soon, they hear the chanting again, and Mr. Lundie comes forward, saying, "Ye mus' really love her! Ye woke me up!" At the curtain, Tommy climbs the hillock that leads to Fiona and Brigadoon.

The score of *Brigadoon* is full of lilting, Scottish melodies and charming lyrics. Perhaps one of the most poetic lyrics Lerner ever wrote is "Come to Me, Bend to Me":

Come to me, bend to me,
Kiss me good day!
Darlin', my darlin',
'Tis all I can say
Jus' come to me, bend to me
Kiss me good day,
Gie me your lips
An' don' take them away.

There was also a rousing, fresh look at romance in "Almost Like Being in Love," which was similar to some of Hammerstein's "negative" love songs:

All the music of life seems to be
Like a bell that is ringin' for me,
And from the way that I feel
When that bell starts to peal,
I would swear I was fallin',
I could swear I was fallin',
It's almost like being in love.

The score of *Brigadoon* also included the alliterative and atmospheric "The Heather on the Hill":

But when the mist is in the gloamin'
An' all the clouds are holdin' still,
If you're not there I won't go roamin'
Through the heather on the hill.

The raucous Scottish fantasy "I'll Go Home with Bonnie Jean" treads lightly into the paranormal with such a delicate step and score that it retains its charm today.

Marion Bell, who played Fiona in the original production of *Brigadoon,* had an affair with Lerner that led to the dissolution of his first marriage in 1947. Loewe's disapproval, coupled with the fact that the composer wanted a long holiday after their first smash success, while Lerner wanted to begin his next show immediately in order to prove that his success had not been a mere fluke, led Lerner to seek out Kurt Weill to write the music for his next show.

Lerner with Marion Bell, who played Fiona in the original 1947 production of Brigadoon *and was married to Lerner from 1947 to 1949 (from Stephen Citron,* The Wordsmiths, *1995)*

Love Life (1948), like *Brigadoon* an original story by Lerner, begins around the time of the American Revolution, when Sam and Susan Cooper move to a new town. The libretto travels through the decades highlighting the changes that industrialization, economic panic, women's suffrage, the Great Depression, and modern times wrought. The story incorporates the couple's separation and eventual tentative reunion. If the plot sounds familiar, it is because it was *Brigadoon* all over again, but with a difference. To foil death and to escape the encroaching witches of society, instead of moving the town and the love affair into the sheltering braes of Scotland, Lerner had the Coopers and their descendants face the buffeting that progress and industrialization bring. Unfortunately, he eliminated his best stock in trade: romance. With songs such as "Economics" and "Progress," it resembled Soviet propaganda or an extended lesson in American history. (Lerner tried the same theme again later in life, with even less success, in *1600 Pennsylvania Avenue.*)

But no amount of political messages could hide Lerner's poetry. In "Here I'll Stay," which has one of Weill's most exquisite melodies, Sam sings about ignoring a "field of gold" or "an isle deep with clover":

For that land is a sandy illusion,
It's the theme of a dream gone astray,

And the world others woo
I can find loving you
And so here I'll stay.

Some of the songs in *Love Life* are saved by Weill's imaginative melodies. "Green-Up Time," a metaphor for spring, has lines such as "Then I began to look around / And in ev'ry field I found / Greens were a-pushing up through the ground." There was also a charming duet, "I Remember It Well," in which the female corrects the male for his braggadocio and faulty memory, a forerunner of the song of the same title in *Gigi,* the greatest duet in the movie.

As was his lifelong habit, when things became difficult, Lerner moved out. With *Love Life* running to half-filled houses and wife, Marion, discontented at home because Nanette Fabray was starring in the musical rather than she, Lerner went to work in Hollywood. Collaborating with Lane, he wrote a screenplay that cashed in on the publicity surrounding the 1947 wedding of the future Queen Elizabeth II and Prince Philip. Called *Royal Wedding* (1951), it told the story, somewhat honestly but heavily updated, of the dissolution of the dancing partnership of Fred Astaire and his sister, Adele, when they came to England. There, Adele married a British peer and retired from the stage. The charming movie had songs of great variety, from the torrid "I Left My Hat in Haiti" to the buoyant "Every Night at Seven" to the number with the longest title in ASCAP history: "How Could You Believe Me When I Said I Loved You When You Know I've Been a Liar All My Life?" Lerner cleverly avoided using the title more than once in the lyric, rhyming it with "How could you believe me when I said we'd marry when you know I'd rather hang than have a wife."

But the loveliest song in the score was the simplest, "Too Late Now":

How could I ever close the door
And be the same as I was before?
Darling, no, no I can't any more—
It's too late now.

While Lerner was in Hollywood for the filming of *Royal Wedding,* he was offered an assignment from M-G-M producer Arthur Freed to write a screenplay about three men pursuing the same girl in Paris. Since it would have a score comprising old songs by George and Ira Gershwin, be directed by Vincente Minnelli, star Leslie Caron and Gene Kelly, and have an almost unlimited budget, Lerner accepted at once. *An American in Paris* (1951) turned out to be one of the glories of American cinema. It won the 1951 Academy Award for best picture, the first movie musical to do so since *The Great Ziegfeld* (1936), and it brought Lerner an Oscar

for best screenplay. With the success of *An American in Paris,* Lerner was riding at the top of his career. To a man like Lerner, who had an almost compulsive need to be married, residing on the West Coast for the several years that it took to complete these two movie projects spelled the end of his relationship with Marion. While in Hollywood, he met and fell in love with movie actress Nancy Olson, whom he married in 1950. The couple had two daughters, Liza and Jennifer.

By this time, perhaps, Lerner's driven work ethic was mellowing, for he was able to reconcile with Loewe. Soon they began working on a "Western musical" to be called *Paint Your Wagon* (1951). The sparse and somewhat confused plot opens in a California town where gold is discovered. The story concerns an uneducated miner who sends his daughter back East to get an education. There she falls in love with an illiterate Mexican, who sings the show's hit song, "I Talk to the Trees," which is composed mostly of monosyllables:

I talk to the trees,
But they don't listen to me,
I talk to the stars,
But they never hear me,
The breeze hasn't time
To hear what I say,
I talk to them all in vain. . . .

Paint Your Wagon is replete with sensitive songs for the miners, such as "They Call the Wind Maria":

Away out there they got a name
For wind and rain and fire:
The rain is Tess, the fire's Jo
And they call the wind Maria.

"Another Autumn," with its chilling ending, fits the psyche of the weary miners:

Another autumn,
So sweet when all is well,
But how it haunts you when all is wrong.
For one thing time has shown
If you're alone
When autumn comes
You'll be alone all winter long.

Lerner's involvement with the 1956 musical *My Fair Lady* began in 1951 with a luncheon invitation from Gabriel Pascal, who controlled the movie rights to George Bernard Shaw's classic *Pygmalion* (1914). Lerner and Loewe were not the first to be asked to try to set this play to music. Dietz and Arthur Schwartz had attempted an adaptation, followed by Rodgers and Hammerstein, who had thrown up their hands, saying that Higgins was a nonsinging character and

Fred Astaire and Jane Powell dancing and singing "How Could You Believe Me When I Said I Loved You When You Know I've Been a Liar All My Life?" in the 1951 movie Royal Wedding, *for which Lerner and Loewe wrote the score (Photofest)*

that the play was all drawing-room comedy with no room for a chorus. But worse, Hammerstein told Lerner, *Pygmalion* had no subplot—essential to musicals of that time.

Lerner and Loewe were as stymied by this classic as were their predecessors, and Lerner, needing activity, turned to composer Lane and began work on a musical based on Al Capp's *Li'l Abner* comic strip. But when Pascal died in 1954 and the rights to the *Pygmalion* property were once more available, Lerner and Loewe were determined to solve Shaw's unsolvable misogynistic comedy. Molding the text of Shaw's play into a libretto, Lerner brought size and humor to the musical by adding flower sellers, costermongers, denizens of London's Covent Garden, and the Ascot attendees for the chorus. Successful subplots were created by including Eliza Doolittle's father, with his reluctance to marry, and the love-struck Freddy, to whom Eliza turns in desperation. The creative team faced a big challenge when Rex Harrison, a nonsinging actor, was chosen to star as Higgins. Harrison was taught to "talk on pitch," using only important notes plucked from the score. With

Harrison's range from falsetto to basso profundo, coupled with his extraordinary sense of rhythm, Higgins became a full-bodied musical-comedy character—paving the way for such nonsingers as Richard Burton and Richard Harris to star in musicals.

My Fair Lady is that rare show with no dead spots. From the outset, the scene in Covent Garden captures both Lerner's and Shaw's great love for the English language, as well as Higgins's imperiousness in his diatribe "Why Can't the English?" This song is contrasted at the end of the scene with Julie Andrews's heartfelt rendering of Eliza's dreams of marital bliss as she mangles the mother tongue in "Wouldn't It Be Loverly?" Lerner created such slang words for her as "abso-bloomin-lutely" and followed them with poetic thoughts: "I would never budge till Spring / Crept over me windowsill." In his soliloquy "I'm an Ordinary Man" Higgins has a chance to explain in rhythmically perfect English why he will never marry:

Let a woman in your life,
And you are plunging in the knife,

*Tony Bavaar singing "I Talk to the Trees" to Olga San
Juan in Lerner and Loewe's 1951 musical,*
Paint Your Wagon *(Photofest)*

Let the others of my sex
Tie the knot around their necks.
I'd prefer a new edition
Of the Spanish Inquisition
Than to ever let a woman in my life!

Lerner worked his magic subtly, for while he showed Higgins's passion for the English language, he also revealed the man's snobbish, uncaring side as he treats Eliza as a mere object to win his bet with Colonel Pickering that he can turn this ragamuffin into a duchess. But Higgins's excitement when Eliza finally masters his assignments in the English broad *a* with the line "The rain in Spain stays mainly in the plain" is palpable, as Loewe's setting progresses from a mild habanera through a fandango to a wild *jota* (a Spanish courtship dance). Eliza, whom Higgins calls "this bit of flotsam," emerges as a living, loving young woman when she sings "I Could Have Danced All Night." The gentle melody, coupled with the lines "I only know when he / Began to dance with me," indicates that the "he" is Higgins, with whom she is falling in love.

A more poetic side of Higgins's character was intended to be displayed in "Come to the Ball," Lerner's own favorite lyric from the score, which was excised from the show. Perhaps it was cut because it gives away the plot, revealing that not even an expert dialectician such as Karpathy, Higgins's former student, can penetrate Eliza's elegant mask and discover the cockney underneath. Regardless of the success of the first act, many musicals bog down in the second act; not so with *My Fair Lady*. Critic Walter Kerr, not noted for gushing, wrote that the show was "so dazzlingly melodic and visually rich in its first act that it scarcely needs a second—and so emotionally blinding in its second that you wonder why you were merely dazzled by the first." From the outset, the second act presents the now-refined Eliza's temperament vis-à-vis Higgins when, after winning his bet, he ignores her and turns to Pickering with "You Did It." She hurls his slippers at him but does not break through his facade. Later, she minces no words when she tells the effete Freddy, "Words! Words! Words! I'm so sick of words / I get words all day through / First from him, now from you!" Only toward the end of the act does the difference emerge between Shaw's and Lerner's interpretations of Eliza. Lerner's version is closer to the mythological story of Pygmalion, in which the sculptor Pygmalion falls in love with his own statue of the ideal woman and prays to the gods to make her human. Higgins has transformed a real woman, but he is too proud to tell Eliza he has fallen in love with her. At first he insults her and imagines how delicious it would be to turn her away from his door on a snowy night. Then, when he senses he is in love, the most he can muster is a sense of habitude, expressed in "I've Grown Accustomed to Her Face":

I've grown accustomed to her face,
She almost makes the day begin.
I've grown accustomed to the tune
She whistles night and noon.

Loewe's exquisite melody will not be denied; Eliza tiptoes in on her former cockney line, "I washed my face and hands before I come. I did." Higgins, knowing all will be well now, slinks down in his chair, asking "Eliza? Where the devil are my slippers?" Lerner gives this stage direction: "*There are tears in Eliza's eyes. She understands*" as the music of "I Could Have Danced All Night" swells up. It was no wonder audiences sat stunned before they dared to applaud; no wonder that at the twentieth-anniversary revival of the show Kerr wrote:

structurally sound of limb, skipping like springtime and living out its winters on wit, *My Fair Lady* isn't an enter-

*Sheet music for a song from Lerner and Loewe's 1956 musical, their greatest
success (Music Library, University of South Carolina)*

tainment that requires certain performers to bring off
the Bernard Shaw based libretto, the leaping Alan Jay
Lerner lyrics, the sweeping Frederick Loewe score; it's
an entertainment that invites any and all performers to
simply lift the lid from its treasure-chest and avail themselves of its glistening baubles.

After the tumultuous success of *My Fair Lady*
Loewe again wanted to sit back and imbibe the life at his
home in the South of France and enjoy dolce far niente.
Lerner, on the other hand, was intent on their working
on a new movie project that he planned to adapt from
Gigi (1944), a novelette by Colette about a young girl,
Gigi, growing up in a family of Parisian courtesans. Gaston, a wealthy and bored young Parisian, thinks of Gigi
as a companion, a child, never realizing that she is growing into womanhood. At last he recognizes that he loves
her and—to his horror—does not want her for a mistress
but for a wife. The songwriters were to integrate a few
numbers (including some of the rejects from *My Fair
Lady*) into the screenplay and add several new ones.

Loewe was won over, and the two set to work. The climactic title song in the 1958 movie *Gigi* is not unlike
"I've Grown Accustomed to Her Face" in *My Fair Lady*.
But whereas Higgins is reserved, Gaston is not afraid to
shout his joy at finding that the girl he carelessly watched
grow up is now the object of his passion:

> She's a child! A silly child!
> Adolescent to her toes,
> And, good heavens, how it shows.
> Sticky thumbs are all the fingers she has got.
> She's a child! A clumsy child!
> She's as swollen as a grape
> And she doesn't have a shape
> Where her figure ought to be, it is not!

Later Gaston observes,

> Of course, I must in truth confess
> That in that brand new little dress
> She looked surprisingly mature,
> And had a definite allure.

*Rex Harrison and Julie Andrews in Lerner and Loewe's
1956 musical,* My Fair Lady *(Museum of
the City of New York)*

Then at last, when he realizes his passion,

> Gigi, am I a fool without a mind,
> Or have I merely been too blind
> To realize?
> Oh, Gigi, why you've been growing up before my eyes.

"Gigi" was Lerner's favorite lyric of all his work. Yet, it is fairly matched with nuggets of wisdom and beauty in other songs in the score, especially those given to Gaston's uncle, a part played by Maurice Chevalier. Inspired by this great French star, Lerner contributed the rewritten lyric "I Remember It Well" (a duet he had first used in *Love Life,* and which worked more successfully with Loewe's nostalgic music than it had with Weill's acerbic score), outlining the details of a liaison that the man has forgotten and the woman, more romantically, remembers.

"Thank Heaven for Little Girls" is an almost too graphic hymn for ogling old lechers. "I'm Glad I'm Not Young Anymore," which Chevalier also sings, is about the dividends of aging. For the latter, Lerner wrote three refrains, only two of which were used in the movie, but the third refrain was used in the stage adaptation, which had a brief run in 1973:

> No desperation,
> No midnight pacing of floors,
> What liberation
> To know that child on all fours
> Couldn't be yours . . .
> Too old for a wedding day in June,
> But not for a weekend honeymoon.
> What better life could heaven have in store?
> Oh I'm so glad that I'm not young any more!

Gigi brought Lerner the 1958 Oscars for best screenplay and best original movie song (the title song). Now forty years old, having won three Academy Awards and with *My Fair Lady* an internationally lauded success, he was at the peak of his career. But his personal life was in chaos, and within a few months he had divorced his third wife, Nancy, to marry a French lawyer, Micheline Muselli Pozzo di Borgo. His three earlier wives had been docile about the separations and divorces, but with Micheline the case was to be quite different.

Perhaps it is not coincidental that Lerner's next project, an adaptation of T. H. White's sprawling tetralogy about King Arthur and his court, *The Once and Future King* (1958), dealt with infidelity and cuckoldry. The 1960 musical *Camelot* almost did not come about because Loewe could see no way to make Queen Guenevere's betrayal of Arthur in the second act acceptable. But he relished the quasimedieval and modal melodies the story afforded and eagerly went to work on the first act. Even the titles—"The Jousts," "The Lusty Month of May," and "If Ever I Would Leave You" (rather than "If I Would Ever Leave You")—give an indication of the mood Lerner was seeking and that Loewe so beautifully supplied. Certainly, Lerner could not lighten the historical fact that Lancelot, Arthur's most trusted knight, and the queen, Guenevere, were embroiled in an adulterous love affair. Their betrayal sends Arthur's utopian Camelot crashing down around him. The action ends on a battlefield, with no hope for Arthur's survival.

Lerner saved the second act of *Camelot* by ennobling the ending in a way Hammerstein would have applauded. He used a reprise of the title song, a martial melody used throughout the show to express Arthur's idealism. In the original production, when "Camelot" was first introduced early in the musical, Burton as Arthur made it sound like the seductive boasting of a young king who has been touched by magic, cajoling a beautiful princess to stay in his country:

> The snow may never slush upon the hillside,
> By nine P.M. the moonlight must appear.
> In short, there's simply not
> A more congenial spot
> For happ'ly-ever-aftering than here
> In Camelot.

By the final reprise of the song, Arthur's dream has passed on to a young boy, Tom of Warwick, who is directed to run behind the lines and escape to recount the Arthurian saga for future generations:

Each evening from December to December
Before you drift to sleep upon your cot
Think back on all the tales that you remember
Of Camelot.
Ask ev'ry person if he's heard the story
And tell it strong and clear if he has not
That once there was a fleeting wisp of glory
Called Camelot. . . .
Where once it never rained till after sundown
By eight A.M. the morning fog had flown.
Don't let it be forgot
That once there was a spot
For one brief shining moment that was known
As Camelot.

Camelot received mixed reviews but mustered a considerable two-year run. It was still touring when President John F. Kennedy was assassinated on 22 November 1963.

For the next few years Lerner's name was not only in the theatrical news—for a collaboration with Rodgers that was doomed to dissolution and recrimination—but also provided extensive fodder for the tabloids. Lerner's marriage to Micheline was stormy, almost from the outset. This marriage produced a son, Michael, and the child's custody was to be hotly contested when divorce proceedings began. After months of front-page courtroom news, accusations, and counteraccusations, as well as Micheline's allegations of Lerner's drug usage and homosexuality, the couple was divorced at last in 1965. Lerner settled down to work with Lane on a story about the paranormal that eventually became *On a Clear Day You Can See Forever,* a difficult assignment for both artists. Lerner was using drugs, and Lane, not noted for his patience, was vociferous—even to the press—about his collaborator's habit. Despite these problems, the two men turned out a splendid score. The imperishability of the title song perhaps owes more to Lane's superb melody than to Lerner's middling lyric. But Lerner's clever handling of "Come Back to Me," a list song, is a tour de force. The speech is contemporary but mixes the possible with the impossible ("Hop a freight, grab a star") to delightful effect:

Hear my voice where you are:
Take a train, steal a car;
Hop a freight, grab a star,
Come back to me.
Catch a plane, catch a breeze,
On your hands, on your knees,
Swim or fly, only please
Come back to me.

*Lerner watching Leslie Caron and Loewe rehearse
"The Parisians," a song in the 1958 movie*
Gigi *(Photofest)*

Although the score was received with acclaim—critics agreed that Lane had written some of his best music in years, and there were kudos for many of Lerner's lyrics—most of the reviewers felt that Lerner overreached in his libretto, and the show had a curtailed run of 280 performances. Because of trouble with the libretto, Lane was publicly critical of Lerner, and they fought bitterly, vowing never to work together again (a promise they kept for fourteen years, until *Carmelina* brought them back together in 1979). *On a Clear Day You Can See Forever* was eventually bought by Paramount as a vehicle for Barbra Streisand, and Lerner went to Hollywood to write the screenplay for the movie, which was released in 1970.

Lerner's next project, *Coco* (1969), a musical built around the life of couturiere Chanel, was inaugurated by Frederick Brisson as a vehicle for his wife, movie actress Rosalind Russell. It was to be a musical about the designer, who had many love affairs but was married only to her career. Again, the story was quite contemporary because Chanel was the prototype of the new, autonomous woman of the 1960s. For the first time in his life, Lerner was planning to write a "star" part suitable for a Mary Martin or a Carol Channing, which could translate into box-office success. Producer Brisson soon signed André Previn to write the score, and he and Lerner began work. When Russell had to withdraw because of acute arthritis, they got the biggest coup of all by casting Katharine

*Julie Andrews and Richard Burton in Lerner and Loewe's
1960 musical,* Camelot *(Jose Abeles Studio)*

Hepburn, the star who was to be the insurance for the show. Cecil Beaton's elegant costumes and Michael Bennett's inventive choreography were also a help. But Lerner and Previn did not write an interesting score, and only Hepburn's personal fame and drawing power (even though she croaked through her songs) kept the show running for ten months. When Hepburn finally left and Danielle Darrieux, who could really sing, took over, Previn said, "it was the first time I heard my songs sung properly in a year."

The best song in *Coco* was the throwaway "When Your Lover Says Goodbye," the kind of artless, seemingly heartless, lyric Lerner did so well:

When your lover says goodbye,
Wise are they who know;
When your lover says goodbye,
Let her go.
When your lover flies away,
Sad are they who learn
There can be a darker day,
Her return. . . .
When your lover says goodbye,
Wise men all agree
There can be but one reply,
"Leave the key."

Even had *Coco* had a remarkable score, it could not be revived today, perhaps because Chanel as she comes off in this musical biography is so disagreeable and irritating.

Lerner's next project was based on Vladimir Nabokov's brilliant, controversial novel *Lolita* (1958). The musical adaptation, *Lolita, My Love* (1971), with music by John Barry, was perceived as Lerner's worst failure to date. This time he got everything right but the timing. Had Nabokov's story of a teenage seductress and her pedophiliac lover, Humbert Humbert, been presented on the musical stage a generation later, when Stephen Sondheim's monsters were common fare, it might have been a resounding success. As it was, mayhem set in when star, cast, and director had to be replaced, and the show eventually closed in Philadelphia, ostensibly for repairs but inevitably for good. Still, there are beautifully extended musical scenes in the Hammerstein tradition that make much dialogue unnecessary and carry the musical to new heights. Perhaps it was a built-in fault of the libretto that the only wholesome character is Lolita's mother, Charlotte, who has the witty and seductive song, "Sur les Quais de Ramsdale, Vermont," but is killed off before the second act. During the interim between *Coco* and *Lolita, My Love,* Lerner was married to journalist Karen Gundersen, his fifth wife. With the demise of *Lolita, My Love,* their marriage faltered.

It might have been the story of the underage Lolita that put Lerner in mind of the seduction scenes in *Gigi*. In any case, he and Loewe reunited in 1972 for a stage production of the classic 1958 movie. They added new numbers, including a long musical scene called "The Contract," in which Gigi's clever courtesan aunt battles with Gaston's lawyer in defining the property that will come to Gigi once she marries Gaston. On stage, *Gigi* boasted a large, capable cast. But the public perceived it as a cheaply staged rehash of the old movie, and, after opening on 13 November 1973, the show barely eked out three months on Broadway.

The reunion of Lerner and Loewe was to bring about another gem, a 1973 animated movie based on Antoine de Saint-Exupéry's *The Little Prince* (1943). Again, it was a failure at the box office because of all its subtleties. What was intended to be a juvenile romp with an interplanetary theme came out as a rather confused allegory for adults:

If you think you are hurting me
By wickedly deserting me
And leaving me to suffer and to cry . . .
And later die
You're very wrong
I'll get along
And so goodbye.

Lerner's next three Broadway shows, as well as two further marriages, were to have brief runs. *1600 Pennsylvania Avenue* seemed like a cannot-fail idea: the librettist-lyricist of *My Fair Lady* working with Leonard Bernstein, the composer of *West Side Story* (1957), on a tribute to America that was to premiere in 1976, the nation's bicentennial year. Bernstein and Lerner planned a springtime opening so that the show would have acquired a patina by that auspicious Fourth of July. It was one of the most enthusiastically awaited theatrical milestones of the decade. It was not the first time Lerner and Bernstein had worked together. They had had a harmonious collaboration back in 1957, when they had written songs for Harvard's benefit concert.

Lerner's libretto for *1600 Pennsylvania Avenue* spans the presidencies of George Washington through Theodore Roosevelt. The action all takes place in the White House, with the presidents, their wives, families, and fictional servants as the main characters. The same players portray the various residents throughout the successive presidencies. The idea was similar to what Lerner had tried to do in *Love Life,* which concerned the succeeding generations of the Cooper family. There, the one constant throughout each of the scenes is love buffeted by changing mores. Here, the constant was to be another, perhaps less chimerical, ideal—that the White House is the symbol of hope and freedom in the world. Again, Lerner overlooked the theatrical axiom that predicts disaster: when a dramatist abandons characters, the audience dismisses them too. He had closed his ears to the critics who had complained about the fragmentation of *On a Clear Day You Can See Forever,* in which the story skips from generation to generation, saying that "Lerner brought us close and then snatched us away from the central plot."

From 1972 to 1975, the years of the writing of *1600 Pennsylvania Avenue,* Lerner was heavily dependent on drugs, and this dependency spelled the end of his marriage to Gundersen. The day after his divorce in 1974, he married British actress Sandra Payne, thirty years his junior. After divorcing her two years later, when he was fifty-eight, he married Nina Bushkin, daughter of cocktail pianist Joe Bushkin. Nina was twenty-six at the time. Both marriages seemed to restore Lerner's youth—his wives were getting younger and younger. So were the forces putting *1600 Pennsylvania Avenue* together. Producers Robert Whitehead and Roger L. Stevens, as well as J. Paul Austin, an angel from the Coca-Cola company whom Lerner had persuaded to invest $1 million in the production, wanted the show to come off its pedestal. They hired Gilbert Moses and choreographer George Faison (both younger black men), who objected to Lerner and Bernstein's "token liberalism" and began cut-

Loewe and Lerner in 1962 (Photofest)

ting Lerner's lines. Soon the play became an incoherent diatribe, and the theater became a battleground, with Lerner and Bernstein barred from attending rehearsals. As might be expected, *1600 Pennsylvania Avenue* was a flop of gigantic proportions and barely eked out seven performances. Yet, the show is full of charming music and at least one extremely moving song, "Take Care of This House," sung to a servant before she leaves the White House by the first first lady to occupy it, Abigail Adams:

Take care of this house.
Keep it from harm.
If bandits break in,
Sound the alarm.
Care for this house.
Shine it by hand.
And keep it so clean
The glow can be seen
All over the land.
Be careful at night.
Check all the doors
If someone makes off with a dream,
The dream will be yours.
Take care of this house.
Be always on call.
For this house is the hope of us all.

John Cullum and Barbara Harris in Lerner and Burton
Lane's 1965 musical, On a Clear Day You
Can See Forever *(Photofest)*

Ever the optimist, Lerner was undaunted by the failure of *1600 Pennsylvania Avenue* and asked Lane to bury the hatchet and work with him again. In 1978 Lerner adapted a 1968 movie, *Buona Sera, Mrs. Campbell,* which he thought could be a sparkling Broadway musical. He titled the new show *Carmelina* (1979). The story concerns a young Italian widow, Carmelina, who has been receiving support checks from three former soldiers, veterans of the Sicilian campaign of World War II. Each man believes he has fathered the illegitimate daughter about whom she has written to them. When they arrive in the village for a reunion, Carmelina tells them that she does not know which of them is the father but that it was "someone in April" (also the title of a song in the score). In spite of her confession, each man revels in his prowess and believes that the daughter looks like him, but the girl is so ashamed of her mother's duplicity that she attempts to elope with a local fisherman, even

though she does not love him. The three "fathers" save the day for the daughter and, of course, for Carmelina.

Although this time Lerner hewed to the story line, and the show had a charming score, it might just as well have been written in 1945, and the critics unanimously said so. *Carmelina* opened on 8 April 1979 and closed ignominiously after only seventeen performances; no original-cast album was made. But one of the songs from the show, the haunting, yearning, if a bit lugubrious "One More Walk around the Garden," has become a favorite of the cabaret set. With the closing of *Carmelina* and the failure of the latest of his many marriages, Lerner was at his lowest ebb since the days of *1600 Pennsylvania Avenue.*

Lerner took off for London to supervise a revival of *My Fair Lady.* Although he did not know it at the time, his relationship with the Eliza of the company, Elizabeth Robertson, thirty-six years his junior, was to bring him the true happiness and love that had eluded him all his life. They were married in 1981, and Lerner began working on a musical to star her. He was attracted to Robert E. Sherwood's creaky play *Idiot's Delight* (1936), ostensibly because of its rumblings of war and annihilation on the horizon (which Lerner equated with the ongoing Cold War). But in his heart he was again drawn to the theme of a woman transformed, as in *My Fair Lady, Gigi,* and even *On a Clear Day You Can See Forever.* In the resulting show, *Dance a Little Closer* (1983), a woman tries to deny her former life. The more than adequate musical score was written by Charles Strouse, but Lerner's book was so obtuse that the songs did not stand a chance. *Dance a Little Closer* closed after a single performance. It became known by the showbiz sobriquet of *Close a Little Faster.*

Lerner and Robertson returned almost immediately to London. They were happy, with Robertson accepting theater roles and Lerner sketching out yet another Cinderella story. This time it was a musical adaptation of the 1936 movie *My Man Godfrey,* which concerns the education of an entire family. He teamed with Gerard Kenney, a young composer and a contemporary of Barry Manilow and Peter Allen, whose music Kenney's resembled. Working with the youthful Kenney, Lerner admitted that "he had never had such fun." The fun was interrupted in 1984 by an urgent call from Andrew Lloyd Webber to write the lyrics for his next project, *The Phantom of the Opera* (1986). Lerner wrote the lyric for the big second-act number, "Masquerade." Then his memory began to fail (from a yet-to-be-diagnosed brain tumor), and he had to inform Lloyd Webber that he wanted to withdraw from work on *The Phantom of the Opera.* Lerner continued to work on the adaptation of *My Man Godfrey* from time to time and dictated to his secretary his book *The Musical Theatre: A Celebration* (1986), on the history of that art form. It was published posthumously to great acclaim.

The winter of 1985 was a particularly brutal one in England, and Lerner took his wife to the Caribbean for a holiday. When they returned in 1986, he was coughing badly. A month later, he was diagnosed with lung cancer and hospitalized. Soon he was moved to the United States, lingering on at Memorial Sloan-Kettering Cancer Center in New York until his death on 14 June 1986. Of the obituaries that began to fill the papers, perhaps *Time* magazine's was the most cruelly honest: "Mr. Lerner's theater work never thrived without Mr. Loewe. His later efforts tended to be daring, flawed, and commercially futile." Yet, in another obituary, New York theater critic Barnes truly understood Lerner's special gift and ended up comparing him with two other great twentieth-century lyricists, Cole Porter and Sondheim. Then he added, "He had a way with a song and could make words cling to melodies like ivy to a wall." Lerner lived his life in a fantasy composed of equal parts of the search for life after death—all the generational scenarios—leavened by a bon vivant's sophistication. His heart-on-the-sleeve romanticism was always saved from becoming maudlin by a touch of irony. His masterful use of English and sense of poetry are his alone.

Interview:

Al Kasha and Joel Hirschhorn, *Notes on Broadway: Conversations with Great Songwriters* (Chicago: Contemporary Books, 1985), pp. 219–229.

Bibliography:

Benny Green, ed., *A Hymn to Him: Lyrics of Alan Jay Lerner* (New York: Limelight, 1987).

Biographies:

Gene Lees, *Inventing Champagne: The Worlds of Lerner and Loewe* (New York: St. Martin's Press, 1990);

Stephen Citron, *The Wordsmiths: Oscar Hammerstein 2nd & Alan Jay Lerner* (New York: Oxford University Press, 1995);

Edward A. Jablonski, *Alan Jay Lerner: A Biography* (New York: Holt, 1996).

References:

Humphrey Burton, *Leonard Bernstein* (New York: Doubleday, 1994);

Maurice Chevalier, *Bravo Maurice! A Compilation from the Autobiographical Writings of Maurice Chevalier* (London: Allen & Unwin, 1973);

Thomas S. Hischak, *Word Crazy: Broadway Lyricists from Cohan to Sondheim* (New York: Praeger, 1991), pp. 95–106;

Agnes de Mille, *Speak to Me, Dance with Me* (Boston: Little, Brown, 1973);

Vincente Minnelli, with Hector Arce, *I Remember It Well* (Garden City, N.Y.: Doubleday, 1974);

Richard Rodgers, *Musical Stages: An Autobiography* (New York: Random House, 1975).

Selected Discography:

Brigadoon, 1988 London cast, First Night, 16, 1988;

Camelot, original Broadway cast (1960), Sony, 60542, 1998;

An Evening with Alan Jay Lerner, First Night, 12, 1987;

Lyrics by Lerner: Alan Jay Lerner Performs His Own Songs, DRG, 5246, 1998;

M.G.M's Brigadoon, motion-picture soundtrack (1954), Rhino, 71965, 1996;

My Fair Lady, motion-picture soundtrack (1954), Sony, 25169, 1994;

My Fair Lady, original Broadway cast (1956), Columbia, 5090, ca. 1990s.

Frank Loesser
(29 June 1910 – 26 July 1969)

Michael Lasser

Unless otherwise indicated, music is by Loesser.

SELECTED SONGS FROM THEATRICAL PRO-
DUCTIONS: *The Illustrators' Show* (1936)–
"Bang–the Bell Rang" (music by Irving Actman);

Where's Charley? (1948)–"At the Red Rose Cotillion";
"Make a Miracle"; "My Darling, My Darling";
"The New Ashmolean Marching Society and Stu-
dents Conservatory Band"; "Once in Love with
Amy"; "The Woman in His Room"; "The Years
Before Us";

Guys and Dolls: A Musical Fable of Broadway (1950)–"Ade-
laide's Lament"; "A Bushel and a Peck"; "Fugue
for Tinhorns"; "Guys and Dolls"; "If I Were a
Bell"; "I'll Know"; "I've Never Been in Love
Before"; "Luck Be a Lady"; "Marry the Man
Today"; "More I Cannot Wish You"; "My Time
of Day"; "The Oldest Established"; "Sit Down,
You're Rockin' the Boat"; "Sue Me"; "Take Back
Your Mink";

The Most Happy Fella (1956)–"Abbondanza"; "Big D";
"Happy to Make Your Acquaintance"; "How
Beautiful the Days"; "Joey"; "My Heart Is So Full
of You"; "Ooh, My Feet"; "Rosabella"; "Standing
on the Corner"; "Warm All Over";

Greenwillow (1960)–"The Music of Home"; "Never Will
I Marry"; "The Sermon"; "Summertime Love";
"Walking away Whistling";

How to Succeed in Business without Really Trying (1961)–
"Brotherhood of Man"; "Coffee Break"; "The
Company Way"; "Happy to Keep His Dinner
Warm"; "I Believe in You"; "A Secretary Is Not a
Toy."

SELECTED SONGS FROM MOTION-PICTURE
PRODUCTIONS: *Postal Inspector* (1936)–"Don't
Let Me Love You" (music by Irving Actman);

Fight for Your Lady (1937)–"Blame It on the Danube"
(music by Harry Akst);

The Hurricane (1937)–"The Moon of Manakoora"
(music by Alfred Newman);

Frank Loesser (from Susan Loesser, A Most
Remarkable Fella, *1993)*

Cocoanut Grove (1938)–"Says My Heart" (music by Burton Lane);

College Swing (1938)–"How'dja Like to Love Me?"
(music by Lane); "I Fall in Love with You Every
Day" (music by Arthur Altman and Manning
Sherwin); "Moments Like This" (music by Lane);

Sing You Sinners (1938)–"Small Fry" (music by Hoagy
Carmichael);

A Song Is Born (1938)–"Heart and Soul" (music by Carmichael);

Spawn of the North (1938)–"I Like Hump-Backed
Salmon" (music by Lane);

Thanks for the Memory (1938)–"Two Sleepy People" (music by Carmichael);

Destry Rides Again (1939), music by Frederick Hollander–"The Boys in the Backroom"; "You've Got That Look";

The Gracie Allen Murder Case (1939)–"Snug as a Bug in a Rug" (music by Matt Malneck);

Hawaiian Nights (1939)–"Hey, Good Lookin'" (music by Malneck);

Man About Town (1939), music by Hollander–"Strange Enchantment"; "That Sentimental Sandwich";

Some Like It Hot (1939)–"The Lady's in Love with You" (music by Lane);

Buck Benny Rides Again (1940), music by Jimmy McHugh–"My! My!"; "Say It (Over and Over Again)";

Dancing on a Dime (1940)–"Dancing on a Dime"; "I Hear Music" (music by Lane);

Moon over Burma (1940)–"Moon over Burma" (music by Hollander);

Seven Sinners (1940)–"I've Been in Love Before" (music by Hollander);

Typhoon (1940)–"Palms of Paradise" (music by Hollander);

Glamour Boy (1941)–"Magic of Magnolias" (music by Victor Schertzinger);

Kiss the Boys Goodbye (1941), music by Schertzinger–"I'll Never Let a Day Pass By"; "Kiss the Boys Goodbye"; "Sand in My Shoes";

Las Vegas Nights (1941)–"Dolores" (music by Louis Alter);

Mr. Bug Goes to Town (1941)–"We're the Couple in the Castle" (music by Carmichael);

Sailors on Leave (1941)–"Since You" (music by Jule Styne);

Sis Hopkins (1941), music by Styne–"If You're in Love"; "Look at You, Look at Me" (music by Styne and George R. Brown); "That Ain't Hay (That's the U.S.A.)";

The Forest Rangers (1942)–"Jingle Jangle Jingle" (music by Joseph J. Lilley);

Priorities on Parade (1942)–"You're in Love with Someone Else (But I'm in Love with You)" (music by Styne);

Seven Days Leave (1942), music by McHugh–"Can't Get Out of This Mood"; "I Get the Neck of the Chicken"; "A Touch of Texas";

Sweater Girl (1942), music by Styne–"I Don't Want to Walk without You"; "I Said 'No'";

Happy Go Lucky (1943), music by McHugh–"Let's Get Lost"; "'Murder' He Says"; "Sing a Tropical Song";

Thank Your Lucky Stars (1943), music by Arthur Schwartz–"The Dreamer"; "How Sweet You Are"; "Love Isn't Born, It's Made"; "They're Either Too Young or Too Old";

Christmas Holiday (1944)–"Spring Will Be a Little Late This Year";

See Here, Private Hargrove (1944)–"In My Arms" (music by Ted Grouya);

Duffy's Tavern (1945)–"Leave Us Face It (We're in Love)" (lyric and music by Loesser and Abe Burrows);

The Perils of Pauline (1947)–"I Wish I Didn't Love You So"; "Poppa, Don't Preach to Me";

Variety Girl (1947)–"Tallahassee";

Neptune's Daughter (1949)–"Baby, It's Cold Outside";

Red, Hot and Blue (1949)–"(Where Are You) Now That I Need You";

Hans Christian Andersen (1952)–"Anywhere I Wander"; "I'm Hans Christian Andersen"; "The Inch Worm"; "The King's New Clothes"; "No Two People"; "Thumbelina"; "The Ugly Duckling"; "Wonderful Copenhagen";

Guys and Dolls (1955)–"A Woman in Love."

SELECTED SONGS PUBLISHED INDEPENDENTLY OF THEATRICAL OR MOTION-PICTURE PRODUCTIONS: "In Love with a Memory of You" (1931), music by William Schuman;

"I Wish I Were Twins" (1934), lyric by Loesser and Eddie DeLange, music by Joseph Meyer;

"Junk Man" (1934), music by Meyer;

"Praise the Lord and Pass the Ammunition" (1942);

"Have I Stayed Away Too Long" (1943);

"What Do You Do in the Infantry" (1943);

"First Class Private Mary Brown" (1944);

"The Sad Bombardier" (1944);

"Salute to the Army Service Forces" (1944);

"The WAC Hymn" (1944);

"Why Do They Call a Private a Private" (1944), lyric by Loesser and Peter Lind Hayes;

"Rodger Young" (1945);

"Bloop, Bleep!" (1947);

"The Feathery Feelin'" (1947);

"A Tune for Humming" (1947);

"What Are You Doing New Year's Eve" (1947);

"On a Slow Boat to China" (1948);

"Hoop-Dee-Doo" (1950), music by Milton De Lugg;

"Just Another Polka" (1953), lyric and music by Loesser and De Lugg;

"Warm and Willing" (1958).

Frank Loesser wrote only five musicals that opened on Broadway, yet they established him as a master of the form. He was an innovator who created everything from musical comedy to Broadway

Sheet music for songs with lyrics by Loesser for two Dorothy Lamour sarong productions (1937, 1940)
(from Marion Short, Hollywood Movie Songs, *1999)*

opera, a self-taught composer who wrote a surprisingly diverse body of melody, and a lyricist with an unsurpassed ear for the great variety and vitality of American speech. Although Loesser was a native New Yorker, he was also one of the few lyricists who established himself in Hollywood before trying his luck on Broadway.

Frank Henry Loesser, the first son and second child of Henry and Julia Ehrlich Loesser, was born in New York on 29 June 1910. Both parents were nonreligious Jews who prized intellect and high culture. In the 1880s Henry Loesser fled to the United States from Prussia to avoid military service and employment with his family's banking business. He initially worked as a grocer and supplemented his income by playing piano. He married Berthe Ehrlich, an Austrian immigrant, in 1892 and began a career as a piano teacher. The couple had a son, Arthur, in 1894. Four years later, when Berthe's sister Julia arrived in America, she moved in with the Loessers. Julia and Henry fell in love soon after her arrival, and she became attached to young Arthur, who remained her

favorite even after her own children were born. Berthe sent Julia to live in Washington, D.C., in order to get her away from Henry, but she returned to New York to keep house for him after Berthe died in childbirth. Julia and Henry married in January 1907. Their first child, Grace, was born in December of that year.

Henry Loesser, who stood only five feet two, had a fiery temper and a didactic manner, yet his wife and children appear to have loved him deeply. Neither parent had any interest in Jewish practices or American culture. As Arthur Loesser explained, "German was the vehicle of culture and loftier thought; English was the medium suitable for purchasing vegetables." To put young Frank to sleep, his parents read to him from Johann Wolfgang von Goethe's works. Julia Loesser was a dedicated amateur pianist, and there was always serious music in the house on West 107th Street, but both parents scorned popular music as something for the lower classes. Arthur Loesser was giving concerts at the age of eighteen, and he eventually became the head of the piano department at the Cleveland Institute of Music.

A well-regarded pianist, critic, and musicologist, he represented the kind of cultural and intellectual success the Loesser family valued.

Frank Loesser, in contrast, taught himself to play the harmonica and the piano, and in his early teens he became smitten with show business. In 1914 Henry Loesser wrote to Arthur that four-year-old Frank was "developing more and more into a musical genius. He plays any tune he's heard and can spend an enormous amount of time at the piano. Always he wants attention and an audience." His parents refused to accept his songwriting ambitions, but he persisted despite their disapproval and lifelong condescension. In *A Most Remarkable Fella: Frank Loesser and the Guys and Dolls in His Life* (1993), her biography of her father, Susan Loesser suggests that even Arthur always looked down on his half brother for not being an intellectual, yet he envied Frank's critical and financial success.

Loesser was also a natural rebel. At two he refused to speak German, the common language in the household. Though he was obviously bright, he was not an especially good student and was often in trouble. He was accepted at Townsend Harris High School, a school for gifted students, but was expelled because he was more interested in playing practical jokes than pursuing his studies. The City College of New York accepted him at the age of fifteen, even though he had no high-school diploma. One night, in his mid teens, Loesser wrote some comic couplets for part of the entertainment at a Lions Club dinner. Some club members encouraged him to continue. A vaudevillian then bought his first song, "Armful of You," for $15.

On 26 July 1926, when Loesser was sixteen, his father died suddenly at the age of sixty-nine. For days Frank walked the streets alone. Arthur gave up concert tours to take a teaching job at the Cleveland Institute of Music, and Frank dropped out of City College after less than a year in order to contribute to the family's upkeep with a series of jobs. He sold classified ads for *The New York Herald Tribune,* worked as the knit-goods editor for *Women's Wear Daily,* drew political cartoons for *The Tuckahoe Record,* and, at the age of eighteen, served as the city editor for the short-lived *New Rochelle News.* He also screwed lids on insecticide bottles, was a process server, and worked for his meals as a restaurant spotter (a person who pretends to be a customer but reports on the food and service).

Loesser's goal, even at this young age, was to succeed in Tin Pan Alley, the home of popular-music publishing. Because New York Jews dominated the songwriting business, Loesser even cultivated a working-class New York accent, sprinkled with Yiddishisms. By the time he was in his mid twenties, he sounded as if he had grown up on the Lower East Side—urban, Jewish, and street-smart.

One of Loesser's earliest collaborators was Joe Brandfonbrenner, a friend with whom he frequented the In Old Algiers Restaurant on Upper Broadway. They took a song to Leo Feist, Inc., where, to their amazement, both of them received contracts for $100 a week for all the songs they could write. Loesser changed his advance into $1 bills and burst into the house, scattering them all over the living room. It was typical of the exuberance and ebullience with which he greeted good news. His emotions were often extreme, and he eventually became as well known for his volatile temper and legendary rages as for his irreverence and warm affection.

The young collaborators wrote dozens of songs in 1928 and 1929, but Feist published none of them, and none of them survives. Loesser had a more significant collaborator in the early 1930s when he worked with his friend William Schuman, who went on to become one of the most esteemed classical composers in America. Schuman served as head of the Juilliard School of Music from 1945 to 1962 and as president of Lincoln Center from 1962 to 1969. One of his choral works, *A Free Song* (1942), won the 1943 Pulitzer Prize in music.

In the early days of the Depression, Loesser and Schuman, just out of their teens, were brimming with ideas for popular songs. They frequented the Feist offices long—and persistently—enough to be given a room to work in. Their one published song together, "In Love with a Memory of You" (1931), was also Loesser's first published song. In later years, Schuman observed, "Frank Loesser has written hits with Hoagy Carmichael, Burton Lane, Jule Styne, and other Hollywood grand dukes, but I have the distinction of having written a flop with him."

Loesser's next collaborator was composer Joseph Meyer, best known for writing the music to such songs as "California, Here I Come" (1924), "If You Knew Susie" (1925), and "A Cup of Coffee, a Sandwich, and You" (1925). In 1934 they wrote "Junk Man," introduced by Benny Goodman, and, with Eddie DeLange, "I Wish I Were Twins," a bouncy, upbeat song with a slangy turn of phrase especially suited to Fats Waller, who recorded it that same year.

Loesser loved the theater, especially musicals, and longed to write for Broadway. He soon got his chance. He had written songs for vaudevillian Lita Grey Chaplin, Charlie Chaplin's second wife. Her accompanist, Irving Actman, became Loesser's next

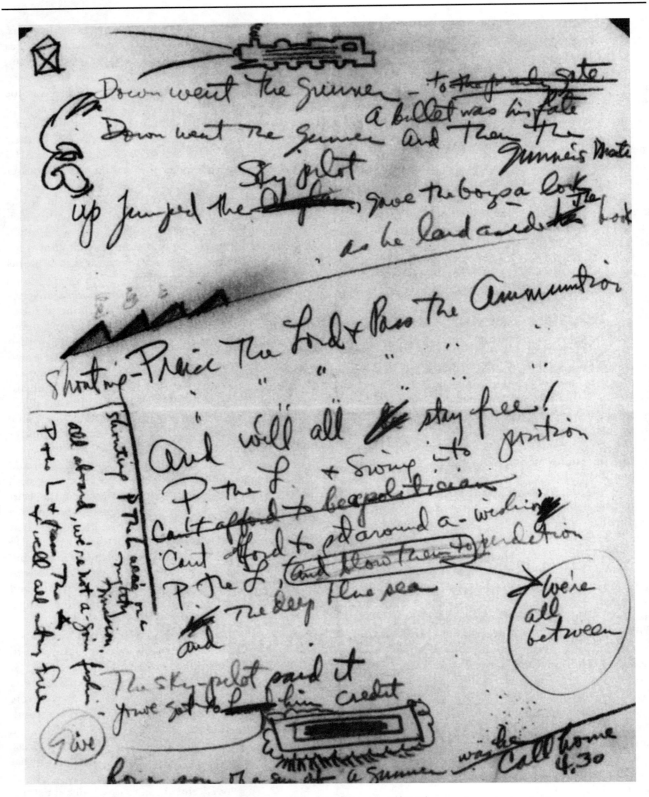

Draft of Loesser's lyric for "Praise the Lord and Pass the Ammunition" (1942), a song he wrote upon hearing an anecdote about a navy chaplain's heroic behavior during the Japanese attack on Pearl Harbor
(from Susan Loesser, A Most Remarkable Fella, *1993)*

collaborator. Loesser and Actman were performing their own songs at a small club called The Back Drop on West Fifty-second Street when a press agent named Ted Weatherly offered to use some of their songs when he found the right property.

Soon after, Weatherly produced the Society of Illustrators' annual revue, known for being especially bawdy. Though it was usually a private production, the police had closed it down the previous year. With that kind of publicity, Weatherly planned to take a new version to Broadway. He used five of Loesser and Actman's songs and had them write the finale as well. Titled *The Illustrators' Show,* it opened on 22 January 1936 and closed five performances later. Loesser and Actman went back to working at The Back Drop. One night, after he sang "Bang–the Bell Rang," one of his and Actman's songs from *The Illustrators' Show,* Loesser met a young woman named Lynn Garland, who had changed her name from Mary Alice Blankenberg when she left Terre Haute, Indiana, for New York and a singing career. They began to date and soon fell in love.

In April 1936 Loesser and Actman signed a six-month contract with Universal Pictures. Loesser was earning $200 a week in Hollywood, more than he had ever earned before. He described his early attempts at writing songs for movies in a letter to his mother: "Right now Irving and I are in the throes, trying to knock off a hit out of a situation where the producer orders a certain title, the musical director orders a certain rhythm, the dance director orders a certain number of bars and the composers order a certain number of aspirin." Based in part on these early frustrations in Hollywood, Loesser learned to control every aspect of a production after he had established himself on Broadway.

Loesser and Actman contributed their first movie song, "Don't Let Me Love You," to *Flying Hostess* (1936), a picture Loesser called "a stinker." Yet, he was enjoying himself even in the midst of the Depression. He thrived on the climate of Hollywood, but he soon learned that Universal would not renew his and Actman's option. He responded by sending money to Lynn so that she could travel to Hollywood, where they married in September 1936. They had two children, Susan and John. Meanwhile, Loesser and Actman continued to work for Universal but were paid only by the individual song.

When composer Burton Lane heard some songs Loesser had written with Manning Sherwin, he was sufficiently impressed to take them to producer Lew Gensler at Paramount Pictures. Gensler offered Sherwin and Loesser a ten-week contract at a time when Loesser was flat broke. For dinner one night, he and

Lynn had nothing to eat but a can of baked beans and a single apple. Paramount paid him $1,500 to write songs for one movie, *Blossoms on Broadway* (1937). In October 1936 the studio gave him a new contract with options for renewal. The next day Lane found him being measured for custom-made suits and shirts, a typical display of extravagance. Loesser remained with Paramount until 1949 and wrote more than one hundred songs for more than sixty movies.

In 1937 Paramount lent Loesser to M-G-M, where he and Alfred Newman collaborated on "The Moon of Manakoora" for Dorothy Lamour in *The Hurricane,* also starring Jon Hall, Mary Astor, and Raymond Massey. Lamour did not sing the song in the movie, but her recording became Loesser's first hit. It was also the first of several "tropical paradise" songs he wrote, including "Moon over Burma" (1940) and "Palms of Paradise" (1940), as well as a satire of tropical songs, "Sing a Tropical Song" (1943).

The year 1938 was one of Loesser's most successful. He and Hoagy Carmichael wrote "Small Fry" for Bing Crosby in *Sing You Sinners,* "Two Sleepy People" for Bob Hope and Shirley Ross in *Thanks for the Memory,* and "Heart and Soul" for the short feature *A Song Is Born.* The two songwriters came up with "Two Sleepy People" after the Loessers had spent an evening at the Carmichaels', where the two men tried unsuccessfully to come up with an idea for a song. Finally, at three in the morning, the Loessers got up to leave. Lynn remarked on her way out, "Look at us, four sleepy people." Loesser and Carmichael said, as if on cue, "That's it." The sheet music reads, "Title suggested by Lynn Garland." Loesser also worked with Lane, collaborating on "Says My Heart" for *Cocoanut Grove* (1938), "How'dja Like to Love Me?" for *College Swing* (1938), "The Lady's in Love with You" for *Some Like It Hot* (1939), and "I Hear Music" and the title song for *Dancing on a Dime* (1940).

In Loesser's songs with Carmichael and Lane, one begins to discern the characteristic qualities of his lyrics. He used colloquial phrases with a sure touch previously undetected in his writing. Like many of his best songs, these offer a surprisingly rich mix of emotion. They are romantic, sensuous, alternately sweet or exuberant, and amusing. This unlikely combination of qualities focuses the emotion rather than easing or diffusing it, especially in the duet "Two Sleepy People," which had the daunting task of following on the heels of Hope and Ross's previous hit, "Thanks for the Memory," from *The Big Broadcast of 1938* (1938). A loving, seductive, bantering conversation between a husband and wife, "Two Sleepy People" was a gentler, less ambiguous song but a worthy successor to "Thanks for the Memory."

Loesser (right) and composer Arthur Schwartz, who collaborated on the songs for Thank Your Lucky Stars *(1943),
a morale-boosting wartime movie musical with an all-star cast (from William Zinsser,* Easy to Remember, *2000)*

During these same years Loesser also collaborated with Frederick Hollander on such songs as "The Boys in the Backroom," sung by Marlene Dietrich in *Destry Rides Again* (1939), and with Victor Schertzinger on "Sand in My Shoes" and other songs for *Kiss the Boys Goodbye* (1941). Ten songs Loesser cowrote before the Japanese attack on Pearl Harbor were featured on the weekly radio program *Your Hit Parade:* "Says My Heart," which reached the number-one position, along with "How'dja Like to Love Me?" "Small Fry," "Two Sleepy People," "Heart and Soul," "The Lady's in Love with You," "I Fall in Love with You Every Day" (1938), "Strange Enchantment" (1939), "Say It (Over and Over Again)" (1940), and "We're the Couple in the Castle" (1941).

By now Loesser had developed his own way of working. A man of uncommon energy, he was a pacer, a heavy smoker, and a compulsive doodler. He often rose at four in the morning to write, and he sometimes wrote in his car. He would have someone else drive because he became so involved in his work that he would drive through stop signs and red lights. He once turned the wrong way on a one-way street and drove past his own house on his way home. Lane described him as secretive. Loesser would sit across the room, away from the piano, holding a pad of paper in front of his face, refusing to tell Lane what he was writing. When he finished, he would set the lyric on the piano.

When Paramount lent Loesser to Republic Pictures in 1940, he was furious. Republic was known for producing B movies, and Loesser thought that such work was beneath his talents. But while he was there, he met composer Jule Styne, who played him a melody he had been working on with another lyricist. Loesser told him it was too good for Republic and said that he ought to save it. Styne agreed, and Loesser later contributed the lyric and the title, "I Don't Want to Walk without You." Introduced by Betty Jane Rhodes in *Sweater Girl* (1942) and made into a hit record by Harry James's Orchestra with singer Helen Forrest, the song was Loesser's most important to date. It extended his range to include the kind of sentimental ballad that Styne, working mainly with lyricist Sammy Cahn, wrote so successfully during World War II. The lyric is repetitive and conventional, but its image of walking alone touched a chord during the war years, when millions of women separated from loved ones bought copies of popular songs about loneliness and longing. The particular Loesser touch comes in a burst of emotion that is also recognizably conversational and slangy:

I don't walk to walk without the sunshine
Why'd you have to turn off all that sunshine?
Oh, baby, please come back
Or you'll break my heart for me,
'Cause I don't want to walk without you,
No siree.

In 1941 Loesser and composer Joseph J. Lilley wrote a song for *The Forest Rangers* (1942), starring Fred MacMurray and Paulette Goddard. Even before the movie was released, the song, "Jingle Jangle Jingle," had risen to the top of *Your Hit Parade,* even though it was strikingly different from Loesser's increasingly sophisticated work. It was his contribution to the fad for cowboy songs, which included Cole Porter's "Don't Fence Me In" (1944), Al Dexter's "Pistol Packin' Mama" (1943), Bob Nolan's "Cool Water" (1936), and Jimmie Davis and Charles Mitchell's "You Are My Sunshine" (1940). In that same year, Loesser and Louis Alter wrote "Dolores" for *Las Vegas Nights.* It was the first of Loesser's five Oscar-nominated songs.

During World War II Loesser began to write melodies as well as lyrics. He found wartime experience an especially rich source of material, as he wrote songs about the home front, military life, the experience of combat, and the themes of parting, loneliness, and the longing to return that dominated the songs of the time. Several of these songs had a distinctive comic twist. Among them were a gripe about military life, "In My Arms" (1944), with music by Ted Grouya; a love song titled "First Class Private Mary Brown" (1944) and "Why Do They Call a Private a Private" (1944), both with music by Loesser himself; and "They're Either Too Young or Too Old" (1943), cowritten with composer Arthur Schwartz.

Loesser and Schwartz wrote nine songs for *Thank Your Lucky Stars* (1943), a typical wartime musical anthology featuring performance numbers by singing and nonsinging stars. Two of the songs became standards: "Love Isn't Born, It's Made" and "They're Either Too Young or Too Old." The latter is a comic lament, bemoaning the absence of available men and

the celibacy forced on women left behind with no hope of romance until the end of the war. Introduced by actress Bette Davis, the song made *Your Hit Parade* and received an Oscar nomination as best original movie song. Loesser's tongue-in-cheek approach to the "problem" comes through most clearly in his playfully forced rhyming:

I'll never never fail ya'
While you are in Australia,
Or out in the Aleutians,
Or off among the Rooshians. . . .

Loesser's most important World War II song was inspired by an incident that occurred during the attack on Pearl Harbor. It was also the first published song for which he wrote both the lyric and the music. He had read a newspaper article about a navy chaplain who had taken over a position in a gun crew after one member had been killed. He apparently urged the men on with a spontaneous battle cry: "Praise the Lord and pass the ammunition!" Loesser thought it was the perfect title for a song. He typically wrote a dummy melody to establish the rhythm for a new lyric until a composer could provide a usable melody. When he played the new song for friends, they urged him to keep his dummy melody. "Praise the Lord and Pass the Ammunition" (1942) sold more than two million recordings and a million copies of sheet music. The song was so popular that the Office of War Information, fearing the public might tire of it too quickly, limited its performances on radio stations to once every four hours.

Despite the wartime jingoism of "Praise the Lord and Pass the Ammunition," the song represents a successful blending of disparate elements: a melody that seems like a combination of a jazzy hymn and a patriotic anthem, and a lyric that draws on the exuberant imagery of the spiritual, the wisecracking irreverence of American slang, and the spontaneous wordplay typical of the best American lyricists:

Yes, the sky pilot said it
You've got to give him credit
For a son of a gun of a gunner was he,
Shouting,
"Praise the Lord, we're on a mighty mission!
All aboard, we're not a-goin' fishin';
Praise the Lord and pass the ammunition
And we'll all be free."

In addition to "Praise the Lord and Pass the Ammunition," Loesser's wartime songs on *Your Hit Parade* included "I Don't Want to Walk without You," "Jingle Jangle Jingle," and "Let's Get Lost" (1943), all of which reached number one, along with "They're Either

Sheet music for a song Loesser wrote in 1943 at the request of the U.S. Army
(from Marion Short, More Gold in Your Piano Bench, *1997)*

Too Young or Too Old," "In My Arms," and "How Sweet You Are" (1943).

By the time Loesser wrote "Praise the Lord and Pass the Ammunition" he had enlisted in the army. Originally assigned to the Radio Productions Unit in Santa Ana, California, he wrote songs and skits for two daily live radio shows featuring top Hollywood stars. His collaborator was nightclub personality Peter Lind Hayes. Loesser was fond of Hayes's wife, singer Mary Healy, and he wrote a song for her, "Once in Love with Mary." Six years later he changed the name in the title to Amy and had the most important song from his first Broadway score, *Where's Charley?* (1948). When Hayes left the outfit in 1943, Loesser bought his half of "Why Do They Call a Private a Private," the lyric to which they had cowritten; Loesser later used the same melody for "Happy to Keep His Dinner Warm," a song in his last stage musical, *How to Succeed in Business without Really*

Trying (1961). He also became friendly with fellow soldier Milton De Lugg, a musician who later became his first musical secretary. Like Irving Berlin, Loesser needed someone to write down the songs he heard in his head but played poorly on the piano. For years he could not notate music. In 1950 Loesser and De Lugg collaborated on "Hoop-Dee-Doo," a lighthearted polka that made it to *Your Hit Parade,* and followed it in 1953 with "Just Another Polka."

In 1943 Loesser transferred to the army's Special Services Unit in New York City, where he wrote a series of "Blueprint Specials," prepackaged camp shows with scripts, sheet music, sketches, and instructions for making costumes and sets from what might be available on an army post. He wrote songs for various branches of the armed services: "The Sad Bombardier" (1944), "The WAC Hymn" (1944), and "Salute to the Army Service Forces" (1944). He wrote another song, "What

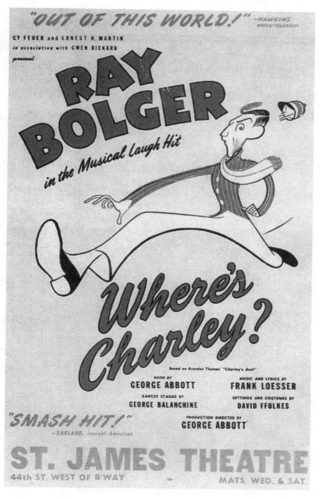

Window card for Loesser's first Broadway musical, based on Brandon Thomas's Charley's Aunt, *which opened in 1948 (from Amy Henderson and Dwight Blocker Bowers,* Red, Hot & Blue, *1996)*

Do You Do in the Infantry" (1943), at the army's request, but because it expressed the ordinary private's gripes about army life, the infantry turned it down. Loesser published the song anyway. Similar in spirit to Berlin's "Oh! How I Hate to Get Up in the Morning" (1918), it became popular, especially among foot soldiers. Loesser was especially proud of being a private, even though he wore custom-tailored uniforms. His wife, Lynn, said he was furious when he was promoted to private first class.

Meanwhile, the infantry kept after Loesser for an acceptable song. In 1945 he wrote "Rodger Young," a ballad about a winner of the Medal of Honor. One of the most memorable songs of the war, it told the story of Young, a private who volunteered to draw the fire of Japanese machine guns so his platoon could escape. Loesser donated the earnings from the song to charities chosen by Young's mother. He also contributed all the other earnings from his war songs to war-related charities.

During his army service Loesser also continued to write songs for Hollywood. Between 1941 and 1945 he had songs in twenty movies, including "Love Isn't Born, It's Made"; the raucous "'Murder' He Says" (1943), with music by Jimmy McHugh; and "Spring Will Be a Little Late This Year" (1944), a romantic ballad so perfectly defined by its melancholy hush that one wonders why Loesser did not write in this vein more often. After a routine verse, the chorus begins:

Spring will be a little late this year,
A little late arriving
In my lonely world over here.
For you have left me,
And where is our April of old?
You have left me,
And winter continues cold,

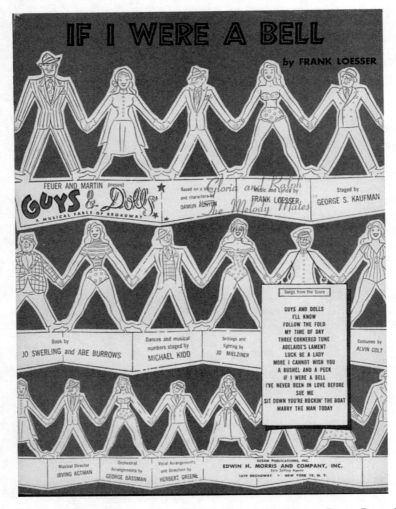

*Sheet music for a song from Loesser's popular 1950 Broadway musical based on Damon Runyon's stories
of New York gamblers and their women (Bruccoli Clark Layman Archives)*

As if to say
Spring will be a little slow to start. . . .

The delay of the seasons, brought on by sadness, is an expansive image, yet Loesser reduces it to human scale—"a little late"—to ponder the absence of "our April of old." Though his later theater ballads have a bravura quality dictated by the idiosyncratic characters who sing them, his touch here is delicate. While the lyric relies heavily on repetition, one of Loesser's favorite rhetorical devices, it also remains true to how people talk.

Loesser was honorably discharged in April 1945 after a serious bout with pneumonia and soon returned to Hollywood. Of the eight movies for which he wrote songs from 1947 to 1952, six were released after he had begun working in New York. Three of these songs made *Your Hit Parade:* "I Wish I Didn't Love You So"

(1947), "Tallahassee" (1947), and "Baby, It's Cold Outside" (1949). "I Wish I Didn't Love You So" reached number one and was nominated for an Oscar. In addition to writing "(Where Are You) Now That I Need You" for *Red, Hot and Blue* (1949), Loesser also appeared in the movie as Hair-Do Lempke, a scarfaced, piano-playing gangster.

The most important of these songs, "Baby, It's Cold Outside," won an Academy Award in 1949. It is an amusingly sexy song of seduction with a catchy title that quickly entered the language. It was also the first of Loesser's contrapuntal duets, written as a dialogue between two people who go back and forth as they would in an ordinary conversation, repeating, interrupting, and changing direction:

SHE: I really can't stay.
HE: But, baby, it's cold outside.

SHE: I've got to go 'way.
HE: But, Baby, it's cold outside.
SHE: This evening has been . . .
HE: Been hoping that you'd drop in.
SHE: So very nice.
HE: I'll hold your hands, they're just like ice.

Among the many pairs of singers who recorded the song were Margaret Whiting and Johnny Mercer, Dinah Shore and Buddy Clark, Ella Fitzgerald and Louis Jordan, Louis Armstrong and Velma Middleton, and Ray Charles and Betty Carter. Loesser wrote other contrapuntal duets, such as "Make a Miracle," from *Where's Charley?;* "Sue Me," from *Guys and Dolls* (1950); "No Two People," from the 1952 movie *Hans Christian Andersen;* and "The Sermon," from *Greenwillow* (1960). Loesser's other successful postwar songs included "Poppa, Don't Preach to Me" (1947), "Bloop, Bleep!" (1947), "A Tune for Humming" (1947), "What Are You Doing New Year's Eve" (1947), and "On a Slow Boat to China" (1948), which reached the number-one spot on *Your Hit Parade.*

Even though Paramount was paying him quite well, Loesser wanted to return to New York. He expressed his desire in "The Delicatessen of My Dreams," an unpublished contrapuntal duet he wrote for his wife and himself to perform at parties. The lyric is both amusing and nostalgic:

HE: Join me, my sweet, for a bite to eat
In the delicatessen of my dreams.
SHE: Tempt me, my prince, with a homemade blintz
In the land where the Russian dressing gleams.

In addition to loving New York, Loesser longed for full control of his artistic and financial life. Paramount was generous, but the studio still held copyrights on most of his songs. When first-time Broadway producers Cy Feuer and Ernest H. Martin approached him in 1948, Loesser was ready to listen.

The producers had in mind a musical adaptation of the classic English stage farce *Charley's Aunt* (1892), by Brandon Thomas. Harold Arlen was to write the music and Loesser, the lyrics. When Arlen had to withdraw from the project, Loesser convinced the producers to let him write the entire score. The imperious George Abbott, known to everyone in the theater as "Mr. Abbott," wrote the adaptation and directed. Never lacking in confidence, Loesser soon started calling him George. George Balanchine served as choreographer. Set at Oxford University in the 1890s, *Where's Charley?* recounts the story of two Oxonians, the girls they fall in love with, and Charley's rich aunt from Brazil. The girls require a proper chaperone, so when the aunt's arrival is delayed,

Charley must assume her identity, periodically racing offstage in a mad scramble to change clothes and avoid detection. Ray Bolger starred as Charley and Allyn Ann McLerie played Amy, the woman Charley loves. The show opened at the St. James Theatre on 11 October 1948.

Although the reviews of *Where's Charley?* were mediocre, the show had a run of 792 performances, thanks to Richard Rodgers and Oscar Hammerstein's word-of-mouth praise for Loesser's score and Bolger's transformation of his solo number, "Once in Love with Amy," into a show-stopping triumph. At first, the vaudeville-like song received little response. Bolger once forgot the words and asked the orchestra leader for a cue. Feuer's seven-year-old son, who had seen several performances and knew the score by heart, called out the words from his orchestra seat. The audience laughed, and Bolger spontaneously asked everyone to sing with him. From that point on, he worked on the number at matinees as a sing-along until he felt it was ready to do at night as well. It evolved over several months into a deliriously joyful celebration, as young Charley imagines his own future happiness: "Once in love with Amy, / Always in love with Amy." By closing night, the song ran for twenty-five minutes, as Bolger performed it "in one" (in front of a closed curtain), singing and dancing a soft-shoe and getting the audience to sing along.

Though the rest of the score lacked the innovation and range of Loesser's later work, it was charming, a little old-fashioned, and surprisingly diverse for a first effort by a songwriter with no Broadway experience. Other songs included "My Darling, My Darling," a lovely ballad that was a throwback to operetta, sung by the second leads, Doretta Morrow and Byron Palmer; "The Woman in His Room," marked by mood swings from outrage to forgiveness to renewed trust to renewed outrage as Amy reacts to the pictures of scantily clad women in Charley's room; and "Make a Miracle," the wittiest number in the score, in which Amy becomes so interested in telling of the miraculous inventions of the future that she fails to hear Charley's proposal of marriage. As is typical in Loesser's contrapuntal duets, the two voices overlap conversationally. Other songs include a waltz, "At the Red Rose Cotillion," a traditional school song, "The Years Before Us"; and a march, "The New Ashmolean Marching Society and Students Conservatory Band."

From Berlin, Loesser learned that his financial security rested on his ability to control and publish his own work. In 1948 he formed Susan Publications with Edwin H. Morris to publish and control his own songs. He started with the score to *Where's Charley?*

Loesser with Abe Burrows, who wrote the book for Loesser's Guys and Dolls *(1950) and* How to Succeed in Business
without Really Trying *(1961) (from Susan Loesser,* A Most Remarkable Fella, *1993)*

along with a few movie songs he got Paramount to
release. In 1950 Loesser formed Frank Music Corp.,
absorbing Susan Publications, adding the songs from
Guys and Dolls and *Hans Christian Andersen* to the catalogue, and signing additional young songwriters.
Among the hit songs and shows not by Loesser but
published by Frank Music are "Unchained Melody"
(1955), by Hy Zaret and Alex North; "Cry Me a
River" (1953), by Arthur Hamilton; *Kismet* (1953), by
Robert Wright and George Forrest; *The Pajama Game*
(1954) and *Damn Yankees* (1955), both by Richard
Adler and Jerry Ross; and Meredith Willson's *The
Music Man* (1957).

Despite his insistence that "I don't write for pos-
terity. I write for the here and now," Loesser demonstrated that he was capable of producing a score that
created a world removed in both time and place from
his own. For each of his shows this practical, profane
man with a violent temper created a solid, believable
place that was also suggestive of the wonder of fairy
tale and fable.

Loesser's shows ranged from the fast-paced confusion of *Where's Charley?* to the flashy but sweet
demimonde, populated by amiable touts and lovable
faded flowers, in *Guys and Dolls;* from the unlikely
May-December romance in *The Most Happy Fella*
(1956), set amid the lush vineyards of rural California, to the equally unlikely story of a young window
washer who rises to the top of a major Manhattan
corporation through intelligence and lovable chica-
nery in *How to Succeed in Business without Really Trying.*
Likewise, from the stylized patois of *Guys and Dolls,* to
the bravura Italian accents of *The Most Happy Fella,* to
the corporate lingo of *How to Succeed in Business without
Really Trying,* Loesser also demonstrated a keen mastery of the rhythms of American speech, no matter
how arcane or stylized.

Guys and Dolls, appropriately subtitled *A Musical
Fable of Broadway,* is arguably the greatest of all musicals about New York. *On the Town* (1944) is more star-
struck, *Gypsy* (1959) tawdrier, *West Side Story* (1957)
more ominous. By the time librettist Jo Swerling fin-

*Sheet music for a song from Loesser's 1956 musical about a middle-aged vineyard owner who courts
a San Francisco waitress by mail (from Lehman Engel,* Their Words Are Music, *1975)*

ished an adaptation of "The Idyll of Miss Sarah Brown" (1933), a short story by New York newspaperman Damon Runyon, Loesser had finished the score as well. Paramount owned the rights to Runyon's stories but released them to producers Feuer and Martin in return for the first refusal of screen rights to the production. When Swerling's book proved unusable, Feuer and Martin hired Abe Burrows on Loesser's recommendation. Burrows, a writer for the popular radio show *Duffy's Tavern,* well known as a wit and raconteur, was a quintessential New Yorker. He and Loesser had first met at a party, where Burrows improvised two of his classic party songs, "The Girl with the Three Blue Eyes" and "I'm Strolling Down Memory Lane without a Thing to Remember."

Burrows was able to use all of Loesser's songs in the libretto, so closely tied were they to the story and the characters. Similarly, Loesser found cues for new songs in Burrows's writing. Burrows retained the story of Sarah Brown, an innocent Salvation Army

sister who wins the heart of big-time gambler Sky Masterson, and then borrowed some of the shady but lovable gamblers, tinhorns, and touts from other Runyon stories, including Nicely-Nicely Johnson, Harry the Horse, Benny Southstreet, and, most notably, Nathan Detroit, lover of Miss Adelaide, the adorable floozy with the incurable head cold. Nathan is also the sole proprietor of "the oldest established permanent floating crap game in New York." The events of the plot concern Masterson's attempts to seduce Sarah in order to win a bet, only to find himself falling in love with her; Nathan's attempt to run a crap game despite a police crackdown; and Miss Adelaide's eagerness to get Nathan to the altar.

Loesser's score combines comedy and skepticism, advances plot, and creates both atmosphere and character. Sarah sings the jubilant romantic ballad, "If I Were a Bell," while drunk, and in "I'll Know" she and Masterson have an argument in song as they are falling in love. Paralleling "I'll Know" is the comic argument between Nathan and Miss Adelaide, "Sue Me." Just as "I'll Know" is serious with a comic undertone, "Sue Me" is comic with a serious undertone.

The songs in *Guys and Dolls* are as diverse as those in any Broadway score, yet they serve the needs of the play perfectly. The opening number, "Fugue for Tinhorns," makes affectionately ironic use of a classical musical form to introduce characters and establish their world. In "Adelaide's Lament," sung in the original production by Vivian Blaine, Miss Adelaide attempts to understand why an "unmarried female, just in the legal sense," is unable to get over what appears to be no more than a common cold. One of the wittiest of all theater songs, it demonstrates Loesser's ability to create character while writing a funny song with heart. The rest of the score also displays his impressive range: "Marry the Man Today," a cynical complaint about men; "Luck Be a Lady," a rousing production number in which Masterson appeals for help in a crap game; "More I Cannot Wish You," a father's loving wish for his daughter's happiness; "A Bushel and a Peck" and "Take Back Your Mink," two parodies of tawdry nightclub acts; "Sit Down, You're Rockin' the Boat," a comic revival number that reforms the sinners at the end of the show; and the title song, the gamblers' boisterous explanation of what a doll can do to a happily independent guy.

Unfortunately, the rehearsals for *Guys and Dolls* were not as happy as the outcome. Loesser was a demanding taskmaster with a notoriously short temper. He expected stars and chorus members alike to perform his songs exactly as written, without embellishment. He once wrote, "Singers love to vocalize beyond the sense of a lyric. They're always so sure you want to hear their goddamned tones." He also wanted them to sing loudly, in the days before shows used microphones. Once Loesser interrupted a rehearsal to scream four-letter words at the chorus for saving their voices while they rehearsed a dance number. Then he strode out of the theater, went next door to buy a huge ice-cream cone, and strolled peacefully back to his hotel room. During one tantrum, he actually leaped to the stage and slapped Isabel Bigley (who played Sarah) in the face when she failed to sing the way he wanted her to. Overcome with remorse, he fell to his knees and begged forgiveness. When Feuer recounted the story years later, he said the incident cost Loesser an expensive piece of jewelry, but it was "the only time I ever saw a guy punch a soprano in the nose."

Guys and Dolls ran for 1,200 performances and won the 1951 Tony Award for best musical. It has been revived on Broadway several times, most notably in 1992, with a cast that included Faith Prince as Miss Adelaide and Nathan Lane as Nathan Detroit.

Paramount declined to make a motion-picture adaptation of *Guys and Dolls,* despite the success of the show, because Burrows had been blacklisted in Hollywood. Instead, Samuel Goldwyn produced a movie version in 1955. Despite Loesser's attempts to control the production, Goldwyn insisted on casting Frank Sinatra as Nathan, and two nonsingers, Marlon Brando and Jean Simmons, as Masterson and Sarah. Goldwyn also cut five songs and had Loesser write three new ones for Sinatra, none of them notable. Loesser disliked Sinatra's silky crooning; he believed Nathan's character required a brassy singing style. As gently as he could, he offered to help Sinatra with "Sue Me," to explain what he had in mind when he wrote the song. He said, "Why don't we meet in my bungalow and rehearse it?" Sinatra replied, "If you want to see me, you can come to my dressing room." Loesser walked outside, literally jumped up and down, swore profusely, and then calmed down. When he went to Sinatra's dressing room, he encountered Sinatra's entourage and a loud radio. That led to a blowup between the two men. Sinatra sang the song his way, but the movie is badly miscast and performed with little sense of the material. The two men never spoke again.

Three years earlier, in 1952, Loesser had returned to Hollywood to write his last screen musical, *Hans Christian Andersen.* Less a biography of the nineteenth-century Danish writer than a fairy tale itself, the movie weaves a sentimental story about an innocent cobbler named Andersen who invents fairy tales for the children of his village. He travels to Copenhagen, falls in love with a beautiful ballerina who is already married, and then wanders off again to tell his stories, sadder but wiser for the experience.

Although playwright Moss Hart wrote the final script, there had already been thirty different treatments, and Gary Cooper was originally supposed to play Andersen. When Goldwyn decided to include a ballet sequence because of the success of the dance movie *The Red Shoes* (1948), he cast ballerina Moira Shearer (who starred in *The Red Shoes*) and, to play the role of Andersen, the nonsinging actor James Stewart. Sylvia Fine, a songwriter and the wife of entertainer Danny Kaye, suggested to Goldwyn that he turn the project into a musical starring her husband. Goldwyn agreed and hired Loesser to write the songs. Four of them—"The Inch Worm," "The King's New Clothes," "The Ugly Duckling," and "Thumbelina"—are musical versions of fairy tales. The rest of the score consists of a sprightly waltz, "Wonderful Copenhagen," a "character" song, "I'm

Hans Christian Andersen," and two lighthearted love songs, "Anywhere I Wander" and the contrapuntal duet "No Two People." Although critics panned the screenplay, they praised Loesser's score and Kaye's performance.

After the unhappy experience of turning *Guys and Dolls* into a movie, Loesser spent the rest of his career writing for the theater. For the first time, he was to write both the book and the score, and he also had contractual approval of literally everything–from casting to the number of musicians in the pit band. He based his new show, *The Most Happy Fella,* on Sidney Howard's 1924 play *They Knew What They Wanted.* Although Loesser's adaptation both added and dropped individual characters and entire scenes, the basic story remained unchanged. A wealthy, middle-aged Napa Valley winegrower named Tony Esposito begins a correspondence with Amy (whom he calls "Rosabella"), a pretty young waitress who once served him in a San Francisco restaurant. Deciding that he loves her, he proposes in one of his letters; fearing rejection, he encloses a photograph of his foreman, Joe, a handsome but restless young man. Thus taken in, Amy travels to Napa Valley for the wedding but learns from Joe of Tony's deception. Meanwhile, Tony is involved in an accident on his way to meet her. Amy agrees to go through with the marriage but has a passionate liaison with Joe. As she nurses Tony back to health, however, she finds herself drawn to his warmth and decency and recognizes the love he feels for her. The problem is that she is pregnant with Joe's child. Despite his sister's opposition, Tony overcomes his own hurt and anger to embrace Amy and the unborn child.

Loesser composed great quantities of music for this intensely melodramatic story. The show became huge: twenty speaking parts, a twenty-four-member chorus, and twelve dancers. Loesser also enlarged the usual twenty-six-piece orchestra to thirty-six. But he never called the show an opera. Instead, he insisted, it was an "extended musical . . . with lots of music." *The Most Happy Fella* includes typical Broadway fare, to which Loesser added arias, duets, trios, quartets, choral passages, even recitative. The result was a combination of Broadway musical and grand opera, a rare "Broadway opera" akin to *Porgy and Bess* (1935), *Street Scene* (1947), *Sweeney Todd* (1979), and *Evita* (1979).

When rehearsals began, *The Most Happy Fella* was four hours long, and 90 percent of it was sung. Loesser eventually replaced much of the recitative with dialogue, and he began to cut songs as well. The show was just under three hours long when it opened at the Imperial Theatre on 3 May 1956, and it ran for 676 performances. Columbia Records also

Rudy Vallee and Robert Morse in a scene from Loesser's 1961 musical How to Succeed in Business without Really Trying *(photograph by Friedman-Abeles)*

made it the first Broadway musical recorded in its entirety. In 1992 a revival as a chamber musical using only two pianos moved successfully to Broadway from the Goodspeed Opera House in East Haddam, Connecticut.

The Most Happy Fella was notable for the richness and variety of its score. The recognizable musical comedy elements included two songs aimed at a popular audience far beyond Broadway, "Big D" and "Standing on the Corner," as well as the comic plaint of a waitress at the end of her shift, "Ooh, My Feet." The score also featured "Abbondanza," an exuberant trio sung by Italian chefs and an intense but reflective song of character, "Joey." Tony, originally played by opera star Robert Weede in his Broadway debut, has the most aria-like songs, especially "Rosabella" and "How Beautiful the Days." He and Amy, originally played by Jo Sullivan, have several duets, including "My Heart Is So Full of You," and one of the Broadway theater's finest charm songs, "Happy to Make Your Acquaintance." By the time *The Most Happy Fella* opened, Loesser and Sullivan had fallen in love. He and Lynn divorced in 1957, and he married Sullivan on 29 April 1959. They had two daughters, Hannah and Emily.

With the 1960 musical *Greenwillow* Loesser had his first major flop. Based on B. J. Chute's short novel *Greenwillow* (1956), it presented the whimsical story of a family of quaint characters in a make-believe village in a faraway time. Although the show resembled Alan Jay Lerner and Frederick Loewe's *Brigadoon* (1947), the story had little drama or conflict. The narrative quality of Chute's novel did not lend itself to dialogue, and the conflicts were mainly within characters rather than between them. After struggling to dramatize the story, Loesser added screenwriter Lesser Samuels as co-librettist. The story concerns the Briggs family, whose sons are wanderers, destined to spend their lives abandoning their families to roam the world, returning home only to impregnate their wives. Young Gideon, knowing he will grow up to wander, vows never to marry. By the time he hears his own call to wander, he has fallen in love with Dorrie but refuses to marry her. However, his call leads him back home to a happy ending.

Loesser's libretto also focuses on two ministers who share a single church; one detests winter as a time of "wretched cold and wild storms," and the other loves it for its "hot plum porridge and merry white snowdrifts." Aside from the ministers' contrapuntal duet, "The Sermon," and some other appealing songs, including "Never Will I Marry" and "The Music of Home," *Greenwillow* failed to come together onstage. Complicating the problems were tensions between Loesser and leading man Tony Perkins. *Greenwillow* closed after ninety-five performances.

After an unsuccessful attempt at something entirely make-believe, Loesser felt much more at home in the here and now, especially since the tone of his upcoming show was irreverent and satirical, much closer to his own outlook. It was based on Shepherd Mead's cynical book *How to Succeed in Business without Really Trying: The Dastard's Guide to Fame and Fortune* (1952), about how to rise to the top in the business world. In 1955 Willie Gilbert and Jack Weinstock adapted Mead's book unsuccessfully for the stage and, in 1960, took it to Feuer and Martin. Burrows agreed to write the libretto and direct, and Loesser, after some initial reluctance, signed on to write the score. He was considering writing musical versions of *Time Remembered* (1958), by French playwright Jean Anouilh, or *The Pearl* (1947), by his good friend John Steinbeck. Loesser also would not have total control over the production but would be part of a collaborative team. Nevertheless, he wrote the score quickly.

As J. Pierrepont Finch rides the scaffold to clean windows, he reads Mead's book and follows its recommendations. Thus begins Finch's meteoric rise at World Wide Wickets, presided over by J. B. Biggley. Finch also falls in love with a secretary and eventually wins the day. Every character in *How to Succeed in Business without Really Trying* is unappealing, and all the songs are satiric. Yet, Loesser wrote with his customary eclecticism, and his lyrics demonstrate his keen ear for corporate blather. "A Secretary Is Not a Toy," "The Company Way," and "Coffee Break" lampoon corporate life; the ironic finale, "Brotherhood of Man," is a parody of a revival hymn; and even the apparently tender "Happy to Keep His Dinner Warm" is a parody of the long-suffering corporate wife. The best-known song in the score, "I Believe in You," is an egotistical self-tribute, sung by Finch as he looks in the mirror.

The show made a star of Robert Morse, who played Finch in the original production, and returned crooner Rudy Vallee to national attention. As Biggley, Vallee was perfect onstage and monstrous off. He complained about everything, made constant demands, and refused to submit to Loesser's insistence that he sing "A Secretary Is Not a Toy" exactly as written, rather than crooning it as he would have done thirty years earlier. Loesser literally wanted Feuer to punch Vallee in the nose, and at one point Loesser took all his music and walked out, but the two managed to paper over their differences and get the show on. Vallee never sang the song as Loesser wanted, and the number was never as effective as it should have been.

How to Succeed in Business without Really Trying opened on 14 October 1961, ran for 1,417 performances, and in 1962 won both the Tony Award for best musical and the Pulitzer Prize in drama, only the fourth time a musical had received the prestigious Pulitzer. The show was successfully revived on Broadway in 1995, with Matthew Broderick in the role of Finch.

In 1963 Loesser began work on his next project, *Pleasures and Palaces* (1965), a period piece about John Paul Jones at the court of Catherine the Great of Russia. After taking the show to Detroit for an out-of-town run, Loesser closed it on the road. He then began to adapt a Budd Schulberg short story, "Señor Discretion Himself," in 1965. After two years of unsuccessful struggle, he set the project aside. In the winter of 1969 Loesser's half brother, Arthur, and his old friend Steinbeck both died. Soon after, Loesser was diagnosed with lung cancer. He died on 26 July

1969 and was cremated. He gave instructions that there was to be no death announcement, funeral, or memorial service. His ashes were scattered over Moriches Bay, off the South Shore of Long Island.

Frank Loesser was inducted into the Songwriters Hall of Fame in 1970. In 1999 the United States Postal Service issued a stamp with his likeness.

Biography:

Susan Loesser, *A Most Remarkable Fella: Frank Loesser and the Guys and Dolls in His Life* (New York: Donald I. Fine, 1993).

References:

Lehmann Engel, *Their Words Are Music: The Great Theatre Lyricists and Their Lyrics* (New York: Crown, 1975), pp. 112–127;

Roy Hemming, *The Melody Lingers On: The Great Songwriters and Their Movie Musicals* (New York: Newmarket Press, 1986), pp. 303–305;

Thomas S. Hischak, *Word Crazy: Broadway Lyricists from Cohan to Sondheim* (New York: Praeger, 1991), pp. 113–118;

William G. Hyland, *The Song Is Ended: Songwriters and American Music, 1900–1950* (New York: Oxford University Press, 1995), pp. 130–142;

Alec Wilder, *American Popular Song: The Great Innovators, 1900–1950* (New York: Oxford University Press, 1972), pp. 153–155;

Max Wilk, "*Guys and Dolls:* Frank Loesser," in *They're Playing Our Song: the Truth Behind the Words and Music of Three Generations* (Mt. Kisco, N.Y.: Moyer Bell, 1991), pp. 248–262;

William Zinsser, *Easy To Remember: The Great American Songwriters and Their Songs* (Boston: Godine, 2000), pp. 199–206.

Selected Discography:

Frank Loesser's The Most Happy Fella: The New Broadway Cast Recording, 1992 revival cast, RCAVictor, 09026-61294-2, 1992;

Greenwillow, original Broadway cast (1960), DRG, 19006, ca. 1995;

Guys and Dolls, 1976 Broadway revival cast, Motown, M6-876S1, 1976;

Guys and Dolls: A Musical Fable of Broadway, original Broadway cast, Decca, 9023, 1950;

Guys and Dolls: The New Broadway Cast Recording, 1992 revival cast, RCA Victor, 09026-61317-2, 1992;

Hans Christian Andersen, on *Hans Christian Andersen/The Court Jester,* motion-picture soundtracks, Varèse Sarabande, 5498, 1994;

How to Succeed in Business without Really Trying: The New Broadway Cast Recording, 1995 revival cast, RCA Victor, 09026-68197-2, 1995;

I Hear Music: Capitol Sings Frank Loesser, Capitol, 8 32567 2, 1995;

I Hear Music: Frank Loesser, Pavilion/Flapper, 7830, 1998;

Frank Loesser, *An Evening with Frank Loesser,* DRG, 5169, 1992;

Loesser, *Frank Sings Loesser: Rare and Unreleased Performances,* Koch International Classics, 3-7241-2H1, 1995;

Loesser by Loesser: A Salute to Frank Loesser, DRG, 5170, 1992;

Where's Charley? 1958 London production, EMI/Broadway Angel, 65701, 1993.

Johnny Mercer

(18 November 1909 – 25 June 1976)

Philip Furia
University of North Carolina at Wilmington

SELECTED SONGS FROM THEATRICAL PRODUCTIONS: *The Garrick Gaieties* (1930)–"Out of Breath (And Scared to Death of You)" (music by Everett Miller);

Americana (1932)–"Wouldja for a Big Red Apple" (lyric by Mercer and Miller, music by Henry Souvaine);

Walk with Music (1940), music by Hoagy Carmichael–"The Rumba Jumps";

St. Louis Woman (1946), music by Harold Arlen–"Any Place I Hang My Hat Is Home"; "Come Rain or Come Shine"; "I Wonder What Became of Me";

Texas Li'l Darlin' (1949), music by Robert Emmett Dolan–"The Big Movie Show in the Sky";

Top Banana (1951), music by Mercer–"Top Banana";

Li'l Abner (1956), music by Gene DePaul–"The Country's in the Very Best of Hands"; "If I Had My Druthers"; "Jubilation T. Cornpone";

Saratoga (1959), music by Arlen–"A Game of Poker";

Foxy (1964), music by Dolan–"Bon Vivant"; "Talk to Me, Baby";

Good Companions (1974), music by André Previn–"Good Companions."

SELECTED SONGS FROM MOTION-PICTURE PRODUCTIONS: *To Beat the Band* (1935)– "Eeny, Meeny, Meiny, Mo" (lyric and music by Mercer and Matt Malneck);

Rhythm on the Range (1936)–"I'm an Old Cowhand from the Rio Grande" (music by Mercer);

Ready, Willing and Able (1937), music by Richard A. Whiting–"Too Marvelous for Words";

Cowboy from Brooklyn (1938), music by Whiting–"Ride, Tenderfoot, Ride";

Garden of the Moon (1938), lyrics by Mercer and Al Dubin, music by Harry Warren–"The Girl Friend of the Whirling Dervish";

Going Places (1938), music by Warren–"Jeepers Creepers";

Hard to Get (1938), music by Warren–"You Must Have Been a Beautiful Baby";

Johnny Mercer (ASCAP)

Hollywood Hotel (1938), music by Whiting–"Hooray for Hollywood";

Naughty but Nice (1939), music by Warren–"Hooray for Spinach";

Birth of the Blues (1941)–"The Waiter and the Porter and the Upstairs Maid" (music by Mercer);

Blues in the Night (1941), music by Harold Arlen– "Blues in the Night"; "Says Who? Says You, Says I!"; "This Time the Dream's on Me";

The Fleet's In (1942), music by Victor Schertzinger– "Arthur Murray Taught Me Dancing in a Hurry"; "I Remember You"; "Tangerine";

Star Spangled Rhythm (1942), music by Arlen—"Hit the Road to Dreamland"; "On the Swing Shift"; "That Old Black Magic";

You Were Never Lovelier (1942), music by Jerome Kern—"Dearly Beloved"; "I'm Old Fashioned"; "You Were Never Lovelier";

The Sky's the Limit (1943), music by Arlen—"My Shining Hour"; "One for My Baby (And One More for the Road)";

True to Life (1943), music by Hoagy Carmichael—"The Old Music Master";

Here Come the Waves (1944), music by Arlen—"Ac-cent-tchu-ate the Positive"; "Let's Take the Long Way Home";

Laura (1944)—"Laura" (music by David Raksin);

To Have and Have Not (1944)—"How Little We Know" (music by Carmichael);

Out of This World (1945), music by Arlen—"Out of This World";

The Harvey Girls (1946), music by Warren—"In the Valley (Where the Evenin' Sun Goes Down)"; "On the Atchison, Topeka and the Santa Fe"; "Wait and See";

Here Comes the Groom (1951)—"In the Cool, Cool, Cool of the Evening" (music by Carmichael);

Seven Brides for Seven Brothers (1954), music by Gene DePaul—"Bless Your Beautiful Hide"; "Lonesome Polecat"; "Sobbin' Women"; "Spring, Spring, Spring!"; "When You're in Love";

Daddy Long Legs (1955), music by Mercer—"Sluefoot"; "Something's Gotta Give";

Bernadine (1957)—"Bernadine" (music by Mercer);

Love in the Afternoon (1957)—"Love in the Afternoon" (music by Malneck);

Breakfast at Tiffany's (1961)—"Moon River" (music by Henry Mancini);

Days of Wine and Roses (1962)—"Days of Wine and Roses" (music by Mancini);

Charade (1963)—"Charade" (music by Mancini);

The Americanization of Emily (1964)—"Emily" (music by Johnny Mandel);

The Great Race (1965), music by Mancini—"The Sweetheart Tree";

Darling Lili (1970), music by Mancini—"Whistling Away the Dark."

SELECTED SONGS PUBLISHED INDEPENDENTLY OF THEATRICAL OR MOTION-PICTURE PRODUCTIONS: "Spring Is in My Heart Again" (1932), music by William Woodin; "Lazybones" (1933), music by Hoagy Carmichael; "Fare-Thee-Well to Harlem" (1934), music by Bernard Hanighen; "Here Come the British" (1934), music by Hanighen;

"Pardon My Southern Accent" (1934), music by Matt Malneck; "When a Woman Loves a Man" (1934), music by Hanighen and Gordon Jenkins; "The Dixieland Band" (1935), music by Hanighen; "I'm Building Up to an Awful Let-Down" (1935), music by Fred Astaire; "Goody-Goody" (1936), music by Malneck; "Jamboree Jones" (1936), music by Mercer; "Bob White (Whatcha Gonna Swing Tonight?)" (1937), music by Hanighen; "The Weekend of a Private Secretary" (1938), music by Hanighen; "And the Angels Sing" (1939), music by Ziggy Elman; "Day In—Day Out" (1939), music by Rube Bloom; "I Thought about You" (1939), music by Jimmy Van Heusen; "You Grow Sweeter as the Years Go By" (1939), music by Mercer; "Air-Minded Executive" (1940), music by Hanighen; "Fools Rush In (Where Angels Fear to Tread)" (1940), music by Bloom; "Mister Meadowlark" (1940), music by Walter Donaldson; "On Behalf of the Visiting Firemen" (1940), music by Donaldson; "Skylark" (1941), music by Carmichael; "Mandy Is Two" (1942), music by Fulton McGrath; "Strip Polka" (1942), music by Mercer; "G.I. Jive" (1943), music by Mercer; "Trav'lin' Light" (1943), music by Jimmy Mundy and Trummy Young; "Dream" (1944), music by Mercer; "(Love's Got Me in a) Lazy Mood" (1947), music by Eddie Miller; "Harlem Butterfly" (1948), music by Mercer; "Autumn Leaves" (1950), original French lyric by Jacques Prevert, music by Joseph Kosma; "When the World Was Young" (1950), original French lyric by Angela Vannier, music by M. Philippe-Gerard; "Early Autumn" (1952), music by Ralph Burns and Woody Herman (1949); "Glow Worm" (1952), original lyric by Lilla C. Robinson, music by Paul Lincke (1907); "Song of India" (1953), music by Nicolai Rimsky-Korsakov; "Midnight Sun" (1954), music by Sonny Burke and Lionel Hampton (1947); "Satin Doll" (1958), music by Duke Ellington and Billy Strayhorn (1953); "I Wanna Be Around" (1959), lyric by Mercer and Sadie Vimmerstedt, music by Mercer;

Newlyweds Johnny and Ginger Meehan Mercer on the Atlantic City boardwalk in 1931 (from Bob Bach and Ginger Mercer, Our Huckleberry Friend, *1982)*

"The Bilbao Song" (1961), original German lyric by Bertolt Brecht, music by Kurt Weill (1929);

"Once upon a Summertime" (1962), original French lyric by Eddie Marnay, music by Michel Legrand and Eddie Barclay (1954);

"Summer Wind" (1965), original German lyric by Hans Bradtke, music by Henry Mayer;

"I'm Shadowing You" (1973), music by Blossom Dearie;

"My New Celebrity Is You" (1977), music by Dearie;

"When October Goes" (1984), music by Barry Manilow.

His fellow songwriters freely acknowledged that Johnny Mercer had the greatest range and versatility of them all. Where other lyricists, such as Oscar Hammerstein 2nd, established a long-term partnership with a single collaborator, Mercer wrote with virtually every great popular-song composer of his day. Because the music always came first, Mercer had to adjust his lyrics to his collaborator's musical idiom, from the lush melodies of Henry Mancini ("Moon River," 1961) and the folksy strains of Hoagy Carmichael ("Skylark," 1941) to the blues and jazz of Harold Arlen ("That Old Black

Magic," 1942) and Duke Ellington and Billy Strayhorn ("Satin Doll," 1958). At the height of his career Mercer wrote with Jerome Kern, his boyhood idol. Near the end of Mercer's life Paul McCartney, who idolized him, wanted to collaborate with him.

Mercer was unique in being the only lyricist of his day who was also a successful singer, prefiguring such singer-songwriters as Paul Simon and Bob Dylan. Mercer sang with Benny Goodman's ensemble and other big bands of the swing era and was a radio star on programs such as *Your Hit Parade* (which often featured his own songs, including, on one program, in the fall of 1942, four of the top ten songs of the week). Mercer was also a powerful force in the music-recording business. In 1942 he helped found Capitol Records and, as its first president and chief talent scout, developed such performers as Jo Stafford, Peggy Lee, and Nat King Cole. Because of his creative guidance, Capitol grew into a major recording company that challenged such big, established firms as Decca and Columbia. Despite his success, Mercer felt like a failure because, for all of his hit songs, he never had a major Broadway musical. At the height of his career, when he was not even fifty years old, rock and roll displaced his kind of music.

While older songwriters such as Ira Gershwin and Cole Porter could retire and rest on the laurels of their great Broadway shows, Mercer, until the day he died in 1976, felt washed up.

Yet today, Mercer, whose songs linked the age of Gershwin and Porter with the era of rock, folk, and country, stands as a pivotal figure in twentieth-century music. At a time when most songwriters were New Yorkers, Mercer grew up in Savannah, Georgia, listening to black and country music. His regional roots also gave him an ear for vernacular speech. From "Ac-cent-tchu-ate the Positive" (1944) to "Jeepers Creepers" (1938), he took the American language and made it sing. No one but Mercer would have heard the music in a phrase such as "On the Atchison, Topeka and the Santa Fe" (1946) or in such an ordinary statement as, "It's quarter to three, / There's no one in the place except you and me," the opening lines of "One for My Baby (And One More for the Road)" (1943). Little wonder that Hammerstein called Mercer "the most perfect American lyricist."

When Mercer was six months old, his aunt told him, she hummed a song to him, and he hummed it right back at her. From then on his life was caught up in song. "It was my sun on a dark day," he wrote in the manuscript of his unpublished autobiography, "My solace in time of pain and disappointment, and if not my life my best friend. I know of no joy like it, outside of sex." Most of his childhood memories were of music. "I can hardly remember there not being music," he recalled, "everything from the lullabies, work songs, and spirituals of black servants to minstrel shows, parlor folk songs, and songs from British music halls and Broadway shows played on the family 'graffola.'" Particularly, Mercer remembered songs his father sang to him in front of the fireplace when he was three or four, such as "When You and I Were Young, Maggie" (1909). "A lot of the songs that I have written over the intervening years," he said, "were probably due to those peaceful moments in his arms."

Mercer's father, George A. Mercer, owned a real-estate firm in Savannah, and when his first wife died in childbirth, he married his secretary, Lillian Ciucevich, who gave birth to John Herndon Mercer on 18 November 1909. The combination of his mother's Slavic heritage and the Mercer family's roots that went back to Scottish nobility gave Johnny a richly varied background. It reflected the changes in American society in the early decades of the twentieth century, as immigrants from eastern and southern Europe were disrupting the traditional WASP establishment. Black culture, too, was entering mainstream American life, at first through music, and Johnny felt its influence. He had a black nurse, learned to speak Geechee (the Savannah

Mercer (left) with bandleader Paul Whiteman, who hired him as a singer in the early 1930s (NBC)

version of the Gullah dialect), and loved to sit outside of black churches and listen to the singing.

Mercer entered his teenage years as America plunged into the Roaring Twenties. He got his own car when he was only eleven, and he loved going to dances, particularly in the summer, when local orchestras played in open-air pavilions. He craved the "hottest" jazz and was sometimes so carried away that he would stand in front of the orchestra and play along on an imaginary trumpet. (He was thus a forerunner, he later noted, of the frenetic rock fans of the 1960s.) Friends remembered Mercer's flair for improvising his own lyrics to songs, sometimes on first hearing a tune. He took his first drink at a country-club dance, prompted by a girl who took a drink first, thus initiating his lifelong problem with drinking. He spent his summer nights driving to dances, drinking in the car, and then ending the night at a party playing records. He developed a taste for what were called "race records," made by blues singers such as Bessie Smith, and would regularly go to stores in the black sections of Savannah to buy them.

Mercer was a choirboy at an Episcopal church in Savannah and later sang in the choir while attending

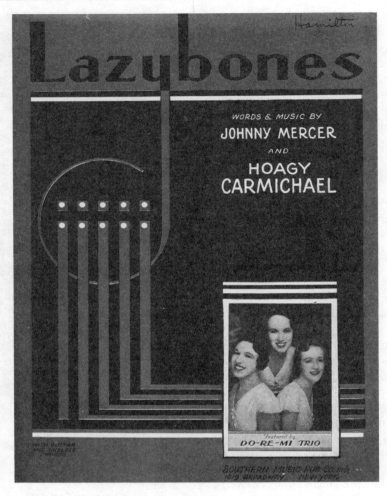

*Sheet music for the 1933 song that became Mercer's first big hit (from Bob Bach
and Ginger Mercer,* Our Huckleberry Friend, *1982)*

Woodbury Forest Preparatory School, a fashionable
school in Orange, Virginia, but he most loved singing
in a quartet with friends. Singing taught Mercer enough
about the craft of songs that he tried writing some of his
own, though he never learned to read music. Smitten
by a girl from New York who was visiting Savannah,
Mercer sang his fledgling effort, "Sister Susie, Strut
Your Stuff," on a double date, accompanied on the ukulele by a friend in the backseat of his Model T Ford.
Mercer's date liked the song, and, as he recalled,
"Songs, such as they were, began to flow from my pen."

Another girl, visiting Savannah from New York
the summer he was eighteen, prompted Mercer's bold-
est adolescent move. Seeing her off on the ship back to
New York, he vowed to visit her. When he heard that
Bing Crosby and the Paul Whiteman Orchestra were
playing in New York at the time, Mercer made good on
his promise. Sneaking aboard another ship as a stowaway, he was caught and put to work, but when they

arrived, he received his first taste of New York. Years
later, he still recalled seeing the skyline at five in the
morning, "a cold wind whipping my gray flannel shirt
as I stood at the railing taking it all in." Though the girl
was so frightened by Mercer's daring that she refused to
see him, his two weeks in New York gave him "another
girl I was really stuck on—New York City."

That trip made Mercer determined to get back to
New York and make it as an actor. He had performed in
plays at school and joined the Savannah Little Theater,
and in 1928 the group made a trip to New York to perform in a drama competition. Encouraged by critical
praise for his performance, Mercer then decided to
remain in the city. The year 1928 was a good one to try
to scale Broadway. At the height of "Coolidge prosperity" more shows opened on Broadway than ever before
or since, and even a youngster from Savannah could
obtain bit parts. After two years in New York, however,
Mercer realized he had little to show "but a three-story

Mercer and composer Richard A. Whiting, with whom he collaborated on movie songs in the late 1930s
(from Bob Bach and Ginger Mercer, Our Huckleberry Friend, *1982)*

walk-up on Jones Street in the Village, with clothes piled in the corner—all dirty—and a stove which let down from a hinge over the bath-tub." There had been long stretches with no acting jobs and nothing to eat but oatmeal. Finally, he began to fear that he was not going to make it as an actor and that the hometown people—one beauty in particular—who believed the "Mercer boy" was thriving would soon find him returning to Savannah with his tail between his legs.

After graduating from Woodbury Forest in 1927, Mercer had been expected to go on to Princeton University and then return home to join the family firm. The short time he had spent working for his father, however, mostly collecting rents in black neighborhoods, soured Mercer on the real-estate business. "Nothing in Savannah was working," he recalled, "No music, no acting, no girls, no future

that I could see, and no fun." What saved him, ironically, was the failure of the company. The mid 1920s were years of unbridled real-estate speculation, and when a huge land-development project collapsed, George Mercer faced the choice of declaring bankruptcy and saving his own investment or trying to repay all the people who had invested with him. With steely Southern honor, he chose the latter course of action, convinced that the boom years of the 1920s would continue and business would pick up again. With the stock-market crash of 1929, his hopes of repaying investors were dashed, but the business failure meant that his son could now continue on his own in New York.

During these years Mercer had continued to write songs, trying to get vaudeville performers to work them into their acts. Talking his way backstage after one

Ruby Keeler and Lee Dixon singing and dancing to Mercer and Whiting's "Too Marvelous for Words" in the 1937 movie Ready, Willing and Able, *choreographed by Busby Berkeley (Warner Bros.)*

show, he rode up in an elevator, surrounded by nearly naked chorus girls, and walked into Eddie Cantor's dressing room to demonstrate one of his comic numbers. Amused at the Southern boy's chutzpah, Cantor gave him a hearing and, although he never used the song, encouraged Mercer to send him more. Mercer kept at songwriting largely, he said, because of that bit of encouragement. One day he showed up at the Theatre Guild in hopes of getting a part in a new revue, the 1930 edition of *The Garrick Gaieties,* but he was told that no more actors were needed—"only songs and pretty girls." He went back to his apartment and set words to a melody a friend, Everett Miller, had given him. Mercer started off with the kind of double, feminine rhymes he admired in W. S. Gilbert and Sir Arthur Sullivan— "When tasks super*human* demand such a*cumen* that only a *few men* possess"—but then veered into the American vernacular: "All you have to do is say 'Boo!'" The song, "Out of Breath (And Scared to Death of You)," got in the revue the next day.

Although he did not abandon his dream of acting, Mercer now turned more of his attention to songwriting. He began hanging around Tin Pan Alley and met some of the great songwriters—Kern, George Gershwin, and Hammerstein, as well as older ones such as Charles Harris, whose 1893 hit "After the Ball" was the first song to sell a million copies of sheet music. These songwriters were amazed that the young Mercer knew the lyrics to all of their songs, even ones that had never become popular. Without trying to ingratiate himself with these elder statesmen, Mercer did just that, and their help began to open doors for him. He obtained a $25-a-week job at Miller Music, and in one of his early songs, "Pardon My Southern Accent" (1934), he reflected on the oddity of a boy from Savannah trying to make it on Tin Pan Alley:

It may sound funny,
Ah, but honey,
I love y'all. . . .

*Mercer with composer Harold Arlen (left) at the Beverly Hills home of George Gershwin
in late 1936 (photograph by George Gershwin; courtesy of the Ira
and Leonore Gershwin Trusts; used by permission)*

While such regionalisms were fine for laughs, for serious love songs Mercer had to strive to emulate the jargon of Tin Pan Alley, avowing in songs such as "Spring Is in My Heart Again" (1932) that "skies are clear" because "you are here." In one early song, "Wouldja for a Big Red Apple" (1932), the linguistic mix ranged from the pomposity of Victor Herbert operettas—"Greater men than I have sought your favor"—to the elegant flippancy of Porter: "you spurn the vermin who offer ermine."

With a steady job, Mercer could get married, but the "beauty" back home in Savannah had given up waiting for him. Heartbroken over news of her marriage, he began dating Ginger Meehan, a dancer he knew from the 1930 *Garrick Gaieties*. A Jewish girl from Brooklyn, Meehan was also being pursued by Crosby, as evidenced by love letters she saved. But Crosby could not match Mercer at words. On the rebound from his first true love, Mercer proposed in several ardent letters, and he and Ginger married on 8 June 1931. Since the Depression continued, the newlyweds moved in with her mother. Ginger took a job sewing

buttons on dresses, and Johnny went to work each day with 25¢: 5¢ for each trip on the subway and 15¢ for a lunch of two hot dogs and an orange drink. Still, with men selling apples on every street corner, the couple felt lucky.

Mercer's first big hit came when a friend put him in touch with Hoagy Carmichael, another songwriter from outside New York. The Indiana-born Carmichael's melody for the 1929 song "Star Dust" was already a jazz standard. He had a much more folksy melody for a tune he called "Snowball," and he patiently waited for months until his new collaborator came up with a lyric that overhauled the title as well. "Lazybones" (1933), which garnered praise from Berlin and Porter, was a refreshing change from the pseudo-regionalism of Tin Pan Alley that had produced "Swanee" (1919) and "Carolina in the Morning" (1922), both by songwriters who had never been south of New Jersey. Mercer's lyric announced its authenticity with lines such as "Long as there is chicken gravy on your rice" and "Lazy bones, sittin' in the shade, / How you 'spec to get your cornmeal made?"

"Lazybones" also gave Mercer's career another turn. He had won an amateur singing contest in 1931, which netted him a radio appearance with the Paul Whiteman Orchestra, and with the success of "Lazybones," Whiteman invited him back as part of the band. There Mercer developed as a songwriter as well as a singer by working with great musicians who went on to become bandleaders on their own—Benny Goodman, Jimmy and Tommy Dorsey, Glenn Miller, and Artie Shaw. Mercer styled his singing after the "jazz" singing of Louis Armstrong and the early Crosby—the only singers at the time who were attuned to what was innovative in jazz, though Mercer despised their "popular" fare such as "I Surrender, Dear" (1931). The drawback of working with Whiteman's band was that Whiteman decided to use the diminutive Mercer with the Texan trombonist Jack Teagarden as a "musical Amos and Andy," with Mercer singing in a comic high voice. The image he projected over the radio as a "cute" black singer dogged him throughout his career, though in the 1940s he found it amusing that a black fraternity voted Mercer its favorite "colored" vocalist.

In 1934 Mercer received what he thought was his big break—a movie contract from RKO that called for him to write songs but also to sing and act in pictures. RKO was a small studio that had been saved from bankruptcy by pairing Fred Astaire with Ginger Rogers. Bringing in such great songwriters as Berlin, Kern, and the Gershwins to supply songs for Astaire and Rogers, RKO musicals had set a new standard for sophisticated stories and elegant songs. Mercer could hardly ask for anything better, and when he arrived in California on the Santa Fe Chief, he was as ecstatic as he had been at his first glimpse of New York:

> It really was a "Rose Room," as you looked at the gardens filled with big cabbage roses and chugged along through the orange groves on either side. Coming into San Bernardino, Monrovia, and Pomona in those days, I'm sure the poor traveler thought that he was really in heaven as he looked out of his train window to see the palms of Arcadia and the green rolling hills filled with orange blossoms and topped by purple mountains with snowy peaks.

Mercer's dreams of triple-threat success as an actor, singer, and songwriter were quickly dashed, however, when his self-conscious screen presence relegated him to roles in B movies. In this period the ugly side of Mercer's character emerged. Outwardly charming and gregarious, he was actually a lonely, insecure, and shy person who, when he drank, would lash out at the people he wanted to please. Knowing his admiration for Helen Hayes, a friend introduced him to the actress at a Hollywood party, only to see Mercer drunkenly insult her.

Still, as a songwriter Mercer thrived in Hollywood. He struck up a friendship with Astaire, and the two collaborated on "I'm Building Up to an Awful Let-Down" (1935), Mercer's first lyric fully in the urbane, casually sophisticated style that Astaire elicited from Porter, the Gershwins, and other songwriters who tailored their songs to his debonair persona: "My one big love affair, is it just a flash? / Will it all go smash? Like the 1929 market crash?" In the telegraphic syntax, the slangy exuberance, and what Bob Bach, in *Our Huckleberry Friend: The Life, Times, and Lyrics of Johnny Mercer* (1982), calls the "nonchalant bravado" of the stock-market simile, Mercer found his own distinctively jazzy version of the colloquial elegance of his lyricist seniors.

Through Ginger the Mercers became friends with Crosby and his family, and Mercer became part of the singer's gang of cronies in Hollywood. Crosby introduced several of Mercer's songs in his movies, such as "I'm an Old Cowhand from the Rio Grande" (1936), in which his deadpan delivery was perfect for Mercer's droll picture of the modern cowboy: "I know ev'ry trail in the Lone Star State, / 'Cause I ride the range in a Ford V-8." At Warner Bros., composer Richard A. Whiting took Mercer under his wing. While Paramount and M-G-M formed the upper echelon of movie studios, Warner Bros. was always known as the gritty, "working-class" studio, and Mercer and Whiting were harangued by studio executives, one of whom threw one of their songs in the trash after the songwriters demonstrated it. Still, the two men clicked and produced "Hooray for Hollywood" (1938), a satirical wink at Tinseltown that has since become its anthem:

> Hooray for Hollywood!
> That screwy bally-hooey Hollywood,
> Where any office boy or young mechanic
> Can be a panic
> With just a good-looking pan. . . .

While the lyric mingles discordant allusions—Tyrone Power, Lassie, Aimee Semple MacPherson, and Donald Duck—with the skill of Porter in one of his "list" songs, it also plays with the very argot of "phony super Coney" Hollywood, "Where you're terrific if you're even good," and people "come from Chilicothes and Paducahs / With their bazookas / To get their names up in lights."

The central figure in Warner Bros. musicals was director-choreographer Busby Berkeley, and Mercer and Whiting were assigned to write a song for one of Berkeley's typically lavish fantasy sequences in the

Sheet music for a 1938 song about the American movie capital
(*from Marion Short,* Hollywood Movie Songs, *1999*)

movie *Ready, Willing and Able* (1937), in which a boy types a love letter on a gigantic typewriter with chorus girls as the types. Inspired by the idea of a song about words, Mercer came up with "Too Marvelous for Words." As Ira Gershwin so frequently did, he made the language of love more his subject than love itself, even alluding to Gershwin's "'S Wonderful" with "that old standby" rhyme of "glamorous" and "amorous":

It's all too wonderful,
I'll never find the words,
That say enough,
Tell enough. . . .

Bedeviled by the language of love songs, Mercer gives vent to his frustrations at having to follow such masters as Lorenz Hart, Gershwin, and Porter. Then, just as he seems to be at the end of his linguistic rope, his own slangy punch comes through: "I mean they just aren't swell enough!" Using another Gershwin (and E. E. Cummings) device, substituting one part of speech for another, Mercer mimes the affected terms of endearment of urbane sophisticates: "You're much too much and just too very very / To ever be in Webster's dictionary." The syntactic play of having adverbs and adjectives modify one another testifies to the paucity not only of spoken but also of the whole written reservoir of words.

Just as it seemed that Whiting and Mercer were poised to become one of the great songwriting teams, Whiting died. At the same time, however, another Warner Bros. team, Al Dubin and Harry Warren, the songwriters for *42nd Street* (1933) and other Berkeley spectaculars, was breaking up over Dubin's alcohol and drug problems. Young Mercer was teamed with

Sheet music for the 1941 song that is one of several standards Mercer wrote with Hoagy Carmichael (Bruccoli Clark Layman Archives)

Warren, and for *Going Places* (1938) they wrote "Jeepers Creepers" (the title inspired by a chance expression of Midwesterner Henry Fonda), the song that brought Mercer his first Academy Award nomination. Mercer wove a lyric out of slang expressions, from the yokelese of "Gosh all git up" to such citified expressions as "How'd they get so lit up?" and "Oh! Those weepers." With everything from an archaic "Woe is me" to the latest slang for spectacles, the lyric is a collage of clashing idioms:

> Golly gee!
> When you turn those heaters on,
> Woe is me!
> Got to put my cheaters on.

Warren's driving melodies provided a perfect setting for turnaround slang phrasing, as Mercer proved in "You Must Have Been a Beautiful Baby" (1938), when he took a remark of his wife, Ginger—"You must have been a beautiful baby"—and followed it with the vernacular comeback "'Cause, baby, look at you now."

Throughout the 1930s Mercer regularly returned to New York to sing with Goodman's group and other big bands of the swing era. He became a popular radio singer on programs such as *Your Hit Parade,* which frequently featured his current hits. Writing lyrics for jazz instrumentals sometimes brought out Mercer's lyrical peccadilloes, such as his penchant for cuteness, as seen in "Goody-Goody" (1936):

> So you think that love's a barrel of dynamite,
> Hooray and hallelujah!
> You had it comin' to ya.

He could also adopt a "poetic" streak, as in "And the Angels Sing" (1939):

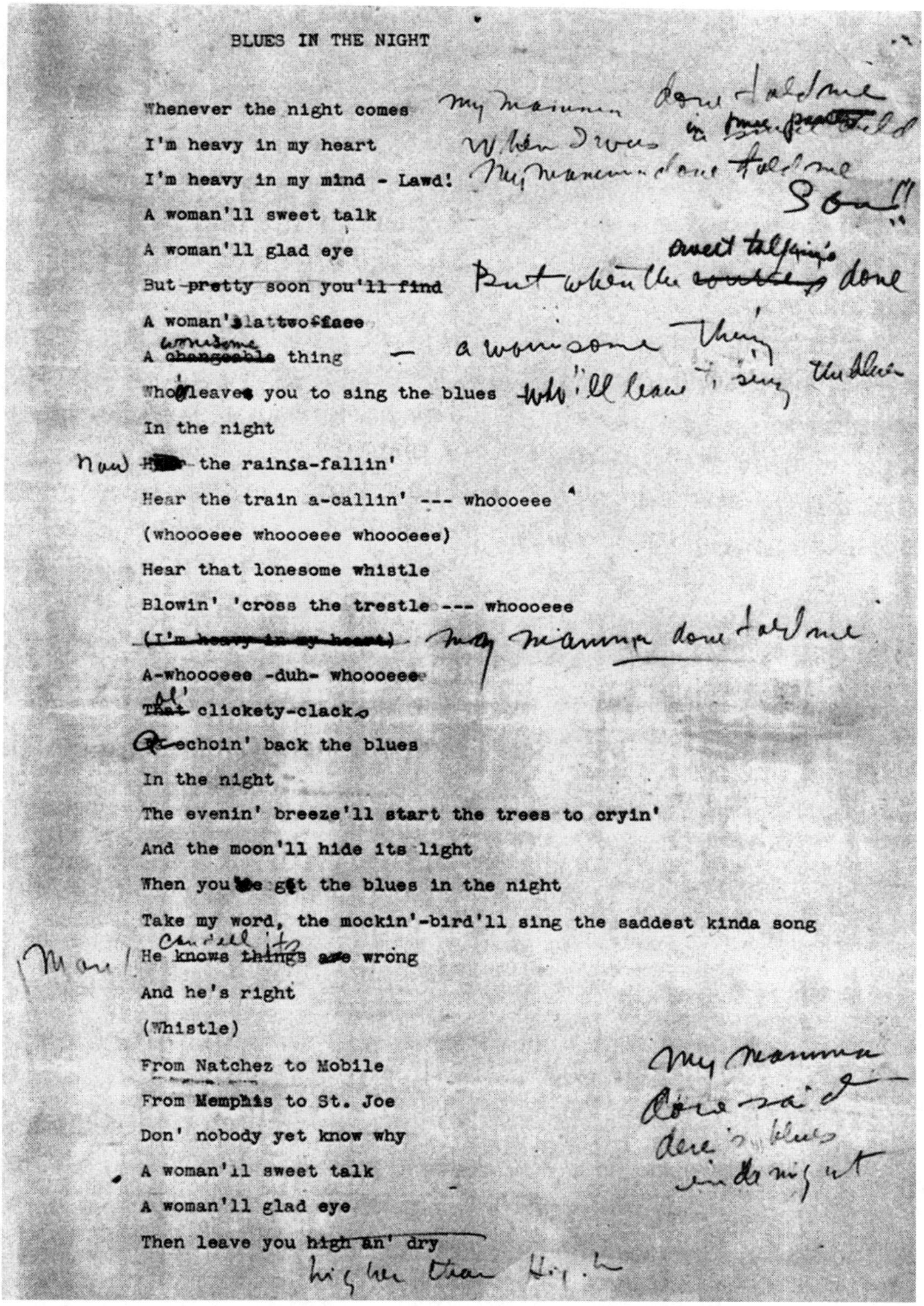

BLUES IN THE NIGHT

Whenever the night comes

I'm heavy in my heart

I'm heavy in my mind - Lawd!

A woman'll sweet talk

A woman'll glad eye

But pretty soon you'll find

A woman'slattwoffaee

A changeable thing

Who leaves you to sing the blues

In the night

Hear the rains a-fallin'

Hear the train a-callin' --- whoooeee

(whoooeee whoooeee whoooeee)

Hear that lonesome whistle

Blowin' 'cross the trestle --- whoooeee

(I'm heavy in my heart)

A-whoooeee -duh- whoooeee

That clickety-clack

echoin' back the blues

In the night

The evenin' breeze'll start the trees to cryin'

And the moon'll hide its light

When you get the blues in the night

Take my word, the mockin'-bird'll sing the saddest kinda song

He knows things are wrong

And he's right

(Whistle)

From Natchez to Mobile

From Memphis to St. Joe

Don' nobody yet know why

A woman'll sweet talk

A woman'll glad eye

Then leave you high an' dry

Mercer's draft of the lyric to his and Arlen's song for a 1941 movie that was to have been titled "Hot Nocturne" but was finally given the same title as the song (Archives Department, Georgia State University)

I can see water and moonlight beaming,
Silver waves that break on some undiscovered shore . . .
Long winter nights with the candles gleaming.

With the right melody, however, Mercer could hit his urbanely earthy stride. Given Rube Bloom's "Day In–Day Out" (1939), Mercer captured the passion of the tune in words by playing with the Porterish paradox of bored excitement. The catchphrase title implies excruciating routine, but Mercer counters it with exotic images of passionate buildup:

Day in–day out,
The same old hoodoo follows me about.
The same old pounding in my heart
Whenever I think of you,
And, darling, I think of you
Day in–and day out.

Given an unusually long refrain and no verse, Mercer skillfully weaves a syntactically driving line of appositions by carrying over phrases—"same old" and "think of you"—from line to line, mirroring the incessant repetition that is the theme of the song.

In the midst of all this success, Mercer's father died on 15 November 1940, a loss he took hard since he had seen his father transformed from a jaunty Southern gentleman into a broken and guilt-ridden man as a result of the losses suffered by people in Savannah when his company failed. When Mercer learned that his father was dying, he put aside his fear of airplanes and took the arduous flight back to Savannah, only to find him already gone. Without telling anyone, Mercer vowed to himself that one day he would repay all of his father's creditors, even though there was no legal obligation to do so.

When he returned to Hollywood, Mercer went into business himself—the record business, which at that time was dominated by three companies: RCA Victor, Columbia, and Decca. Teamed with songwriter and movie producer Buddy DeSylva, who put up the money, and record-store owner Glen Wallichs, who handled manufacturing and distribution, Mercer founded Capitol Records in 1942. Nominally the company president, Mercer was actually the talent scout who decided what songs would be recorded, who would sing them, and how they would be performed. Mercer developed Peggy Lee and Jo Stafford, and he discovered Nat King Cole playing piano in a Hollywood nightclub. In the early years of the company Mercer decided on every song to be recorded, and his artistic standards were high (he refused to record Cole's version of "Mona Lisa" on his label). He also recorded many of his own songs, such as "Strip Polka" (1942, the company's first million-seller),

"Tangerine" (1942), and "Dream" (1944), one of several songs for which Mercer wrote the music as well as the lyric. Capitol was, as he put it, "a modern success story. It was unthinkable to compete with the big, established firms then, but we did, and succeeded, and now everybody does!"

As a lyricist, Mercer was now able to work with the top composers, such as Kern, his boyhood idol, with whom he wrote, fittingly, "I'm Old Fashioned" (1942). But he found his perfect contemporary match in Arlen, whose feel for blues and jazz corresponded with Mercer's vernacular way with words. During the 1940s they collaborated on some of the greatest standards in popular music. The Oscar-nominated "Blues in the Night" (1941) was written for a movie originally to be titled "Hot Nocturne," but the song, sung by a black man in a jail cell, was so good that the producers changed the title of the movie to fit that of the song. Like W. C. Handy's "St. Louis Blues" (1914), "Blues in the Night" opens with a twelve-bar blues phrase, and Mercer follows suit with some equally bluesy repetitions:

My mama done tol' me,
When I was in knee pants,
My mama done tol' me–son. . . .

The abrupt musical drop on "son" gives weight to the maternal voice, and just as repetition informed "Day In–Day Out," here Mercer's strategy of "echoing" runs through the lyric—an echoing that reflects the image of a train: "Ol' clickety-clack's / A-echoin' back / The blues in the night." The singer has been echoing his mother's voice, and when the song returns to the "Now" of the present, nature is resounding as well. The "rain's a-fallin'," echoing the incessant "whooee-duh-whooee" of the train whistle. Even the verbs reverberate: the mother's warning of what a "woman'll" do is echoed by such contractions as "breeze'll start" and "moon'll hide," and the singer declares that the mimicking "mocking bird'll / Sing."

From the blues Mercer and Arlen turned to what might be called the "witchcraft" genre with "That Old Black Magic," an Oscar-nominated 1942 song inspired, Mercer said, by Porter's "Do do that voodoo that you do so well," from "You Do Something to Me" (1929). Arlen's melody is rife with repeated notes and sudden octave drops, and Mercer's phrasing mimes the musical motion with a comfortably familiar "same old tingle that I feel inside." But suddenly, "then that elevator takes its ride," and "down and down" and "'round and 'round" goes the lyric, "like a leaf that's caught in the tide."

Sheet music for the Mercer-Arlen song for a movie about jazz musicians
(Bruccoli Clark Layman Archives)

In "One for My Baby (And One More for the Road)," introduced in the 1943 movie *The Sky's the Limit,* Mercer and Arlen rang their changes upon another pop form, the torch song. Mercer cast the lyric as a dramatic monologue set in a bar between the singer and the bartender. What might have been a lugubrious lament takes a witty turn when the singer drunkenly alludes to a story he never really tells. Despite his protests that "I've gotta lotta things to say" and "You simply gotta listen to me / Until it's talked away," he never really tells the bartender the "little story you oughta know." His not telling that tale, of course, is more moving than any story that he could have told.

Arlen and Mercer's affinities ran deeper than music and words. Both men felt trapped in unhappy marriages. Whereas Arlen stoically resigned himself to misery, Mercer sought to escape and thought that he

had finally found happiness with Judy Garland. He had followed Garland when she was a child star in vaudeville, and he was enchanted with her image of youthful innocence. They had an affair when she was engaged to David Rose, but friends intervened and Garland broke the relationship off and married Rose. By then Mercer was a father. He and Ginger had adopted a daughter, Amanda, and he felt trapped for the rest of his life. Out of that pain came some of Mercer's best songs with Arlen, such as "One for my Baby (And One More for the Road)" and "Blues in the Night."

If the songs of the Gershwins captured the Roaring Twenties and Porter's reflected the Art Deco glitter of the 1930s, then Mercer's songs bring back the 1940s, the era of what has been called "the greatest generation": the wartime humor of "G.I. Jive" (1943); the great age of train travel, evoked in "On the Atchison,

Topeka and the Santa Fe"; and the haunting melody of the title song to the film noir motion picture *Laura* (1944). Mercer saw World War II change American song—and American culture. Ever since the advent of radio, songwriters such as Berlin worried that the medium would destroy the quality of popular songs by creating an insatiable appetite for new hits. They also resented the huge profits radio stations made by playing their songs for a small annual payment to the American Society of Composers, Authors, and Publishers (ASCAP), the songwriters' licensing organization.

In 1941 ASCAP, with Mercer on its executive board, squared off against radio broadcasters over licensing fees and refused to let stations play its members' songs. Radio stations countered by setting up a rival songwriters' organization, Broadcast Music Incorporated (BMI), for which they recruited black and country songwriters who had long been relegated to the fringe of the popular-music industry. With his Savannah roots, Mercer was receptive to these regional styles, and he could even write a countryish song such as "In the Cool, Cool, Cool of the Evening" (1951), which brought him his second Academy Award for best original movie song. Still, he was conscious of a drop-off in the quality of songwriting, as numbers were marketed on gimmicks, such as the cracking whip of "Mule Train" (1949). Any power he had to stem the tide of artistic deterioration was lost in 1952 when Capitol Records was sold by his partners. Mercer had wanted Capitol to remain a small company that turned out only high-quality recordings, and he was appalled at how huge the company had become. He also disliked the crassly commercial practice it had adopted of "covering" hits of other record companies instead of developing its own songs.

The huge profit Mercer made on the sale did, however, help him to make good on his vow to repay his father's debts. Trying to avoid publicity, he sent a Savannah bank a check for $300,000 and instructed it to pay off every investor in full without disclosing his name. (Characteristically, Mercer forgot to sign the check and had to send the bank another one.) Word got out, however, and the media picked up the story of Mercer's display of a kind of honor and integrity that were becoming increasingly rare in postwar America. No one felt that loss more sharply than Mercer. "Little did we dream," he reflected, "what a change the Second World War was to make upon our neighborly, friendly, leisurely America." The transformation was most vivid in southern California, with its smog, freeways, and overcrowding. "I really don't know how we let America get away from us," he lamented, "when just a little discipline and a few

restrictions, inaugurated at the proper time, could have kept it comparatively like it was."

After the war Mercer tried to write for the Broadway stage, and there he experienced his worst professional failures. What should have been his greatest achievement, the production of the 1946 musical *St. Louis Woman,* initially had all the right ingredients. The songs were by Mercer and Arlen, and the book was by the black writers Countee Cullen and Arna Bontemps. Rouben Mamoulian, who had staged *Porgy and Bess* (1935) and *Oklahoma!* (1943), was the director, and Lena Horne was to star. But the NAACP found the characterization of blacks in the musical demeaning (despite the involvement of Cullen and Bontemps). The organization pressured Horne into withdrawing. The NAACP picketed the show, and it closed after only 113 performances, carrying most of Mercer and Arlen's songs—except for one—to oblivion. The surviving song, Mercer's only hit from a Broadway show, was "Come Rain or Come Shine," a phrase he had used in both "Day In—Day Out" and "Dearly Beloved," an Oscar-nominated song that he and Kern had written for *You Were Never Lovelier* (1942). Arlen's music is full of his characteristic repeated notes and octave drops, and Mercer's lyric is equally characteristic, full of driving, mirror-like phrases: "Happy together, unhappy together," "We're in or we're out of the money," and "I'm gonna love you. . . . / You're gonna love me." Despite the success of "Come Rain or Come Shine," the failure of *St. Louis Woman* was a sign that Mercer would never achieve the kind of success he longed for on Broadway.

In part, Mercer was a victim of a major historical shift in the nature of the Broadway musical, ushered in by Rodgers and Hammerstein's *Oklahoma!* Before that landmark show, the emphasis in Broadway musicals had been on good, commercial songs that would go on to become independently popular. Like the great songwriters of the preceding era, such as Berlin and Porter, Mercer thought in terms of the song rather than the show. With *Oklahoma!* however, "integration" between song and story became the watchword on Broadway; songs had to be tailored to characters and advance the story line. Mercer tried Broadway again and again, achieving mild success with *Top Banana* (1951) and *Li'l Abner* (1956), but he was clearly out of place in the musical theater of his day.

Given his personality, Mercer was also temperamentally unsuited for the kind of intensive collaboration that went into a Broadway musical. Even though his was the most collaborative of professions, he was a loner. Other teams of composers and lyricists normally hammered out a song side by side, but Mercer usually waited until his collaborator finished a melody and then

Sheet music for the Mercer-Arlen song that was nominated for
an Academy Award in 1943 (Collection of Paul Talbot)

went off by himself to work on the lyric. "I don't like to get too close to a composer," he said, and one way to avoid such closeness was to work with a variety of collaborators. This method gave his songs the greatest range of any lyricist, but it prevented Mercer from developing the kind of deep, ongoing relationship Rodgers and Hammerstein had, the kind of partnership that was required for a major Broadway musical. Not only composers and lyricists but also librettists, choreographers, directors, and the rest of a company work together as a show is "doctored" through rehearsals. Mercer said that he hated the person he became in the intense artistic tug-of-war that goes into pulling a show together. With his equally characteristic inability to turn people down, he often agreed to write for a show even when his instincts told him that the book was not strong; he then hated himself all the more once he became involved in a doomed project. For all his individual hit songs, Mercer's Broadway flops made him

feel increasingly like a failure—the boy from Savannah who had never truly made it in New York.

Mercer continued to flourish, however, in Hollywood, where songwriters worked much more in isolation. Instead of being a central part of the creative team, as on Broadway, Hollywood songwriters were usually given a script (or sometimes only the outline of a script) and simply told to go off and write songs for certain spots in the story. Given his temperament, Mercer was perfectly at home in the great era of the Hollywood musical in the late 1940s and early 1950s, particularly at M-G-M, where Arthur Freed oversaw production of movie musicals that rivaled the best Broadway shows. Mercer and Warren wrote the songs for *The Harvey Girls* (1946), including "On the Atchison, Topeka and the Santa Fe," for which Mercer earned his first Academy Award. Mercer's songs in *The Harvey Girls* and other movies, such as *Seven Brides for Seven Brothers* (1954), were as "integrated" into the story as those of any

Sheet music for the title song of a 1944 murder-mystery movie
(from Marion Short, Hollywood Movie Songs, *1999)*

Broadway musical. In 1954 Mercer wrote the lyrics and music for the songs in *Daddy Long Legs* (1955). When the production team was stymied over the May-December romance between Astaire and Leslie Caron, Mercer was asked to resolve the situation with a song. What he came up with was "Something's Gotta Give":

When an irresistible force such as you
Meets an old immovable object like me,
You can bet as sure as you live,
Something's gotta give,
Something's gotta give,
Something's gotta give.

The great era of motion-picture musicals ended in the mid 1950s. Faced with competition from television, the big movie studios stopped producing original musicals and turned instead to making movie versions of proven Broadway shows, such as *South Pacific* (1949) or *My Fair Lady* (1956), with only casting changes to distinguish them from the stage originals. The real deathblow

to Mercer's musical world, however, came with the emergence of rock and roll. Elvis Presley and Chuck Berry were the next wave of that influx of black and country music into mainstream popular song that had started in the 1940s. At first Mercer, who was always closer to those musical sources than his older songwriting colleagues, was more welcoming to the new music. He admired songs such as Berry's "School Days" (1957), made an album with Bobby Darin, and encouraged such younger talents as Jimmy Webb, Marvin Hamlisch, and Paul Simon. Mercer even gamely tried writing in the new idiom and had a hit when Pat Boone recorded "Bernadine" (1957). But as melodies became more simplistic and lyrics more inane, Mercer grew despondent. "I can't get a job," he would tell people, "Nobody wants me anymore." Though still in his forties, he would say, "I'm an old man, I'm through, it's over." Most of the other great songwriters, such as Porter and Berlin, were near the end of their careers (and had Broadway successes to look back on) when rock arrived, but Mercer was still at the top of his creative form. Drinking more and more heavily, he would lash out at friends and then send them his trademark apology of roses delivered to their door the next morning. He was particularly vicious to Ginger; at parties he would ad-lib cutting lyrics about her or simply curse at her and pour his drink over her head.

So desperate for work that he would collaborate with practically anybody, Mercer let second-rate composers take advantage of him, and what resulted were inferior songs, leaving him feeling that he was everybody's "lyric boy." As an alternative, he tried setting words to existing jazz instrumentals. Driving down a California freeway one morning in 1954, he heard "Midnight Sun" (1947), by Lionel Hampton and Sonny Burke. Pulling over to a gas station, Mercer called the radio station and asked them to play it again so he could set words to it. As he listened a second time, he came up with his lyric:

Your lips were like a red and ruby chalice,
Warmer than the summer night.
The clouds were like an alabaster palace
Rising to a snowy height.
Each star its own aurora borealis,
Suddenly you held me tight.

In 1958 Mercer worked a much different, but equally poetic, vernacular magic with Duke Ellington and Billy Strayhorn's 1953 instrumental "Satin Doll":

Cigarette holder
Which wigs me.
Over her shoulder
She digs me.
Out cattin',
That satin doll.

The poetic touch lies in the way Mercer weaves the *at* rhyme through "s*at*in," "c*at*tin'," "L*at*in" (in a later line of the song), and that most prosaic term, "th*at*."

In these same years Mercer wrote some of his best lyrics by taking on assignments that many lyricists shunned because it meant diminished royalties—writing English lyrics to successful foreign songs. "Glow Worm" (1907), based on a German melody by Paul Lincke, received a stunning update from Mercer in 1952: "Thou aer-o-nau-tic-al boll weevil, / Il-lu-mi-nate yon woods primeval." Mercer's lyric wittily balances the archaic and the contemporary, as befits such a "modernization" of an old song.

In 1950 Mercer crafted a sparse, imagistic lyric to Joseph Kosma's melody for "Autumn Leaves":

The falling leaves
Drift by the window,

The autumn leaves
Of red and gold.

With the wit of a haiku poet, Mercer reworked a seasonal metaphor—"Since you went away / The days grow long"—to underscore the lover's impression of what are in fact the increasingly shorter days of autumn.

Mercer worked a similar transformation on M. Philippe-Gerard's melody for "When the World Was Young" (1950):

Ah, the apple trees,
Blossoms in the breeze
That we walked among,
Lying in the hay,
Games we used to play,
While the rounds were sung,
When the world was young.

These nostalgic reminiscences of a sophisticated "boulevardier, the toast of Paris," amid "the noise, the talk, the smoke" of a Parisian café, could easily describe the Savannah-born Mercer himself.

Mercer's refusal to accept change, so characteristic of Savannah natives, paralyzed him. He clung to the little house he had bought when he first moved to Hollywood. As his income grew, he had made additions to it rather than move to a bigger one. When the neighborhood grew increasingly commercial and industrial, Mercer spent a year trying to have his house moved to a better part of town. Finally, he had to accept the fact that, after all the additions, it was too flimsy to be moved.

In the 1960s Mercer found new professional life with Henry Mancini. Mancini was primarily a movie-score composer rather than a songwriter, but his background melodies lent themselves to adaptation as individual "theme" songs in dramatic movies. When Mercer set a lyric to Mancini's theme for *Breakfast at Tiffany's* (1961), the result was "Moon River," which won Mercer his third Academy Award for best original movie song. Their title song for *Days of Wine and Roses* (1962), which brought Mercer a fourth Oscar, sent chills through Jack Lemmon when Mercer demonstrated it on a darkened sound stage:

The days of wine and roses
Laugh and run away
Like a child at play.
Through the meadowland
Toward a closing door,
A door marked "Nevermore"
That wasn't there before.

With such colloquial simplicity Mercer takes images from Ernest Dowson's poem "Non sum qualis eram bonae sub regno Cynarae" (1891), from which the title

Sheet music for the only hit song from the 1946 Mercer-Arlen musical (from Bob Bach and Ginger Mercer, Our Huckleberry Friend, *1982)*

phrase was taken, and distills them into sentiments confined by the strictures of the popular song.

Mercer's working relationship with Mancini was as distant as any of his earlier collaborations. He would take the completed melody and go off on his own to work on the lyric. Mancini caught a blast of Mercer's temper when he called one day to see if a lyric were finished. Hollywood gave Mercer and Mancini piecework through the 1960s, but occasional hits could not salve the lyricist's bitterness over the course of American song. Listening to the increasingly raucous and aggressive rock music of the 1970s, Mercer would moan, "I can't write for this generation."

Even though Mercer's own behavior sometimes exemplified the crassness he saw in American culture, with its spreading pollution and violence, he could also embody the gentility and honor that were becoming

things of the past. A niece recalls that when she visited the Mercers as a child, her aunt and uncle spent most of the time screaming at one another and that in later years Mercer made a drunken pass at her in his car. In contrast, a cousin walking with him in New York was surprised when Mercer darted into a church to pray—not to ask something of God, but, as always in his prayers, simply to express thanks.

Only Savannah seemed to Mercer to have resisted the changes that had ruined America after World War II. As the country was torn apart by civil rights and Vietnam War protests, Savannah retained the "sweet indolence" he remembered from his youth. Mercer could be blindly protective of his native city—and the South as a whole. When composer Jule Styne proposed that they collaborate on a musical based on Tennessee Williams's 1951 play

Mercer (right) and composer Henry Mancini, holding their Oscars for "Moon River" from Breakfast at Tiffany's,
*backstage with Debbie Reynolds at the 1961 Academy Awards ceremony (from Bob Bach
and Ginger Mercer,* Our Huckleberry Friend, *1982)*

The Rose Tattoo, Mercer read the script and then hurled it down a staircase at Styne, screaming that writers such as Williams distorted the South with images of decadent sensationalism.

To the end Mercer longed to have one smash Broadway musical, and he was working in London with the young composer André Previn on a show titled *Good Companions* (1974) when he began having headaches, dizzy spells, and blackouts. A lifelong aversion to doctors kept Mercer from seeking medical help, but after he fell off of a London bus and afterward remained unconscious for days, he was forced to return to the United States for a diagnosis. When he learned he had a brain tumor, despite the pleas of Ginger and their friends, he refused to undergo an operation, fearing it would leave him "a vegetable." As spasms sent him reeling and crashing into walls, he finally had no choice but surgery. At this time Mercer learned that Paul McCartney wanted to collaborate with him in what would have been an extraordinary merger of the best of two different songwriting traditions. When doctors operated on Mercer, their discovery confirmed his worst fear—the tumor was so deep it could not be removed. He spent months in his hospital room, so ashamed of his condition that he refused to see anyone but family and a few close friends, such as Astaire. Before Mercer died on 25 June 1976, in a bitter end for one of the world's greatest lyricists, he lost the power of speech.

For all his fears of failure, Johnny Mercer's songs stand firmly in the great American songbook beside those of Porter, Berlin, and the Gershwins. Fresh as ever, they are heard in Broadway revues, movies such as *Midnight in the Garden of Good and Evil* (1997), and even television commercials. So distinctive are his lyrics that people speak of a "Mercer song" as readily as they refer to a "Kern song," a "Gershwin song," or a song by another well-known composer. No other lyricist, usually the forgotten half of a songwriting team, enjoys this distinction. As Frank Sinatra put it, "A Johnny

Mercer song is all the wit you wished you had and all the love you ever lost."

Interviews:

Henry Kane, *How to Write a Song* (New York: Macmillan, 1962), pp. 69–87;

Max Wilk, *They're Playing Our Song: From Jerome Kern to Stephen Sondheim—the Stories behind the Words and Music of Two Generations* (New York: Atheneum, 1973), pp. 134–148.

References:

Bob Bach and Ginger Mercer, eds., *Our Huckleberry Friend: The Life, Times, and Lyrics of Johnny Mercer* (Secaucus, N.J.: Lyle Stuart, 1982);

Philip Furia, *The Poets of Tin Pan Alley: A History of America's Great Lyricists* (New York: Oxford University Press, 1990), pp. 263–282;

Gene Lees, *Singers and the Song II* (New York: Oxford University Press, 1998), pp. 69–89.

Papers:

Johnny Mercer's papers are in the Johnny and Ginger Mercer Archive of the William Russell Pullen Library at Georgia State University, Atlanta.

Selected Discography:

The Belle of New York, on *The Band Wagon; The Belle of New York,* motion-picture soundtracks, Blue Moon, 7011, 1995;

Blues in the Night: The Johnny Mercer Songbook, Verve, 314553 268-2, 1997;

Rosemary Clooney, *Rosemary Clooney Sings the Lyrics of Johnny Mercer,* Concord, 4333, 2000;

Bobby Darin and Johnny Mercer, *Two of a Kind: Bobby Darin and Johnny Mercer,* ATCO, 90484-2, 1990;

An Evening with Johnny Mercer, DRG, 5176, 1977;

Ella Fitzgerald, *The Johnny Mercer Songbook,* Verve, 823 247-2, 1984;

The Good Companions: Original London Cast (1974), DRG, 15020, ca. 1992;

Great American Songwriters, volume 2: Johnny Mercer, Rhino, R2 71504, 1993;

The Harvey Girls: Original Motion Picture Soundtrack, Rhino, R2 72151, 1996;

Johnny Mercer, American Songbook Series, Smithsonian, 048-11, 1993;

Johnny Mercer, Great American Composers, Columbia, C21 8017 / C22 8017, 1991;

The Johnny Mercer Songbook, RCA/BMG, 9788-2-R, 1989;

Li'l Abner: Original Broadway Cast Recording (1956), Sony, 87700, 2002;

Susannah McCorkle, *The Songs of Johnny Mercer,* Inner City, 1101, 1980;

Johnny Mercer, *Johnny Mercer,* Capitol Collector's Series, Capitol, CDP-7 92125 2, 1989;

Mercer, *Johnny Mercer Sings,* CEMA, S21 17505, 1993;

Mercer, *My Huckleberry Friend: Johnny Mercer Sings the Songs of Johnny Mercer,* DRG, 5244, 1974;

Mercer, *Our Huckleberry Friend: Johnny Mercer Sings Blues in the Night and other Great Hits,* Blue Moon, 3041, 1995;

Mostly Mercer, Painted Smiles, 103, 1989;

The Old Music Master, Flapper, 7094, 1996;

Saratoga, original Broadway cast (1959), RCA Victor, 09026 63690-2, 2000;

Seven Brides for Seven Brothers: Original Motion Picture Soundtrack (1954), Rhino, R2 71966, 1996;

Frank Sinatra, *Frank Sinatra Sings the Select Johnny Mercer,* Capitol, CDP 0777 7 80326 2 5, 1995;

The Stars Salute Johnny Mercer, Charly, 1238, 1995;

St. Louis Woman, 1998 revival cast, Mercury, 314 538 148-2, 1998;

St. Louis Woman: Original Broadway Cast Recording (1946), Angel, ZDM 764662 24, 1992;

Sylvia Syms, *A Jazz Portrait of Johnny Mercer,* DRG, 91433, 1995;

Too Marvelous for Words: Capitol Sings Johnny Mercer, Capitol, CDP 7 96791 2, 1991;

Top Banana, original Broadway cast (1951), Angel, ZDM 0777 7 64772 2 0, 1993;

Marlene VerPlanck, *Marlene VerPlanck Loves Johnny Mercer,* Audiophile, 138, 1988;

Margaret Whiting, *Too Marvelous for Words,* Audiophile, 152, 1995;

Nancy Wilson, *With My Lover beside Me: Music by Barry Manilow, Lyrics by Johnny Mercer,* Columbia, CK 48665, 1991.

Mitchell Parish

(10 July 1900 – 31 March 1993)

Tony L. Hill
University of Minnesota

SELECTED SONGS FROM THEATRICAL PRO-
DUCTIONS: *Blackbirds of 1933* (1933)–"Christ-
mas Night in Harlem" (music by Raymond
Scott);
Continental Varieties (1934)–"Hands across the Table"
(music by Jean Delettre).

SELECTED SONG FROM MOTION-PICTURE
PRODUCTION: *Ruby Gentry* (1953)–"Ruby"
(music by Heinz Roemheld).

SELECTED SONGS PUBLISHED INDEPEN-
DENTLY OF THEATRICAL OR MOTION-
PICTURE PRODUCTIONS: "Where the Jack
O'Lanterns Glow" (1920), music by Neuman
Fier;
"Carolina Rolling Stone" (1921), music by Harry
Squires and Eleanor Young;
"Sweet Lorraine" (1928), music by Cliff Burwell;
"Star Dust" (1929), music by Hoagy Carmichael;
"Mood Indigo" (1931), music by Duke Ellington and
Barney Bigard;
"Corrine, Corrina" (1932), original lyric and music by
J. Mayo Williams and Bo Chatman;
"Take Me in Your Arms" (1932), original lyric and
music by Fritz Rotter and Alfred Markush;
"Sophisticated Lady" (1933), lyric by Parish and Irving
Mills, music by Ellington;
"One Morning in May" (1933), music by Carmichael;
"Stars Fell on Alabama" (1934), music by Frank Per-
kins;
"Does Your Heart Beat for Me?" (1936), music by
Arnold Johnson;
"Don't Be That Way" (1938), music by Edgar Samp-
son;
"Moonlight Serenade" (1939), music by Glenn Miller;
"Stairway to the Stars" (1939), music by Matt Malneck
and Frank Signorelli;
"The Lamp Is Low" (1939), music by Peter De Rose
and Bert Shefter, based on Maurice Ravel's
Pavanne pour une Infante Défunte;

Mitchell Parish (Collection of Tony L. Hill)

"Deep Purple" (1939), music by De Rose;
"Lilacs in the Rain" (1939), music by De Rose;
"Mademoiselle de Paris" (1948), music by Paul
Durand;
"The Blue Skirt Waltz" (1948), music by Vaclav Blaha;
"Serenata" (1950), music by Leroy Anderson;
"Sleigh Ride" (1950), music by Anderson;
"The Syncopated Clock" (1950), music by Anderson;
"Tzena, Tzena, Tzena" (1950), music by Issachar Miron
and Julius Grossman;
"All My Love" (1950), music by Durand, based on
Ravel's *Bolero;*

"Belle of the Ball" (1951), music by Anderson;
"Blue Tango" (1952), music by Anderson;
"Dream, Dream, Dream" (1954), music by Jimmy McHugh;
"Forgotten Dreams" (1954), music by Anderson;
"Moonlight Love" (1956), music by Claude Debussy;
"Volaré" (1958), music by Domenico Modugno.

BOOK: *For Those in Love* (New York: Richmond Organization, 1965).

OTHER: "Writing the Song Lyric," in *How to Write for Pleasure and Profit*, edited by Warren Bower (Philadelphia: Lippincott, 1951), pp. 303–311.

Mitchell Parish achieved fame as one of the most talented and versatile writers of popular song lyrics. His career is singular for four things. First, he wrote the words to "Star Dust" (1929), supposedly the most recorded song in history, the title of which is synonymous with the word *standard*. Second, he achieved his success without being a show writer; with the exception of an occasional song added to a stage show and several movies near the end of his career, Parish's entire output consists of straight popular songs, or what a theater-minded musicologist would call independent songs. Third, many of his lyrics consist of what can be called adaptations. Many of these adaptations are English lyrics to songs that had already been published in other languages. Many others were lyrics that were newly added to instrumental pieces that already had some popularity in that format ("Star Dust" and "Deep Purple" [1939]–Parish's two biggest successes–both fall into that category). Finally, Parish wrote continuously for almost forty years–compiling a catalogue of more than six hundred songs–without ever developing a regular collaborative relationship with a composer.

Michael Hyman Peretz was born in Lithuania on 10 July 1900 to Meyer and Rose Peretz. The family immigrated to the United States and settled in Louisiana when Michael, then the only child, was seven months old. (A brother and two sisters were born in the United States.) It is not known exactly when the family name became *Parish*–the whole family, even Meyer's brothers, took the name. Some speculate the parishes of Louisiana were the inspiration. The family relocated to the Lower East Side of Manhattan, where an uncle owned a dry-goods store, when Michael was three years old. Parish grew up in relative poverty. His father got a job washing the windows in skyscrapers in the days when the job meant walking out on the ledge without so much as a rope.

When he was old enough, Parish got a job hawking newspapers–the *Jewish Daily Forward* and the *New York Journal*. He attended the High School of Commerce on a five-dollar-a-week scholarship granted by the Henry Street Settlement. He took an early interest in poetry and claimed Algernon Swinburne, Percy Bysshe Shelley, and Lord Byron as his favorites. He dabbled in the light verse of his age and wrote poems and short stories. While these early literary efforts might seem a natural path to songwriting, Parish nevertheless was determined to become a doctor and enrolled at Columbia University. Although his off-campus job as a hospital aid fit into his medical ambition, his hobby of writing for the campus magazine foreshadowed his future as a lyricist, and the two came together through a neat set of circumstances. His entrée to songwriting came when some amateur songs he had written for a benefit show at the hospital turned up in the hands of music publishing baron Irving Mills. Mills was impressed with the young man's work and offered him a job as a staff writer and song plugger. The twelve-dollar-a-week offer was apparently sufficiently lucrative that Parish immediately dropped out of Columbia and permanently forsook his goal of practicing medicine. (He later reported having bought a flashy vest with some of his first earnings as a badge of how proud he was to be in show business.) He also changed his first name to Mitchell at the behest of his new employer.

Despite his auspicious discovery by Mills, Parish did not achieve success immediately. His first published song, copyrighted on 2 January 1920, was "Where the Jack O'Lanterns Glow," with music by Neuman Fier. "Carolina Rolling Stone" (1921), with music by Harry Squires and his wife, Eleanor Young, attracted some attention in 1922 but was not a major hit. Also in 1922 Parish married Molly Lillienfeld, an Austrian native. The pair stayed together until her death on 18 October 1979. They had three children: twin daughters Ruth (who was known as Ricky from a young age) and Helen, born in 1924, although Helen lived only a few months, a tragedy her parents never overcame; and a son, Lawrence, born in 1930.

Parish's primary function at Mills's company was not songwriting but writing for vaudeville–a task more akin to writing stand-up comedy than anything resembling elegant song lyrics. His first real hit came in 1928–after nine years in the Mills firm–when he set the lyric "Sweet Lorraine" to a melody by Cliff Burwell. Years later, when asked to provide the story behind this song, Parish described its inspiration as a girl he had known on the Lower East Side named Sadie Moscovitz. (Parish was also known to denigrate the notion that songwriters needed "inspiration," telling an interviewer in 1991 "the only time a songwriter gets up in the middle of the night is to go to the bathroom.")

Sheet music for Parish's first hit, published in 1928
(Bruccoli Clark Layman Archives)

Mills owned an instrumental piece by Hoagy Carmichael called "Star Dust," which had been introduced in 1927 by Don Redman and his orchestra without notable success. The tune had already undergone some overhauling; arranger Jimmy Dale had persuaded Carmichael to slow the piece down to showcase the broad melody. A new recording by Emil Seidel and his orchestra, with the composer at the piano, had spurred Mills's interest in vocalizing the piece. The firm sought to exploit the greater commercial potential "Star Dust" would have as a popular song and called upon Parish to do the job. "Star Dust" is an exceedingly complex melody—its verse is nearly as outstanding melodically as its chorus—and Parish had to deal with the obvious drawback that the piece already had a title that somehow had to be incorporated into the lyric. As has often been pointed out, the lyric uses the title only once, and even then not in a prominent part of the melody:

Sometimes I wonder why I spend the lonely night
Dreaming of a song,
The melody haunts my reverie,
And I am once again with you,
When our love was new
And each kiss an inspiration,
But that was long ago,
Now my consolation is in the star dust of a song.

Parish did a masterful job, wedding poetic lyrics to a soaring melody. "I had a gut feeling it was something special," he said later.

Published in 1929, "Star Dust" was initially a hit in a recording by Mills himself. The song took off in 1931, when it was number one on the music charts in a recording by Isham Jones and his orchestra. Other hit versions that year were recorded by Bing Crosby, Louis Armstrong, Wayne King, and Lee Sims. Despite all of this initial attention, "Star Dust" did not become a

Sheet music for one of the most-recorded songs in history. Parish added lyrics to the instrumental in 1929
(from William Zinsser, Easy to Remember, *2000).*

standard until the era of the great swing bands. Like Irving Berlin's "Marie"–largely unknown since it was first heard in the 1928 silent movie *The Awakening* but transformed into a hit by Tommy Dorsey and Jack Leonard nearly a decade later–"Star Dust" was largely forgotten until Jimmie Lunceford made it a hit again in 1935. Big-band greats Benny Goodman and Dorsey recorded it the next year, and someone at Victor Records had the idea to put the two versions on the same 78 RPM record–a sure sign that they did not think either version would be particularly successful. Sammy Kaye had a modest hit with the number in 1939, but "Star Dust" was perhaps established as one of the great standards when Artie Shaw and his orchestra released their landmark recording on Victor in 1941, a success that inspired "cover" recordings by Dorsey (with a young singer named Frank Sinatra) and Glenn Miller that same year.

There was also renewed interest in Crosby's 1931 recording. Relatively few solo male vocalists–as opposed to those singing with bands–have done the song over the years, perhaps because of Crosby's outstanding recording. Recording "Star Dust" while Crosby's versions–he cut it more than once–were keen in the ears of musicians and listeners would have required an intrepid singer, since such a recording would obviously invite comparisons to the great crooner. When Sinatra recorded it as a solo performer in 1962–the time in his career when he was close to overtaking Crosby as the greatest vocalist of the twentieth century–even he did not enter Crosby's domain, choosing instead to record merely the verse. "Star Dust" may be the only popular song in history that has had its verse recorded by itself.

The dearth of purely vocal versions is part of the reason Parish's contribution to the song has been under-

Sheet music for a 1934 hit song by Parish and Frank Perkins (Bagaduce Music Lending Library)

valued; the composer's name comes to the mind of many more music fans than that of the lyricist. Carmichael was a performer as well as a composer and thus gained added prominence. Carmichael developed his own mythology about the song, claiming he wrote it on a return visit to Indiana University, his alma mater, when he recalled a lost love. Perhaps this anecdote led Parish to choose a melancholy feeling about young love as the lyrical theme for the song; in any event, it was a theme he returned to many times over the years. Oscar Hammerstein 2nd once analyzed the enduring appeal of the song in a letter to Parish, saying it "rambles and roars like a truant schoolboy in a meadow. Its structure is loose, its pattern complex. It has repose and wistfulness. It is something special all by itself. What has it got? I'm not certain. I know only that it is beautiful and I like to hear it."

Around the time Parish created "Star Dust," he was felled by an episode of blood poisoning stemming from a heel infection. "I was quite small at the time," his daughter

Ricky recalled. "He was laid up in bed, so Duke Ellington and Cab Calloway came to the house to work with him. I remember answering the door and there was this huge black man standing in the hall." Parish's next hit after "Star Dust" was "Mood Indigo" (1931), but few people are aware that Parish is the lyricist of the song, since the lyric credit went to Mills. Toward the end of his life, Parish told Ricky Goldstein that he was rueful but no longer bitter about losing the song. "My father didn't dwell on his past problems," Lawrence Parish said, "and he often said 'If I'd stood up to them, maybe I wouldn't be [in this business] now.'" This instance was the only one in which Parish was denied a songwriting credit. Two years later he wrote the lyric for another of Ellington's greatest hits, "Sophisticated Lady," and got most–but not all–of the credit.

Parish's next important song was the 1932 reworking of "Corrine, Corrina," a song that had greater success in the burgeoning country-and-western field. That same year he had his first of many successes with an import song, writing a new lyric for a German song by Fritz Rotter and Alfred Markush called "Liebe War Es Nie." Parish rewrote it as "Take Me in Your Arms." (His lyric includes a reference to "Star Dust": the singer urges her lover to use "all the star dust in the sky" to woo her.) The following year Parish had his biggest hit in the jazz field. There was not much emphasis on lyric writing in the early days of jazz, as might be expected from an area of music in which improvisation was the key. As jazz became more commercial, publishers sought to develop a product that could transfer from the originating jazz band to popular singers. After all, the jazz band was only recorded on a single label, and the goal in song plugging had always been to get each of the recording companies to come out with a version of the hit song—perhaps more than one version. With the help of Mills, the Ellington band originated more standards than any of the other jazz bands, an accomplishment stemming in no small part from the Mills organization's ability to expand the boundaries of the music beyond the narrow audience the bands were reaching in those days.

Mills turned Ellington's "Sophisticated Lady" over to Parish. The lyric he created is one of the most evocative to come out of any jazz band. The opening of the chorus is arresting—Parish sets up a story of a woman who was swept up in the Jazz Age, and Ellington rouses the listener's attention with his broad chromatic sweep. Although inversion of word order is a tool many berate, Parish's inversions in "Sophisticated Lady"—such as "in this heart of yours burned a flame"—slink up on the listener without being jarring to the ear (as is Cole Porter's "so easy to idolize all others above" in his 1936 "Easy to Love"). At the bridge of the song Parish's lyric enumerates the lady's bad habits, which effectively evokes a specific image of her and her surroundings:

Smoking, drinking, never thinking of tomorrow,
Diamonds shining, dancing, dining
With some man in a restaurant,
Is that all you really want?

"He was always proud that he had come up with a rhyme for 'restaurant,'" his son Lawrence said with a laugh.

Since the success of "Sweet Lorraine," Parish had repeatedly demonstrated his skill at writing lyrics to already-existing melodies. Essentially, Parish was assigned by his superiors to write specific songs at the publishing house. While most writers had to adapt to this way of working early in their careers, in the days when much of American musical output was written by staff writers at publishing houses, few of these in-house

compositions became standards; nothing, for example, that Berlin wrote when he was first on Ted Snyder's payroll is still remembered. Despite the enormous egos many creative people amass as a result of their success, Parish reportedly did not become overly defensive when Mills demanded changes in his lyrics, although he usually did not give in without arguing for his original. Songwriter Ervin Drake, a friend of Parish's, recalled that "He respected his publishers in terms of that they were the boss. If there was something they wanted, he produced it. It was as simple as that."

By the time Parish was still taking on assignments at Mills in the early 1930s, most of his contemporaries—many with far less skill at weaving words with music—were working as freelance songwriters, moving with ease from project to project and hawking their independent songs to various publishers. Many experienced songwriters reject the opportunity to write English lyrics to foreign songs out of hand, even though the song may already be a hit abroad and thus may have more ready-made potential to be successful than an original song, because the majority of the royalties goes to the original lyricist. For Parish, however, such an assignment was also a philological challenge, since he was conversant in several languages. He found the conditions of the 1930s worse than he had experienced in the poverty of his Lower East Side childhood and took solace within the walls of the New York Public Library. (This venue was not a new one for the lyricist, because as a teen he had often walked from the Lower East Side to the main library at 42nd Street and Fifth Avenue.) He believed that people in show business faced less misery than many. Years later he joked that songwriters were not likely to jump from their windows because they probably lived in the basement apartment and were apt to land on their feet.

As the Depression dragged on, Parish was unable to live on his songwriting income alone, and in 1935 he took a job as a bailiff in the New York City Court of Special Sessions, traveling from borough to borough with the panel of judges, swearing in witnesses. Technically, his title was that of plainclothes patrolman with the New York Police Department. Undoubtedly, the meticulous and erudite Parish had more in common with the judges he served than the litigants who came to court. This job went on for ten years, spanning a period when "Star Dust" was becoming nearly omnipresent and Parish's other songs grew more popular as well. When asked why he needed the second job, Parish replied, "I don't trust the music business." The courtroom job underscored Parish's no-nonsense approach to life. Dick Dorrance, in "America Sings His Songs," wrote, "He lives without dash, without flourish." Ricky Parish noted, "He kept us out of the theatri-

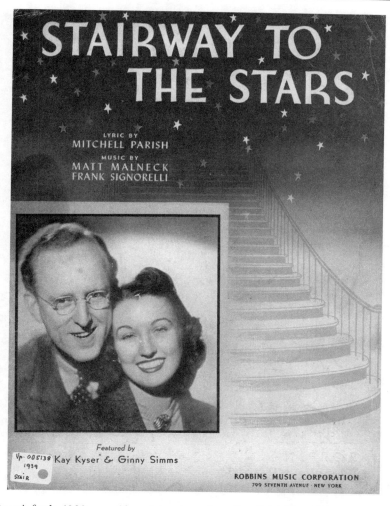

Sheet music for the 1939 song with music based on a theme from Frank Signorelli's instrumental suite
Park Avenue Fantasy (1935) (Bagaduce Music Lending Library)

cal part of his life. He wanted a more cultural life for us. He took us to the ballet, the Philharmonic, sent us to private schools. He wanted his children to be well educated. He didn't have a department store to leave us, so we had to be prepared to make our own way."

Despite his comfort with writing adaptations, beginning in 1933 Parish had a short string of hits that were original songs: "One Morning in May" (1933), "Stars Fell on Alabama" (1934), and "Does Your Heart Beat for Me?" (1936) were all big hits in the mid 1930s, although "Stars Fell on Alabama"–another Parish lyric reminiscent of "Star Dust"–is the only true standard of the group. Parish felt "Does Your Heart Beat for Me?" did not fare as well as it deserved because its adoption by Russ Morgan as his orchestra's theme song dissuaded other bands from playing it lest they seem to be plugging their competitor. Also in 1933, Parish, a fifteen-year veteran of the business, wrote his first lyric for the stage; "Christmas Night in Harlem" was featured in

Blackbirds of 1933. The only song that he wrote for the stage that has endured is "Hands across the Table," introduced in the 1934 revue *Continental Varieties*. This song is another of Parish's adaptations, its music having been composed by the French composer Jean Delettre.

With the boom in swing music in the period from 1935 to 1937, some of Parish's older songs were enjoying a renaissance, especially "Star Dust" and "Sweet Lorraine." The latter song, according to some accounts, was important to Nat King Cole's career as a vocalist. The King Cole Trio performed an instrumental version of the song, and a drunken customer demanded that Cole sing the lyric. Cole acquiesced; from then on audiences demanded that his singing be the centerpiece of his performances, and the trio was eventually phased out. Meanwhile, in 1938 the up-and-coming bandleader Benny Goodman persuaded Parish to write a lyric to an instrumental that Edgar Sampson had composed a few years earlier, "Don't Be That Way." The tune

Sheet music for the 1939 song that was, after "Star Dust," Parish's biggest success
(Bagaduce Music Lending Library)

became one of Goodman's signature pieces and proved that Parish, who had been reluctant to put his name on swing music when he first heard a swing version of "Star Dust," had now accepted the new style. Parish's next big hit turned out to be one of the defining songs of the swing era, Glenn Miller's "Moonlight Serenade" (1939), which became the bandleader's theme song. Although the best-known recording is Miller's instrumental version, many people know the words, which are among Parish's most poignant.

In 1939 Parish collaborated with Peter De Rose. De Rose had written some piano music in 1934 that was not aimed at the popular market, but he sat down with Parish to see if his jazz-oriented music could be popularized. De Rose sought to have one particular melody made into a song, but Parish demurred and wanted to write a lyric to the countermelody instead. The resulting song, "Deep Purple," is replete with references to "Star Dust," even referring to "garden walls."

"Deep Purple" has seen many revivals over the years. Parish also gave what De Rose intended as the main melody another chance, and he wrote a lyric for it called "Lilacs in the Rain." The song was a popular hit and has been featured by jazz musicians over the years, but it did not become a standard on the scale of its original countermelody. Parish provided a lyric for another highbrow jazz piece that year, a theme from Frank Signorelli's *Park Avenue Fantasy* (1935). Matt Malneck adapted the music, and, with Parish's words, the theme became the song "Stairway to the Stars." Parish hypothesized over the years that he came up with so many lyrics alluding to stars because he could not see them from the Lower East Side growing up.

One of the big trends in popular music starting around 1939 was writing songs based on classical melodies. Although popular songs have long derived from the classics, a surprisingly large number of them were written in the period from 1939 to 1945. Among the classical adaptations that became standards are "Tonight We Love" (1941), with lyric by Bobby Worth and music by Freddy Martin and Ray Austin, based on Pyotr Ilich Tchaikovsky's Piano Concerto no. 1 in B-flat Minor; "The Story of a Starry Night" (1942), adapted by Jerry Livingston, Al Hoffman, and Mann Curtis from Tchaikovsky's *Pathétique* Symphony in B Minor; "Till the End of Time" (1945), adapted by Ted Mossman and Buddy Kaye from Frédéric Chopin's Polonaise no. 6 in A-flat Major; "My Reverie" (1938), adapted by Larry Clinton from Claude Debussy's "Reverie"; "The Things I Love" (1941), adapted by Harold Barlow and Lew Harris from Tchaikovsky's Melody op. 43, no. 3; and "Full Moon and Empty Arms" (1946), Kaye and Mossman's adaptation of Sergey Rachmaninoff's Piano Concerto no. 2. There was even a song parodying the whole fad, Les Brown's "Everybody's Making Money But Tchaikovsky" (1941). Parish's contribution to the genre was "The Lamp Is Low" (1939), based on Maurice Ravel's *Pavane pour une Infante Défunte* (Pavane for a Dead Princess). In 1956 he adapted Debussy's *Clair De Lune* as "Moonlight Love."

Parish was an active sonneteer for most of his life. He struck up a close friendship with Walter Winchell, who published Parish's sonnets in his nationally syndicated column from time to time. In 1965 a volume of these sonnets, *For Those in Love,* was published. Parish's friend and fellow songwriter Vic Mizzy remarked that "Mitch was a real poet. There were only two genuine poets on Tin Pan Alley, Johnny Burke and Mitchell Parish."

Although Parish continued to be active as a songwriter and continued to have modest hits into the 1940s, it was nearly a decade before another of his songs became a standard. During the buildup to World War II, Parish considered becoming an officer in the army. He spent much of the summer of 1941 at Camp Drum with the Civilian Military Training Corps, which did not train men to fight overseas but to run the United States in the event of an enemy invasion. After training, however, Parish decided not to enlist. "He was too much of a perfectionist to be in the Army," his son notes. "If he had gone, we'd still be fighting World War II today because there would have been something about it that didn't end right."

After World War II, Parish picked up from where he had been at the end of World War I: he went back to college, enrolling at New York University. "There isn't much done in Tin Pan Alley until noon anyhow," he noted. At age forty-eight he was elected to Phi Beta Kappa, and at age fifty he graduated summa cum laude in literature and history. Parish had always been an avid reader; his apartment was filled with thousands of books. As a young man, the intellectual Parish had been an amateur prizefighter, and in reading he developed strong opinions on a range of subjects. "If he

took exception to something, he was ready with a fist," noted Drake. The Parishes lived variously in the Bronx, White Plains, and New Rochelle, but they returned to the city, where Parish lived his last years on the fourth floor at 400 East 56th Street. One of his close friends was composer Sammy Fain. "When Sammy's son was born," their mutual friend Edward Cramer explains, "Mitch told him to name the kid Farfel. That's a kind of egg barley used in Eastern European cooking. Sammy couldn't believe it. But Mitch said 'You're music. I know about how words sound. Trust me, Farfel Fain, it's a great sounding name.'" (Fain named his son Frank.)

In 1948 Parish wrote an English lyric to a song by French composer Paul Durand called "Mademoiselle de Paris," and this light and lilting ballad became the theme song for chanteuse Jacqueline François. Parish later said that images of Paris at the turn of the century were among his favorite scenes. In 1948 he also wrote the English words to a Czech song by Vaclav Blaha, "The Blue Skirt Waltz." In 1950 Parish began the closest thing he had to long-term collaboration, writing words to the music of Leroy Anderson. Anderson was known for sound-effect-based compositions such as "The Syncopated Clock" rather than popular songs, but Parish helped him expand his audience by adding words to his melodies. Of the many Anderson-Parish songs, only one is as well known for its words as its music: "Sleigh Ride" (1950). Some of the others are "Serenata" (1950), "Belle of the Ball" (1951), and "Forgotten Dreams" (1954). One of the problems Parish faced popularizing these lyrics was that the leading proponent of Anderson's music was Arthur Fiedler of the Boston Pops Orchestra, an ensemble that did not include vocalists. "He was always very proud of 'Sleigh Ride,'" said Stanley Mills, son of Jack. "That's a very difficult melody line, and Mitch thought his lyric was one of his better works. He took a lot of satisfaction as that song became a standard, being recorded by people like Johnny Mathis."

Besides the Anderson collaborations, Parish pursued other fruitful projects in the early 1950s. One of his memorable hits during this period–because of its title, if nothing else–was "Tzena, Tzena, Tzena" (1950), which Parish had the opportunity to write only because of another lyricist's inadvertent copyright problem. The song was the first international hit to come out of the new nation of Israel. Gordon Jenkins wrote an English lyric for the song, but it turned out the composer had already sold the American rights to Mills. Jenkins's version was pulled from the market, and Parish's became a modest hit. He also wrote his only hit to come out of a motion picture during this period, in 1953. "Ruby," with music by European composer Heinz Roemheld, is one of the more

Sheet music for Parish's last big hit, a popular Italian song for which he supplied English lyrics in 1958 (Bagaduce Music Lending Library)

sophisticated movie themes to come out of the decade, and its best-known recording is the one made by Ray Charles. Parish claimed ambiguity was a secret ingredient in his songwriting: "I want them to wonder what I mean," he told *The New York Times* in 1991. The ambiguity in "Ruby" was encapsulated in its first two words, *They say,* since the pronoun has no clear reference in the lyric. Parish used the same two words to begin "Sophisticated Lady," to the same ambiguous effect. In 1954 Parish wrote "Dream, Dream, Dream," which became the theme song of Fred Waring and the Pennsylvanians.

With the advent of the long-playing record, there came an increased demand for the standards of the first half of the century, and the songs of Parish and his contemporaries received considerable attention by recording artists. Sinatra recorded most of Parish's standard ballads on his LPs for Capitol Records. Parish's personal favorite of the thousands of recordings of "Star Dust" was Cole's 1957 rendition on his album *Love Is*

the Thing, which features a lush arrangement by Jenkins. This recording was played at Parish's funeral. As a special tribute to the wide popularity of "Star Dust," RCA Victor once issued an LP collecting twelve different recordings of the song. In 1978 Willie Nelson, in one of his attempts to cross over from country to pop, recorded an album of standards for Columbia with "Star Dust" as the title track. The album sold some three million copies.

Parish's last important hit was an Italian song that became popular in North America both in its original language and in English. "Volaré," under its original title, "Nel Blu, Dipinto di Blu," was an international hit for its Italian composer, Domenico Modugno. A new version with Parish's English lyric was recorded by Dean Martin in 1958 and has remained a popular number. When "Volaré" became a hit in 1958, four decades had passed since Parish left his premed studies at Columbia to join the ranks of Tin Pan Alley. He had written not only major hits but also some of the great standards of the genre, in each of four consecutive decades. Few songwriters can claim to have written standards over such a span. "Being a straight pop writer as opposed to a show or film writer, Mitch was not restrained by the conventions of the theatre," said Drake. "His songs have that florid quality, that grace, because Mitch wrote them to his inner music."

Parish kept writing commercially into the 1960s but lamented the decline in the quality of lyric writing that he saw over the course of his career. "He was among the most brilliant people I ever knew," entertainment industry lawyer Edward Cramer said, "and I've known presidents. He acted like a curmudgeon when others were in the room—he had to put on a show so everyone would believe he was like that, but it was wonderful to be alone with him. He was a different person then." Rick Smith, who befriended Parish late in life, agreed. "He was tough on the outside but soft on the inside." In 1986 a revue was mounted on Broadway to celebrate Parish and his music. It was called *Stardust*—a single word in order to distinguish it from the song title—even though many record labels had long since abandoned this nuance and adopted the one-word version. Although he was never as well-known as Berlin, Porter, Lorenz Hart, Hammerstein, Johnny Mercer, or even Alan Jay Lerner, Parish did not complain, except when people spelled his name "Parrish." At one time he was listed in the phone book both ways but gave up when his daily delivery of junk mail doubled. "When the National Arts Club honored Mitch, I saw that they had spelled his name wrong on the invitation," said Cramer. "I called them up and said they'd have to issue a new invitation, because Mitch wouldn't come if he saw that."

Parish lived to be ninety-two years old, and in his final years he received many of the accolades that had not been bestowed upon him during his years as an active songwriter—the National Arts Club tribute, the New York revues, programs at the 92nd Street Y, occasional updates in *The New York Times,* and induction into the Songwriters Hall of Fame. He was also feted by the French consulate. Parish was confined to a wheelchair for his last years, but he remained alert and communicative. Following his death from complications of a stroke, at New York Hospital on the evening of 31 March 1993, friends said there was nothing bad anyone could say about him. Parish was buried at Beth David Cemetery in Elmont, New York, and the first two lines of the verse to "Star Dust" grace his tombstone. Parish insisted that the ellipsis that opens the song be carved into stone.

Although he toiled in relative anonymity—relative both to the fame of his more publicized colleagues and to the enormous popularity of his greatest songs—Mitchell Parish's contributions to American popular song have not gone unnoticed. Many of Parish's standards are better known as instrumentals, but the use of those songs would have been considerably less frequent—and altogether different—without his lyrics. A great Parish lyric makes for "a song that will not die."

Interviews:

Stephen Holden, "Mitchell Parish: A Way with Words," *The New York Times,* 1 February 1987;

Douglas Martin, "Barks and Coos from a Master of Tin Pan Alley," *The New York Times,* 6 February 1991.

References:

Dennis Duggan, "Mitchell Parish at 89: Kissed by the 'Star Dust of a Song,'" *Newsday,* 10 September 1989;

George W. Goodman, "Jazz Festival: Bittersweet Memories of the 1930's," *The New York Times,* 3 July 1983;

Stephen Holden, "Effervescent Standards Available around City," *The New York Times,* 28 November 1986;

Holden, "Mitchell Parish, 92, the Lyricist of 'Star Dust' and 'Volaré,' Dies," *The New York Times,* 2 April 1993;

David Jasen, *Tin Pan Alley: The Composers, the Songs, the Performers, and Their Times: The Golden Age of American Popular Music from 1886 to 1956* (New York: Fine, 1988), pp. 210–212;

Irv Lichtman, "Parish's Poetry Recalled . . . ," *Billboard,* 105 (13 April 1993): 13;

Lichtman, "The Prolific Songwriting Career of Mitchell Parish," *Billboard,* 104 (29 February 1992): 14;

Lichtman, "An Unlikely Meeting of Writers: Jerry Garcia & Mitchell Parish," *Billboard,* 107 (9 September 1995): 62;

Elizabeth Montgomery, *The Story behind Popular Songs* (New York: Dodd, Mead, 1958), pp. 99–105;

"Parish of 'Stardust' [sic] Fame Still Writing Foxy Lyrics," *Billboard,* 92 (12 July 1980): 41.

Selected Discography:

Duke Ellington: Greatest Hits, CBS Special Products, A 21512, 1990;

Ella Fitzgerald Sings the Duke Ellington Song Book, Verve, V-4008-2, V-4009-2, 1956;

Star Dust: The Music of Hoagy Carmichael, North Star, NS0064, 199?.

Cole Porter

(9 June 1891 – 15 October 1964)

Frederick Nolan

Unless otherwise indicated, music is by Porter.

SELECTED SONGS FROM THEATRICAL PRO-
DUCTIONS: *Cora* (1911)–"Saturday Night";
The Pot of Gold (1912)–"Longing for Dear Old Broad-
way"; "My Houseboat on the Thames";
Paranoia (1914)–"I've a Shooting Box in Scotland";
Hands Up (1915), lyrics by E. Ray Goetz, music by Sig-
mund Romberg–"Esmerelda" (interpolation);
Miss Information (1915), music by Jerome Kern–"Two
Big Eyes" (interpolation);
See America First (1916), lyrics and music by Porter and
Thomas Lawrason Riggs–"See America First";
Hitchy-Koo of 1919 (1919)–"Old-Fashioned Garden";
Mayfair and Montmartre (1922)–"The Blue Boy Blues";
The Greenwich Village Follies (1924)–"I'm in Love Again";
"Two Little Babes in the Wood";
Paris (1928)–"Let's Do It, Let's Fall in Love"; "Let's
Misbehave" (unused);
Fifty Million Frenchmen (1929)–"You Do Something to
Me"; "You've Got That Thing";
Wake Up and Dream (1929)–"I Loved Him but He
Didn't Love Me"; "I'm a Gigolo"; "Looking at
You"; "What Is This Thing Called Love?";
The New Yorkers (1930)–"Let's Fly Away"; "Love for
Sale";
Gay Divorce (1932)–"After You, Who?"; "Night and
Day";
Nymph Errant (1933)–"The Physician"; "Solomon";
Anything Goes (1934)–"All through the Night"; "Any-
thing Goes"; "Blow, Gabriel, Blow"; "I Get a
Kick out of You"; "You're the Top";
Ever Yours, unproduced (1934)–"Miss Otis Regrets";
"Thank You So Much, Mrs. Lowsborough-
Goodby";
Jubilee (1935)–"Begin the Beguine"; "Just One of Those
Things"; "Me and Marie"; "A Picture of Me
without You"; "When Love Comes Your Way";
"Why Shouldn't I?";
O Mistress Mine (1936)–"Goodbye, Little Dream, Good-
bye" (interpolation);

Cole Porter *(photograph by Horst; courtesy of* Vanity Fair;
© *1934 [renewed 1962] by Condé Nast Publications, Inc.)*

Red, Hot and Blue (1936)–"Down in the Depths"; "It's
De-Lovely"; "Ridin' High";
Leave It to Me (1938)–"From Now On"; "Get Out of
Town"; "Most Gentlemen Don't Like Love";
"My Heart Belongs to Daddy"; "Tomorrow";
You Never Know (1938)–"At Long Last Love"; "For No
Rhyme or Reason"; "Maria"; "You Never
Know";
Du Barry Was a Lady (1939)–"But in the Morning, No";
"Do I Love You?"; "Friendship"; "It Ain't Eti-
quette"; "Well, Did You Evah!";
Panama Hattie (1940)–"Let's Be Buddies"; "Make It
Another Old-Fashioned, Please";

Sheet music for a ballad Porter wrote for a revue early in his career
(from Marion Short, From Footlights to "The Flickers," *1998)*

Let's Face It (1941)–"Farming"; "Let's Not Talk about Love";

Something for the Boys (1943)–"By the Mississinewah"; "Hey, Good-Lookin'";

Mexican Hayride (1944)–"I Love You";

Seven Lively Arts (1944)–"Ev'ry Time We Say Goodbye";

Kiss Me, Kate (1948)–"Always True to You in My Fashion"; "Another Op'nin', Another Show"; "Brush Up Your Shakespeare"; "I've Come to Wive It Wealthily in Padua"; "So in Love"; "Too Darn Hot"; "We Shall Never Be Younger" (unused); "Were Thine That Special Face"; "Where Is the Life That Late I Led?"; "Why Can't You Behave?"; "Wunderbar";

Out of This World (1950)–"Cherry Pies Ought to Be You"; "From This Moment On" (unused); "Nobody's Chasing Me"; "You Don't Remind Me";

Can-Can (1953)–"Allez-Vous-En"; "Can-Can"; "C'est Magnifique"; "I Love Paris"; "It's All Right with Me";

Silk Stockings (1955)–"All of You"; "As On through the Seasons We Sail"; "Paris Loves Lovers"; "Siberia"; "Silk Stockings"; "Stereophonic Sound."

SELECTED SONGS FROM MOTION-PICTURE PRODUCTIONS: *The Battle of Paris* (1929)–"Here Comes the Bandwagon"; "They All Fall in Love";

Adios, Argentina, unproduced (1934)–"Don't Fence Me In";

Born to Dance (1936)–"Easy to Love"; "I've Got You under My Skin";

Rosalie (1937)–"In the Still of the Night"; "Rosalie";

Broadway Melody of 1940 (1940)–"I Concentrate on You"; "I've Got My Eyes on You";

You'll Never Get Rich (1941)–"So Near and Yet So Far"; "The Wedding Cakewalk";

Something to Shout About (1943)–"You'd Be So Nice to Come Home To";

The Pirate (1948)–"Be a Clown"; "Love of My Life";

Adam's Rib (1949)–"Farewell, Amanda";

The Dolly Sisters, Rosie and Jennie, performing Porter's
"Two Little Babes in the Wood" in the 1924 show
Greenwich Village Follies, which also
featured four other Porter songs

High Society (1956)—"I Love You, Samantha"; "Little One"; "Mind if I Make Love to You?"; "Now You Has Jazz"; "True Love"; "Well, Did You Evah!" (revised); "Who Wants to Be a Millionaire?"; "You're Sensational";
Les Girls (1957)—"Ça, c'est l'Amour"; "Les Girls";
Silk Stockings (1957)—"The Ritz Roll and Rock."

SELECTED SONGS FROM TELEVISION PRO-
DUCTION: *Aladdin* (1958)—"Come to the Supermarket in Old Peking"; "Wouldn't It Be Fun?"

SELECTED SONGS PUBLISHED INDEPEN-
DENTLY OF THEATRICAL OR MOTION-
PICTURE PRODUCTIONS: "Bingo Eli Yale"
(1910);
"Bridget McGuire" (1910);
"Bull Dog" (1911);
"The Laziest Gal in Town" (1927).

BOOK: *The Complete Lyrics of Cole Porter,* edited by Robert
Kimball (New York: Knopf, 1983).

Even though, with the exception of *Kiss Me, Kate* (1948) and *Anything Goes* (1934), few of Cole Porter's shows are now revived, the best of his songs live on. The Porter style—the impudence, the wit, that sense of being allowed a peek into a privileged world, and, in the best of his love songs, the intensity of the passion—is instantly recognizable. If, of all the Broadway masters, he is one of the few perceived to have been happy with "legs and laffs" shows—there is no *Show Boat* (1927), no *Carousel* (1945), no *Most Happy Fella* (1956) in the Porter catalogue—he was unquestionably the one who most constantly pushed the taboos, challenging what could or could not be said or sung.

He might have been able to push beyond those boundaries because, in an era when many songwriters were born into poverty on New York's Lower East Side, Porter had a wealthy background. Born Cole Albert Porter on 9 June 1891 to Samuel Fenwick Porter and Kate Cole Porter in Peru, Indiana, he was the grandson of James Omar "J. O." Cole, a coal and lumber magnate who saw to it that his daughter and her son had every privilege his money could give them. Samuel Porter, a handsome but parvenu druggist, played only a background role in his son's life. As one commentator observed, Samuel "seems to have been crushed to death between the fiercely go-getting mother and his powerful, contemptuous father-in-law, neither of whom made any bones about preferring the cheerful son to the sorry father."

Even if Samuel Porter was perceived as "sorry," Cole apparently inherited his talent from his father, who loved Robert Browning and the English Romantic poets, played the guitar and piano, and had a charming singing voice. At first Cole's gifts seemed modest enough: he took his first violin lessons at age six, and at eight he began studying the piano. A year later he wrote the words and music for an extended six-section piece called "The Song of the Birds," and when he was eleven, one of his songs, "The Bobolink Waltz" (1902), was published by a vanity press in Chicago at his mother's expense.

J. O. Cole's money enabled Kate Porter to make special arrangements for her son and only surviving child. Early in Cole's life she had the official records amended, altering his age from six to four, reasoning that a four-year-old playing the violin would seem a prodigy, whereas a six-year-old doing so would be no more than an unremarkable beginner. When he went to Peru Grammar School, she also financed its student orchestra and reportedly influenced the media's reviews of the concerts in which Cole played his violin solos and piano pieces. His mother also decided on the educational environment that was to affect his later life most profoundly. J. O. Cole thought the boy was too "sissified" and wanted to send him to a military academy or a business school where he

William Gaxton and chorus girls in Porter's 1929 musical Fifty Million Frenchmen
(*from Robert Kimball, ed.,* Cole, *1971*)

could learn to manage the family interests. But Kate Porter wanted her son to go to an eastern preparatory school and then on to an Ivy League college.

Kate's insistence so alienated her father that they did not speak again for two years, but in 1905 Cole entered Worcester Academy in Worcester, Massachusetts. The piano installed in his room by his mother—the first such in the history of the school—made it possible for him to entertain his classmates with his own songs, among them "The Tattooed Gentleman" and "The Bearded Lady," compositions doubtless inspired by a love of the circus born of his childhood in Peru (the winter quarters of a large circus), and early prototypes of the "naughty" songs, studded with double entendres, that he wrote in later years. By the time he was a senior, Porter was much in demand: he was the star of the class play, the pianist for the glee club, and editor of the school newspaper.

Having failed the preliminary test for entrance to Yale University, Porter passed the second and last-chance examination in his senior year at Worcester,

where he was class valedictorian. As a reward, his grandfather offered him any present he wished; Porter asked for, and got, a trip to Paris. It was to be the beginning of a lifelong love affair with the French capital in particular and luxury travel in general.

At Yale, deploying his exceptional talents and intelligence to obtain what he wanted and sidestep what he disliked, Porter became an accomplished charmer. He formed friendships with scions of the "old money" families or young men who had notable standing in society, such as Vanderbilt Webb, Edgar Montillion "Monty" Woolley, and Howard Sturges. Porter was a member of the glee club, the Dramatic Association, the Corinthian Club, the Yacht Club, the University Club, the Wigwam and Wrangler Debating Club, the Hogans, the Whiffenpoofs, the Pundits, the Grill Room Grizzlies, the Mince Pie Room, Delta Kappa Epsilon (Dekes), and Scroll and Key, a senior or "secret society." He was even a football cheerleader.

Porter continued writing his clever songs. In his freshman year at Yale he managed to sell an Irish

Lilly Tosch, Toni Birkmayer, and (in background) William Cavenagh in Porter's London revue Wake Up and Dream *(1929) (from Robert Kimball, ed.,* Cole, *1971)*

Phi Theatre on York Street when the Phi Opera Company presented "a musical farce in two acts" called *Cora,* which featured such Porter numbers as "Saturday Night":

Saturday night, Saturday night,
This is the one time we all get plenty of
Liquor, liquor, just a wee flicker
So order a gallon and don't stop to bicker
We'll all sing something
Any old tune's all right
I love, I love the rest of the week
But oh, you Saturday night!

After *Cora* came *And The Villain Still Pursued Her* (1912), starring Porter's close friend Woolley, which spoofed Harriet Beecher Stowe's *Uncle Tom's Cabin* (1852), and *The Pot of Gold* (1912), which might be called Porter's first "book" show, with a libretto by Almet Jenks, a winner of the Yale Dramatic Association Prize. Included in the score was the George M. Cohan–esque "Longing for Dear Old Broadway" and "My Houseboat on the Thames," a lampoon of the languid lifestyle of the upper-class British:

On my houseboat on the Thames
It's a jolly ripping vessel to relax on,
For it's deuced dull and deadly Anglo-Saxon.
We'll have Punch on board, I think,
One to read and one to drink. . . .

Not until he left Yale in 1913—graduating only thanks to some judicious bending of the rules by the faculty—and transferred to Harvard Law School did Porter begin to be seen as a potential writer of Broadway shows. The first indications of this ability came when he and fellow Yale alumnus, Thomas Lawrason Riggs, produced another college show, *Paranoia* (1914), notable mainly for having in its score what was to be Porter's first recorded song, another of his lampoons of upper-class British life, called "I've a Shooting Box in Scotland."

When it became clear that Porter was never going to become a lawyer, another intercession, as at Yale, saved him. The dean of the Harvard Law School got him transferred to the Graduate School of Arts and Sciences, thereby allowing the continuation of the generous allowance from J. O. Cole that supported Porter's lavish lifestyle. One of those who admired his songs was Elizabeth "Bessie" Marbury, a former literary agent who had become a successful theatrical producer by backing the shows at Broadway's Princess Theatre written by Guy Bolton, P. G. Wodehouse, and Jerome Kern. Marbury was instrumental in having a Porter song, "Esmerelda," interpolated into *Hands Up,* a 1915 revue with a score mostly by Sigmund Romberg. A few

"story song" called "Bridget McGuire" (1910) to Remick, a New York music-publishing firm. His "football songs"—"Bingo Eli Yale" (1910) and "Bull Dog" (1911)—are still popular in New Haven. In 1911 Porter's first musical-comedy score was heard at the

months later Porter's song "Two Big Eyes" was performed in the Kern musical *Miss Information* (1915).

Marbury now decided to give Porter and Riggs a Broadway show of their own, a musical based on the flag-waving career of Cohan called *See America First*, which opened at the Maxine Elliott Theatre on 28 March 1916. It lasted less than two weeks. Riggs's libretto was weak; the "star" was a socialite who could not sing; and, instead of creating a completely new score, Porter used some of his earlier songs. Speaking of this show in later years, actor Clifton Webb observed, "I played a cowboy and an autumn flower. Others had roles not so believable."

Porter moved to New York, where he proceeded to throw glittering parties. In this milieu he met society matron Nina Larrey Smith Duryea and, soon after the United States entered World War I, became her personal assistant and adjutant of the Duryea Relief Party, set up to distribute food to needy villagers in France. Now that it was apparent that Porter had no intention of becoming a lawyer, J. O. Cole bowed to the inevitable and set up a trust for his grandson, which meant that Porter would never want for money. When Cole died, Porter would become a millionaire. In July 1917 Porter sailed for Europe.

Porter's war record remains a mystery. After three months in France he apparently became bored with his position in the Duryea organization and left for Paris, where he installed himself in a large and comfortable house. According to Woolley, Porter had "more changes of uniform than Maréchal Foch and wore them with complete disregard to regulation." Porter himself said he served with the French army and was later detailed to the Bureau of the U.S. Military Attaché; he even boasted that he had been awarded the croix de guerre. No records have ever been found to authenticate these claims, however. About the only contribution he seems to have made to the war effort was to write a parody of Kern's "They Didn't Believe Me" (1914) that became immensely popular with the troops in the trenches:

And when they ask us, and they're certainly going to ask us
Why on our chests we do not wear the Croix de Guerre
We never will tell them
We never will tell them
There was a front, but damned if we knew where.

Porter's two closest friends in Paris were Woolley (then an army lieutenant) and the rich, alcoholic, and gay Sturges, whose friendship was instrumental in helping Porter advance in society. At the end of January 1918, at a breakfast reception following the wedding of Henry Russell and Ethel Harriman (a sister of Porter's Yale classmate Averell Harriman), Porter met Linda Lee Thomas, the former wife of sportsman-playboy Edward Thomas, whose family owned the *New York Telegram*.

Said at the time to have been the most beautiful woman in America, Linda was a decade—perhaps more, for her birth date is given variously—older than Porter. Born in Louisville, Kentucky, she had married Edward Thomas when she was eighteen; on the occasion of their marriage, he had given her a town house on Fifty-seventh Street in New York, a mansion in Palm Springs, a cottage in Newport, a box at the opera, and a substantial collection of jewelry. His philandering was frequently reported in the newspapers, and Linda finally named the showgirl involved in one of his affairs and won an unconditional divorce. To avoid any further exposure in the press, Thomas's parents settled $1 million in stocks and bonds on her, and she became known in Parisian circles as "the alimony millionairess."

When Linda and Porter decided to marry, Porter sailed for home, intending to go to Peru to ask his grandfather to increase his allowance. On the ocean liner he met Raymond Hitchcock, a former comedian turned producer of Broadway revues; in a play on his own name Hitchcock had called the first of these *Hitchy-Koo of 1917*, and it was quite successful. When Porter played for him, Hitchcock was apparently so enamored of his songs that he said, "I'll take the lot!"

Hitchy-Koo of 1919 opened at New York's Liberty Theatre on 6 October 1919; the first week's gross was a surprising $16,000. Even more surprising in that time of flappers and the Charleston, Porter's untypical ballad "Old-Fashioned Garden"—said to have been written only because producers A. L. Erlanger and Charles Dillingham had purchased some flower costumes from an unsuccessful Florenz Ziegfeld production and needed a song to go with them—became a hit, selling one hundred thousand copies of sheet music.

In Peru, when J. O. Cole refused to increase Porter's allowance in order for him to marry, Kate Porter stepped in and shared her own considerable income with her son. That money, along with advances from his new music publisher, Max Dreyfus of T. B. Harms, and a $10,000 loan from his Yale friend Bill Crocker (whom Porter used as the model for the lead character in *Anything Goes* in 1934), made the wedding possible. On 19 December 1919 Porter and Linda were married at the city hall in Paris's Eighteenth Arrondissement prior to departing on a honeymoon that took them to the French and Italian Rivieras, the first in a series of extensive excursions they were to make over the next decade.

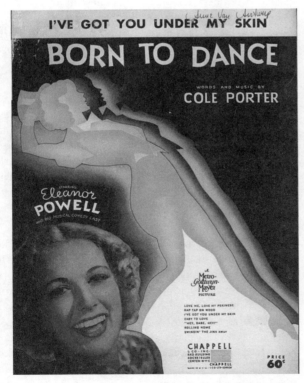
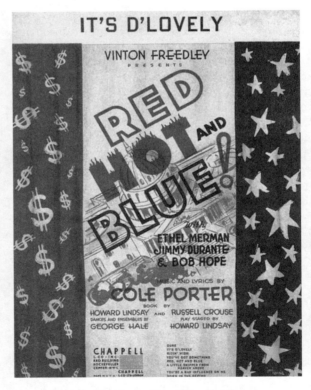

Sheet music for four of Porter's successful songs of the 1930s (clockwise from top left: from Marion Short, From Footlights to "The Flickers," *1998; Short,* Hollywood Movie Songs, *1999; William Zinsser,* Easy to Remember, *2000; Bruccoli Clark Layman Archives)*

Ethel Merman with Marshall Smith, Ray Johnson, Dwight Snyder, and Del Porter in Cole Porter's 1934 musical
Anything Goes *(Van Damm Photos, Billy Rose Theatre Collection,*
New York Public Library for the Performing Arts)

For each the marriage was one of convenience. After her brutalizing marriage to Thomas, a sexless relationship understandably appealed to Linda, while for Porter a glamorous and talented wife would be a perfect cover for his frequent homosexual relationships. In addition, their tastes, interests, and ambitions were identical. The *Coleporteurs,* as they became known, spent most of the next two decades in Europe, establishing a lushly elegant permanent residence in Paris on the rue Monsieur, where the social, political, and theatrical elite were frequently in attendance. There were trips up the Nile, to Venice, Morocco, Biarritz, Spain, the Riviera, and London, where Porter contributed some songs—among them, "The Blue Boy Blues"—to an ill-fated revue produced by Charles B. Cochran, *Mayfair and Montmartre* (1922).

J. O. Cole died on 3 February 1923 but did not include Porter in his will. He did leave Kate Porter $2 million, and she gave half of it to her son. At Linda's insistence (for she believed her husband capable of more-serious work than his musical-comedy songs), Porter studied music at the Schola Cantorum, founded by Vincent d'Indy in Paris. Partly as a result of that classical training, in October 1923 Porter produced a

score for a pantomime ballet called *Within the Quota,* a satire on American life with a libretto by Gerald Murphy.

In 1924 five of Porter's songs were used in a New York show, *The Greenwich Village Follies,* including "Two Little Babes in the Wood," an archly witty tale sung by the sisters Rosie and Jennie Dolly. Also in the score was "I'm in Love Again," a song that perfectly defined the Porter style. It was beginning to seem that, although he was passionate to be a successful songwriter, Porter so feared the kind of public failure that had attended *See America First* that he hid behind the facade of a playboy who wrote clever songs merely to entertain his wealthy friends. He wrote some excellent songs for a 1927 revue staged at the Café des Ambassadeurs in Paris—among them "The Laziest Gal in Town" and "Let's Misbehave" (later intended for Porter's 1928 show *Paris* but dropped before the New York opening)—but none gave him the recognition he sought. Then, suddenly, dramatically, Porter successfully emerged on Broadway.

In 1926, when Irving Berlin married Ellin Mackay in the teeth of bitter opposition from her tycoon father, the Porters warmly supported the new

Porter and Moss Hart working on the 1935 musical Jubilee,
for which Hart wrote the libretto (from Stanley Green,
The World of Musical Comedy, *1962)*

bride and groom and welcomed them to their Paris home. A grateful Berlin recommended Porter to producer E. Ray Goetz, who was mounting a show to star his wife, Irene Bordoni. Goetz liked Porter's work and hired him to write the score. The show, *Paris,* opened in Atlantic City in February 1928, but Goetz kept it on the road for eight months, working it into shape. Meanwhile, Porter shuttled back and forth across the Atlantic, working simultaneously on another show, *La Revue des Ambassadeurs,* which opened in May of that year, and adding to or excising songs from both.

Paris opened on 8 October 1928 in New York at Berlin's Music Box Theatre, and with it Porter's three-decade Broadway career was launched. The precise moment of that launch came when Bordoni undulated onto the stage to sing "Let's Do It, Let's Fall in Love":

Old sloths who hang down from twigs do it,
Though the effort is great,
Sweet guinea-pigs do it,
Buy a couple and wait.
The world admits bears in pits do it,
Even Pekineses at the Ritz do it,
Let's do it, let's fall in love.

"Let's Do It, Let's Fall in Love" established Porter as the premier writer of the catalogue or "list" song, in which a witty list of images, each funnier than the preceding, unravels itself over a series of refrains.

Porter's next venture was a score for *Wake Up and Dream* (1929), another Cochran revue in London starring Jessie Matthews and her husband, Sonnie Hale. In addition to "Let's Do It, Let's Fall in Love" (on the zoological research for which the British censor congratulated Porter), the songs included the wistful "I Loved Him but He Didn't Love Me"; the sad tale of a paid lover, "I'm a Gigolo"; and–danced with sensual verve by Tillie Losch and sung by Elsie Carlisle–what was to become one of Porter's best-known ballads, "What Is This Thing Called Love?"

Despite mixed reviews, *Wake Up and Dream* ran for 263 performances at the London Pavilion and, at the end of 1929, transferred to New York. In the wake of the stock-market crash, it managed only 136 performances, but when Walter Winchell singled out "What Is This Thing Called Love?" as one of the best specimens of the newer breed of love song, Porter was established as the Broadway success he had always wanted to be.

As the Depression reduced the number of musicals produced on Broadway, Porter, like many other songwriters, responded to the demand for songs for Hollywood musicals after the advent of the "talkies." Paramount Pictures invited him to write songs for *The Battle of Paris* (1929), a musical comedy to star Gertrude Lawrence in her first screen appearance. Porter's two songs, "They All Fall in Love" and "Here Comes the Bandwagon," were written in New York and sent out to Hollywood. The movie was a complete failure, remembered today only for having prompted one critic to coin the term "floperetta" to describe it.

Porter signed with Goetz to score a new musical with a book by Herbert Fields, who had hitherto been indivisibly associated with the shows of Richard Rodgers and Lorenz Hart. Porter worked extremely hard; between his arrival in New York on 20 August 1929 and opening night on 27 November, he wrote some thirty songs. But even though critic Gilbert Seldes found *Fifty Million Frenchmen* "as near to a perfect musical as you are likely to see," and Gilbert Gabriel called it "the best thing in seven years," the reviews were largely tepid, and it looked as if the show would close. Again, Berlin came to Porter's aid, taking out paid newspaper advertisements trumpeting *Fifty Million Frenchmen* as "the best musical comedy I have seen in years. . . . It's worth the price of admission to hear Cole Porter's lyrics." As a result, receipts picked up, and the show went on to a highly respectable run of 254 performances. Although most of the score was unexceptional, it added another standard to Porter's catalogue, "You Do Something to Me," and again showed his virtuosity with an elegantly witty and sensual release, or bridge: "Let me live 'neath your spell. / Do do that voodoo that you do so well. . . ."

The 1930s turned out to be Porter's most successful decade, and he began it in typical style, by taking a four-month trip around the world, sailing via Hollywood, Hawaii, China, and Japan to Venice, where he had already agreed to write a new Goetz show with Fields. *The New Yorkers* (1930) had a typically lighthearted Fields book about a socialite and her romance with a bootlegger, but Porter seems to have found plots such as this a convenient clothesline on which to hang his songs. With a cast that included Hope Williams, Jimmy Durante, and the Fred Waring Orchestra, *The New Yorkers* opened at the Broadway Theatre on 8 December 1930, and almost immediately the best song in the show, "Love for Sale," became a cause célèbre that was to generate controversy for years. There were many guardians of the public morals on hand to pillory anything that went "too far," and "Love for Sale" certainly did that. In a scene one critic dubbed "filthy," a prostitute sings,

When the only sound in the empty street
Is the heavy tread of the heavy feet
That belong to a lonesome cop,
I open shop.
When the moon so long has been gazing down
On the wayward ways of this wayward town
That her smile becomes a smirk,
I go to work.
Love for sale,
Appetizing young love for sale,
Love that's fresh and still unspoiled,
Love that's only slightly soiled,
Love for sale.

Once again, Porter had created a lyric that was both sensuous and colloquially elegant. The song, however, was immediately banned from the airwaves by the Federal Communications Commission (FCC), much to Porter's professed chagrin. "I can't understand it," he complained. "You can write a novel about a harlot, paint a picture of a harlot, but you can't write a song about a harlot." Recordings of the song by Elizabeth Welch, Fred Waring, and Libby Holman ensured a widespread audience.

The following year, 1931, Porter scored a musical called *Star Dust*. The songs included "I Get a Kick out of You" and "The Physician." Produced by Goetz, with a book by Fields and Peggy Wood cast as the star, the show ought to have been a hit, but it never had the chance: with the economic picture daily becoming

June Knight singing "Begin the Beguine" in Jubilee *(Van Damm Photos, Billy Rose Theatre Collection, New York Public Library for the Performing Arts)*

bleaker, the principal backer pulled out, and *Star Dust* was withdrawn. Porter's fine songs went into the trunk, but some of them reappeared the following year when he wrote the score for *Gay Divorce* (1932), which starred Fred Astaire in his first Broadway role without his sister, Adele, as costar.

Gay Divorce was bright, brittle, and mildly naughty. The character played by Astaire is a writer who comes to interview a woman (originally played by Claire Luce) who mistakes him for the corespondent she has hired so she can obtain a divorce. Smitten from an earlier meeting with her, he goes along with the plot until they work it all out. Astaire was uncertain about taking on the role until Porter sat down at the piano and played "After You, Who?" It is one of Porter's most attractive songs, simple yet touching, but it—and everything else he wrote for the show—was swamped by the huge success of "Night and Day."

Legends about Porter's writing the melody of "Night and Day" after hearing an Islamic call to prayer in Morocco are just that: legends. Porter, an inveterate

Mary Martin, with Gene Kelly (immediate left of Martin) and unidentified cast members, singing "My Heart
Belongs to Daddy" in Porter's 1938 musical Leave It to Me *(Van Damm Photos, Billy Rose*
Theatre Collection, New York Public Library for the Performing Arts)

and skillful hoaxer, was living at the Ritz-Carlton when he composed the melody, which, unusually for him, came before the lyric. Weekending at Mrs. Vincent Astor's estate in Newport, Rhode Island, he played it for Woolley, who told him, "Throw it away; it's terrible!" Next day at lunch, during a steady downpour, Mrs. Astor remarked that she had to have one of the eaves repaired. "That drip, drip, drip is driving me mad," she said, and Porter leaped to his feet with a shout of joy: there was the line his verse could take. Once he had "Like the drip drip drip of the raindrops," "the beat beat beat of the tom-tom" and "the tick tick tock of the stately clock" followed rapidly.

Gay Divorce opened at the Ethel Barrymore Theatre on 29 November 1932, "the most brilliant gathering of the season," according to one critic. The libretto was criticized, but there was nothing but praise for the songs. Porter's music, Burns Mantle said, "sets him apart as a modest Gershwin," while the lyrics had "wit

and form and a provocative lilt. He can be audacious without being offensive, bold without being cheap." The show ran on Broadway for 248 performances and moved with the same cast to further success in London. By February 1933 more than thirty artists had recorded "Night and Day," including Astaire, Leslie "Hutch" Hutchinson, and Morton Downey. It is still one of the top twenty-five most-played songs in the catalogue of the American Society of Composers, Authors, and Publishers (ASCAP).

Porter was already writing a new show for London producer Cochran. *Nymph Errant* (1933), which starred Lawrence, was a story about an English girl named Evangeline who travels the world trying to lose her virginity, only to return from her travels unsullied. "Fantasy *indeed*," as one critic remarked. In spite of the lavish production and risqué songs, *Nymph Errant* ran for only 154 performances at London's Adelphi Theatre and did not make the Atlantic crossing. Probably the best-known song in the show was the wailing, bluesy "Solomon," which Elizabeth Welch introduced, although Porter had some naughty fun with medical terminology in "The Physician" and grew even saucier with "Si Vous Aimez Les Poitrines" (If You Love Breasts):

> Si vous voulez d'la ten-dresse
> Et d'la volupté,
> Let me give you my ad-dresse
> For a rainy day.
> And when zat feeling comes a-stealing
> You know what I mean?
> Mais oui, Monsieur,
> Come and play wiz me in gay Paree
> Si vous aimez les poitrines.

Back in New York, producers Alex Aarons and Vinton Freedley were in trouble. Their most recent production, *Pardon My English* (1933), with a score by Ira and George Gershwin, had closed after only forty-six performances, leaving the producers so deeply in debt that they had to flee the country. Aarons was never to return to Broadway, but during their enforced vacation, Freedley considered doing a different sort of musical: instead of coming up with an idea, commissioning a libretto, putting together a cast, and finding a director, he wondered,

> What if you just sat down and put together a set of components the public would clamor for? Something with, say, Ethel Merman, star of the smash-hit 1930 show *Girl Crazy*, teamed with top leading man William Gaxton, and maybe dithering Victor Moore, famous for his performance as Throttlebottom in *Of Thee I Sing*. Get Cole Porter to do the songs and there it was—a sure-fire, platinum-plated hit.

The result of Freedley's dreams, when he returned to America, was the 1934 show *Anything Goes*. After many tribulations with the book, Russel Crouse and Howard Lindsay came up with a scenario in which Merman, Gaxton, and Moore played, respectively, Reno Sweeney, a former evangelist turned nightclub hostess; Billy Crocker, a penniless playboy in pursuit of Bettina Hall; and Moonface Martin, Public Enemy No. 13, disguised as a clergyman. With such Porter songs as "I Get a Kick out of You," "Blow, Gabriel, Blow," "All through the Night," "You're the Top," and the title song, *Anything Goes* was destined to be a hit.

Opening at the Alvin Theatre on 21 November 1934, *Anything Goes* was an instant success that ran, in the darkest days of the Depression, for 420 performances and a further 260 in London. Porter later said, "*Anything Goes* was the first of my two 'perfect' shows—musicals that had no tinkering whatever on them after

Betty Grable, Bert Lahr, and Merman in Porter's 1939 musical Du Barry Was a Lady *(Museum of the City of New York, Theatre and Music Collection)*

opening night. The other, *Kiss Me, Kate,* was a tribute to the assembled stagecraft of those associated with me."

With the success of *Anything Goes,* the Porters were the toast of New York. Rich, famous, talented, and successful, the couple seemed to have everything anyone could possibly wish for. As a headline in *The New York Herald Tribune* indicated just a few months after the opening of *Anything Goes,* Porter was undertaking a new Broadway show in lavish style: "BALLADEER, WITH MOSS HART, TO PASS FIVE MONTHS SEEKING NEW MUSICAL COMEDY." Hart, who had already written the play *Merrily We Roll Along* (1934) with George S. Kaufman and supplied the sketches for Berlin's hit revue *As Thousands Cheer* (1934), and Porter were off around the world on the Cunard ocean liner *Franconia* with Linda Porter, Woolley, and Sturges. "When Messrs. Porter and Hart return to New York," the newspaper said, "they expect to have on paper a complete score and book for a new show."

The travelers first went to Jamaica (where Porter appropriated the name of a local bird, the Kling-Kling, for a song), then to Los Angeles and Hawaii, bypassing Tahiti because of typhoons, and on to Samoa, the Fiji Islands, New Zealand, Australia, Papua, Bali, Singapore, Colombo, Calcutta, Mombasa, Zanzibar, Durban, and Cape Town. While they were crossing the

all of these romantic entanglements, the king is perfecting a magic trick.

For this whimsical story Porter fashioned a score that ranged from the fervent "Begin the Beguine" with its 108-bar refrain and its passionate, Latin American tempo, to "Me and Marie," a beer-garden-style waltz the king and queen "remember" from their courting days. With such other songs as "Just One of Those Things," "A Picture of Me without You," and "Why Shouldn't I?" the score for *Jubilee* promised to make the show as big a success as *Anything Goes,* but when *Jubilee* opened at the Imperial Theatre on 12 October 1935, although the critics liked it, the public's reaction was tepid. Neither "Just One of Those Things" nor "Begin the Beguine" became popular at first (it was another three years before clarinetist and bandleader Artie Shaw put an instrumental version of the latter into *Your Hit Parade*). Then the death of George V on 20 January 1936 cast a pall over the entire proceedings, and when Mary Boland, who played the queen in *Jubilee,* left the cast in February, ticket sales fell off so much that the show had to be closed after twenty-one weeks.

By that time, however, Porter and his entourage had moved to Hollywood, where he had signed (for a $75,000 fee) to write a movie musical. Porter enjoyed working in Hollywood, and for the rest of his life he spent between four and six months a year there. Linda disliked their time in Hollywood: it was all too easy for Porter to indulge himself sexually there, and she was constantly afraid that his homosexuality would become public knowledge.

In the labyrinthine fashion of Hollywood, the project Porter had come to write ended up as *Born to Dance* (1936), a vehicle for the pyrotechnical tap dancer Eleanor Powell and James Stewart. The plot was flimsy: a lonely-hearts-club hostess, Nora Paige (Powell), meets and falls in love with Coast Guard seaman Ted Barker (Stewart), but Lucy James (played by Broadway star Virginia Bruce) obstructs their romance until the inevitable happy ending. Porter partially rewrote the lyric for "Easy to Love"—originally composed for *Anything Goes* but dropped because Gaxton was uncomfortable with its wide vocal range (Stewart also had difficulty with the song)—and created a couple of specialty numbers for Powell, but Bruce sang the big hit of the movie, "I've Got You under My Skin." Once again, Porter broke all the songwriting rules, composing a fifty-six-bar chorus (instead of the standard thirty-two bars) and an extended bridge that frames the singer's impatience with her own folly:

> I'd sacrifice anything, come what might,
> For the sake of having you near, in spite
> Of the warning voice that comes in the night

Porter with Danny Kaye during a rehearsal for Porter's Let's Face It *(1941) (from Robert Kimball, ed.,* Cole, *1971)*

Atlantic, they received news by ship's radio of the twenty-fifth-anniversary celebrations of the coronation of England's King George V and Queen Mary, and there was the title for their show: *Jubilee* (1935). As the *Franconia* sailed into the harbor at Rio de Janeiro, Porter reportedly exclaimed, "It's delightful!"; Linda echoed, "It's delicious"; and Woolley completed the title with "It's de-lovely," which Porter filed away for future use.

Jubilee had the kind of plot "clever college boys . . . develop for their varsity shows," as one critic put it. A king with a somewhat wandering eye and his flirtatious queen are about to celebrate their jubilee but are fed up with their cosseted life. When the threat of revolution looms, they decide to "hide" by passing as commoners. The queen flirts with Charles Rausmiller (whose character was based on Johnny Weissmuller, who played Tarzan in movies). The royal couple's daughter, Princess Diana, has a brief romance with the celebrated writer Eric Dare (a caricature of Noel Coward). The older of the two princes, James, falls in love with nightclub dancer Karen O'Kane, and, amid

Advertisement in the May 1948 issue of Screen Stories

And repeats and repeats in my ear,
"Don't you know, little fool, you never can win,
Use your mentality,
Wake up to reality."
But each time I do, just the thought of you
Makes me stop before I begin,
'Cause I've got you under my skin.

M-G-M's Louis B. Mayer was so enamored of the score for *Born to Dance* that Porter returned to New York with a $100,000 contract in his pocket for another movie, *Rosalie* (1937).

First, however, Porter was to write the score for another Freedley production, again to star Porter's favorite Broadway performer, Merman. But although the same team was involved, there were clashes of temperament: everyone involved was now a star, and every one of them—Porter included—wanted things his

or her way. Gaxton, overhearing a conversation in which librettists Lindsay and Crouse assured Merman that hers was the star part, walked out. Freedley tried to replace him with Eddie Cantor, who was not available, and quickly hired Durante, whereupon another argument began because both stars wanted their names above the title. Bob Hope, then a promising young juvenile actor, was added to the cast, but Merman feuded with him, too. As a result of all the backstage bickering, the show, titled *Red, Hot and Blue* (1936), suffered and closed after only 183 performances.

If the failure bothered Porter, he gave little sign of it. It may well be, as he himself said, that once a show opened, he no longer felt the same way about it. "For some reason, the moment the curtain rises on opening night, I say to myself: 'There she goes' and I've bid goodbye to my baby. . . . The minute that it is

Librettist Bella Spewack, Porter, and director Jack Wilson at a rehearsal for
Kiss Me, Kate *(1948) (from Charles Schwartz,* Cole Porter, *1979)*

exposed to its premiere audience, . . . I feel that it's no longer mine." Porter probably felt satisfied that he had done a good job: he had managed finally to squeeze "It's De-Lovely" into a score and produced a darkly beautiful lament for Merman in "Down in the Depths," as well as "Ridin' High," an exuberant "belter" of the kind Merman could perform better than anyone else on Broadway.

Eager to get back to Hollywood, Porter wrote the score for his second Powell movie during the first half of 1937. *Rosalie* was a motion-picture adaptation of a 1928 Ziegfeld extravaganza of the same title that had starred Marilyn Miller. The plot concerned a romance between a West Point cadet (played by Nelson Eddy in the movie) and a Ruritanian princess (Powell). Porter wrote twelve songs, only eight of which were used. The best of these was "In the Still of the Night." When Eddy claimed it was impossible to sing, Porter took the song to Mayer, who, legend has it, burst into tears when he heard it and ordered Eddy to sing it. Porter struggled with the title song for *Rosalie:* he wrote five versions of it before settling on a sixth as the final version. For the rest of his life he complained that it was one of the dreariest songs he had ever written, but Berlin gave him

some good advice: "Never hate a song that has sold half a million copies, kid."

Porter had other, more serious problems. His wife, Linda, was incensed to learn that he had signed to write songs for yet another movie. She disliked the blatant antics of the largely homosexual crowd with which Porter surrounded himself in Hollywood. She left for Paris, and although Porter eventually followed her there, the estrangement lasted into the fall of 1937. Insouciantly, Porter went on a European walking tour with his close friends Sturges and architect Edward Tauch. When they returned, Linda was still unrelenting, so Porter sailed to New York to work on a new show, *You Never Know* (1938).

In October 1937 Porter accepted an invitation to weekend with his old friend "Tookie," Countess Edith di Zoppola, at her home at Oyster Bay, Long Island. On Sunday 24 October he arranged a riding party with the nearby Piping Rock Club in Locust Valley. Ignoring a groom's advice that the horse he had chosen was skittish, Porter mounted and led the way into the woods. Cresting a rise, his horse shied, then reared so high it fell over. Porter was crushed beneath the animal, shattering the bones in his right leg. As the

It's Too Darn Hot
refrain.
It's tough to cavort
For the Diary report
                    vive L'Amour
                        temperature
Is 90 in the shade   hot but
It's a tragic   when the weather is hot
Adam + Eve are not.
thermoter - barometer.
Swet - perspire
E   Mister Adam
          MISTRESS
+ his Missus or Miss -- Madam
Are not.
Mister/Adam + his Madame
+ his girl friend & her boy friend
Are not.
Cause it's too darn hot.
famous indoor sport
  Mister Adam, poor Adam)
Is not.
Mister Adam for his Madam
Is not

Porter's manuscript for a song in his 1948 musical Kiss Me, Kate *(The Cole Porter Collection, Yale University)*

Porter with his wife, Linda Lee Porter, in 1948
(AP/Wide World Photos)

the surgeon handling Porter's case told her his legs were so badly shattered that he feared gangrene might set in, and he recommended immediate amputation. Both Linda and Porter's mother, Kate, rejected the proposition, knowing amputation would completely crush Porter's spirit. Instead, they brought in an eminent specialist, Dr. John Moorhead, who had Porter moved to Doctors' Hospital in Manhattan, where the first of many operations was performed. Through months of excruciating pain Porter maintained a courageous stoicism and even a sense of humor. He began by naming his ruined right leg Geraldine and the slightly less ruined left leg Josephine. Josephine, he said, was mostly sweet and accommodating, but Geraldine was "a hellion, a bitch, a psychopath." In January 1938 Porter was allowed to return to his apartment at the Waldorf-Astoria Hotel. There was a white-tie gala to welcome him home, and he was carried in by his valet and a caretaker.

In February there were further operations, and Moorhead urged Porter to adopt a positive approach to his disabilities and go back to work. Dropping plans to write songs for a show to be titled "Greek to You," Porter returned to *You Never Know,* the project he had been working on before his accident, a show that was to star Webb, Holman, and Lupe Velez (the "Mexican Spitfire"). It was produced by Lee and J. J. Shubert, who sent the show out on an extended series of tryouts beginning 3 March 1938.

Feuding between the two leading ladies, a weak libretto, and songs that—apart from "At Long Last Love"—were not Porter at his best (in all, he wrote twenty-one numbers, of which only twelve were used), *You Never Know* floundered so badly that even George Abbott, then considered the best "fixer" in the theater business, could not help. When it opened in New York on 21 September 1938, it attracted the worst notices Porter had received in years and disappeared after seventy-eight performances.

Before *You Never Know* ended its short run, Porter was already hobbling about on crutches, hard at work on another show, once again for Freedley and again featuring Gaxton and Moore, this time with Sophie Tucker, "the Last of the Red-Hot Mamas." The book, by Samuel and Bella Spewack, who also directed, was a silly story about Alonzo P. "Stinky" Goodhue, homesick American ambassador to Russia, who tries to have himself recalled by kicking the Nazi ambassador, shooting a counterrevolutionary, and performing other foolish acts. But the book turned out to be irrelevant. *Leave It to Me* (1938) is remembered not for such Porter songs as "Get Out of Town" or "Most Gentlemen Don't Like Love" but for Mary Martin, making her Broadway

panicked horse tried to get up, it fell again, this time crushing Porter's left leg. Afterward, he claimed to have worked on a lyric while he waited for help. "When this horse fell on me, I was too stunned to be conscious of great pain," he recalled. "But until help came, I worked on the lyrics for a song called 'At Long Last Love.'" In fact, Porter went into shock on the way to the hospital and remained unconscious for two days.

Linda Porter, who was in Paris making plans to divorce her husband, was sent for; when she arrived,

debut (as was chorus boy Gene Kelly) doing a coy mock striptease to "My Heart Belongs to Daddy."

Not wishing to be seen being carried into the theater, Porter did not attend the 9 November 1938 opening night. Linda Porter did, however, and she telephoned him excitedly at the end of the show to tell him he had a hit. He had believed that the big number would be the gospel song "Tomorrow," which he had written for Tucker, but Martin, Linda told him, had stopped the show (as she continued to do for another 306 performances). *Leave It to Me,* said critic Richard Watts, boasted "one of Cole Porter's choicest scores." John Mason Brown found Porter "at his topnotch best."

Reenergized by being back in the celebrity spotlight, Porter made plans for a trip to Cuba and then set out to explore the ruins of Machu Picchu in the South American Andes, while Linda Porter, sensing the end of an era, closed down their house on rue Monsieur and shipped all of its furnishings to California. At this time Porter was downcast to learn from Moorhead that he had contracted osteomyelitis, a rarely curable disease of the bone marrow, and that the full recovery he had hoped for would probably never materialize, but he was not going to let it slow him down.

From 1939 to 1944 Porter had five hit shows—*Du Barry Was a Lady* (1939), *Panama Hattie* (1940), *Let's Face It* (1941), *Something for the Boys* (1943), and *Mexican Hayride* (1944), each of which ran for more than four hundred performances. In addition, he composed three successful movie scores—*Broadway Melody of 1940* (1940), *You'll Never Get Rich* (1941), and *Something to Shout About* (1943), as well as seventeen songs for a fourth, to be titled "Mississippi Belle," which was never produced. The roster of songs from this amazing outpouring of creativity includes "I Concentrate on You" and "I've Got My Eyes on You," from *Broadway Melody of 1940;* "Do I Love You?" "But in the Morning, No," "Friendship," and "Well, Did You Evah!" from *Du Barry Was a Lady;* "Let's Be Buddies" and "Make It Another Old-Fashioned, Please" (which gave Merman a rare chance to do a torch song), from *Panama Hattie;* "So Near and Yet So Far," from *You'll Never Get Rich,* which starred Fred Astaire and Rita Hayworth; "Let's Not Talk about Love," a tour de force for Danny Kaye in *Let's Face It;* "You'd Be So Nice to Come Home To," sung by Janet Blair and Don Ameche in *Something to Shout About;* "Hey, Good-Lookin'" and "By the Mississinewah," from *Something for the Boys,* Porter's fifth show starring Merman; and "I Love You," from *Mexican Hayride.* In addition to these songs, Porter had written others for lesser-known or unproduced shows or movies. "Goodbye, Little Dream, Goodbye" was originally intended for *Born to Dance* but ended up being

Lilo singing "I Love Paris" in Porter's 1953 musical
Can-Can *(photograph by Graphic House)*

interpolated into the London musical *O Mistress Mine* (1936). For the unproduced musical *Ever Yours* (1934) Porter wrote "Miss Otis Regrets" and "Thank You So Much, Mrs. Lowsborough-Goodby," which perfectly caught the horror of a ghastly weekend visit:

Thank you so much, Mrs. Lowsborough-Goodby, . . .
For the clinging perfume
And that damp little room,
For those cocktails so hot
And the bath that was not,
For those guests so amusing and mentally bracing
Who talked about racing and racing and racing,
For the ptomaine I got from your famous tin salmon,
For the fortune I lost when you taught me backgammon, . . .
And for making me swear to myself there and then
Never to go for a weekend again.

By 1944 a great deal had changed in Porter's life. Before he had completed the score for *Panama Hattie,* Linda had purchased—with her own money—an elegant country house called Buxton Hill in the Berkshires in Williamstown, Massachusetts. At first, Porter found it remote and lonely, but after a few months he enjoyed working there, as well as throwing lavish weekend parties for the large number of guests that the house could accommodate. He topped *Your Hit Parade* in 1944 with "Don't Fence Me In," a song he had written in 1934

*Ann Miller, Howard Keel, and Kathryn Grayson in a publicity still for the 1953
3-D movie version of* Kiss Me, Kate *(Collection of Paul Talbot)*

(for the unproduced movie *Adios, Argentina*) that had been revived by singing cowboy Roy Rogers. Billy Rose persuaded Porter to write the score for a star-spangled revue that was to feature Beatrice Lillie, Bert Lahr, Dolores Gray, and Benny Goodman. Rose had commissioned sketches by Kaufman, Moss Hart, and Ben Hecht, and even an Igor Stravinsky ballet danced by Alicia Markova and Anton Dolin. Despite enormous advance sales of $350,000, however, *Seven Lively Arts* (1944) closed after only twenty weeks.

Porter, scheduled for more surgery on his legs, slipped into a deep depression. Critics were implying that his work had been declining ever since *Anything Goes*. Reviewing *Seven Lively Arts,* a critic for *The New York Times* said (in spite of the presence in the score of one of Porter's finest ballads, "Ev'ry Time We Say Goodbye"), "the tunes are definitely not Cole Porter's best," and a reviewer for the *New York World-Telegram* wrote, "Cole Porter seems to have lost his inspiration." Such reviews fixed themselves in Porter's mind, and nothing Linda could say or do would persuade him to take a trip and forget his troubles, as he had done so often in the past. Perhaps at this time the only thing that kept him going was his vanity, which was being vastly

indulged by Warner Bros.; the movie studio had been trying for a decade to obtain Porter's permission to film his life story. He had agreed to the proposition a year earlier and accepted a $300,000 arrangement that gave the studio "the right to select from his musical catalogue thirty-five musical compositions to be used in a motion picture," *Night and Day* (1946), based on his life. Arthur Schwartz, himself a successful songwriter, was assigned the producer's role and clearly envisioned the movie as an all-star vehicle, with Cary Grant (Porter's choice) playing Porter and Alexis Smith (Linda Porter's choice) playing his wife.

By the time production on *Night and Day* began in April 1945, several scripts had been written and rejected, and as filming proceeded, disagreements between Grant and director Michael Curtiz escalated. Ignoring these tribulations, Porter plunged into another project, a score for *Around the World in Eighty Days* (1946), a musical produced by Mike Todd and directed by Orson Welles. Porter wrote fifteen songs, none of which was strong, and Welles treated them so ruthlessly that the disenchanted composer left New York the day before the show opened at the Adelphi Theatre on 31 May 1946. It was a dismal, seventy-five-performance failure.

Night and Day, released in August 1946, was a box-office success, and it gave Porter a new prominence even if, to quote *The San Francisco News,* it was "no more the story of Cole Porter's life than a two-cent stamp is of Washington's." In spite of the celebrity generated by the success of the movie, however, Porter's reputation was languishing, and the next project he undertook did little to improve it. Although it later achieved cult status, M-G-M's *The Pirate* (1948), starring Judy Garland and Kelly, attracted tepid reactions from the critics and the public. Porter had written most of the score before the movie, directed by Vincente Minnelli, began production in February 1947. It was not completed until November, mainly because of Garland, who suffered from frequent bouts of "nervous exhaustion." The best song in the movie is one Porter wrote during filming, when Kelly complained about the lack of a "knockabout" song-and-dance number. Porter, drawing on his childhood love of the circus, quickly came up with "Be a Clown":

If you become a doctor, folks'll face you with dread,
If you become a dentist, they'll be glad when you're dead,
You'll get a bigger hand if you can stand on your head,
Be a clown, be a clown, be a clown! . . .
Why be a great composer with your rent in arrears,
Why be a major poet and you'll owe it for years,
When crowds'll pay to giggle if you wiggle your ears?
Be a clown, be a clown, be a clown!

With no new projects on the horizon, Porter was approached by Arnold Saint-Subber, who had been a stage manager for a production of William Shakespeare's *The Taming of the Shrew* starring Alfred Lunt and Lynn Fontanne. Their backstage bickering during the production had given Saint-Subber the idea of creating a musical featuring just such a quarrelsome pair. Enlisting Lemuel Ayers as his coproducer, he had first approached Burton Lane to write the music, but Lane, famously irresolute, said no.

Temporarily abandoning his search for a composer, Saint-Subber approached Samuel and Bella Spewack to write a libretto. Bella Spewack was as dubious about the project as Lane had been, unable to see *The Taming of the Shrew* as a Broadway musical, until she came up with a play-within-the-play idea. She then approached Porter to write the music, but he was just as adamantly against the idea as she herself had first been. She culled the text and brought him titles that included "I've Come to Wive It Wealthily in Padua," "Where Is the Life That Late I Led?" and "Were Thine That Special Face"—and still Porter was unconvinced. He was finally won over, however, and *Kiss Me, Kate* became his biggest hit. By confining Porter to a single dramatic milieu, the libretto forced him to maintain a consistency

of tone; as a result his score was, for the first time, a score, as opposed to a string of unconnected or even interchangeable numbers. The finished product was a tapestry of hits—"Wunderbar"; "Always True to You in My Fashion"; a big romantic number, "So in Love"; a sizzling dance routine, "Too Darn Hot," which opens the second act; and everyone's favorite, "Brush Up Your Shakespeare," presenting the sometimes raunchy advice of two gangsters:

Brush up your Shakespeare
And the women you will wow.
Just declaim a few lines from "Othella"
And they'll think you're a helluva fella. . . .
If she says your behavior is heinous,
Kick her right in the "Coriolanus.". . .
When your baby is pleading for pleasure
Let her sample your "Measure for Measure.". . .
And if still she won't give you a bonus
You know what Venus got from Adonis!

Even more amazing is the fact that throughout the period he was writing the songs for *Kiss Me, Kate,* Porter was suffering "complete agony" from ulcers and an abscess on his right leg. Despite his pain he attended rehearsals, immaculate as always, carrying a gold-topped cane and wearing a whistle around his neck, which he would use to stop the dancers so he could suggest changes. By the time *Kiss Me, Kate* opened for tryouts in Philadelphia, it was almost "in." Five minutes of dialogue were cut to allow for encores of "Brush Up Your Shakespeare," and the nostalgic "We Shall Never Be Younger" was dropped.

Opening in New York to a wild welcome at the New Century Theatre on 30 December 1948, *Kiss Me, Kate* was a triumph for everyone involved, a perfect marriage of book, lyrics, and music that works as well now as it did that star-spangled first night. All the reviews were unqualified raves, and the show settled in for a record-breaking run of 1,077 performances, winning the 1949 Tony Award for best musical (beating out *South Pacific*) and another Tony—Porter's first—for the remarkable score.

Porter did not long enjoy his success, remaining unconvinced that he had shaken off his jinx. Suffering constant pain, insomnia, and blinding headaches; convinced he was going broke, and ever more concerned over the health of his constantly ailing wife, he immersed himself in another show with Ayers and Saint-Subber. Porter was now to be cursed with his own success. Thus, despite the deliciously fey "Nobody's Chasing Me" and "From This Moment On" (ignored by every out-of-town reviewer and dropped before the New York opening) and despite frantic rewriting and cutting on the part of play "fix-

Sheet music for a song from the 1956 movie musical based on Philip Barry's play The Philadelphia Story
(*from Marion Short,* Hollywood Movie Songs, *1999*)

ers" Abbott and F. Hugh Herbert, *Out of This World* ran for only 157 performances.

For almost two years Porter sank into deeper and deeper depression. Not a single offer came his way after *Out of This World,* and he was convinced that none ever would. Thinking to cheer him up, Linda—in failing health herself and unable to accompany him—arranged a six-week vacation for him in Paris. He was there only a week. After electroshock therapy at Doctors' Hospital, Porter showed enough improvement to appear in a two-hour salute to him on *The Ed Sullivan Show* in February 1952 before returning to California. There he worked sporadically on *Boy Meets Girl,* a show the Spewacks were putting together for Ray Bolger, but Porter withdrew because "the subject matter, even though it may be excellent, does not appeal to me." He also turned down a musical version of Rudolf Besier's 1931 play *The Barretts of Wimpole Street.* There was wis-

dom as well as apathy in Porter's decisions. On Broadway, people were queuing up to see *Guys and Dolls* (1950), *The King and I* (1951), *Wish You Were Here* (1952), and *Wonderful Town* (1953). In order to compete with these shows, one needed a strong libretto. To Porter's joy, one came along.

Ernest H. Martin and Cy Feuer, producers of Frank Loesser's *Where's Charley?* (1948) and *Guys and Dolls,* had been nursing an idea about a show set in Montmartre in the 1890s and featuring La Goulue, a dancer in Henri Toulouse-Lautrec's paintings. Although Martin and Feuer did not know Porter, they approached him and were delighted when he welcomed their idea. When Abe Burrows was brought in to write the book, however, his research led the producers to abandon the original idea and opt for Burrows's plot about the real-life attempts of Parisian puritans to censor the cancan. Porter set to work immediately, and within a month, after daily phone calls in which Burrows read him his latest dialogue, much of the score of *Can-Can* (1953) was written.

On 29 July 1952 Kate Porter suffered a cerebral hemorrhage and went into a coma. Cole Porter flew out to Peru and remained there, working on the title song for *Can-Can* as his mother lay dying. The results are a chilling testament to his ability to compartmentalize his emotions:

If in Deauville ev'ry swell can,
It is so simple to do,
If Debussy and Ravel can,
'Twill be so easy for you.
If the Louvre custodian can,
If the Garde Republican can,
If Van Gogh and Matisse and Cézanne can,
Baby you can can-can too!

Kate Porter died on 2 August 1952 and was buried in the family plot. Cole Porter stayed on in Peru to clear up her estate–apart from a few minor bequests, she left him all her money and property–and then returned to New York to resume work. "Generally speaking," Feuer said of Porter's working method, "He would have nothing to do with the book." He recalled once telling the composer they were going to have a production meeting. "I don't want to go," Porter said. "I have nothing to contribute to that. I don't want to be uncomfortable. Just tell me what you want written and I'll write it."

On 23 March 1953 *Can-Can* began tryouts in Philadelphia with the largest advance sale–$195,000–that that city had ever seen for a musical; at the end of its six-week run the gross was more than $300,000, and New York knew a hit was coming. Once again, Porter's score was an embarrassment of riches that resulted in the jettisoning of thirteen songs. At the beginning of the project Martin had told Porter he did not want any Paris songs in the score, but Porter went ahead and wrote one anyway. When he first played "I Love Paris" for Feuer, a Juilliard School graduate, the producer was amazed by the release (bridge), which suddenly went from C minor to C major and stayed there. When Feuer in turn played the song later for his wife, Posy, she said "For God's sake, it's a Jewish song!" "Not in the middle," Feuer told her.

Opening on 7 May 1953, *Can-Can* was immediately pronounced a hit. The brilliant choreography of Michael Kidd and the sinuously sexy dancing of Gwen Verdon, who stopped the show, won enormous praise, although critics were less than enthusiastic about the book and tepid about Porter's songs. By the end of the year, however, five of the songs were ranked by *Variety* among the top tunes of the year, and *Can-Can* went on to run for 892 performances, making it the second-longest-running of Porter's shows.

Porter left for the West Coast two days after the premiere of *Can-Can* to work on M-G-M's movie version of *Kiss Me, Kate*, released in 1953. It suffered some distortion through being filmed in what was then called 3-D, but the sheer swagger of the story and the brilliance of the score–into which "From This Moment On" was interpolated–ensured the success of the movie. On 26 July 1953 *The New York Times* reported that Porter was working on another Feuer and Martin show, this time an adaptation by Kaufman (who was also to direct) and his wife, Leueen McGrath, of the Garbo movie *Ninotchka* (1939). But on 20 May 1954 Linda Porter died of complications caused by emphysema. She left her husband just under $2 million and two houses, the one at Buxton Hill and the other on rue Monsieur in Paris. She was buried, not in Williamstown as she had wished, but in the Porter family plot at Mount Hope Cemetery in Peru. Linda's one fear had been that she would soon be forgotten after her death. "If only I was [important enough] so a flower or something would be named for me," she had said just before she died. As soon as it could be done, Porter commissioned horticulturists to develop an especially large pink rose called the "Linda Porter" rose.

Porter immersed himself in the score for *Silk Stockings* (1955), the stage adaptation of *Ninotchka*. Rehearsals began on 18 October 1954 and at first went badly. "It looks disastrous," Porter wrote to a friend, "slow, gloomy, and most of the numbers very badly done." During the Philadelphia tryouts, Kaufman threw up his hands and quit, taking his wife with him. The producers brought in Burrows to fix the book, while Feuer took over the director's role. The result, as Walter Kerr said, reviewing the opening-night performance, was "the end product of a fabulous out-of-town sortie in which the authors were changed, the choreographers were changed, and the changes were changed." Nonetheless, *Silk Stockings* was a success, and the reason was undoubtedly Porter's score. Although nowhere near as good as the score for *Can-Can*, it was good enough for a healthy run of 477 performances, for RCA Victor to release an original-cast album, and for M-G-M to buy the movie rights. The hit song was "All of You," in which fast-talking agent Steve Canfield (played by Ameche) maps out a physical tour of commissar Ninotchka (Hildegarde Neff). But the comedy numbers were admirable, too, notably "Paris Loves Lovers," crooned by Canfield as Ninotchka interjects "Capitalistic!" "Anti-Communistic," and "Not at all collectivistic"; and the sly "Siberia," about the place where "When it's cocktail time 'twill be so nice / Just to know you'll not have to phone for ice." Porter decided not to attend the opening night, leaving for a long European trip on 19 February 1955.

Immediately after returning from his trip, Porter learned that his oldest, dearest male friend, Sturges, had died. To assuage his grief, Porter once again buried himself in work, this time a score for a movie musical based on Philip Barry's 1939 play *The Philadelphia Story*. The stellar cast of M-G-M's *High Society* (1956) included Bing Crosby, Grace Kelly, Frank Sinatra, Celeste Holm, and Louis Armstrong, all of whom turned in enjoyable performances. Porter's score included "I Love You, Samantha" (his favorite); "You're Sensational"; "Who Wants to Be a Millionaire?"; "Mind if I Make Love to You?"; "Now You Has Jazz"; a revised version of "Well, Did You Evah!" from *Du Barry Was a Lady* (with updated lyrics contributed by associate producer Saul Chaplin, who became Porter's musical amanuensis); and the untypically (for Porter) gentle, if forgotten, "Little One":

Little one, life was gloomy,
Felt that life would sure undo me,
Till, one night, you happened to me,
My little one.
Little one, no controversy,
You're my downfall, you're my Circe
I'm a good guy, show me mercy,
My little one.
I have such love for you
Our future could be
Heaven above for you
And paradise for me.
Little one, fate might miscarry,
Little one, why do you tarry?
Little one, when may I marry you,
My little one?

To Porter's surprise, when *High Society* was released in August 1956, "True Love," written for Crosby to sing to Kelly, turned into a major hit and was nominated for an Academy Award. That November, Max Dreyfus, Porter's publisher, wrote that in all his years of music publishing, "nothing has given me greater pleasure than the extraordinary success of your 'True Love.' It is truly a simple, beautiful, tasteful composition, worthy of a Franz Schubert."

In February 1957 Porter went on a tour of Europe and the Near East, tacking on a cruise around the Greek Islands before heading out to California to work on two more movies for M-G-M, a screen adaptation of *Silk Stockings* and *Les Girls,* both released that same year. The adaptation needed little input from him, other than two serviceable new numbers, but he produced no less than fourteen songs for *Les Girls,* starring Gene Kelly and Mitzi Gaynor. In the final print only five were used, of which "Ça, c'est

l'Amour" (essentially a retread of "C'est Magnifique," from *Can-Can*) was the only one to catch on.

There was to be only one more Porter show, and a poor one at that, an adaptation of the story of Aladdin from *The Thousand and One Nights,* with a script by S. J. Perelman, produced by Richard Lewine for the CBS network's *Du Pont Show of the Month. Aladdin* was broadcast on 21 February 1958. Porter's nine songs from the show have not lasted, although Barbra Streisand's 1963 recording of "Come to the Supermarket in Old Peking" had brief popularity. Before the show was even broadcast, however, Porter was hospitalized again for the treatment of a duodenal ulcer and the thirty-second operation on his right leg. Despite massive doses of antibiotics, the leg refused to heal, and in April he was rushed back to the hospital to have it amputated.

For six more years, lonely, angry, and driven to despair by the conviction that he was no longer a composer, a lyricist, or for that matter even a man, Porter struggled to maintain some semblance of his previous lifestyle and keep abreast of professional matters; it was a brave, but inevitably rearguard, action. Although honors were heaped on him, although tributes and birthday celebrations were held to mark his reaching the age of seventy, he no longer wrote songs and no longer played the piano, eating less and less and drinking more and more. There were several more hospitalizations, the final one coming on 13 October 1964, when Porter was operated on for the removal of a kidney stone. Two days later he was dead.

In the popular mind Cole Porter remains the debonair party entertainer singing his slightly risqué songs at the piano. Less frequently is it acknowledged that he was a painstakingly meticulous craftsman and as natural a melodist as Rodgers or George Gershwin. Wealthy beyond most peoples' dreams, Porter drove himself like a galley slave, producing scores for twenty-seven Broadway shows and nearly as many movies, always trying to do that most impossible thing of all, improve on the best he could do. More remarkably still, he occasionally succeeded. The best of his work not only survives but shows no signs of losing its charm. No songwriter could possibly ask for more than that.

Letters:

Jean Howard, *Travels with Cole Porter* (New York: Abrams, 1991).

Interviews:

David Grafton, *Red, Hot and Rich! An Oral Biography of Cole Porter* (New York: Stein & Day, 1987).

Biographies:

Richard G. Hubler, *The Cole Porter Story* (New York: Holt, Rinehart & Winston, 1965);

Charles Schwartz, *Cole Porter: A Biography* (New York: Dial, 1977);

Stephen Citron, *Noel and Cole: The Sophisticates* (New York: Oxford University Press, 1993);

William McBrien, *Cole Porter: A Biography* (New York: Knopf, 1998).

References:

Philip Furia, *The Poets of Tin Pan Alley: A History of America's Great Lyricists* (New York: Oxford University Press, 1990), pp. 153–180;

Thomas S. Hischak, *Word Crazy: Broadway Lyricists from Cohan to Sondheim* (New York: Praeger, 1991), pp. 55–62;

Robert Kimball, ed., *Cole* (New York: Holt, Rinehart & Winston, 1971);

Walter Rimler, *A Cole Porter Discography* (San Francisco: Charles Sylvan, 1995).

Selected Discography:

Anything Goes, 1962 revival cast, Epic, EK 15100, ca. 1986;

Anything Goes: Capitol Sings Cole Porter, Capitol, 7 96361 2, 1991;

Ben Bagley's Cole Porter Revisited, Painted Smiles, 121, 1990;

Born to Dance, motion-picture soundtrack (1936), Classic International Filmusicals, 3001, ca. 1970s;

Broadway Melody of 1940, motion-picture soundtrack, Classic International Filmusicals, 3002, ca. 1970s;

Can-Can, motion-picture soundtrack, Capitol, SW-1301, 1960;

Cole Porter's Aladdin, original television cast (1958), Sony, SK 48205, 1992;

Cole Porter's Anything Goes, original Broadway cast (1934), Smithsonian, R 007, 1977;

Cole Porter's Out of This World, original Broadway cast (1951), Sony, SK 48223, 1992;

Ethel Merman in Something for the Boys, selections, AEI, 004, 1992;

Fifty Million Frenchmen, 1991 studio cast recording, New World, 80417-2, 1991;

Ella Fitzgerald, *Ella Fitzgerald Sings the Cole Porter Song Book* (1956), Verve, 314 537 257-2, 1997;

Fitzgerald, *Ella Loves Cole*, Atlantic, 1631, 1972;

From This Moment On: The Songs of Cole Porter, Smithsonian, RD 047, 1992;

High Society, motion-picture soundtrack (1956), Capitol, 93787, ca. 1999;

Kiss Me, Kate, original Broadway cast (1948), Columbia, CK 4140, ca. 1973;

Let's Face It; Red, Hot and Blue; Leave It to Me, selections, Smithsonian, R 016, 1979;

Mary Martin, *Decca Presents Mary Martin in an Album of Cole Porter Songs*, Decca, 123, ca. 1940;

Mabel Mercer, *Mabel Mercer Sings Cole Porter*, Rhino, R2 71690, 1994;

Panama Hattie, selections (1940), on *12 Songs from Call Me Madam, with Selections from Panama Hattie*, MCA, 10521, 1992;

The Pirate, motion-picture soundtrack (1948), Sony, AK 48608, 1991;

Cole Porter, *Cole Porter, 1924–1944*, JJA, 19732, 1973;

Porter, *Cole Sings Porter: Rare and Unreleased Songs from Can-can and Jubilee*, Koch, 7171, 1994;

Red, Hot and Blue, selections, on *Red, Hot and Blue; Stars in Your Eyes*, AEI, 1147, 1991;

Red, Hot and Blue: A Tribute to Cole Porter, Chrysalis, F2 21799, 1990;

Bobby Short, *Bobby Short Loves Cole Porter*, Atlantic, SD 2-606, 1971;

Frank Sinatra, *Frank Sinatra Sings the Select Cole Porter*, Capitol, 7 96611 2, 1991;

Kiri Te Kanawa, *Kiri Sings Porter*, EMI, CDQ 55050, 1994;

Unpublished Cole Porter, Painted Smiles, PS 1358, n.d.;

Lee Wiley, *Lee Wiley Sings: The Songs of George and Ira Gershwin; The Songs of Cole Porter*, Audiophile, ACD-1, 1989.

Andy Razaf

(16 December 1895 – 3 February 1973)

Barry Singer

Music is by Thomas "Fats" Waller unless otherwise indicated.

SELECTED SONGS FROM THEATRICAL PRO-
DUCTIONS: *The Passing Show of 1913* (1913)–
"Baltimo'" (music by Andy Razaf);

Keep Shufflin' (1928)–"Willow Tree";

Load of Coal (1929)–"Honeysuckle Rose"; "My Fate Is
in Your Hands"; "Zonky";

Hot Chocolates (1929), music by Waller and Harry
Brooks–"Ain't Misbehavin'"; "(What Did I Do to
Be So) Black and Blue";

Kitchen Mechanic's Revue (1930), music by James P.
Johnson–"Go Harlem"; "A Porter's Love Song to
a Chamber Maid";

Blackbirds of 1930 (1930), music by Eubie Blake–"Memories of You"; "My Handy Man Ain't Handy No
More"; "You're Lucky to Me";

Cotton Club Parade of 1933 (1933)–"That's What I Like
'bout the South" (interpolation, music by Razaf);

Hot Chocolates (1935)–"What Harlem Is to Me" (music
by Paul Denniker and Russell Wooding);

Tan Manhattan (1941), music by Blake–"I'd Give a Dollar for a Dime" (originally "I'll Take a Nickel for
a Dime").

SELECTED SONGS PUBLISHED INDEPEN-
DENTLY OF THEATRICAL OR MOTION-
PICTURE PRODUCTIONS: "Squeeze Me"
(1925), music by Waller and Clarence Williams;

"Goin' Crazy with the Blues" (1927), music by J. C.
Johnson;

"My Special Friend Is Back in Town" (1927), lyric by
Razaf and Bob Schafer, music by Johnson;

"Do What You Did Last Night" (1928), music by
Johnson;

"Dusky Stevedore" (1928), music by Johnson;

"Guess Who's in Town? (Nobody but That Gal of
Mine)" (1928), music by Johnson;

"Lonesome Swallow" (1928), music by Johnson;

*Andy Razaf, 1924 (Schomburg Center
for Research in Black Culture)*

"Louisiana" (1928), lyric by Razaf and Schafer, music
by Johnson;

"My Handy Man" (1928), music by Razaf;

"Take Your Tomorrow (And Give Me Today)"
(1928), music by Johnson;

"Ain't-Cha' Glad?" (1929);

"Find Out What They Like, and How They Like It" (1929);

"S'posin'" (1929), music by Paul Denniker;

"Blue Turning Grey over You" (1930);

"On Revival Day" (1930), music by Razaf;

"Concentratin' on You" (1931);

"How Can You Face Me?" (1932);

"If It Ain't Love" (1932), music by Waller and Don Redman;

"Keepin' Out of Mischief Now" (1932);

"Strange as It Seems" (1932);

"Christopher Columbus" (1936), music by Leon "Chu" Berry;

"Make Believe Ball Room" (1936), music by Denniker;

"The Milkmen's Matinee" (1936), lyric and music by Razaf, Denniker, and Joe Davis;

"Stompin' at the Savoy" (1936), music by Benny Goodman, Chick Webb, and Edgar Sampson;

"Cryin' Mood" (1937), music by Webb;

"The Joint Is Jumpin'" (1938), lyric by Razaf and Johnson;

"In the Mood" (1939), music by Joe Garland;

"I'm Gonna Move to the Outskirts of Town" (1942), lyric by Razaf and William Weldon, music by Weldon;

"Knock Me a Kiss" (1942), lyric by Razaf and Mike Jackson, music by Jackson;

"Massachusetts" (1942), music by Charles "Luckey" Roberts;

"Gee Baby, Ain't I Good to You?" (1944), lyric by Razaf and Redman, music by Redman.

Race has always played a disproportionate role in American popular music. Certainly, in the pantheon of American popular music, the place of Andy Razaf is assured, irrespective of color. Yet, it remains impossible to assess Razaf's achievements without addressing also the pigmentation of his skin. No black lyricist was more talented or accomplished nor finally more important. In fact, few lyricists of any race wrote as successfully as Razaf did during the years between the world wars. His collaborators included just about every black composer of significance, along with an impressive number of white composers. Primarily, though, Razaf is remembered for his work with two songwriting giants, both black: the ragtime pianist Eubie Blake and the Harlem stride piano player Thomas "Fats" Waller. The songs that Razaf wrote in collaboration with these two men—including, among many others, "Ain't Misbehavin'" (1929), "(What Did I Do to Be So) Black and Blue" (1929), "Honeysuckle Rose" (1929), "Memories of You" (1930), and "You're Lucky to Me" (1930)—are not just timeless standards; they remain benchmarks in the

The future Andy Razaf, Andreamenentania Paul Razafinkeriefo, age ten, with his mother, Jennie Waller Razafinkeriefo (Schomburg Center for Research in Black Culture)

evolution of both popular music and racial equality in the United States.

Razaf was born Andreamenentania (pronounced *Andrea-men-tania*) Paul Razafinkeriefo (pronounced *Ra-zahf-keer-yef*) on 16 December 1895 in Washington, D.C., the son of an unusual union—his father was a Madagascan of royal blood, and his mother was an American-born daughter of freed slaves. The catalyst behind this exotic coupling was Razaf's Missouri-born maternal grandfather, John Louis Waller, a notable figure in his own right, a self-educated lawyer who, after settling his family in Kansas following their liberation from slavery, launched himself into Republican politics at first the local and soon the national level.

In 1890, as a direct result of his campaign effort for the newly elected Republican President Benjamin Harrison, Waller received a patronage appointment as U.S. consul to Madagascar. Arriving in Madagascar the following year, he aligned himself quickly with the local royal rulers, marrying off his sixteen-year-old daughter, Jennie, to Henry Razafinkeriefo, purportedly a nephew of the reigning Madagascan queen. Waller also received valuable land grants from the queen at this time, land that he planned to develop as a back-to-Africa colony for American blacks. These machinations brought Waller into a dangerous con-

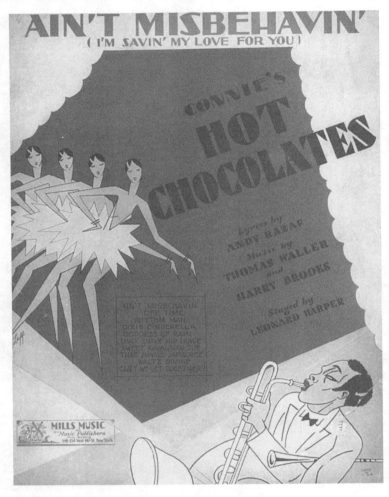

Sheet music for Razaf's best-known song, published in 1929
(Bruccoli Clark Layman Archives)

frontation with the French governors of Madagascar, who had long sought to annex the country as a protectorate. When, in 1895, the French finally invaded and conquered the island, they also arrested Waller, though his family, including the by-now-pregnant Jennie, managed to escape. Within months Waller was hastily convicted by a French court and imprisoned, Henry Razafinkeriefo was killed in battle with the French, and Jennie Waller, upon her arrival in the United States, gave birth to a son, Andrea.

The ensuing hue and cry around the world for Waller's release was an unprecedented phenomenon in American history: an international incident on behalf of a former slave. In the ugly denouement to the case, the American government ultimately secured Waller's release from prison by acceding to the specious French evidence asserting his guilt in providing information to France's enemies. When Waller at last returned in 1896 to resume his life in the United States, he did so under a

cloud of unjustified suspicion from which he never quite emerged.

Andy Razaf grew up in the home of his grandfather, absorbing there a profound sense of pride mingled with righteous indignation about race, as well as a driving ambition laced with a powerful desire for vindication. The focus for this ambition became the written word; family legend records Razaf writing his first original verse at the age of ten. Members of Razaf's immediate family, including his mother, both grandparents, and an aunt, all wrote verse inveterately, for pleasure. Razaf later acknowledged to an interviewer that he had in fact hoped to become a poet but recognized early on the need to make a living, to support himself and his widowed mother. He decided therefore, in his own words, to "versify for music."

Razaf's first song lyric was written as early as 1909, at the end of an initial era of opportunity for blacks in the American song business. The deaths of

Ernest Hogan in 1908 and George Walker in 1909, followed by Bob Cole in 1911—three black songwriters who had dominated Broadway and Tin Pan Alley during the previous decade—brought this period to an abrupt halt.

With characteristic aggressiveness, Razaf sent his early song efforts out for approval, not to any of the black songwriters of the moment but rather to Charles K. Harris, the dominant white songwriting figure of the period, both as a publisher and as the composer of, among other songs, "After the Ball" (1892). Harris returned the submission with a personal reply that Razaf saved: "Dear Andrea," he wrote. "Your lyrics show great merit but I would advise you to go into some other field."

Four years later Razaf was working as an elevator operator in a Tin Pan Alley office building, pitching his songs to anyone in the business who might listen. Though the song industry, by 1913, was no longer especially welcoming to black creators, the notion of buying something tuneful from a young black elevator boy apparently proved acceptable to someone in the Shubert theatrical organization. Razaf's song "Baltimo'," for which he wrote both words and music, was acquired that year by the Shuberts and interpolated into their Broadway production *The Passing Show of 1913*. Andrea Razaf, his last name truncated for professional purposes, was, at seventeen, a published Broadway songwriter.

In April 1915 he married Annabelle Miller, age twenty-four, a housemaid in the employ of an opera singer named Eleanor Kent. The couple settled in the newly burgeoning uptown Manhattan black neighborhood of Harlem. Over the ensuing five years, however, Razaf found little success as a lyricist, working instead at various odd jobs, including a stint as Madame Kent's butler. This deeply frustrating period perhaps not coincidentally paralleled Razaf's development into something of a race radical; a rabble-rousing activist in the spirit of his grandfather Waller. Throughout the years of World War I and then in its immediate wake, Razaf regularly published incendiary writings celebrating the "New Negro" in a variety of "New Order" African American periodicals, including *The Messenger, The Emancipator,* and *The Crusader.* One example from these feverish outpourings characterizes the lot:

Beware! Race hater how you play with fire,
For there are limits to your mad desire;
Too long we've stood your hanging and your burning
But you are nearing where the road is turning!
We love the law but love of life is stronger,
We cannot play the "gentle lambs" much longer;
Soon comes the day when you must find out whether
Twelve million blacks will live—or die together!

Ethel Waters and Eubie Blake performing "You're Lucky to Me" in Razaf and Blake's revue Blackbirds of 1930

Razaf, by the beginning of 1920, was well known in Harlem, not merely as a name in print but as a secular street-corner preacher who, from a soapbox at Harlem's "Speaker's Corner"—135th Street and Lenox Avenue—hectored daily on the same racial themes that he wrote about so fiercely. Yet, Razaf was wearying of this dead-end existence as a thwarted songwriter in New York. By May 1920 he and his wife were living in Cleveland, where Razaf played semiprofessional baseball for a season.

The monumental success of Mamie Smith's seminal blues recording "Crazy Blues," released later that year, put an end to this respite, however. As of January 1921 Razaf was back in Harlem, writing blues songs for the suddenly wide-open "Race" music market, working with such talented black songwriters as Jack Palmer, Maceo Pinkard, and both Spencer and Clarence Williams, as well as the young pianist and composer J. C. Johnson. He quickly established himself as one of the more clever and prolific writers of so-called bawdy blues—catchy, suggestive, double-entendre, black genre tunes for which the American music-buying public now exhibited an inexhaustible appetite.

Sometime in 1921 or 1923 (a precise dating remains speculative), Razaf attended a piano contest at the Roosevelt Theater in Harlem and afterward felt

Sheet music for a song from a Razaf and Blake revue (from Marion Short,
The Gold in Your Piano Bench, *1997)*

compelled to introduce himself to the winner, a teenage prodigy of impressive girth and astounding keyboard virtuosity named Waller, known to his friends and, increasingly, to his fans around Harlem, as "Fats." The two, though seemingly dissimilar in almost every respect, hit it off and soon were writing songs together.

It has been said that Razaf and Fats Waller were opposites who counterbalanced beautifully, disparate partners in a perfect if unlikely marriage. "During their years together," Waller's son Maurice later observed in *Fats Waller* (1977), "Andy's methodic planning and discipline served as a necessary balance for his partner's instability." Certainly, Waller was as wildly carefree as Razaf was intensely focused. Yet, beneath the surface, the two men were oddly alike. As impractical as Waller often was, he proved far more diplomatic than his more business-wise but often artlessly outspoken partner. As levelheaded as Razaf was, his sense of injustice could move him to behavior that was as volatile and self-destructive as that which made Waller famous.

Both men also wrote quickly and hardly ever rewrote. For Razaf and Waller, songwriting was an act of spontaneous creation.

It seems appropriate that their first published song together remains shrouded in a cloak of questionable attribution. Over the years Razaf, on occasion, but especially Waller sold songs outright to other Tin Pan Alley composers—sometimes black but more often white men and women whose names would then appear on the published tunes as sole authors. This practice was as much a function of the ruthless business ethic of Tin Pan Alley as it was an issue of racial discrimination, though certainly both factors played significant roles. In any case, tracing the work of Razaf and Waller frequently descends to the level of detective work. Such is the case with the tune "Squeeze Me" (1925).

Waller's mentor was a Harlem piano giant named James P. Johnson, one of the fathers of the "stride piano" style that Waller employed so brilliantly.

On a Harlem piano circuit that included bravura solo performing in clubs, bars, and all-night "rent parties" hosted in local apartments, Johnson was the acknowledged king, alongside such stride masters as Charles "Luckey" Roberts and Willie "The Lion" Smith (Razaf, in time, worked with all three). In this musical world of fluid, ongoing, improvisational give-and-take, one of Johnson's signature pieces, which he called "Fascination," had been reworked by other circuit pianists into a vulgar, bawdy blues number known as "The Boys in the Boat." Waller, in turn, had taken the limerick-like cadence of "The Boys in the Boat" and created something that he called "The Boston Blues."

Ever on the lookout for promising new talent, the New Orleans–born Clarence Williams—a pianist and composer in his own right and an all-around music business entrepreneur, one of a handful of ambitious black music men who had capitalized on the new 1920s vogue for black music by forming their own publishing companies—seized upon Waller and his incipient song. Rendering the young pianist's "The Boston Blues" from twelve-bar blues form to sixteen-bar Tin Pan Alley song form, Williams added a lyric written, it would seem, by Razaf in a for-hire arrangement. This lyric parodied a popular Victor Herbert waltz from the 1906 operetta *Mlle. Modiste,* a song called "Kiss Me Again." When Herbert's music publishers threatened legal action, Williams apparently reengaged Razaf to transform the lyric further. This new song was finally published in 1925 as "Squeeze Me," by Waller and Williams only. The song went on to achieve fairly substantial success. Razaf would not even acknowledge the lyric as his own until the 1960s when, most offhandedly, he at last did so to an inquiring journalist.

Of all the songwriters to emerge from Harlem in the 1920s, Razaf and Waller, as a team, became the most prolific, the most indigenously representative of black Harlem and its music during this period, and, in that respect, the most important. That they also wound up, in many ways, the most victimized professionally by the dubious business practices of Tin Pan Alley only confirms how symbolic their partnership was to the decade. "Squeeze Me" remains clouded enough in its history and exceptional enough in overall quality to qualify as Razaf and Waller's first official collaboration, although it might have been preceded by other songs.

From 1923 through 1930 they published more than forty songs, a number that does not reflect the unknowable quantity of uncredited tunes the pair also sold outright. Engaged during this period as an in-house songwriting team for the legendary Harlem nightspot Connie's Inn, they began turning out entire scores for Connie's Inn floor shows two or three times a year, scores that yielded such gems as "Zonky," "My

Razaf (right) with pianist-composer James P. Johnson, with whom he wrote the Kitchen Mechanic's Revue *in 1930 (Andy Razaf Estate)*

Fate Is in Your Hands," and one of their signature songs, "Honeysuckle Rose," all written for the show *Load of Coal* (1929). They also composed, in 1928, approximately half of a Broadway score, sharing credit with James P. Johnson and his lyricist, Henry Creamer (alongside supplementary contributing songwriters Clarence Todd and Con Conrad), for *Keep Shufflin',* one of the better and more successful black musicals to emerge in the wake of Blake and Noble Sissle's landmark "colored" Broadway breakthrough in 1921, *Shuffle Along.*

The most significant event of Razaf and Waller's career together was the Connie's Inn floor show that they scored in early 1929, initially known during its uptown nightclub run as *Hot Feet.* Razaf's preliminary work on the score began with Waller still in prison for nonpayment of alimony, a frequent occurrence in Waller's life. Collaborating with Harry Brooks, resi-

Performers on the stage of Connie's Inn in Harlem, where Razaf and Thomas "Fats" Waller were the in-house songwriting team from 1923 to 1930 (Schomburg Center for Research in Black Culture)

dent pianist for the Connie's Inn house band, Razaf prepared verses for a handful of songs that Waller, upon his release, then supplied with refrains. Other songs, however, Razaf and Waller created wholly on their own for this score, with no help from Brooks, who nevertheless was generously credited by the pair for all the songs. *Hot Feet* proved such a success uptown that, with the silent backing of gangster Dutch Schultz, the show was transferred to Broadway under the new, brazenly stereotyping title *Hot Chocolates*. For this transfer Razaf and Waller, in a matter of weeks, composed two new numbers (again sharing credit with Brooks) that proved to be among the finest and most enduring of their partnership: "Ain't Misbehavin'" and "(What Did I Do to Be So) Black and Blue."

In a sense, "Ain't Misbehavin'" constituted Razaf's lyric retort to all the endlessly suggestive, bawdy blues variations he had been compelled to compose since the onset of the 1920s. The song is a double entendre that does not even try to be naughty, ingenuously affirming home, heart, and devotion to one love, set against the undercutting drollery of Waller's melody:

> No one to talk with,
> All by myself,
> No one to walk with
> But I'm happy on the shelf,

Ain't misbehavin',
I'm savin' my love for you.

Razaf's words are the sincere words of a reformed man, but, matched with Waller's music, they reverberate with double-edged whimsy:

> Like Jack Horner
> In the corner,
> Don't go nowhere,
> What do I care?
> Your kisses are worth waiting for,
> Believe me–
> I don't stay out late,
> Don't care to go,
> I'm home about eight,
> Just me and my radio,
> Ain't misbehavin'
> I'm savin' my love for you.

The song remains the team's quintessential expression, an evocation of Razaf's stolid reliability and Waller's irresistible unreliability, conjoined and everlasting. "Ain't Misbehavin'" became, almost instantaneously upon its introduction, the most enduringly popular hit of their collaboration.

"Black and Blue" was another matter. Over the years many have cited it as the first American racial-protest song. Certainly, Razaf's lyric bared essences of racial discontent that had rarely if ever been addressed

Waller in 1935 (Andy Razaf Estate)

by any African American musically. According to Razaf, the song was written during the pre-Broadway tryout of the show, in response to an order from Schultz for a "comedy number" addition to the existing score: "something," in Schultz's words (according to Razaf), "for a little colored girl singing how tough it is being colored." Evading the base intent of Schultz's premise, Razaf wrote a lyric that outwardly, at least, addressed intraracial prejudice between lighter- and darker-skinned blacks, a fact of African American life that Razaf loathed and was no doubt glad to skewer in passing. His true intentions for "Black and Blue" could not have been clearer: to compose a lyric that confronted how tough it was in a white world to be black. Nor could his execution have been more deft. It took considerable courage, moreover, to express these intentions on the stage of a Broadway-bound black musical revue in 1929, particularly under the eye of Schultz.

Razaf's lyric for the verse and opening chorus of the song mask his intent with coarse, whimsical, almost minstrel-like references: "old empty bed, / Springs hard as lead / Pains in my head, / Feel like old Ned, / All my life through, I've been so black and blue." The bridge, however, offers a raw, frank pronouncement:

I'm white inside,
It don't help my case,
'Cause I can't hide
What is on my face.

With those words Razaf resolutely fractured the repressed traditions of black entertainment expression in the United States. "Just 'cause you're black, folks think you lack," he continued. "They laugh at you and scorn you too / What did I do to be so black and blue? / How will it end? / Ain't got a friend, / My only sin is in my skin, / What did I do to be so black and blue?"

Louis Armstrong, who made the classic recording of Razaf, Waller, and Harry Brooks's "(What Did I Do to Be So) Black and Blue" (1929) (from Barry Singer, Black and Blue, *1992)*

"Black and Blue" remains an achievement of consummate lyric-writing craft, of cunning, of cleverness, of musical empathy on the part of Razaf's collaborator, Fats Waller, and of profound, adamant pride and conviction on Razaf's own. That the song also wound up something of a hit owes a great deal to the riveting performance "Black and Blue" received from the greatest of all jazz trumpeters and jazz vocalists, Louis Armstrong, who recorded the tune in July 1929, as well as to Edith Wilson's highly theatrical premiering of the song onstage in *Hot Chocolates* and her own subsequent "Black and Blue" recording in November 1929.

Though white appetite for black entertainment had been greatly diminished by excess over the course

of the 1920s, audiences still turned out for *Hot Chocolates* in gratifying numbers after the show opened at the Hudson Theater on 20 June 1929. *Hot Chocolates* was the final great "Negro" revue of the 1920s, and its impact on the careers of both Razaf and Waller, to say nothing of Armstrong, was enormous, establishing all three in the white mass-entertainment market beyond the confines of black Harlem.

Over the course of the 1920s Razaf had written extensively with a host of collaborators, independent of Waller. His songs with J. C. Johnson, including "My Special Friend Is Back in Town" (1927), "Louisiana" (1928), "Dusky Stevedore" (1928), "Take Your Tomorrow (And Give Me Today)" (1928), and "Guess Who's in Town? (Nobody but That Gal of Mine)"

Razaf in the late 1930s at the piano on which he and Waller wrote "Honeysuckle Rose" (1929)
and other songs (Schomburg Center for Research in Black Culture)

(1928), had generated substantial sales. His work with Paul Denniker, a London-born white songwriter, especially their song "S'posin'" (1929), shattered a ludicrous music-business canard by proving that a black writer could in fact compose a heartfelt, yet witty, love lyric. In the wake of the Broadway success of *Hot Chocolates,* however, it seemed—to Razaf as much as anyone—that his future now lay in turning out more hits with Waller. It was therefore devastating for Razaf to discover during the mid 1930s that Waller's proven hit-making abilities as a composer and, increasingly, his talent as a performer, only inspired the white music-industry professionals now staking out an interest in Waller's future to distance the pianist as much as possible from his black songwriting partner in order to market him more easily to mainstream white audiences. Razaf was simply too feisty a commodity, too much the race renegade for

Waller's music-business handlers. Over the course of the 1930s he and Waller continued to work together but far more sporadically and largely at a remove. They never again wrote a full Broadway score, and their songs together—for example, "Ain't-Cha' Glad?" (1929), "Blue Turning Grey over You" (1930), "Concentratin' on You" (1931), "Keepin' Out of Mischief Now" (1932), and "How Can You Face Me?" (1932)—though of an ongoing superb quality, were composed at a diminishing rate.

Forced to turn elsewhere for musical collaborators, Razaf did so, with stellar results. Waller's old mentor, piano great James P. Johnson, became a frequent partner. As early as 1930 Razaf wrote a memorable revue score with Johnson for the Harlem nightspot Small's Paradise under the title *Kitchen Mechanic's Revue,* a production that in its giddy romanticizing of the com-

Newspaper advertisement for a 1941 Razaf-Blake revue at the Apollo, the top theater in Harlem

mon menial laborers of Harlem—including one song hit, "A Porter's Love Song to a Chamber Maid"—nearly constituted a Razaf sociopolitical tract in itself. On his own, Razaf wrote both words and music for two hits, "On Revival Day" in 1930 and "That's What I Like 'bout the South" in 1933. He was also called upon to transform existing big-band instrumentals into pop-song hits with lyrics written to order—from the Fletcher Henderson band's "Christopher Columbus" (1936) to Chick Webb's and then Benny Goodman's "Stompin' at the Savoy" (1936) to Glenn Miller's "In the Mood" (1939).

Another positive by-product for Razaf of the dawning Swing Era was the rediscovery of a song from his and Waller's immediate past, "Honeysuckle Rose," their once-neglected tap number written for *Load of Coal*. Though "Honeysuckle Rose" had been sporadically, if indifferently, recorded over the intervening years, its adoption in the mid 1930s as a favorite riffing jam theme by such jazz-centered big-band swing musicians as Goodman and Count Basie brought the song new currency. Eventually, vocalists embraced Razaf's effortlessly lighthearted, suggestive lyric as well:

Don't buy sugar,
You just have to touch my cup,
You're my sugar,
So sweet when you stir it up.

When I'm takin' sips
From your tasty lips,
Seems the honey fairly drips,
You're confection, goodness knows,
Honeysuckle Rose.

While Waller's melody contributes enormously to the fresh and frolicsome nature of the song, Razaf's lyric gives "Honeysuckle Rose" its bawdy sophistication, which is a lyric portrait of his songwriting partner.

Razaf's most important collaborative relationship beyond Waller was also initiated in the 1930s. Eubie Blake was still a musical power on black Broadway in 1930, despite having recently separated from Noble Sissle, his lyricist and performing partner of fifteen years. One of the greatest of all early-ragtime pianist-composers, Blake blended the robust bawdiness of formative years spent pounding pianos in East Coast

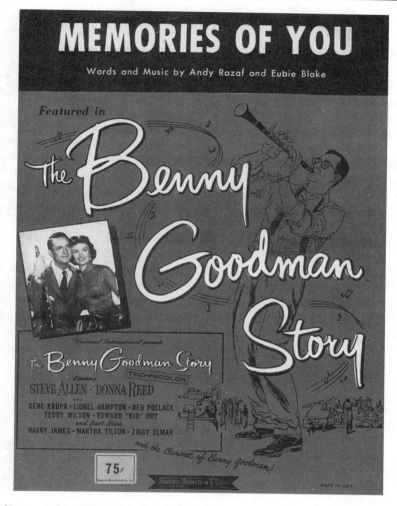

Sheet music for a 1930 song by Razaf and Blake that was used in the 1955 movie about the bandleader and jazz clarinetist Benny Goodman (Bruccoli Clark Layman Archives)

saloons and dance halls with a cultivation and refinement bred in his long association with "society" bandleader James Reese Europe's prewar Clef Club Orchestras. Blessed with a lustrous, theatrical melodic sense and a compositional facility on a par with Waller's, Blake also freed Razaf from the constraint of Waller's oversized performing personality.

Razaf and Blake wrote two major scores together, the first in 1930 for Broadway impresario Lew Leslie's *Blackbirds* revue series and the second in 1941, an intended Broadway revue, *Tan Manhattan,* that never reached its destination. Razaf and Blake's *Blackbirds* debut also suffered because it appeared on Broadway at the onset of the Depression. Despite its song riches, including "You're Lucky to Me," "My Handy Man Ain't Handy No More," and "Memories of You," all

performed by a first-rate ensemble led by Ethel Waters, and despite costumes designed by a young Vincente Minnelli, vocal arrangements by the venerable J. Rosamond Johnson, and Blake in the pit conducting, *Blackbirds of 1930* opened on Broadway on 22 October 1930 at the Royale Theatre and closed fifty-seven performances later.

Razaf's lyric writing nevertheless assumed new dimension with *Blackbirds of 1930,* inspired by Blake's melodic adventurousness. The subtly fractured line scans of his "You're Lucky to Me" lyric are rife with interior rhymes poised elegantly against the meter:

Whenever you're near
All my fears disappear, dear,
It's plain as can be
You're lucky to me.

"My Handyman Ain't Handy No More" offers Razaf's further, perhaps final, comment on the brazen impotency of bawdy blues writing:

> He don't perform his duties like he used to do,
> He never hauls his ashes, 'less I tell him to,
> Before he hardly gets to work he says he's through,
> My handyman ain't handy no more.

In another musical highlight, the poignant "Memories of You" (written to display the three-octave vocal range of *Blackbirds* co-star Minto Cato), Razaf's lyric ornaments Blake's soaring melody with aplomb:

> Waking skies at sunrise,
> Every sunset too,
> Seems to be bringing me
> Memories of you,
> Here and there, ev'rywhere,
> Scenes that we once knew,
> And they all just recall
> Memories of you.

Razaf and Blake's short-lived *Blackbirds of 1930* was followed by a handful of nightclub revue scores that they composed throughout the 1930s, leading finally to *Tan Manhattan,* in many ways the last great gasp of Razaf's career. Written with the express purpose of restoring the Negro musical revue to a position of prominence on Broadway, the show teemed with talent, its cast a veritable who's who of black entertainment luminaries, from the actress and singer Nina Mae McKinney to the song-and-dance legend Avon Long. The score, moreover, is filled with Razaf and Blake songs of distinction, more than twenty in all. Perhaps the best-remembered remains "I'd Give a Dollar for a Dime" (inflated by Razaf in later years from his original title of "I'll Take a Nickel for a Dime"). Despite all of these attainments, however, *Tan Manhattan* stalled after a promising out-of-town run-through in Washington, D.C., never progressing beyond Harlem's Apollo Theater. Its failure was a devastating blow to all concerned.

For Razaf, though, there was worse to come. On 16 December 1943 Waller died of pneumonia on a New York–bound train from Los Angeles passing through Kansas City. He was thirty-nine years old, weakened by a crushing tour schedule compounded by the increasingly chronic dimension of his alcoholism. The last great song of Razaf and Waller's collaboration had been written with J. C. Johnson some six years earlier, their ebullient evocation of Harlem rent parties past, "The Joint Is Jumpin'" (1937). Since then, Razaf and Waller had grown more estranged professionally, though never personally.

The final loss of his dearest collaborator left Razaf bereft. Newly married (for the fourth time), he opted in 1948 for semiretirement on the West Coast, relocating to Los Angeles, only to be struck down three years later by an illness that left him paralyzed from the waist down. Over the ensuing twenty years, often in pain, Razaf continued to write as best he could: a column for local newspapers, the occasional song with local collaborators. Drifting into an enforced obscurity that he sorely resented, he nevertheless maintained his dignity under the circumstances and, to some extent, even thrived.

Early in May 1972, after an absence of nearly twenty-five years, Razaf returned to New York for induction into the Songwriters Hall of Fame, a new institution that had nominated him in the second year of its existence. "My color made life interesting," he maintained in an interview shortly thereafter. "With it came a sense of humor and the gift of laughter and a soul. It has given me something to strive for and shown me every advantage over thousands of white men, born with every advantage, who turned out to be nobodies."

Andy Razaf died of kidney failure on 3 February 1973 at Riverside Hospital in North Hollywood, California. He was seventy-seven years old and was acknowledged, if only among his peers, as one of the finest lyric writers that this country has produced.

Biography:

Barry Singer, *Black and Blue: The Life and Lyrics of Andy Razaf* (New York: Schirmer, 1992).

References:

David A. Jasen and Gene Jones, *Spreadin' Rhythm Around: Black Popular Songwriters, 1880–1930* (New York: Schirmer, 1998), pp. 201–220;

Robert Kimball and William Bolcom, *Reminiscing with Sissle and Blake* (New York: Viking, 1973);

Maurice Waller and Anthony Calabrese, *Fats Waller* (New York: Schirmer, 1977).

Papers:

Andy Razaf's papers are in the Schomburg Center for Research in Black Culture, New York Public Library, and at Howard University.

Selected Discography:

The Complete Fats Waller, Bluebird/RCA, 5511;

Fats Waller Favorites, RCA Victor, LPT-14, 1956;

Maxine Sullivan and Her All-Stars, *A Tribute to Andy Razaf,* DCC Jazz, DJZ-610, 1956;

Dinah Washington, *The Fats Waller Songbook,* EmArcy, 818930-2, 1957.

Leo Robin
(6 April 1895 – 29 December 1984)

Bryan A. Oesterreich
University of North Carolina at Wilmington

POPULAR SONGS FROM THEATRICAL PRO-
DUCTIONS: *By the Way* (1925)–"I've Found a
Bluebird" (interpolation; music by Richard
Myers); "Looking Around" (interpolation; music
by Myers);

Hit the Deck (1927), lyric by Robin and Clifford Grey,
music by Vincent Youmans–"Hallelujah!";

Gentlemen Prefer Blondes (1949), music by Jule Styne–
"Diamonds Are a Girl's Best Friend"; "Bye, Bye,
Baby"; "A Little Girl from Little Rock."

POPULAR SONGS FROM MOTION-PICTURE
PRODUCTIONS: *Innocents of Paris* (1929), music
by Richard Whiting–"Louise";

The Dance of Life (1929), lyric by Robin and Sam
Coslow, music by Whiting–"True Blue Lou";

Monte Carlo (1930), music by Whiting and W. Franke
Harling–"Beyond the Blue Horizon";

Playboy of Paris (1930), music by Whiting and Newell
Chase–"My Ideal";

The Big Broadcast (1932), music by Ralph Rainger–
"Please"; "Here Lies Love";

One Hour with You (1932), music by Whiting–"One
Hour with You"; "What Would You Do?";

Torch Singer (1933), music by Rainger–"Don't Be a Cry
Baby"; "Give Me Liberty or Give Me Love";
"The Torch Singer";

She Loves Me Not (1934)–"Love in Bloom" (music by
Rainger);

Here Is My Heart (1934)–"June in January" (music by
Rainger); "Love Is Just Around the Corner"
(music by Lewis E. Gensler);

Jungle Princess (1936)–"Moonlight and Shadows"
(music by Frederick Hollander);

Artists and Models (1937)–"Whispers in the Dark" (music
by Rainger);

Waikiki Wedding (1937), music by Rainger–"Blue
Hawaii";

The Big Broadcast of 1938 (1938), music by Rainger–
"Thanks for the Memory";

Leo Robin (AP/Wide World Photos)

Gulliver's Travels (1939), music by Rainger–"Faithful
Forever";

My Gal Sal (1942), music by Rainger–"Here You Are" (music by
Rainger);

Wonder Man (1945)–"So-o-o in Love" (music by David
Rose);

Casbah (1948), music by Harold Arlen–"For Every Man
There's a Woman"; "Hooray for Love"; "It Was
Written in the Stars"; "What's Good about
Goodbye?";

That Lady in Ermine (1948), music by Hollander–"This
Is the Moment";

Sheet music for the song that became a signature number for the French actor who introduced it in a 1929 movie (from Marie-Reine A. Pafik and Anna Marie Guiheen, The Sheet Music Reference and Price Guide, *1995)*

Just for You (1952), music by Harry Warren—"Zing a Little Zong."

SELECTED SONGS PUBLISHED INDEPENDENTLY OF THEATRICAL OR MOTION-PICTURE PRODUCTIONS: "My Cutey's Due at Two to Two Today" (1926), music by Irving Bibo and Albert Von Tilzer;

"Prisoner of Love" (1931), lyric and music by Robin, Clarence Gaskill, and Russ Columbo.

Leo Robin, one of the wittiest and most literate Hollywood lyricists, was born in Pittsburgh on 6 April 1895 to Max and Fannie (Finkespearl) Robin. The Robins lived a meager existence in one of the bleaker neighborhoods of Pittsburgh, which may account for young Leo's fierce determination to succeed. He went to New York City to break into show business, found success, was lured to California by Paramount, and achieved further success writing and collaborating on many songs. Robin accomplished what few other lyricists could—he began on Broadway, went to California, wrote successfully, and returned to Broadway triumphantly.

Robin entered the University of Pittsburgh after high school and studied law in 1915–1916. He had given thought to becoming an attorney but soon became unhappy with the course work. He went to a theatrical production in Pittsburgh and was filled with a

*Sheet music for a romantic song that was performed by Bing Crosby in a 1932 movie
(from Marion Short,* More Gold in Your Piano Bench, *1997)*

new ambition—the theater. From 1917 though 1918 he studied dramatics at the Carnegie Institute of Technology while working nights at a local steel mill. He also worked from 1916 to 1920 as a reporter for the *Pittsburgh Chronicle Telegraph.* Robin disliked the rigidly structured journalistic guidelines—there was not much room at the paper for creative writing—but he needed to help support his family.

When he finished his dramatic and journalistic studies, he took a job as a social worker for the Jewish Big Brothers club that worked with young criminal offenders, perhaps a surprising place for a talented young man to initiate a successful career in the entertainment field. Robin was the first director of the club. He enjoyed working with troubled boys and soon found a way to help his charges while experimenting

with his newfound love: he established a small dramatic repertory at the Settlement House in Pittsburgh. His collection of young actors put on small productions for the local residents in his impoverished neighborhood, and they were well received. This first exposure to the footlights increased Robin's appetite for the stage. For months he battled with a major decision. His parents needed him and the young boys looked up to him, but he had to try to follow a career in the theater.

Robin left the Big Brothers in 1923 and took the train to New York City, where he hoped to find work as a director. When he reached New York, he managed to arrange an interview with George Kaufman, also from Pittsburgh. Kaufman, at that time, was the assistant dramatic editor of *The New York Times,* although he soon became a major force in American theater; at first

Robin with other songwriters at the Trocadero in Hollywood in 1938: (back row) Al Dubin, Mack Gordon, Robin, Harry Revel, and Harry Warren; (front row) Lorenz Hart and Hoagy Carmichael (from Tony Thomas,
Harry Warren and the Hollywood Musical, *1975)*

he did his best to send young Robin back to Pittsburgh with the $600 he had brought with him. He told Robin he would need years of apprenticeship to break into the competitive world of Broadway. Robin, however, would not be deterred, and through persistence (and faith in his poetic ability) he finally persuaded Kaufman to look at the lyric of a song he had written with Irving Bibo and Albert Von Tilzer, called "My Cutey's Due at Two to Two Today," which was published in 1926. When Kaufman read the lyrics, he said, "That's it—that's what you should be doing!"

Kaufman sent Robin to his friend, composer Lewis Gensler. Gensler was impressed with Robin's work and gave him his chance to write lyrics, although Robin officially became a professional lyri-

cist in 1925, when two of his songs with composer Richard Meyers, "I've Found a Bluebird" and "Looking Around," found their way to the Broadway stage in the musical *By the Way*. Robin had arrived on Broadway, just not through the door he had expected. In 1926 he entered into collaboration with Clifford Grey on lyrics for Vincent Youmans's music for *Hit the Deck*. This Broadway musical, which opened 25 April 1927, was a commercial success. One of the songs, "Hallelujah!," became a Youmans standard. Youmans had written the melody years earlier, during World War I, as a Navy song, but when Robin and Grey added lyrics to it for *Hit the Deck*, "Hallelujah!" became an enormous hit that established Robin as a lyricist.

Sheet music for the Oscar-winning 1938 number that became Bob Hope's theme song
(from Marion Short, More Gold in Your Piano Bench, *1997)*

During the following year Robin wrote lyrics with other composers for three 1927 Broadway productions—*Judy, Allez-Oop,* and *Just Fancy*—all failures. Max Dreyfus, the head of the Harms music publishing firm, had Robin under contract for $25 a week and thought his young lyricist might do better in California, where the movie studios were introducing sound and music in movies. Paramount was impressed with Robin, signed him to a contract, and paired him with the well-known composer Richard Whiting. Robin connected with Whiting at once, and the two writers found themselves in demand. The original writing contract with Dreyfus was for three months—Whiting would not agree to anything longer—but Robin ended up staying in Hollywood for more than forty years. Over the next three years Robin and Whiting created an impressive array

of successful and evocative romantic songs for popular performers. For example, the writing duo created songs for a newcomer to the American screen—Maurice Chevalier—for the motion picture *Innocents of Paris* (1929). The movie was Chevalier's American debut, but he came to the United States an established star of the great music halls of Paris. Although Robin and Whiting worked on several Chevalier movies, one of their first songs written for him, "Louise," stayed with Chevalier throughout his lengthy career.

The composer and lyricist had checked in to the Hotel Roosevelt, where, according to Robin, "everybody who is anybody in Hollywood stayed." Whiting was searching for a tune on the piano in the room, when Robin, from another room, heard the melody and yelled to Whiting that he had found a combination

427

for a song. The result became the French performer's signature song. When *Innocents of Paris* was released in 1929, to Chevalier's surprise, the tune audiences were humming on their way out of theaters was not one of the interpolated Parisian songs but "Louise."

Robin's first encounter with Chevalier was a story he loved to retell. Robin and Whiting were on the Paramount set when Chevalier was rehearsing the song. At first, Robin was awed by the international star. When Chevalier began to gesticulate with the same arm and hand movements in each chorus, however, Robin turned to Whiting and said, "Dick, that's wrong, doing the same gestures in both choruses. The second chorus isn't an anti-climax, it should be *the* climax." Whiting told Robin that if it bothered him that much, he should tell Chevalier himself. At first Chevalier scoffed at the young lyricist's suggestion to hold his hand gestures until the second chorus, but, moments later, he called Robin back onstage and told him, "Robin, you are right!"

At Paramount, Robin and Whiting were involved in a picture many consider to be one of the most inventive of the time in marrying a song to a movie—*Monte Carlo* (1930), which featured Jeanette MacDonald and Jack Buchanan. The most memorable number in the movie is "Beyond the Blue Horizon." Director Ernst Lubitsch used the song to build the first "Big Number" in an American movie musical—the first extended scene in a musical in which the elements of style, song, story, and meaning were blended with pyrotechnics to display state-of-the-art cinematic technology. Rapidly cut images of the driving pistons on a locomotive engine were synthesized, musically, with the rolling wheels of the train, some percussive blasts from its whistle, and the billowing puffs from its smokestack. MacDonald sings the song from inside her compartment and the song is married to the sounds of the train engine. The expansive visual scene is mirrored by Whiting's soaring melody and Robin's deft manipulation of verbal sounds. Long *i* and *e* vowels, as well as subtle internal rhymes, underscore MacDonald's rising exultation: "My life has only begun! Beyond the blue horizon lies a rising sun." "Beyond the Blue Horizon" was the first big hit song that Robin and Whiting wrote for Paramount. The song is instrumental in showing the leading lady's passion to raise herself out of financial adversity—a common theme in the United States during the Depression. After the release of *Monte Carlo* the song climbed up the *Variety* Top Ten song chart and remained there for sixteen weeks. The song remained popular for decades and was recorded by many performers.

One of the contrasts that Robin noted between Hollywood and New York was in the casual Hollywood attitude toward the art of songwriting. While Robin was under contract at Paramount, Adolph Zukor, the president of the studio, called the writer over and told him he "liked his lyrics." This compliment made an impression on Robin, who said, "that's the first time I heard the word 'lyrics' in Hollywood, because nobody knew what the hell a lyric meant. They'd refer to *the words*." The growing interest in Hollywood musicals matched Robin's growing songwriting interest and ability.

In 1931 he began a lengthy writing association with Ralph Rainger. The list of credits for Robin and Rainger is impressive—and lengthy. The principal movies they wrote for include *Torch Singer* (1933), *She Loves Me Not* (1934), *Waikiki Wedding* (1937), *The Big Broadcast of 1938, Gulliver's Travels* (1939), and *My Gal Sal* (1942). Rainger was known for his torch songs, which suited Robin's lyrical style. One of the team's early efforts was "Please," for *The Big Broadcast* (1932). The song is a straightforward romantic plea to "tell me that you love me, too" and was written especially for Bing Crosby's relaxed style of singing. "Please" differs from other popular songs of the era because it begins with the highest note of the melody. *The Big Broadcast* was a hit movie, solidifying Crosby's movie career, and the team of Robin and Rainger was offered a long-term contract with Paramount.

Paramount kept them busy churning out songs "to order" for B movies as well as bigger productions. Typically, Rainger would write the music, then Robin would write the lyrics. Robin was noted for his clever titles, and he insisted his ideas came after hearing Rainger's melodies. In 1934 they were assigned to write music for another Crosby movie, *Here Is My Heart* (1934), featuring Kitty Carlisle. The biggest song of the movie, "June in January," stayed on the *Variety* Top Ten list for ten weeks and remained a pop standard for many seasons. Unusually, Robin wrote the title before Rainger wrote the melody. The title has persisted as a phrase used to describe warm weather in January, though most people have probably forgotten Robin's romantic lyrics:

It's June in January because I'm in love;
It's always spring in my heart, with you in my arms.
The snow is just white blossoms that fall from above,
And here is the reason my dear, your magical charms.

Robin collaborated with Gensler, the composer who had first encouraged his fledgling efforts at lyrics, on another song that Crosby sang in *Here Is My Heart,* the

Sheet music published in conjunction with Perry Como's million-selling 1946 recording of a 1931 song (Bruccoli Clark Layman Archives)

clever "Love Is Just Around the Corner." Taking their title from Herbert Hoover's prediction of imminent prosperity, which was by then widely mocked, Robin came up with a series of comic, feminine rhymes: *corner, mourner,* and *forlorner.* In the release, he concocted a witty turn of metaphor:

But strictly between us, you're cuter than Venus,

And what's more—you got arms!

The literate allusion, the archly casual "strictly between us," and the resounding slang of "what's more—you got arms" balance elegance and earthiness in the manner of the best lyrics of the era.

"Thanks for the Memory," another Robin and Rainger hit, emerged from the annual *Big Broadcast*

movies produced at Paramount, which featured radio personalities so audiences could see what their favorite stars looked like. The formula for these movies was a minimal plot and a series of variety acts. Robin and Rainger were working on a *Big Broadcast* picture when director Mitchell Leisen approached the writing team to say that he had six different writers working on a scene, but that they had been unable to get it right. If Robin and Rainger put that scene into words and music, Leisen thought, perhaps a song could solve the problem. He then explained that the scene involved a couple who had been married but were now separated. They meet on an ocean liner, and Leisen wanted them to show each other that they are still in love without saying it. Robin and Rainger accepted the challenge. They knew Bob Hope would be singing it with Shirley Ross and that Hope would be expected to be funny, but that the scene also called for a regretful, melancholy tone.

After three weeks Robin felt he found the right combination in a work with a complex set of lyrics. He had used Cole Porter's list songs for inspiration and combined classy European images with prosaic American ones:

Thanks for the memory
Of Candlelight and wine,
Castles on the Rhine,
The Parthenon, and moments on
The Hudson River Line.

Robin created a character for Hope who is an intricate transformation of the insouciant, brokenhearted lover of Porter's "Just One of Those Things" (1935)—an urbane sophisticate who feels he must keep up his debonair guard. In the release Robin allows Hope's figure to come close to direct emotional expression while maintaining his cavalier image.

We said good-bye with a high-ball,
Then I got as high as a steeple,
But we were intelligent people,
No tears, no fuss. Hurray for us.

Rainger took Robin's lyrics and wrote the accompanying music. When told the song was ready, Leisen anxiously hurried into the studio to hear the results. The director was so moved by the song, he began to cry midway through the performance. He used it in *The Big Broadcast of 1938,* and the tune has stayed with Hope ever since. "Thanks for the Memory" won Robin and Rainger an Academy Award for best song—over, among others, two Irving Berlin compositions.

Hope and Crosby were not the only entertainers to benefit from the artistic talents of this writing team. Some of the best names in the movie business found success with Robin and Rainger's material—performers such as Eddie Cantor, Jack Benny, and Danny Kaye.

Robin also worked with successful collaborators other than Whiting and Rainger. He collaborated with other composers, sometimes in a spontaneous manner. In 1931 Robin was on vacation in New York when he received a frantic phone call from Con Conrad. "Con called and said he needed a song written for Helen Morgan within the hour for a Ziegfeld Broadway production. I told him I was on vacation and that he was nuts." Ten minutes later Conrad knocked on the door of his hotel room,

along with crooner Russ Columbo, who, with Clarence Gaskill, had composed a melody. While Robin finished shaving, Columbo sat at the small piano in the hotel room and began trying out tunes. Robin liked what he heard, and suddenly lyrics came to him, and he started shouting them to Columbo. During the next hour they wrote "Prisoner of Love." The next day Ziegfeld turned the song down, but Columbo sang the song on his radio show two days later, and it was an overnight hit. Perry Como revived the song in 1946, and it sold more than a million copies. "Prisoner of Love" was also performed by James Brown, "the Godfather of Soul," in 1963. An explanation for the timelessness of the song may be found in the lyric, which portrays a character helplessly enthralled by an unfaithful lover:

Someone, that I belong to, doesn't belong to me;
Someone, who can't be faithful, knows that I have to be.

That romantic twist, together with the interwoven motif of chains and shackles, lifts the lyric above the usual heartbroken lament.

In 1939 Robin and Rainger came back to New York to work on a musical called *Nice Goin'.* The writing team thought they had connected with a winning show. The production featured Mary Martin, who had gained notice the previous year in *Leave It to Me,* singing Porter's "My Heart Belongs to Daddy." In spite of the young and talented Martin, the show flopped during tryouts in Boston and closed out of town in what Jule Styne called "a typical Boston massacre." The collaborators were surprised and dejected by the poor run of the show. They knew they faced an uphill battle in trying to return to Broadway, but they were at a loss to explain their failure. Robin speculated at the time that the specter of bad reviews from the New York theater critics might have pressured Rainger enough to affect his creative processes.

In 1942 Robin and Rainger were asked to come to New York for a meeting of movie executives to discuss planned productions. Robin was uncomfortable flying and decided to take a train to New York. Rainger chose to spend a little extra time at home and fly later to join Robin. On 24 October 1942, shortly after takeoff, Rainger's plane collided with a military aircraft over Palm Springs. All passengers were killed. Rainger had just celebrated his forty-first birthday. Robin was shattered by the death of his close friend, and it took some time for him to recover from the loss. He continued to write for movies and the theater, and on 3 March 1947 he married Fran English; she bore him one son.

Sheet music for the show-stopping song performed by Carol Channing in the 1949 Broadway musical based on Anita Loos's 1926 novel (from Marion Short, Covers of Gold, *1998)*

"The luckiest thing that happened to me after Rainger passed away," Robin said, "was a Broadway show called *Gentlemen Prefer Blondes,*" which opened on 8 December 1949. Robin, always modest, attributed many of his successes to good luck rather than taking credit himself. After the failure of *Nice Goin'* he was leery of trying to scale the heights of Broadway again with another Hollywood composer. Styne recalled that Robin felt he was making enough money writing movie songs. In the case of *Gentlemen Prefer Blondes,* another young and talented actress was employed, but this time with much different results: Carol Channing emerged as a Broadway star. Robin was attracted to the production because it was based on Anita Loos's successful 1926 play, and because the main character, Lorelei Lee—who was "terribly sexy, erotic, and a cheap, kept-lady"—intrigued him, since writing for her would give him a chance to mix slang and wit, as in the showstopping catalogue song, "Diamonds Are a Girl's Best Friend":

> But square-cut or pear-shape,
> These rocks don't lose their shape. . . .

Gentlemen Prefer Blondes not only ran for years on Broadway, it also became a movie showcase for another rising actress, Marilyn Monroe. Many critics felt the movie was one of the few times the blonde starlet was given strong comedic material to work with, and her performance of

"Diamonds Are a Girl's Best Friend" has remained one of her most memorable scenes. While he was writing those well-known lyrics, Robin was doubtful he could write in the theatrical style that delineated character with literate wit—he said he thought of himself as "a writer of love songs and ballads only."

Robin's only subsequent Broadway assignment was not as successful as *Gentlemen Prefer Blondes*. He wrote lyrics for a Sigmund Romberg show, *The Girl in Pink Tights* (1954), a musical about the mounting of the nineteenth-century production of *The Black Crook* (1866), the show that was the genesis of American musical theater. Romberg died before their collaboration began, however, and his score was completed by Don Walker from the composer's sketches and notes. It opened at the Mark Hellinger Theater but closed after only fifteen weeks.

Robin had accomplished what few other Hollywood lyricists could do—return to New York and write successfully for Broadway. He had also gained a personal reputation that few in his business could match. He was regarded by most as a modest artist, known for giving credit for successful songs to his collaborators, to the artist who recorded his work, or just plain luck. Those in the entertainment business who knew Robin considered him a member in the select, and unofficial, "Sweet Fellas Club." He married a second time, to the former Estelle Clark, an actress, and the two had a daughter. Robin retired to North Maple Drive in Beverly Hills, where he died of a heart attack on 29 December 1984.

When asked, Leo Robin said that, while he felt his best lyrical composition was "Thanks for the Memory," his favorite combination of lyric and music was "June in January." Robin's favorite pastime was trying to improve on lyrics he had written but never liked. He had a hard time satisfying himself, but throughout his lengthy career he satisfied millions of people with his ability to put love into words in a style not many could match.

Interview:

Max Wilk, *They're Playing Our Song: From Jerome Kern to Stephen Sondheim—The Stories Behind the Words and Music of Two Generations* (New York: Atheneum, 1973), pp. 98–111.

References:

Philip Furia, *The Poets of Tin Pan Alley: A History of America's Great Lyricists* (New York: Oxford University Press, 1990), pp. 223–230;

Roy Hemming, *The Melody Lingers On: The Great Songwriters and Their Movie Musicals* (New York: Newmarket, 1986), pp. 187–210.

Selected Discography:

Carol Channing and original Broadway cast, *Gentlemen Prefer Blondes,* Sony Broadway, SK 48013, 1991;

Susannah McCorkle, *Thanks for the Memory: Songs of Leo Robin,* Pausa, PR 7175, 1985.

Harold Rome
(27 May 1908 – 26 October 1993)

Thomas S. Hischak
State University of New York College at Cortland

Music is by Rome unless otherwise indicated.

SELECTED SONGS FROM THEATRICAL PRO-
DUCTIONS: *Pins and Needles* (1937)–"Sing Me
a Song with Social Significance"; "Sunday in
the Park"; "Chain Store Daisy"; "Nobody
Makes a Pass at Me"; "It's Better with a Union
Man"; "Four Little Angels of Peace"; "Doin'
the Reactionary"; "One Big Union for Two";
"It's Not Cricket to Picket"; "Mene, Mene,
Tekel";

Sing Out the News (1938)–"F. D. R. Jones"; "One of
These Fine Days";

Sing for Your Supper (1939)–"Papa's Got a Job" (lyric
by Rome, as "Hector Troy," and Robert Sour,
music by Ned Lehac);

Streets of Paris (1939)–"History Is Made at Night";

The Little Dog Laughed (1940)–"Easy Does It";

Let Freedom Sing (1942)–"It's Fun to Be Free";

Stars and Gripes (1943)–"Jumping to the Jukebox";

Call Me Mister (1946)–"Call Me Mister"; "Along with
Me"; "South America, Take It Away"; "The
Red Ball Express"; "Goin' Home Train"; "The
Face on the Dime"; "Military Life (The Jerk
Song)";

Alive and Kicking (1950)–"Love, It Hurts So Good";

Michael Todd's Peep Show (1950)–"Gimme the
Shimmy"; "(I've Got a) Pocketful of Dreams";

Bless You All (1950)–"Little Things (Meant So Much
to Me)"; "You Never Know What Hit You
(When It's Love)";

Wish You Were Here (1952)–"Wish You Were Here";
"Where Did the Night Go?"; "Don Jose of Far
Rockaway"; "Social Director";

Fanny (1954)–"Fanny"; "Be Kind to Your Parents";
"Welcome Home"; "I Have to Tell You";
"Restless Heart";

Destry Rides Again (1959)–"Anyone Would Love
You"; "I Say Hello"; "Are You Ready, Gyp
Watson?"; "Ring on the Finger";

Harold Rome (photograph by Alfredo Valente)

I Can Get It for You Wholesale (1962)–"Have I Told
You Lately?"; "Miss Marmelstein"; "The
Sound of Money"; "Too Soon"; "A Funny
Thing Happened"; "Eat a Little Something";

The Zulu and the Zayda (1965)–"Rivers of Tears";
"It's Good to Be Alive";

La Grosse Valise (1965), music by Gerard Calvi–"A
Big One"; "Delilah Done Me Wrong (The No
Haircut Song)"; "La Grosse Valise"; "La Java";
"Sandwich for Two"; "Slippy Sloppy Shoes";

Gone with the Wind (1973)–"Bonnie Gone"; "Lonely
Stranger".

433

Berni Gould as Adolf Hitler and Harry Clark as Joseph Stalin in Rome's 1937 revue Pins and Needles

SELECTED SONG FROM MOTION-PICTURE PRODUCTION: *Anchors Aweigh* (1945)–"All of a Sudden My Heart Sings" (English lyric by Rome, French lyric by Jean Marie Blanvillain, music by Jamblan Herpin).

SELECTED SONG PUBLISHED INDEPENDENTLY OF THEATRICAL OR MOTION-PICTURE PRODUCTIONS: "Meadowland" (1943), lyric by Rome and Victor Gusev, music by Lev Knipper.

During the decades before and after World War II, no American lyricist captured the sentiments of working-class people as vividly as Harold Rome. Whether in his musicals or revues, whether protesting against the short-comings of democracy or celebrating the American spirit, Rome found a way of expressing the voice of the common people. He often achieved this goal with humor and dignity rather than through speechifying or bitterness.

Harold Jacob Rome was born in Hartford, Connecticut, on 27 May 1908, the son of Louis Rome, owner of the Connecticut Coal and Charcoal Company, and Ida (Aronson) Rome. As a young boy he showed a musical talent at the piano, but the family had more-serious plans for him. After being graduated from high school in 1924, he attended Trinity College for two years and played piano in local dance bands in Hartford. He attended Yale University from 1926 through 1929, where he studied law and, later, architecture. He also studied music and played piano with the Yale Collegians.

After graduation from Yale Law School and the Yale School of Architecture, Rome was working as a draftsman when the Depression hit, earning extra money by playing piano for parties and receptions. Hired one summer to accompany amateur theatricals at Green Mansions, an adult summer camp in upstate New York, Rome began writing original pieces as well, mostly bright, topical songs that were used in the musical revues put on by the camp. He found little success when he tried to interest Broadway producers in his songs, most of whom

*Betty Garrett with Alan Manson, Chandler Cowles, George Hall, and Harry Clark in Rome's 1946
Broadway revue* Call Me Mister *(photograph by Ellen Darby, Graphic House)*

believed that escapism was the only way to entertain audiences during the Depression.

Louis Schaffer, the head of the theatrical division of the International Ladies Garment Workers Union (ILGWU), had heard Rome's songs at Green Mansions, however, and was impressed by their sly lyrics and tuneful melodies, so he hired the young songwriter in 1935 to work on an unusual project. The ILGWU was one of the most vocal and successful unions in the United States. The members had fought against management on several fronts and had eliminated many of the sweatshop conditions that had made the garment industry infamous. The large and active membership of the union, many of whom barely spoke English, now had some leisure time on their hands, and the ILGWU took it upon themselves to educate and provide cultural enrichment for them. In the area of theater, some factions wanted to present hard-hitting social drama such as what Clifford Odets was writing at the time. Schaffer and others, however, argued for a musical revue about union topics that could both entertain and enlighten its audiences. Rome played some of his songs for the union leaders in 1936 and convinced them to proceed with the show.

Because the cast consisted of working union members, rehearsals were held three evenings a week over a period of a year and a half. It was strictly an amateur production, for few of the performers had any stage experience at all, so the revue was slated for weekends only in a small Broadway house, the Princess Theatre. Once the home of witty and tuneful musical comedies by the celebrated trio of Guy Bolton, P. G. Wodehouse, and Jerome Kern, the theater was renamed the Labor Stage, and the new revue, called *Pins and Needles,* opened there in late 1937. The three hundred seats at the Labor Stage were

*Sheet music for the title song from the 1954 musical based
on a trilogy of plays (and their movie adaptations) by
Marcel Pagnol (Bruccoli Clark Layman Archives)*

self selling women's foundation garments at Macy's, and
"Nobody Makes a Pass at Me."

"Nobody Makes a Pass at Me" is in a long line of
comic female laments in the musical theater. While less
political than most of that score, this number is just as
pointed. The forlorn singer, a dressmaker, has tried all of
the products advertised on the radio in order to improve
her love life, but still she remains untouched. She is not
aching for love or even fantasized romance but rather
"kissing" and "more of what I'm missing." In the verse she
also proclaims her availability ("nobody comes knocking
at my front door") and desperation ("if they don't come
soon there won't be any more!"). The refrains then list all
the name brands she has tried, from Lux laundry soap to
Pond's skin cream, from reading Margaret Mitchell's *Gone
with the Wind* (1936) to get cultured to eating Ry-Krisp to
stay thin. Each experiment ends, however, with the title
phrase and the question "Oh, dear what can the matter
be?" There is even a patter section in which the product
names are rushed together, and her plea becomes more
direct: "So why ain't I got sex?" Rome's special talent is to
allow the audience to laugh at the woman's misfortune
without sacrificing her dignity and believability. The lyric
is beautifully sustained, and its effectiveness has outlasted
many of the actual products listed in the number.

"Sunday in the Park" reveals the sentiments of factory workers who treasure "the one day I can call my
own," and socialist ideas provide the basis for a swinging
dance number, "Doin' the Reactionary." Rome's lyric
work could be silly and inventive, as in the sportive "It's
Not Cricket to Picket," as well as stingingly serious, as in
the cautionary "Mene, Mene, Tekel," which was added
after war broke out in Europe. During its long run, *Pins
and Needles* went on tour and then returned with the subsequent titles *Pins and Needles 1939* and *New Pins and Needles*.
Rome's career was secured by the success of the show,
and he found many offers during the next decade.

Rome's next musical revue, *Sing Out the News*
(1938), lasted only four months in a traditional Broadway house, but it had much to recommend it and
received favorable reviews. Another topical revue, it
had leftist leanings that made some Broadway audiences nervous. Yet, the most remembered song from
the show was the patriotic "F. D. R. Jones," in which
an African American family in Harlem christens their
newborn son and names him after the current president.
The number caught on and was popular with American
troops some years later, during World War II. Though
less known, another fine Rome song from the revue was
the soulful "One of These Fine Days," which expressed
the frustration of some Harlem residents hoping to better
themselves. Rome contributed a few songs to several other
Broadway revues and book musicals in the late 1930s and
early 1940s. On 3 February 1939 he married Florence

not filled the first few weekends, and getting nonunion
audiences to see an amateur show was difficult, but *Pins
and Needles* gradually caught on and soon became a popular attraction, playing eight times a week and running
1,108 performances, an astounding record even for so
small a house.

While several writers contributed to the songs and
sketches, most of the revue was the work of Rome. His
"Sing Me a Song with Social Significance" set the tone for
the show, combining self-mockery with sincere intent.
Some numbers used union terms to express personal feelings, such as the love song "One Big Union for Two,"
while others tackled worldwide issues, as in the satiric
"Four Little Angels of Peace," in which Adolf Hitler,
Benito Mussolini, Anthony Eden, and a Japanese diplomat merrily claim to love each other and the rest of the
world. (As the show continued to run, the characters
changed in order to remain topical–Emperor Hirohito
and Neville Chamberlain replacing the diplomat and Eden
after the Munich Agreement.) Also in the varied and
clever score were some seriocomic character songs, such
as "Chain Store Daisy," in which a Vassar grad finds her-

Jack Cassidy, Patricia Marand, and Sheila Bond in Rome's musical Wish You Were Here, *produced in 1952 (photograph by Slim Aarons)*

Miles. They had a son, Joshua, and a daughter, Rachel. Rome's career seemed stalled as war broke out. He was inducted into the army in 1943 and spent the next few years scoring wartime propaganda revues for the troops.

Rome often collaborated with Arnold Auerbach, a former radio scriptwriter also in uniform, and together they planned a topical revue about GIs returning to civilian life after V-J Day. *Call Me Mister* opened on Broadway in the spring of 1946 and immediately caught on with audiences, running 734 performances. The cast comprised mostly former servicemen and USO women, and, like *Pins and Needles,* the show manages to maintain a bright and optimistic tone, even though the readjustment to civilian life was not always a laughing matter. Among the more somber moments in the revue are "The Face on the Dime," a hymn-like tribute to the recently deceased President Roosevelt, and "The Red Ball Express," a stirring narrative ballad sung by an African American who worked in the Transportation Unit during the war but in the civilian world is refused a job because of his race. On the lighter side, the mocking "South America, Take It Away" spoofs the then-current rage for Latin songs, and "Military Life (The Jerk Song)" points out that the jerk who went off to war was more than likely to return still a jerk.

After a handful of near misses and outright flops, Rome had his first successful book musical in 1952 with

Wish You Were Here, which received less-than-kind notices, but its working swimming pool on stage attracted publicity. The pleasant musical comedy found patrons for nearly six hundred performances. Set in an adult camp not unlike Green Mansions, the show dealt with a series of summer romances between staff members and guests. Rome was on familiar ground, not only with the setting but also with the urban, working-class Jewish characters who populate the tale. The title song was a hit and has remained a standard, but also delightful are such comic numbers as "Don Jose of Far Rockaway" and such heartfelt ballads as "Where Did the Night Go?"

Different in subject matter but also deeply felt was *Fanny* (1954), a musical based on a trilogy of French movies by Marcel Pagnol. This bittersweet tale of a French fisherman, his yearning for the sea, and the events that occur when he leaves his pregnant girlfriend behind gave Rome his first opportunity to write a score without topical subjects or a satiric tone of voice. "Welcome Home," "Be Kind to Your Parents," and "I Have to Tell You" are potent, sincere, and moving, and once again the title song became a hit. "Restless Heart" is a short but potent song for the young, confused hero, Marius. Bored with village life and yearning to go to sea, Marius expresses his restlessness in simple imagery: a "silver bird that streaks the sky," a cloud dancing out of view, and a ship heading out to sea. Rome's lyric-writing skills are so polished that the

Andy Griffith, Scott Brady, and Dolores Gray in Rome's 1959 musical comedy Destry Rides Again,
based on the 1939 Western movie (photograph by Friedman-Abeles)

simplicity is disarming. He uses personification well, with each ship seeming to call out to Marius and even his own restless heart having its own character and speaking aloud. The recurring phrase "my restless heart and I" speaks volumes for its character. *Fanny* was the first musical produced by David Merrick, a shrewd showman who kept the show running for 888 performances.

Destry Rides Again (1959) ran about half as long but provided first-class entertainment, even if Rome's score was artificial in comparison with his previous work. The Wild West comedy, based on a popular movie, was more noted for its boisterous dance numbers, staged by Michael Kidd, than for any of its songs.

In 1962 Rome was back in his milieu with *I Can Get It for You Wholesale,* an unsentimental look at a young cutthroat businessman who climbs the ladder of the garment industry, stepping on anyone in his way. In some ways the score is the culmination of Rome's talents, dealing with Jews, business, family, and self-mockery—all subjects he excelled at. While many of the songs are antiromantic,

there is still plenty of comedy, as well as a sincerity that is sometimes uncomfortable. The duet "The Sound of Money," in which two ambitious lovers admit the ugly truth about their dreams, is uncompromising in its honesty. "A Funny Thing Happened" reveals a character broken and bitter as he admits his failure, while "Eat a Little Something" is a painful reconciliation between mother and son, with layers of unspoken pain implied between the lines. The most-remembered number from the score is "Miss Marmelstein," a witty lament sung by an overlooked and overly romantic secretary, made famous because Barbra Streisand sang it in her Broadway debut. *I Can Get It for You Wholesale* was a moderate hit at three hundred performances, but in many ways it is Rome's best score.

The rest of Rome's career was filled with curiosities: he composed both Jewish and African songs for the odd *The Zulu and the Zayda* (1965); an English score for the French revue *La Grosse Valise* (1965); and a lush set of songs for a 1973 stage version of *Gone with the Wind* that played in Tokyo, London, and Los Angeles but never made it to Broadway. Like many veteran songwriters faced with the shrinking Broadway market for musicals (revues, in particular), Rome retired in 1973 and rarely saw his works revived during the last two decades of his life. He painted as a hobby and acquired a large collection of African sculpture. He died on 26 October 1993.

Rome was among the handful of Broadway lyricists who tackled sociopolitical issues in their work, considered alongside Marc Blitzstein, Maxwell Anderson, Paul Green, Langston Hughes, and E. Y. "Yip" Harburg. Yet, only Rome and Harburg dealt with musical comedy, the others preferring serious book musicals and even operas, so comparisons between the two men are unavoidable. Both Rome and Harburg made names for themselves writing topical revues in the 1930s and 1940s before moving on to book musicals. Both also dealt with social and economic subjects with a leftist point of view. There are significant differences between the two, however. Rome often abandoned the political attack as he expanded into book musicals, while Harburg's librettos and lyrics got sharper and more pointed in his later book shows. Rome's strength was realism, whereas Harburg excelled at fantasy. Yet, Rome's satire was sometimes lightweight and less piercing than Harburg's humor, which was often deadly accurate. Most important, Harburg attempted subjects that were deeply controversial and not easily solvable, while Rome's targets were often one-sided and safe. It took less courage to lampoon Hitler or sneer at antiunionists, as Rome did, than to confront contemporary bigotry and capitalism, as Harburg did. Rome was a man of strong and sincere beliefs, but he usually preached to the converted, and his songs made people laugh freely. Harburg presented unpopular ideas, cloaked them in fantastical satires, and the audience laughed nervously.

Such a comparison is not to take away from Rome's superior talent in portraying working-class men and women as funny, human, and worthy of attention. He does not idealize the laborer nor romanticize the laboring class. Such people are not just interested in human rights and justice; they crave love, affection, serenity, and even silliness. When the garment workers demand "Sing Us a Song of Social Significance," they wanted their economics dressed in "the best harmonics" or "we won't love you." When the father in *Fanny* greets his son with "Welcome Home," he points out the simple little details—a friendly door, a chair with arms outstretched, the floorboards that talk to his shoe—that are achingly real. Rome's lyrics go far beyond the satirical revue songs that avoid the specific and revel in the vague. Even in a plot-free revue, his words painted vivid characters who cannot be classified as types.

The "Chain Store Daisy" is a living, breathing creation, just as are the driver on "The Red Ball Express" and the youth with a "Restless Heart."

Rome rarely wrote about people who are sophisticated or even articulate. They cannot express themselves poetically or academically; yet, they still express themselves, and in Rome's hands they do so with humor and pathos. Without sentiment or exaggeration, they simply are. His range is not as wide as Oscar Hammerstein, nor is he as verbally dexterous as Ira Gershwin or Lorenz Hart; but when he is in his milieu, Rome is a master lyricist, as proficient as he is distinctive.

References:

Lehman Engel, *Their Words Are Music: The Great Theatre Lyricists and Their Lyrics* (New York: Crown, 1975), pp. 97–111;

Stanley Green, *Broadway Musicals of the 1930s* (New York: Da Capo Press, 1982), pp. 148–154;

Green, *The World of Musical Comedy: The Story of the American Musical Stage as Told Through the Careers of Its Foremost Composers and Lyricists* (San Diego: Barnes, 1980), pp. 189–195;

Thomas S. Hischak, *Word Crazy: Broadway Lyricists from Cohan to Sondheim* (New York: Praeger, 1991), pp. 90–93.

Papers:

Harold Rome's papers are held at the Yale University Music Library.

Selected Discography:

Call Me Mister, original Broadway cast, Columbia Special Products, X 14877, 1946;

Call Me Mister, motion picture soundtrack, Titania, 510, 1951;

Fanny, original Broadway cast, Decca, DL 79075, 1954;

Harold Rome, *And Then I Wrote,* Coral, CRL 57082, 1957;

Rome, *A Touch of Rome,* Heritage, LP-H-0053, 1964;

I Can Get It for You Wholesale, original Broadway cast, Columbia, AKOS 2180, 1962;

Pins and Needles: 25th Anniversary Edition of the Hit Musical Revue, Columbia, OL 5810, 1962;

Wish You Were Here, original Broadway cast, RCA, LOC 1108, 1960;

Wish You Were Here, 1953 London cast, Stet, DS 15015, 1980;

The Zulu and the Zayda, original Broadway cast, Columbia, KOS 2880, 1965.

Ned Washington

(15 August 1901 – 20 December 1976)

Tony L. Hill
University of Minnesota

SELECTED SONGS FROM THEATRICAL PRODUCTIONS: *Vanities of 1928* (1928)–"Getting the Beautiful Girls" (music by Michael H. Cleary); "My Arms Are Wide Open" (music by Cleary);

Murder at the Vanities (1933)–"Sweet Madness" (music by Victor Young);

Blackbirds of 1933 (1933)–"A Hundred Years from Today" (lyric by Washington and Joe Young, music by Victor Young).

SELECTED SONGS FROM MOTION-PICTURE PRODUCTIONS: *The Show of Shows* (1929)–"Singin' in the Bathtub" (lyric and music by Washington, Herb Magidson, and Michael H. Cleary);

A Night at the Opera (1935)–"Cosi Cosa" (music by Bronislau Kaper and Walter Jurmann);

Here Comes the Band (1935)–"You're My Thrill" (music by Burton Lane);

Tropic Holiday (1938), music by Agustín Lara–"The Lamp on the Corner"; "Tonight Will Live";

Romance in the Dark (1938)–"The Nearness of You" (music by Hoagy Carmichael);

Pinocchio (1940), music by Leigh Harline–"Give a Little Whistle"; "Hi-Diddle-Dee-Dee (An Actor's Life for Me)"; "Jiminy Cricket"; "When You Wish upon a Star";

Dumbo (1941), music by Frank Churchill–"Baby Mine"; "Casey Junior"; "Pink Elephants on Parade"; "Look Out for Mister Stork"; "When I See an Elephant Fly" (music by Oliver Wallace);

Saludos Amigos (1943)–"Saludos Amigos" (lyric by Washington, Edmundo Santos, and Louis Alyosio Oliveria, music by Charles Wolcott);

For Whom the Bell Tolls (1943)–"A Love Like This" (music by Victor Young);

Hands across the Border (1943)–"Hands across the Border," music by Carmichael;

Brazil (1944)–"Rio de Janeiro" (music and original lyric by Ary Barroso);

Ned Washington (AP/Wide World Photos)

I Walk Alone (1947)–"Don't Call It Love" (music by Allie Wrubel);

My Foolish Heart (1949)–"My Foolish Heart" (music by Young);

The Greatest Show on Earth (1952)–"The Greatest Show on Earth" (music by Young);

High Noon (1952)–"High Noon (Do Not Forsake Me)" (music by Dimitri Tiomkin);

Return to Paradise (1953)–"Return to Paradise" (music by Tiomkin);

Miss Sadie Thompson (1953)–"The Blue Pacific Blues (Sadie Thompson's Song)" (music by Lester Lee);

The Adventures of Hajji Baba (1954)–"Hajji Baba" (music by Tiomkin);

The High and the Mighty (1954)–"The High and the Mighty (The Whistling Song)" (music by Tiomkin);

The Man from Laramie (1955)–"The Man from Laramie" (music by Lee);

The Eddy Duchin Story (1956)–"To Love Again" (music by Morris Stoloff and George Sidney);

Wild Is the Wind (1957)–"Wild Is the Wind" (music by Tiomkin);

Search for Paradise (1957)–"Search for Paradise" (lyric by Washington and Lowell Thomas, music by Tiomkin);

Fire Down Below (1957)–"Fire Down Below" (music by Lee);

The Young Land (1959)–"Strange Are the Ways of Love" (music by Tiomkin);

The Unforgiven (1960)–"The Need for Love" (music by Tiomkin);

The Guns of Navarone (1961)–"They Call It Love" (music by Tiomkin); "Yassu" (music by Tiomkin);

The Last Sunset (1961)–"Pretty Little Girl in the Yellow Dress" (music by Tiomkin);

Town without Pity (1961)–"Town without Pity" (music by Tiomkin);

Advise and Consent (1962)–"Heart of Mine" (music by Jerry Fielding);

Circus World (1965)–"Circus World" (music by Tiomkin).

SELECTED SONGS PUBLISHED INDEPENDENTLY OF THEATRICAL OR MOTION-PICTURE PRODUCTIONS: "Can't We Talk It Over?" (1931), music by Victor Young;

"(I Don't Stand) A Ghost of a Chance" (1932), lyric by Washington and Bing Crosby, music by Young;

"I'm Gettin' Sentimental over You" (1932), music by George Bassman;

"Love Me Tonight" (1932), lyric by Washington and Crosby, music by Young;

"Waltzing in a Dream" (1932), lyric by Washington and Crosby, music by Young;

"Somebody Stole Gabriel's Horn" (1932), lyric by Washington and Irving Mills, music by Edgar Hayes;

"Got the South in My Soul" (1932), lyric by Washington and Lee Wiley, music by Young;

"Love Is the Thing" (1933), music by Young;

"Smoke Rings" (1933), music by H. Eugene Gifford;

"Stella by Starlight" (1946), music by Young;

"On Green Dolphin Street" (1947), music by Bronislan Kaper;

"Rawhide" (1958), music by Dimitri Tiomkin.

Ned Washington excelled as a writer of popular songs in the 1930s, and in the 1940s he established himself as a premier writer of movie songs. Although he wrote all of the lyrics for such memorable animated Walt Disney features as *Pinocchio* (1940) and *Dumbo* (1941), his specialty was not the full score for a musical but rather the individual title or "theme" song for a dramatic motion picture. Washington was the lyricist of such motion-picture songs as "The Nearness of You" (from *Romance in the Dark,* 1938) and "When You Wish upon a Star" (from *Pinocchio*), as well as for such popular standards as "(I Don't Stand) A Ghost of a Chance" (1932) and "I'm Gettin' Sentimental over You" (1932).

Ned Washington was born in Scranton, Pennsylvania, on 15 August 1901, the next to youngest of the two sons and five daughters born to Michael Washington and Catharine Stone Washington. Ned Washington was the only one of these children who did not receive musical training. He attended the Charles Sumner School and Scranton Technical High School but left after the ninth grade, when his father died, and went to work to support the family. He began writing poetry and submitting it to the Scranton newspapers. The family soon relocated to Norfolk, Virginia, and Washington continued to write and publish poems in newspapers and magazines.

In 1922 he went to New York and broke into show business, at age twenty-one, by booking theatrical acts for vaudeville houses. He went on to serve as a master of ceremonies in vaudeville and also wrote what was called "special material"–comic sketches and monologues–for various performers. After several years in vaudeville, he began writing songs and, with composer Michael H. Cleary, placed "Getting the Beautiful Girls" and "My Arms Are Wide Open" in the *Vanities of 1928.*

With the advent of sound motion pictures, which soon put vaudeville out of business, Washington moved to California in 1928, where he was hired by Warner Bros. to write songs for motion pictures. His first hit was "Singin' in the Bathtub" (1929), written with co-lyricist Herb Magidson and composed by Cleary. It was sung by Winnie Lightner in *The Show of Shows* and then recorded by Guy Lombardo and His Royal Canadians. Washington's first tenure in Hollywood was brief, however. The novelty of talking pictures soon wore off, and the public soured on musicals, whose "backstager" plots served as an excuse for actors to sing (because they were rehearsing or performing a stage musical) but relied on a handful of show business clichés. By 1930, *Variety* magazine reported, customers were inquiring at the box office if a motion picture was a musical and turning away if it was. With the initial boom for movie musicals over, Washington returned to

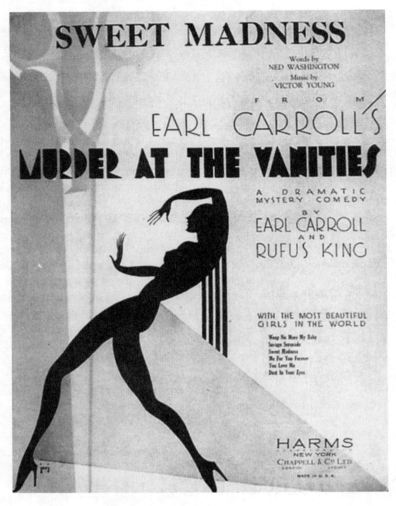

Sheet music for the song by Washington and Victor Young that was interpolated into a 1933 musical
(from Marion Short, Covers of Gold, *1998)*

New York, where he developed his craft in the milieu of Tin Pan Alley.

He established a collaborative relationship with composer Victor Young, and one of their first successes was "Can't We Talk It Over?" in 1931, which was recorded by torch singer Lee Wiley. In 1932 Washington and Young wrote three songs, "(I Don't Stand) A Ghost of a Chance," "Waltzing in a Dream," and "Love Me Tonight" with Bing Crosby. (Although Crosby shares the credit, it is unclear what, if anything, he contributed to the song; it was a frequent practice in those days for top performers to receive writing credit–and a share of the royalties– on the songs they introduced.) "(I Don't Stand) A Ghost of a Chance" is perhaps Washington's most sophisticated early lyric. It is laced with double and internal rhymes, such as the "stand" and "chance" in its vernacular title phrase:

I need your love so badly
I love you, oh, so madly
But I don't stand a ghost of a chance with you. . . .
If you'd surrender
For a tender
Kiss or two,
You might discover
That I'm the lover
Meant for you . . .
And I'll be true.

Such subtly repeated lines, as phrased by a radio crooner like Crosby, insinuated the lyric into the listener's mind.

In 1932 Washington also wrote the lyrics to "Got the South in My Soul" with Young (Wiley, who recorded it, is also listed as co-lyricist) and "Someone Stole Gabriel's Horn" with composer Edgar Hayes and co-lyricist Irving Mills, which was recorded by Jack

*Sheet music for the song by Washington and Leigh Harline that received the 1940 Academy Award
for best original movie song (Bruccoli Clark Layman Archives)*

Teagarden and his orchestra. With the Big Band era in full swing, Washington wrote the lyrics to two songs that were adopted by bandleaders as their theme songs. "Smoke Rings" (1932), with music by H. Eugene Gifford, became the theme of Glen Gray and the Casa Loma Orchestra, and "I'm Gettin' Sentimental over You," music by George Bassman, was recorded by the Dorsey Brothers, then adopted by Tommy Dorsey as his theme song. Washington's lyric for "I'm Gettin' Sentimental over You" uses the casually vernacular "I'm Gettin'" to relieve the sentimentality of the rest of the title phrase and again creates subtle internal rhymes—"Be gentle with me because I'm sentimental over you"—that give the lyric the same flowing drive as the long melodic line.

In 1933 Washington wrote, again with Young, a few of his songs that were introduced on stage:

"Sweet Madness" was interpolated into the musical *Murder at the Vanities,* and "A Hundred Years from Today" (with co-lyricist Joe Young) was introduced by Kathryn Perry in the Broadway revue *Blackbirds of 1933,* then recorded by Wiley with Glen Gray and the Casa Loma Orchestra as well as by Ethel Waters with the Benny Goodman Orchestra.

With the success of *42nd Street* at Warner Bros. in 1933 and Fred Astaire and Ginger Rogers in *The Gay Divorcee* at RKO in 1934, the movie musical revived, and Washington returned to Hollywood in 1935 as a staff writer at M-G-M. For the Marx Brothers movie *A Night at the Opera* he wrote the hit "Cosi Cosa," with music by Bronislau Kaper and Walter Jurmann. With composer Hoagy Carmichael, Washington wrote "The Nearness of You" for *Romance in the Dark.* Once again, he demonstrated his skill at

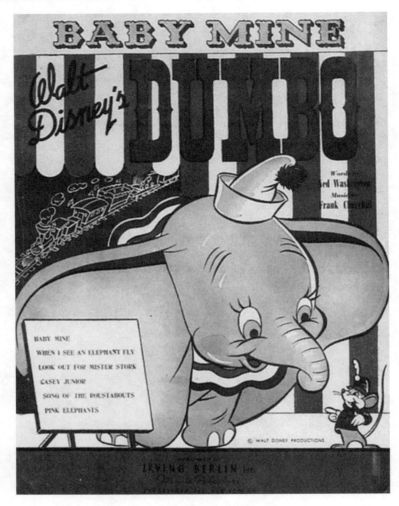

Sheet music for a song from the 1941 Walt Disney animated movie about a flying elephant
(from Marion Short, Covers of Gold, *1998)*

using double and internal rhymes to match the flow of a long melodic line:

> It's not that pale moon that excites me,
> That thrills and delights me,
> Oh, no, it's just the nearness of you. . . .
> I need no soft lights to enchant me
> If you'll only grant me
> The right to hold you ever so tight
> And to feel in the night
> The nearness of you.

"The Nearness of You" was the first song with lyrics by Ned Washington to be featured on the radio program *Your Hit Parade*.

A two-year contract with Walt Disney Studios that commenced in 1938 led to Washington's establishment as a permanent fixture in the screen songwriting business. At Disney he wrote lyrics for three animated movies: *Pinocchio, Dumbo,* and *Saludos Amigos* (1943). Washington won two Academy Awards for *Pinocchio*, the first for best song, for "When You Wish upon a Star," and another for best complete score. He also won the Box Office Blue Ribbon Award for his lyrics for that animated feature. "When You Wish upon a Star" is a beautifully simple lyric, appropriate to the character of Jiminy Cricket, who sings it, and the childhood setting of the movie. Instead of the more intricate internal rhymes he created in other lyrics, Washington relies upon the simplest sound repetitions in a lyric composed largely of monosyllables: "When you wish upon a star, makes no difference who you are / Anything your heart desires will come to you."

In *Pinocchio* "When You Wish upon a Star" is sung on the soundtrack by Cliff "Ukulele Ike"

Sheet music for Washington and Young's title song for the 1949 movie based on J. D. Salinger's
1948 short story "Uncle Wiggily in Connecticut" (Bruccoli Clark Layman Archives)

Edwards; it was also recorded by Frances Langford, Kate Smith, and, more recently, Linda Ronstadt.

Washington could also create lyrics that introduced sophistication into a Disney musical. In *Dumbo*, for example, he weaves a clever catalogue of puns into "When I See an Elephant Fly": "I saw a peanut stand, heard a rubber band, . . . But I think I will have seen everything when I see an elephant fly." Such witty wordplay is balanced by the tender maternal sentiments of the lullaby "Baby Mine" and the innocently sprightly "Look Out for Mister Stork."

While many songwriters found Walt Disney difficult to work for—he tended to be less than effusive in his appraisal of their work, and they took this reticence for disinterest—Washington thought Disney was a brilliant man. When Washington pitched a new song, he

tantalized Disney until he would say, "For crying out loud, Ned, let me listen to the song!"

After writing complete scores for Disney musicals, Washington went on to work on individual theme songs for dramatic motion pictures. He also married Mildred Allen, and in 1945 the couple had a daughter, Catharine. One of Washington's most successful standards, "Stella by Starlight" (1946), was derived from theme music used in the 1944 motion picture *The Uninvited,* and Washington's lyrics were added later. "Stella by Starlight" was Washington's favorite among his lyrics. The lyric is a masterpiece in light of the sparseness of the melody. As opposed to the typical musical phrases of seven or eight notes, the musical phrases in "Stella by Starlight" consist of only two to four notes, calling for an equally parsimonious number of syllables:

Sheet music for the 1952 movie title song that brought Washington his third Academy Award
(Collection of Paul Talbot)

The song
A robin sings
Through years
Of endless springs.
The murmur of a brook
At eventide
That ripples through a nook
Where two lovers hide.
A great
Symphonic theme
That's Stella by Starlight
And not a dream.

One of his last hit songs with Young was written as the title song for the 1949 motion picture *My Foolish Heart*. It was recorded by Billy Eckstein and was featured for eighteen weeks on *Your Hit Parade,* three times as the number one song.

Washington's approach to songwriting was to start with the music, as was the habit of most popular lyricists. He was a fast writer, often finishing a lyric in less than a day, but he then would withhold the finished song until his contract with the studio was almost up. This increased his bargaining ability for the next picture. He also did not want the studios to know he was as quick a writer as he was.

Washington's wife died suddenly in 1951, and in 1953 he married Patti Jackson Page (no relation to the singer). Washington was Roman Catholic, which made him something of a novelty in the songwriting business. "We were the only family on our block that wasn't Jewish," his daughter, Catharine, said.

During the 1950s Washington continued to write title songs and theme songs for motion pictures—often Westerns—rather than scores for movie musicals. His most frequent collaborator until the early 1950s was Young, and then Washington began writing with Dimitri Tiomkin. Tiomkin had scored motion pictures, but he was one of the first composers to insist that he also be given the lucrative assignment of writing the songs for his motion pictures. One of their first efforts together was "High Noon (Do Not Forsake Me)" (1952), which garnered Washington his third Academy Award. "High Noon (Do Not Forsake Me)" is a seminal part of *High Noon,* as is Washington and Tiomkin's title song for *The High and the Mighty* (1954), which is whistled throughout the film by the main character. Both songs were hit records at the time and achieved the goal of a title song—to promote the movie, which in turn promotes the song. In 1958 Washington and Tiomkin also wrote the theme song for the television series *Rawhide.*

Apart from their songs for Westerns, Washington and Tiomkin wrote such romantic ballads as the title song for the 1957 movie *Wild Is the Wind,* which became an early hit recording for Johnny Mathis. The lyric includes some of Washington's more exotic imagery and passionate entreaties:

> Love me, love me, say you do
> Let me fly away with you
> For my love is like the wind
> And wild is the wind.
> Give me more than one caress
> Satisfy this hungriness
> Let the wind blow through your heart
> For wild is the wind.

This rhapsodic lyric is different from the child-like sentiments of a song such as "Give a Little Whistle," from *Pinocchio.* Perhaps if Washington had written more lyrics such as "Wild Is the Wind" and fewer cartoon songs and Western ballads, he would have emerged as a more prominent lyricist.

Washington also proved useful to the studios as a troubleshooter, someone who could revise songs by other songwriters. He chose to do this work anonymously, not getting or even wanting credit for songs he "fixed." He did not want the songwriters whose work he doctored to know he was their editor.

Washington's career—along with those of most of his colleagues—declined in the 1960s as the movie studios focused more on using contemporary performers to provide music in their films rather than relying on established songwriters. Washington was furious at United Artists for the studio's treatment of "Town without Pity" (1961), a title song he and Tiomkin had written that was modified as a vehicle to suit singer Gene Pitney. Pitney's arrangement was completely different in tempo and style from the writers' conception, and Washington came to hate the song. It was his last hit. He won the Golden Globe Award for best song for

it, and four years later he won another Golden Globe for the title song from *Circus World* (1965).

Washington was not bitter about his premature retirement prompted by the changes in the music industry. He was proud of the three Oscars he had in his studio and did not worry about his dearth of current work. Washington was also a horseman, and he won many prizes for his horse training. At one time he owned a racehorse whose name was also Ned Washington.

He kept active with his fellow songwriters; he lunched frequently at the Swiss Chalet in Beverly Hills with Sammy Fain, L. Wolfe Gilbert, Sammy Cahn, Harry Ruby, and Jimmy McHugh. (Their favorite place when in New York was the Diner's Club.) People who knew Washington say he did not think of the screen lyricists as rivals, although there were inevitably the same names on the shortlists for many years. "Ned had no enemies," reported one acquaintance. "He got along with everyone. He said 'You don't win three Oscars unless you get along with people.' The songwriters were all friends. They all knew each other and they all talked and commiserated. It was not competition at all. You got hired and you did it." Washington was also in the habit of lending money to songwriters who could not wait for their royalty checks.

Ned Washington was on the board of directors of ASCAP from 1957 to 1976 and served the licensing organization as its vice president from 1964 to 1976. Afraid to fly, he commuted to New York for the monthly board meetings by train. "He'd be three days on the train out, four days in New York, and then three days back," his daughter recalled. Washington was inducted into the Songwriters Hall of Fame in 1972. In reflecting on his career, he told an interviewer in the 1960s that he thought he had a gift for writing lyrics, but nothing more than that. He was modest about his successes and did not complain about the studios (as some of his contemporaries did). Those who knew him described him as the most perfect gentleman they had ever known.

Ned Washington contracted leukemia in the early 1970s and died of a heart attack in a Los Angeles hospital on 20 December 1976. He was honored as a "Disney Legend" in 2001 by the Walt Disney Company on the occasion of the one-hundredth anniversary of Walt Disney's birth. "When You Wish upon a Star" is the single piece of music most associated with the Walt Disney Company; it was the theme song of the Sunday night Disney television show for decades and is used often in commercials for the company's amusement parks.

Reference:

"Behind the Scenes with Ned Washington," *Box Office,* 16 March 1956, p. 3.

Paul Francis Webster

(20 December 1907 – 22 March 1984)

Tony L. Hill
University of Minnesota

SELECTED SONGS FROM THEATRICAL PRO-
DUCTIONS: *Kill That Story* (1934)–"Two Ciga-
rettes in the Dark" (music by Lew Pollack);
Jump for Joy (1941), music by Duke Ellington–"The
Brown-Skin Gal in the Calico Gown"; "The
Chocolate Shake"; "I Got It Bad (And That Ain't
Good)"; "Jump for Joy."

SELECTED SONGS FROM MOTION-PICTURE
PRODUCTIONS: *Rainbow on the River* (1936)–
"Rainbow on the River" (music by Louis Alter);
Breaking the Ice (1938)–"Good-bye My Dreams, Good-
bye" (music by Victor Young); "Happy as a
Lark" (music by Frank E. Churchill);
How Green Was My Valley (1941)–"How Green Was My
Valley" (music by Alfred Newman);
To Have and Have Not (1942)–"Baltimore Oriole"
(music by Hoagy Carmichael);
Minstrel Man (1944)–"Remember Me to Carolina"
(music by Harry Revel);
The Stork Club (1945)–"Doctor, Lawyer, Indian Chief"
(music by Carmichael);
The Great Caruso (1950)–"The Loveliest Night of the
Year" (music by Irving Aaronson, adapted from
"Over the Waves" by Juventino Rosas);
The Student Prince (1952)–"I'll Walk with God" (music
by Nicholas Brodszky); "Beloved" (music by
Brodszky);
Calamity Jane (1953), music by Sammy Fain–"The
Deadwood Stage"; "The Black Hills of Dakota";
"Just Blew In from the Windy City"; "Secret
Love";
Young at Heart (1954)–"There's a Rising Moon (For
Every Falling Star)" (music by Fain);
Love Is a Many-Splendored Thing (1955)–"Love Is a
Many-Splendored Thing" (music by Fain);
Friendly Persuasion (1956)–"Friendly Persuasion (Thee I
Love)" (music by Dimitri Tiomkin);
Anastasia (1956)–"Anastasia" (music by Newman);
A Farewell to Arms (1957)–"Love Theme from *A Farewell
to Arms*" (music by Mario Nascimbene);

Paul Francis Webster (AP/Wide World Photos)

April Love (1958)–"April Love" (music by Fain);
Mardi Gras (1958), music by Fain–"I'll Remember
Tonight"; "The Mardi Gras March";
Marjorie Morningstar (1958)–"A Very Precious Love"
(music by Fain);
A Certain Smile (1958)–"A Certain Smile" (music by
Fain);
The Alamo (1960)–"The Ballad of the Alamo" (music by
Tiomkin); "The Green Leaves of Summer"
(music by Tiomkin);
The Counterfeit Traitor (1961)–"Marianna" (music by
Newman);
El Cid (1961)–"Love Theme from *El Cid* (The Falcon
and the Dove)" (music by Miklós Rósza);

448

Tender Is the Night (1962)—"Tender Is the Night" (music by Fain);

Mutiny on the Bounty (1962)—"Follow Me" (music by Bronislau Kaper);

55 Days at Peking (1963)—"So Little Time" (music by Tiomkin);

The Seventh Dawn (1964)—"The Seventh Dawn" (music by Riz Ortolani);

The Sandpiper (1965)—"The Shadow of Your Smile" (music by Johnny Mandel);

The Bible (1966)—"In the Beginning" (music by Toshiro Mayuzumi);

An American Dream (1966)—"A Time for Love" (music by Mandel);

The Naked Runner (1967)—"You Are There" (music by Harry Sukman);

Airport (1970)—"Winds of Chance" (music by Newman);

Nicholas and Alexandra (1971)—"Too Beautiful to Last" (music by Richard Rodney Bennett);

The Stepmother (1971)—"Strange Are the Ways of Love" (music by Fain);

Half a House (1976)—"A World That Never Was" (music by Fain).

SELECTED SONGS PUBLISHED INDEPENDENTLY OF THEATRICAL OR MOTION-PICTURE PRODUCTIONS: "Birthday of a Kiss" (1931), music by John Jacob Loeb and Rudy Vallee;

"Two Little Blue Little Eyes" (1931), music by Loeb and Vallee;

"Masquerade" (1932), music by Loeb;

"Got the Jitters" (1933), lyric by Webster and Billy Rose, music by Loeb;

"My Moonlight Madonna" (1933), music by William Scotti, based on "Poème" by Zdenko Fibich;

"The Lamplighter's Serenade" (1942), music by Hoagy Carmichael;

"My Christmas Song for You" (1944), lyric and music by Webster, Carmichael, and Furniss T. Peterson;

"Black Coffee" (1948), music by Sonny Burke;

"The Merry Christmas Polka" (1949), music by Burke;

"The Sleigh Bell Serenade" (1952), music by Burke;

"Watermelon Weather" (1952), music by Carmichael;

"Christmas in Rio" (1955), music by Ben Oakland;

"The First Snowfall" (1955), music by Burke;

"The Christmas Waltz" (1956), music by George Cates;

"Invitation" (1956), music by Bronislau Kaper from the motion-picture score for *Invitation;*

"The Twelfth of Never" (1956), music by Jerry Livingston;

"Padre" (1957), original lyric by Jacques Larue, music by Alain Romans;

"Like Young" (1958), music by André Previn;

"Theme from *Maverick*" (1958), music by David Buttolph;

"Mostly for Lovers" (1959), music by Henry Mancini;

"Sweet Thursday" (1961), music by Newman;

"That's My Kind of Christmas" (1961), music by Livingston;

"The Gift (Recado Bossa Nova)" (1962), music by Luis Antonio and Djalma Ferreira;

"Christmas Star" (1963), music by Ben Weisman;

"The Sounds of Christmas" (1963), music by Livingston;

"Lullaby for Christmas Eve" (1964), music by Pete King;

"The Mood I'm In" (1964), music by King;

"The Snows of Yesteryear" (1965), music by Doug Talbert;

"Somewhere, My Love" (1965), music by Maurice Jarre, "Lara's Theme," from the motion picture score of *Dr. Zhivago;*

"The Summer of Our Love" (1966), music by Marty Paich;

"A World of Whispers" (1967), music by Percy Faith;

"A Lonely Place" (1969), music by Johnny Mandel;

"To America with Love" (1970), music by Cates;

"The First Family of Christmas Time" (1971), music by Burke.

Paul Francis Webster stands as one of the finest movie lyricists in the history of the genre. Although not as well-known as some of his contemporaries, mostly because of his reserved nature, Webster wrote some classic movie songs. His "Love Is a Many-Splendored Thing" (1955) is one of the most popular songs to emerge from the decade of the 1950s, and "The Shadow of Your Smile" (1965) is one of the five most popular songs from the 1960s, exceeded only by the likes of Johnny Mercer and Henry Mancini's "Moon River" (1961) and the Beatles' "Yesterday" (1965). "Love Is a Many-Splendored Thing" and "The Shadow of Your Smile" came late in the career of a man who wrote lyrics successfully from the 1930s into the 1970s.

Paul Francis Webster was born 20 December 1907 in Long Island, New York, the younger of the two sons of Michael and Blanche Webster. The Websters were an upper-middle-class family who owned a successful clothing store. Webster's father wanted Paul to enter the family business, and it galled him that his son chose instead to be a scholar, poet, and songwriter. (Despite Webster's success, his parents always regarded him as the "black sheep," much preferring the course taken by their older son, Morton, who commanded a ship in World War II and later

Sheet music for the 1941 song that was Webster's first standard (Bruccoli Clark Layman Archives)

became a successful lawyer and businessman.) After graduating from the public schools in Lawrence, New York, Webster enrolled at Cornell University and New York University, although it is doubtful that he received a degree from either.

While still studying journalism in Ithaca, Webster, who already fancied himself a poet (and published some poems in a campus organ), was recruited by his classmate Johnny Loeb to serve as a lyricist. Loeb had written a piece based on the work of art-song composer Zdenko Fibich, and with Webster's words, it became the song "My Moonlight Madonna" (1933). While few amateur songs historically have become hits, the pair achieved success, aided no doubt by their own bravado. Paul Whiteman—riding high in those days as the so-called King of Jazz—introduced their song "Masquerade" (1932). Rudy Vallee recorded their "Two Little Blue Little Eyes" (1931) and took a share of the credit for composing the song, as he did on other Webster and Loeb works such as "Birthday of a Kiss" (1931). They also collaborated with

Billy Rose, who is credited as co-lyricist on such songs as "Got the Jitters" (1933).

Throughout this apprenticeship Webster's passion for poetry helped him become a popular songwriter. The earliest Webster song that has remained well known is "Two Cigarettes in the Dark" (1934), with music by Lew Pollack. The song was introduced in the stage play *Kill That Story*. Soon, Webster was called to Hollywood to write songs for motion pictures. Some of Webster's earliest movie credits are for RKO musicals featuring Bobby Breen, including *Rainbow on the River* (1936) and *Breaking the Ice* (1938). Not long after his arrival in Los Angeles, Webster met and married Gloria Leonore Benguiat. They had two sons: Guy was born in 1939 and Roger in 1941. In Hollywood, Webster became acquainted with—albeit briefly—George Gershwin. Eventually he got to know nearly all of his fellow songwriters, but the friendship with Gershwin is significant because there was such little overlap in the time the two men were in California before Gershwin's death in 1937.

Sheet music for Webster and Hoagy Carmichael's novelty hit from a 1945 movie
(Bruccoli Clark Layman Archives)

Webster's first standard was "I Got It Bad (And That Ain't Good)" (1941), with music by Edward K. "Duke" Ellington. It was an odd creation from the man whose name later became synonymous with formal, flowery lyrics. The lyric was well suited to the vocal stylings of the Ellington band, and it was a marked improvement over some of the lyrics the band had been creating in-house. Some other Ellington songs with Webster lyrics are "The Chocolate Shake," "The Brown-Skin Gal In the Calico Gown," and "Jump for Joy," the last the title song of a revue staged to feature the music of the Ellington band.

Also that year, Webster and Hoagy Carmichael wrote "The Lamplighter's Serenade," which has the distinction of being recorded at the first solo session by a young singer named Francis Albert Sinatra. (Sinatra and Webster did not cross paths much; the singer recorded

only a few Webster standards, and the only song Webster wrote for Sinatra was "You Are There" for the 1967 film *The Naked Runner*.) Known to Sinatra's fans as "The Stordahl Session," the 18 January 1942 recordings were not especially big hits but are much treasured by collectors. Glenn Miller and His Orchestra, with Ray Eberle on vocal, enjoyed a bigger hit with the song. (Sinatra also recorded the song with Tommy Dorsey and His Orchestra before finally going solo.) Another big 1942 hit for Webster and Carmichael was "Baltimore Oriole," which is a favorite with vocal groups.

Webster received his first Academy Award nomination for the 1944 song "Remember Me to Carolina" from *Minstrel Man*, with music by Harry Revel. In 1948 Webster and Sonny Burke put together "Black Coffee," which became one of Peggy Lee's signature tunes and a favorite of jazz musicians from Maynard Ferguson to Ella Fitzgerald. Webster and Carmichael had a huge novelty hit in 1945 with "Doctor, Lawyer, Indian Chief," which was recorded most successfully by Betty Hutton.

One of Webster's best songs from the early 1950s had a melody based on the classical theme "Over the Waves" by Juventino Rosas. Remade by Webster and composer Irving Aaronson as "The Loveliest Night of the Year" (1950), it was a signature song for Mario Lanza and features some of Webster's most evocative lines, including "words fall into rhyme anytime you are holding her near." Webster even paid tribute to "Over the Waves" with the line "waltzing along in the blue." More important, "The Loveliest Night of the Year" was the first of Webster's emphatically affectionate songs, a style that was to become his trademark.

Songs featuring religious themes were popular in the 1950s, in part a result of the resurgence of Communism and the reaction seen in Joseph McCarthy's congressional hearings. There were songs that intimated religion, such as Jill Jackson and Sy Miller's "Let There Be Peace on Earth" (1955), discussed it forthrightly, and openly proselytized, such as Geoff Love's "He's Got the Whole World in His Hands" (1958). There were songs about miracles, such as Gladys Gollahon and Samuel M. Lewis's "Our Lady of Fatima" (1950) and Eula Parker's "The Village of St. Bernadette" (1959). Webster's contribution to this genre includes "I'll Walk with God," a small hit in 1952, a collaboration with Nicholas Brodszky. That same year, Webster and Carmichael teamed up for "Watermelon Weather," which was a minor hit as a duet for Perry Como and Eddie Fisher, and it was also recorded as a duet by Bing Crosby and Peggy Lee.

Western musicals reached a peak in the early 1950s, in terms of quality if not quantity. (Western musicals had been produced by boilerplate since the 1930s, although most were forgettable.) The popularity of this genre is apt to have been inspired by the success of Irving Berlin's score for *Annie Get Your Gun* (1946), and it led to the production of the Doris Day vehicle *Calamity Jane* (1953). While the score included several numbers of note by Webster and Sammy Fain, the outstanding one is "Secret Love," an intriguing and beguiling song. Even a cursory reading of the lyric reveals it to be a song for a woman, filled with much feminine imagery. Nevertheless, the song has become a standard not only from Day's recording but also by those of Frank Sinatra, Andy Williams, Johnny Mathis, and Pat Boone. (The song's popularity has continued; Neil Diamond recorded it in 1998 and George Michael did so in 2000.) It won Webster his first Academy Award.

Webster and Day were next-door neighbors on Crescent Drive in Beverly Hills. Webster and Day's husband, Marty Melcher, were friends, and Webster's sons were friends of Day's son, Terry Melcher. "Paul loved

Beverly Hills and California, living next door to Doris Day," Frank Fain, Sammy's son, recalled. "He didn't travel much. If you wanted him to go to Vermont Avenue, you might as well ask him to go to the moon." The Webster home was bordered on the back by that of Sammy Cahn, who was both a friend and a rival. "Whenever a project came up in this town for a lyricist, two of the first guys that got called were Paul Francis Webster and Sammy Cahn," says Danny Gould of the Warner Bros. music department and a former copyist to Webster before that. It is rather startling to believe that someone in the movie business could equivocate between Webster's poetic formality and Cahn's lighthearted irreverence. Not only are the words and music of the songs that go into movies shaped by their writers, however; so are the general tone and theme, and the competition among writers for the contract on a movie occurs before the songs are written. Frank Fain points out that Webster was tone-deaf, which meant some additional steps were needed in the songwriting process, because Webster and his collaborators could not simply work at a piano, as was customary. Webster needed a copyist. Gould explained how he handled the job in the mid 1950s: "I would get the song down from the composer, and then I would go over to Paul's home and lay it out for him. I'd record it for him, and he'd write the lyric from that recording. He'd play it on a child's phonograph over and over until he had it down."

For the movie version of *The Student Prince* (1952) Webster and Brodszky contributed "Beloved." In his brief career, Lanza also recorded Webster's "You Are My Love," a collaboration with Constantine Callinicos. Day introduced one of Webster and Fain's best songs, "There's a Rising Moon (For Every Falling Star)," in the motion picture *Young at Heart* (1954). Webster scored the biggest hit of his career with the title song from the 1955 film *Love Is a Many-Splendored Thing*, starring William Holden and Jennifer Jones. Fain's melody is soaring; its first strain is on the same dramatic melodic level as Harold Arlen and E. Y. "Yip" Harburg's "Over the Rainbow" (1939), and the extended opening note rivets the listener's attention as does the initial note of Richard Rodgers and Oscar Hammerstein's "Oklahoma!" (1943). The song was an instant hit in 1955 and has continued to receive treatment by singers and orchestras. The only arguable shortcoming to Webster's lyric is the masculine specificity at the end of the first B section ("makes a man a king"), which undoubtedly discourages women from singing it. Webster and Fain won their second Oscar in two years for the song.

Webster's songs have been characterized as "Elizabethan" by Johnny Mandel, one of his musical collaborators, and no song of his fits this description more than the 1956 Pat Boone hit "Friendly Persuasion (Thee I Love)." Filled with language evocative of the King James Bible and such convoluted constructions as "thee is mine," the song

Sheet music for the 1955 song that was the biggest hit of Webster's career
(Bruccoli Clark Layman Archives)

was nevertheless nominated for an Academy Award and became one of Boone's biggest hits. In fact, both of the biggest songs Boone introduced had words by Webster. "April Love" (1958) is the title song of a movie that has become much less known than the song. While Boone (who originally rejected the song) recorded it in a triplet-enhanced arrangement, Mathis recorded it in a setting that better displays its touching lyric (and also features its little-known verse). Webster also wrote "Anastasia" (1956), "I'll Remember Tonight," and "The Mardi Gras March" (the latter two from the 1958 movie musical *Mardi Gras*) for Boone.

Mathis also benefitted from other Webster lyrics. One of the singer's first hits was a song Webster and Jerry Livingston adapted from the folk song "The Riddle Song (I Gave My Love a Cherry)." "The Twelfth of Never" was not only a big hit in 1956, it has become a standard and remains one of Mathis's signature tunes.

Mathis is also identified with Webster and Fain's "A Certain Smile," an Academy Award nominee that was the title song of a 1958 film. Webster also wrote some of Mathis's minor hits, including "Sweet Thursday" (1961) and "Marianna" (1961).

In what was his closest contact with jazz since working with the Ellington band in the 1940s, Webster wrote a lyric to André Previn's "Like Young" (1958). The piece was the biggest contribution Previn, one of the few people to successfully migrate from jazz to classical music, made in the jazz world. It continues to be a favorite of jazz musicians. Few popular singers have recorded the song, among them Perry Como, who is usually not associated with jazz or even swing. Como recorded it as part of a 1961 concept album, *For the Young at Heart,* on which all of the songs included the word *young.*

Another Webster-Fain collaboration to get an Oscar nomination was "A Very Precious Love" (1958), best

Sheet music for the 1956 song by Webster and Dimitri Tiomkin that was nominated for an Academy Award (from Marion Short, Hollywood Movie Songs, *1999)*

known for a recording by the Ames Brothers. Gene Kelly introduced the song in the movie *Marjorie Morningstar.*

One of Webster's most poignant lyrics was written to one of Dimitri Tiomkin's most unusual melodies. While the great motion-picture composer frequently strayed from the usual diatonic keys, "The Green Leaves of Summer" sounds modal. The song, written for the John Wayne movie *The Alamo* (1960), was nominated for an Academy Award and was a hit for the folk quartet the Brothers Four. It has been recorded by musicians as disparate as Mahalia Jackson and Herb Alpert. "The Ballad of the Alamo," another song from the movie, was treated by no less diverse a selection of performers. Among those who have recorded it are Marty Robbins, Frankie Avalon, and the Easy Riders.

Webster and Miklós Rózsa were nominated for an Oscar for the "Love Theme from *El Cid* (The Falcon and the Dove)" (1961), and Webster and Fain earned yet another Oscar nomination for what is perhaps their best song, "Tender Is the Night," the title song for the 1962

motion-picture adaptation of the F. Scott Fitzgerald novel, starring Jennifer Jones and Jason Robards. Tony Bennett introduced it in an understated rendition, while Andy Williams took a completely different approach with a soaring treatment reminiscent of "Love Is a Many-Splendored Thing." Webster wrote two of the five songs up for an Oscar that year; his and Bronislau Kaper's "Follow Me," from *Mutiny on the Bounty,* was also nominated.

Another of Webster and Kaper's songs, "Invitation" (1956), is what is known as a "back door" standard. The song was never a popular hit but became a standard over the years through repeated recordings by top artists (usually those who appeal to the adult market) and frequent nightclub performances. "Invitation" has been recorded by a variety of artists, including George Benson, Rosemary Clooney, John Coltrane, Bill Evans, and Caterina Valente.

In 1965 Webster was brought in to write "The Shadow of Your Smile" for the movie *The Sandpiper* only after Mercer tried to do the lyric and found Mandel's melody not to his liking. Webster's lyric was as striking for its simplicity as its elegance. One subtle trick the adept lyricist uses is putting every rhyme (but one) on a one-syllable word. He also deftly manages to turn the song into a circle by both starting and ending the lyric with the title. The hit recording by Tony Bennett was only the first of many. Mandel still speaks well of his senior collaborator. "You couldn't find a better guy," he said in 2000. "Paul was ideal to work with. It was almost too easy. I moved in with him and Gloria and we did our work right there." Mandel says Webster's lyrics have similarities to those of Oscar Hammerstein 2nd. Mandel can count "The Shadow of Your Smile" among his biggest hits. "But it wasn't until after it was a hit, someone told me, 'John, those opening bars sound a lot like Hoagy Carmichael's song "New Orleans."' That's when I realized what I'd done. 'Oops!' I said. Looking back, I'm glad Hoagy didn't sue me!" Webster and Mandel followed up "The Shadow of Your Smile" with "A Time for Love," for the movie *An American Dream* (1966), and it became the title song of Bennett's next album. While it earned an Academy Award nomination and became a favorite among the singer's legion of fans, it did not equal its predecessor in becoming a standard. Bennett is yet another singer for whom Webster provided at least a trilogy of songs; he and Mandel also wrote "A Lonely Place," which the singer recorded in 1969.

One of Webster's outstanding little-known songs of the 1960s was "The Summer of Our Love" (1966), written for the B side of an Andy Williams record. The lyric was written for the teenage market, while the song as a whole was much too sophisticated for that. Webster did a magnificent job crafting an evocative lyric to an unusually complex melody by Marty Paich, who was Jack Jones's musical director at that time. (Jones recorded at least three Webster originals: "Lullaby for Christmas Eve" and "The Mood I'm In," both from 1964, and "The Snows of Yesteryear" from 1965.) The song has the unusual melodic structure *abaca*. Webster's lyric includes pleasing internal rhymes such as "starry eyed and *young* we walked a*mong* the willows," but it remains a specialty piece.

Webster's other major 1960s hit, "Somewhere, My Love" (1965), had already been published as "Lara's Theme from *Dr. Zhivago*" before the lyric was added. Webster was thus ineligible for an Academy Award (since the song has to be written for and used in the movie in order to be nominated), and he received no royalty payments on instrumental recordings of the tune. Most songs created in that manner have no chance at becoming hits, since the novelty of the melody is exhausted by the popularity of the original instrumental version. Nonetheless, a recording of "Somewhere, My Love" by Ray Conniff and the Singers became a huge international hit, and many other vocalists covered the song, too. Webster also collaborated with Henry Mancini on several minor songs.

One of their early works together was "Mostly for Lovers" (1959) an independent song. One of their few movie songs was "The Hills of Yesterday," introduced in *The Molly Maguires* (1970).

In the 1970s Webster did not repeat the success he had enjoyed in earlier years. There were some bright spots: a revival of "The Twelfth of Never" by Donny Osmond and the placement of "Love Is a Many-Splendored Thing" in the movie *Grease* (1978) helped the popularity of those songs with the younger generation. ("Love Is a Many-Splendored Thing" was also used as the theme song of the daytime soap opera of the same name from 1967 to 1973.) Some of Webster's last hits suffered from the decline of song as an important element in the motion pictures. *Airport* was one of the most successful movies of all time when it was made in 1970, and Webster wrote the words to its love theme, "Winds of Chance." One has to strain to hear the words at the end of the movie, however, while the music is quite familiar. There is no single outstanding vocal version of "Winds of Chance"; a few easy-listening orchestras recorded it with a vocal chorus. Webster's last important song was for the 1971 motion picture *Nicholas and Alexandra*. "Too Beautiful to Last" is one of Webster's most sensitive lyrics, but it too is less familiar than the music by Richard Rodney Bennett. Engelbert Humperdinck recorded an excellent vocal rendition. Two more Webster-Fain songs were nominated for Academy Awards in the 1970s: "Strange Are the Ways of Love" from *The Stepmother* (1971), and "A World That Never Was" from the 1976 movie *Half a House*.

Webster wrote lyrics for several Christmas songs: "My Christmas Song for You" (1944), "The Merry Christmas Polka" (1949), "The Sleigh Bell Serenade" (1952), "Christmas in Rio" (1955), "The First Snowfall" (1955; recorded by the Carpenters, among others), "The Christmas Waltz" (1956; not to be confused with the Cahn-Jule Styne opus of the same name), "That's My Kind of Christmas" (1961), "Christmas Star" (1963), "The Sounds of Christmas" (1963), "Lullaby for Christmas Eve" (1964), and "The First Family of Christmas Time" (1971). None of these songs has joined the enduring seasonal repertoire along with Irving Berlin's "White Christmas" (1942), Leroy Anderson and Michell Parish's "Sleigh Ride" (1950), and Hugh Martin and Ralph Blane's "Have Yourself a Merry Little Christmas" (1943).

Webster had some success writing English lyrics for foreign songs. In 1957 he provided the English lyric to "Padre," a French song recorded by Marty Robbins and Elvis Presley, and in 1962 he wrote an English lyric for "The Gift (Recado Bossa Nova)," a Latin American song recorded by Eydie Gorme. Webster also wrote lyrics for television. He wrote the words to the theme from the James Garner series *Maverick,* which premiered in 1958. To Franz Waxman's music, he

Sheet music for Webster and Sammy Fain's title song for the 1962 motion-picture adaptation of F. Scott Fitzgerald's 1934 novel (Matthew J. and Arlyn Bruccoli Collection of Fitzgerald, University of South Carolina Library)

wrote several pieces for the 1960s soap *Peyton Place,* and he wrote the words to the theme for the animated series *Spider-Man.*

Beyond his career, Webster's passion was English literature. He owned a collection of first editions, including a copy of William Shakespeare's First Folio. Among his other acquisitions were original copies of the Magna Carta, the Emancipation Proclamation, and the lyrics to "Battle Hymn of the Republic." "My father wasn't a social man," Guy Webster explained. "He wasn't a party person. He didn't like to leave the house much. My parents' house was a fine English Tudor, and he never understood why he'd want to leave the house where he had everything the way he wanted it." As Guy Webster put it in a song-

book he compiled of his father's songs, "he rarely wanted to leave the house except to play tennis, to find a good lemon meringue pie, or to pick up an Academy Award."

Paul Francis Webster died at his Beverly Hills home on 22 March 1984. He was buried at Hillside Memorial Park in Culver City, California.

Selected Discography:
Calamity Jane, studio cast recording, Jay Records, CD2 1234, 1996;
Doris Day Sings Songs from Calamity Jane and The Pajama Game, Columbia, 63032, 1957;
Andy Williams, *Dear Heart / The Shadow of Your Smile,* Collectables Records, COL-CD-6048, 1999.

Meredith Willson

(18 May 1902 – 15 June 1984)

Thomas S. Hischak
State University of New York College at Cortland

Music is by Willson unless otherwise indicated.

SELECTED SONGS FROM THEATRICAL PRO-
DUCTIONS: *The Music Man* (1957)–"Rock
Island"; "Trouble"; "Goodnight, My Someone";
"Seventy-Six Trombones"; "Marian the Librar-
ian"; "Shipoopi"; "Lida Rose"; "Gary, Indiana";
"Till There Was You"; "Piano Lesson"; "The
Sadder-but-Wiser Girl"; "Iowa Stubborn"; "Will I
Ever Tell You?"; "Pick-a-Little, Talk-a-Little";
"Sincere"; "It's You";

The Unsinkable Molly Brown (1960)–"I Ain't Down Yet";
"Colorado, My Home"; "Belly Up to the Bar,
Boys"; "I'll Never Say No"; "Are You Sure?";

Here's Love (1963)–"Pine Cones and Holly Berries";
"Here's Love"; "That Man Over There."

SELECTED SONGS FROM MOTION-PICTURE
PRODUCTIONS: *The Cavalier* (1928)–"My
Cavalier" (music by Hugo Riesenfeld);

The Great Dictator (1940)–"Falling Star" (lyric and music
by Willson, Charles Chaplin, and Eddie
DeLange);

The Little Foxes (1941)–"Never Feel Too Weary to
Pray";

The Music Man (1962)–"Being in Love";

The Unsinkable Molly Brown (1964)–"He's My Friend."

SELECTED SONGS PUBLISHED INDEPEN-
DENTLY OF THEATRICAL OR MOTION-
PICTURE PRODUCTIONS: "You and I"
(1941);

"Two in Love" (1941);

"May the Good Lord Bless and Keep You" (1950);

"It's Beginning to Look Like Christmas" (1951).

BOOKS: *And There I Stood with My Piccolo* (Garden City,
N.Y.: Doubleday, 1948);

Who Did What to Fedalia? (Garden City, N.Y.: Doubleday, 1952);

Eggs I Have Laid (New York: Holt, 1955);

Meredith Willson (from David Ewen,
American Songwriters, *1987)*

"But He Doesn't Know the Territory" (New York: Putnam,
1957).

Meredith Willson's career did not follow the usual
pattern of Broadway songwriters. A successful musician,
conductor, musical arranger, and composer of instrumental and background music, Willson did not embark on his
first Broadway score until he was well into his fifties.
When he did start to write musical comedies, though, his
work was as fresh and innovative as any young prodigy;
he brought his years of musical (and worldly) experience
to his stage projects and, in the case of *The Music Man*
(1957), created a distinctive Broadway musical.

The setting and people of his most famous stage work provide the details for Willson's early years. He was born Robert Meredith Reiniger Willson on 18 May 1902 in Mason City, Iowa, where his father, John David Willson, was a lawyer and businessman and his mother, Rosalie (Reiniger) Willson, was a piano teacher. As a boy he studied both flute and piccolo as well as the piano, and by his high-school years he was earning money playing for school dances, county fairs, and other local amusements. Willson was graduated from Mason City High School in 1919, married Elizabeth Wilson on 29 August 1920, and left his small-town world to study music at Juilliard (then called the Institute of Musical Art). By the time he was nineteen years old, Willson was hired as first flutist for John Philip Sousa's band, then in 1924 he left Sousa to play with the New York Philharmonic under conductor Arturo Toscanini.

In 1929 he moved to the West Coast and worked in Hollywood scoring music for such movies as *Peacock Alley* (1922) and *The Lost Zeppelin* (1929). He also worked as music director for ABC radio in Seattle, and then at KFRC radio in San Francisco for three years, conducting the studio orchestra for such programs as *The Blue Monday Jamboree.* Willson moved over to NBC in 1932 and remained there as conductor and musical arranger for more than two decades. There he directed *The George Burns and Gracie Allen Show, Maxwell House Good News,* and *The Big Ten,* a forerunner of *Your Hit Parade.*

During that time Willson turned to composing as well. He wrote Symphony no. 1 in F-minor (*San Francisco*) when he was thirty-six, and he premiered it as guest conductor of the San Francisco Symphony on 19 April 1936. His second symphony, *The Missions of California,* was performed by the Los Angeles Philharmonic on 21 April 1940. In 1941 he had his first successful popular song, "You and I," for which he provided the lyric as well as the music, a practice he continued with his popular-music projects. Willson's credits also included writing the background music for Lillian Hellman's Broadway drama *The Little Foxes* (1939) and the film soundtracks for Charles Chaplin's *The Great Dictator* (1940) and the movie version of *The Little Foxes* (1941).

During World War II, Willson served as music director of the Armed Forces Radio Service. He composed several songs for radio shows, such as "Mail-Call March" and "America Calling," as well as a symphonic work, *The Jervis Bay,* as a memorial to the crew of an Australian freighter. After the war he continued to work in radio as a conductor, composer, and occasional performer. In 1947 he divorced his first wife, and on 13 March 1948 he married a singer named Ralina Zarova.

Of his Tin Pan Alley hits, none was more popular than "May the Good Lord Bless and Keep You" (1950), which was written as the theme song for Tallulah Bankhead's radio program, *The Big Show* (for which Willson also served as music director). The song went on to become a national favorite during the Korean War years. Willson also tried television in 1949, presenting a half-hour program called *The Meredith Willson Show,* but he was not successful in the new medium and returned to radio with his own show, *Meredith Willson's Music Room.*

Having been in show business for many years, Willson knew many Broadway songwriters but never considered writing a musical himself until composer-lyricist Frank Loesser, who enjoyed Willson's reminiscences about growing up in rural Iowa after the turn of the century, suggested that there was material in Willson's youth for a musical comedy. It took eight years and many rewrites before *The Music Man* opened in 1957. Since he wanted to write the libretto, music, and lyrics himself, Willson struggled with various versions of his Iowa days before creating the con man Harold Hill, the most fictitious aspect of the show, though Willson was familiar with traveling salesmen of the period. His mother became the piano teacher and librarian Marian Paroo, and the rest of the characters fell into place, all based on people he recalled from Mason City. The role that gave him the most trouble was the moody youth Winthrop, originally a severely handicapped child with a cleft palate, then rewritten with various other physical abnormalities before he was given a lisp.

Willson went through thirty-two drafts of the story and many songs before he admitted he needed help, and Franklin Lacey was hired to help shape the book. Despite Willson's popularity in the entertainment business, producers were not eager to present the nostalgic musical. Even after Kermit Bloomgarden agreed to produce, they found difficulty getting a star to play Hill; Danny Kaye, Phil Harris, Dan Dailey, and Gene Kelly were among the performers to turn it down. Musical director Herbert Greene and director Morton DaCosta strongly suggested Western-movie actor Robert Preston for the role, even though his stage and singing experience were limited.

The Music Man proved to be one of the most successful Broadway shows of the decade, running 1,375 performances, inspiring a popular 1962 movie version, and remaining on the list of the most frequently produced musicals for the rest of the century. Willson's considerable musical knowledge is evident in the score, which includes rhythm numbers, barbershop quartets, ballads, vaudeville pieces, ragtime, patter songs, and, of course, marches. The homespun, gently satiric dialogue he wrote for the book flowed seamlessly into the lyrics. While "Seventy-Six Trombones" and "Till There Was You" were the standout hits, all of the musical numbers are exceptional. *The Music Man* is proudly old-fashioned and yet, at the same time, is surprisingly original. While the spirit of the piece recalled George M. Cohan and the raucous musical comedies of

Sheet music for a love ballad from Willson's hit 1957 musical (Bruccoli Clark Layman Archives)

the early decades of the century, there had never been a show quite like it.

Willson's next project, *The Unsinkable Molly Brown* (1960), was also set in the early 1900s, but this time Willson forsook the woes of writing another libretto and had Richard Morris fashion the book. A fanciful fable about true-life backwoods girl Molly and her rise in society, the plot again features a strong leading character. Molly is reminiscent of the Annie Oakley of *Annie Get Your Gun* (1946), and Tammy Grimes's quicksilver performance was commendable, but the supporting characters are not as engaging as the Iowa residents of *The Music Man.* The show includes Molly's best-known deed, taking command of a lifeboat during the sinking of the *Titanic,* but the story of Molly's troublesome marriage to lucky prospector Leadville Johnny Brown is less gripping. Willson's score often has the energy and spirit of *The Music Man,* with "I Ain't Down Yet," "Belly Up to the Bar, Boys," and other

numbers conveying joyous abandon. The gospel number "Are You Sure?" compares favorably with Harold Hill's "Trouble," and "I'll Never Say No" is a full-voiced ballad suitable for Johnny. Too much in the show seems manufactured rather than inspired. Perhaps Willson's sincerity and familiarity of subject matter in *The Music Man* could not be repeated. Nonetheless, *The Unsinkable Molly Brown* was a moderate success at 532 performances.

Even more disappointing was *Here's Love* (1963), a musical version of the 1947 holiday movie classic *Miracle on 34th Street* that Willson adapted himself and for which he provided the score, which utilizes his popular "It's Beginning to Look Like Christmas" (1951). Few of the other songs are memorable, however, and the expensive production ran 334 times only because of its healthy advance sale. After *Here's Love,* Willson went into retirement, making only one other attempt at Broadway with *1491* (1969), an operetta about Christopher Columbus

Sheet music for a song from the 1964 movie version of Willson's 1960 musical about the eccentric philanthropist and actress who survived the sinking of the Titanic *(from Marion Short,* Hollywood Movie Songs, *1999)*

that closed out of town. With its quick failure, he retired again to California and contented himself with the continued popularity of *The Music Man*.

Willson wrote three autobiographical works—*And There I Stood with My Piccolo* (1948), *Eggs I Have Laid* (1955), and *"But He Doesn't Know the Territory"* (1957)—and a novel, *Who Did What to Fedalia?* (1952). For John F. Kennedy's 1960 presidential campaign he wrote the song "Ask Not," and for Gerald Ford's 1976 campaign he wrote "WIN WIN WIN." After his second wife died in 1966, Willson married Rosemary Sullivan, his secretary, on 14 February 1968. He had no children.

Willson's talent as a lyricist merits attention because he thought of words as extensions of music. In fact, he often relegated melody to the background and depended on rhythm and words to carry the song. *The Music Man* is filled with innovative uses for words. The opening, "Rock Island," is done without orchestra, the salesmen creating the changing tempos of a train going from one station to another by building up phrases, sometimes only single words used in repetition. The mother-daughter argument in "Piano Lesson" is set to rising and descending scales played by Marian's piano student. "Trouble" is part salesman spiel, part revivalist patter that only breaks into melody on the refrain. Willson also manages the tricky feat of keeping both sets of lyrics clear in the contrapuntal duets "Lida Rose/Will I Ever Tell You?" and "Pick-a-Little, Talk-a-Little/Goodnight, Ladies." Words pile up in the soft-shoe number, "The Sadder-but-Wiser Girl," just as they do in the patter leading up to "Seventy-Six Trombones." That march lyric that seems so vigorous uses the same melody as Marian's yearning lullaby, "Goodnight, My Someone," one of Willson's most imaginative transformations of a melody.

The Music Man is such a verbal show that it seems to create its own language. No other Broadway musical number has ever employed the vocabulary found in "Trouble"—"cistern," "beefsteak," "iron-clad leave,"

Sheet music for the lullaby from the 1962 movie version of Willson's 1957 musical (from Lehman Engel, Their Words Are Music, *1975)*

"libertine," "pinch-back suit," "screen door," "dime novel," "corn crib," "shirt-tail young ones," "balk line game," and "Sen Sen." Equally rich is the argot of items and salesmen's terms used in "Rock Island." Nuances of language create the self-mocking tone of "Iowa Stubborn" and the wordy serenade "Marian the Librarian," with its long vowels. Willson can hang on to a word endlessly, as in the Buffalo Bill quartet's "Sincere" and "It's You," or chop the words into syllabic pieces, as with "Pick-a-Little, Talk-a-Little." For a man who spent most of his life in instrumental music, Willson was a master craftsman of words.

Two of Willson's lyrics from *The Music Man* illustrate both his dexterity with the conventions of lyric writing and his willingness to break convention. As in many musicals, the big hit in *The Music Man* was the love ballad, in this case "Till There Was You." Arriving late in the second act, sung by the leading characters, and positioned so that it will stand out, the song easily established itself as an independent hit. (Even the Beatles recorded the ballad in 1963 and included it on one of their early albums.) It is at once the most conventional and surprising number in the whole score. Willson's lyric construction in the song is old-fashioned. While "Till There Was You" has no verse, its AABA pattern is so typical of Tin Pan Alley love songs that it almost seems out of place in such a character-driven show as *The Music Man*. Each section uses the phrases "there was" or "there were" to set up an image, then does a reverse on that image in order to turn it into an exclamation of love. "Bells were ringing," the lyric states, but until love came along Marian never heard them. Realistically speaking, it is a far-fetched notion, but the hyperbole works. Harold Hill has somehow opened her ears.

The second section does the same thing with the time-worn image of birds in the sky. Again, she never saw them until loving him opened her eyes. And the fact that she finally sees them "winging" (to rhyme with the bells *ringing*), rather than "flying," underscores the old-fashioned vocabulary of the lyric that sets it in turn-of-the-century Iowa. The release, a lovely and flowing section that rises and falls with the lyric description of roses, fragrant meadows, dawn, and dew, continues the list of things Marian was unaware of until she fell in love. Willson even adds the pointed phrase "they tell me," to emphasize Marian's past experience of living life through hearsay.

The final section moves from specifics to a generalization about love itself, but the word *love* is only used once in the whole lyric, and it is used as a noun rather than as a verb: "there was love all around." Like the other items in this romantic list song, however, she never noticed it "till there was you"–the title phrase used for the third time. The whole lyric evokes Irving Berlin in its simplicity, conciseness, clarity, and unpretentiousness.

By contrast, "Marian the Librarian" is a mocking love song: a seduction song sung by an insincere lover. Not until Stephen Sondheim's scores in the 1970s was a lyric so intentionally phony and subversive. Harold Hill has no affection at all for Marian at this point, though he would willingly bed her to protect his scam. Even before he meets the attractive but uptight Marian, Harold confesses he would seduce any piano teacher if necessary, even an unappealing one. This song is sung in the local library where Marian works; she has walked away from him on earlier attempts but now she is forced to stay and hear his callow and comic serenade. Just holding one syllable of her name for seemingly endless counts is clever mockery. Further, the images he presents–the library burning down, his falling and lying on the floor until his body starts to decay–are as ridiculous as they are unromantic.

Only in the release, when he paints a picture of two traditional lovers in the moonlight, does the lyric ever turn the least bit lyrical. Much of the rest of it consists of bold and meaningless proclamations of love. The word barely used in "Till There Was You" is bantered easily in this song. "I love you madly, madly," he almost immediately announces, and "I need you badly, badly" is more true that the naive librarian can understand. Willson lets the music provide the subtext for the song. The words argue sincere passion, but the melody is careless, hapless, and even nonchalant, as though the love-making is all routine and part of any con man's job. The lyric even has fun with the unusual setting for the song. Harold calls it an "unforgivable sin" to speak of love aloud in a library, almost admitting that his approach is more business than passion. It is a deft, sharp, and clever lyric and shows a master craftsman using the musical-theater song in unprecedented fashion.

While he rarely equaled the brilliance of *The Music Man*, Meredith Willson did retain some similar elements throughout his three Broadway scores. All three are unabashedly optimistic. No one since Cohan celebrated affirmation and life in his songs as Willson did. In all three shows, the major character takes over and mesmerizes the crowd with his or her strong convictions and promises of happiness. Con man Harold Hill, ambitious Molly Brown, and Santa Claus himself are each leading their own parade, sometimes literally. The power of music to transform an Iowa town, the gumption for survival that survives a sinking ship, and the triumph of genuine holiday cheer over commercialism are the themes of Willson's shows. The words offer the possibilities of miracles, and each musical produces its miracle on cue. Perhaps the optimism was in Willson, and it came out in his lyrics.

References:

Stanley Green, *The World of Musical Comedy: The Story of the American Musical Stage as Told through Its Foremost Composers and Lyricists* (San Diego: Barnes, 1980), pp. 273–277;

Thomas S. Hischak, *Word Crazy: Broadway Lyricists from Cohan to Sondheim* (New York: Praeger, 1991), pp. 153–155;

Ethan Mordden, *Coming Up Roses: The Broadway Musical in the 1950s* (New York: Oxford University Press, 1998), pp. 195–198;

Peter Waddington, "Meredith Willson: Young Man with Ideas," *Opera and Concert* (September 1948): 16–17;

Dixie Willson, "The Man Behind *The Music Man*," *American Weekly* (4 May 1958): 15–16.

Papers:

Meredith Willson's papers, comprising manuscripts and musical compositions, are held at the Special Collections Department of the University of Iowa Libraries.

Selected Discography:

Here's Love, original Broadway cast, Columbia, KOS 2400, 1963;

The Music Man, original Broadway cast, Capitol, SW 990, 1958;

The Music Man, original London cast, Stanyan, 10039, 1961;

The Music Man, motion-picture soundtrack, Warner Bros., WS 1459, 1962;

The Music Man, 2000 Broadway revival, Atlantic/Q Records, 92915-2, 2000;

The Unsinkable Molly Brown, original Broadway cast, Capitol, SW 2152, 1960;

The Unsinkable Molly Brown, motion-picture soundtrack, M-G-M, SE 4232 ST, 1964.

Jack Yellen

(6 July 1892 – 17 April 1991)

Michael Lasser

Unless otherwise indicated, music is by Milton Ager.

**SELECTED SONGS FROM THEATRICAL PRO-
DUCTIONS:** *High Jinks* (1913)–"All Aboard for
Dixieland" (music by George L. Cobb);
Frivolities of 1920 (1920)–"Peaches" (music by Albert
Gumble);
What's in a Name? (1920)–"A Young Man's Fancy";
Bombo (1922)–"Who Cares?" (interpolation);
The Bunch and Judy (1922)–"Lovin' Sam, the Sheik of
Alabam'" (interpolation);
Innocent Eyes (1924)–"Hard-Hearted Hannah, the Vamp
of Savannah" (lyric by Yellen and Charles Bates,
music by Ager and Robert Bigelow);
Rain or Shine (1928)–"Falling Star"; "Feelin' Good"
(music by Owen Murphy); "Forever and Ever";
"Rain or Shine" (music by Ager and Murphy);
Whoopee (1928)–"Hungry Women" (interpolation);
John Murray Anderson's Almanac (1929)–"I Can't Remem-
ber the Words";
Follow a Star (1930), music by Vivian Ellis–"Follow a
Star";
You Said It (1931), music by Harold Arlen–"Sweet and
Hot"; "You Said It";
George White's Scandals (1939), music by Sammy Fain–
"Are You Havin' Any Fun?"; "Something I
Dreamed Last Night" (lyric by Yellen and Herb
Magidson);
Boys and Girls Together (1940), lyrics by Yellen and
Irving Kahal, music by Fain–"I Want to Live";
Sons o' Fun (1941), music by Fain–"Happy in Love";
Ziegfeld Follies of 1943 (1943), music by Ray Hender-
son–"Love Songs Are Made in the Night."

**SELECTED SONGS FROM MOTION-PICTURE
PRODUCTIONS:** *Honky Tonk* (1929)–"He's a
Good Man to Have Around"; "I'm Doing What
I'm Doing for Love"; "I'm Feathering a Nest (For
a Little Bluebird)"; "I'm the Last of the Red Hot
Mamas";

*Jack Yellen (from David Ewen,
American Songwriters, 1987)*

Glad Rag Doll (1929)–"Glad Rag Doll" (music by Ager
and Dan Dougherty);
Chasing Rainbows (1930)–"Happy Days Are Here
Again"; "Lucky Me, Lovable You";
King of Jazz (1930)–"A Bench in the Park"; "Happy
Feet"; "I Like to Do Things for You";
George White's Scandals (1934)–"Nasty Man" (lyric by
Yellen and Irving Caesar, music by Ray Hender-
son);
George White's 1935 Scandals (1935), music by Joseph
Meyer–"According to the Moonlight" (lyric by
Yellen and Herb Magidson); "Hunkadola" (lyric
by Yellen and Cliff Friend); "Oh, I Didn't Know

(You'd Get That Way)" (lyric by Yellen and Friend);

King of Burlesque (1935)—"I Love to Ride the Horses on a Merry-Go-Round" (music by Lew Pollack);

Sing, Baby, Sing (1936)—"Sing, Baby, Sing" (music by Pollack).

SELECTED SONGS PUBLISHED INDEPENDENTLY OF THEATRICAL OR MOTION-PICTURE PRODUCTIONS: "Alabama Jubilee" (1915), music by George L. Cobb;

"Are You from Dixie?" (1915), music by Cobb;

"How's Every Little Thing in Dixie?" (1916), music by Albert Gumble;

"Playmates" (1917), music by Gumble;

"Southern Gals" (1917), music by Gumble;

"There's a Lump of Sugar Down in Dixie" (1918), lyric by Yellen and Alfred Bryan, music by Gumble;

"Alexander's Band Is Back in Dixieland" (1919), music by Gumble;

"Don't Put a Tax on the Beautiful Girls" (1919);

"Down by the O-Hi-O" (1920), music by Abe Olman;

"Louisville Lou, the Vampin' Lady" (1923);

"Mamma Goes Where Papa Goes, or Papa Don't Go Out Tonight" (1923);

"Big Bad Bill Is Sweet William Now" (1924);

"Big Boy" (1924);

"I Wonder What's Become of Sally" (1924);

"Cheatin' on Me" (1925), music by Lew Pollack;

"My Yiddishe Momme" (1925), music by Yellen and Pollack;

"Could I? I Certainly Could" (1926);

"Ain't She Sweet?" (1927);

"Ain't That a Grand and Glorious Feeling?" (1927);

"Crazy Words, Crazy Tune" (1927);

"Dream Kisses" (1927), music by M. K. Jerome;

"I'm Waiting for Ships That Never Come In" (1927), music by Olman;

"Is She My Girl Friend?" (1927);

"My Pet" (1928);

"I'm Doing What I'm Doing for Love" (1929);

"Let's Get Friendly" (1931), lyric by Yellen and Sid Silvers, music by Dan Dougherty.

Lyricist Jack Yellen was a skillful journeyman songwriter who plied his trade, providing songs for sheet music, recordings, Broadway musicals, and Hollywood movies, for more than forty years. Though the songs he wrote with composer Milton Ager played an important role in establishing the popular music styles of the 1920s, Yellen's most important lyric, "Happy Days Are Here Again" (1930), became one of the rallying cries of the Depression.

Jacob Selig "Jack" Yellen was born on 6 July 1892 in Razcki, Poland, to Abraham Yellen and Bessie Wallens Yellen. The family migrated to the United States in 1897, settling in Buffalo, New York, where the father worked as a pawnbroker and Jack attended public schools. A chronically tardy student, Yellen wrote his first song, "You'll Have to Come to Old Central High," (1907) in an attempt to placate the principal. He earned a B.A. degree from the University of Michigan, where he wrote songs—both words and music—to earn pocket money. By the end of his sophomore year, Yellen was writing only lyrics and had begun a brief collaboration with Buffalo composer George L. Cobb. They sold their songs to small local publishers. One of their songs, "All Aboard for Dixieland" (1913), was interpolated into Otto Harbach and Rudolf Friml's 1913 operetta *High Jinks*. Yellen and Cobb published "Are You from Dixie?" and "Alabama Jubilee" in 1915.

Like other untutored songwriters, Yellen later wrote that he "learned by imitating current popular hits. Songs about the South were then the rage, and eventually [we] wrote 'All Aboard for Dixieland.'" Songs about a gentle, bucolic South had been popular in the United States at least since the rise of minstrel shows in the first half of the nineteenth century. By the early twentieth century these songs had found a new lease on life, as young people from the farms and small towns of the South and Midwest flocked to New York and other burgeoning northern cities. Though some songs celebrated the excitement of urban life, others conjured up nostalgic memories of hometowns, country lanes, and mothers and sweethearts left behind. Because most of the songs of the day were so rigidly formulaic, Yellen, a Polish-born Jew raised in Upstate New York, had no trouble writing them. His songs from this period were easy to sing and just as easy to remember, but they did little more than rework already familiar material, with no particular freshness or invention.

After college Yellen was a reporter on the police beat and eventually an assistant sports editor for the *Buffalo Courier-Express* before moving to New York to pursue a full-time career as a songwriter. He plugged songs in Coney Island dives, lived in a $5-a-week furnished room, and ate meals at free lunch counters in saloons. Yellen's first collaborator after the move was composer Albert Gumble, with whom he wrote such nostalgic songs as "How's Every Little Thing in Dixie?" (1916) and "There's a Lump of Sugar Down in Dixie" (1918). Gumble and Yellen's postwar song "Alexander's Band Is Back in Dixieland" (1919) was one of several deriving from Irving Berlin's massive 1911 hit "Alexander's Ragtime Band" and was obviously a direct response to Cliff Hess, Alfred Bryan, and Edgar Leslie's

*Sheet music for two 1915 Yellen songs that capitalized on the popularity of nostalgic songs about
the South (Music Library, University of South Carolina; Marie-Reine A. Pafik and Anna
Marie Guiheen,* The Sheet Music Reference and Price Guide, *1995)*

hit of 1918, "When Alexander Takes His Ragtime Band to France." That was the way Tin Pan Alley worked: songwriters either came up with a gimmick of their own or "borrowed" an already successful one from somebody else. Like so many other songwriters, Yellen had no personal style, no approach to sentiment or imagery that was distinctly his own. He wrote what people wanted to hear.

Although his success eventually required him to move back and forth between Manhattan and Hollywood, Yellen maintained lifelong ties to Buffalo. After serving in the army during World War I, he returned to his hometown, where he plugged his own songs in a local five-and-ten until his close friend Marion Healy urged him to try New York again. Yellen and Gumble placed "Peaches" in the Broadway revue *Frivolities of 1920,* but the young lyricist had his first major success that same year when he and band leader Abe Olman collaborated on "Down by the O-Hi-O" (1920). The song switched the focus from the South to the Midwest, but the nostalgic point of view remained unchanged. Sophie Tucker plugged the song so often in vaudeville that Broadway headliners Gus Van and Joseph Schenck

soon interpolated it into the *Ziegfeld Follies of 1920,* and Lou Holtz sang it in *George White's Scandals of 1920.*

At about this time comedy writer Al Boasberg introduced Yellen to Ager. Their first song was a comic number popularized by Eddie Cantor, "Don't Put a Tax on the Beautiful Girls" (1919). Director John Murray Anderson had hired Ager to write the score for the Broadway revue *What's in a Name?* (1920), and Ager insisted on having the unknown Yellen as his lyricist. Their songs marked the beginning of one of the major songwriting collaborations of the 1920s. Yellen and Ager–along with Buddy DeSylva, Lew Brown, Ray Henderson, Gus Kahn, and Walter Donaldson–defined the frisky, carefree sound of that decade. When flappers rouged their knees and college boys sported raccoon coats, they often danced the night away to songs by Yellen and Ager. By 1922 the collaborators had established their own publishing company, Ager, Yellen, and Borenstein. Specializing in comedy numbers rather than ballads, for the next six years they turned out such jazzy hits as "Who Cares?" (1922); "Lovin' Sam, the Sheik of Alabam'" (1922); "Louisville Lou, the Vampin' Lady" (1923); "Hard-Hearted Han-

Sheet music for the 1927 song that is the best known of Yellen's 1920s songs
(Bruccoli Clark Layman Archives)

nah, the Vamp of Savannah" (1924); "Big Bad Bill Is Sweet William Now" (1924); "Ain't She Sweet?" (1927); and "Crazy Words, Crazy Tune" (1927). Yellen and Ager's songs reflected the flippant assurance of the young–their heady embrace of pleasure for its own sake and their madcap defiance of convention.

Yellen and Ager also had a hit with the charmingly old-fashioned "I Wonder What's Become of Sally" (1924), which sold more than a million copies; working with Olman again, Yellen wrote the pensive "I'm Waiting for Ships That Never Come In" (1927). On the cusp of the Great Depression, Ager and Yellen wrote (with composer Dan Dougherty) their last important 1920s song, "Glad Rag Doll" (1929). It was also one of their best. Lacking the breeziness of their other successes, the song told a bluesy, rueful story of virtue compromised, in the tradition of such tales of women fallen, abandoned, or betrayed as James F. Hanley and Grant Clarke's comic "Second Hand Rose" (1921) and

Hanley and Ballard Macdonald's "Rose of Washington Square" (1922). Yellen's lyric plays the elegance of the "doll's" attire off against the absence of someone who truly loves her:

Admired, desired,
By lovers who soon grow tired,
Poor little glad rag doll.
You're just a pretty toy
They like to play with.
You're not the kind they choose
To grow old and gray with.

Of all Yellen's songs of the 1920s, none has endured longer than "Ain't She Sweet." The simple, direct lyric is typical of Yellen's artless style. Its charm rests on the enthusiasm of a young man watching his sweetheart approach and inviting someone confidentially to "look her over once or twice." The short, ungrammatical title phrase is repeated to create the

Sheet music for the title song by Yellen and Milton Ager for a 1929 movie
(from Marion Short, Hollywood Movie Songs, *1999)*

youthfulness and crowing delight of the song. The simple phrase is contrasted with the few longer words that form the climax of the lyric, which nonetheless retains its slangy drive: "Just cast an eye in her direction. / Oh, me! Oh, my! Ain't that perfection?"

Despite their success with individual songs, most of Yellen and Ager's Broadway efforts of the 1920s flopped, including such shows as *Zig Zag* (1922), *Ted Lewis' Frolic* (1923), and *John Murray Anderson's Almanac* (1929). Their one hit show was *Rain or Shine* (1928), which starred comic Joe Cook. The title song and "Forever and Ever" were the most successful numbers in the score.

By the time Yellen and Ager left New York for Hollywood (they were among the first songwriters to write for the talkies), Yellen had contributed songs to ten different Broadway shows, almost all of them revues. That is, even when he was writing for the stage, he was writing individual songs rather than complete scores. He also designed several of his songs for specific performers—"Who Cares?" for Al Jolson in *Bombo* (1922) and the amusing, slightly surreal "Hungry Women" for Cantor in *Whoopee* (1928). Even though Kahn and Donaldson wrote the score to *Whoopee,* Cantor interpolated comic numbers by other songwriters for his "star turn" in the second act. In "Hungry Women" the singer bemoans the cost of dating because his girlfriends are always hungry:

> I met a girl,
> She had two teeth.
> I took her to supper.
> 'Twas just my luck,
> Her lower tooth
> Met with the upper.

In 1925 Yellen wrote both words and music to "My Yiddishe Momme" as a tribute to his mother, who had died the previous year. It was the most personal

*Sheet music for the 1930 Yellen-Ager song that was the theme song for Franklin D. Roosevelt's
1932 presidential campaign (Bruccoli Clark Layman Archives)*

song he ever wrote and clearly the one that meant the most to him. (When he later dissolved his partnership with Ager, "My Yiddishe Momme" was the only song to which he retained the rights.) Though he had not intended to publish it, Yellen asked composer Lew Pollack to polish the melody. Yellen then took the finished version to Tucker, who wept when he sang it to her. She suggested that he change the title to "My Jewish Momme" or "My Hebrew Momme." Not only did he refuse, but he also persuaded Tucker to sing one chorus of the song in Yiddish. When she introduced "My Yiddishe Momme" at the Palace Theatre in 1925, it stopped the show. It became one of Tucker's most popular numbers after her theme song, "Some of These Days" (1910). In *Some of These Days: The Autobiography of Sophie Tucker* (1945), which she dedicated to Yellen, she wrote of his song, "I was always careful to use it only when I knew the majority of the house would under-

stand Yiddish. However, I have found whenever I have sung 'My Yiddishe Momme,' in the U.S.A., or in Europe, Gentiles have loved the song and have called for it. They didn't need to understand the Yiddish words. They knew, by instinct, what I was saying, and their hearts responded. . . ."

The melody to "My Yiddishe Momme" suggests that Yellen never entirely forgot the melancholy cadences he heard as a young man at Buffalo's B'rith Sholem synagogue, but it is also clear that he continued to work within the constraints of Tin Pan Alley even in this song. "My Yiddishe Momme" is firmly in the tradition of the sentimental "mammy song" made popular by Jolson and several other performers. Because he wrote about his own mother, Yellen coated the familiar material with a Yiddish rather than a Southern accent, and he set it in a Lower East Side tenement rather than somewhere in the Carolinas or Alabama. The few touches of realism in the song–the three flights of stairs, the dirt–provide whatever respite there is from the self-conscious sentimentality of the lyric:

And as I sit in the comfort of a cozy chair,
My fancy takes me to a humble Eastside tenement,
Three flights in the rear to where
My childhood days were spent.
It wasn't much like paradise,
But amid the dirt and all,
There sat the sweetest angel,
One that I fondly recall.
My Yiddishe Momme,
I need her more than ever now. . . .

Yellen and Ager were already working in Hollywood by 1928, when they wrote "I'm the Last of the Red Hot Mamas" and "He's a Good Man to Have Around" for Tucker to sing in the movie *Honky Tonk* (1929). The former song became one of the signature numbers she sang for the rest of her career. Beginning with his early songs for Jolson and Cantor, Yellen demonstrated a gift for crafting lyrics to suit the vivid, larger-than-life personalities of the stars of the 1920s and 1930s. They had emerged from the rough-and-tumble world of burlesque and vaudeville and were now appearing on Broadway and in the movies. The same Yellen who had been writing nostalgic songs about Dixie only a decade earlier was now writing for a star who presented herself as tough, outspoken, and sexually knowing. His ear was perfectly tuned to Tucker's bawdy high jinks:

I can warm the cold ones
And give the old ones
Back their flaming youth.
Say, I was born in the hot Bahamas,
Right now I'm in lovin' prime.
Others pet and kiss and hug
And don't know what it's all about,
Say, when I kiss men
They feel they've had their tonsils taken out.
'Cause I'm the last of the red hot mamas,
I'm gettin' hotter all the time.

During their first years in Hollywood, Yellen and Ager also collaborated on "Happy Feet" and "A Bench in the Park" for *King of Jazz* (1930), starring Paul Whiteman and his Orchestra, and on "Happy Days Are Here Again" for *Chasing Rainbows* (1930). "Happy Days Are Here Again" remains the most important lyric Yellen wrote, and the song was one of the great popular anthems of the Depression. Initially, Ager's bouncy tune and Yellen's feel-good lyric had nothing to do with bad times. *Chasing Rainbows* was nearly finished when Irving Thalberg, M-G-M's head of production, told Yellen he wanted a song for a new scene in which

World War I doughboys celebrated the Armistice. Ager grumbled about having to collaborate on another song with Yellen, since their relationship had soured and was about to end, despite their many successes. But he agreed to stop at Yellen's house that afternoon. "Got a title?" he groused when he arrived. "Happy Days Are Here Again," Yellen answered. He later swore that the words came to him at that moment. Half an hour later they had finished the song. Two days later M-G-M filmed the scene, even though the movie was still so poor that it was not released for more than a year.

Ager and Yellen published "Happy Days Are Here Again" anyway, and a New York song plugger took it to George Olsen, whose well-known orchestra was playing at Manhattan's Hotel Pennsylvania. By coincidence, the plugger showed up on 29 October 1929, the day the stock market crashed. Yellen later wrote about the reaction:

In the big dining room of the hotel, a handful of gloom-stricken diners were feasting on gall and wormwood. Olsen looked at the title of the song and passed out the parts. "Sing it for the corpses," he said to the soloist. The diners broke into a roar of laughter. The band played on, and one couple after another rose from their tables, stomped to the bandstand and sardonically yelled the words with the vocalist. Before the night was over, the hotel lobby resounded with what had become the theme song of ruined stock speculators as they leaped from hotel windows.

The Democratic Party adopted "Happy Days Are Here Again" as its theme song during Franklin D. Roosevelt's 1932 presidential campaign; it continued to be associated with Democrats through John F. Kennedy's campaign in 1960. Yellen, however, was a lifelong Republican.

Perhaps the success of "Happy Days Are Here Again" as a campaign song and a Depression anthem derives from its directness and naiveté. The brief lyric has only two words of more than one syllable. The sentiments are as simple as the words, but the bubbly assertion of good times in the face of the contradictory evidence soon had people singing along. The narrow melodic range of the song, the insistent repetition of the title phrase, and the triple rhymes made the chorus infectious. What started as an unintentionally ironic comment on the Depression soon became a widely known expression of optimism. In 1963 the American Society of Composers, Authors, and Publishers (ASCAP) named "Happy Days Are Here Again" as one of sixteen songs on its All-Time Hit Parade.

In 1930 Yellen and Ager dissolved their partnership. Yellen soon accompanied Tucker to London to write songs with composer Vivian Ellis for a musical to

Sheet music for Yellen and Lew Pollack's title song for a 1936 movie
(Bruccoli Clark Layman Archives)

be called *Follow a Star* (1930). The best song from the score was the title number. When Yellen returned to New York, he began to write with other composers. He and fellow Buffalonian Harold Arlen wrote the score for *You Said It* (1931), a Broadway musical that Yellen coproduced with comedian Lou Holtz and that ran for 192 performances. The show included the song "Sweet and Hot."

Back in Hollywood in 1935, Yellen worked on screenplays for several movies but only occasionally wrote lyrics. For *George White's Scandals* (1934) Yellen and Irving Caesar wrote the lyric and Henderson, another Buffalonian, wrote the music for "Nasty Man," a good example of the tough, sassy songs typical of the 1930s.

In August 1939 Yellen collaborated with composer Sammy Fain on the songs for that year's edition of the Broadway revue *George White's Scandals.* Their most memorable song in the show was "Are You Havin' Any Fun?" made popular by Ella Logan. Yellen and Fain also collaborated on two more Broadway musicals: *Boys and Girls Together* (1940), with co-lyricist Irving Kahal, which ran for 191 performances; and *Sons o' Fun* (1941), which ran for 742 performances. Yellen and Henderson wrote the score for the *Ziegfeld Follies of 1943,* which had a run of 553 performances. During these years the exuberance of Yellen's 1920s songs gave way to the tender, often melancholy romanticism characteristic of the 1930s and 1940s. Though he was never a writer of distinguished ballads, his later work included "According to the Moonlight," for the movie *George White's 1935 Scandals;* "Something I Dreamed Last Night," for the 1939 *George White's Scandals* on Broadway; and "Love Songs Are Made in the Night," for the *Ziegfeld Follies of 1943.*

In the 1950s Yellen wrote additional special material for Tucker and for The Versailles, a Manhattan nightclub. He had joined ASCAP in 1917 and was a director of the organization from 1951 to 1969. During these years, however, he was essentially retired. On 13 September 1944 Yellen married his second wife, Lucille Hodgeman. (There is little information available about his first wife.) The couple lived in New York before moving to Melody Acres, a farm in Springville, a village near Buffalo, in the late 1940s. Yellen operated an egg business from the farm for several years. According to Lucille Yellen, her husband was content to be out of show business and never considered his work to be of any lasting quality. He kept few private papers from his years as a lyricist, even though he wrote more than 130 songs over a span of four decades. Yellen died at home on 17 April 1991, at the age of ninety-eight.

Like many other successful lyricists, Jack Yellen was something of a chameleon. He wrote in the language of the day to express the attitudes of the day, yet many of his lyrics became standards because of their humor, their engaging deftness, and their broad appeal. Yellen's song titles suggest that he was always keeping track of any approach or angle that produced a hit. Like many second-rank lyricists, he was a skillful imitator, frequently reworking whatever was popular. He accepted whatever was current and apparently never tried to break out of the constraints of Tin Pan Alley; it

is impossible to know whether he could have. At their best, his lyrics were natural, easy, and straightforwardly conversational. Yellen was, in other words, a highly professional "Alley man."

Interview:
James Greico, "A Conversation with Mrs. Jack Yellen," Buffalo and Erie County Public Library, February 1980.

Reference:
Jack Yellen, "The Songwriter and the Redhead," *Buffalo Courier-Express,* 15–22 March 1970.

Selected Discography:
Fanny Brice and Eddie Cantor, *Makin' Whoopee: The Best of Fanny Brice and Eddie Cantor,* Fanfare, 460, 1989;

Ruth Etting, *Love Me or Leave Me,* Pearl, 7061, 1996;

Annette Hanshaw, *Lovable and Sweet,* ASV, 5220, 1997;

Looking on the Bright Side, ASV, 5255, 1998;

Music from the New York Stage, volume 4 (1917–1920), Pearl, 9059-61, 1993;

Maxine Sullivan, *Singin' Sweet,* Concord, 4351, 1988;

Sophie Tucker, *Some of These Days,* Flapper, 7807, 1996.

Appendix:
Additional Lyricists: 1920–1960

Appendix:
Additional Lyricists: 1920–1960

In addition to the lyricists included in this volume, there were others who wrote important lyrics during the period from 1920 to 1960. The following lyricists were not given full entries because of the relatively small number of important songs they wrote or because of a paucity of available biographical information. Unless indicated otherwise, songs were published independently of theatrical or motion-picture productions. Only selected songs are given.

—Philip Furia

Tom Adair
(15 June 1913 –   )

Music is by Matt Dennis unless otherwise indicated.

"Everything Happens to Me" (1941);
"Let's Get Away from It All" (1941);
"Violets for Your Furs" (1941);
"The Night We Called It a Day" (1942);
"There's No You" (1944), music by Hal Hopper.

Steve Allen
(26 December 1921 – 30 October 2000)

Music is by Allen unless indicated otherwise.

"South Rampart Street Parade" (1939), music by Ray Bauduc and Bob Haggart;
"Let's Go to Church (Next Sunday Morning)" (1950);
Picnic (motion picture, 1955)–"Theme from *Picnic*" (music by George Duning);
"Impossible" (1956);
"This Could Be the Start of Something Big" (1956);
"Pretend You Don't See Her" (1957).

Maxwell Anderson
(15 December 1888 – 28 February 1959)

Knickerbocker Holiday (show, 1938), music by Kurt Weill–"It Never Was You"; "September Song";

Lost in the Stars (show, 1949)–"Lost in the Stars" (music by Weill).

Ralph Blane (Hunsecker)
(26 July 1914 – 13 November 1995)

Music is by Hugh Martin unless indicated otherwise.

Best Foot Forward (show, 1941)–"Buckle Down, Winsocki";
Meet Me in St. Louis (motion picture, 1944)–"The Boy Next Door"; "Have Yourself a Merry Little Christmas"; "The Trolley Song."

Jack Brooks
(14 February 1912 – 8 November 1971)

Music is by Harry Warren unless indicated otherwise.

Canyon Passage (motion picture, 1946)–"Ole Buttermilk Sky" (lyric and music by Brooks and Hoagy Carmichael);
Summer Stock (motion picture, 1950)–"You, Wonderful You" (lyric by Brooks and Saul Chaplin);
The Caddy (motion picture, 1953)–"That's Amore";
Artists and Models (motion picture, 1955)–"Innamorata (Sweetheart)."

Hoagy Carmichael
(22 November 1899 – 27 December 1981)

Music is by Carmichael unless indicated otherwise.

"Rockin' Chair" (1930);
"Lazy River" (1931), lyric and music by Carmichael and Sidney Arodin;
"I Get Along without You Very Well" (1939).

Sidney Clare
(15 August 1892 – 29 August 1972)

The Midnight Rounders (show, 1921)–"Ma! (He's Makin' Eyes at Me)" (music by Con Conrad); "(I Wanna Go Where You Go, Do What You Do) Then I'll Be Happy" (1925), lyric by Clare and Lew Brown, music by Cliff Friend; "Please Don't Talk about Me When I'm Gone" (1931), music by Sam H. Stept; *Bright Eyes* (motion picture, 1934)–"On the Good Ship Lollipop" (lyric and music by Clare and Richard Whiting).

Grant Clarke
(14 May 1891 – 16 May 1931)

"Ragtime Cowboy Joe" (1912), music by Maurice Abrahams and Lewis F. Muir; *Ziegfeld Follies of 1921* (show, 1921)–"Second Hand Rose" (music by James F. Hanley); *On with the Show* (motion picture, 1929)–"Am I Blue?" (music by Harry Akst).

Gordon Clifford
(29 March 1902 – 11 June 1968)

"I Surrender, Dear" (1931), music by Harry Barris.

Larry Conley
(29 November 1895 – 29 February 1960)

"Cottage for Sale" (1930), music by Willard Robison.

Sam Coslow
(27 December 1902 – 2 April 1982)

Music is by Arthur Johnston unless indicated otherwise.

Dance of Life (motion picture, 1929)–"True Blue Lou" (lyric by Coslow and Leo Robin, music by Richard Whiting); *Honey* (motion picture, 1930)–"Sing, You Sinners" (music by W. Franke Harling); "Just One More Chance" (1931); *Hello, Everybody!* (motion picture, 1933)–"Moon Song (That Wasn't Meant for Me)"; *Murder at the Vanities* (motion picture, 1934)–"Cocktails for Two";

Belle of the Nineties (motion picture, 1934)–"My Old Flame."

Benny Davis
(21 August 1895 – 20 December 1979)

"Margie" (1920), music by Con Conrad and J. Russel Robinson; "I'm Nobody's Baby" (1921), music by Milton Ager and Lester Santly; "Baby Face" (1926), music by Harry Akst; "Lonesome and Sorry" (1926), music by Conrad.

Eddie DeLange
(12 January 1904 – 13 July 1949)

Blackbirds of 1934 (show, 1934)–"Moonglow" (lyric and music by DeLange, Will Hudson, and Irving Mills); "Solitude" (1934), lyric by DeLange and Mills, music by Duke Ellington; *Swingin' the Dream* (show, 1939)–"Darn That Dream" (music by Jimmy Van Heusen); "A String of Pearls" (1941), music by Jerry Gray.

Mort Dixon
(20 March 1892 – 23 March 1956)

"That Old Gang of Mine" (1923), lyric by Dixon and Billy Rose, music by Ray Henderson; "Bye Bye Blackbird" (1926), music by Henderson; "I'm Looking over a Four-Leaf Clover" (1927), music by Harry Woods; *Billy Rose's Crazy Quilt* (show, 1931)–"I Found a Million Dollar Baby (In a Five and Ten Cent Store)" (lyric by Dixon and Billy Rose, music by Harry Warren).

Dorothy Donnelly
(28 January 1880 – 3 January 1928)

The Student Prince (show, 1924), music by Sigmund Romberg–"Deep in My Heart, Dear"; "Drinking Song (Drink! Drink Drink!)"; "Golden Days."

Vernon Duke
(10 October 1903 – 16 January 1969)

Thumbs Up (show, 1935)–"Autumn in New York."

Raymond B. Egan
(14 November 1890 – 13 October 1952)

"Till We Meet Again" (1918), music by Richard Whiting;

Midnight Rounders of 1920 (show, 1920)—"I Never Knew (I Could Love Anybody Like I'm Loving You)" (lyric and music by Egan, Roy K. Marsh, and Tom Pitts);

"Ain't We Got Fun?" (1921), lyric by Egan and Gus Kahn, music by Whiting;

"Sleepy Time Gal" (1925), lyric by Egan and Joseph R. Alden, music by Whiting and Ange Lorenzo.

Edward Eliscu
(2 April 1902 – 18 June 1998)

Great Day (show, 1929), lyrics by Eliscu and Billy Rose, music by Vincent Youmans—"Great Day"; "More than You Know"; "Without a Song";

Flying Down to Rio (motion picture, 1933), lyrics by Eliscu and Gus Kahn, music by Youmans—"Carioca"; "Flying Down to Rio"; "Music Makes Me"; "Orchids in the Moonlight."

Ralph Freed
(1 May 1907 – 13 February 1973)

Babes on Broadway (show, 1941)—"How about You?" (music by Burton Lane).

Nancy Hamilton
(27 July 1908 – 18 February 1985)

Two for the Show (show, 1940)—"How High the Moon" (music by Morgan Lewis).

Edward Heyman
(14 March 1907 – 16 October 1981)

Music is by John Green unless indicated otherwise.

Three's a Crowd (show, 1930)—"Body and Soul" (lyric by Heyman, Robert Sour, and Frank Eyton);

Here Goes the Bride (show, 1931)—"Hello, My Lover, Goodbye";

I Cover the Waterfront (motion picture, 1933)—"I Cover the Waterfront";

"Easy Come, Easy Go" (1934);

Ziegfeld Follies of 1934 (show, 1934)—"You Oughta Be in Pictures" (music by Dana Suesse);

One Minute to Zero (motion picture, 1952)—"When I Fall in Love (It Will Be Forever)" (music by Victor Young).

DuBose Heyward
(31 August 1885 – 16 July 1940)

Porgy and Bess (show, 1935), music by George Gershwin—"Oh Bess, Oh Where's My Bess?"; "Bess, You Is My Woman Now" (lyric by Heyward and Ira Gershwin); "I Got Plenty o' Nuthin'" (lyric by Heyward and Ira Gershwin); "I Loves You, Porgy" (lyric by Heyward and Ira Gershwin); "My Man's Gone Now"; "Summertime"; "A Woman Is a Sometime Thing."

Walter Hirsch
(10 March 1891 –   )

"'Deed I Do" (1926), music by Fred Rose.

Herman Hupfeld
(1 February 1894 – 8 June 1951)

Lyrics and music composed by Hupfeld.

Everybody's Welcome (show, 1931)—"As Time Goes By";

George White's Music Hall Follies (show, 1932)—"Let's Put Out the Lights and Go to Sleep."

Irving Kahal
(5 March 1903 – 7 February 1942)

"Let a Smile Be Your Umbrella" (1927), lyric by Kahal and Francis Wheeler, music by Sammy Fain;

"Wedding Bells Are Breaking Up That Old Gang of Mine" (1929), lyric by Kahal and Willie Raskin, music by Fain;

The Big Pond (motion picture, 1930)—"You Brought a New Kind of Love to Me" (music by Fain and Pierre Norman);

Billy Rose's Casa Manana (show, 1936)—"The Night Is Young and You're So Beautiful" (lyric by Kahal and Billy Rose, music by Dana Suesse);

Right This Way (show, 1938), music by Fain—"I Can Dream, Can't I"; "I'll Be Seeing You."

Jack Lawrence
(7 April 1912 –   )

"If I Didn't Care" (1939), music by Lawrence;

"All or Nothing at All" (1940), music by Arthur Altman;

"Tenderly" (1946), music by Walter Gross;

"Beyond the Sea" (1947), French lyric by Charles Trenet, music by Albert Lasry.

Sam M. Lewis
(25 October 1885 – 22 November 1959)
and
Joe Young
(4 July 1889 – 21 April 1939)

"Dinah (Is There Anyone Fin-ah?)" (1925), music by Harry Akst;

"Five Foot Two, Eyes of Blue (Has Anybody Seen My Girl?)" (1925), music by Ray Henderson;

"I'm Sitting on Top of the World" (1925), music by Henderson;

"In a Little Spanish Town" (1926), music by Mable Wayne.

Herbert Magidson
(7 January 1906 – 2 January 1986)

The Gay Divorcee (motion picture, 1934)–"The Continental" (music by Con Conrad);

"Gone with the Wind" (1937), music by Allie Wrubel;

"Music, Maestro, Please!" (1938), music by Wrubel;

"Enjoy Yourself (It's Later than You Think)" (1948), music by Carl Sigman.

Irving Mills
(16 January 1894 – 21 April 1985)

"When My Sugar Walks Down the Street" (1924), lyric and music by Mills, Gene Austin, and Jimmy McHugh;

"Washboard Blues" (1925), lyric by Mills and Fred B. Callahan, music by Hoagy Carmichael;

"Minnie the Moocher (The Ho De Ho Song)" (1931), lyric and music by Mills, Cab Calloway, and Clarence Gaskill;

"Mood Indigo" (1931), lyric by Mills and Albany Bigard, music by Duke Ellington;

"It Don't Mean a Thing (If It Ain't Got That Swing)" (1932), music by Ellington;

"Sophisticated Lady" (1933), lyric by Mills and Mitchell Parish, music by Ellington;

Blackbirds of 1934 (show, 1934)–"Moonglow" (lyric and music by Mills, Eddie DeLange, and Will Hudson);

"Solitude" (1934), lyric by Mills and DeLange, music by Ellington;

"In a Sentimental Mood" (1935), lyric by Mills and Manny Kurtz, music by Ellington;

"Caravan" (1937), music by Ellington and Juan Tizol;

"I Let a Song Go Out of My Heart" (1938), lyric by Mills, Henry Nemo, and John Redmond, music by Ellington;

"Straighten Up and Fly Right" (1944), lyric by Mills and Nat King Cole, music by Cole.

Ogden Nash
(19 August 1902 – 19 May 1971)

One Touch of Venus (show, 1943), music by Kurt Weill–"Speak Low"; "West Wind."

Don Raye
(16 March 1909 – 29 January 1985)

"Beat Me Daddy, Eight to the Bar" (1940), lyric and music by Raye, Hughie Prince, and Eleanore Sheehy;

"This Is My Country" (1940), music by Al Jacobs;

Buck Privates (motion picture, 1941)–"Boogie Woogie Bugle Boy (Of Company B)" (music by Prince);

Keep 'Em Flying (motion picture, 1941)–"You Don't Know What Love Is" (lyric and music by Raye and Gene de Paul);

Ride 'Em Cowboy (motion picture, 1942)–"I'll Remember April" (lyric by Raye and Patricia Johnston, music by de Paul);

Reveille with Beverly (motion picture, 1943)–"Cow Cow Boogie" (lyric and music by Raye, de Paul, and Benny Carter;

"The House of Blue Lights" (1946), music by Freddie Slack;

A Song Is Born (motion picture, 1948)–"Daddy-O (I'm Gonna Teach You Some Blues)" (lyric and music by Raye and de Paul).

Ann Ronell
(1908 – 25 December 1993)

"Willow, Weep for Me" (1932), music by Ronell;

The Three Little Pigs (motion picture, 1933)–"Who's Afraid of the Big Bad Wolf?" (lyric and music by Frank Churchill, additional lyric by Ronell).

Billy Rose
(6 September 1899 – 10 February 1966)

"Barney Google" (1923), music by Con Conrad;

"That Old Gang of Mine" (1923), lyric by Rose and Mort Dixon, music by Ray Henderson;

"Don't Bring Lulu" (1925), lyric by Rose and Lew Brown, music by Henderson;

"Me and My Shadow" (1927), music by Dave Dreyer and Al Jolson;

The Singing Fool (motion picture, 1928)–"There's a Rainbow 'round My Shoulder" (lyric and music by Rose, Jolson, and Dreyer);

Great Day (show, 1929), lyrics by Rose and Edward Eliscu, music by Vincent Youmans–"Great Day"; "More Than You Know"; "Without a Song";

Billy Rose's Crazy Quilt (show, 1931)–"I Found a Million Dollar Baby (In a Five-and-Ten-Cent Store)" (lyric by Rose and Mort Dixon, music by Harry Warren);

The Great Magoo (show, 1932)–"It's Only a Paper Moon" (lyric by Rose and E. "Yip" Harburg, music by Harold Arlen);

The Ziegfeld Follies of 1934 (show, 1934)–"The House Is Haunted (By the Echo of Your Last Good-Bye)" (music by Basil G. Adlam);

Billie Rose's Casa Manana (show, 1936)–"The Night Is Young and You're So Beautiful" (lyric by Rose and Irving Kahal, music by Dana Suesse).

Bob Russell
(25 April 1914 – 18 February 1970)

"Don't Get Around Much Anymore" (1942), music by Duke Ellington;

"Brazil" (1943), Portuguese lyric and music by Ary Barroso;

"Do Nothin' till You Hear from Me" (1943), music by Ellington;

"No Other Love" (1950), music by Paul Weston, based on Frédéric Chopin's Etude no. 3 in E, op. 10.

Carl Sigman
(24 September 1909 – 26 September 2000)

"Pennsylvania 6-5000" (1940), lyric and music by Sigman, William Finegan, and Jerry Gray;

"Shangri-La" (1946), music by Matt Malneck and Robert Maxwell;

"My Heart Cries for You" (1950), music by Percy Faith;

"It's All in the Game" (1951), music by Charles Gates Dawes;

"Ebb Tide" (1953), music by Maxwell;

"Dream Along with Me, I'm on My Way to a Star" (1955), music by D. J. LaRocca and Larry Shields;

"Goodbye to Rome (Arrivederci Roma)" (1955), music by Renato Rascel;

"What Now My Love?" (1966), French lyric by Pierre Dalanoe, music by Gilbert Becaud.

Noble Sissle
(10 July 1889 – 17 December 1975)

Shuffle Along (show, 1921), music by Eubie Blake–"I'm Just Wild about Harry"; "Love Will Find a Way"; "Shuffle Along."

Roy Turk
(20 September 1892 – 30 November 1934)

"Gimme a Little Kiss, Will Ya Huh?" (1926), lyric and music by Turk, Jack Smith, and Maceo Pinkard;

"Are You Lonesome Tonight?" (1926), music by Lou Handman;

"I'll Get By (As Long as I Have You)" (1928), music by Fred Ahlert;

"Mean to Me" (1929), music by Ahlert;

"Walkin' My Baby Back Home" (1931), music by Ahlert;

The Big Broadcast (motion picture, 1932)–"Where the Blue of the Night Meets the Gold of the Day" (lyric and music by Turk, Ahlert, and Bing Crosby).

George Whiting
(16 August 1884 – 18 December 1943)

"My Blue Heaven" (1925), music by Walter Donaldson.

Richard Whiting
(12 November 1891 – 10 February 1938)

"(I Got a Woman Crazy for Me) She's Funny That Way" (1928), music by Neil Moret.

Robert Wright
(25 September 1914 –   )
and
George Forrest
(31 July 1915 – 10 October 1999)

Music in My Heart (motion picture, 1940)–"It's a Blue World";

Kismet (show, 1953)–"And This Is My Beloved"; "Baubles, Bangles, and Beads"; "Stranger in Paradise."

Checklist of Further Readings

ACE on the Web <http://www.ascap.com/ace>.

All Music Guide <http://www.allmusic.com>.

Altman, Rick. *The American Film Musical*. Bloomington: Indiana University Press, 1987.

American Society of Composers, Authors, and Publishers. *ASCAP Biographical Dictionary,* fourth edition. New York: R. R. Bowker, 1980.

Barrios, Richard. *A Song in the Dark: The Birth of the Musical Film*. New York: Oxford University Press, 1995.

Benjamin, Ruth, and Arthur Rosenblatt. *Movie Song Catalog: Performers and Supporting Crew for the Songs Sung in 1460 Musical and Nonmusical Films, 1928–1988*. Jefferson, N.C.: McFarland, 1993.

Berlin, Edward A. *Reflections and Research on Ragtime*. Brooklyn, N.Y.: Institute for Studies in American Music, 1987.

Block, Geoffrey. *Enchanted Evenings: The Broadway Musical from "Show Boat" to Sondheim*. New York: Oxford University Press, 1997.

Bloom, Ken. *American Song: The Complete Musical Theatre Companion,* second edition. 4 volumes. New York: Schirmer, 1996–2001.

Bloom. *Hollywood Song: The Complete Film and Musical Companion*. 3 volumes. New York: Facts on File, 1995.

Bordman, Gerald. *American Musical Theatre: A Chronicle*. New York: Oxford University Press, 1978.

Bradley, Edwin M. *The First Hollywood Musicals: A Critical Filmography of 171 Features, 1927 through 1932*. Jefferson, N.C.: McFarland, 1996.

Brahms, Caryl, and Ned Sherrin. *Song by Song: The Lives and Work of 14 Great Lyric Writers*. Bolton, U.K.: Ross Anderson, 1984.

Braun, D. Duane. *Toward a Theory of Popular Culture: The Sociology and History of American Music and Dance, 1920–1968*. Ann Arbor, Mich.: Ann Arbor, 1969.

Burton, Jack. *The Blue Book of Tin Pan Alley: A Human Interest Anthology of American Popular Music*. Watkins Glen, N.Y.: Century House, 1951.

Colbert, Warren E. *Who Wrote That Song?; or, Who in the Hell Is J. Fred Coots?: An Informal Survey of American Popular Songs and Their Composers*. New York: Revisionist Press, 1975.

Coslow, Sam. *Cocktails for Two: The Many Lives of Giant Songwriter Sam Coslow*. New Rochelle, N.Y.: Arlington House, 1977.

Craig, Warren. *Sweet and Lowdown: America's Popular Songwriters*. Metuchen, N.J.: Scarecrow Press, 1978.

Davis, Sheila. *The Craft of Lyric Writing*. Cincinnati: Writer's Digest Books, 1985.

Douglas, Ann. *Terrible Honesty: Mongrel Manhattan in the 1920s*. New York: Farrar, Straus & Giroux, 1995.

Engel, Lehman. *The American Musical Theater: A Consideration*. New York: Macmillan, 1967.

Engel. *Their Words Are Music: The Great Theatre Lyricists and Their Lyrics*. New York: Crown, 1975.

Erenberg, Lewis. *Steppin' Out: New York Nightlife and the Transformation of American Culture, 1890–1930*. Westport, Conn.: Greenwood Press, 1981.

Ewen, David. *All the Years of American Popular Music: A Comprehensive History*. Englewood Cliffs, N.J.: Prentice-Hall, 1977.

Ewen. *American Songwriters*. New York: Wilson, 1987.

Ewen. *Complete Book of the American Musical Theater: A Guide to More than 300 Productions of the American Musical Theater from The Black Crook (1866) to the Present, with Plot, Production History, Stars, Songs, Composers, Librettists, and Lyricists*. New York: Holt, 1958.

Ewen. *Great Men of American Popular Song: The History of the American Popular Song Told through the Lives, Careers, Achievements and Personalities of Its Foremost Composers and Lyricists–from William Billings of the Revolutionary War through Bob Dylan, Johnny Cash, Burt Bacharach*. Englewood Cliffs, N.J.: Prentice-Hall, 1972.

Ewen. *The Life and Death of Tin Pan Alley: The Golden Age of American Popular Music*. New York: Funk & Wagnalls, 1964.

Ewen. *New Complete Book of the American Musical Theater*. New York: Holt, Rinehart & Winston, 1970.

Ewen, ed. *American Popular Songs: From the Revolutionary War to the Present*. New York: Random House, 1966.

Feinstein, Michael. *Nice Work if You Can Get It: My Life in Rhythm and Rhyme*. New York: Hyperion, 1995.

Feuer, Jane. *The Hollywood Musical*. Bloomington: Indiana University Press, 1993.

Forte, Alan. *The American Popular Ballad of the Golden Era, 1924–1950*. Princeton: Princeton University Press, 1995.

Friedwald, Will. *Jazz Singing: America's Great Voices from Bessie Smith to Bebop and Beyond*. New York: Scribners, 1990.

Furia, Philip. *The Poets of Tin Pan Alley: A History of America's Great Lyricists*. New York: Oxford University Press, 1990.

Gänzl, Kurt. *The Encyclopedia of the Musical Theatre*. 3 volumes. New York: Schirmer, 1994.

Goldberg, Isaac. *Tin Pan Alley: A Chronicle of the American Popular Music Racket*. New York: John Day, 1930.

Gottfried, Martin. *Broadway Musicals*. New York: Abradale, 1984.

Green, Stanley. *Broadway Musicals of the 1930s*. New York: Da Capo Press, 1982.

Green. *Broadway Musicals, Show by Show*. Milwaukee: Hal Leonard, 1987.

Green. *The World of Musical Comedy: The Story of the American Musical Stage as Told through the Careers of Its Foremost Composers and Lyricists*. New York: DaCapo Press, 1984.

Hamm, Charles. *Yesterdays: Popular Song in America*. New York & London: Norton, 1979.

Hemming, Roy. *The Melody Lingers On: The Great Songwriters and Their Movie Musicals.* New York: Newmarket, 1986.

Henderson, Amy, and Dwight Blocker Bowers. *Red, Hot, and Blue: A Smithsonian Salute to the American Musical.* Washington, D.C.: Smithsonian Institution Press, 1996.

Hirschhorn, Clive. *The Hollywood Musical.* New York: Crown, 1981.

Hischak, Thomas S. *Word Crazy: Broadway Lyricists from Cohan to Sondheim.* New York: Praeger, 1991.

Hyland, William G. *The Song Is Ended: Songwriters and American Music, 1900–1950.* New York: Oxford University Press, 1995.

Jasen, David A. *Tin Pan Alley: The Composers, the Songs, the Performers, and Their Times: The Golden Age of American Popular Music from 1886 to 1956.* New York: Donald I. Fine, 1988.

Jasen and Gene Jones, *Spreadin' Rhythm Around: Black Popular Songwriters, 1880–1930.* New York: Schirmer, 1998.

Kane, Henry. *How to Write a Song: As Told to Henry Kane.* New York: Macmillan, 1962.

Kanter, Kenneth. *The Jews on Tin Pan Alley: The Jewish Contribution to American Popular Music, 1830–1940.* New York: Ktav / Cincinnati: American Jewish Archives, 1982.

Kasha, Al, and Joel Hirschhorn. *Notes on Broadway: Conversations with the Great Songwriters.* Chicago: Contemporary Books, 1985.

Kinkle, Roger D. *The Complete Encyclopedia of Popular Music and Jazz, 1900–1950.* New Rochelle, N.Y.: Arlington House, 1974.

Kobal, John. *Gotta Sing Gotta Dance: A Pictorial History of Film Musicals.* London & New York: Hamlyn, 1971.

Krasker, Tommy, and Robert Kimball. *Catalog of the American Musical: Musicals of Irving Berlin, George and Ira Gershwin, Cole Porter, Richard Rodgers, and Lorenz Hart.* Washington, D.C.: National Institute for Opera and Musical Theater, 1988.

Kreuger, Miles. *Show Boat: The Story of a Classic American Musical.* New York: Oxford University Press, 1977.

Lax, Roger, and Frederick Smith. *The Great Song Thesaurus,* second edition. New York: Oxford University Press, 1989.

Lees, Gene. *Singers and the Song II.* New York: Oxford University Press, 1998.

Lissauer, Robert. *Lissauer's Encyclopedia of Popular Music in America: 1888 to the Present.* New York: Paragon House, 1991.

Marks, Edward B. *They All Sang: From Tony Pastor to Rudy Vallée.* New York: Viking, 1934.

Mast, Gerald. *Can't Help Singin': The American Musical on Stage and Screen.* Woodstock, N.Y.: Overlook, 1987.

Montgomery, Elizabeth. *The Story behind Popular Songs.* New York: Dodd, Mead, 1958.

Mordden, Ethan. *Better Foot Forward: The History of American Musical Theatre.* New York: Grossman, 1976.

Mordden. *Coming Up Roses: The Broadway Musical in the 1950s.* New York: Oxford University Press, 1998.

Mordden. *The Hollywood Musical.* New York: St. Martin's Press, 1981.

Palmer, Tony. *All You Need Is Love: The Story of Popular Music,* edited by Paul Medlicott. New York: Grossman, 1976.

Rosenberg, Bernard, and Ernest Harburg. *The Broadway Musical: Collaboration in Commerce and Art.* New York & London: New York University Press, 1993.

Sanjek, Russe. *American Popular Music and Its Business: The First Four Hundred Years.* 3 volumes. New York: Oxford University Press, 1988.

Scheurer, Timothy E. *Born in the U.S.A.: The Myth of America in Popular Music from Colonial Times to the Present.* Jackson: University Press of Mississippi, 1991.

Shaw, Arnold. *The Jazz Age: Popular Music in the 1920s.* New York & Oxford: Oxford University Press, 1987.

Sheward, David. *It's a Hit: The Back Stage Look at the Longest-Running Broadway Shows: 1884 to the Present.* New York: Back Stage, 1994.

Spaeth, Sigmund. *The Facts of Life in Popular Song.* New York: Whittlesey House/McGraw-Hill, 1934.

Spaeth. *A History of Popular Music in America.* New York: Random House, 1948.

Stubblebine, Donald J. *Broadway Sheet Music: A Comprehensive Listing of Published Music from Broadway and Other Stage Shows, 1918–1993.* Jefferson, N.C.: McFarland, 1996.

Suskin, Stephen. *Berlin, Kern, Rodgers, Hart, and Hammerstein: A Complete Song Catalogue.* Jefferson, N.C.: McFarland, 1990.

Suskin. *Opening Night on Broadway: A Critical Quotebook of the Golden Era of the Musical Theatre, "Oklahoma!" (1943) to "Fiddler on the Roof" (1964).* New York: Schirmer, 1990.

Suskin. *Show Tunes, 1905–1991: The Songs, Shows, and Careers of Broadway's Major Composers,* revised and expanded edition. New York: Limelight, 1992.

Swain, Joseph P. *The Broadway Musical: A Critical and Musical Survey.* New York: Oxford University Press, 1990.

Tawa, Nicholas E. *The Way to Tin Pan Alley: American Popular Song, 1866–1910.* New York: Schirmer, 1990.

Taylor, William, ed. *Inventing Times Square: Commerce and Culture at the Crossroads of the World.* New York: Russell Sage Foundation, 1991.

Tormé, Mel. *My Singing Teachers: Reflections on Singing Popular Music.* New York: Oxford University Press, 1994.

Tyler, Don. *Hit Parade: An Encyclopedia of the Top Songs of the Jazz, Depression, Swing, and Sing Eras.* New York: Quill, 1985.

Whitburn, Joel. *Pop Memories, 1890–1954: The History of American Popular Music.* Menomonee Falls, Wis.: Record Research, 1986.

White, Mark. *"You Must Remember This . . .": Popular Songwriters 1900–1980.* New York: Scribners, 1985.

Wilder, Alec. *American Popular Song: The Great Innovators, 1900–1950.* New York & Oxford: Oxford University Press, 1972.

Wilk, Max. *They're Playing Our Song: From Jerome Kern to Stephen Sondheim—The Stories behind the Words and Music of Two Generations.* New York: Atheneum, 1973.

Witmark, Isidore, and Isaac Goldberg. *The Story of the House of Witmark: From Ragtime to Swingtime.* New York: Furman, 1939.

Contributors

Stephen Citron . . . . *Beverly Hills, California*
Philip Furia . . . . *University of North Carolina at Wilmington*
Anna Wheeler Gentry . . . . *Tuscaloosa, Alabama*
Tony L. Hill . . . . *University of Minnesota*
Thomas S. Hischak . . . . *State University of New York College at Cortland*
Michael Lasser . . . . *Penfield, New York*
Shannon D. McCreery . . . . *University of North Carolina at Wilmington*
Harold Meyerson . . . . *Los Angeles, California*
Marty Minchin . . . . *University of North Carolina at Wilmington*
Frederick Nolan . . . . *Chalfont St. Giles, England*
Bryan A. Oesterreich . . . . *University of North Carolina at Wilmington*
Deena Rosenberg . . . . *New York University*
Rachel Scharfman . . . . *New York University*
Barry Singer . . . . *New York, New York*
Deborah Grace Winer . . . . *New York, New York*
Graham Wood . . . . *Coker College*
Paul Woodbury . . . . *University of North Carolina at Wilmington*

Permissions

Renewal Term in the U.S. controlled by Warner Bros Inc., Ray Henderson Music, and Stephen Ballentine Music. All Rights Reserved. Used by Permission. Warner Bros. Publications U.S. Inc., Miami, FL 33014.

"Do It Again." Lyric by DeSylva. Music by George Gershwin. © 1922 (Renewed) WB Music Corp. Rights for Extended Renewal Term controlled by WB Music Corp. and Stephen Ballentine Music. All Rights Reserved. Used by Permission. Warner Bros. Publications U.S. Inc., Miami, FL 33014.

"Don't Bring Lulu." Lyric by Brown and Billy Rose. Music by Ray Henderson. © 1925 (Renewed) Warner Bros. Inc. Rights for Extended Renewal Term in the U.S. controlled by Warner Bros. Inc. and Ray Henderson Music. All Rights Reserved. Used by Permission. Warner Bros. Publications U.S. Inc., Miami, FL 33014.

"If You Knew Susie." Lyric by DeSylva. Music by Joseph Meyer. © 1925 Renewed, terminated, and assigned to JoRo Music Corp., New York, NY. All Rights Reserved. Used by Permission.

"It All Depends on You." Lyric and music by DeSylva, Brown, and Ray Henderson. © 1926 (Renewed) Chappell & Co., Stephen Ballentine Music, and Ray Henderson Music. All Rights Reserved. Used by Permission. Warner Bros. Publications U.S. Inc., Miami, FL 33014.

"Last Night on the Back Porch." Music by Carl Schraubstader. Copyright © 1923 Skidmore Music Co. Inc., New York. Copyright Renewed. International Copyright Secured. All Rights Reserved.

"Somebody Loves Me." Lyric by DeSylva and Ballard MacDonald. Music by George Gershwin. © 1924 (Renewed) WB Music Corp. Rights for Extended Renewal Term in the U.S. controlled by WB Music Corp. and Stephen Ballentine Music. All Rights Reserved. Used by Permission. Warner Bros. Publications U.S. Inc., Miami, FL 33014.

"Three Times a Day." Lyric by DeSylva and Ira Gershwin. Music by George Gershwin. © 1925 (Renewed) WB Music Corp. All Rights Reserved. Used by Permission. Warner Bros. Publications U.S. Inc., Miami, FL 33014.

"You Try Somebody Else and I'll Try Somebody Else." Music by Ray Henderson. © 1931 (Renewed) Chappell & Co., Ray Henderson Music, and Stephen Ballentine Music. All Rights Reserved. Used by Permission. Warner Bros. Publications U.S. Inc., Miami, FL 33014.

HOWARD DIETZ

"That's Entertainment." Music by Arthur Schwartz. © 1953 (Renewed) Chappell & Co. All Rights Reserved. Used by Permission. Warner Bros. Publications U.S. Inc., Miami, FL 33014.

AL DUBIN

"Dancing with Tears in My Eyes." Music by Joe Burke. Copyright © 1930 (Renewed) Warner Bros. Inc. All Rights Reserved. Used by Permission. Warner Bros. Publications U.S. Inc., Miami, FL 33014.

"42nd Street." Music by Harry Warren. Copyright © 1932 (Renewed) Warner Bros. Inc. All Rights Reserved. Used by Permission. Warner Bros. Publications U.S. Inc., Miami, FL 33014.

"I'll String Along with You." Music by Harry Warren. Copyright © 1934 (Renewed) Warner Bros. Inc. All Rights Reserved. Used by Permission. Warner Bros. Publications U.S. Inc., Miami, FL 33014.

"Lullaby of Broadway." Music by Harry Warren. Copyright © 1935 (Renewed) Warner Bros. Inc. All Rights Reserved. Used by Permission. Warner Bros. Publications U.S. Inc., Miami, FL 33014.

"Lulu's Back in Town." Music by Harry Warren. Copyright © 1935 (Renewed) Warner Bros. Inc. All Rights Reserved. Used by Permission. Warner Bros. Publications U.S. Inc., Miami, FL 33014.

"Remember My Forgotten Man." Music by Harry Warren. Copyright © 1933 (Renewed) Warner Bros. Inc. All Rights Reserved. Used by Permission. Warner Bros. Publications U.S. Inc., Miami, FL 33014.

"September in the Rain." Music by Harry Warren. Copyright © 1937 (Renewed) Warner Bros. Inc. All Rights Reserved. Used by Permission. Warner Bros. Publications U.S. Inc., Miami, FL 33014.

RAY EVANS AND JAY LIVINGSTON

"A Square in the Social Circle." Lyric and Music by Evans and Livingston. Copyright © 1945 (Renewed 1973) Famous Music Corporation. International Copyright Secured. All Rights Reserved. Used by Permission.

"Mona Lisa." Lyric and Music by Evans and Livingston. Copyright © 1949 (Renewed 1976) Famous Music Corporation. International Copyright Secured. All Rights Reserved. Used by Permission.

"Never Let Me Go." Lyric and Music by Evans and Livingston. Copyright © 1956 (Renewed 1984) Famous Music Corporation. International Copyright Secured. All Rights Reserved. Used by Permission.

"To Each His Own." Lyric and Music by Evans and Livingston. Copyright © 1946 (Renewed 1973) Paramount Music Corporation. International Copyright Secured. All Rights Reserved.

DOROTHY FIELDS
"A Fine Romance." Music by Jerome Kern. Copyright © 1936 Universal–PolyGram International Publishing, Inc. (ASCAP). All Rights Reserved. Used by Permission.

"April Fooled Me." Music by Jerome Kern. Copyright © 1956 Universal–PolyGram International Publishing, Inc. On behalf of T.B. Harms Co. (ASCAP). All Rights Reserved. Used by Permission.

"He Had Refinement." Music by Arthur Schwartz. Copyright ©1951 Universal–PolyGram International Publishing, Inc. On behalf of Putnam Music, Inc. (ASCAP). All Rights Reserved. Used by Permission.

"I Can't Give You Anything But Love." Music by Jimmy McHugh. Copyright © 1928 (Renewed) EMI Mills Music, Inc. Rights for Extended Renewal Term in the U.S. controlled by Aldi Music Co. and Universal–MCA Music Publishing, a division of Universal Studios, Inc. All Rights Reserved. Used by Permission. Warner Bros. Publications U.S. Inc., Miami, FL 33014.

"It's Not Where You Start." Music by Cy Coleman. Copyright © 1972, 1973 (Renewed) Notable Music Co., Inc. and Aldi Music Company. All Rights administered by WB Music Corp. All Rights Reserved. Used by Permission. Warner Bros. Publications U.S. Inc., Miami, FL 33014.

"Make the Man Love Me." Music by Arthur Schwartz. Copyright © 1951 Universal–PolyGram International Publishing, Inc. On behalf of Putnam Music, Inc. (ASCAP). All Rights Reserved. Used by Permission.

"On the Sunny Side of the Street." Music by Jimmy McHugh. Copyright ©1930 (Renewed) Shapiro, Bernstein & Co., Inc. New York and Cotton Club Publishing for the U.S.A. All Rights for Cotton Club Publishing controlled and administered by EMI April Music Inc. International Copyright Secured. All Rights Reserved. Used by Permission.

"Pick Yourself Up." Music by Jerome Kern. Copyright © 1936 Universal–PolyGram International Publishing, Inc. (ASCAP). All Rights Reserved. Used by Permission.

"You Should See Yourself." Music by Cy Coleman. Copyright © 1965, 1969 (Renewed) Notable Music Co., Inc. and Lida Enterprises Inc. All Rights administered by WB Music Corp. All Rights Reserved. Used by Permission. Warner Bros. Publications U.S. Inc., Miami, FL 33014.

ARTHUR FREED
"Broadway Melody." Music by Nacio Herb Brown. Copyright © 1929 (Renewed) EMI Robbins Catalog Inc. All Rights Reserved. Used by Permission. Warner Bros. Publications U.S. Inc., Miami, FL 33014.

"I Cried for You." Music by Gus Arnheim and Abe Lyman. Copyright © 1923 (Renewed) EMI Miller Catalog Inc. All Rights Reserved. Used by Permission. Warner Bros. Publications U.S. Inc., Miami, FL 33014.

Ira Gershwin
"Back Bay Polka." Music by George Gershwin. Copyright © 1946 (Renewed) Chappell & Co. All Rights Reserved. Used by Permission. Warner Bros. Publications U.S. Inc., Miami, FL 33014.

"Bess, You Is My Woman." Lyric by Ira Gershwin and DuBose Heyward. Music by George Gershwin. Copyright © 1935 (Renewed 1962) George Gershwin Music, Ira Gershwin Music, and DuBose and Dorothy Heyward Memorial Fund. All Rights administered by WB Music Corp. All Rights Reserved. Used by Permission. Warner Bros. Publications U.S. Inc., Miami, FL 33014.

"Fascinating Rhythm." Music by George Gershwin. Copyright © 1924 (Renewed) WB Music Corp. All Rights Reserved. Used by Permission. Warner Bros. Publications U.S. Inc., Miami, FL 33014.

"I Can't Get Started." Music by Vernon Duke. Copyright © 1935 (Renewed) Ira Gershwin Music & Chappell and Co. All rights o/b/o Ira Gershwin Music administered by WB Music Corp. All Rights Reserved. Used by Permission. Warner Bros. Publications U.S. Inc., Miami, FL 33014.

"I Got Rhythm." Music by George Gershwin. Copyright © 1930 (Renewed) WB Music Corp. All Rights

Reserved. Used by Permission. Warner Bros. Publications U.S. Inc., Miami, FL 33014.

"It Ain't Necessarily So." Lyric and music by Ira Gershwin, George Gershwin, and Dubose and Dorothy Heyward. Copyright © 1935 (Renewed 1962) George Gershwin Music, Ira Gershwin Music and Dubose and Dorothy Heyward Memorial Fund. All rights administered by WB Music Corp. All rights reserved. Used by permission. Warner Bros. Publications U.S. Inc., Miami, FL 33014.

"Liza." Lyric by Ira Gershwin and Gus Kahn. Music by George Gershwin. Copyright © 1929 (Renewed) WB Music Corp. Rights for Extended Renewal Term in U.S. controlled by WB Music Corp. And Gilbert Keyes Music. All Rights Reserved. Used by Permission. Warner Bros. Publications U.S. Inc., Miami, FL 33014.

"Love Is Here to Stay." Music by George Gershwin. Copyright © 1938 (Renewed) George Gershwin Music and Ira Gershwin Music. All rights administered by WB Music Corp. All Rights Reserved. Used by Permission. Warner Bros. Publications U.S. Inc., Miami, FL 33014.

"The Man I Love." Music by George Gershwin. Copyright © 1924 (Renewed) WB Music Corp. All Rights Reserved. Used by Permission. Warner Bros. Publications U.S. Inc., Miami, FL 33014.

"The Man that Got Away." Music by Harold Arlen. Copyright © 1954 (Renewed) New World Music Company Ltd. And Harwin Music Corp. All Rights o/b/o New World Music Company Ltd. Administered by WB Music Corp. All Rights Reserved. Used by Permission. Warner Bros. Publications U.S. Inc., Miami, FL 33014.

"Mine." Music by George Gershwin. Copyright © 1933 (Renewed) WB Music Corp. All Rights Reserved. Used by Permission. Warner Bros. Publications U.S. Inc., Miami, FL 33014.

"'S Wonderful." Music by George Gershwin. Copyright © 1927 (Renewed) WB Music Corp. All Rights Reserved. Used by Permission. Warner Bros. Publications U.S. Inc., Miami, FL 33014.

"Someone to Watch Over Me." Music by George Gershwin. Copyright © 1926 (Renewed) WB Music Corp. All Rights Reserved. Used by Permission. Warner Bros. Publications U.S. Inc., Miami, FL 33014.

"Song of the Rhineland." Music by Kurt Weill. Copyright © 1945 (Renewed) Chappell & Co. and TRO-Hampshire House Publ. Corp. All Rights Reserved. Used by Permission. Warner Bros. Publications U.S. Inc., Miami, FL 33014.

"Tschaikowsky." Music by Kurt Weill. Copyright © 1941 (Renewed) Ira Gershwin Music (administered by WB Music Corp.) & TRO-Hampshire House Publ. Corp. Canadian Rights controlled by Chappell and Co. All Rights Reserved. Used by Permission. Warner Bros. Publications U.S. Inc., Miami, FL 33014.

"That Certain Feeling." Music by George Gershwin. Copyright © 1925 (Renewed) WB Music Corp. All Rights Reserved. Used by Permission. Warner Bros. Publications U.S. Inc., Miami, FL 33014.

"Things Are Looking Up." Music by George Gershwin. Copyright © 1937 (Renewed) George Gershwin Music and Ira Gershwin. All Rights administered by WB Music Corp. All Rights Reserved. Used by Permission. Warner Bros. Publications U.S. Inc., Miami, FL 33014.

"This Is New." Music by Kurt Weill. Copyright © 1941 (Renewed) Chappell & Co. and TRO-Hampshire House Publ. Corp. All Rights Reserved. Used by Permission. Warner Bros. Publications U.S. Inc., Miami, FL 33014.

"You're a Builder-Upper." Lyric by Ira Gershwin and E.Y. Harburg. Music by Harold Arlen. Copyright © 1934 (Renewed) New World Music Corporation. Rights for Extended Term in U.S. controlled by WB Music Corp., SA Music and Glocca Morra Music. All Rights Reserved. Used by Permission. Warner Bros. Publications U.S. Inc., Miami, FL 33014.

HAVEN GILLESPIE
"You Go to My Head." Music by J. Fred Coots. Copyright © 1938 (Renewed) Haven Gillespie Music and Toy Town Tunes. All Rights Reserved. Used by Permission.

"The Old Master Painter." Music by Beasley Smith. Copyright © 1945 WB Music Corp. All Rights Reserved. Used by Permission. Warner Bros. Publications U.S. Inc., Miami, FL 33014.

MACK GORDON
"Did You Ever See a Dream Walking?" Music by Harry Revel. Copyright © 1933 DeSylva, Brown & Henderson, Inc. Copyright Renewed, Assigned to Chappell & Co. International Copyright Secured. All Rights Reserved.

"You Make Me Feel So Young." Music by Josef Myrow. Copyright © 1946 (Renewed) WB Music Corp. All Rights Reserved. Used by Permission. Warner Bros. Publications U.S. Inc., Miami, FL 33014.

"You'll Never Know." Music by Harry Warren. © 1943 (Renewed) WB Music Corp. All Rights Reserved. Used by Permission. Warner Bros. Publications U.S. Inc., Miami, FL 33014.

OSCAR HAMMERSTEIN 2ND

"All in Fun." Music by Jerome Kern. Copyright © 1939 Universal– PolyGram International Publishing, Inc. On behalf of T.B. Harms Co. (ASCAP). All Rights Reserved. Used by Permission.

"I Am Going to Like It Here." Music by Richard Rodgers. Copyright © 1958 (Renewed) Richard Rodgers and Oscar Hammerstein II. Williamson Music owner of Publication and Allied Rights throughout the World. International Copyright Secured. All Rights Reserved. Used by Permission.

"Shall We Dance?" Music by Richard Rodgers. Copyright © 1951 (Renewed) Richard Rodgers and Oscar Hammerstein II. Williamson Music owner of Publication and Allied Rights throughout the World. International Copyright Secured. All Rights Reserved. Used by Permission.

"Sixteen Going on Seventeen." Music by Richard Rodgers. Copyright © 1959 (Renewed) Richard Rodgers and Oscar Hammerstein II. Williamson Music owner of Publication and Allied Rights throughout the World. International Copyright Secured. All Rights Reserved. Used by Permission.

"Soliloquy." Music by Richard Rodgers. Copyright © 1945 (Renewed) Williamson Music. International Copyright Secured. All Rights Reserved. Used by Permission.

"The Big Black Giant." Music by Richard Rodgers. Copyright © 1953 (Renewed) Williamson Music owner of Publication and Allied Rights throughout the World. International Copyright Secured. All Rights Reserved. Used by Permission.

"The Desert Song." Lyric by Hammerstein and Otto Harbach. Music by Sigmund Romberg. Copyright © 1926 (Renewed) Warner Bros. Inc. All Rights Reserved. Used by Permission. Warner Bros. Publications U.S. Inc., Miami, FL 33014.

"The Folks Who Live on the Hill." Music by Jerome Kern. Copyright © 1937 Universal–PolyGram International Publishing, Inc. (ASCAP). All Rights Reserved. Used by Permission.

"Twin Soliloquies." Music by Richard Rodgers. Copyright © 1949 (Renewed) Richard Rodgers and Oscar Hammerstein II. Williamson Music owner of Publication and Allied Rights throughout the World. International Copyright Secured. All Rights Reserved. Used by Permission.

"You've Got To Be Carefully Taught." Music by Richard Rodgers. Copyright © 1949 (Renewed) Richard Rodgers and Oscar Hammerstein II. Williamson Music owner of Publication and Allied Rights throughout the World. International Copyright Secured. All Rights Reserved. Used by Permission.

E.Y. "YIP" HARBURG

"Adrift on a Star." Music by Jacques Offenbach, arranged by Jay Gorney. Copyright © 1961. All Rights Reserved. Used by Permission. Warner Bros. Publications U.S. Inc., Miami, FL 33014.

"Ain't It De Truth." Music by Harold Arlen. Published by Glocca Morra Music (ASCAP). Administered by Next Decade Entertainment, Inc. All Rights Reserved. Used by Permission.

"April in Paris." Music by Vernon Duke. Published by Glocca Morra Music (ASCAP). Administered by Next Decade Entertainment, Inc. All Rights Reserved. Used by Permission.

"Brother, Can You Spare a Dime?" Music by Jay Gorney. Published by Glocca Morra Music (ASCAP). Administered by Next Decade Entertainment, Inc. All Rights Reserved. Used by Permission.

"A Butler In the Abbey." Music by Jule Styne. Published by Glocca Morra Music (ASCAP). Administered by Next Decade Entertainment, Inc. All Rights Reserved. Used by Permission.

"Fun To Be Fooled." Lyric by Harburg and Ira Gershwin. Music by Harold Arlen. Published by Glocca Morra Music (ASCAP). Administered by Next Decade Entertainment, Inc. All Rights Reserved. Used by Permission.

"How Are Things in Glocca Morra?" Music by Burton Lane. Published by Glocca Morra Music (ASCAP).

by Next Decade Entertainment, Inc. All Rights Reserved. Used by Permission.

"When I'm Not Near the Girl I Love." Music by Burton Lane. Published by Glocca Morra Music (ASCAP). Administered by Next Decade Entertainment, Inc. All Rights Reserved. Used by Permission.

"When the Idle Poor Become the Idle Rich." Music by Burton Lane. Published by Glocca Morra Music (ASCAP). Administered by Next Decade Entertainment, Inc. All Rights Reserved. Used by Permission.

SHELDON HARNICK

"She Loves Me." Music by Jerry Bock. Copyright © 1962 (Renewed 1990) Mayerling Productions, Ltd. Administered by R&H Music and Jerry Bock Enterprises (U.S.A.). All Rights Reserved. Used by Permission.

"When Messiah Comes." Music by Jerry Bock. Copyright © 1964 (Renewed 1990) Mayerling Productions, Ltd. Administered by R&H Music and Jerry Bock Enterprises (U.S.A.). All Rights Reserved. Used by Permission.

LORENZ HART

"At the Roxy Music Hall." Music by Richard Rodgers. Copyright © 1938. All Rights Reserved. Used by Permission. Warner Bros. Publications U.S. Inc., Miami, FL 33014.

"Den of Iniquity." Music by Richard Rodgers. Copyright © 1941, 1950, 1962 (copyrights Renewed) Chappell & Co. Rights for Extended Renewal Term in the U.S. controlled by The Estate of Lorenz Hart (administered by WB Music Corp.) and The Family Trust U/W Richard Rodgers and The Family Trust U/W Dorothy F. Rodgers (administered by Williamson Music). All Rights Reserved. Used by Permission. Warner Bros. Publications U.S. Inc., Miami, FL 33014.

"I Wish I Were in Love Again." Music by Richard Rodgers. Copyright © 1937 (Renewed) Chappell & Co. Rights for Extended Renewal Term in the U.S. controlled by The Estate of Lorenz Hart (administered by WB Music Corp.) and The Family Trust U/W Richard Rodgers and The Family Trust U/W Dorothy F. Rodgers (administered by Williamson Music). All Rights Reserved. Used by Permission. Warner Bros. Publications U.S. Inc., Miami, FL 33014.

"Johnny One Note." Music by Richard Rodgers. Copyright © 1937 (Renewed) Chappell & Co. Rights

for Extended Renewal Term in the U.S. controlled by The Estate of Lorenz Hart (administered by WB Music Corp.) and The Family Trust U/W Richard Rodgers and The Family Trust U/W Dorothy F. Rodgers (administered by Williamson Music) All Rights Reserved. Used by Permission. Warner Bros. Publications U.S. Inc., Miami, FL 33014.

"Manhattan." Music by Richard Rodgers. Copyright © 1925 (Renewed) Piedmont Music Company. All Rights Reserved. Used by Permission.

"My Funny Valentine" Music by Richard Rodgers. Copyright © 1937 (Renewed) Chappell & Co. Rights for Extended Renewal Term in the U.S. controlled by The Estate of Lorenz Hart (administered by WB Music Corp.) and The Family Trust U/W Richard Rodgers and The Family Trust U/W Dorothy F. Rodgers (administered by Williamson Music). All Rights Reserved. Used by Permission. Warner Bros. Publications U.S. Inc., Miami, FL 33014.

"Nobody's Heart." Music by Richard Rodgers. Copyright © 1942 (Renewed) Chappell & Co. Rights for Extended Renewal Term in the U.S. controlled by The Estate of Lorenz Hart (administered by WB Music Corp.) and The Family Trust U/W Richard Rodgers and The Family Trust U/W Dorothy F. Rodgers (administered by Williamson Music). All Rights Reserved. Used by Permission. Warner Bros. Publications U.S. Inc., Miami, FL 33014.

"Sing." Music by Richard Rodgers. Copyright © 1926 (Renewed) Warner Bros. Inc. Rights for Extended Renewal Term in the U.S. controlled by The Estate of Lorenz Hart (administered by WB Music Corp.) and The Family Trust U/W Richard Rodgers and The Family Trust U/W Dorothy F. Rodgers (administered by Williamson Music). All Rights Reserved. Used by Permission. Warner Bros. Publications U.S. Inc., Miami, FL 33014.

"Thou Swell." Music by Richard Rodgers. Copyright © 1927 (Renewed) Warner Bros. Inc. Rights for Extended Renewal Term in the U.S. controlled by The Estate of Lorenz Hart (administered by WB Music Corp.) and The Family Trust U/W Richard Rodgers and The Family Trust U/W Dorothy F. Rodgers (administered by Williamson Music). All Rights Reserved. Used by Permission. Warner Bros. Publications U.S. Inc., Miami, FL 33014.

"Where or When." Music by Richard Rodgers. Copyright © 1937 (Renewed) Chappell & Co. Rights for Extended Renewal Term in the U.S. controlled by The Estate of Lorenz Hart (administered by WB Music Corp.) and The Family Trust U/W Richard Rodgers and The Family Trust U/W Dorothy F. Rodgers (administered by Williamson Music). All Rights Reserved. Used by Permission. Warner Bros. Publications U.S. Inc., Miami, FL 33014.

"Where's That Rainbow." Music by Richard Rodgers. Copyright © 1926. All Rights Reserved. Used by Permission. Warner Bros. Publications U.S. Inc., Miami, FL 33014.

"Zip." Music by Richard Rodgers. Copyright © 1951, 1962 (Copyrights Renewed) Chappell & Co. All Rights Reserved. Used by Permission. Warner Bros. Publications U.S. Inc., Miami, FL 33014.

"Spring Is Here." Music by Richard Rodgers. Copyright © 1938 (Renewed) EMI Robbins Catalog Inc. All Rights Reserved. Used by Permission. Warner Bros. Publications U.S. Inc., Miami, FL 33014.

"The Lady Is a Tramp." Music by Richard Rodgers. Copyright © 1937 (Renewed) Chappell & Co. Rights for Extended Renewal Term in the U.S. controlled by The Estate of Lorenz Hart (administered by WB Music Corp.) and The Family Trust U/W Richard Rodgers and The Family Trust U/W Dorothy F. Rodgers (administered by Williamson Music). All Rights Reserved. Used by Permission. Warner Bros. Publications U.S. Inc., Miami, FL 33014.

GUS KAHN
"Ain't We Got Fun." Lyric by Kahn and Raymond B. Egan. Music by Richard A. Whiting. Copyright © 1921 (Renewed) Warner Bros. Inc. Rights for Extended Renewal Term in the U.S. controlled by Warner Bros. Inc. and Gilbert Keyes Music. All Rights Reserved. Used by Permission. Warner Bros. Publications U.S. Inc., Miami, FL 33014.

"Carolina in the Morning." Music by Walter Donaldson. © 1922 Copyright Renewed 1949. Donaldson Publishing Co. and Gilbert Keyes Music Co. International Copyright Secured. All Rights Reserved. Used by Permission.

"Liza (All the Clouds'll Roll Away)." Lyric by Kahn and Ira Gershwin. Music by George Gershwin. Copyright © 1929 (Renewed) WB Music Corp. Rights for Extended Renewal Term in the U.S. controlled by WB Music Corp. and Gilbert Keyes Music. All Rights

Reserved. Used by Permission. Warner Bros. Publications U.S. Inc., Miami, FL 33014.

"Love Me or Leave Me." Music by Walter Donaldson. Copyright © 1928 Copyright Renewed 1955. Donaldson Publishing Co. and Gilbert Keyes Music Co. International Copyright Secured. All Rights Reserved. Used by Permission.

"Makin' Whoopee." Music by Walter Donaldson. Copyright © 1928 Copyright Renewed 1955. Donaldson Publishing Co. and Gilbert Keyes Music Co. International Copyright Secured. All Rights Reserved. Used by Permission.

"Pretty Baby." Music by Tony Jackson and Egbert Van Alstyne. Copyright © 1916. All Rights Reserved. Used by Permission. Warner Bros. Publications U.S. Inc., Miami, FL 33014.

Bert Kalmar
"California Skies." Music by Harry Ruby. Copyright © 1926 (Renewed) Warner Bros. Inc. and Harry Ruby Music. All Rights Reserved. Used by Permission. Warner Bros. Publications U.S. Inc., Miami, FL 33014.

"Hooray for Captain Spaulding." Music by Harry Ruby. Copyright © 1936 (Renewed) Warner Bros. Inc. All Rights Reserved. Used by Permission. Warner Bros. Publications U.S. Inc., Miami, FL 33014.

"I Wanna Be in Love With You." Music by Herbert Stothart and Harry Ruby. Copyright © 1928 (Renewed) Warner Bros. Inc. Rights for Extended Renewal Term in U.S. controlled by Warner Bros. Inc., Harry Ruby Music and Edwin H. Morris & Co., a division of MPL Communications. All Rights Reserved. Used by Permission. Warner Bros. Publications U.S. Inc., Miami, FL 33014.

"Moonlight on the Rhine." Lyric by Kalmar and Edgar Leslie. Music by Ted Snyder. Copyright © 1914. All Rights Reserved. Used by Permission. Warner Bros. Publications U.S. Inc., Miami, FL 33014.

"So Long! Oo-long (How Long You Gonna Be Gone?)" Music by Harry Ruby. Copyright © 1920. All Rights Reserved. Used by Permission. Warner Bros. Publications U.S. Inc., Miami, FL 33014.

"Three Little Words." Music by Harry Ruby. Copyright © 1930 Warner Bros. Inc. © Renewed 1958 Edwin H. Morris & Co., A Division of MPL and Harry Ruby Music. All Rights for Harry Ruby Music Administered by The Songwriters Guild of America. All Rights Reserved.

"Who's Sorry Now." Lyric by Kalmar and Harry Ruby. Music by Ted Snyder. Copyright © 1923 (Renewed) EMI Mills Music, Inc. Warner Bros. Inc. All Rights Reserved. Used by Permission. Warner Bros. Publications U.S. Inc., Miami, FL 33014.

TED KOEHLER

"Between the Devil and the Deep Blue Sea." Music by Harold Arlen. Copyright © 1931 (Renewed 1958). Administered by The Fred Ahlert Music Company on behalf of Ted Koehler Music and by SA Music on behalf of Harold Arlen. All Rights Reserved. Used by Permission.

"Stormy Weather." Music by Harold Arlen. Copyright © 1933 (Renewed 1961). Administered by The Fred Ahlert Music Company on behalf of Ted Koehler Music and by SA Music on behalf of Harold Arlen. All Rights Reserved. Used by Permission.

CAROLYN LEIGH

"Don't Ask a Lady." Music by Cy Coleman. Copyright © 1982 Notable Music Company, Inc. (ASCAP) and Junes Tunes (ASCAP). All Rights o/b/o Notable Music Company, Inc. administered by WB Music Corp. All Rights Reserved. Used by Permission. Warner Bros. Publications U.S. Inc., Miami, FL 33014.

"I'm Flying." Music by Mark Charlap. Copyright © 1954. All Rights Reserved. Used by Permission. Warner Bros. Publications U.S. Inc., Miami, FL 33014.

"It Amazes Me." Music by Cy Coleman. Copyright © 1958 (Renewed) Notable Music Co., Inc. and EMI Carwin Catalog Inc. All Rights o/b/o Notable Music Co., Inc. administered by WB Music Corp. All Rights Reserved. Used by Permission. Warner Bros. Publications U.S. Inc., Miami, FL 33014.

"I've Gotta Crow." Music by Mark Charlap. Copyright © 1954 (Renewed) Carolyn Leigh and Mark Charlap. All Rights Controlled By Edwin H. Morris & Co., A Division of MPL Communications, Inc. All Rights Reserved.

"I Want to be Yours." Music by Cy Coleman. Copyright © 1982. All Rights Reserved. Used by Permission. Warner Bros. Publications U.S. Inc., Miami, FL 33014.

"I Won't Grow Up." Music by Mark Charlap. Copyright © 1954. All Rights Reserved. Used by Permission. Warner Bros. Publications U.S. Inc., Miami, FL 33014.

"Real Live Girl." Music by Cy Coleman. Copyright © 1962 (Renewed) Notable Music Co., Inc. and EMI Carwin Catalog Inc. All Rights o/b/o Notable Music Co., Inc. administered by WB Music Corp. All Rights Reserved. Used by Permission. Warner Bros. Publications U.S. Inc., Miami, FL 33014.

"Young at Heart." Music by Johnny Richards. Copyright © 1953. All Rights Reserved. Used by Permission. Warner Bros. Publications U.S. Inc., Miami, FL 33014.

ALAN JAY LERNER

"Almost Like Being in Love." Music by Frederick Loewe. Copyright © 1947 (Renewed) Alan Jay Lerner and Frederick Loewe. World Rights assigned to Chappell & Co. and EMI U Catalog Inc. All Rights Reserved. Used by Permission. Warner Bros. Publications U.S. Inc., Miami, FL 33014.

"Another Autumn." Music by Frederick Loewe. Copyright © 1950. All Rights Reserved. Used by Permission. Warner Bros. Publications U.S. Inc., Miami, FL 33014.

"Camelot." Music by Frederick Loewe. Copyright © 1960 (Renewed) Alan Jay Lerner and Frederick Loewe. Publication and Allied Rights assigned to Chappell & Co. All Rights Reserved. Used by Permission. Warner Bros. Publications U.S. Inc., Miami, FL 33014.

"Come Back to Me." Music by Burton Lane. Copyright © 1965 Alan Jay Lerner and Burton Lane. © Renewed. Publication and Allied Rights assigned to Chappell & Co. All Rights Reserved. Used by Permission. Warner Bros. Publications U.S. Inc., Miami, FL 33014.

"Come to Me, Bend to Me." Music by Frederick Loewe. Copyright © 1947 (Renewed) Alan Jay Lerner and Frederick Loewe. World Rights assigned to Chappell & Co. And EMI U Catalog Inc. All Rights Reserved. Used by Permission. Warner Bros. Publications U.S. Inc., Miami, FL 33014.

"Come to the Ball." Music by Frederick Loewe. Copyright © 1956. All Rights Reserved. Used by Permission. Warner Bros. Publications U.S. Inc., Miami, FL 33014.

"Forever Young." Music by Frederick Loewe. Copyright © 1945. All Rights Reserved. Used by Permission. Warner Bros. Publications U.S. Inc., Miami, FL 33014.

"Gigi." Music by Frederick Loewe. Copyright © 1957, 1958 (Copyrights Renewed) Chappell & Co. All Rights Reserved. Used by Permission. Warner Bros. Publications U.S. Inc., Miami, FL 33014.

"Heather on the Hill." Music by Frederick Loewe. Copyright © 1947 (Renewed) Alan Jay Lerner and Frederick Loewe. World Rights assigned to Chappell & Co. World Rights assigned to and administered by EMI U Catalog Inc. All Rights Reserved. Used by Permission. Warner Bros. Publications U.S. Inc., Miami, FL 33014.

"Here I'll Stay." Music by Kurt Weill. Copyright © 1948 (Renewed) TRO-Hampshire House Publishing Corp. and Chappell & Co. All Rights Reserved. Used by Permission. Warner Bros. Publications U.S. Inc., Miami, FL 33014.

"I Talk to the Trees." Music by Frederick Loewe. Copyright © 1951 Alan Jay Lerner and Frederick Loewe. © Renewed. Publications and Allied Rights assigned to Chappell & Co. All Rights Reserved. Used by Permission. Warner Bros. Publications U.S. Inc., Miami, FL 33014.

"I'm an Ordinary Man." Music by Frederick Loewe. Copyright © 1956 Alan Jay Lerner and Frederick Loewe. © Renewed. Chappell & Co. Owner of Publication and Allied Rights throughout the World. All Rights Reserved. Used by Permission. Warner Bros. Publications U.S. Inc., Miami, FL 33014.

"I'm Glad I'm Not Young Anymore." Music by Frederick Loewe. Copyright © 1957, 1958 (Renewed) Chappell & Co. All Rights Reserved. Used by Permission. Warner Bros. Publications U.S. Inc., Miami, FL 33014.

"I've Grown Accustomed to Her Face." Music by Frederick Loewe. Copyright © 1956 Alan Jay Lerner and Frederick Loewe. © Renewed. Chappell & Co. Owner of Publication and Allied Rights throughout the World. All Rights Reserved. Used by Permission. Warner Bros. Publications U.S. Inc., Miami, FL 33014.

"One More Walk Around the Garden." Music by Burton Lane. Copyright © 1979. All Rights Reserved.

Used by Permission. Warner Bros. Publications U.S. Inc., Miami, FL 33014.

"Take Care of This House." Music by Leonard Bernstein. Copyright © 1976 Universal–PolyGram International Publishing, Inc. On behalf of Leonard Bernstein Music Publishing (ASCAP). All Rights Reserved. Used by Permission.

"They Call the Wind Maria." Music by Frederick Loewe. Copyright © 1951 Alan Jay Lerner and Frederick Loewe. © Renewed. Publications and Allied Rights assigned to Chappell & Co. All Rights Reserved. Used by Permission. Warner Bros. Publications U.S. Inc., Miami, FL 33014.

"Too Late Now." Music by Burton Lane. Copyright © 1949. All Rights Reserved. Used by Permission. Warner Bros. Publications U.S. Inc., Miami, FL 33014.

"When Your Lover Says Goodbye." Music by Andre Previn. Copyright © 1970 (Renewed) Chappell & Co. and Maird Music Inc. All Rights administered by Chappell & Co. All Rights Reserved. Used by Permission. Warner Bros. Publications U.S. Inc., Miami, FL 33014.

FRANK LOESSER
"Baby, It's Cold Outside." Music by Loesser. Copyright © 1948. Used By Permission of Frank Music Corp.

"Spring Will Be a Little Late This Year." Copyright © 1944. Used By Permission of Frank Music Corp.

"I Don't Want to Walk Without You." Music by Jule Styne. Copyright © 1941 (Renewed 1968) Paramount Music Corporation. International Copyright Secured. All Rights Reserved.

"Praise the Lord and Pass the Ammunition." Copyright © 1942 (Renewed 1969) Famous Music Corporation. International Copyright Secured. All Rights Reserved. Used by Permission.

"They're Either Too Young or Too Old." Music by Arthur Schwartz. Copyright © 1943 (Renewed) Warner Bros. Inc. All Rights Reserved. Used by Permission. Warner Bros. Publications U.S. Inc., Miami, FL 33014.

JOHNNY MERCER
"Autumn Leaves." Original French lyric by Jacques Prevert. Music by Joseph Kosma. Copyright © 1947, 1950 (Renewed) Enoch Et Cie. Sole Selling Agent for

Morris & Co., A Division of MPL Communications, Inc. All Rights Reserved. Used by Permission. Warner Bros. Publications U.S. Inc., Miami, FL 33014.

"I'm the Last of the Red Hot Mamas." Music by Milton Ager Copyright © 1926 (Renewed) Warner Bros.

Inc. All Rights Reserved. Used by Permission. Warner Bros. Publications U.S. Inc., Miami, FL 33014.

"My Yiddishe Momme." Music by Yellen and Lew Pollack. Copyright © 1925 (Renewed) Cappell & Co. and Lew Pollack Music. All Rights Reserved. Used by Permission. Warner Bros. Publications U.S. Inc., Miami, FL 33014.

Cumulative Index

Dictionary of Literary Biography, Volumes 1-265
Dictionary of Literary Biography Yearbook, 1980-2001
Dictionary of Literary Biography Documentary Series, Volumes 1-19
Concise Dictionary of American Literary Biography, Volumes 1-7
Concise Dictionary of British Literary Biography, Volumes 1-8
Concise Dictionary of World Literary Biography, Volumes 1-4

Cumulative Index

DLB before number: *Dictionary of Literary Biography,* Volumes 1-265
Y before number: *Dictionary of Literary Biography Yearbook,* 1980-2001
DS before number: *Dictionary of Literary Biography Documentary Series,* Volumes 1-19
CDALB before number: *Concise Dictionary of American Literary Biography,* Volumes 1-7
CDBLB before number: *Concise Dictionary of British Literary Biography,* Volumes 1-8
CDWLB before number: *Concise Dictionary of World Literary Biography,* Volumes 1-4

Cumulative Index

O'Shea, Patrick [publishing house] DLB-49

Osipov, Nikolai Petrovich
1751-1799 .... DLB-150

Oskison, John Milton 1879-1947........DLB-175

Osler, Sir William 1849-1919 .... DLB-184

Osofisan, Femi 1946- DLB-125; CDWLB-3

Ostenso, Martha 1900-1963 .... DLB-92

Ostrauskas, Kostas 1926- DLB-232

Ostriker, Alicia 1937- DLB-120

Osundare, Niyi 1947- DLB-157; CDWLB-3

Oswald, Eleazer 1755-1795 .... DLB-43

Oswald von Wolkenstein
1376 or 1377-1445 ....DLB-179

Otero, Blas de 1916-1979 .... DLB-134

Otero, Miguel Antonio 1859-1944 .... DLB-82

Otero, Nina 1881-1965 .... DLB-209

Otero Silva, Miguel 1908-1985 .... DLB-145

Otfried von Weißenburg
circa 800-circa 875? DLB-148

Otis, Broaders and Company.......... DLB-49

Otis, James (see Kaler, James Otis)

Otis, James, Jr. 1725-1783 .... DLB-31

Ottaway, James 1911- DLB-127

Ottendorfer, Oswald 1826-1900........ DLB-23

Ottieri, Ottiero 1924- DLB-177

Otto-Peters, Louise 1819-1895 .... DLB-129

Otway, Thomas 1652-1685 .... DLB-80

Ouellette, Fernand 1930- DLB-60

Ouida 1839-1908 .... DLB-18, 156

Outing Publishing Company DLB-46

Outlaw Days, by Joyce Johnson DLB-16

Overbury, Sir Thomas
circa 1581-1613 .... DLB-151

The Overlook Press DLB-46

Overview of U.S. Book Publishing,
1910-1945....................... DLB-9

Ovid 43 B.C.-A.D. 17 ...... DLB-211; CDWLB-1

Owen, Guy 1925- DLB-5

Owen, John 1564-1622.............. DLB-121

Owen, John [publishing house]......... DLB-49

Owen, Peter, Limited DLB-112

Owen, Robert 1771-1858 ....DLB-107, 158

Owen, Wilfred
1893-1918........ DLB-20; DS-18; CDBLB-6

The Owl and the Nightingale
circa 1189-1199 .... DLB-146

Owsley, Frank L. 1890-1956 .... DLB-17

Oxford, Seventeenth Earl of, Edward
de Vere 1550-1604................DLB-172

Ozerov, Vladislav Aleksandrovich
1769-1816..................... DLB-150

Ozick, Cynthia 1928- DLB-28, 152; Y-83

First Strauss "Livings" Awarded to Cynthia
Ozick and Raymond Carver
An Interview with Cynthia Ozick Y-83

P

Pace, Richard 1482?-1536 .... DLB-167

Pacey, Desmond 1917-1975 .... DLB-88

Pack, Robert 1929- DLB-5

Packaging Papa: *The Garden of Eden* Y-86

Padell Publishing Company DLB-46

Padgett, Ron 1942- DLB-5

Padilla, Ernesto Chávez 1944- DLB-122

Page, L. C., and Company DLB-49

Page, Louise 1955- DLB-233

Page, P. K. 1916- DLB-68

Page, Thomas Nelson
1853-1922 ....DLB-12, 78; DS-13

Page, Walter Hines 1855-1918...... DLB-71, 91

Paget, Francis Edward 1806-1882 ..... DLB-163

Paget, Violet (see Lee, Vernon)

Pagliarani, Elio 1927- DLB-128

Pain, Barry 1864-1928 ....DLB-135, 197

Pain, Philip ?-circa 1666 .... DLB-24

Paine, Robert Treat, Jr. 1773-1811 ...... DLB-37

Paine, Thomas
1737-1809 .... DLB-31, 43, 73, 158; CDALB-2

Painter, George D. 1914- DLB-155

Painter, William 1540?-1594 ...... DLB-136

Palazzeschi, Aldo 1885-1974 ...... DLB-114, 264

Paley, Grace 1922- DLB-28, 218

Paley, William 1743-1805............. DLB-251

Palfrey, John Gorham 1796-1881 .. DLB-1, 30, 235

Palgrave, Francis Turner 1824-1897...... DLB-35

Palmer, Joe H. 1904-1952.............DLB-171

Palmer, Michael 1943- DLB-169

Palmer, Nettie 1885-1964............ DLB-260

Palmer, Vance 1885-1959............ DLB-260

Paltock, Robert 1697-1767............. DLB-39

Paludan, Jacob 1896-1975............ DLB-214

Pan Books Limited DLB-112

Panama, Norman 1914- and
Frank, Melvin 1913-1988........... DLB-26

Panaev, Ivan Ivanovich 1812-1862...... DLB-198

Panaeva, Avdot'ia Iakovlevna
1820-1893 .... DLB-238

Pancake, Breece D'J 1952-1979......... DLB-130

Panduro, Leif 1923-1977............. DLB-214

Panero, Leopoldo 1909-1962 .... DLB-108

Pangborn, Edgar 1909-1976 .... DLB-8

"Panic Among the Philistines": A Postscript,
An Interview with Bryan Griffin Y-81

Panizzi, Sir Anthony 1797-1879........ DLB-184

Panneton, Philippe (see Ringuet)

Panshin, Alexei 1940- DLB-8

Pansy (see Alden, Isabella)

Pantheon Books DLB-46

Papadat-Bengescu, Hortensia
1876-1955 .... DLB-220

Papantonio, Michael (see Kohn, John S. Van E.)

Paperback Library DLB-46

Paperback Science Fiction.............. DLB-8

Papini, Giovanni 1881-1956........... DLB-264

Paquet, Alfons 1881-1944............. DLB-66

Paracelsus 1493-1541 ....DLB-179

Paradis, Suzanne 1936- DLB-53

Páral, Vladimír, 1932- DLB-232

Pardoe, Julia 1804-1862 .... DLB-166

Paredes, Américo 1915-1999 .... DLB-209

Pareja Diezcanseco, Alfredo 1908-1993 .. DLB-145

Parents' Magazine Press DLB-46

Parfit, Derek 1942- DLB-262

Parise, Goffredo 1929-1986 ....DLB-177

Parisian Theater, Fall 1984: Toward
A New Baroque Y-85

Parish, Mitchell 1900-1993........... DLB-265

Parizeau, Alice 1930- DLB-60

Park, Ruth 1923- DLB-260

Parke, John 1754-1789 .... DLB-31

Parker, Dan 1893-1967............. DLB-241

Parker, Dorothy 1893-1967 ...... DLB-11, 45, 86

Parker, Gilbert 1860-1932 .... DLB-99

Parker, J. H. [publishing house] DLB-106

Parker, James 1714-1770............... DLB-43

Parker, John [publishing house] DLB-106

Parker, Matthew 1504-1575 .... DLB-213

Parker, Stewart 1941-1988............ DLB-245

Parker, Theodore 1810-1860 .... DLB-1, 235

Parker, William Riley 1906-1968...... DLB-103

Parkes, Bessie Rayner (Madame Belloc)
1829-1925 .... DLB-240

Parkman, Francis
1823-1893 ....DLB-1, 30, 183, 186, 235

Parks, Gordon 1912- DLB-33

Parks, Tim 1954- DLB-231

Parks, William 1698-1750............. DLB-43

Parks, William [publishing house] DLB-49

Parley, Peter (see Goodrich, Samuel Griswold)

Parmenides
late sixth-fifth century B.C. DLB-176

Parnell, Thomas 1679-1718 .... DLB-95

Parnicki, Teodor 1908-1988.......... DLB-215

Parr, Catherine 1513?-1548 .... DLB-136

Parrington, Vernon L. 1871-1929.....DLB-17, 63

Parrish, Maxfield 1870-1966......... DLB-188

Parronchi, Alessandro 1914- DLB-128

Parton, James 1822-1891 .... DLB-30

Parton, Sara Payson Willis
1811-1872...........DLB-43, 74, 239

Partridge, S. W., and Company........ DLB-106

Parun, Vesna 1922- DLB-181; CDWLB-4

Pasinetti, Pier Maria 1913- DLB-177

Pasolini, Pier Paolo 1922- DLB-128, 177

Pastan, Linda 1932- DLB-5

Paston, George (Emily Morse Symonds)
1860-1936 ....DLB-149, 197

The Paston Letters 1422-1509 .... DLB-146

Pastorius, Francis Daniel
1651-circa 1720 .... DLB-24

Cumulative Index

ISBN 0-7876-6009-4

90000

9 780787 660093